The Trans-Canada Writer

A Rhetoric, Reader, Handbook

First Canadian Edition

The Trans-Canada Writer
A Rhetoric, Reader, Handbook
First Canadian Edition

Mark Connelly
Milwaukee Area Technical College

Wendy Shilton
University of Prince Edward Island

Greg Doran
University of Prince Edward Island

NELSON / EDUCATION

NELSON EDUCATION

The Trans-Canada Writer: A Rhetoric, Reader, Handbook
First Canadian Edition
by Mark Connelly, Wendy Shilton, and Greg Doran

Associate Vice President, Editorial Director:
Evelyn Veitch

Editor-in-Chief, Higher Education:
Anne Williams

Executive Editor:
Laura Macleod

Marketing Manager:
Amanda Henry

Developmental Editor:
Roberta Spinosa-Millman

Photo Researcher and Permissions Coordinator:
Paula Joiner

Content Production Manager:
Susan Wong

Production Service:
ICC Macmillan Inc.

Copy Editor:
Karen Rolfe

Proofreader:
Karen Rolfe

Indexer:
Maura Brown

Production Coordinator:
Ferial Suleman

Design Director:
Ken Phipps

Managing Designer:
Katherine Strain

Interior Design:
Dianna Little

Cover Design:
Peter Papayanakis

Cover Image:
Dave Reede/First Light

Compositor:
ICC Macmillan Inc.

Printer:
Webcom

Library and Archives Canada Cataloguing in Publication Data

Connelly, Mark, 1951- The trans-Canada writer / Mark Connelly, Wendy Shilton, Greg Doran. — 1stCanadian ed.

Includes index.
ISBN 978-0-17-610344-6

1. English language—Rhetoric. 2. English language—Grammar. 3. College readers. 4. Report writing. I. Shilton, Wendy, 1955- II. Doran, Gregory Killen, 1967- III. Title.

PE1408.C578 2009   808'.0427
C2008-900195-8

ISBN-10: 0-17-610344-9
ISBN-13: 978-0-17-610344-6

"To all our students,
past, present, and future . . ."

Brief Table of Contents

Table of Contents

10 Editing and Proofreading   113

PART TWO   Critical Reading and Writing

11 Becoming a Critical Reader: Reading with a "Writer's Eye"   128

Prager uses a variety of modes, including comparison, description, narration, and cause and effect, to develop her essay about the Barbie doll.

16 Comparison and Contrast: Analyzing Similarities and Differences   261

    Directed to a general audience, Catton's essay seeks to contrast the two most famous generals of the Civil War.

    This preface to *Silent Spring* is intended for a general audience and is an imaginative rendering of the eventual consequences of continued indifference to the environment.

    In her essay Ephron explores society's growing fascination with haute cuisine and compares this trend to a form of pornography.

17 Process: Explaining How Things Work and Giving Directions   297

19 Cause and Effect: Determining Reasons and Measuring Results   377

In this classic essay Orwell argues that to guard against political deception, the public must arm itself with a strong vocabulary and precise writing.

Using George Orwell's 1946 essay "Politics and the English Language," Fawcett discusses how Orwell's fundamental principles of clear thinking and honest expression are still relevant even though the political scene has changed.

PART THREE   Research and Writing

21   Conducting Research   454

22 Writing the Research Paper   482

PART FOUR   Special Writing Situations

23 Writing with Visuals   518

24 Writing for Professional, Collaborative, and Oral Purposes   540

25   Writing for Essay Examinations and Literary Purposes   556

PART FIVE   Grammar and Handbook

Preface

Welcome to the *The Trans-Canada Writer*. This textbook is a comprehensive guide to writing in English for composition courses in Canadian universities and colleges. Its blend of concepts and practical strategies, intellectual rigour and readability, critical thinking and emphasis on writing for the "real world" make it a flexible learning tool for strengthening writing skills. In addition to offering instruction on the writing process, rhetorical modes, and grammar and mechanics, it presents exemplary and relevant readings for Canadian audiences as well as strategies for professional writing, conducting research, analyzing and using images, and interpreting literature.

The Trans-Canada Writer takes its title from a rich but complex metaphor of the Canadian experience: the Trans-Canada Highway. On a literal level, the Trans-Canada (known variously in different locales as the Trans Can, T-Can, TCH, Route One, la Transcanadienne, the Queensway, and many other informal names) is an important means of interprovincial travel from sea to sea, linking mountains, prairies, and wetlands. At the same time, however, it also has become a symbol of national unification, connecting diverse Canadian geographical, economic, social, and cultural forces. Writing, as a means of inquiry, discovery, analysis, explanation, and argumentation, also can be viewed as a multifaceted journey. It often involves travel from one position to another, one state of understanding to another, establishing a direction, arriving at a destination, and using one rhetorical form or another appropriate to particular contexts and conditions. Also like the phases of a journey, the writing process involves unfolding stages—from the generation, formulation, and organization of ideas to the drafting, revision, and editing of the whole.

Writing, like the Trans-Canada Highway, is a technological artifact as well as a process. It is capable of being undertaken independently or collaboratively. It is inseparable from the politics of competing interests. And it possesses the power to transform the environments it touches. And just as the cohesiveness of the Trans-Canada contains gaps (Yukon, the Northwest Territories, and Nunavut) and discontinuities (punctuated by ferries, tunnels, causeways, and bridges), so too is writing frequently challenged by contradictory logic and structural weaknesses. Both the Trans-Canada Highway and writing are far from simple phenomena. They each require ample knowledge and skills for determining goals and successful outcomes, accessing and navigating routes, and negotiating one's perspective and rights interdependently with others'.

The Trans-Canada Highway is foundational to the Canadian experience. Given the central, even urgent, importance of writing and communication in the global knowledge economy, *The Trans-Canada Writer* will help Canadian students develop a strong writing foundation in critical literacy to enhance their chances of personal and professional success.

KEY FEATURES

The Trans-Canada Writer focuses on critical stages in the writing process, providing students with techniques to improve their writing and overcome common problems. It encourages students to see a composition course in highly practical terms, giving them the important critical thinking and writing skills they need in future classes and in any field or occupation they pursue: the ability to reason logically, organize ideas, and communicate effectively.

The Trans-Canada Writer is divided into five parts: The Rhetoric, Critical Reading and Writing, Research and Writing, Special Writing Situations, and Grammar and Handbook.

The Rhetoric

Writing does not occur in a vacuum but in a context that consists of the writer's objective, the reader, the shared context or discourse community, and the nature of the document. After introducing strategies for establishing context and enhancing critical thinking, *The Trans-Canada Writer* guides students in developing a thesis and creating supportive structures for ideas. Students also are given practical directions for revising and editing.

Critical Reading and Writing

Organized by rhetorical mode, this section presents both classic and contemporary essays by Canadian and international authors such as George Orwell, Lester B. Pearson, Margaret Atwood, Alice Munro, Carol Shields, and Drew Hayden Taylor. Women and people of ethnic minority are well represented, and the subjects cover a range of issues: postsecondary education, Canadian politics, employment, and the homeless.

The wide variety of reading topics on science, law, culture, business, and social issues make *The Trans-Canada Writer* suitable for thematic courses. In addition, this textbook has several features that make it a useful teaching tool for instructors:

A range of readings   Each chapter opens with brief, easy-to-read entries that clearly demonstrate the rhetorical mode, followed by longer, more challenging essays. Instructors have the flexibility to assign readings best suited to their student populations.

Brief entries suitable for in-class reading   Many of the essays are short enough to be read in class and used as writing prompts, thus reducing the need for handouts.

An emphasis on critical thinking   *The Trans-Canada Writer* stresses critical thinking by including essays such as Samuel Scudder's "Take This Fish and Look at It," which dramatizes the importance of detailed observation.

Research and Writing

The Trans-Canada Writer offers students a complete discussion of conducting research and writing research papers, initially addressing common student misconceptions. Defining *what a research paper is not* is very effective in preventing students from embarking on misguided, time-consuming endeavours. *The Trans-Canada Writer* gives guidelines to help students locate, evaluate, and document material, including electronic sources.

Special Features

- Strategies for selecting and evaluating sources
- Strategies for overcoming problems with research
- Strategies for evaluating Internet sources
- Strategies for conducting interviews and surveys
- Strategies for locating and evaluating visual images
- Separate MLA and APA research papers

Special Writing Situations

The Trans-Canada Writer includes chapters on analyzing and using photographs, graphs, tables, and charts in both academic and business writing. In addition, *The Trans-Canada Writer* provides strategies for writing effective e-mail, résumés, letters, and business reports. Strategies are also presented to communicate in a range of special writing contexts:

- collaborative writing
- online writing groups
- writing as the representative of others
- writing to mass audiences
- writing to multiple readers
- giving multimedia and oral presentations

The Trans-Canada Writer also includes chapters on writing for special academic purposes, such as essay examinations and writing about literature.

Special Features

- Sample essay examination questions and responses
- An introduction to major literary terms
- A complete short story, two poems, and a dramatic scene
- Sample literary essays

Grammar and Handbook

The Trans-Canada Writer presents an overview of grammar, explaining the parts of speech and basic sentence structure in a separate review chapter. Grammar and Handbook is designed for easy use and focuses on the most common problems in grammar and mechanics.

Special Features

- Strategies for detecting and revising sentence fragments, run-ons, dangling modifiers, faulty parallelism, unnecessary commas, and other errors
- Lists of commonly confused and misspelled words

Writing beyond the classroom   *The Trans-Canada Writer* places a unique emphasis on the practical value of writing skills. Each chapter ends with a sample of "real-world" writing that illustrates how professionals use the modes in different fields.

Blending the modes   Each chapter highlights an essay that demonstrates how writers use different modes to relate a narrative, make a comparison, or outline a definition.

Opposing viewpoints   Paired essays present different opinions on critical issues: ethnic identity, the "abuse excuse," and slavery reparations.

Student papers for each mode   Samples of student writing offer models of common assignments.

Collaborative writing   Each reading concludes with directions for group writing.

Responding to images   Classic and contemporary photographs prompt student writing, class discussion, and collaborative analysis.

COMPANION WEBSITE

http://www.transcanadawriter.nelson.com

The *Trans-Canada Writer* website serves as a supplement for the *Trans-Canada Writer*, providing students with an online study guide divided into five sections:

1. The Writing Process
2. Modes of Exposition
3. Research and the Research Paper
4. Special Kinds of Writing
5. Grammar/Sentence Skills

   Interactive quizzes offer self-graded support for students in 12 key areas:

1. commonly confused words
2. commonly misspelled words
3. problems with modifiers
4. pronoun agreement
5. parallelism
6. fragments and run-ons

7. punctuation

8. history of English

9. the writing process

10. the comma

11. MLA citations

12. subject-verb agreement

Students receive immediate evaluations and can e-mail results to their instructor.

Sample student papers demonstrate each stage of the writing process from instructor's assignment and prewriting notes through rough and edited drafts to the final essay.

Above all, *The Trans-Canada Writer* has been designed to encourage students to read critically and develop confidence as writers.

ACKNOWLEDGMENTS

The authors would like to express their appreciation to all who contributed to the creation of this textbook. We want to thank the following reviewers for their many useful questions and suggestions:

Hasan Malik, *Sheridan College Institute of Technology*

Peter Lovrick, *George Brown College*

Sheila Hancock, *Kwantlen University College*

Anita Agar, *Sheridan College Institute of Technology*

We are especially grateful to Laura Macleod, Executive Editor, Roberta Spinosa-Millman, Development Editor and their many colleagues at Nelson who provided helpful guidance, meticulous feedback, and unwavering support throughout the production process.

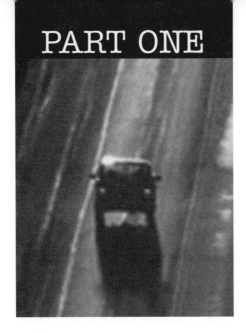

PART ONE

The Rhetoric

CHAPTER 1

About Writing: An Overview

This chapter explores why writing matters today and provides an overview of how to think of yourself as a writer and go about writing confidently. It looks at the relationship between the writing process and the final product, and it discusses strategies that produce good writing.

I'm inspired every morning at half-past nine. Writing is a habit and once you get into it something inside helps you to go on.

—MADGE MACBETH,
LEADING CANADIAN JOURNALIST AND LITERARY WRITER
BETWEEN 1920 AND 1945

WRITING MATTERS

Why write? This may seem like a simple question, but is it? Many students assume that writing (essays, essay examinations, research assignments, lab reports, and the like) is a major part of the academic experience, but few really consider why writing matters. The answer is powerful: strong writers have far greater chance today of succeeding in their personal, academic, and professional lives. Writing is an essential skill in our world of information, knowledge, technology, and communication.

When students think of writers, they often picture professional writers: people who write for a living, such as novelists, playwrights, and reporters. But the reality is that all people who write are writers. More important, all professionals—all educated men and women, in fact—use writing to achieve their goals:

- Police officers document their daily activities in reports and charts, knowing whatever they write may be introduced in court as evidence months or years in the future.

- Lawyers devote much of their time writing motions, drafting appeals, and composing letters.

- Psychiatrists take notes while interviewing patients and later record a diagnosis and outline a course of treatment.

- Business lobbyists, labour leaders, environmentalists, and consumer advocates write members of Parliament to support or reject proposed legislation.

- Salespeople send streams of e-mail messages and faxes to announce new products, intro-duce themselves to new customers, respond to buyers' questions, and inform management of their progress.

- Stockbrokers publish investor newsletters and post recommendations on the Internet.

- A young couple opening a bed and breakfast will find themselves writing to secure financing, contact travel agents, address concerns raised by building inspectors, create sales brochures, and train employees.

Men and women entering any profession soon realize they depend on writing to share ideas, express opinions, and influence people. When you think about your future career, you probably envision yourself in action—perhaps as a doctor treating patients, an architect walking through a construction site, or a choreographer directing a rehearsal. But whether your goal is Bay Street or CUSO, whether you want to help the homeless or develop accounting software, writing will be critical to your success.

In this age of communication, nearly all jobs involve exchanging data. Computers and fax machines link individuals to a global economy. The Internet has created a world community in which nearly everyone can communicate through Web pages, e-mail, chat rooms, or blogs. Sitting at a keyboard, you write to the world, reaching out to people to share your ideas, values, and interests. Writing, in other words, is far more than an academic exercise; it is a vocational tool useful in every job. After graduation you will have to write a convincing letter and résumé to secure job interviews. In fact, throughout your career you will encounter challenges and problems that demand a written response.

Learning to write well sharpens your critical thinking skills, improving your ability to communicate. The strategies you learn in a composition course can also enhance your performance in oral arguments, presentations, job interviews, meetings, and telephone calls. By learning to think more clearly, analyze your audience, and organize your ideas, you will be a more effective communicator in any medium and in any context.

THE WRITING PROCESS
Writing as a Directed Activity

Now that we know why writing matters, we need to ask another deceptively simple question: What is writing? Because writing is so integral to academic life, it is worth taking the time to inquire a little into its nature. To begin with, writing is a *process* (the activity of composing ideas in written form) that usually is intended to lead to a *product* (the result of a writer's activity). Many factors are required to produce good writing, but key among them are language skills, a clear sense of purpose and audience, strong time management skills, effort, and practice.

Like building a table or creating a computer program, good writing (and the confidence and pleasure of producing good writing) emerges through know-how and careful preparation. Don't be fooled by television shows or novels that glamorize writers as people who work in bursts of inspiration—poets, for example, who dash out masterpieces in a flash of creativity, or tough reporters who rush to typewriters and pound out flawless stories without changing a line.

Writing is a craft. Like any craft, writing must be honed through motivation, concentration, and determination. Even professional writers can struggle with the same problems students face in composition: setting the right tone, explaining complicated ideas, sharing experiences that are difficult to put into words, deciding which details to add and which to delete, and often toughest of all—getting started.

Most writers don't have time to wait until inspiration strikes, hoping for a sudden insight to automatically guide them. *The best way to begin writing is to write.* As writer Pearl S. Buck wrote, "I don't wait for moods. You accomplish nothing if you do that. Your mind must know it has got to get down to work."

Developing Effective Composing Habits

Is there a single or ideal method for producing good writing? No, writing is deeply personal, and different writers develop different composing styles and work habits that work best for them. Every writer needs to take the time and initiative to discover an approach to writing.

Some writers can work only in the quiet of a library, whereas others are able to plug in their laptops and write in crowded airports and noisy restaurants. Many writers prefer to work at certain times of day, in specific rooms, or in a favourite coffee shop, and use pencils, an antique fountain pen, or a computer. Some writers work in two- or three-hour blocks; others work in fits and starts, continually interrupting themselves to study for a quiz or run an errand.

When it comes to formulating and organizing ideas, some writers take extensive notes and develop intricate outlines before writing. Others simply plunge into their subjects and write in all directions, knowing they will discard much of what they produce. Some writers agonize over the first page, unable to move on until the first three or four paragraphs are complete. Others race through half a dozen drafts, slowly revising and reshaping a loose, illogical, misspelled mass of writing into refined prose.

If you are not accustomed to writing, it may take you a while to discover when, where, and how you will be most productive. As you get more practice, you may learn that you do your best work under conditions your friends would find impossible. Most people try to find quiet, non-distracting spaces in which to write, such as the hushed silence of a book-lined study, whereas you might find yourself thinking and writing best with a television, radio, or headset on.

Be aware, however, that you may have developed bad habits that hamper your ability to write. If you find writing difficult, or even dread it, reflect seriously on your writing approach and work habits. Consider changing the time, place, and conditions in which you write. Even if you achieve high grades, you may wish to examine the way you compose to see if you can improve the process. The sooner you discover your own personal approach to writing, the more likely you will enjoy writing and avoid potential traps in the writing process.

The Writing Stages as a Recursive Process

Fortunately, to assist in developing a composing style, there are general composing principles and guidelines that can benefit all writers. In the past, composition manuals promoted the idea that writing occurred in fixed stages, encouraging students to follow these stages in strict, linear order. Current research recognizes that writing is a recursive process: that is, writers repeat steps and sometimes carry out two or three simultaneously. Writing on a computer, moreover, makes it easier to scroll up and down, jotting down ideas for a conclusion, say, and then moving back to change a word or two to polish the introduction.

It is possible to identify six common stages in the writing process, and even though good writers may not follow them in a strict or particular order, most rely on them.

Discover	Explore topics, develop ideas.
Plan	Establish context and outline points.
Write	Get your ideas on paper.
Cool	Put your writing aside.
Revise	Review your draft and rewrite.
Edit	Check your final document.

At first glance, a six-step process may appear complex and time consuming, but mastering these strategies can improve the speed and quality of your writing:

1. **DISCOVER—Explore topics, develop ideas.** Good writing does more than record what you "feel" about a subject—it explores issues, asks questions, engages readers, and moves beyond the obvious. Writing starts with critical thinking—observing details, testing commonly held assumptions, and distinguishing between fact and opinion. Discovery writing takes many forms—brainstorming, freewriting, making lists, sketching ideas, and noting facts. Discovery writing helps you look at the world with new eyes, prompting you to develop fresh ideas and establish a point of view.

2. **PLAN—Establish context and outline points.** Once you have established your goal, develop your thesis—your main idea—and supporting ideas in the context formed to meet the needs of your reader, the standards of the discourse community (a particular discipline, profession, community, culture, or situation), and the conventions or requirements of the document. If you are responding to an assignment, ensure your plan addresses the instructor's requirements. Develop an outline listing the items you need to achieve your goal and the best way to arrange them. Your opening should attract attention, announce the topic, and prepare readers for the ideas presented in the body of the document. The conclusion should bring the paper to a logical end, using a final observation, quote, or question to make a lasting impression. An outline does not have to be a formal plan using Roman numerals and capital letters—it can be a list or a diagram that allows you to visualize the essay on a single sheet of paper. Outlining helps to organize ideas, spot missing information, and prevent writing in circles or going off topic.

Long projects should include a budget or timeline. If you are working on a research paper that will take weeks to complete, consult a calendar to break the process into steps. Don't spend six weeks conducting research and expect to write and revise a twenty-page paper over a weekend. Make sure you allot enough time for each stage in the writing process.

3. **WRITE—Get your ideas on paper.** After reviewing your plan, write as much as possible without stopping. As you write, new ideas may occur to you. Record all your thoughts. It is easier to delete ideas later than to try to recover something you forgot to include. Do not pause to check spelling or look up a fact, because these interruptions may break your train of thought. Instead, make notes as you go. Underline words you think are misused or misspelled. Leave gaps for missing details. Write quick reminders in parentheses or the margins. Place question marks next to passages that may be inaccurate, unclear, or ungrammatical. Above all, keep writing!

4. **COOL—Put your writing aside.** This is the easiest, but one of the most important, steps in the writing process. It is difficult to evaluate your work immediately after writing because much of what you wish to say is still fresh in your mind. Set your draft aside. Work on other assignments, run an errand, watch television, or read a book to clear your mind. Afterward, you can return to your writing with more objectivity. If you have a letter to send out by the end of the day, try to write the first draft in the morning so you can revise it after lunch. When responding to an e-mail request, set your writing aside for five minutes. Make a telephone call or do some other work. Just ten minutes of "cooling" can help you gain a new perspective on your work, remember missing details, and eliminate errors you may have overlooked.

5. **REVISE—Review your draft and rewrite.** Before searching your paper for misspelled words or fragments, evaluate it holistically. Review your assignment and your plan. Does what you have created meet the needs of your audience? Does it suit the discourse community? Does it follow the format expected in this document? If you have developed new ideas, are they relevant? You may find that your first attempt has failed and you must start fresh. On the other hand, your first draft may be so well crafted that you can move directly to editing without rewriting. Remember that an essay should have a clear focus—it is not a collection of everything you can think of. Don't be afraid to delete ideas that do not directly support your thesis. You may have developed some interesting points, but they may not belong in this assignment.

6. **EDIT—Check your final document.** When you have completed your last revision, examine it for missing details, grammatical errors, and misspelled words. In addition, review your diction. Eliminate wordy phrases and reduce repetition. Make sure your ideas flow evenly and have clear transitions. Reading a paper aloud can help spot errors and awkward passages.

Each writing assignment is unique. For example, a narrative requires attention to chronology, while a division paper demands clear organization, and persuasion depends on the skillful use of logic. Each discipline represents a distinct discourse community. In literature courses students are expected to provide original interpretations of a play or novel.

In the sciences students are required to follow strict standards of gathering data, analyzing results, and presenting conclusion. Undoubtedly, you may find some papers more challenging than others. Because it is often difficult to determine how hard a particular assignment may be, it is advisable to start writing as soon as possible. Just ten minutes of discovery writing will quickly reveal how much time and effort you need to devote to this paper.

WRITING ON A COMPUTER

If you have never written on a computer, use whatever opportunities your campus offers to learn word processing. Modern programs are simple to use and will help to make your academic experience easier while preparing you for your future career. Almost every business and profession today requires computer literacy. If you find yourself overwhelmed by technology, as many professional writers do, consider taking a computer course. Many colleges and universities offer one-credit courses or free seminars. You also can ask a friend or classmate to show you how he or she uses a computer to write.

WRITING **ACTIVITIES**

1. Choose a topic from the list on pages 650–651 and use the six-step method described in this chapter to draft a short essay. As you write, note which stages of the process pose the greatest challenges. Alter your composing style in any way that improves your writing.

2. Select an upcoming assignment and write a rough draft. Use this experience to identify areas that require the most attention. Save your notes and draft for future use.

3. Write a letter or e-mail to a friend about a recent experience. Before sending it, set the letter aside, letting it "cool." After two or three days, examine your draft for missing details, awkward or confusing phrases, misspelled words, or repetitious statements. Notice how revision and editing can improve your writing.

E-WRITING

Exploring Writing Resources Online

The Internet offers an ever-growing variety of resources for student writers: dictionaries, encyclopedias, grammar drills, databases of periodicals, library catalogues, editing exercises, and research guides.

1. Review the Companion website for *The Trans-Canada Writer* at http://www.transcanadawriter.nelson.com.

2. Review your library's electronic databases, links, and search engines. Locate online dictionaries and encyclopedias you can use as references while writing assignments.

3. Using a search engine such as AltaVista, Google, or Yahoo!, enter key words such as *prewriting, proofreading, narration, capitalization, thesis statement, comma exercises, editing strategies,* and other terms that appear throughout the book, the index, or your course syllabus. In addition to formal databases, many schools and instructors have constructed online tutorials that can help you improve your writing, overcome troubling grammar problems, and aid in specific assignments.

4. Ask your instructors for useful websites. Keep a list and update it when you find a useful source.

 ## COMPANION WEBSITE

See **http://www.transcanadawriter.nelson.com** for further information on the writing process.

CHAPTER 2

Writing and Context

This chapter explores the important relationship between writing and the surrounding context. It explains why meaningful writing is inseparable from context and provides an overview of how context works, including four main factors: the writer's purpose, audience, situation, and document type.

The skill of writing is to create a context in which other people can think.

—EDWIN SCHLOSSBERG

CONTEXT AND MEANINGFUL WRITING

Writing can be understood accurately only when it is produced and interpreted in context. Think of writing that deliberately breaks the "rules" of standard English grammar and style. Advertisements include slang. Journalism and fiction contain sentence fragments. Scientific articles run multisyllabic terms into long sentences, and government reports are studded with indecipherable acronyms. Should these grammatical and stylistic differences be considered flaws? Within the context of strict academic writing, they would be. But when judged within their respective contexts, they are understood as appropriate. Meaningful writing is inseparable from context.

Context refers to the circumstances that surround a situation or event and the way in which language is used in that situation. Context explains, for example, why a story about an airplane crash in *The Globe and Mail* differs from a NAVCANADA report or the airline's condolence letter to the victims' families. A newspaper account, stated simply and printed in narrow columns for easy skimming, briefly describes the event for general readers. In contrast, a NAVCANADA investigation, directed to aviation safety experts, produces multivolume reports, including extensive test results and testimony of survivors and witnesses in highly technical language. In further contrast, the airline's letter to victims' families—addressing people experiencing confusion, grief, loss, and anger—is drafted carefully by crisis communications experts and reviewed by attorneys in an attempt to inform without admitting liability or appearing falsely sympathetic.

Writing can be successful in one context but unacceptable in another. The notes you write to prepare for an upcoming examination may be useless to other students. An essay on the theme of sexual harassment in a novel might be viewed as insightful in an English course but "too wordy" for the university paper or lacking research on male and female sexual behaviour for a psychology course. Context determines reception: how readers make meaning of writing.

The way you communicate shifts, often unconsciously, depending on context. Suppose that on your way to class, a van runs a red light and rams into your front fender. For the police officer who arrives on the scene, you relate your version of the accident as accurately as possible, providing details about the position of the vehicles and realizing that your comments will become part of an official record. As you tell the physician at the hospital about the accident, you focus on the nature of your injuries. Calling your parents, you explain what happened while reassuring them that you are all right. Meeting friends at the student union, you smile at your slight exaggeration of events for dramatic effect. Seeking comfort that night, you e-mail your best friend, telling her how upset you are by the accident and urging her to call. Later, sitting alone with your diary, you reflect on the fragility of life. Each context is related to the accident but creates its own shifts of emphasis and meaning.

There is no standard form of "good writing" that suits all circumstances. Understanding the role of context will help you achieve your goals in writing.

Questions for Reflection

1. Can you recall times where you had difficulty expressing yourself because you were unsure how your reader would react? How did this uncertainty affect your writing process? Did you have problems finding the right word or getting your ideas on paper? Did you compromise the truth in some way or significantly modify the facts?

2. Have you found that professors have different attitudes about what constitutes "good writing"? How is writing a paper in English literature different from writing one in psychology or economics?

3. Have you noticed that magazines have strikingly different writing styles? What do articles in *The Walrus, World of Wheels, Tessera, Canadian Living, Maclean's, Elle,* and *Opus* reveal about their readers?

THE FOUR MAIN FACTORS OF THE WRITING CONTEXT

In writing, context is shaped by four main factors, each of which is examined in detail:

1. the writer (purpose, role, and mode)
2. the audience (the knowledge base, attitudes, needs, expectations, and biases of the reader)
3. the surrounding or framing situation (the profession, disciplines, community, culture, or event in which the writing takes place)
4. the document type

Context and the Writer

Purpose

Everything you write has a goal or purpose. The note you scribble on a Post-It and stick on your computer screen reminds you of an upcoming test. Research essays demonstrate your academic knowledge and skills. The résumé you submit to employers is designed to secure an interview. The announcement stapled on campus bulletin boards alerts students to an upcoming rally, sporting event, or concert. Good writing has a clear purpose.

Purpose Expressed through Modes

Most writing goals, or purposes, aim to inform, to entertain, or to persuade. Purpose determines in part the way in which all writers—whether students or professionals—represent their ideas, use language, and produce the physical appearance of the finished document. And a writer's purpose usually is expressed through the patterns provided by different *modes*:

DESCRIPTION	PROCESS
Narration	Division
Example	Classification
Definition	Cause and Effect
Comparison and Contrast	Argument and Persuasion

DESCRIPTION	Purpose: To create a picture or impression of a person, place, object, or condition.

Description is an element in all writing and usually serves to support the writer's main goal. Descriptions can be wholly factual and objective, as in an accident report, encyclopedia article, or parts catalogue. In other instances, descriptions are highly personal and subjective, offering readers a writer's impression of a person or subject.

NARRATION	Purpose: To relate a series of events, usually in chronological order.

Biographies, histories, and novels use narration. Business and government reports often include sections called narratives that provide a historical overview of a problem, organization, or situation. Narration can be fictional or factual, and it can be related in first or third person.

EXAMPLE	Purpose: To highlight a specific person, place, object, event, or situation as representative or symbolic of a larger element.

A writer may isolate a particular event and describe it in detail so readers can have a fuller appreciation of a larger or more abstract subject. For instance, the fate of a single business may be related in detail to illustrate an economic or technological trend.

DEFINITION	Purpose: To explain a term, condition, topic, or issue.

In many instances, definitions are precise and standard, such as a country's definition of second-degree murder or a biology book's definition of a virus. Other definitions, such as the definition of a good teacher or parent, may be based on a writer's personal observation, values, experience, and opinion.

COMPARISON AND CONTRAST	Purpose: To examine the similarities and differences between two or more subjects.

Textbooks often employ comparison or contrast to discuss different scientific methods, theories, or subjects. Comparisons may be made to distinguish items or to recommend one theory as superior. Consumer magazines, for example, frequently compare competing products.

PROCESS	Purpose: To explain how something occurs or to demonstrate how to accomplish a specific task.

Writers can explain how nuclear power plants generate power, how the Internet works, or how the liver functions by breaking down the respective processes into a series of events or stages. Writers also use process to provide directions. Recipes, operator's manuals, and first-aid books provide step-by-step instructions to accomplish specific tasks.

DIVISION	Purpose: To name subgroups in a broad class.

Writers seek to make complex topics understandable or workable by dividing them in smaller units. Insurance can be divided into life, health, homeowners, and auto policies. Biology and medical texts divide the human body into the respiratory, nervous, digestive, and other systems. Writers can develop their own divisions, often creating labels to describe three types of jobs or four kinds of customer.

CLASSIFICATION	Purpose: To place subjects in different classes or levels according to a standard measurement.

Writers use classification to rate subjects. Teachers assign higher grades based on the quality of submitted assignments. Homicides are classified as first, second, or third degree according to circumstances and premeditation. As with division, writers often establish subjective classifications, creating a personal system to rate people, products, or ideas.

CAUSE AND EFFECT	Purpose: To trace the reasons for an occurrence or predict the results of an event.

A writer can explain the causes for a decrease in crime, a rise in the stock market, the election of a mayoral candidate, or the extinction of a species. Similarly, he or she could detail the effects that a decrease in crime will have on property values, how rising stock values will impact pension funds, how the new mayor will influence the business community, or what effect the loss of a species will have on the environment.

ARGUMENT AND PERSUASION	Purpose: To influence opinion and motivate actions.

Writers persuade readers using logical appeals based on evidence and reasoning, ethical appeals based on values or belief, and emotional appeals that arouse feelings to support their views. Fundraising letters persuade readers to donate to charities or political campaigns. Advertisements encourage consumers to try new products. Essayists, columnists, and commentators try to influence readers to accept their views on issues ranging from abortion to casino gambling.

Questions for Reflection

1. Consider how you have employed these modes in the past. How often have you used them to achieve your goals in communicating with people? Can you think of essay questions that directed you to demonstrate your knowledge by using comparison or cause and effect?

2. How often do you use modes such as comparison or classification in organizing your ideas and solving problems? Before you buy a product, do you compare it to others? Do you classify the courses you would like to take next semester by their relevance to your major, their difficulty, or their general interest value? Do you seek solutions to problems by applying cause-and-effect reasoning?

About Blending the Modes

Modes, as you have seen, give form to a writer's goal or purpose. Few writing tasks, however, call for the use of a single mode. Although a dictionary entry is pure definition and an auto parts catalogue lists simple descriptions, in most instances writers blend modes to achieve their goals. A biographer, for example, might tell his subject's life story by relying mainly on *narration* of the events, but the author also may use *cause and effect* to explain the forces that modelled the subject's childhood, *comparison* to illustrate how the person differed from his or her peers, and *argument* to persuade readers to accept the subject as an example or role model.

When you write, select the mode or modes that suit your purpose. Don't feel obligated to "fit" your paper into a single pattern. Most writers, as you will see in reading the essays in *The Trans-Canada Writer*, develop their ideas using a number of modes.

The Writer's Role

The way writers design their writing is greatly shaped by their role. In an academic context, your role is somewhat like that of a freelance writer: that is, your essays, reports, and research papers are expected to reflect only your own efforts for each project. The grades you receive in psychology should have no effect on the way your English papers will be examined. A low grade on your midterm essay should not influence how your final will be evaluated. In a composition class, your papers are likely to be graded as much by how you state your views as by what your views are.

The academic environment is unique and very different from what you will encounter after graduation. Beyond the classroom, your role may be more complicated. Instead of seeking high grades through your writing ability, you will be asking readers to invest money, buy a product, give you a job, accept your idea, or change their opinions on an important issue. In some cases, you may have an ongoing relationship with your reader. If you give a client bad news in November, you cannot expect that he or she will read your December business letter with much enthusiasm. It is important to consider how one message will affect the way future messages will be evaluated. In many instances, your profession dictates a role that greatly influences the kind of writing you will be expected to produce. Police officers and nurses, for example, are required to provide objective and impersonal records of their observations and actions. Fashion designers, decorators, and advertising copywriters, who are judged by their creativity and originality, are more likely to offer personal insights and write in the first person.

Questions for Reflection

1. Consider the jobs you have had in the past and the organizations you have worked for. What writing style would be considered appropriate for employees in these

fields? Was objective reporting more important than personal opinion? What image did the organization try to project in its memos, ads, brochures, and other communications to employees and the public? Can you think of instances where an employee could jeopardize his or her job by making inappropriate statements to customers or clients?

2. What kind of writing would be effective in your future career? How does writing in engineering or medical malpractice law differ from writing in sales, hotel management, or charities? Does your future profession demand strict adherence to government or corporate regulations or allow for personal expression?

Context and Audience

Writing is more than an act of self-expression; it is an act of communication. To be effective, your message must be understood by readers. The content, form, style, and tone of your writing are largely shaped by the needs, expectations, and attitudes of your audience. A medical researcher announcing a new AIDS treatment would word an article for the *Canadian Medical Association Journal* very differently from one for *Maclean's* or *Chatelaine*. Each magazine represents a different audience, knowledge base, and set of concerns. Fellow immunologists would focus on the writer's research methods and demand detailed data, precise descriptions of experiments and testing methods, and proof of his or her claims. Readers of non-medical publications would be interested in a range of issues such as cost, government policy, and insurance coverage. They have limited tolerance for scientific terms, require definitions, and need brief summaries of data they are unable to interpret. Subscribers to a so-called women's magazine might wonder if the treatment works equally well for both sexes or would be suitable for pregnant women with HIV.

As a writer you will have to determine how much knowledge your readers have about your subject. Are you writing to a broad general audience or specialized readers from the same discipline, profession, or area of interest? Do technical terms require definition? Are there common misunderstandings that should be explained? Do you make historical or biographical references that are unfamiliar to readers? In addition to your readers' level of knowledge about your subject, you must consider your readers' goals, needs, and expectations. What information do your readers want? Is your audience reading for general interest, curiosity, or entertainment? Or do your readers demand specific details in order to make decisions and plan future actions?

It is also important to take into account how your readers will respond to your ideas. Who are your readers? Are they likely to be friendly, uninterested, or hostile to you, your ideas, or the organization you might represent? What are their interests and concerns? Defence lawyers and police officers have different attitudes toward informer testimony. Environmentalists and real estate developers have conflicting philosophies of land use. Liberals and conservatives have opposing concepts of the proper role of government.

When presenting ideas to audiences with undefined or different attitudes, you will have to work hard to overcome their natural resistance, biases, and suspicions.

Context and Individual Readers

The papers you write in high school and university or college postsecondary institutions are usually read by a single instructor evaluating your work within the context of a specific course. Teachers and professors form a special audience because they generally provide clear instructions outlining requirements for each assignment. They are obligated to read your writing and are usually objective in their evaluations.

Beyond the classroom, you may have to persuade people to read your work. No one is required to read your résumé or proposal. Your readers will be expected to do more than evaluate how effective your writing is. You will be asking your readers to hire you, adopt ideas or products, commit to policies, or accept your opinions about controversial issues. You may ask readers to invest substantial resources on your behalf, conceivably placing their careers in your hands. In writing to individuals, you will have to carefully analyze their needs, concerns, and objections.

The more you learn about the individual you are writing to, the better equipped you will be to shape an effective message. If possible, contact this person to gain greater insight about his or her background, needs, interests, and concerns. Before submitting a long report, you may be able to "test" your ideas by sending a letter or preliminary draft for consideration and discussion before committing yourself to a final document.

Extended Audiences

In college and university, most of your papers are graded and returned. Beyond the classroom, there are often two audiences: immediate readers, who receive your documents; and a second, extended audience. In most professional situations, letters, reports, and memos are retained for future reference. The angry letter you send to an irate customer may be passed on by the consumer to your supervisor, the Canadian Competition Bureau, or a lawyer. At a trial, it may be entered into evidence and read to a jury. The safety inspection report you write in March may be routinely skimmed and filed. But if a serious accident occurs in April, this report will be retrieved and closely examined by insurance investigators, provincial inspectors, and attorneys for the injured. The handouts you give to high school students may be read by parents and members of the school board. Whenever you write beyond the classroom, realize that many people other than your immediate readers may see your documents. In all cases, avoid making remarks that may be misunderstood out of context.

Context and the Reader's Perceptual World

Readers also bring background contexts to their reading. To fully appreciate the way readers will respond to your ideas, it is useful to understand what communications experts call the *perceptual world*—the context in which people respond to new information and experiences. As individuals, and as members of groups, readers base their responses on a range of cultural influences that have varying significance.

The perceptual world is often depicted as a circle to indicate that its elements are not ranked in any particular order and often operate interdependently. Advertising and marketing executives analyze the perceptual world of consumers to design new products and commercials. Trial lawyers assess the perceptual world of jurors to determine their most persuasive arguments. Biographers and psychologists often construct the perceptual world of an individual to explain past actions or predict future behaviour. Political candidates take polls, conduct interviews, and operate focus groups to establish the perceptual worlds of voters in key ridings.

The following are among the more influential elements of the perceptual world:

Past experiences	Age
Values	Status
Class	Social roles
Gender	Reference groups
Education	Race and ethnicity
Professional experiences	

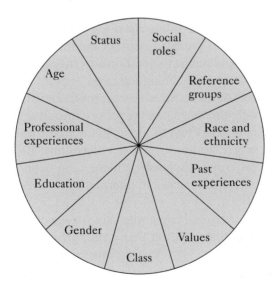

The Perceptual World

Past experiences influence how people react to new information and situations. Readers who have lost money in the stock market will be more skeptical of an advertisement for brokerage services than those who have enjoyed substantial profits. People who have a history of conflict with law enforcement may view police officers differently from those who rely on their services to protect their property. The way people behave as parents is often determined by the nature of their own childhood and the way they were treated.

Values, whether religious, political, or cultural, shape how readers react to ideas. Although often unspoken, these values may be deeply held. People's attitudes about money, sexual behaviour, drug use, politics, technology, and child rearing frequently stem from a core set of beliefs.

Class (economic position) influences attitudes. In general, people with greater incomes have more opportunities for education, travel, and leisure activities. Wealthier people tend to socialize with members of upper-income groups, those who have enjoyed economic success. They may be more optimistic about the economic system that has worked for them, whereas less economically advantaged people may feel constrained or oppressed, seeing fewer examples of success among their peers.

Gender has been proven to affect people's judgments. Polls about a prime minister's popularity, for example, often show a "gender gap" between men and women. Although gender may have no impact on how people evaluate their pension plans or the introduction of computers in the workplace, it can influence how readers respond to issues such as child care, divorce laws, and sexual harassment.

Education, both formal and informal, shapes the intellectual background against which new ideas are examined and tested. Readers with greater academic training are in a stronger position to measure ideas, evaluate evidence, and analyze the validity of a writer's conclusions. Education in specific disciplines will influence how readers consider the evidence writers present. Scientists and mathematicians, for example, are more likely than the general public to question advertising claims using statistics.

Professional experiences, along with training and career responsibilities, form people's attitudes about a number of issues. An economics professor with tenure (the right to job security) may more easily embrace a new tax policy than a struggling business owner worrying about meeting next week's payroll. Occupations expose readers to a range of situations, problems, and people, leading them to develop distinct attitudes and values about the government, success, crime, relationships, money, and technology.

Age affects how people look at the world and interpret experiences. An 18-year-old naturally views life differently from a 50-year-old. In addition, people's attitudes are influenced by their experiences. People who came of age during the 1960s may have different views of using military power than a younger generation whose experience of war has been limited to viewing television images of conflicts such as Operation Desert Fox.

Status influences people's responses, especially to change. A proposed modification in social welfare policies will be of little interest to high school students but of immediate importance to those collecting benefits. An entry-level employee with little invested in a corporation may feel less threatened by rumours of a merger than a senior executive whose position may be eliminated.

Social roles, such as being a parent, civic leader, or homeowner, influence how people interpret new ideas. A 30-year-old with two small children has different concerns than someone of the same age with no dependants. Board members of charitable organizations may feel an obligation to represent the interests of those less fortunate than themselves.

Reference groups refer to people or institutions that readers generally respect and defer to in making judgments. A physician unsure about prescribing a new drug may base his or her decision on recommendations from the Canadian Medical Association. Before leaving college to take a job offer, a student might discuss her decision with friends or advisers.

Race and ethnicity are constantly evolving social categories, applied to distinguish members of a group or tribe who derive from the same common heritage. Categories of race and ethnicity easily can become dangerous if used to stereotype or discriminate against people, or to establish one group (for example, "white" people) as a cultural norm. Canada considers itself multicultural, but many Canadian minorities continue to feel discriminated against; for example, studies show that most hate crimes are committed on the basis of race and ethnicity and that visible minorities have cause to feel threatened. Writers need to be aware of the historical, political, and economic forces that influence the race and ethnic lenses of their readers.

Other aspects of the perceptual world can include physical stature, religion, and geography. In determining your readers' perceptual world, it is important to realize that in some instances people will respond to your ideas based on their entire life experiences. In other circumstances, they may react in solely a professional role or because your ideas trigger a specific reaction. In assessing perceptual worlds, avoid basing your assumptions on stereotypes. Not all older people are conservative, and not all minorities support employment equity. Some Roman Catholics support women's rights to obtain an abortion, and some feminists consider themselves pro-life. Many elements of a reader's perceptual world are unconscious and cannot be easily ascertained. But by learning as much as you can about your readers, you can better determine which strategies will influence them to accept your ideas.

Questions for Reflection

1. How would you describe your own perceptual world? Which factors do you think most influence the way you respond to new ideas?

2. How would you describe the perceptual world of your parents, coworkers, and friends? Are there sharp individual differences? Are there shared values and experiences that might lead them to respond as a group in some circumstances? How would they respond to a letter urging them to donate money to a homeless shelter, support gun legislation, or outlaw smoking citywide? Which issues would be difficult to present to them? Why?

3. Have you ever tried to understand someone you hoped to influence in some way? In practising a presentation, preparing for a job interview, or seeking the right words to discuss a difficult issue with family or friends, do you consider how your audience will react? Is understanding people's perceptual worlds something we engage in every day?

4. Examine the photographs on pages 163, 196, 222, 259, 294, 295, 326, 374, 375, 408, and 450. How do your attitudes, experiences, social roles, and values affect the way you perceive these images? Can you predict how other people might respond to them?

Evaluating Readers and Context

In many instances, you will be unable to learn much about your readers. A want ad may offer only a box number to respond to. Foundations and government agencies sometimes have strict policies that limit information given to applicants. However, in most cases, you can learn something about your audience that will aid you in shaping your writing.

General Readers

1. Envision your readers. Who is your audience? What kind of person or people are you addressing? How do you want them to respond to your ideas?

2. Consider your purpose. What are you asking your readers to accept or do? What objections might they have to your main idea or thesis? How can you answer their questions or address their concerns? Play the devil's advocate (by looking for holes in an argument) and list all the possible objections people may have to your thesis, evidence, and style. How can you overcome these objections?

3. Test your writing. Before printing or mailing an announcement, ad, or brochure, present it to a small group of people who represent your wider audience. Even a group of friends sometimes can detect errors, misleading statements, or inappropriate comments you may have overlooked.

Individual Readers

1. If you are writing for a specific person, who is it? What type of person are you addressing, and what is his or her perceptual world? How do you want this person to respond to your ideas?

2. Ask your instructor for further guidelines about an upcoming assignment or request comments on an outline or rough draft.

3. In writing beyond the classroom, learn as much as you can about your reader. If you cannot obtain personal information, learn what you can about the organization he or she is associated with. What does your reader's profession suggest about his or her perceptual world?

4. Before submitting a résumé or proposal, call ahead and see if you can speak to the person who will evaluate your work. Even a brief conversation with a receptionist or assistant can often give you valuable clues about your reader.

Extended Readers

1. Determine who may see your writing in addition to your intended audience. How would your friends or parents respond to your essays? Beyond the classroom, will your superiors or peers find your messages to employees or customers, for example, acceptable?

2. Review your writing to see if it reflects the kind of image you want to convey to your organization or professional peers. Is it appropriate?

3. Realize that your writing may surface months or years later. Consider how what you write today will affect your future options. How do you wish to represent yourself? What values do you wish to project in your career? Can anything you write today blemish your future?

Context and the Surrounding or Framing Situation

Communication between writer and reader usually occurs within a context that has its own particular culture: academic disciplines, for example, or professions, neighbourhoods, events, publications, and so forth. Each context has its own communication style or use of language, creating a "discourse community." Effective writers are sensitive to the role that discourse communities have on how their ideas will be received and evaluated. In many instances, the discourse community will have a greater influence on how readers respond to messages than their own perceptual worlds. When in court, lawyers, no matter what their personal beliefs, values, or gender, must follow standard procedures and judicial rulings. Members of labour unions, similarly, have shared views of corporate behaviour, the role of government, and international trade. The discourse community, like the perceptual world of the reader, may contain several forces operating simultaneously with varying degrees of influence: discipline, profession, community, culture, and situation.

Discipline　Each academic discipline has a unique history that can dictate how writers collect information, evaluate evidence, measure results, and propose ideas. Some disciplines such as philosophy and mathematics have evolved over thousands of years. Computer science and genetic engineering, in contrast, are such recent discoveries that their founders are still actively developing the nature of the discipline. In the humanities, research usually involves an individual's interpretation of specific works. Fields such as physics, biology, and chemistry demand that a thesis results from experiments using standard scientific methods that can be replicated by independent researchers.

Profession　Each profession has its own context of historical experience, technical training, areas of concern, responsibilities, and political outlooks. The success of advertising executives and designers, for example, may depend on a willingness to be individualistic, radical, daring, and inventive. In contrast, accountants and engineers must follow government regulations. Law enforcement, in a case of suspected child abuse, seek to determine evidence indicating that a crime has been committed, whereas mental health professionals are more interested in the well-being of the child, whether or not the situation meets the legal definition of abuse.

Community   People are influenced by those around them. A community may be a geographic region, organization, or collection of people with shared interests. Residents of downtown Toronto have different interests, concerns, and challenges from those who live in remote farming or fishing communities. The Canadian Navy, IBM, the National Action Committee for the Status of Women, the Canadian Labour Congress, and the Canadian Space Agency each form a distinct community with an individual history, values, problems, and philosophies. Communities form when people share a common interest. AIDS patients, Google users, peacekeeping veterans, Employment Insurance recipients, French speakers, and adopted children have unique concerns leading them to develop common attitudes toward government regulations and public policy.

Culture   National, regional, religious, and ethnic groups have common histories and values that influence how ideas are expressed and evaluated. Traditions and rituals vary between cultures. Although Canadians generally respect individuality, other nationalities may value conformity. What may appear to Westerners as frank and honest writing may be viewed by others as brash and disrespectful. Attitudes about immigration, the role of women, or education can be culturally based.

Situation   Specific events can create a discourse community. The way a manager writes to employees will be altered during a strike. An international crisis will influence the way the prime minister addresses parliamentary ministers opposed to his policies. A crisis may bring writer and reader together as they face a common threat, or it may heighten differences, creating mutual suspicion and hostility.

Questions for Reflection

1. Examine your textbooks from different courses. What do they indicate about the values, standards, and practices in each discipline? Do sociologists write differently than psychologists? What do the books' glossaries reveal about how terms are defined?

2. Consider your future career. What values, attitudes, and skills are important? How will they influence the way you would write to peers? What kind of writing would be considered unprofessional or inappropriate?

3. Think of places where you have worked in the past. Did each form a specific community or culture? Did one office, warehouse, or restaurant have a different atmosphere or spirit than others? Would you word a memo to employees in one business differently than in another?

4. How can a dramatic event shape the way messages are written and evaluated? How would you word a statement announcing the death or injury of a fellow classmate, teammate, or employee?

Context and the Document Type

The nature of the document influences reader expectations. Memos and e-mail sometimes include informal statements, even slang, that would be unacceptable in an essay or formal report. Readers expect that newspaper articles will be brief, simply stated, and accurate, but the same readers likely would have even higher expectations for accuracy from a magazine or a book because the writers have weeks or even years to check their stories and verify facts.

Certain documents (for example, research papers, résumés, wills, legal briefs, military action reports, dissertations, and press releases) have unique styles and formats. Writers who fail to follow the standard forms may alienate readers by appearing unprofessional or lacking in credibility.

Strategies for Writing Specialized Documents

1. **Make sure you understand the form, style, and rigour expected in the document.** Legal documents, grant proposals, and academic dissertations have distinct standards. If no formal directions or guidelines exist, review existing samples or ask the reader what is expected.

2. **Determine if the document suits your purpose.** The importance of your message, the amount of information, and the style of writing should match the form. Memos are suited for routine information and reminders; however, announcing salary changes or job reclassifications in such an informal document will strike readers as callous and impersonal.

3. **Use more than one document to achieve your goals.** If an accident prompts you to immediately alert employees about new safety regulations, you can state them in a short memo. If, however, you find yourself producing pages of text, consider writing a formal report or set of guidelines. Use a memo to quickly alert readers to the most important actions they should take and tell them to expect detailed regulations in the near future. Sometimes formal documents restrict your ability to highlight what you consider significant. Attach a cover letter or send a preliminary report that allows greater freedom of expression.

WRITING IN CONTEXT

Former prime minister Pierre Elliott Trudeau was considered by many Canadians to be one of the country's greatest statesmen, though his actions often incited controversy. On September 28, 2000, he died. Among the eulogies presented at his funeral were one by his son, Justin, and another by former senator Jacques Hébert.

Eulogy by Justin Trudeau*

Friends, Romans, countrymen.

———————————————

1   I was about six years old when I went on my first official trip. I was going with my father and my grandpa Sinclair to the North Pole. It was a very glamorous destination.

But the best thing about it was I was going to be spending lots of time with my dad because in Ottawa he just worked so hard.

One day, we were in Alert, Canada's northernmost point, a scientific military installation that seemed to consist entirely of low shed-like buildings and warehouses.

Let's be honest. I was six. There were no brothers around to play with and I was getting a little bored because dad still somehow had a lot of work to do.

I remember a frozen, windswept Arctic afternoon. And I was bundled up into a Jeep and
10 hustled out on a special top-secret mission.

I figured I was finally going to be let into the reason for the existence of this high-security Arctic base.

I was exactly right.

We drove slowly through and past the buildings, all of them very grey and windy. And we rounded a corner and came upon a red one.

We stopped. I got out of the Jeep and started to crunch across towards the front door but I was told, no, to the window.

So I clambered over the snowbank, boosted up onto the window, rubbed my sleeve against the frosty glass to see inside, and as my eyes adjusted to the gloom, I saw a figure,
20 hunched over one of many worktables that seemed very cluttered.

He was wearing a red suit with a furry white trim. And that's when I understood just how powerful and wonderful my father was.

Pierre Elliott Trudeau. The very words convey so many things to so many people.

Statesman, intellectual, professor, adversary, outdoorsman, lawyer, journalist, author, prime minister.

But more than anything, to me, he was dad.

And what a dad.

He loved us with passion and a devotion that encompassed his life. He taught us to believe in ourselves. To stand up for ourselves. To know ourselves and to accept responsibility
30 for ourselves.

We knew we were the luckiest kids in the world, and that we had done nothing to actually deserve it.

It was instead something that we would have to spend the rest of our lives to work very hard to live up to. He gave us a lot of tools.

We were taught to take nothing for granted. He doted on us but didn't indulge.

*Trudeau, Justin, "Eulogy by Justin Trudeau" reprinted by permission of Justin Trudeau.

Many people say he didn't suffer fools gladly, but I'll have you know he had infinite patience with us.

He encouraged us to push ourselves, to the limits. To challenge anyone and anything, but there were certain basic principles that could never be compromised.

As I guess it is for most kids, in Grade 3, it was always a real treat to visit my dad at work. As on previous visits this particular occasion included a lunch at the parliamentary restaurant, which always seemed terribly important and full of serious people that I didn't recognize.

But at eight, I was becoming politically aware. And I recognized one whom I knew to be one of my father's chief rivals.

Thinking of pleasing my father, I told a joke about him. A generic, silly little grade school thing.

My father looked at me sternly with that look I would learn to know so well.

And said: Justin, [begin translation] we never attack the individual. We can be in total disagreement with someone without denigrating them as a consequence, and saying that, he stood up, took me by the hand and brought me over to introduce me to this man.

He was a nice man, who was eating there with his daughter, a nice-looking blond girl, a little younger than I was.

He spoke to me in a friendly manner for a bit, and it was at that point that I understood that having opinions that are different from another does not preclude being deserving of respect as an individual.

Because simple tolerance, mere tolerance, is not enough.

We need genuine and deep respect for each and every each human being, notwithstanding their thoughts, their values, their beliefs, their origins.

That's what my father demanded of his sons, and that's what he demanded of his country. He demanded this out of a sense of love. Love of his sons. Love of his country, and that's why we love him so.

The letters, the flowers, the dignity shown by the crowds in bidding their farewells—all of this as a thank you for having loved us so much [end translation].

My father's fundamental belief in the sanctity of the individual never came from a textbook. It stemmed from his deep love for and faith in all Canadians and over the past few days, with every card, every rose, every tear, every wave and every pirouette, you returned his love.

It means the world to Sacha and me. Thank you.

We have gathered from coast to coast to coast. From one ocean to another, united in our grief to say goodbye. But this is not the end. He left politics in '84, but he came back for Meech, he came back for Charlottetown, he came back to remind us of who we are and what we're all capable of.

But he won't be coming back any more. It's all up to us—all of us—now.

The woods are lovely, dark and deep. He has kept his promises and earned his sleep.

Je t'aime Papa. ∎

Eulogy by Jacques Hébert*

1   [begin translation] Pierre Trudeau loved very much this thought written by Aristotle: The main goal of society is that its members be able to collectively and individually live a full life.

Throughout his years as head of government, he tenaciously tried to achieve this goal. He was convinced that it was a priority to help young people blossom.

During the past few days, a lot has been said about his more spectacular endeavours—the *Charter of Rights and Freedoms,* the *Constitution* and official languages, et cetera—but we also heard mention of his immense compassion for the youth of this country. He never hesitated to put to the fore programs aimed at youth such as youth opportunities, Katimavik, Canada World Youth. He still spoke to me fondly about Katimavik 10 days before his death
10   in a barely audible voice as if it were already coming from another world, another place.

Hundreds of thousands of young people are now living fruitful and full lives thanks to one or the other of Pierre Trudeau's undertakings toward young people. This voiceless minority who up until that time had never seemed to interest or concern politicians.

One day in 1959, a long time before his entry into politics, I had asked him for his help to help with a young orphan who was having trouble with the rotten system that existed at the time. He was an orphan at that time, one of Duplessis's orphans, as we'd say today.

Pierre Elliott Trudeau threw himself heart and soul into this struggle that lasted for many months until this young, 19-year-old youth was able to recover, both his freedom and dignity. One example among thousands of the generosity of this man.

20   When he was young and free, some would call him a playboy because once and a while we would see him on the ski slopes—Saturdays, perhaps—but the rest of the week, and his friends can testify to that, he worked doggedly to write articles, memoirs that were going to feed the Quiet Revolution and come to task with received ideas.

He was one of the most ardent defenders of the young labour movement in Quebec, which was hardly tolerated at the time, and civil liberties that were often infringed.

For those who admire Pierre Trudeau, he remains a hero and a giant among men. A kind of superman, proud, courageous, a knight in shining armour of immense culture, uncommon intelligence, that was placed at the disposal of Quebec and Canada, both the province and country that he loved passionately.

30   And those who had the privilege and joy of being a friend of his, recall Pierre Trudeau much differently than the public figure that the media never tires of.

For his friends, Pierre Trudeau was, first and foremost, a good and happy friend, a simple human being with a delicacy of nature, generous, attentive, which might surprise those who never knew him and had been known to use the word arrogance.

He had an exquisite sense of what friendship meant, and that is why the illness and death of his friend, Gérard Pelletier, our common friend, was a great blow to him. After the funeral, he sighed and said—quite an incredible expression coming from such a discreet man—"I just have lost a bit of my soul."

*Hébert, Jacques, "Eulogy by Jacques Hébert" reprinted by permission of Jacques Hébert.

And the day we learned of his own death, an expected moment, how many among us felt the same thing—that a little bit of ourselves had just flown away. [end translation]   40

He taught us to question ourselves and debate ideas rather than feelings.

Because of Pierre Trudeau, we have become better human beings, and Canada is now a more generous and caring country. As he once said, a country can be influential in the world by the size of its heart and the breadth of its mind, and this is the role that Canada can play.

Among Pierre Trudeau's qualities, there is one on which everyone is unanimous. Until his last breath, he was an admirable father who gave the best of himself to his children. He could have allowed himself to become distracted, overwhelmed by the duties of being prime minister. He adored his three boys and his daughter, and with infinite patience he communicated his values to them. His love of culture, his love of nature, his sense of discipline.   50

When I think of Pierre Trudeau, I always see him surrounded by his three boys at various stages of their lives, such as in the numerous photographs that line the walls of his office and home.

We can all rejoice in one thing, at least. He died in peace, lucid, serene, accepting his fate, happy and surrounded by Justin, Sacha, and Margaret, and he well deserved this final moment.

It is perhaps not correct to quote an agnostic in this church, but Trudeau loved Baudelaire so much: "Happy is the man who can run in serene and happy fields, those whose thoughts like larks fly in the morning, fly over life and understand without effort the language of both flowers and things unspoken."   60

Goodbye, O brother, rest in peace. And we will all continue to love you. ■

Questions for Reflection

1. Compare the writer's purpose in each of the respective eulogies. How are they similar? How do they differ? What does each writer seek to do? What is the role of each writer—are they the same? What are the different modes used by each writer, and for what purpose?

2. Who is the audience for these eulogies? What are the perceptual worlds of the readers which each writer must consider? Does each writer consider these lenses well? What effect on the audience does each piece strive for, and how?

3. Describe the situation for which these pieces were written. How do the writers take into consideration the context of the situation?

CHAPTER 3

Critical Thinking: Seeing with a Writer's Eye

This chapter explores the relationship between good writing and good thinking. You will learn the definition of critical thinking and how to see with a writer's eye while acquiring strategies for developing critical thinking and how to avoid common thinking errors.

It is part of the business of the writer . . . to examine attitudes, to go beneath the surface, to tap the source.

—JAMES BALDWIN

WHAT IS CRITICAL THINKING?

Good writing and good thinking go hand in hand. Effective writing requires more than paraphrasing what you have read or seen on television. It is more than a rush of thoughts and feelings. Too often we respond to ideas and experiences without examining our assumptions. We allow runaway emotions to colour our judgment and guide our decisions. We buy a product because we like the name or admire the celebrity featured on the box. We confuse opinions with facts, accept statistics without question, and allow stereotypes to influence our evaluations. In short, we let our existing perceptual world short-circuit our thinking and rush to judgment:

Ted had a heart attack; he should have stopped smoking ten years ago.

Rahmin's parents sent him to an Islamic school in Pakistan; I had no idea they supported terrorism.

These statements probably made sense to the people who made them, but close inspection reveals flaws in logic. Smoking is bad for the heart, but it is not the only cause of heart disease. Ted's weight or an inherited condition may be more to blame for his heart attack than smoking. Madrassahs in Pakistan have been known to be operated by radical Islamists, but not all Islamic schools in Pakistan are extremist and not everyone who sends a child to a religious school in Pakistan supports terrorism.

Good writing goes beneath the surface to see things others may have overlooked or misunderstood. To determine your purpose, analyze the perceptual world of your readers, develop effective strategies, and achieve your goals, you will have to develop critical thinking skills. Critical thinking moves beyond casual observation and immediate reactions. Instead of simply responding with what you *believe* or *feel* about a subject, critical thinking guides you to *think*—to examine issues fully and objectively, test your own assumptions for bias, seek additional information, consider alternative interpretations, ask questions, and delay judgment.

How to See with a Writer's Eye

Good writers are not passive—they don't simply record immediate responses. They *look closely, ask questions, analyze, make connections,* and *think*. Learning to see with a writer's eye benefits not just those who write for a living but all professionals. In any career you choose, success depends on keen observation and in-depth analysis. An information-driven society depends on people who can examine and solve problems instead of simply responding with memorized behaviours learned from strict training. A skilled physician, for example, detects minor symptoms in a physical or follows up on a patient's complaint to ask questions that lead to a diagnosis others might miss. A successful stockbroker observes overlooked trends and conducts research to detect new investment opportunities.

Close observation is the first step in critical thinking. Detailed observation helps not only novelists but also scientists. In his essay "Take This Fish and Look at It" (page 171), Samuel Scudder relates the lesson taught him by Professor Louis Agassiz. Instead of lecturing, Agassiz told his new student to take a fish from a specimen jar, stating, "Look at it . . . by and by I will ask what you have seen." After examining the specimen for ten minutes, Scudder felt he "had seen all that could be seen in that fish" and sought out his professor. Learning that Agassiz had left the building, he returned to the fish and looked at it for over an hour. When Agassiz came back to question Scudder, the professor was unimpressed with his student's observations. "You have not looked very carefully . . . you haven't even seen one of the most conspicuous features of the animal, which is plainly before your eyes as the fish itself; look again, look again!" Still dissatisfied with his student's observations, Agassiz instructed Scudder to try the next day and the next:

> For three long days he placed that fish before my eyes, forbidding me to look at anything else, or to use any artificial aid. "Look, look, look," was his repeated injunction.
>
> This was the best . . . lesson I ever had—a lesson whose influence has extended to the details of every subsequent study; a legacy the Professor had left to me, as he has left it to so many others, of inestimable value, which we could not buy, with which we cannot part.

By examining his subject closely, moving beyond first impressions, Scudder was able to identify the subtle complexities of his specimen.

Asking questions can also stimulate critical thinking. Questions can help you become a critical consumer of information and a better writer as you test the validity of assumptions. Consider a passage from a first-year student essay:

Canada must restrict immigration. Thousands of people are coming to this country, taking jobs and running businesses while Canadians are out of work. A lot of these people don't even speak English. With a recession deepening, this country should promise jobs to people who have lived here and paid taxes, not to new arrivals who are willing to work cheap.

The thesis—that Canada must restrict immigration—is clearly stated. But where is the proof? The student mentions "millions of immigrants"—but is there a more precise number? Just how many people are we talking about? What evidence is there that immigrants "take jobs" from others? Could they create jobs that others wouldn't take? Does the country "promise" jobs to anyone? What relationship is there between paying taxes and being qualified for a job? Do immigrants really "work cheap"? A thesis makes an assertion; it states a point of view. But without credible support, it remains only an opinion.

Strategies for Increasing Critical Thinking

There is no quick method of enhancing critical thinking, but you can challenge yourself to develop a writer's eye by asking questions to improve your prewriting, drafting, and editing skills.

1. **Why have you selected this topic?** Be wary of writing about "important" issues such a capital punishment, gun control, or global warming. Unless you have developed a unique angle, you are likely only to reproduce previously stated ideas. Look around and write about topics that might have been forgotten or ignored.

2. **Have you looked at your topic closely?** First impressions can be striking but misleading. Examine your subject closely, asking questions, probing beneath the surface. Look for patterns; measure similarities and differences.

3. **Have you rushed to judgment?** Postpone making evaluations or judgments until you have examined your subject objectively. Collect evidence but avoid drawing conclusions until you have analyzed your findings and observations.

4. **Do you separate facts from opinions?** Don't confuse facts, evidence, and data with opinions, claims, and assertions. Opinions are judgments that must be supported with adequate proof; they are not evidence.

5. **Are you aware of your assumptions?** Assumptions are ideas we accept or believe to be true. It is nearly impossible to divorce ourselves from what we have been taught, but you can sharpen your critical thinking skills if you acknowledge your assumptions. Avoid relying too heavily on a single assumption—that IQ tests measure intelligence, that poverty causes crime, that television is a bad influence on children.

If Canada limited immigration, would the unemployed be hired in the place of immigrants? Do immigrants become valuable consumers? Do immigrants help to sustain multicultural values and Canada's appreciation of linguistic diversity? Do they help us to communicate and compete in a global marketplace? Do immigrant-run businesses create jobs for Canadian-born citizens?

Critical thinking reveals that the student needs to conduct research and refine his or her arguments. In addition, the writer should consider what opponents will say. Can he or she call for restrictions on immigration without appearing to be racist? What proof can be offered to support the need for restrictions?

Critical thinking can help generate insight into even minor subjects. Instead of commenting on "more important" women's issues such as sexual harassment or abortion, Emily Prager considers the Barbie doll (see page 132). In analyzing the significance of a popular toy, she reveals much about the way females are programmed to identify themselves as women. This short piece about a plastic toy is of more interest than a two-page article about sexual assault that only repeats widely held opinions.

COMMON ERRORS IN CRITICAL THINKING

When you attempt to understand problems, evaluate evidence, draw conclusions, and propose solutions, it is easy to make mistakes. These lapses in critical thinking include logical fallacies. In establishing your reader's perceptual world, developing your ideas, and interpreting information, avoid the following common mistakes.

Ignoring the Role of Coincidence

The degree of coincidence in life is usually underestimated. Random or accidental occurrences are often viewed as being significant, evidence of a cause-and-effect relationship, an ability to predict the future, or proof of some grand conspiracy:

> "Tom has flipped that coin ten times and each time it came up heads. I'll bet a hundred dollars next time it comes up tails." (Each toss of a coin provides a 50/50 chance of one side facing up. Because each flip of the coin is a separate event, one toss or a thousand previous tosses have no influence on future attempts. The chance that the coin will turn up tails on the eleventh try is still 50 percent.)

Mathematicians use this simple example to show how frequently coincidences occur. Counting February 29, there are 366 possible birthdays. To have a 100 percent guarantee that at least two people in a group share the same birthday, the smallest number of people needed is 367. With 367 people, it is clear that at least two people must have the same birthday since there are only 366 days to go around. If you ask a class, "What's the smallest number of people needed to guarantee that there is a 50 percent probability that two people share the same birthday?"

most students would guess 184, or half of 367. The actual number is only 23. With only 23 people there is a 50/50 chance that two people in the group were born on the same day. Coincidence occurs far more often than the general public and many experts realize.

Hasty Generalizations or Jumping to Conclusions

If we believe or suspect something to be true, we may be tempted to make a rash judgment based on limited evidence:

> "My new Toyota needs brakes after 1,000 kilometres. My cousin's Nissan is six months old and needs a new transmission. The quality of Japanese cars has slipped." (Japan manufactured millions of vehicles last year. This conclusion is based on two cars and fails to consider owner misuse. A fast check of the ratings in *Consumer Reports* might disprove this conclusion.)

> "Cuba is a rip-off! Everyone I know who has vacationed there had a terrible time." (The evidence seems overwhelming because "everyone" you know who has visited Cuba regrets the trip. But just how many people does "everyone" amount to—3, 5, even 50? Because Cuba is a popular Canadian tourist destination, can we automatically assume that it is a "rip-off"?)

To avoid jumping to conclusions, ask yourself if you have assembled enough data, then examine alternative interpretations. *Don't rush to judgment.*

Relying on Anecdotal Evidence

One form of jumping to conclusions often appears in misleading advertisements and fraudulent claims:

> "Smoking can't be that bad for your health. Both my grandfathers were heavy smokers, and they lived past 80 and never developed cancer or heart disease." (These grandfathers may be among the lucky smokers—for example, Winston Churchill. But a few exceptions fail to counter the overwhelming evidence that smoking causes fatal diseases. The fact that some people win at Russian roulette does not diminish its danger.)

Avoid relying on testimonials or a parade of test cases. Individual stories can be impressive but misleading. You might unearth a half-dozen homeless McGill University graduates and argue that higher education is worthless. Likewise, the fact that a number of celebrities dropped out of high school does not prove that dropouts face a successful future. A collection of exceptions does not refute a general truth or trend. The majority of people who gamble lose—no matter how many winners are featured in casino commercials.

Mistaking Time Relationships for Cause and Effect (*post hoc, ergo propter hoc*)

Events occur in time, whether measured in nanoseconds or millions of years. Just because something precedes an event does not mean it was a causal factor. This mistake, often referred to by the Latin phrase *post hoc, ergo propter hoc (after this, therefore because of this)*, is easy to make because dramatic events or compelling evidence appear to support a claim:

> "Don't take your car to Quikee Lube! I took my car in for an oil change and the transmission went out three days later." (The evidence seems clear-cut. Your car ran fine until those mechanics at Quikee Lube touched it. Now it needs major repairs. But changing the oil would have nothing to do with the transmission—which may have been destined to fail in a few days.)

As with hasty generalizations, look for alternative explanations.

Making Faulty Comparisons (False Analogies)

Comparisons are the weakest form of argument. Because no two situations are exactly alike, avoid making judgments based on limited or selected evidence:

> "If we can fly to the moon, why can't we cure AIDS?" (This reasoning ignores the complex differences between engineering and medicine.)

> "We should legalize marijuana because Prohibition failed against alcohol." (The same reasoning could be used to justify legalizing anything—crack, child pornography, machine guns, or prostitution.)

Assuming Trends Will Continue, Making "Slippery Slope" Judgments

We often look to past performance to judge future events: good students can be counted on to do well on upcoming tests; a winning CFL team can be predicted as a serious Grey Cup contender. But conditions and individuals change, and trends cannot be assumed to continue without alteration:

> "My baseball card collection is worth more than $2,000. Think how much it will be worth when our three-year-old is ready for college!" (Perhaps a baseball card collection is a good investment for college. But what gives those pieces of cardboard their value is demand. The fact that a baseball card collection has soared in value in the past is no guarantee that its value will continue to rise.)

Creating "Either-Or" Constructions

Often complex issues are oversimplified and only two alternatives are given, when in fact there are many others:

> "Employees must accept a 10 percent pay cut or the company will go bankrupt and close. A pay cut is better than losing a job." (The company may have problems and need more money, but cutting wages is only one remedy. Raising prices, increasing sales, selling assets, and limiting hours could also be solutions.)

False dualisms are often used to coerce people into accepting something unpleasant by making it appear to be the lesser of two evils.

Relying on False Authorities, Attacking Personalities, and Guilt by Association

Celebrity endorsements often attempt to use a person's image or popularity to lend credibility to an issue or product:

> "Vote for Maria Lafontaine. Her anticrime proposals were supported by Angelina Jolie, Avril Lavigne, and Stephen King." (An actress, a singer, and a novelist may be authorities in their fields, but they are not experts in law enforcement. Endorsements by lesser-known lawyers, police officers, and judges might carry more weight.)

Often negative associations are used to discredit something without genuine proof:

> "How can we consider accepting a budget offered by a man who just pleaded guilty to drunk driving?" (The issue at hand is the budget, not the behaviour of the person who developed it.)

Using Circular Reasoning (Begging the Question)

Neither assume that a premise is true nor offer a definition as proof:

> "This inefficient plant should be closed to save energy costs." (No proof is offered to demonstrate that the plant is inefficient.)

Making Emotional and Irrelevant Statements (Red Herrings)

The term *red herring* comes from the ancient practice of farmers dragging fish across their fields to disrupt fox hunts. Chasing the scent of the fox, hunting dogs would be confused by the pungent smell and run in circles, putting an end to the stampede of hunters about to trample a farmer's crop. People sometimes attempt to dodge issues by raising emotionally charged but unrelated issues:

> "Requiring public school students to wear uniforms is repulsive in a democracy. We should encourage individual expression, not conformity. We don't need a nation of brown-shirted Hitler Youth goose-stepping on our playgrounds." (Conjuring up images of Nazism offers no proof that school uniforms have a negative influence on students or society.)

Red-herring arguments often stem from desperation. Losing one argument, people will raise issues from past arguments, usually ones where they have been proven right, to distract attention.

WRITING **ACTIVITIES**

1. Select a recent editorial and examine it for lapses in critical thinking. Does the writer make statements that rest on untested assumptions, false analogies, or insufficient data? Write a critique, commenting on the writer's use of logic to support his or her views.

2. Select a topic from the list on pages 650–651 and identify the types of errors in critical thinking you might face in addressing this issue.

3. Examine an evening or two of news talk shows. How many guests engage in arguments that are laced with errors in critical thinking? Can you identify people who attack personalities, use anecdotal evidence, and make faulty comparisons? Do interviewers or guests try to persuade viewers by using circular reasoning or creating false "either-or constructions"?

✔ CRITICAL THINKING **CHECKLIST**

Examine Your Writing for Evidence of Critical Thinking

✔ Have you carefully examined your subject or relied solely on casual observation?

✔ Is your main idea clearly and logically stated?

✔ Have you collected enough information to make judgments?

✔ Are your sources reliable and unbiased?

✔ Have you considered alternative interpretations?

✔ Have you avoided errors in critical thinking such as imprudent, hasty generalizations?

E-WRITING

Exploring Critical Thinking Online

The Internet presents a range of sources dedicated to critical thinking, ranging from sites maintained by academic organizations to those created by individual teachers posting information for their students.

1. Using InfoTrac® College Edition or one of your library's databases, enter *critical thinking* as a search term and locate articles that may assist you in your writing course and other classes.

2. Locate the online version of a national or local newspaper and review recent editorials. Can you detect any lapses in critical thinking? Do any editorials rely on hasty generalizations, anecdotal evidence, faulty comparisons, circular reasoning, or false authorities?

3. To learn more about critical thinking, enter *critical thinking* as a search term in a general search engine, such as AltaVista, Google, or Yahoo!, or enter one or more of the following terms:

coincidence	anecdotal evidence
post hoc	circular reasoning
red herrings	guilt by association
hasty generalizations	fact and opinion

FOR FURTHER READING

Barnet, Sylvan, and Hugo Bedau. *Critical Thinking: Reading and Writing.*

Dauer, Francis Watanabe. *Critical Thinking: An Introduction to Reasoning.*

Hirschberg, Stuart. *Essential Strategies of Argument.*

Packer, Nancy Huddleston, and John Timpane. *Writing Worth Reading: The Critical Process.*

Paulos, John Allen. Innumeracy: *Mathematical Illiteracy and Its Consequences.*

Rosenwasser, David, and Jill Stephens. *Writing Analytically.*

E-SOURCES

The Critical Thinking Community
http://www.criticalthinking.org/resources/articles/

Logical Fallacy
http://www.answers.com

York University Counselling and Development Centre
http://www.yorku.ca/cdc/lsp/readingonline/read4.htm

COMPANION WEBSITE

See **http://www.transcanadawriter.nelson.com** for additional information on critical thinking.

CHAPTER 4

Pre(liminary) Writing: Getting Started

This chapter explores the importance of preliminary writing in developing ideas. It discusses a variety of prewriting strategies, such as freewriting and brainstorming, to help you generate ideas while focusing toward a topic.

WHAT IS PREWRITING?

Prewriting refers to preliminary, exploratory, or experimental writing—writing that helps you get started, identify new ideas, sharpen your skills of observation, and indicate areas requiring further research. Writing is more than a means to show what you know or to create a document. It also can be a method for discovering topics and exploring ideas. Like an artist making quick sketches before beginning a mural, you can test ideas, explore a range of topics, list ideas, and get a feel for your subject. Prewriting can help you save time by quickly determining which ideas are worth developing and which should be discarded. *Prewriting puts critical thinking into action.*

PREWRITING STRATEGIES

People think in different ways, so it is not surprising that writers use a number of strategies to discover and develop ideas. Prewriting can be highly focused or totally open. Review these methods and experiment with them. Feel free to combine strategies to create your own method.

Freewriting

Freewriting records your thoughts, ideas, impressions, and feelings without interruption and without any concern for spelling, grammar, punctuation, or even logic. Don't confuse freewriting with writing a rough draft of an essay. Freewriting is a method of discovering ideas, rather like talking to yourself. It has no direction: it can skip from one topic to another without rational transitions; it may contain contradictory statements. Freewriting produces "running prose," like the tape recording of a rambling telephone conversation. The goal is to sketch out ideas as fast as you can write.

Sit down with a piece of paper or at a computer and start writing. Some experts suggest writing nonstop for at least five minutes. If you can't think of anything to write, draw Os and Xs or type gibberish. The main thing is to keep the process going until you can think of something to say, and don't worry about errors. Let one idea remind you of another. Stay open and remember, at this stage there are no bad ideas.

Having spent the evening searching the Internet for material for a paper, a student switched to a word processing program and rapidly recorded her thoughts on the Internet:

> The Internet links anyone to the world. A university student, sitting in a dorm or libary, can connect to sources in New York, London, or Tokyo. Web pages link you to sources you would never find on your own or now about. Within fifteen minutes tonight I printed off twenty pages of information that would take hours to find in a conventional library. The interent is the ultimate consumer guide. I could find online catalogs and read product descriptions and prices for things I thought about buying for xmas gifts and presents. I could even check sticker prices on new cars. Xxxxxxxxxxxxxxxx xxxxxxxxx.

> But switching from web page to web page, bieng hit with all kinds of data from around the owrld wears off after a while. The internet is exciting but like having cable TV, you get used to having 80 channels instead of four or five.

> But one wonders. If children have trouble reading, what will the internet provide books don't? The internet bombards us with statistics and facts. The real question is can people analyze it? Do we have the wisdom to know what to make of all this material. I see students in the lib. Get excited as they see the stacks of information slipping from the printers. But like students forty years ago who were the first to be able to use a Xerox machine and copy an article instead of haivng to take notes—I wonder what will they do with all this informaiton when they get home?

> Wisdom vs. Knowledge. X xxxxxxxx x xxxx x Being able to synehisize data. xxxxxxxxxx

This freewriting is a loose, repetitive, and misspelled collection of ideas, switching from the Internet to cable television without connection. But within the text there are the germs of ideas that could lead to a good essay about the Internet.

Advantages

- Freewriting is a good technique to help you overcome writer's block. By giving yourself the freedom to write anything—even meaningless symbols—you can force yourself to overcome the idea that every time you sit down to write you must come up with significant insights and flawless prose.

- Freewriting is useful when you simply have no idea what to write about. It can help you discover a subject by free association.

Disadvantages

- Because of its unrestricted nature, freewriting can spin off a lot of interesting but inappropriate ideas. You may find yourself writing off track. Keep in mind your instructor's guidelines, and write with your reader in mind.

- Freewriting can be tiring. Feel free to list or cluster ideas to save time. Don't feel obligated to write in complete sentences.

WRITING **ACTIVITY**

Freewriting

Select one of the following issues and write about it for at least five minutes without stopping. Don't worry about making sense, keeping on topic, or connecting ideas. Remember, this is an exploration of ideas. The topic is simply a catalyst, a jumping-off point. Let your free associations flow.

your hometown	campus child care	roommates	reality TV shows
job interviews	blind dates	student loans	death penalty
best friends	success	cable news	first day at work
gay rights	binge drinking	the Internet	outsourcing

Brainstorming

Brainstorming is another method of finding ideas to write about. Brainstorming can take different forms, the most simple being making lists. As in freewriting, there is no attempt to be selective. You write down every idea you can come up with, whether it makes sense or not. The purpose is not to plan a paper but to develop ideas. As with freewriting, there is no need to worry about spelling and grammar at this point.

You can use brainstorming to discover ideas for a personal essay or a research paper. A psychology student searching for a subject for a term paper might begin listing thoughts and topics:

mental illness—schizophrenia

inability to function in society

insanity defence

mental illness/homelessness

mentally ill off medication

public disturbances by mental patients

institutions/group homes

commitment laws decision to protect patients against their will

human rights versus incarceration without trial

committing the homeless to mental health institutions for their own safety

Through brainstorming the student moves from the general topic of mental illness and legal issues to a subject suitable for a research paper—institutionalizing homeless mentally ill patients. With further prewriting, he or she can develop this topic to compare past and present practices, argue for more group homes, study the causes of homelessness, or debate the merits of a local ordinance.

Brainstorming can help you develop writing even when the topic is clearly defined and the context is fixed.

Advantages

- Like freewriting, brainstorming can help you get started when you have no topic in mind.
- Brainstorming allows you to jot down ideas rapid fire, freeing you from the need to write complete sentences.
- Brainstorming can quickly identify information needed to support your point of view.

Disadvantages

- You may find that brainstorming produces nothing more than a shopping list of unrelated ideas. Remember, you can combine other techniques such as freewriting, to flesh out superficial ideas, and clustering, to organize and prioritize ideas.
- Brainstorming can lead you far astray from an assigned topic. Keep your syllabus or instructor's guidelines in front of you to help focus your train of thought.

WRITING **ACTIVITY**

Brainstorming

Select a column of topics from below and build on it, adding your own ideas. Jot down your thoughts as quickly as possible. Allow your thoughts to flow freely. Do not worry about changing direction or coming up with an entirely different subject.

men/women	success	campus housing
attitudes about relationships	careers	dorms/off campus
ending relationships	salaries	having your own apt.
how men and women cope with failed relationships	the perfect first job	advantages/disadvantages of living alone

Asking Questions

Asking questions is another method of exploring ideas. Questions can help you focus your thoughts, identify a thesis, and discover needed support. For over a century reporters, writers who work with tight deadlines, have been trained to approach a news story by asking the Five W's—Who? What? Where? When? Why? Asking questions can help you avoid writing in circles while highlighting important issues.

A student in a literature class has been assigned to write about Willa Cather's short story "Paul's Case":

Why did Paul commit suicide at the end?

Why didn't Paul have any friends?

Why did Paul like his job at the opera house?

Cather tells readers that Paul had sisters, but he never thinks about them—what does that reveal about his character?

What kind of relationship does Paul have with his father?

Was Paul's father a good parent?

Was Paul gay?

Cather wrote this story about a teenage suicide in 1904—what relevance does it have today?

Asking questions can help identify ideas and focus assignments such as description, narration, or persuasion. Asking questions also can help target other forms of prewriting, giving direction to your freewriting and brainstorming. In addition, questions can help spark critical thinking. Exploring the "why's" and "how's" of people, places, and events can help you move beyond simply recording first impressions and superficial observations.

Advantages

- Asking questions can help transform a topic into a thesis by directing you to state an opinion or take a position.
- Questions, if carefully worded, force you to think and test your preconceived notions and attitudes.
- Questions reveal needed information, guiding you to conduct research.

Disadvantages

- Questions are not necessarily effective in provoking thought. Pat questions can lead to simple answers. If your answers simply restate what you already know or believe, write tougher questions or try another prewriting method.
- Asking too many questions can lead you on a scattered mission. Edit your questions when you complete your list. Don't feel obligated to consider every question you develop.

Clustering

Clustering is a visually oriented type of freewriting that explores ideas diagrammatically on a sheet of paper or computer screen. It is a form of directed doodling or informal charting. Instead of listing ideas or writing in paragraphs, sketch your ideas on paper, as if arranging

▣ WRITING **ACTIVITY**

Asking Questions

Select one of the topics below and develop as many questions as you can. If you find yourself blocked, choose another topic or create one of your own. List as many questions as you can and don't worry about repeating yourself.

campus crime	credit cards	computers	health care
prisons	stalking laws	online dating	fashion
mobile phone etiquette	health clubs	divorce	media images of women

Look over your questions and circle those that suggest interesting topics for papers.

index cards on a table. People who use clustering often develop unique visual markers—using rectangles, arrows, and circles to diagram their ideas.

Thinking about his sister's decision to adopt a baby from China, a student clustered a series of observations and questions:

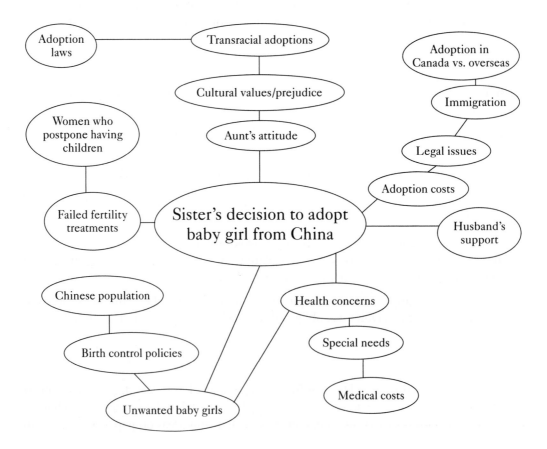

In this case clustering helps chart the positive and negative elements of transracial adoptions.

Advantages

- Clustering is suited to people who think spatially and find it easier to draw rather than write.
- Clustering is a good method to explore topics for comparison or classification papers.
- Clustering can save time. Freewriting, brainstorming, and asking questions list ideas in the order in which they occur to the writer rather than in relationship to each other. These ideas have to be examined and reorganized. Clustering allows you to create several lists or groupings, ranking ideas in importance and immediately showing links between related ideas.
- Clustering can help place ideas in context. You can group ideas in columns to contrast advantages and disadvantages or create a spectrum, showing the range of ideas.

Disadvantages

- The creative design elements of clustering can distract from ideas and organization. Keep the design simple. Don't waste your time using rulers to draw arrows or make perfect squares and circles. If you prewrite on a computer, don't bother using clip art.
- Clustering can be an excellent device for organizing ideas but may not help you get started. Use freewriting or ask questions to start the flow of ideas, then arrange them with clustering techniques.

WRITING **ACTIVITY**

Clustering

Select one of the following topics. Use a blank sheet of paper to record and arrange your ideas. You may wish to list pros and cons in separate columns or use a simple pie chart to split up a complex or confusing topic. Connect related ideas with arrows. Use different shapes and colours to distinguish contrasting ideas. Remember, clustering is a means to an end. Don't allow your artwork to get in the way of your thinking or take too much time. Neatness does not count.

computer hackers	being laid off	worst/best jobs
role models	airport security	teen pregnancy
violence on TV	singles' bars	fast food
the stock market	poverty	eating disorders
diets	having children	electronic games

Strategies for *Prewriting*

1. Write as often as you can.
2. Get in the habit of asking questions and listing ideas and observations.
3. Make notes of interesting subjects you see on television and clip newspaper and magazine articles that could serve as writing prompts.
4. Review upcoming assignments and make lists of possible topics.
5. Experiment with different forms of prewriting and feel free to blend them to develop your own style.
6. Save your notes. Ideas that you might discard for one paper might aid you in developing a topic for a future assignment.

E-WRITING

Exploring Prewriting Strategies Online

The Internet offers a number of valuable prewriting resources. Websites range from those maintained by academic organizations to those created by individual teachers posting information for their students.

1. Using InfoTrac® College Edition or one of your library's databases, enter *prewriting strategies* as a search term to locate articles that may assist you in your writing course and other classes.
2. Using a search engine such as AltaVista, Google, or Yahoo!, enter key words such as *prewriting, freewriting,* and *brainstorming* to locate current websites.
3. Familiarize yourself with your library's online databases and resources, such as encyclopedias. Checking a fact or reference can often help trigger ideas for an assignment or prevent you from wasting time.

FOR FURTHER READING

Lamm, Kathryn. *10,000 Ideas for Term Papers, Projects, Reports, and Speeches.*

E-SOURCES

University of Guelph Online Learning Commons
http://www.learningcommons.uoguelph.ca/ByTopic/Writing/WritingPaper/index.html

The University of Kansas Writing Center
http://www.writing.ku.edu/students/guides/.shtml

Online Writing Lab at Purdue University
http://owl.english.purdue.edu/handouts/general

University of Toronto—Advice on Academic Writing
http://www.utoronto.ca/writing/essay.html

COMPANION WEBSITE

See **http://www.transcanadawriter.nelson.com** for additional information on prewriting strategies.

CHAPTER 5

The Thesis

This chapter focuses on the importance of a strong thesis and how to produce one. It first defines a thesis and distinguishes strong thesis statements from weak ones. It then discusses where to locate the thesis in the context of the essay as a whole and the difference between explicit, evolving, and implied thesis statements. After providing tips on ways to develop a thesis, it then explores how to support a thesis statement.

I write because there is some lie I want to expose, some fact to which I want to draw attention, and my initial concern is to get a hearing.

—GEORGE ORWELL

WHAT IS A THESIS?

Most students are familiar with the term "thesis," but few can define or explain it accurately. Remember, effective writing has a clear purpose. An essay is never just "about" something. Whether the subject is global warming, your first job, Iraq, a high school coach, or Dance of the Happy Shades, your writing should make a point or express an opinion. The thesis is a writer's main or controlling idea. A thesis statement presents the writer's position in a sentence or two and serves as the document's mission statement. A thesis is more than a limited or narrowed topic; it expresses a specific point of view. It is a declaration, summarizing your purpose.

TOPIC	NARROWED TOPIC	THESIS STATEMENT
gun control	handgun ban	The city's proposed handgun ban will not prevent gang violence.
computer crime	consumer fraud	Consumers will resist shopping on the Internet until credit card security is assured.
campus housing	rehabbing dorms	Given the demand for more on-campus housing, the fifty-year-old men's dorm should be rehabilitated.
terrorism	cyber-terrorism	Security agencies must take steps to protect the Internet from cyber-terrorism.

◻ WRITING **ACTIVITY**

Develop a thesis statement for each of the following topics. Use prewriting techniques such as asking questions and clustering to explore ideas. Remember, your thesis should state a viewpoint, express an opinion, make an appeal, or suggest a solution, not simply make a factual statement or limit the subject.

1. Stem cell research

2. The aging baby boomers

3. Canada's role in the 21st century

4. The current job market for university graduates

5. DNA testing and criminal investigations

ELEMENTS OF A THESIS STATEMENT

An effective thesis statement comprises the following characteristics:

■ **It is usually stated in a single sentence.** This statement forms the core of the paper, focusing your point of view and clearly presenting it. Writing a thesis statement can be a critical part of the prewriting process, helping you move from a list or cluster of ideas to a specific paper. Thesis statements direct your writing.

■ **It asserts a considered viewpoint, not a topic.** A thesis statement expresses an informed opinion; it does not announce a subject or topic. The statement "There is a serious shortage of campus parking" describes a problem, but it does not express a thoughtful perspective on that problem. "Shuttle bus service should be expanded to alleviate the campus parking problem" serves as a thesis statement, clearly asserting a considered point of view.

■ **It limits the topic.** A thesis statement focuses the paper, limiting the scope of the writer's area of concentration. "Television is bad for children" states an opinion, but the subject is so broad that any essay would probably be limited to a list of superficial observations. A thesis such as "Television action heroes teach children that violence is an acceptable method of resolving conflicts" is limited enough to create a far more engaging paper.

■ **It indicates the kind of support to follow.** Opinions require proof. "Because of declining enrollment, the cinema course should be cancelled" indicates a clear cause-and-effect argument based on factual evidence, leading readers to expect a list of enrollment and budget figures.

■ **It often organizes supporting material.** The thesis statement "Exercise is essential to control weight, prevent disease, and maintain mental health" suggests that the body of the paper will be divided into three segments.

■ **It is precisely worded.** Because it expresses the writer's point of view in a single sentence, a thesis statement must be accurately stated. General terms such as *good, bad, serious,* and *important* weaken a thesis. Absolute statements can suggest that the writer is proposing a panacea. "Deadbolt locks should be installed in all dorm rooms to prevent crime" implies that a single mechanism is a foolproof method of totally eradicating all crime. "Deadbolt locks should be installed in all dorm rooms to deter break-ins" is far more accurate and easier to support.

WRITING **ACTIVITY**

Revise the following thesis statements, increasing their precision.

1. Global competition is a challenge for many businesses.
2. Public schools must prepare students for the 21st century.
3. The media stereotypes minorities.
4. Canadians pride themselves on understanding other cultures.
5. Peer pressure can be negative.

LOCATING THE THESIS

Academic writing almost always requires a thesis statement "up-front"—that is, in the introduction, as opposed to a "detective novel approach," as it were, in which the main point is left to the end. In more general forms of writing, thesis statements are strategically placed, appearing where they will be most effective. Students are strongly encouraged to practise producing strong thesis statements in the introductions of essays.

■ **Placing the thesis at the opening** starts the essay with a strong statement, providing it with a clear direction and an outline of the supporting evidence. However, if the thesis is controversial, it may be more effective to open with supporting details and confront readers' objections before formally announcing the thesis. An essay that opens with the statement "We must legalize heroin" might easily be dismissed by people who would think the writer must be naive or insensitive to the pain of addiction, the spread of HIV, and other social problems stemming from drug abuse. However, if the essay first demonstrates the failure of current policies and argues that addiction should be treated as a medical rather than a legal issue, more readers might be receptive to the writer's call for legalization.

    In non-academic writing, thesis statements can emerge in the middle or at the end.

■ **Placing the thesis in the middle of the essay** allows a writer to introduce the subject, provide support, raise questions, and guide the reader into accepting a thesis that is then explained or defended. However, placing the thesis somewhere within the essay may weaken its impact because reader attention is strongest at the opening and closing paragraphs.

Writers sometimes highlight a thesis statement in the middle of an essay by placing it in a separate paragraph or using italics.

- **Placing the thesis at the end** allows a writer to close the essay with a strong statement. Delaying the thesis allows the writer to address reader objections and bias by providing narratives, examples, and statistics to support the conclusion. However, postponing the thesis will disappoint some readers who want a clear answer. Delaying the thesis can suggest to some readers that the writer's position cannot stand on its own and depends on a great deal of qualification.

Again, however, academic writing on the whole encourages thesis statements in the introductory paragraphs.

EXPLICIT, EVOLVING, AND IMPLIED THESES

Most writers present explicit thesis statements, but some use a series of sentences to develop their claims. In some instances, the writer's thesis is not formally stated but only implied or suggested.

Explicit Thesis Statements

In "Wasp Waists and Lotus Buds: The Corset Looks at Footbinding," Marni Stanley discusses a contradiction that arises in the work of 19th-century British women travel writers who became indignant about Chinese footbinding but ignored their own oppression through corseting. In the introduction, she presents an explicit thesis statement:

> While they campaigned hard to stop the mutilation caused by footbinding, they simultaneously denied any connection between it and the practices in their own culture—such as tight-lacing—which could also injure women in the name of beauty and marriage-marketability.

Explicit theses are best used in writing in the modes of argument and persuasion, comparison, and division and classification.

Advantages

- An explicit thesis statement is clear and concise. The writer's purpose is stated directly so that readers are not confused.
- An explicit thesis can be used to make a strong opening or closing statement.
- A concise, strongly worded statement is easily understood so that even a casual reader will quickly grasp the writer's main idea.

Disadvantages

- Explicit thesis statements can present a narrow interpretation or solution to a complex situation or problem. In many instances an evolving or implied thesis gives the writer greater freedom to discuss ideas and address possible objections.

- Because they are clear and direct, explicit theses can easily alienate readers with differing opinions. An evolving thesis allows the writer to explain or qualify opinions.

Evolving Thesis Statements

In "The Role of New Media in Social Change," Marshall McLuhan discusses the evolving impact on social conditions through technology's extension of the human body. But instead of stating his thesis in a single sentence, he develops his controlling ideas in a series of statements. He begins:

> From the Neolithic age until the advent of electromagnetic technology men have been extending their bodies technologically.

McLuhan then focuses on the distinctly different kind of extensions produced by the impact of electromagnetism on social organization, expanding his thesis:

> Whereas in the previous technologies of fragmented extensions of the body there had been typically a considerable gap in time between social action and the ensuing consequences and reactions, this gap of time has almost disappeared. . . . I suggest that the sensory typology of an entire population is directly altered by each and every new extension of the body or of the senses.

McLuhan concludes his essay with a final controlling statement that focuses on the relationship between social literacy and technology:

> I suggest that if we value this legacy of literacy, we shall need to take steps to maintain its existence by a fuller understanding of the role of new media in social change. Autonomy and freedom are best secured by a grasp of the new parameters of our condition.

Evolving thesis statements are best suited for complex or controversial subjects. They allow you to address an issue piece by piece or to present a series of arguments.

Advantages

- An evolving thesis lets a writer present readers with a series of controlling ideas, allowing them to absorb a complex opinion point by point.

- An evolving thesis can be useful in presenting a controversial opinion by slowly convincing readers to accept less threatening ideas first.

- An evolving thesis can help a writer tailor ideas to suit different situations or contexts. An evolving thesis can also be organized to address separate reader objections.

Disadvantages

- Because the statements are distributed throughout an essay, they can appear "scattered" and have less impact than a single direct sentence.

- Evolving theses can make a writer appear unsure of his or her points, as if he or she is reluctant to state a direct opinion.

Implied Thesis Statements

Essays with implied thesis statements do not have clear controlling ideas. They work best when the writer's evidence is so compelling that it does not require an introduction or explanation. Writers also use an implied thesis to challenge readers by posing an idea or presenting a problem without suggesting an interpretation or solution. Although you may not state a clear thesis statement in writing a description or telling a story, your essay should have a clear purpose, a direction. A thesis statement, though it may not appear on the page, can prevent an essay from becoming a list of random facts or a chain of unrelated events.

Advantages

- An implied thesis allows the writer's images and observations to represent his or her ideas. Implied thesis statements are common in descriptive and narrative writing.

- An implied thesis does not dictate an opinion but allows readers to develop their own responses.

- An implied thesis does not confront readers with bold assertions but allows a writer to slowly unfold controlling ideas.

Disadvantages

- Writing without an explicitly defined thesis can lead readers to assume ideas unintended by the writer.

- Writing that lacks a clear thesis statement requires careful reading and critical thinking to determine the writer's purpose. A strong thesis sentence in the introduction or closing of an essay makes the author's goal very clear.

Strategies for Developing Thesis Statements

1. **Develop a thesis statement while planning your essay.** If you cannot state your goal in a sentence or two, you may not have a clear focus regarding your purpose. Even if you decide to use an implied thesis, a clearly worded statement on your outline or at the top of the page can help keep your writing on track.

2. **Write your thesis statement with your reader in mind.** The goal of writing is not only to express your ideas but also to share them with others. Choose your words carefully. Be sensitive to your readers' perceptual world. Avoid writing biased or highly opinionated statements.

3. **Ensure that your thesis statement expresses a viewpoint.** Don't confuse making an announcement or a factual statement with establishing a thesis. Review the wording of the statement to see if it includes action verbs. Direct readers to take action, change their ideas, or alter their behaviour.

4. **Determine the best location for your thesis.** If you believe that most of your readers will be receptive to your views, placing the thesis at the opening may be appropriate. If your position is controversial or depends on establishing a clear context of support, delay your thesis by placing it in the middle or at the conclusion.

5. **Ensure that your thesis matches your purpose.** Persuasive arguments demand a strongly worded thesis statement, perhaps one that is restated throughout the essay. If your position is complex, you may wish to develop it by making partial thesis statements throughout the essay. If you are not motivating your readers to take specific action, you may wish to use an implied thesis. State your observations or evidence, and permit readers to develop their own conclusions.

6. **Test your thesis.** Ask a friend or acquaintance to consider your thesis statement. Is it precise? Does it seem logical? What kind of evidence would be needed to support it? Are there any words or phrases that seem awkward, unclear, or offensive? If your thesis statement seems weak, review your prewriting notes. You may need to further limit your topic or choose a new subject.

7. **Avoid making simple announcements or presenting narrowed topics.** The most common errors writers make in developing thesis statements include simply announcing the subject of a paper or presenting a narrowed topic:

ANNOUNCEMENTS:	My paper is about racial profiling.
	Snowboarding is a popular sport.
NARROWED TOPICS:	Police departments have been accused of racial profiling.
	Snowboarders are regarded as outlaws by traditional skiers.
IMPROVED THESIS STATEMENTS:	Police departments must develop methods to combat crime and prevent terrorism without resorting to racial profiling.
	Snowboarders and traditional skiers must learn to respect each other on the slopes.

▣ WRITING **ACTIVITIES**

1. Select three to five topics from pages 650–651 and write thesis statements to guide possible rough drafts. Ensure that your statements are opinions, not merely narrowed topics.

2. Skim through the entries in the Reader section of the book and locate thesis statements. Note where they are located and whether they are explicit, implied, or evolving.

3. Select an issue you have considered over a period of time and write a series of thesis statements illustrating your evolving viewpoints.

SUPPORTING A THESIS

What Is Support?

A thesis must be supported with evidence. Readers will appreciate your views only if you provide sufficient proof to convince them. The type of evidence you select depends on context: your goal, your reader, the discourse community, and the nature of the document. All writers—even those composing personal essays or memoirs—provide support for their ideas.

A student proposing a new computer system would have to provide factual support to create a convincing argument:

> ***The university must improve its computer system.*** This semester 400 students did not receive midterm grades because of a computer breakdown. The university e-mail system, which is critical to the distance learning department, malfunctioned for two weeks, preventing students from electronically submitting research papers. The eight-year-old system simply does not have the speed and capacity needed to serve the faculty, students, and administration. If the university is to attract students, maintain its programs, and offer new services, it must upgrade its computers.

The same student writing a personal narrative would use supporting details to paint a picture, set a mood, and express a feeling.

Writers verify their theses using various types of evidence, ranging from personal observations to statistics. Because each type of evidence has limitations (as you will see in the following sections), writers usually present a blend of personal observations and experience, examples, facts, testimony, and analogies.

Personal Observations

Personal observations are descriptive details and sensory impressions about a person, place, object, or condition. Writers can support a thesis or controlling idea by supplying readers with specific details. The thesis that "Westwood High School must be renovated" can be supported with detailed observations about leaking roofs, faulty wiring, broken windows, and defective plumbing.

Advantages

- Personal observations can be powerful as long as they are carefully selected and well organized. To be effective, writers must choose words carefully, being aware of their connotations.

- Personal observations can be used to balance objective facts by adding human interest and personal narratives, allowing the writer to inject himself or herself into the writing.

Disadvantages

- Personal observations are subjective. They often require outside evidence such as facts, statistics, or testimony to be convincing.

- Personal observations may be inappropriate in objective reports. Writers often include material they observed without using first-person references such as "I" or "me."

Personal Experiences

Like personal observations, accounts of your own life can be convincing support. For example, as a university student, you have great authority in discussing higher education.

Advantages

- Personal experiences can be emotionally powerful and commanding because the writer is the sole authority and expert.

- Personal experiences are effective support in descriptive and narrative writing.

- Individual accounts can humanize abstract issues and personalize objective facts and statistics.

Disadvantages

- Personal experience, no matter how compelling, is only one person's story. As with personal observations, personal experience can be supported with the introduction of outside evidence such as expert testimony, facts, and statistics.

- Personal experience, unless presented carefully, can seem self-serving and can weaken a writer's argument. Before including your own experiences, consider whether readers will think you are making a self-serving appeal, asking readers to accept ideas or take actions that primarily benefit only you.

Examples

Examples are specific events, individuals, or situations that represent a general trend, type, or condition. A writer supporting the right to die might relate the story of a single terminally ill patient to illustrate the need for euthanasia. The story of a single small business could illustrate an economic trend.

Advantages

- Specific cases or situations can illustrate an issue and humanize a complex or abstract problem. They often make effective introductions.
- Examples can be used to demonstrate facts and statistics that tend to be static lists.
- Examples allow you to introduce narratives that can make a fact-filled paper more interesting and readable.

Disadvantages

- Examples can be misleading or misinterpreted. Examples must be representative. For instance, a single mugging, no matter how violent, does not prove that a crime wave is sweeping a campus. Avoid selecting isolated incidents or exceptions to a general condition.
- Because they are highlighted, examples can sometimes be distorted into being viewed as major events instead of illustrations. Another danger is that examples can create false generalizations and overlook complex subtleties. Examples should be placed in context with statistics or a disclaimer.

Facts

Facts are objective details that are either directly observed or gathered by the writer. The need to renovate a factory can be demonstrated by presenting evidence from inspection reports, maintenance records, and a manufacturer's repair recommendations.

Advantages

- Facts provide independent support for a writer's thesis, suggesting that others share his or her conclusions.

- Facts are generally verifiable. A reader who may doubt a writer's personal observations or experiences can check factual sources.

- Because of their objectivity, facts can be used to add credibility to personal narratives.

Disadvantages

- Facts, like examples, can be misleading. Don't assume that a few isolated pieces of information can support your thesis. Citing a list of celebrities who dropped out of high school does not disprove the value of education.

- Facts, in some cases, must be explained to readers. Lengthy or technical explanations of facts may distract or bore readers.

Testimony (Quotations)

Testimony, the observations or statements by witnesses, participants, or experts, allows writers to interject other voices into their document, whether in the form of direct quotations or paraphrases.

Advantages

- Testimony, like factual support, helps verify a writer's thesis by showing that others share his or her views and opinions.

- Testimony by witnesses or participants adds a human dimension to facts and statistics.

- Expert testimony, usually in the form of quotations, enhances a writer's credibility by indicating that highly respected individuals agree with his or her thesis.

Disadvantages

- Comments by people who observed or participated in an event are limited by the range of their experiences.

- Witnesses and participants interpret events based on their perceptual worlds and may be less than objective.

- Expert testimony can be misleading. Don't take quotes out of context. Don't assume that you can impress readers by simply sprinkling a paper with quotations from famous people. Statements by experts must be meaningful, relevant, and accurate.

Analogies (Comparisons)

Analogies compare similar situations, people, objects, or events to demonstrate the validity of the thesis. The thesis "AIDS prevention programs will reduce the incidence of infection" can be supported by pointing to the success of similar programs to combat sexually transmitted diseases or teenage pregnancy.

Advantages

- Analogies can introduce new topics by comparing them to ones readers find familiar or understandable.

- Comparisons can counter alternative theses or solutions by showing their failures or deficiencies in contrast to the writer's ideas.

Disadvantages

- Analogy is a weak form of argument. Because no two situations are exactly alike, analogy is rarely convincing in itself.

- Comparisons depend on readers' perceptual worlds. Suggesting that an urban planner's design should be adopted because it will transform a city's green space into another High Park assumes that readers know Toronto's High Park and find it desirable.

Statistics

Statistics are factual data expressed in numbers and can validate a writer's thesis in dramatic terms readers can readily appreciate. However, although statistics represent facts and not an opinion, they can be very deceptive. Numbers can be used to provide strikingly different perceptions.

Advantages

- Statistics can distill a complex issue into a single dramatic statement:

  Each cigarette takes seven minutes off a smoker's life.

- Statistics can be easily remembered and repeated to others. Readers may be unable to remember lengthy paragraphs or sophisticated reasoning but can easily recall a statistic and share it with others.

Disadvantages

- Because they are often misused, statistics are often distrusted by readers. Whenever you quote statistics, be prepared to explain where you obtained them and why they are reliable.

■ Although statistics can be dramatic, they can quickly bore readers. Long lists of numbers can be difficult for readers to absorb. Statistics can be easier to understand if presented in graphs, charts, and diagrams.

Strategies for Using Statistics

In gathering and presenting statistics, consider these questions:

1. **Where did the statistics come from?** Who produced the statistics? Is the source reliable?

2. **When were the statistics collected?** Information can become obsolete very quickly. Determine whether the numbers are still relevant.

3. **How were the statistics collected?** Public opinion polls are commonly used to represent support or opposition to an issue. How was the question worded? Was it objective or did it provoke a desired response? Did the polled students reflect the attitudes of the entire student body?

4. **Are the units being counted properly defined?** All statistics count some item— drunk-driving arrests, housing starts, defaulted loans, student dropouts, teenage pregnancies, or AIDS patients. In some cases confusion can occur if the items are not precisely defined.

5. **Do the statistics measure what they claim to measure?** The units being counted may not be accurate indicators. Comparing students' LSAT scores assumes that the tests accurately measure achievement.

6. **Are enough statistics presented?** A single statistic may be accurate but misleading.

7. **How are the statistics being interpreted?** Numbers alone do not tell the whole story.

WRITING ACTIVITY

List the types of evidence needed to support the following thesis statements.

1. Consumers will resist shopping on the Internet until credit card security is assured.

2. Greater gun control will reduce gang violence in Canada's large cities.

3. Transforming North America's "car culture" will go a long way toward reducing Canadian and American consumption of fossil fuels.

DOCUMENTING SOURCES

No matter how dramatic, evidence is not likely to impress readers unless they know its source. Chapter 22 details methods of using academic documentation styles, such as MLA (Modern Language Association) and APA (American Psychological Association) formats.

Documentation, usually mandatory in research papers, is useful even in short essays. Even informal notations can enhance your credibility.

Strategies for Using Evidence

Use these questions to evaluate the evidence you have assembled to support your thesis.

1. **Is the evidence suited to your thesis?** Review the writing context to determine what evidence is appropriate. Personal observations and experiences would support the thesis of an autobiographical essay. However, these subjective elements could weaken the thesis of a business report. The thesis "My aunt taught me the meaning of courage" can be supported by personal observations and narratives. But a thesis such as "Canada must protect itself from the threat of biological terrorism" demands expert testimony, statistics, and factual data to be convincing.

2. **Is the evidence accurate?** It may be possible to find evidence that supports your thesis—but are these quotations, facts, and statistics accurate? Are they current?

3. **Are the sources reliable?** Evidence can be gathered from innumerable sources but not all proof is equally reliable or objective. Many sources of information have political biases or economic interests and produce only data that support their views.

   In some instances, reliable and objective evidence is difficult to obtain. Highly partisan and controversial issues generate a great deal of information, much of it produced to support a particular viewpoint. You can persuade readers to accept your thesis if you balance sources and openly state that some evidence may be biased and subject to alternative interpretations.

4. **Is sufficient evidence presented?** To convince readers, you must supply enough evidence to support your thesis. A few isolated facts or quotations from experts are not likely to be persuasive.

   Examine your thesis carefully to see whether it can be separated into parts, and determine whether you have adequate proof for each section:

   The university should offer more Internet courses to increase enrollment.

   - The thesis suggests the current enrollment is unacceptable and must be increased—is there enough factual support to document this view?
   - Internet courses are offered as a proposed solution—are sufficient data offered to indicate their success in attracting new students?
   - Does the essay document why Internet courses are a better vehicle for increasing enrollment than alternative proposals such as advertising existing courses, expanding night school offerings, or creating new classes?

5. **Is the evidence representative?** To be intellectually honest, writers have to use evidence that is representative. You can easily assemble isolated facts, quotations taken out of context, and exceptional events to support almost any thesis.

   If you can support your thesis only with isolated examples and atypical instances, you may wish to question your conclusions.

   (Continued)

6. **Is the evidence presented clearly?** Although evidence is essential to support your thesis, long quotations and lists of statistics can be boring and counterproductive. Evidence should be readable. Outside sources should blend well with your own writing.

   Read your paper aloud to identify awkward or difficult passages.

7. **Does the evidence support the thesis?** Finally, ask yourself if the evidence you have selected really supports your thesis. In listing personal observations, collecting statistics, or searching for quotations, it is easy to be led astray from your original goal. Before including a particular piece of evidence, test it against your thesis.

   If your evidence does not directly support your thesis, review your prewriting notes and consider revising your thesis statement.

▣ WRITING **ACTIVITIES**

1. If you developed any thesis statements in the exercises on page 47, list the types of sources that would prove the best support.

2. Select a topic from pages 650–651 and list the kind of evidence readers would expect writers to use as support.

E-WRITING

Exploring Thesis Support Online

You can use the Internet to learn more about supporting a thesis.

1. Locate resources about specific types of evidence online or in your library's databases by using *statistics* and *personal testimony* as search terms.

2. Search newspapers and journals online and select a few articles and editorials. After identifying the theses, note how the authors presented supporting evidence.

3. Ask instructors in your various courses for websites to locate useful sources in various disciplines.

Exploring Thesis Statements Online

You can use the Internet to learn more about developing thesis statements.

1. Using a search engine such as AltaVista, Google, or Yahoo, enter *thesis statement* as a term and review the range of sources. You may wish to print out helpful websites.

2. Locate one or more newspapers online and scan through a series of recent editorials. Select a few articles on topics you are familiar with and examine the thesis statements.

Which sentence summarizes the editorial's main point or assertion? Where is it placed? Are the thesis statements explicit, evolving, or implied? Are they carefully worded?

3. Using InfoTrac® College Edition or one of your library's online databases, search for articles on gun control, abortion, capital punishment, or any other controversial topic. Can you identify the writers' thesis statements? Are they effective?

E-SOURCES

Using Thesis Statements
http://www.utoronto.ca/writing/thesis/html

How to Write a Thesis Statement
http://www.indiana.edu/~wts/ pamphlets/thesis_statement.shtml

Developing a Thesis Statement
http://www.wisc.edu/writing/Handbook/Thesis.html

Supporting Your Thesis
http://www.powa.org/thesis/supporting.html

Evaluating Web Pages
http://www.lib.berkeley.edu/TeachingLib/Guides/Internet/Evaluate.html

Evaluating Information Found on the Internet
http://www.library.jhu.edu/researchhelp/general/evaluating

COMPANION WEBSITE

See **http://www.transcanadawriter.nelson.com** for information on supporting a thesis.

CHAPTER 6

Organizing Ideas

This chapter looks at the importance of planning in the writing process. You will learn about formal and informal outlines as well as different patterns of arrangement, according to purpose and context. You will also learn about the differences in purpose and structure among the introduction, the body section, and the conclusion of an essay, with guidance on how to develop each. Finally, you will learn how to overcome organizational problems.

Planning a work is like planning a journey.

—H. J. TICHY

WHAT IS ORGANIZATION?

Whenever you write, you take readers on a journey—presenting facts, relating stories, sharing ideas, and creating impressions. Readers can follow your train of thought only if you provide them with a clear road map that organizes your thesis and evidence. Even the most compelling ideas will fail to interest readers if placed in a random or chaotic manner. The way you arrange ideas depends on context: your purpose, the audience, and the conventions of the discourse community. Some formal documents dictate a strict format that readers expect you to follow. But in most instances you are free to develop your own method of organization.

As you review the readings in this book, notice how writers organize their essays, providing transitions from one idea to another.

Once you have written a thesis statement and collected supporting material, create a plan for your paper. Prewriting techniques such as brainstorming, writing lists, and clustering can help establish ways to structure your essay. You do not have to develop an elaborate outline with Roman numerals and letters for every paper; a plan can be a simple list of reminders, much like a book's table of contents or a shopping list. A short narrative recalling a recent experience may require only a few notes to guide your first draft. But a complex research paper with numerous sources usually demands a more detailed outline to help you avoid getting lost. Like an artist making a sketch before attempting to paint a large mural, you can use an outline to get an overall view of your essay. Sketching out your ideas can help you identify potential problems, spot missing information, reveal irrelevant material, and highlight passages that would make a good opening or final remark.

INFORMAL AND FORMAL OUTLINES

Your outline is a means to an end, and often no one but you sees it. If your prewriting has clearly established the ideas in your mind, you may simply need a few notes to keep your writing on track. The student who worked for an insurance agency for a number of years needs only a few reminders to draft a comparison of two types of policies:

Whole Life and Term Insurance

Whole Life

—explain premiums

—savings & loan options

Term

—no savings

—lower rates

Conclusion—last point

A formal outline, however, can serve to refine your prewriting so that your plan becomes a detailed framework for the first draft. Formal outlines organize details and can keep you from drifting off topic. In addition, they provide a document an instructor or peer reviewer can work with. Few people may be able to decipher the rough notes you make for yourself, but a standard outline creates a clear picture of your topic, thesis, and evidence for others to review and critique:

Whole Life and Term Insurance

  I. Introduction: Whole life and term insurance

 II. Whole life insurance

    A. General description

      1. History

      2. Purpose

        a. Protection against premature death

        b. Premium payments include savings

    B. Investment feature

      1. Cash value accrual

      2. Loans against cash value

III. Term insurance

    A. General description

      1. History

      2. Purpose

         a. Protection against premature death

         b. Premium payments lower than whole life insurance

   B. Investment feature

      1. No cash value accrual

      2. No loans against cash value

   C. Cost advantage

      1. Lower premiums

      2. Affordability of greater coverage

IV. Conclusion

   A. Insurance needs of consumer

      1. Income

      2. Family situation

      3. Investment goals & savings

      4. Obligations

   B. Investment counselors' advice about coverage

Whether your plan is a simple list or a formal outline, it serves as a road map for the first draft and should focus on four main elements:

> Title
> Introduction
> Body or Development Section
> Conclusion

Because new ideas can occur throughout the writing process, your plan does not have to detail each element perfectly. You may not come up with an appropriate title or introduction until final editing. In planning, however, consider the impact you want each part of your paper to make. Consider the qualities of an effective title, introduction, body, and conclusion. Develop as complete a plan as you can, leaving blank spaces for future changes.

The Title

Titles play a vital role in creating effective essays. A strong title attracts attention, prepares readers to accept your thesis, and helps focus the essay. If you find developing a title difficult, simply label the paper (described in the next section) until you complete the first draft. As you write you may discover an interesting word or phrase that captures the essence of your essay and would serve as an effective title.

Writers use a variety of types of titles, including labels, thesis statements, questions, and creative statements.

Labels

Business reports, professional journals, student research papers, and government publications often have titles that clearly state the subject by means of a label:

> Italian Industrial Production—Milan Sector
> Bipolar Disorders: Alternative Drug Therapies
> Northrop Frye's Theory of the Imagination

- Labels should be as precisely worded as possible. Avoid vague or extremely general titles that simply announce a broad topic. Titles should reflect your focus.
- Labels are best suited for reports that are addressed to specific audiences, such as a professional association, corporate management, or government agency. Such titles usually fail to generate interest in general readers.
- Labels are generally objective and suited to documents that have to reflect the views and values of a large group. Although undramatic, accurate labels are not likely to confuse or alienate readers.

Thesis Statements

Titles can state or summarize the writer's thesis:

> Legalizing Drugs Will Not Deter Crime
> Why We Need to Understand Science

- Thesis statements are frequently used in editorials and political commentaries to openly declare a writer's point of view.
- Bold assertions attract attention but can also antagonize readers. If you sense that readers may not accept your thesis, it is better to first build your case through introducing background information or supporting details before stating a point of view.

Questions

Writers use questions to arouse interest without revealing their positions:

> Does Recycling Protect the Environment?
> Should This Student Have Been Expelled?

- Questions stimulate readers' interest, motivating them to consider the writer's answer. Because questions imply different responses, they can spark critical thinking and prompt readers to analyze their existing knowledge, values, and opinions.

- Questions are useful for addressing controversial issues because readers must evaluate the writer's evidence before learning his or her answer.

- Questions have to be carefully worded to be effective. Placing a question mark after a label will not make a topic more interesting.

Creative Statements

Writers sometimes use an attention-getting word or creative phrase to attract readers:

Pink Mafia: Women and Organized Crime
Sharks on the Web: Consumer Fraud on the Internet

- Creative titles, like questions, grab attention and motivate people to read items they might ignore. Magazine writers often use clever, humorous, or provocative titles to stimulate interest.

- Creative titles are usually unsuited to formal documents or reports. Creative wording may appear trivial, inappropriate, or biased and should be avoided in objective writing.

- The language used in a title should match the style and tone established by the publication and discourse community.

The Introduction

Introductions are crucial elements in essay writing. They often require a great deal of crafting and revision to get right because they serve a double function. Just as an entrance to a building both receives people from the outside and directs them to points inside, so too does an introduction meet readers coming from other social contexts and redirect their attention and expectations toward the discussion at hand. In other words, introductions require special attention to reader needs because of their double, transitional function. Effective introductions arouse attention, state what the essay is about, and prepare readers for what follows. In addition to stating the topic, the introduction can present background information and provide an overview of the entire essay.

Many writers find the first draft of an introduction difficult. If you don't have a strong introduction in mind, we suggest that you freewrite a working introduction with a thesis statement (see next section) to focus the remainder of the essay draft. This way you can revise the introduction as often as necessary.

In reviewing your initial version, look for quotes, facts, statements, or examples that will make a strong first impression. Avoid making general opening statements that serve as diluted titles: *This paper is about a dangerous trend happening in Canada today.*

Writers use a number of methods to introduce essays. You can begin with a thesis statement, a striking fact or statistic, a quotation, a brief narrative or example, or a question, among other possibilities.

Open with a Thesis Statement

- Opening with a thesis statement creates a strong first impression so that even a casual reader quickly understands the message. Declaring your thesis at the outset can inform or persuade an audience that is likely to skim or ignore much of the document's text.

- Like a title summarizing the writer's thesis, however, introductions that make a clear assertion may alienate readers, particularly if your topic or position is controversial. You may wish to present evidence or explain reasons before openly announcing your thesis.

Begin with Facts or Statistics

- In prewriting and planning, you may have come across an interesting fact or example that can quickly demonstrate the importance of your subject.

- The fact or statistic you select should be easy to comprehend and stimulate reader interest.

Use a Quotation

- Quotations allow you to present another voice, giving a second viewpoint. You can introduce expert opinion, providing immediate support for the upcoming thesis.

- Select quotations by authorities readers respect or people they can identify with. Quotations can humanize an issue by presenting a personal experience or opinion.

- Select relevant quotations. Avoid using famous sayings (by Shakespeare or Grey Owl, for example) because out of context they can be used to justify almost any point of view.

Open with a Brief Narrative or Example

- A short narrative personalizes complex topics and helps introduce readers to subjects that they might not initially find interesting.

- Narratives should be short and representative. An engaging example may distort readers' understanding and should be balanced with facts and statistics to place it in context.

Pose a Question

- An opening question, like one posed in the title, arouses attention by challenging and engaging readers, prompting them to consider your topic.

- Questions can introduce discussion of controversial topics without immediately revealing your opinion.

Body or Development Section

Once you introduce the subject, there are three basic methods of organizing the body of the essay: chronological, spatial, and emphatic. Just as writers often have unique composing styles, they often have different ways of viewing and organizing their material. The way you organize the body of the essay should reflect your thesis and train of thought. *Remember, place your most important ideas at the opening or ending of your paper. Do not bury the most important information in the middle of the document, which readers are most likely to skip or skim.* Within these general methods of organization, you may include portions using different modes. For example, an essay that primarily uses spatial organization may contain chronological sections.

Chronological: Organizing by Time

The simplest and often the most effective way of structuring an essay is to tell a story, relating events as they occurred. Narrative, process, cause-and-effect, and example essays commonly follow a chronological pattern, presenting evidence on a timeline. Biographies, history books, accident reports, and newspaper articles about current events are often arranged chronologically.

A student discussing the causes of Canada's Confederation might explain the gradual uniting of provinces, colonies, and territories as the result of a historical process, the outcome of a chain of events.

Thesis: The coalition of British colonies that became known as Canada's Confederation resulted from a growing economic, cultural, and ideological desire for security, independence, and government reform.

Outline

I. Introduction

II. The expanding colonies of British North America

    A. Rebellion in Upper Canada

    B. French–English tensions in Lower Canada

III. Responsible Government
    A. The old colonial system
    B. The new responsible system
IV. Economic Expansion and the Reciprocity Treaty
    A. The Reciprocity Treaty
        1. American trade
        2. British trade
    B. The railways
    C. Western promise
 V. The Union of the Canadas
    A. The coalition government
    B. The American threat: Civil War and the northern armies
    C. The Dominion of Canada
    Conclusion

Advantages of Chronological Order

■ Readers are accustomed to reading information placed in chronological order. Using a narrative form allows writers to demonstrate how a problem developed, relate an experience, or predict a future course of action.

■ Chronological organization does not have to follow a strict timeline. Dramatic events can be highlighted by using flash forwards and flashbacks.

Disadvantages of Chronological Order

■ Arranging evidence in a chronological pattern can mislead readers by suggesting cause-and-effect relationships that do not exist.

■ Chronological order may be cumbersome if many unrelated events occur simultaneously.

Spatial: Organizing by Division

Writers frequently approach complex subjects by separating them into parts. Comparison, division, and classification essays are spatially arranged. Instead of using chronology, another student explaining the causes of the Confederation might address each cause separately.

Thesis: The Confederation of Canada was a unifying strategy of response to increasing economic, cultural, and ideological threats posed by three main sources of tension: the oligarchies under British imperial rule; the proximity of American power; and British North American French–English conflict.

Outline

I. Introduction

II. The Colonies and British Imperial Rule

   A. Colonial government

      1. The old colonial system

      2. The oligarchies and the "family compact"

   B. Responsible government

      1. Reform and Toryism in Upper Canada

      2. William Lyon Mackenzie and rebellion

      3. The meaning of the *Durham Report* for Upper Canada

III. British North America and French–English Conflict

   A. The *Constitution Act* of 1791

   B. French–English cultural differences

   C. Papineau and rebellion

   D. The meaning of the *Durham Report* for Lower Canada

IV. The Proximity of American Power

   A. Rebellion and American sympathy

   B. The commercial revolution

      1. The Reciprocity Treaty

      2. Maritime–New England in-shore fishing rights

      3. Self-defined trade and tariff policies

      4. The railways

      5. American intrusions into the west and the 54th parallel

   C. Civil War and U.S. northern armies

V. The Great Coalition
  Conclusion: The Dominion of Canada

Advantages of Spatial Order

- Spatial organization can simplify complex issues by dividing them into separate elements. By understanding the parts, readers can appreciate the nature of the whole.

- Spatial organization is useful if you are addressing multiple readers. Those with a special interest can quickly locate where a specific issue is discussed. In a chronological paper, this information would be distributed throughout the essay and require extensive searching.

Disadvantages of Spatial Order

- Divisions in a spatially organized paper must be carefully assigned. Minor ideas can be overemphasized if placed in separate sections, and significant concepts overshadowed or overlooked if merged with other topics.

Emphatic: Organizing by Importance

If you believe that some ideas are more notable than others, you can arrange information in order of importance. Because readers' attention is greatest at the beginning and end of an essay, open or conclude with the most important points.

Advantages: Most Important to Least Important

- Starting with the most important idea places the most critical information in the first few paragraphs or pages. Readers unable to complete the entire document will absorb the most essential ideas. This can be useful for long, detailed papers or documents that you suspect may not be read in their entirety.
- You are likely to devote less space and detail to minor ideas, so the reading will become easier to follow and will counter reader fatigue. Because the sections will be shorter and less dense, readers will have the impression of picking up momentum as they read the final sections.

Disadvantages: Most Important to Least Important

- The principal disadvantage of this method is that the paper loses emphasis and can trail off into insignificant details. An effective conclusion that refers to the main idea can provide the paper with a strong final impression.
- In some instances, important ideas cannot be fully appreciated without introductory information.

Advantages: Least Important to Most Important

- Papers concluding with the most important idea build intensity, taking readers to ideas of increasing significance, building a stronger and stronger case for the writer's thesis.
- Concluding with the most important information is effective in leaving readers with a dominant final impression.

Disadvantages: Least Important to Most Important

- Readers' attention naturally diminishes over time, so that the ability to concentrate weakens as you present the most important ideas. Because you are likely to devote more space to the significant points, the sentences become more complex and the paragraphs longer, making the essay more challenging to read. Subtitles, paragraph breaks, and transitional statements can alert readers to pay particular attention to your concluding remarks.

■ Readers who are unable to finish the paper will miss the most important ideas. However, you can use the introduction to signal where important ideas are located so that readers unable to read the entire paper will skip ahead to the conclusion.

The Conclusion

All writing should end with an emphatic point, final observation, or memorable comment, but not all essays require a lengthy conclusion. Do not simply repeat the opening statement of ideas.

Summarize the Thesis and Main Points

A long, complex essay can benefit from a thoughtful summary that reminds readers of your thesis and principal considerations:

■ Ending with a summary or reminder of the thesis leaves readers with your main point.

■ In short papers, however, summaries can be redundant and weaken rather than strengthen an essay.

End with a Question

Just as an introductory question can arouse reader interest, so concluding with a question can prompt readers to consider the essay's main points or challenge readers to consider a future course of action:

■ Questions can be used to provoke readers to ponder the issues raised in the essay, guiding them to take action or reconsider their views.

■ Questions can lead readers to pause and consider the writer's points. Readers may be tempted to skim through an essay, but a final question provides a test—prompting them to think about what they have just read. A question can lead a reader to review the essay or even read it a second time.

Conclude with a Quotation

A quotation allows writers to introduce a second opinion or conclude with remarks by a noted authority or compelling witness:

■ Select quotations that are striking, relevant, and that emphasize the main points of the essay.

- Avoid irrelevant or generic quotations by famous people. Unless it directly addresses your thesis, a quotation by a celebrity or historic figure will not impress readers.

End with a Strong Image

Narrative and descriptive essays can have power if they leave readers with a compelling fact or scene:

- Choose an image that will motivate readers to consider the essay's main points.
- Concluding images and statements should be suited to the conventions of the discourse community and the nature of the document.

Finish with a Challenging Statement

Writers of persuasive essays frequently end with an appeal, prediction, warning, or challenge aimed directly at the reader:

- Direct challenges are effective if you want readers to take action. Ensure that any appeal you use is suited to both your goal and your audience.
- Avoid making statements that are hostile or offensive. Consider possible extended audiences. If you are writing as the agent of others, determine if the remark you make reflects the attitudes, values, and tone of those you represent.

MOVING FROM PREWRITING TO PLANNING

The plan you develop builds upon your prewriting, pulling the relevant ideas into meaningful order. Having read and discussed several essays concerning criminal justice, a student decided to write a short essay debating the merits of a current legal issue. At first she listed topics, then used clustering, freewriting, and questioning to narrow her topic and develop her thesis:

Topics:

Criminal justice (issues)

Capital punishment pro/con

Gun control

Court TV

Teenage shootings

Gangs

How does the media influence juries?

Jury nullification—moral or unjust?

Victims of crime—are they forgotten?

Who speaks for victims? (victims' rights movement)

Do prosecutors represent victims or the state?

Victims	TV coverage
Privacy issues	Rape cases
Addresses to judge	Impact statements

Victim impact statements are increasingly a feature of modern trials as people are allowed to state their feelings about the crime and the criminal after he/she has been convicted. Judges can consider the impact of the crime on the victim in sentencing. Sometimes victims ask for harsh punishment and sometimes they even ask for leniency and give criminals, especially the young, a second chance.

Who is most impressive?
What about victims who can't speak well or don't know English?
What about families of homicide victims?
Victims without mourners? Less important?

Topic: Victim impact statements

Thesis: Although victim impact statements are designed to empower the victims of crime, they may serve only to further marginalize the most helpless among us.

After reviewing her prewriting notes, she created an outline organizing her essay spatially, presenting positive and then negative effects of victim impact statements. To give her paper a strong conclusion, she decided to end the paper with her thesis.

Outline

I. Introduction
   A. Background of victim impact statements
   B. Definition of victim impact statements
II. Goals of victim impact statements (pro)
   A. Victims granted a voice
   B. Therapeutic benefits for victims
   C. Recommendations for sentencing

III. Negative effects of victim impact statements (con)

    A. Inarticulate victims ignored

    B. Benefits limited to the affluent

IV. Conclusion
    Thesis: Victim impact statements marginalize the poor and helpless

WRITING **ACTIVITIES**

1. Write a brief plan for the following topics, using each of the three basic methods of organization.

   Topic: Television violence

       Chronological   Spatial   Emphatic

   Topic: Teen smoking

       Chronological   Spatial   Emphatic

   Topic: Canada's role in the 21st century

       Chronological   Spatial   Emphatic

2. Review the following prewriting notes and assemble the ideas into an effective outline. (You may use more than one organizational method.)

   Topic: Telemarketing fraud
   Thesis: Federal and provincial agencies must take greater steps to stem the rapid increase in telemarketing fraud.

   NOTES:
   Thousands of victims defrauded of their life savings
   Failure of police and courts to investigate and prosecute
   History of telemarketing fraud
   Case of Nancy Sims—defrauded of $75,000 in investment scam
   Statements by former telemarketer who admitted preying on the elderly
   Need to change attitudes that fraud is "nonviolent crime"
   Telemarketing scams use long distance to avoid local victims
   Failure of existing federal and provincial laws
   Telemarketing scams rarely lead to convictions or harsh sentences

PLANNING **CHECKLIST**

After you have completed your plan, consider these questions.

✓ **Does your plan fulfill the needs of the writing task?** Review notes, comments, or instructor's guidelines to ensure you have clearly understood the assignment. Are there standard formats that should be followed or are you free to develop your own method of organization? Does your plan address the needs of readers?

(Continued)

✓ **Is your thesis clearly stated?** Does your thesis state a point of view or is it simply a narrowed topic?

✓ **Have you developed enough evidence?** Is the thesis clearly supported by examples, details, facts, quotations, and examples? Is the evidence compelling and clearly stated? Are the sources accurate? Will readers accept your evidence? Should outside sources be documented?

✓ **Have you selected an appropriate method of organization?** Will readers be able to follow your train of thought? Are transitions clearly indicated?

✓ **Does your plan help overcome customary problems?** Review previous assignments or comments instructors have made about your writing in the past. Does your plan provide guidelines for a stronger thesis or more organized support?

✓ **Does your opening arouse attention and introduce readers to your topic? Does your conclusion end the paper with a strong point or memorable image?**

✓ **Does your plan give you a workable guideline for writing your first draft?** Does it include reminders, references, and tips to make your job easier? Do you use a format that you can easily amend? *(Note: Leave space between points so you can make changes as you work.)*

Strategies for Overcoming Problems in Organization

If you have problems organizing your ideas and developing a plan for your paper, review your prewriting.

1. **Examine your thesis and goal.** The subject and purpose of your writing can suggest an organizational method. Would your ideas be best expressed by telling a story or separating them into parts? Are some ideas more important than others?

2. **Use prewriting strategies to establish a pattern.** Make a list of your main ideas. Use clustering to draw relationships between points. What pattern best pulls these ideas together?

3. **Discuss your paper with your instructor or fellow students.** Like someone who cannot see the forest for the trees, you may be so focused on details that you cannot obtain an overall view of your paper. Another person may be able to examine your notes and suggest a successful pattern.

4. **Start writing.** Although writing without a plan may feel like starting a journey without a map, plunging in and starting a draft may help you discover a way of organizing ideas. Although you are writing without a plan, try to stay on target. Review your thesis and focus on your goal. If the introduction gives you trouble, start with the body or conclusion. Developing connections between a few ideas may help you discover a method of organizing your entire essay.

E-WRITING

Exploring Organization Online

You can use the Internet to learn more about organizing an essay.

1. Using a search engine such as AltaVista, Google, or Yahoo!, enter terms such as *organizing an essay, topic outline, sentence outline,* or *writing introductions* to locate current sites of interest.

2. Using InfoTrac® College Edition or one of your library's databases, look up recent editorials or brief articles and notice how authors organized their ideas. Did writers use a chronological or spatial method? Where did they locate the thesis, the most important evidence? How did they begin and end the article? Could any parts be improved to make the article easier to read or more effective?

E-SOURCES

Introductions and Conclusions
http://www.powa.org/thesis/intros.html

Developing an Outline
http://owl.english.purdue.edu/handouts/genereal/gl_outline.html
http://www.utoronto.ca/writing/advise.html

COMPANION WEBSITE

See **http://www.transcanadawriter.nelson.com** for additional information on organizing ideas.

CHAPTER 7

Developing Paragraphs

This chapter explains the role of paragraphs in defining, organizing, and relating your ideas. It provides tips on how to develop clear, logical, and unified paragraphs. It also will help you to create topic sentences and to blend the use of modes within paragraphs for greater coherence and expressive range.

Just as the sentence contains one idea in all its fullness, so the paragraph should embrace a distinct episode; and as sentences should follow one another in harmonious sequence, so the paragraphs must fit on to one another like the automatic couplings of railway carriages.

—WINSTON CHURCHILL

WHAT ARE PARAGRAPHS?

How would you describe a paragraph? Many students are uncertain about the purpose and function of paragraphs, so they avoid paragraphing or they make arbitrary indentations every half page or so to break up the essay. But a paragraph is more than a cluster of sentences or a random pause in a block of text. *Paragraphs are groups of sentences unified by a single idea.* Paragraphs operate much like chapters in a book: they organize related ideas and form cohesive units. Paragraphs have specific functions: they introduce a subject, explain a point, tell a story, compare two ideas, support a thesis, or summarize a writer's main points.

The importance of paragraphs can be demonstrated by removing them from a text. Printed without paragraphs, Walter Lord's foreword to *A Night to Remember* is difficult to comprehend and becomes an unimaginative jumble of facts and numbers:

> In 1898 a struggling author named Morgan Robertson concocted a novel about a fabulous Atlantic liner, far larger than any that had ever been built. Robertson loaded his ship with rich and complacent people and then wrecked it one cold

April night on an iceberg. This somehow showed the futility of everything, and in fact, the book was called Futility when it appeared that year, published by the firm of M. F. Mansfield. Fourteen years later a British shipping company named the White Star Line built a steamer remarkably like the one in Robertson's novel. The new liner was 66,000 tons displacement; Robertson's was 70,000. The real ship was 882.5 feet long; the fictional one was 800 feet. Both vessels were triple screw and could make 24–25 knots. Both could carry about 3,000 people, and both had enough lifeboats for only a fraction of this number. But, then, this didn't seem to matter because both were labeled "unsinkable." On April 12, 1912, the real ship left Southampton on her maiden voyage to New York. Her cargo included a priceless copy of the Rubaiyat of Omar Khayyam and a list of passengers collectively worth two hundred fifty million dollars. On her way over she too struck an iceberg and went down on a cold April night. Robertson called his ship the Titan; the White Star Line called its ship the *Titanic*. This is the story of her last night.

Presented as Lord wrote it, the foreword is far more striking:

In 1898 a struggling author named Morgan Robertson concocted a novel about a fabulous Atlantic liner, far larger than any that had ever been built. Robertson loaded his ship with rich and complacent people and then wrecked it one cold April night on an iceberg. This somehow showed the futility of everything, and in fact, the book was called *Futility* when it appeared that year, published by the firm of M. F. Mansfield.

Fourteen years later a British shipping company named the White Star Line built a steamer remarkably like the one in Robertson's novel. The new liner was 66,000 tons displacement; Robertson's was 70,000. The real ship was 882.5 feet long; the fictional one was 800 feet. Both vessels were triple screw and could make 24–25 knots. Both could carry about 3,000 people, and both had enough lifeboats for only a fraction of this number. But, then, this didn't seem to matter because both were labeled "unsinkable."

On April 12, 1912, the real ship left Southampton on her maiden voyage to New York. Her cargo included a priceless copy of the *Rubaiyat of Omar Khayyam* and a list of passengers collectively worth two hundred fifty million dollars. On her way over she too struck an iceberg and went down on a cold April night.

Robertson called his ship the *Titan*; the White Star Line called its ship the *Titanic*. This is the story of her last night.

Each paragraph signals a shift, breaking up the text to highlight the parallels between the fictional ocean liner and the real one. The conclusion dramatizes the eerie similarity between the ships' names by placing the final two sentences in a separate paragraph.

Remember, although it is important to provide breaks in your text, random and erratic paragraph breaks interrupt the flow of ideas and create a disorganized list of sentences.

WRITING **ACTIVITY**

Read the following student essay and indicate where you would make paragraph breaks.

Disneyland Dads

Like half the members of my generation, I am the product of what used to be called a "broken home." My parents divorced when I was eight. I lived with my mother and saw my father on alternate weekends and two weeks during the summer. My father, like many of *his* generation, was a classic Disneyland Dad. The Disneyland Dad is usually found at malls, little league fields, upscale pizza restaurants and ice cream parlors. He is usually accompanied by a child busily eating food forbidden by Mom, trying on clothes, or playing with new toys. The Disneyland Dad dispenses cash like an ATM and provides an endless supply of quarters for arcade games. Whether they are motivated by guilt, frustration, or an inability to parent, Disneyland Dads substitute material items for fatherly advice, guidance, and discipline. While my mother furnished the hands-on, day to day parenting, my father remained distant. My mother monitored my eating habits, my friends, my grades, even the programs I watched on television. But without daily contact with my mother, my father found it difficult to make decisions about my upbringing. He was afraid of contradicting Mom. So he showered me with gifts and trips. He expanded my wardrobe, gave me my first pieces of real jewelry, introduced me to Broadway shows, and took me to Disneyland—but he did not help me with school, teach me about the job market, give me insight into boys, or allow me to be anything more than a spoiled consumer. As I grew older, my relationship with my father became strained. Weekends with him were spent shopping, going to movies, playing tennis, and horseback riding—activities I loved, but activities that limited opportunities for anything but casual conversation. Like most of my friends, I came to view my father as more of an uncle than a parent. He was a beloved family figure, someone who could be counted on for some extra cash, new clothes, or a pizza. And like most of my friends, I was troubled by the gulf that widened between my father and myself. I talked, argued, and made up with my mother as I went through my teens. Both of us changed over the years. But my father remained the same—the generous but distant Disneyland Dad. The Disneyland Dad is a neglected figure. While books and daytime talk shows focus on the plight of single moms, few people offer advice to the fathers. Men in our society are judged by success and conditioned to dispense tokens of their achievement to their children. We kids of divorce want all the things the Disneyland Dad can offer, but we really need his attention, his guidance, his experience, his mentoring. Someone has to help Disneyland Dads become fathers. ■

DEVELOPING PARAGRAPHS

Paragraphs can be developed in different ways. Effective paragraphs develop in ways that suit the context, so try experimenting with different development strategies to determine which way best fits your writing context.

Creating Topic Sentences

A topic sentence serves as the thesis statement of a paragraph, presenting the writer's main point or controlling idea. Like a thesis statement, the topic sentence announces the subject and indicates the writer's stance or opinion. The text of the paragraph explains and supports the topic sentence.

Writing about the status of France following the First World War, Anthony Kemp uses strong topic sentences to open each paragraph and organize supporting details:

> **The French won World War I—or so they thought.** In 1918, after four years of bitter [topic sentence] conflict, the nation erupted in joyful celebration. The arch-enemy, Germany, had [supporting] been defeated and the lost provinces of Alsace and Lorraine had been reunited [details] with the homeland. The humiliation of 1870 had been avenged and, on the surface at least, France was the most powerful nation in Europe. Germany was prostrate, its autocratic monarchy tumbled and the country rent by internal dissension.
>
> **The reality was different.** The northern provinces, as a result of the fighting, [topic sentence] had been totally devastated and depopulated. The treasury was empty and saddled with a vast burden of war debt. The French diplomat, Jules Cambon, [supporting] wrote prophetically at the time, "France victorious must grow accustomed to [details] being a lesser power than France vanquished."
>
> **The paradox was that Germany had emerged from the war far stronger.** France [topic sentence] had a static population of some 40 million, but was confronted by 70 million Germans whose territory had not been ravaged and who had a higher birth-rate. The [supporting] Austro-Hungarian Empire had been split up into a number of smaller units, none [details] of which could pose a serious threat to Germany. Russia, once the pillar to the Triple Entente, forcing Germany to fight on two fronts, had dissolved into internal chaos. The recreation of an independent Poland after the war produced a barrier between Russia and Germany which meant that the old ally of France no longer directly threatened German territory.

The topic sentence does not always open a paragraph. Like an essay's thesis statement, the topic sentence can appear in the middle or end. Often a writer will present supporting details, a narrative, or a description before stating the topic sentence:

> The airline industry has suffered dramatic losses in the last two years. Lucrative [supporting] business travel has ebbed, and overseas tourist bookings have dropped by a [details] third. In addition, rising fuel prices and an inability to increase fares has eroded the profit margin on most domestic flights. Reflecting the ongoing concern with terrorism, insurance costs have soared. Four of the largest airlines have announced plans to lay off thousands of employees. **The federal government** [topic sentence] **must take steps to save airlines from bankruptcy.**

Not all paragraphs require an explicit topic sentence, but all paragraphs should have a controlling or central idea, a clear focus or purpose. Even if no single topic sentence can be identified in a paragraph, its topic should be clearly implied. Each paragraph has a clear purpose, a controlling idea:

> *I did not know whether to laugh or to cry. So I sat down on the edge of one of the great whalebones, took out my sketchbook, and tried to capture the scene. I felt like laughing in sheer delight because of the bones' great forms—like an exhibition of Henry Moore sculptures I hadn't known about. But I felt like crying inside because of what they represented—the wholesale slaughter of so many majestic sea creatures—and I was also saddened by the gentoo penguin chicks huddled nearby.*

ROBERT BATEMAN,
"MESSAGE IN THE BONES"
FROM *THINKING LIKE A MOUNTAIN*

Using Modes

Just as writers organize essays using modes such as narration and definition, they can use the same patterns of development to unify paragraphs. In writing a comparison, you can use definition, cause and effect, or classification to organize individual paragraphs. You can also number points to make your train of thought easier to follow.

In *On Equilibrium*, John Ralston Saul blends several modes to analyze the relationship between impatience and ideology:

topic sentence quotation definition contrast example description	The constant challenge of trying to balance our qualities does seem a difficult, time-consuming business. The Koran summarizes this nicely—"Impatience is the very stuff man is made of." Writer after writer comes back to this challenge. We'd rather have the illusion of certainty. We don't want to hear, as Rohinton Mistry puts it, that we "cannot draw lines and compartments and refuse to budge beyond them." The great Japanese novelist Soseki Matsume created a hero who was a highly domesticated cat. With a sharp tongue he commented on his owners and others.
example description	Consider human eyes. They are embedded in pairs within a flat surface, yet their owners cannot simultaneously see to both their left and right . . . Being thus incapable of seeing in the round even the daily happenings of life in his own society, it is perhaps not surprising that man should get so excited about certain one-sided aspects of his limited view of reality. . . .

Slightly later, Ralston Saul addresses the tension between self-determination and social responsibility:

topic sentence statistics examples contrast	The romantic illusion that we could all walk away from the reality of society is fed by the reality that some do. A small percentage of any population will, as they always have done, abandon it. One, three, five per cent. They walk out into the desert, physically or figuratively. They reject the shared knowledge. Or rather, they opt

not to share the knowledge and its implication. This is a healthy phenomenon. We need a percentage who stand on the outside. But if all of us, one by one, walked away, the whole would collapse. Society does not exist in the abstract. Our shared knowledge exists as a continuation of citizens and their recognition of the *other*.   example

Emphasizing Transitions

Just as writers use exclamation points to dramatize a sentence, a paragraph break can serve to highlight a transition or isolate an important idea that might be buried or overshadowed if placed in a larger paragraph. In some instances writers will use a one- or two-sentence paragraph to dramatize a shift or emphasize an idea:

> *He could remember a time in his early childhood when a large number of things were still known by his family name. There was a Zhivago factory, a Zhivago bank, Zhivago buildings, a Zhivago necktie pin, even a Zhivago cake which was a kind of baba au rhum, and at one time if you said "Zhivago" to your sleigh driver in Moscow, it was as if you had said: "Take me to Timbuctoo!" and he carried you off to a fairy-tale kingdom. You would find yourself transported to a vast, quiet park. Crows settled on the heavy branches of firs, scattering the hoarfrost; their cawing echoed and re-echoed like crackling wood. Pure-bred dogs came running across the road out of the clearing from the recently constructed house. Farther on, lights appeared in the gathering dusk.*
>
> **And then suddenly all that was gone. They were poor.**
>
> BORIS PASTERNAK

Organizing Dialogue

Dialogue can be difficult to follow unless paragraph breaks show the transition between speakers. Paragraph breaks make dialogue easier to follow and allow you to avoid repeating "he said" or "I said." In "The Fender-Bender," Ramón "Tianguis" Pérez reproduces a conversation that occurred after a minor traffic accident:

> I get out of the car. The white man comes over and stands right in front of me. He's almost two feet taller.
>
> "If you're going to drive, why don't you carry your license?" he asks in an accusatory tone.
>
> "I didn't bring it," I say, for lack of any other defense.
>
> I look at the damage to his car. It's minor, only a scratch on the paint and a pimple-sized dent.
>
> "I'm sorry," I say. "Tell me how much it will cost to fix, and I'll pay for it; that's no problem." I'm talking to him in English, and he seems to understand.
>
> "This car isn't mine," he says. "It belongs to the company I work for. I'm sorry, but I've got to report this to the police, so that I don't have to pay for the damage."
>
> "That's no problem," I tell him again. "I can pay for it."

Paragraph Style

A writer's style or the style of a particular document is shaped by the length of the paragraphs as well as the level of vocabulary. Newspaper articles, which are meant to be skimmed, use simple words, short sentences, and brief paragraphs. Often a paragraph in a newspaper article will contain only two or three sentences. E-mail and memos also use short paragraphs to communicate quickly. Longer and more detailed writing tends to have paragraphs containing 50 to 250 words. In some specialized books, paragraphs will fill an entire page. No matter what their length, however, paragraphs should be well organized and serve a clear purpose.

Strategies for Developing Paragraphs

1. **Use topic sentences to organize supporting details.** A strong topic sentence can give meaning to details, preventing a paragraph from becoming simply a list of facts and numbers.

   topic sentence / supporting details — *The French won World War I—or so they thought. In 1918, after four years of bitter conflict, the nation erupted in joyful celebration. The arch-enemy, Germany, had been defeated and the lost provinces of Alsace and Lorraine had been reunited with the homeland. The humiliation of 1870 had been avenged and, on the surface at least, France was the most powerful nation in Europe. Germany was prostrate, its autocratic monarchy tumbled and the country rent by internal dissension.*

   ANTHONY KEMP

2. **Use modes to unify paragraphs.** Consider unifying paragraphs by using any of the following modes: description, narration, example, definition, comparison and contrast, process, division and classification, cause and effect, and argument and persuasion.

3. **Use paragraphs to highlight transitions.** A paragraph break can highlight a transition or isolate an important idea that might be less noticeable otherwise. One- or two-sentence paragraphs can also create drama or emphasis.

4. **Use paragraphs to distinguish speakers in dialogue.**

   I get out of the car. The white man comes over and stands right in front of me. He's almost two feet taller.

   "If you're going to drive, why don't you carry your license?" he asks in an accusatory tone.

   "I didn't bring it," I say, for lack of any other defense.

   I look at the damage to his car. It's minor, only a scratch on the paint and a pimple-sized dent.

   RAMÓN "TIANGUIS" PÉREZ

WRITING **ACTIVITIES**

1. Select one or more of the subjects listed below and write a paragraph about it. Your paragraph may or may not have a topic sentence, but it should have a controlling idea. It should have a clear purpose and focus, and should not simply contain a number of vaguely related ideas. After drafting your paragraph, review it for missing details or irrelevant material. Underline your topic sentence or list your controlling thought.

   - Describe your first car.
   - Compare high school and university or college instructors.
   - State one or more reasons to explain why you admire a certain actor, singer, athlete, or politician.

2. Develop paragraphs using the topic sentences provided below. Use each topic sentence as a controlling idea to guide your selection of supporting details and examples.

   - Living off-campus provides students with many opportunities.
   - However, distractions and unexpected responsibilities can interfere with studying.
   - Students who plan to live off-campus should think carefully before signing a lease.

3. Write a paragraph supporting the following topic sentences:

   - University and college students must develop self-discipline to succeed.
   - The central problem in relationships is a failure to communicate.
   - Three steps must be taken to curb teenagers from smoking.

4. Write a paragraph organized chronologically about a personal experience.

5. Write a paragraph using comparison to discuss two of your best friends, two local bands, two popular restaurants, or two athletic teams.

6. Write a paragraph that uses division to enumerate at least three points on one of the following topics:

best friends	effects of divorce on children
health care	the Internet
first dates	talk shows

E-WRITING

Exploring Paragraphs Online

You can use the Internet to learn more about developing paragraphs.

1. Using a search engine such as AltaVista, Google, or Yahoo!, enter terms such as *paragraph structure* and *topic sentence* to locate current sites of interest.

2. Using InfoTrac® College Edition, or one of your library's databases, look up recent editorials or brief articles and notice how authors developed paragraphs. Did they use

paragraph breaks to signal important transitions, group related ideas, and make the text easier to follow? Were individual paragraphs organized by specific modes such as comparison, process, or cause and effect? How many had topic sentences you could underline?

E-SOURCES

Paragraphs
http://www.utoronto.ca/writing/parag.html
http://www.unc.edu/depts/wcweb/handouts/paragraphs.html

COMPANION WEBSITE

See **http://www.transcanadawriter.nelson.com** for additional information on developing paragraphs.

CHAPTER 8

Writing the First Draft

This chapter explores the importance of the drafting stage in the writing process. It examines the nature of drafting while offering tips on how to do so. It also addresses the serious topic of writing with academic integrity and avoiding plagiarism. Finally, it explores the element of choice in every writing act: from word choice to effective sentence structures.

Try simply to steer your mind in the direction or general vicinity of the thing you are trying to write about and start writing and keep writing.

—PETER ELBOW

WHAT IS A FIRST DRAFT?

Do you often find yourself expecting to produce a perfect or near-perfect draft the first time around? If so, you are like many students who try to function under a similar illusion about writing—a dangerous illusion because it can lead straight to writer's block, which can severely undermine your confidence. The truth is that effective writing takes work and emerges in stages. Even highly successful professional writers realize that good writing requires rewriting—sometimes many times. This is why drafting is an essential part of the writing process. The first draft refers to the preliminary attempt to capture your ideas on paper and produce a rough version of the final essay. A first draft likely will be far from perfect and no doubt will include awkward sentences, redundant passages, irrelevant ideas, and misspelled words—but this is valuable: it gives you something to build on and refine.

There is no single method of transforming your outline into a completed draft, but there are techniques that can improve your first efforts.

Strategies for Writing the First Draft

1. **Review your plan.** Examine your outline, prewriting notes, and any instructions to make sure your plan addresses the needs of the writing assignment. If you have developed a formal outline, you can follow it as a road map to keep your writing focused.

2. **Focus on your goal.** As you write, keep your purpose in mind. What is your objective—to entertain, inform, or persuade? Do you plan to tell a story, make a comparison, motivate readers to change their behaviour, or explain a process?

3. **Write to your reader.** Writing is an act of communication, an exchange between writer and reader. Your job is not simply to fill a computer screen with words but to address people. Ask, Who is my reader? and then determine an answer. Consider the readers' perceptual world. What information do readers need to grasp and accept your thesis? Anticipate how readers will respond to your ideas. Will they be interested, bored, supportive, or hostile? How can your paper arouse their interest, build on their current knowledge, or address their objections?

4. **Visualize the completed document.** Consider the writing context and what the final product should look like. Are you writing a 500-word personal essay, a ten-page research paper, or a three-paragraph letter? Thinking about the finished document can help you determine whether your plan is suited to the task. Considering how the text should look can guide your decisions about word choice, sentence structure, and paragraph length. Determine whether your document should include photographs, figures, or tables.

5. **Support your thesis.** What evidence will convince your readers to accept your ideas? Determine what appeal will best suit your audience—logical, ethical, or emotional?

6. **Amend your plan if needed.** Sometimes you will discover new ideas while drafting. Be willing to make changes, but keep your goal, reader, and the nature of the document in mind to keep your writing on course. New ideas that occur to you while writing the first draft may lead you to return to prewriting to expand or limit the topic, alter your approach, or develop a new thesis.

7. **Start writing.** The most important goal in writing a first draft is getting your ideas on paper. Start writing and produce as much copy as you can. Don't pause to check your spelling or look up a statistic. Focus on your main points.

   - Start with the easiest parts. Don't feel obligated to write the introduction first. You may find it easier to begin with the body or conclusion.

   - Give yourself room for changes. You can easily insert text on a computer, but if you are writing on paper, you may wish to skip lines or leave wide margins for last-minute additions.

   - Don't edit as you write. Pausing to look up facts or check spelling can interrupt your train of thought, but you can make notes as you write to identify items for future revisions. Underline words you think might be misspelled or misused. Make notes in parentheses to signal missing details.

   - Break the paper into manageable parts. Instead of attempting to write a complete draft, you may find it more effective to focus on one section, especially if your paper is long and complex.

- If you get stuck, return to passages you have written and revise them. Keep writing.

8. **Read your work aloud.** Hearing your words can help you evaluate your writing and test the logic of your ideas.

9. **Lower your standards.** Keep writing even if your ideas seem clumsy or repetitive. Don't expect to write flawless copy—this is a rough draft.

10. **Anticipate problems.** Recall comments instructors have made about your writing in the past. Focus on overcoming weaknesses or bad habits.
    - You may not be able to address problem areas during the first draft, but you can make notes in the margin as you write to guide future revisions.

11. **Save everything you write.** Ideas that may seem unrelated to your topic could prove to be valuable in future drafts or other assignments.
    - Make sure you save your work on a disk if working on a computer. If you print a hard copy, you may wish to double- or triple-space the text for easier editing.

ACADEMIC HONESTY: AVOIDING PLAGIARISM

Workload stress, personal problems, anxiety about an assignment deadline, insecurity about the quality of your ideas or writing, ease of Internet access—all these factors and more underlie the temptation to download a paper from the Internet, copy another student's essay, or plunder passages from a book without attributing the source. Whatever the cause, you need to know that presenting another writer's work as your own is plagiarism. Plagiarism is a form of cheating or academic dishonesty, and it is considered a serious crime of intellectual property. If it is detected, you will face serious consequences. Most colleges and universities have strict policies about plagiarism. Students caught cheating may automatically fail the course or be expelled. Outside academia, plagiarism involves *piracy* and *copyright infringement*—two very serious offences that expose violators to prosecution and litigation. Individuals and corporations have filed multimillion-dollar lawsuits against people who plagiarize.

If you are having difficulty with writing, talk to your instructor or seek tutorial help before you risk terminating your postsecondary career by cheating. Plagiarism involves not only stealing someone's entire essay but also taking and using his or her sentences and paragraphs. Whenever you use outside material, indicate its source. If you copy the speech or writing of another directly, it should be placed in quotation marks:

ORIGINAL STATEMENT: It is good to see this Government recognizes our impaired driving laws need to be more effective. (Andrew Murie, Mothers Against Drunk Driving [MADD] Canada's Chief Executive Officer, speaking in response to new Ontario measures.)

> **STUDENT PAPER:** Responding to new measures introduced by the Ontario government, MADD's Andrew Murie remarked, "It is good to see this Government recognizes our impaired driving laws need to be more effective."

When you paraphrase, or put the idea in your own words, you should indicate the source:

> Andrew Murie has remarked that the Ontario Government's new measures to address impaired driving are encouraging.

Even an informal acknowledgment can protect you from a charge of plagiarism:

> According to the CEO of MADD, the Ontario Government's new impaired driving measures are encouraging.

Under no circumstances should your desperation to complete an assignment on time or get a good grade lead you to copy another's work.

Outside sources should be documented—see Chapter 22 for guidelines on incorporating outside sources into your work. If you are unsure how to document correctly, it is your responsibility to get the guidance you need.

MAKING WRITING DECISIONS

In writing the first draft, you will make a series of decisions about how you want and need to express your ideas. You will choose words, construct sentences, and develop paragraphs and transitions. The more thought you put into these decisions, the better your rough draft will reflect what you want to say and the less rewriting it will require.

Choosing the Right Words

Words have power. The impact of your writing greatly depends on the words you choose to express your ideas. In writing your first draft, select words that represent your stance and will influence readers. Because the goal of the first draft is to record your ideas, don't stop writing to look up words; instead, underline items for further review.

Use Words Precisely

Many words are easily confused. Should a patient's heart rate be monitored *continually* (meaning at regular intervals, such as once an hour) or *continuously* (meaning without interruption)? Is the city council planning to *adapt* or *adopt* a budget? Did the mayor make an *explicit* or *implicit* statement?

Your writing can influence readers only if you use words that accurately reflect your meaning. There are numerous pairs of frequently confused words:

allusion	An indirect reference
illusion	A false or imaginary impression
infer	To interpret
imply	To suggest
conscience	A sense of moral or ethical conduct
conscious	To be awake or aware of something
principle	A basic law or concept
principal	Something or someone important, as in school principal
affect	To change or modify
effect	A result

See pages 645–648 for a longer list of commonly confused or misused words.

Use Concrete Words

Concrete words communicate more information and make clearer impressions than abstract words, which express only generalized concepts.

ABSTRACT	CONCRETE
motor vehicle	pickup truck
modest suburban home	three-bedroom colonial
individual	boy
protective headgear	helmet
residential rental unit	studio apartment
digestive ailment	heartburn
educational facility	high school

Concrete words make a greater impact on readers:

ABSTRACT: Wherever we went, malnourished individuals lined the road in serious need of assistance.

CONCRETE: Wherever we walked, starving children lined the road like skeletons silently holding empty bowls with bony fingers.

As you write, try to think of effective images and specific details that will suit your purpose and your reader.

Use Verbs that Create Action and Strong Images

Linking verbs (such as *is* and *are*) join ideas but do not suggest action or present compelling images. Like abstract nouns, generalized verbs, such as *move, seem,* and *appear,* make only vague impressions. Use verbs that express action and create strong images.

WEAK VERBS	STRONG VERBS
The children *were* homesick and *experienced* sadness.	The children *ached* with homesickness and *cried*.
The landlord *expressed* little interest in his tenants and *did not repair* the building.	The landlord *ignored* his tenants and *refused to repair* the building.
The firefighters *moved* quickly to the accident scene and then *moved* slowly through the debris *to look* for victims.	The firefighters *raced* to the accident scene then *crept* slowly through the debris *searching* for victims.

Use an Appropriate Level of Diction

The style and tone of your writing are shaped by the words you choose. Your goal, your readers, the discourse community, and the document itself usually indicate the kind of language that is appropriate. Informal language that might be acceptable in a note to a coworker may be unsuited to a formal report or article written for publication.

FORMAL: Sales representatives are required to maintain company vehicles at their own expense. (employee manual)

STANDARD: Salespeople must pay for routine maintenance of their cars. (business letter)

INFORMAL: Remind the reps to change their oil every 3,000 miles. (e-mail memo)

Slang expressions can be creative and attention getting, but they may be inappropriate and detract from the credibility of formal documents.

Appreciate the Impact of Connotations

All words *denote,* or indicate, a particular meaning. The words *home, residence,* and *domicile* all refer to where someone lives. Each has the same basic meaning or *denotation,* but the word *home* evokes personal associations of family, friends, and favourite belongings. *Domicile,* on the other hand, has a legalistic and official tone devoid of personal associations.

Connotations are implied or suggested meanings. Connotations reflect a writer's values, views, and attitudes toward a subject. A resort cabin can be described as a *rustic cottage* or a *seedy shack*. The person who spends little money and shops for bargains can be praised for being *thrifty* or ridiculed for being *cheap*. The design of a skyscraper can be celebrated as being *clean and streamlined* or criticized for appearing *stark and sterile*.

The following pairs of words have the same *denotation* or basic meaning but their *connotations* create strikingly different impressions:

young	inexperienced
traditional	old-fashioned
brave	ruthless
casual	sloppy
the homeless	bums
residential care facility	nursing home
unintended landing	plane crash
teenage prank	vandalism
uncompromising	stubborn
strong	dictatorial
delicate	effeminate
street art	graffiti

In selecting words, ensure that your connotations are suited to your task, role, and readers. Avoid terms that your readers may find inappropriate or offensive.

WRITING **ACTIVITIES**

1. Review papers you have written in previous classes and examine your use of words. Read passages aloud. How does your writing sound? Are there abstract terms that could be replaced by concrete words? Are there connotations that detract from your goal? Does the level of diction fit the assignment?

2. Write a description of your hometown, using as many concrete words as possible to provide sensual impressions. Avoid abstract words like "pleasant" or "noisy" and offer specific details.

3. Use connotations to write a positive and negative description of a controversial personality such as a local politician.

4. Translate this negative description into a positive one by substituting key words:

   Frank Kelso is a reckless, money-grubbing gossip who eagerly maligns celebrities. He is impulsive, stubborn, and insulting. He refuses to show restraint and will exploit anyone's personal misfortune to get ahead while claiming to serve his readers' desire for truth.

Writing Effective Sentences

Writing well is more than a matter of avoiding grammatical errors such as fragments and run-ons. Sentences express thoughts. Your sentences should be clear, logical, and economical. Several techniques can increase the power of your sentences.

Emphasize Key Words

Words placed at the beginning and end of sentences receive more attention than those placed in the middle.

Cumulative sentences open with the main idea or key word:

> *Computer literacy* is mandatory for today's high school students.
> *Alcoholism and drug addiction* are contributing causes of child neglect.

Periodic sentences conclude with a key word or major idea:

> For today's high school student, success demands *computer literacy*.
> Child neglect often stems from two causes: *alcoholism and drug addiction*.

Both cumulative and periodic sentences are more effective than those that bury important words in the middle:

> In today's world *computer literacy* is mandatory for high school students to succeed.
> The problem of child neglect often has *alcoholism and drug addiction* as contributing causes.

Use Parallel Structures to Stress Equivalent Ideas

You can demonstrate that ideas have equal value by placing them in pairs and lists:

> *Coffee and tea* are favourite beverages for dieters.
> His doctor suggested that *diet and exercise* could *lower his blood pressure and reduce his risk of stroke*.
> A new study revealed that the chief causes of air pollution are *vehicle exhaust, industrial emissions, and agricultural pesticides*.

Subordinate Secondary Ideas

Secondary ideas that offer background information such as dates and figures should be subordinated or merged into sentences that stress primary ideas. Combining ideas into single sentences allows writers to demonstrate which ideas they consider significant.

PRIMARY IDEA: Nancy Chen was accepted into Osgoode Law School.

SECONDARY IDEA: Nancy Chen did not learn English until she was 12.

COMBINED VERSIONS: Although she did not learn English until she was 12, Nancy Chen was accepted into Osgoode Law School.

Nancy Chen, who did not learn English until she was 12, was accepted into Osgoode Law School.

Secondary ideas can be placed at the beginning, set off by commas in the middle, or attached to the end of a sentence:

PRIMARY IDEA: Bayport College will close its doors.

SECONDARY IDEAS: Bayport College has served this community for 100 years.

Bayport College was forced to declare bankruptcy.

Bayport College will close on June 15.

COMBINED VERSIONS: On June 15, Bayport College, forced to declare bankruptcy, will close its doors, after serving this community for 100 years.

After serving this community for 100 years, Bayport College, forced to declare bankruptcy, will close its doors on June 15.

Forced to declare bankruptcy, Bayport College, which served this community for 100 years, will close its doors on June 15.

Stress the Relationship between Ideas

You can make your train of thought easier for readers to follow if your sentences stress how one idea affects another. Coordinating conjunctions—words that join ideas—demonstrate relationships:

and joins ideas of equal importance:

The prime minister urged Canadians to conserve oil, *and* he denounced Parliament for failing to pass an energy bill.

or indicates choice, suggesting that only one of two ideas is operative:

The university will raise tuition *or* increase class size.

but indicates a shift or contrast:

The company lowered prices, *but* sales continued to slump.

yet   also demonstrates a contrast, often meaning nevertheless:

>He studied for hours *yet* failed the exam.

so   implies cause and effect:

>Drivers ignored the stop sign, *so* authorities installed a traffic light.

Transitional expressions also establish the relationship between ideas.
To establish time relationships:

before	after	now	then
today	further	once	often

To demonstrate place relationships:

above	below	over	under
around	inside	outside	nearby
next	beyond	to the left	

To indicate additions:

again	also	moreover	too
in addition			

To express similarities:

alike	likewise	in the same way

To stress contrasts:

after all	different	on the other hand
although	however	still
unlike	in contrast	

To illustrate cause and effect:

as a result	because	therefore

To conclude or summarize:

finally	in conclusion	in short

When you write the first draft, emphasize the relationships between ideas as clearly as you can. But if trying to determine the best way to link ideas slows your writing, simply underline related items to signal future revisions and move on to the next point.

Understand How Structure Affects Meaning

Just as the connotations of the words you choose shape meaning, so does the structure of your sentences. The way you word sentences can create both dramatic effects and make subtle distinctions. Although the basic facts are the same in the following sentences, notice how altering the words that form the subject (in italics) affects their meaning:

> *Dr. Green and a group of angry patients* are protesting the closing of the Fairview Clinic.

(This sentence suggests the doctor and patients are of equal significance.)

> *Dr. Green,* flanked by angry patients, is protesting the closing of the Fairview Clinic.

(This sentence emphasizes the role of the doctor. The singular verb "is protesting" highlights the actions of a single person. Set off by commas, the "angry patients" are not even considered part of the subject.)

> *Angry patients,* supported by Dr. Green, are protesting the closing of the Fairview Clinic.

(In this version the angry patients are emphasized, and the doctor, set off by commas, is de-emphasized, reduced to the status of a bystander.)

> Despite protests by Dr. Green and angry patients, *the Fairview Clinic* is being closed.

(This wording suggests the protests are futile and that the closing of the clinic is inevitable.)

> *The closing of the Fairview Clinic* has sparked protests by Dr. Green and angry patients.

(This sentence indicates a cause-and-effect relationship, implying that the final outcome may be uncertain.)

▣ WRITING **ACTIVITIES**

1. Combine the following items into a single sentence that emphasizes what you consider the most significant idea.

   A. Arthur Conan Doyle created Sherlock Holmes.
      Arthur Conan Doyle modelled his detective after Dr. Bell.
      Dr. Bell was famous for his diagnostic ability.
      Arthur Conan Doyle was an eye specialist.

   B. Dr. James Naismith was born in Canada.
      He was a YMCA athletic director.
      He invented the game of basketball.
      Naismith wanted to develop a new recreation.

(Continued)

2. Combine the following facts into a single sentence and write three versions, placing emphasis on different elements.
   A. The student council proposed a freeze on tuition.
      The faculty accepted the student proposal.
      The alumni accepted the student proposal.
   B. The city was devastated by an earthquake.
      The public responded with calm determination.
      The mayor urged citizens to help authorities.
   C. Job interviews are stressful.
      Applicants fear rejection.
      Interviewers fear hiring the wrong employee.
3. Select a topic from the list on pages 650–651 and freewrite for ten minutes. Set the draft aside and then analyze your use of sentences. Do they emphasize primary ideas? Are minor ideas given too much significance? Are the relationships between ideas clearly expressed?

Writing Paragraphs

Paragraphs are the building blocks of an essay. If writing the entire paper seems like a confusing or overwhelming task, focus on writing one paragraph at a time.

Use Topic Sentences or Controlling Ideas to Maintain Focus

It is easy to become sidetracked when you write a first draft. Focus your draft by using a topic sentence or controlling idea as a goal. Consider what you want to accomplish in that paragraph. Even if your paragraph does not have a topic sentence, it should have a controlling idea, a clear purpose.

Use the Modes to Organize Paragraphs

Generally, your outline or notes will list *what* you want to write but not *how* to express or organize the ideas. As you develop paragraphs, consider using one or more of the modes. In writing a narrative about moving into your first apartment, for instance, you might use *cause and effect* in one paragraph to explain why you decided to get your own apartment and *comparison* in another paragraph to show how your initial expectations about living alone contrasted with the reality. Later paragraphs in this narrative might be organized by using *process* or *classification*.

Note New Ideas Separately

As you write a first draft, new ideas may come to you. If they do not directly relate to the paragraph you are writing, jot them down on a separate piece of paper or scroll down the computer screen and record them apart from your essay. This way they will not clutter up the paragraph you are working on but remain available for future versions.

Note Possible Paragraph Breaks

Some people find it difficult to make paragraph breaks in the first draft. Narrative and descriptive essays, for example, often seem like a seamless stream of events or details. Because the main goal of the first draft is to get your thoughts on paper, don't agonize over making paragraph breaks. As you write, you might insert a paragraph symbol (¶) or even a pair of slashes (//) to indicate possible breaks.

MOVING FROM PLAN TO FIRST DRAFT

A writer's plan serves as a guide for the first draft, a framework or blueprint that is expanded into a rough version of the final essay. A student writing about victim impact statements used her outline as a guideline for her first draft. In writing her draft, she introduced new ideas, departing from the original plan. At this stage, she does not worry about spelling—the purpose of writing the first draft is not to produce flawless prose, but to get your ideas down on paper.

Outline

   I. Introduction
      A. Background of victim impact statements
      B. Definition of victim impact statements
  II. Goals of Victim Impact Statements (pro)
      A. Victims granted a voice
      B. Therapeutic benefits for victims
      C. Recommendations for sentencing
 III. Negative Effects of Victim Impact Statements (con)
      A. Inarticulate victims ignored
      B. Benefits limited to the affluent
  IV. Conclusion
      Thesis: Victim impact statements marginalize the poor and helpless

First Draft

Across Canada today more and more victims of crime are being allowed to address the court in terms of making what is called a victim impact statment. This written or oral presentation to the court allows victims to express their feelings to the judge after someone has been convicted of a crime.

Advocates of victim impact statements point to key advantages. First, these statements give victims' a voice. For years, victims have felt helpless. Prosecutors represent the state, not the crime victim. Victims have been dismayed when prosecutors have arranged pleas bargains without their knowledge. Some victims are still recovering from their injuries when they learn the person who hurt them has plead to a lesser charge and received probation.

Therapists who work with victims also say that being able to address the court helps with the healing process. Victims of violent crime can feel powerless and vulnerable. Instead of suffering in silence, they are given the chance to address the criminal, to clear their chests, and get on with the rest of their lives.

Impact statements allows judges to consider what sentences are apropppriate. In one case a judge who planned to fine a teenager for shoplifting excepted the store owners suggestions to waive the fine if the defendent completed high school.

But giving victims a change to speak raises some issues. What about the victim who is not articulate, who doesn't even speak English? In murder cases the victim's relatives are given a chance to speak? Does this mean that a middle class professional victim with a circle of grieving friends and family members will be granted more signifiacne than the homeless murder victim who leaves no one behind?

Victim impact statements may help empower victims who are educated, personally impressive, and socially promient. But they may also allow forgotten victims to remain voiceless.

Strategies for Overcoming Problems in the First Draft

When you write the first draft, you may encounter several problems. Remember, your goal is to sketch out your main ideas, not to write flawless prose. Write as well as you can in the first draft—but keep in mind that your objective is to just get your ideas on paper.

1. **Getting started.** You may find yourself unable to write. Perhaps the task seems imposing, your outline too complex, your thoughts unclear.
   - Freewrite on your topic to loosen up and get in the mood to write.
   - Break your essay into parts and start with the easiest section.
   - Flesh out your plan. Write a new version, turning words into phrases and expanding into full sentences. Let the draft emerge from the outline.

2. **Running out of time.** Often you will be writing well, discovering new thoughts as you go. If you cannot write fast enough to capture these ideas or if you run out of time, make notes. A rough draft does not have to be stated in complete sentences.
   - Jot down a list of numbered points so you won't forget new ideas.
   - Use a tape recorder as you work to record ideas you don't have time to write.

3. **Writing in circles.** Even with the best map, you can sometimes get lost and find yourself repeating ideas—discovering on page 3 that you are restating your introduction.
   - Stop writing and read your introduction. Does it set up the rest of the essay? Does it try to say too much? An introduction indicates forthcoming ideas but should not summarize every point.
   - List your main ideas or use a diagram to create a pattern you can follow.

4. **Running out of ideas.** Sometimes you may find yourself running out of ideas on the first page of a five-page essay.
   - Review your goal and plan. Could you add details to support your points? Do not add "extra" ideas just to increase the length of your paper. Whatever you write should relate to your thesis.

- If you can't think of anything else, stop writing and put the draft aside. Do other work, read something about your topic, and let the draft cool. Return to it later and try adding more details. You may find it beneficial to start fresh with a new draft rather than working with an unsuccessful attempt.

5. **Your draft becomes too long.** You might find that the writing goes very well. One idea leads to another. Details and examples come easily. Then you discover that at this rate you will need 15 pages to cover all the points you planned to discuss in a five-page paper.

  - Read your draft aloud. Are you recording interesting ideas, developing needed support, or merely summarizing the obvious or repeating yourself?
  - Concentrate on capturing main points or continue writing, realizing that much of what you write will be deleted.
  - Narrow the scope of your paper. You may have to limit your subject and refine your thesis. Look over what you have written and determine what section would make the best topic for a more sharply defined essay.

E-WRITING

Exploring Writing the First Draft Online

You can use the Internet to learn more about writing first drafts.

1. Using a search engine such as AltaVista, Google, or Yahoo!, enter terms such as *writing process* and *writing first drafts* to locate current sites of interest.

2. Write the draft of an e-mail to a friend. Relate an interesting story about something that happened at school or at work recently. Write a full draft if you can, but do not send it.

E-SOURCES

Preparing to Write and Drafting the Paper
http://www.utoronto.ca/writing/organizing.html
http://writing-program.uchicago.edu/resources/collegewriting

Avoiding Plagiarism
http://owl.english.purdue.edu/handouts/research/r_plagiar.html

COMPANION WEBSITE

See **http://www.transcanadawriter.nelson.com** for further information on writing the first draft.

CHAPTER 9

Revising and Rewriting

This chapter explores the nature of revision as "reseeing": gaining fresh perspective on your draft to help clarify ideas and strengthen your power of communication. It addresses the importance of developing a revising style while adopting various revision strategies to help you with both the macro- and micro-elements of an essay.

Rewriting is the essence of writing well . . .

—WILLIAM ZINSSER

WHAT IS REVISION?

After completing the first draft, you may be tempted to start rewriting immediately—rewording awkward sentences, inserting a good quotation, checking spelling. But wait: revision is more than correcting mistakes and plugging in missing details. Revision means "to see again." Before you start rewriting, it is important to examine your draft and look at it the way your readers will.

DEVELOPING A REVISING STYLE

Revision methods, like composing styles, often are distinctly personal. Some writers produce a first draft, and then without reading it write a second and perhaps a third. Just as photographers will shoot a series of pictures and then select a single exposure, good writers prefer to make a number of attempts, using different styles, wordings, and approaches to their subject. Later they choose the best version, often blending in elements of the other drafts. Other writers work in sections, revising and rewriting the introduction before moving on to the body, perfecting the essay paragraph by paragraph. Still other writers prefer to revise the body of an essay first, then rewrite the introduction and conclusion.

We suggest you experiment with different revision methods and devise your own rewriting style. Some papers will dictate a specific technique. If the introduction establishes an argument or creates a framework for setting up the evidence, you may find it necessary to concentrate on the opening paragraph in order to make decisions about what should follow. However, it might be impossible to revise the introduction of a narrative until you determine which events and details will appear in the final essay.

102

Nevertheless, despite personal revision methods, most writers follow a standard pattern for revising. They begin by examining the larger elements—reading through the draft for content and rewriting the paragraphs—before making corrections at the sentence and word levels.

Strategies for Revising

1. **Let your writing "cool."** Before you can look at your writing objectively, it is important to set it aside. Let some time pass between writing and revising. Take a walk, watch television, or work on other assignments before attempting to revise.

2. **Print your draft.** Although some students are skilled at revising on a computer, many find it easier to work with hard copy. Printing the draft can allow you to spread out the pages and see the entire text. It helps to double- or even triple-space the document to provide room for notes and corrections.

3. **Review your goal.** Before looking at your draft, review your plan and instructor's guidelines.
   - Review models of the kind of writing you are attempting.
   - If you decide your draft is off target, it may be easier to review your notes, create a new outline, and write a new draft rather than spend time rewriting a failed attempt.

4. **Examine your draft globally.** Revising is not copyediting. Don't immediately begin to correct spelling and punctuation. Instead, focus on the larger elements of the draft.
   - Review the writing context—does the draft reflect your role, address readers' needs, and suit the discipline or profession?
   - Is the thesis clearly stated?
   - Is the supporting evidence sufficient?
   - Is the paper logically organized?
   - Does the introduction arouse interest and prepare readers for what follows?
   - Does the conclusion leave readers with a strong final impression, question, or challenge?
   - Are sections "off-topic" or redundant?
   - Does this draft meet the needs of the writing assignment?
   - What are the strong and weak points of the essay? What problems should be given priority?

5. **Examine your paper with a "reader's eye."** Consider your readers' perceptual world. What existing knowledge, experiences, values, or attitudes will shape their responses to your paper?
   - Are readers likely to be receptive, indifferent, or hostile to your views? What details will arouse interest or defend your thesis?
   - Do you expect reader objections? Do you anticipate differing opinions?
   - Do readers need any additional background information to appreciate your views? Are there any misunderstandings or misconceptions that should be clarified or dispelled? Do terms or concepts require definitions?
   - Will readers respond favourably to the style and tone of the paper?

(Continued)

6. **Analyze your critical thinking.** In the rush of creating a first draft it can be easy to make lapses in critical thinking. New ideas spring to mind, and you may make connections that lack logical foundation. Review Common Errors in Critical Thinking (pages 31–35).

7. **Consider the nature of the document.** Documents often dictate specific styles and formats. The choppy sentences and short paragraphs expected in a newspaper article are inappropriate for a research paper. The subjective impressions that add colour to a personal essay are unsuited to a business report.
   - Does your draft suit the needs of the document?
   - Are the language, style, and "look" of your writing appropriate?

8. **Read your draft aloud.** Hearing how your draft sounds increases your ability to evaluate your draft for clarity, logic, and tone. Awkward sentences, illogical statements, redundant passages, and missing details are far easier to "hear" than read.

9. **Have others read your draft.** Many instructors encourage students to engage in peer review. If you have the opportunity to participate in a writing group, ask fellow classmates to review your work.
   - Let others read your work "cold." If you preface their reading by telling them what you are trying to say, they will have a harder time evaluating your work objectively.
   - If you ask people outside your composition class to read your paper, however, explain the assignment first. People cannot provide advice if they read your draft in a vacuum. The more they know about your goal and the intended audience, the more valuable their responses will be.
   - Avoid being defensive. Encourage people to react to your work.
   - Encourage feedback by asking targeted questions. If you simply ask, "Do you like it?" or "Is my paper any good?" you are likely to receive polite compliments or vague assurances that your work is "okay." To get helpful advice ask peers specific questions.
   - Ask readers what they consider the paper's strong and weak points.
   - Make notes of their remarks and ask how your draft could be improved.

10. **Revise and rewrite.** If you are fortunate, your first attempt will be well written enough to require only minor revisions. In fact, you may be able to make a few improvements and move on to final editing. But most writers, especially those working on complex or challenging assignments, usually discover enough flaws to require extensive revising.
    - Revising is an ongoing process. If you write on a computer, it is easy to make subtle changes to your work with each reading.
    - In the light of your first draft, you may wish to review your plan to see whether any changes should be made.
    - If your draft is very unsatisfactory, it may be better to return to your plan and start a fresh draft. Try writing from a different angle, start with a new introduction, use different examples, or select different words and images. Often it will take you less time to write a fresh first draft than to revise and repair an existing one.
    - If you included images or visual aids in your draft, review their use. Do photographs support your points or simply supply illustrations? Avoid images that will distract or offend readers. Ensure that figures and tables are accurate and do not oversimplify or distort data.

Strategies for Peer Review

Feedback from others is important to the revising process. It provides a fresh perspective, greater distance, and objectivity—other eyes often can see what you can't because you are too immersed in the writing process. Just as professional writers receive reactions from editors and reviewers who analyze their work for factual errors, lapses in judgments, and mechanical mistakes, you likely will be asked to engage in peer review—feedback from classmates—by your instructors. Peer review is not about offering negative criticism; it is about providing another perspective on how effectively you have communicated your ideas. Good peer reviewers analyze your draft to see where your writing works and where it could use revision for greater clarity, logic, evidence, and so forth.

1. **Understand the role of a peer reviewer.** A peer reviewer's job is not to tell others how he or she would write the paper. It is to provide thoughtful reader response and offer suggestions for making a document stronger. Work with the writer to identify weaknesses and errors and to suggest improvements.

2. **Understand the writer's goal and the assignment.** If you are not familiar with the assignment, ask to see any directions the student received from his or her instructor. Read the instructions carefully so that you can provide meaningful advice. Does the paper meet the instructor's requirements?

3. **Review the document globally, then look at specifics.** Before pointing out grammar and spelling errors, focus on the big picture.
   - Does the topic suit the assignment?
   - Does it need to be more clearly focused or limited?
   - Does the paper have a clear thesis?
   - Is the thesis effectively supported with details?
   - Are there irrelevant details that can be deleted?
   - Do paragraphs adequately organize the paper? Could the paragraph structure be more effective?
   - Can you detect sentences that are unclear, illogical, or awkward?
   - Does the paper need proofreading for spelling and grammar errors? As a peer reviewer, your job is not to correct mechanical errors but indicate to the writer whether the paper needs proofreading.

4. **Be positive.** Make constructive, helpful comments. Don't simply point out errors but indicate how they might be corrected or avoided.

5. **Ask questions.** Instead of stating that a sentence or paragraph does not make sense, ask the writer what he or she was trying to say. Asking questions can prompt a writer to rethink what he or she wrote, remember missing details, or consider new alternatives.

REVISING ELEMENTS OF THE FIRST DRAFT

Although you can correct errors in spelling and punctuation at any point, your main objective in revising is to study the larger elements of your essay, especially the paragraphs.

Look at the Big Picture

Review the Entire Essay

Read the paper aloud. How does it sound? What ideas or facts are missing, poorly stated, or repetitive? Highlight areas that need improvement and delete paragraphs that are off-topic or redundant.

- How does your draft measure up against your goal?
- What prevents this draft from meeting the needs of the writing assignment?
- What are the most serious defects?
- Have you selected an appropriate method of organizing your essay? Would a chronological approach be better than division? Should you open with your strongest point or reserve it for the conclusion?

Examine the Thesis

Most importantly, focus on the thesis or controlling idea of the essay. Does your paper have a clear thesis, a controlling idea—or is it simply a collection of facts and observations? Does the essay have a point?

- If your paper has a thesis statement, read it aloud. Is it clearly stated? Is it too general? Can it be adequately supported?
- Where have you placed the thesis? Would it be better situated elsewhere in the essay? Remember, the thesis does not have to appear in the opening.
- If the thesis is implied rather than stated, does the essay have a controlling idea? Do details and your choice of words provide readers with a clear impression of your subject?

Review Topic Sentences and Controlling Ideas

Each paragraph should have a clear focus and support the thesis.

- Review the controlling idea for each paragraph.
- Do all the paragraphs support the thesis?
- Are there paragraphs that are off-topic? You may have developed some interesting ideas, recalled an important fact or quote, or detailed a compelling story—but if they don't directly relate to the thesis, they do not belong in this essay.

Review the Sequence of Paragraphs

While writing, you may have discovered new ideas or diverted from your plan, altering the design of the essay. Study the list of topic sentences and determine whether their order serves your purpose.

- Should paragraphs be rearranged to maintain chronology or to create greater emphasis?
- Does the order of paragraphs follow your train of thought? Should some paragraphs be preceded by those offering definitions and background information?

Revise the Introduction

The opening sentences and paragraphs of any document are critical. They set the tone of the paper, announce the topic, arouse reader interest, and establish how the rest of the essay is organized. Because you cannot always predict how you will change the body of the essay, you should always return to the introduction and examine it before writing a new draft.

✔ INTRODUCTION **CHECKLIST**

- ✔ Does the introduction clearly announce the topic?
- ✔ Does the opening paragraph arouse interest?
- ✔ Does the opening paragraph serve to limit the topic, preparing readers for what follows?
- ✔ If the thesis appears in the opening, is it clearly and precisely stated?
- ✔ Does the language of the opening paragraph set the proper tone for the paper?
- ✔ Does the introduction address reader concerns, correct misconceptions, and provide background information so that readers can understand and appreciate the evidence that follows?

Revise Supporting Paragraphs

The paragraphs in the body of the essay should support the thesis, develop ideas, or advance the chronology.

✔ PARAGRAPH **CHECKLIST**

- ✔ Does the paragraph have a clear focus?
- ✔ Is the controlling idea supported with enough evidence?
- ✔ Is the evidence easy to follow? Does the paragraph follow a logical organization? Would a different mode be more effective in unifying the ideas?
- ✔ Are there irrelevant ideas that should be deleted?
- ✔ Are there clear transitions between ideas and between paragraphs?
- ✔ Do paragraph breaks signal major transitions? Should some paragraphs be combined and others broken up?

Revise the Conclusion

Not all essays require a separate paragraph or group of paragraphs to conclude the writing. A narrative may end with a final event. A comparison may conclude with the last point.

☑ CONCLUSION **CHECKLIST**

✔ Does the conclusion end the paper on a strong note? Will it leave readers with a final image, question, quotation, or fact that will challenge them and lead them to continue thinking about your subject?

✔ Does the conclusion simply repeat the introduction or main ideas? Is it necessary? Should it be shortened or deleted?

✔ If your purpose is to motivate people to take action, does the conclusion provide readers with clear directions?

Improving Paragraphs

First drafts often produce weak paragraphs that need stronger topic sentences and clearer support:

First Draft

The automobile changed Canada. Development increased as distances were reduced. People moved outward from the city to live and work. Highways and bridges were built. Travel increased and greater mobility led to rapid population shifts, causing growth in some areas and declines in others. Cars created new industries and demands for new services.

Revision Notes

too vague, need tighter topic sentence too general
The automobile changed Canada. Development increased as distances were
        lack of sentence variety
reduced. People moved outward from the city to live and work. Highways
          explain
and bridges were built. Travel increased and greater mobility led to rapid
    what areas?
population shifts, causing growth in some areas and declines in others. Cars
   give examples
created new industries and demands for new services.

Improved

The automobile reshaped the Canadian landscape. As millions of cars jammed crowded streets and bogged down on unpaved roads, drivers demanded better highways. The cities pushed beyond rail and trolley lines, absorbing farms, meadows, and marshland. The middle class abandoned the polluted congestion of the city for the mushrooming suburbs that offered greater space and privacy. Gas stations, garages, parking structures, and drive-in movies appeared across the country. Motels, chain stores, and fast food restaurants catered to the mobile public. Shopping malls, office towers, factories, and schools appeared in the new communities, all of them surrounded by what the cities could not offer—free parking.

Search subsequent drafts for overwritten paragraphs cluttered with redundant statements, needless or irrelevant details, or wordy sentences.

REVISING THE FIRST DRAFT

The student writing about victim impact statements reviewed her first draft and read it to several classmates, who offered suggestions. As she listened to them, she added notes in the margins and developed a checklist to guide her second draft. At this point, the writer is focusing on the big picture, as well as making some adjustments at the level of word choice. Copyediting and proofreading will come later.

Revision

Across Canada today more and more victims of crime are being allowed to address the court in terms of making what is called a victim impact statment. This written or oral presentation to the court allows victims to express their feelings to the judge after someone has been convicted of a crime.   *wordy/weak*

Advocates of victim impact statements point to key advantages. First, these statements give victim's a voice. For years, victims have felt helpless. Prosecutors represent the province, not the cirme victim. Victim have been dismayed when prosecutors have arranged pleas bargains without their knowledge. Some victims are still recovering from their injuries when they learn the person who hurt them has plead to a lesser charge and received probation.

Therapists who work with victims also say that being able to address the court helps with the healing process. Victims of violent crime can feel powerless and vulnerable. Instead of suffering in silence, they are given the chance to address the criminal, to <u>clear their chests</u>, and get on with the rest of their lives.   *cliché*

Impact statements allows judges to consider what sentences are apropriate. In one case a judge who planned to fine a teenager for shoplifting excepted the store owners suggestions to waive the fine if the defendent completed high school.

But giving victims a change to speak raises some issues. What about the victim who is not articulate, who doesn't even speak English? In murder cases the victim's relatives are given a chance to speak? Does this mean that a middle class professional victim with a circle of grieving freinds and family members will be granted more significance than the homeless murder victim who leaves no one behind?

Victim impact statements may help empower victims who are educated, personally impressive, and socially promient. But they may also allow forgotten victims to remain voiceless.

Revision Notes

Needs stronger opening—needs attention-getter

Sharper definition

Too short/superficial discussion

Clearer examples/Use real-life trials

Tighter conclusion

Second Draft

The courtroom scene was riveting. One by one, the survivors of a deadly shooting took the stand and addressed the man who had maimed them. Their voices quivering with emotion, they told the court how the gunman's actions changed their lives forever. Spouses and parents of the dead spoke of loss. There were tears, moments of intense anger, and quiet despair. Victim impact statements have become a common feature of criminal proceedings. Spoken in court or submitted in writing, these statements provide an opportunity for victims to be heard before sentencing.

Advocates of victims impact statements believe these declarations give victims a voice, an opportunity to be heard. Traditionally, victims have appeared in court only as witnesses subject to cross-examination. Prosecutors, victims soon learn, represent the state and not individuals. Still hospitalized after a brutal beating, a Vancouver restaurant owner learned from reading a newspaper that his assailants had plea-bargained to lesser charges and received probation. Joining with other victims, he became an advocate for victims' rights, including impact statements.

Therapists who counsel victims of crime believe that addressing the court and taking an active role in the legal process helps people recover from a sense of helplessness and regain a measure of self-respect.

Impact statements allow judges to consider appropriate sentences. In an American case, a judge who intended to fine a teenager for shoplifting agreed with the store owner's suggestion that the fine be waived if the defendant completed high school.

But giving victims a chance to speak has led to ugly courtroom scenes that seem inappropriate in a democracy. The relative of one murder victim shouted that he would execute the killer himself. Bailiffs had to restrain him as he begged the judge, "Just gimme five minutes with him!" Defence attorneys argue these harangues are unnecessary. What need is there to heap abuse upon a person about to lose his or her life or liberty? Can anger and harassment be considered healing?

But even restrained, well-reasoned impact statements raise troubling questions. What about the victim who is too impaired, too frightened, or too wounded to speak? Is his or her absence to be judged as indifference? What about those whose English is limited? What of those without friends or family? Should the drunk driver who kills a young professional missed by friends, family, and colleagues receive a tougher sentence than the drunk driver who kills a homeless man who dies unmourned, unmissed, and uncounted? Do we really want our courts and society to suggest that some lives are more significant than others?

Victim impact statements may help empower victims, especially the educated, the personally impressive, and the socially prominent. But these statements, unintentionally, may also further marginalize the most helpless among us, allowing forgotten victims to remain voiceless.

Strategies for Overcoming Problems in Revising

Revising a draft can be challenging. Writers encounter a range of common problems.

1. **The draft remains unfocused.** If your writing remains too general and seems to lack direction, review your thesis statement.
   - Does your thesis limit the scope of the paper?
   - Does your thesis provide a method of organizing the evidence?
   - Apply prewriting techniques such as lists and clustering to map out the ideas in the draft. Often a list will help you discover a new organizational method and identify ideas that are off-topic.

2. **The draft remains too short.** If, after extensive reading, revising, and rewriting, your essay remains too short or too superficial, return to your plan.
   - Review your thesis and return to prewriting to develop more evidence.

3. **The draft is too long and seems incomplete.** Examine your thesis. Have you attempted to cover too broad a topic given the limit of the assignment?
   - Review your goal and any instructor's guidelines for methods of limiting the paper.
   - An essay that offers an in-depth view of a narrow topic is far more interesting than a longer piece that provides a superficial examination of a broader subject.

E-WRITING

Exploring Revision Online

You can use the Internet to learn more about revising first drafts.

1. Using a search engine such as AltaVista, Google, or Yahoo!, enter terms such as *writing process* and *revision* to locate current sites of interest.

2. If you wrote an e-mail to a friend (see page 101), review and revise your draft. What ideas did you forget to add? Are there irrelevant details that could be deleted? Could

paragraphs be stronger, better organized? Does your e-mail have the focus and the impact you intended?

3. Review past e-mails you have sent. What changes would you make now? Do you find awkward and wordy sentences? Are there missing details?

FOR FURTHER READING

Cook, Claire Kehrwald. *Line by Line: How to Improve Your Writing.*
Venolia, Jan. Rewrite *Right! How to Revise Your Way to Better Writing.*

E-SOURCES

A Strategy for Analyzing and Revising a First Draft
http://www.utoronto.ca/writing/organizing.html
http://writing-program.uchicago.edu/resources/collegewriting

Editing and Proofreading Strategies for Revision
http://owl.english.purdue.edu/handouts/general

COMPANION WEBSITE

See **http://www.transcanadawriter.nelson.com** for additional information on revising.

CHAPTER 10

Editing and Proofreading

This chapter focuses on the final, polishing stage of the writing process: editing and proofreading. It defines both terms and discusses the differences between them and the prior stage of drafting. It offers tips on strategies for editing and proofreading, looking in particular at screening out problems in word usage, mechanics, and format.

All good essays are not only fine-tuned but also waxed and polished—they are edited and proofread repeatedly for errors until they shine.

—JEAN WYRICK

WHAT ARE EDITING AND PROOFREADING?

Editing and proofreading are the final steps in the writing process. In the editing stage, you focus on improving the impact of sentences, correcting errors, eliminating needless phrases, and improving the style and clarity of your writing. Proofreading checks the visual appearance of your document, reviewing the paper for spelling, proper format, pagination, margins, and accuracy of names, dates, and numbers.

Editing and proofreading, though often seen as final steps, can occur throughout the writing process. While writing and revising, you can fix mechanical errors, provided they do not distract you from focusing on the larger elements.

A number of tools can assist you in editing and proofreading:

- Dictionary—to check spelling and definitions
- Thesaurus—to find alternatives for overused or imprecise words
- Handbook—to check grammar, punctuation, mechanics, and documentation styles
- Encyclopedia—to check names, dates, facts, and historical and biographical references

If you compose on a computer, you may have easy access to online and CD-ROM resources.

Strategies for *Editing*

1. **Read your paper aloud.** Listen to your words and sentences. Missing and misspelled words, awkward and redundant phrases, and illogical constructions are easier to hear than see.

2. **Use peer editing.** It is far easier to detect errors in someone else's writing. Switch papers with another student if you can. Read the student's paper aloud if possible, noting mistakes and areas needing revision.

3. **Use spell-check and other computer tools.** Almost all word processing programs include spell-check, which detects items it does not recognize as words.

   ■ Spell-check systems have limitations. They will not find missing words or distinguish between homonyms such as "their" and "there." In addition, they will not always be able to detect errors in proper names such as "Kowalski" or "Nunavut."

4. **Edit backward.** By this time in the writing process, you may have read and reread your paper so many times that it is difficult to look at your sentences objectively. An effective way of spotting errors is to start with the last line and read backward, moving from the conclusion to the introduction. Working in reverse order isolates sentences so that you can evaluate them out of context.

5. **Focus on identifying and correcting habitual errors.** Students often have habitual errors. You may frequently make spelling errors, forget needed commas, or continually confuse *its* and *it's*.

   ■ Review previously written papers and instructor comments to identify errors you are likely to repeat.

Common Grammatical Errors

When editing drafts, look for these common grammatical errors.

Fragments

Fragments are incomplete sentences. Sentences require a subject and a verb and must state a complete thought:

Tom works until midnight.	**sentence**
Tom working until midnight.	**fragment (incomplete verb)**
Works until midnight.	**fragment (subject missing)**
Because Tom works until midnight.	**fragment (incomplete thought)**

Note that even though the last item has a subject, *Tom,* and a verb, *works,* it does not state a complete thought.

See pages 594–596 for more on fragments.

Run-ons and Comma Splices

Run-ons and comma splices are incorrectly punctuated compound sentences. Simple sentences (independent clauses) can be joined to create compound sentences in two ways:

1. Link with a **semicolon** [;]
2. Link with a **comma** [,] followed by ***and, or, yet, but,*** or ***so***

I was born in Hull, Quebec, but I grew up in Montreal.	correct
I studied Italian; Jacques took Spanish.	correct
We have to take a cab my battery is dead.	run-on
We have to take a cab; my battery is dead.	correct
George is sick, the game is cancelled.	comma splice
George is sick, so the game is cancelled	correct

See pages 597–598 for more about run-ons and comma splices.

Subject and Verb Agreement

Subjects and verbs must match in number. Singular subjects use singular verbs. Plural subjects use plural verbs:

The boy *walks* to school.	Singular
The boys *walk* to school.	Plural
The cost of drugs *is* rising.	Singular (the subject is "cost")
Two weeks *is* not enough time	Singular (amounts of time and money are singular)
The jury *is* deliberating.	Singular (group subjects are singular)
The teacher or the students *are* invited.	Plural (when two subjects are joined with "or" the subject nearer the verb determines whether it is singular or plural)

See pages 602–606 for more on subject and verb agreement.

Pronoun Agreement

Pronouns must agree with or match the nouns they represent:

Everyone should cast *his* or *her* vote.	Singular
The children want *their* parents to call.	Plural

The most misused pronoun is *they*. *They* is a pronoun and should clearly refer to a noun. Avoid unclear use of pronouns as in, "Crime is rising. Schools are failing. They just don't care." Who does *they* refer to?

See pages 606–608 for more on pronoun agreement.

Dangling and Misplaced Modifiers

To prevent confusion, modifiers—words and phrases that add information about other words—should be placed next to the words they modify.

Rowing across the lake, the moon rose over the water.	(dangling, who was *rowing*? the *moon*?)
Rowing across the lake, we saw the moon rise over the water.	(correct)
She drove the car to the house which was rented.	(misplaced, which was rented?)
She drove the car to the rented house.	(correct)

See pages 616–619 for more about dangling and misplaced modifiers.

Faulty Parallelism

Pairs and lists of words and phrases should match in form:

Karem is tall, handsome, and an athlete.	(not parallel, list mixes adjectives and a noun)
Karem is tall, handsome, and athletic.	(parallel, all adjectives)
We need to paint the bedroom, shovel the walk, and the basement must be cleaned.	(not parallel, the last item does not match with *to paint* and (to) *shovel*.
We need to paint the bedroom, shovel the walk, and clean the basement.	(parallel, all verb phrases)

See pages 599–601 for more on faulty parallelism.

Awkward Shifts in Person

Avoid illogical shifts in person:

We climbed the tower and you could see for miles.	(illogical shift from *we* to *you*)

We climbed the tower and we could see for miles.	(correct)
If a student works hard, you can get an A.	(illogical shift from *student* to *you*)
If you work hard, you can get an A.	(correct)

Awkward Shifts in Tense

Avoid illogical shifts in tense (time):

Hamlet hears from a ghost, then he avenged his father.	(awkward shift from present to past)
Hamlet heard from a ghost, then he avenged his father.	(correct, both past)
Hamlet hears from a ghost, then he avenges his father.	(correct, both present)

Editing Sentences

After revising the larger elements of your draft, examine the sentences in each paragraph. Read each sentence separately to ensure it expresses the thoughts you intended.

☑ SENTENCE **CHECKLIST**

- ✔ Does the sentence support the paragraph's controlling idea? Could it be eliminated?
- ✔ Are key ideas emphasized through concrete words and active verbs?
- ✔ Are secondary ideas subordinated?
- ✔ Are the relationships between ideas clearly expressed with transitional expressions?
- ✔ Do the tone and style of the sentence suit your reader and nature of the document?

Be Brief

Sentences lose their power when cluttered with unnecessary words and phrases. When writing the rough draft, it is easy to slip in expressions that add nothing to the meaning of the sentence.

ORIGINAL: In today's modern world computer literacy is essential to enter in the job market.

IMPROVED: Computer literacy is essential to get a job.

Phrases that begin with *who* is or *which* were can often be shortened:

ORIGINAL: Viveca Scott, who was an ambitious business leader, doubled profits, which stunned her stockholders.

IMPROVED: Viveca Scott, an ambitious business leader, stunned her stockholders by doubling profits.

Delete Wordy Phrases

Even skilled writers use wordy phrases in trying to express themselves in a first draft. When editing, locate phrases that can be replaced with shorter phrases or single words:

WORDY	IMPROVED
at that period of time	then
at the present time	now
in the near future	soon
winter months	winter
round in shape	round
blue coloured	blue
for the purpose of informing	to inform
render an examination of	examine
make an analysis	analyze
in the event of	if

Eliminate Redundancy

Repeating or restating words and ideas can have a dramatic effect, but it is a technique that should be used sparingly and only when you wish to emphasize a specific point.

REDUNDANT: The computer has revolutionized education, revolutionizing delivery systems, course content, and teaching methods.

IMPROVED: The computer has revolutionized educational delivery systems, course content, and teaching methods.

REDUNDANT: He took his medicines, but poor nutrition, bad eating habits, his lack of exercise, and sedentary lifestyle hampered his recovery.

IMPROVED: He took his medicines, but his bad eating habits and sedentary lifestyle hampered his recovery.

Limit Use of Passive Voice

Most sentences state ideas in active voice—the subject performs the action of the verb. In passive voice the order is reversed and the sentence's subject is acted on:

ACTIVE	**PASSIVE**
Mr. Shiwak towed the car.	The car was towed by Mr. Shiwak.
The hospital conducted several tests.	Several tests were conducted by the hospital.
The mayor's office announced a new round of budget cuts.	A new round of budget cuts was announced by the mayor's office.

Passive voice is used when the actor is unknown or less important than the object:

My car was stolen.
The door was locked.
His chest was crushed by a rock.

Passive voice, however, can leave out critical information:

After the plane crash, several photographs were taken.

Who took the photographs—investigators, reporters, the airline, survivors, bystanders? Use passive voice *only* when it emphasizes important elements in a sentence.

Vary Your Use of Sentence Types

You can keep your writing interesting and fresh by altering types of sentences. Repeating a single kind of sentence can give your writing a monotonous predictability. A short sentence isolates an idea and gives it emphasis, but a string of choppy sentences explaining minor details robs your essay of power. Long sentences can subordinate minor details and show the subtle relationships between ideas, but they can become tedious for readers to follow.

UNVARIED: Andrea Borrow was elected to the assembly. She worked hard on the budget committee. Her work won her respect. She was highly regarded by the mayor. People responded to her energy and drive. She became popular with voters. The mayor decided to run for provincial party leader. He asked Andrea Borrow to manage his campaign.

VARIED: Andrea Borrow was elected to the assembly. Her hard work on the budget committee won her respect, especially from the mayor. Voters were impressed by her drive and energy. When the mayor decided to run for provincial party leader, he asked Andrea Borrow to manage his campaign.

UNVARIED: The mayor believed he could unseat Mike Koepple by attacking what he believed were the premier's two weak points: his failure to reduce taxes and his reluctance to commit money to education. Andrea Borrow conducted in-depth focus groups with voters across the province, devising a series of clever commercials that highlighted Koepple's shortcomings and extolling the mayor's achievements in lowering taxes and supporting schools. Premier Koepple, startled at the mayor's strong showing in the polls, was disappointed by his campaign staff. Fearing a brutal assault in the media, Koepple quietly announced that he would not seek a second term and would accept the prime minister's offer of becoming ambassador to New Zealand.

VARIED: The mayor believed he could unseat Mike Koepple by attacking the premier's two weak points: his failure to reduce taxes and his reluctance to commit money to education. After conducting in-depth focus groups with voters across the province, Andrea Borrow devised a series of clever commercials. Mike Koepple's shortcomings were compared to the mayor's achievements in lowering taxes and supporting schools. Premier Koepple, startled by the mayor's strong showing in the polls, was disappointed by his campaign staff. Fearing a brutal assault in the media, Koepple quietly announced that he would not seek a second term. The prime minister had offered him a better job—ambassador to New Zealand.

WRITING **ACTIVITY**

Edit the following sentences by eliminating wordy and redundant phrases and emphasizing main ideas.

1. In many ways students must learn to teach themselves to be successful.
2. The Canadian automotive industry, still overpowered by Japan and the United States, nonetheless is the eighth largest in the world and competes well in the global car market.
3. Illness and disease can be prevented through proper diet, appropriate exercise, and moderation in the consumption of alcohol.
4. In my personal opinion, the calculus course is too tough for the majority of first-year students.
5. The exams were distributed by the professor after a brief introduction.

Edit the sentences in the following paragraph to reduce clutter and increase clarity and variety:

Three years ago the writing lab was opened by the English Department. This lab was designed to assist students taking first-year composition courses. The lab was at first staffed by four paraprofessionals with extensive experience in teaching writing and editing. But the budget was cut by the dean of liberal arts. Now only two part-time graduate students serve the students. Neither has teaching nor editing experience. The students are no longer getting the assistance they need to improve their writing. The lab is no longer crowded. Often students are found using the computers to send e-mail to friends. Some play solitaire or minesweeper between classes. This should change.

Editing Words

✔ DICTION **CHECKLIST**

✔ Are the words accurate? Have you chosen words that precisely reflect your thinking?

✔ Is the level of diction appropriate? Do your word choices suit the tone and style of the document?

✔ Do connotations suit your purpose or do they detract from your message?

✔ Are technical terms clearly defined?

✔ Do you use concrete rather than abstract words?

Avoid Sexist Language

Sexist language either ignores the existence of one gender or promotes negative attitudes about men or women.

Replace sexist words with neutral terms:

SEXIST	NONSEXIST
mankind	humanity
postman	letter carrier
policeman	police officer
Frenchmen	the French
Men at Work	Workers Ahead
manmade	synthetic
everyman	everyone
fireman	firefighter
man in the street	average person
chairman	chairperson

Avoid nouns with "female" endings or adjectives. Although the words *actress* and *waitress* are still used, other words designating female professionals are considered largely obsolete:

SEXIST	NONSEXIST
poetess	poet
authoress	author
lady lawyer	lawyer
woman judge	judge

Avoid using male pronouns when nouns refer to both genders. The single noun *man* takes the single male pronoun *he*. If you are writing about a boys' school, it is appropriate to substitute "he" for the noun "student." But if the school includes both males and females, both should be represented:

Every student should try *his* or *her* best.
All students should try *their* best.

Plural nouns take the pronouns *they* and *their*, avoiding wordy *he or she* and *his or her* constructions.

Avoid Clichés

Clichés are worn-out phrases. Once creative or imaginative, these phrases, like jokes you have heard more than once, have lost their impact. In addition, clichés allow simplistic statements to substitute for genuine thought.

white as snow	light as a feather	acid test
Mr. Big	in the thick of it	on pins and needles
evil as sin	dead heat	crushing blow
viable option	bottom line	all that jazz
crack of dawn	calm before the storm	dog-tired

WRITING **ACTIVITY**

Edit the wording of the following sentences to avoid sexism, clichés, awkward phrases, and misused words.

1. Every student should bring his books to class.
2. He jogged at the crack of dawn every morning.
3. The university has listed three mandatory requirements for future revision.
4. We had better get down to brass tacks if we want to get a fresh start.
5. Threatened by drug dealers, the witness required continual security.
6. This dispute must be settled by an uninterested judge.
7. He could manage to explain a difficult problem with childish simplicity.
8. The computer company began to flounder in debt.
9. The prime minister's speech was vague but most implied he favoured a tax hike.
10. A voter should use his best judgment.

Strategies for Proofreading

Proofreading examines writing for errors and concerns itself with the physical appearance—the "look"—of the finished document.

1. **Make a last check for errors in the text.** Read the paper through to make last-minute corrections in grammar, numbers, dates, spellings, usage, punctuation, and capitalization.

2. **Use an appropriate form.** Instructors often dictate specific styles and requirements about paging, margins, spacing, and cover sheets. Business, government, and professional documents may have precise guidelines.

3. **Use standard formats.** Unless you are given specific instructions, follow these standard guidelines.

   - Use standard-size 8½" x 11" white paper. Avoid using onionskin or easily smeared paper.
   - Remove any perforated edges.
   - Use standard typeface or fonts. Avoid script or fonts smaller than 10 point. Use fonts larger than 14 only for titles and headings.
   - Double-space your text, leaving ample margins.
   - Use a title page or headline listing your name, instructor's name, course, date, and assignment.

4. **Keep a copy of all your papers.** Papers do get lost. Always keep a copy in case your instructor fails to get your assignment.

COMMON MECHANICAL ERRORS

Spelling and Usage Errors

Spell-check programs may not distinguish between words like *there* and *their* or *affect* and *effect*.

Review dictionaries and see pages 645–650.

Punctuation

Use **commas** to separate items in a list, set off introductory and nonrestrictive elements, and join clauses in complex and compound sentences:

> We bought pens, pencils, paper, and ink.
> After losing the game, we met with the coach to discuss strategy.
> My brother, who was born in Halifax, took us to Peggy's Cove.
> Because it was hot, the game was cancelled.
> We bought the plane tickets, but Hector paid for the hotel.

Use **semicolons** to separate independent clauses in compound sentences:

I flew to Nunavut; Louis took the train.

Use **apostrophes** to indicate contractions and possessives:

Don't let Karl's truck leave the garage.

See pages 620–636 for more on punctuation.

Capitalization

Capitalize proper nouns such as names of products, organizations, geographical places, and people:

Buick   Simon Fraser University   Toronto   Rockies   Jim Wilson

Capitalize titles when used before a name:

We called for a doctor just as Dr. Green walked in.

Capitalize *East, North, West, South* when they refer to regions, not directions:

We drove south to the airport and grabbed a flight to the East.

See pages 636–638 for more about capitalization.

Strategies for Overcoming Problems in Editing and Proofreading

1. **Sentences remain awkward.** Even after revising and editing, many sentences may still be awkward or garbled.
   - Think about the ideas you were trying to express and write new sentences without looking at your paper. Try restating your ideas with different words.
   - Use peer review if possible. You can use e-mail or even a phone call to test your sentence with someone else.
2. Sentences contain redundant phrases and repeated words.
   - Search a thesaurus for alternative words.

- Examine your text to see whether headings and subheadings could substitute for repeating phrases.
- Read aloud or use peer review to detect needless or awkward repetitions.

3. **You are unable to determine the final format of the document.** Even when your text is perfected, you may find yourself unable to decide whether your paper should be single- or double-spaced, whether figures or tables should be included, or whether citations should appear at the bottom of the page, within the text, or on a separate page.

- Review instructions for guidelines or talk with your instructor.
- Examine any existing examples for guidance.
- Review official sources such as *The Chicago Manual of Style* or *The MLA Handbook*.

E-WRITING

Exploring Editing Online

You can use the Internet to learn more about editing.

1. Using a search engine such as AltaVista, Google, or Yahoo!, enter terms such as *editing drafts* and *editing process* to locate current sites of interest.

2. If you wrote an e-mail to a friend, review and edit your draft. Can you locate any grammar errors such as fragments, run-ons, or dangling modifiers? Have you used standard forms of punctuation and capitalization?

FOR FURTHER READING

Fulwiler, Toby, and Alan R. Hayakawa. *The College Writer's Reference.*

Sabin, William A. *The Gregg Reference Manual.*

Stilman, Anne. *Grammatically Correct: The Writer's Essential Guide to Punctuation, Spelling, Style, Usage, and Grammar.*

Sutcliffe, Andrea, ed. *The New York Public Library Writer's Guide to Style and Usage.*

Wilson, Kenneth G. *The Columbia Guide to Standard American English.*

E-SOURCES

Answers.com—online dictionary and encyclopedia
http://www.answers.com

Advice on Academic Writing
http://www.utoronto.ca/writing/advise.html#style

COMPANION WEBSITE

See **http://www.transcanadawriter.nelson.com** for further information about editing and proofreading.

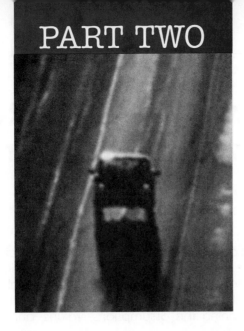

PART TWO

Critical Reading and Writing

Becoming a Critical Reader: Reading with a "Writer's Eye"

This chapter focuses on reading from a writer's perspective. It discusses how to move beyond mere reading comprehension to see how a text builds meaning through its language and organization. The chapter emphasizes the importance of summary skills and suggests strategies for suspending judgment initially while analyzing what a text is saying as well as how it says it. It then offers strategies for shifting to a critical position, questioning the assumptions, values, and interests that inform a text's stance or argument.

WHAT IS CRITICAL READING?

Often students misunderstand reading as a passive activity. It isn't. Reading requires making sense of a text, and that depends on an active process of construing meaning.

Reading can have different purposes. As a student, you likely are accustomed to reading analytically for information. *Analysis,* simply put, refers to the process of inquiring into the nature and relationship of parts to wholes. So, studying for examinations, you review textbooks, highlighting facts, dates, statistics, quotations, and concepts that you expect to be tested on.

As a composition student, you need to focus the analytical reading process further, reading critically, with a "writer's eye" to examine *how* a text is written. In this way, you analyze a text to understand how a writer uses language to build meaning, according to purpose, audience, and context.

Reading gives you the opportunity to watch other writers at work. When you read, note the way other writers use words, form sentences, and develop paragraphs. Focus on techniques that you can use in your own assignments. How did the author limit the subject? Where did the writer place the thesis statement? What kind of support is used? What kinds of visuals are used? How did the writer organize ideas? What sentence opens the essay? What thought, image, question, or fact did the author choose for the conclusion?

HOW TO ANALYZE A TEXT WITH A WRITER'S EYE

When you pick up a magazine, you rarely read every article. Flipping through the pages, you allow your eyes to guide you. A headline, a photograph, a chart, or a famous name makes you pause and begin reading. Reading as a writer, however, you examine familiar works differently from readers seeking information. Even if you know a particular essay well, read it closely, observing how it is constructed. As a writer, you read to learn, seeing the essays as models demonstrating strategies that you can use in your own work.

Like writing, critical reading occurs best in stages.

First Reading

1. **Look ahead and skim selections.** Do not wait until the night before a class discussion to read assigned essays. Check your syllabus and skim through upcoming readings to get a general impression.

2. **Study the headnote and introduction.** Consider the author, the issue, and the writing context. What readers does the writer seem to be addressing? Consider your existing knowledge about the author and subject.

3. **Suspend judgment.** Try to put your personal views aside as you read. Even if you disagree with the author, read the essay objectively. Remember, your goal is to understand *how* the writer states his or her point. Even if you reject an author's thesis, you can still learn useful techniques.

4. **Consider the title.** Titles often provide clues about the author's attitude toward his or her subject. Does the title label the essay, state a thesis, pose a question, or use a creative phrase to attract attention?

5. **Read the entire work.** It is important to complete the entire essay in one sitting if possible.

6. **Focus on understanding the writer's main point.** If possible, summarize the writer's thesis in your own words.

7. **Examine any images or visual aids.** If the author includes photographs, figures, tables, or illustrations, note whether they serve to arouse attention, provide an illustration, or offer supporting evidence.

8. **Write down your first impressions.** What do you think of this work? Do you like it? If so, why? If you find it dull or disturbing, ask why. What is lacking? Be sure to explain your reactions fully.

If possible, put the essay aside and let two or three days pass before returning to the assignment. If the assignment is due the next day, read the selection early in the day and then turn to other work or run an errand, so that you can come back to it with a fresh outlook.

Second Reading

1. **Review your first impressions.** Determine whether your attitudes are based on biases rather than the writer's ability. An essay that supports your views is not necessarily well written. If you disagree with the author's thesis, put your opinions aside to evaluate how well the writer presented his or her point of view. Don't allow your personal views to cloud your critical thinking. Appreciating an author's writing ability does not require you to accept his or her opinion.

2. **Read with a pen in your hand.** Reread the essay, making notes and underlining passages that strike you as interesting, odd, offensive, or disturbing. Reading with a pen will prompt you to be an active reader rather than a passive consumer of words.

3. **Look up unfamiliar words.** Paying attention to words can increase your vocabulary.

4. **Analyze passages you found difficult or confusing during the first reading.** A second reading can help you understand complex passages. If you still have difficulty understanding the writer's point, ask why.

5. **Review the questions at the end of the selection.** When available, the questions can help you focus on a closer, more analytical reading of the work. This book's questions are arranged in three groups:

   ■ *Understanding Context:*
     What is the writer's purpose?
     What is the thesis?
     What audience is the writer addressing?
     What is the author trying to share with his or her readers?

   ■ *Evaluating Strategy:*
     How effective is the title?
     How does the writer introduce the essay?
     What evidence supports the thesis?
     How does the writer organize ideas?
     Where does the author use paragraph breaks?
     What role does the writer play? Is the writer's approach subjective or objective?
     How does the writer address possible objections or differing opinions?
     How does the writer conclude the essay?
     Does the author use any special techniques?

   ■ *Appreciating Language:*
     How does the writer use words?
     What does the language reveal about the intended readers?
     What connotations do the words have?
     How do the words establish the writer's tone?

6. **Analyze the use of any visuals.** Do they illustrate an idea or provide support? Are they designed to arouse an emotional response or provide objective evidence? Do they represent what the author claims they do? Are there other interpretations? Does the author explain the context or source of the images? Are figures and tables accurate or misleading?

7. **Summarize your responses in a point or two for class discussion.** Consider how you will express your opinions of the essay to fellow students. Be prepared to support your remarks by citing passages in the text.

8. **Most importantly, focus on what this essay can teach you about writing.** How can this writer's style, way of organizing ideas, or word choice enrich your own writing?

Though you may not wish to imitate everything you see, you can learn techniques to broaden your personal composing style.

9. **Think of how writers resolve problems that you have encountered.** If you have trouble making an outline and organizing ideas, study how the essays in this book are arranged.

Before Class Discussion

1. **Before class discussion of an assigned essay, review the reading and your notes.** Identify your main reactions to the piece. What do you consider the essay's strongest or weakest points?

2. **Ask fellow students about their reactions to the writing.** If their responses to the writer's thesis, tone, approach, and technique differ from yours, review your notes to get a fresh perspective.

3. **Be prepared to ask questions.** Ask your instructor about unfamiliar techniques or passages that you find confusing.

Analyzing a Text through Summary

The ability to summarize—concisely and precisely—is central to critical reading. Readers first need to grapple with what a text says to ensure a fair and accurate representation of an author's viewpoint *before* the interpretive processes of individual reader response takes over. Too often students leap to conclusions about what a text means before fair and rigorous assessment of the text itself. *What* is an author actually saying? *How* does the author say it? Summaries help to "nail" an accurate understanding of a text through abridging or condensing its substance.

Much of ordinary communication depends on the ability to summarize information: recounting a movie to a friend, reporting the morning news to someone who missed it, or describing a recent triumph or disappointment. When it comes to academic writing, the ability to summarize—pithily, accurately, using one's own words—is essential to nearly all forms of writing, including definition, description, instruction, reporting, explanation, argumentation, and so on. Effective reading and writing, whether academic or professional, depends on the ability to extrapolate and condense information reliably—from taking notes to writing scientific or business abstracts to producing lawyers' briefs.

A summary is an analysis of a text that extracts the main point and purpose along with the most important details, examples, and evidence. Summaries usually are much briefer than the original version; they usually reduce the original material to about 10 percent of its length. They also require the use of your own language, not that of the original. Because the main task of a summary is to provide the core point(s) of the original text, it should be organized with the main point at the outset, followed by the most essential elements that explain and support the main point. Note: Summaries do not reproduce the original structure of the original.

Steps toward producing an effective summary:

1. Read the text to obtain the general sense.

2. Reread the text again, noting cues to central and secondary points (headings, topic sentences, etc.). Make margin notes.

3. Identify the central point and secondary points (ensure that you do not select too many points).

4. Carefully reread the areas noted in the margins, underlining explicit statements of central and secondary points.

5. Draft the main point *in your own words* in one or two sentences.

6. Draft the main supportive points *in your own words.*

7. Assess your statements to see that if they accurately represent the original meaning, without distortion.

8. Integrate your draft statements of the main point and secondary points within a logical, well-structured paragraph. In this draft, aim for slightly more than the desired length.

9. Revise to meet the length requirement, carefully eliminating secondary points, details, and examples. Choose the material to be discarded in order from the smallest details to the main points.

10. Edit for conciseness and polish for clarity, logic, and coherence.

EXAMPLE OF CRITICAL READING

Read the following essay by Emily Prager and study how it has been marked during a critical reading. Notice how the student used the essay to generate ideas for upcoming assignments.

EMILY PRAGER

Emily Prager graduated from Barnard College with a degree in anthropology. She has written pieces for **National Lampoon** as well as several screenplays. Prager has also appeared in several films. For four years she was a star on **The Edge of Night,** a popular soap opera. She has published three books of fiction: **A Visit from the Footbinder and Other Stories, Clea and Zeus Divorce,** and **Eve's Tattoo.**

Our Barbies, Ourselves*

Notice how Prager uses a variety of modes, including comparison, description, narration, and cause and effect, to develop her essay about the Barbie doll. As you read the piece, consider her choice of topics. Is a popular toy a fitting subject to prompt thoughts about gender roles? Is it too trivial? Does Prager give a doll too much significance?

*Prager, Emily, "Our Barbies, Ourselves" copyright © 1991 by Emily Prager. Reprinted by permission of the Wylie Agency.

1   I read an astounding obituary in *The New York Times* not too long ago. It concerned the introduction (obituary as writing prompt)
death of one Jack Ryan. A former husband of Zsa Zsa Gabor, it said, Mr. Ryan had been an
inventor and designer during his lifetime. A man of eclectic creativity, he designed Sparrow
and Hawk missiles when he worked for the Raytheon Company, and the notice said, when
he consulted for Mattel he designed Barbie.

  If Barbie was designed by a man, suddenly a lot of things made sense to me, things I'd description WHY? female/ feminist reaction?
wondered about for years. I used to look at Barbie and wonder, What's wrong with this
picture? What kind of woman designed this doll? Let's be honest: Barbie looks like someone
who got her start at the Playboy Mansion. She could be a regular guest on *The Howard Stern*
10 *Show*. It is a fact of Barbie's design that her breasts are so out of proportion to the rest of her
body that if she were a human woman, she'd fall flat on her face.

  If it's true that a woman didn't design Barbie, you don't know how much saner questions cause and effect
that makes me feel. Of course, that doesn't ameliorate the damage. There are millions
of women who are subliminally sure that a thirty-nine inch bust and a twenty-three
inch waist are the epitome of lovability. Could this account for the popularity of breast
implant surgery?

  I don't mean to step on anyone's toes here. I loved my Barbie. Secretly, I still believe that
neon pink and turquoise blue are the only colors in which to decorate a duplex condo. And
like so many others of my generation, I've never married, simply because I cannot find a
20 man who looks as good in clam diggers as Ken.

  The question that comes to mind is, of course, Did Mr. Ryan design Barbie as a weapon? Barbie as a weapon? cause and effect
Because it is odd that Barbie appeared about the same time in my consciousness as the
feminist movement—a time when women sought equality and small breasts were king.
Or is Barbie the dream date of a weapons designer? Or perhaps it's simpler than that:
Perhaps Barbie is Zsa Zsa if she were eleven inches tall. No matter what, my discovery of
Jack Ryan confirms what I have always felt: There is something indescribably masculine (modern ideal of a hard body!)
about Barbie—dare I say it, phallic. For all her giant breasts and high-heeled feet, she lacks
a certain softness. If you asked a little girl what kind of doll she wanted for Christmas, I just
don't think she'd reply, "Please, Santa, I want a hardbody."

30   On the other hand, you could say that Barbie, in feminist terms, is definitely her own Barbie as role model?
person. With her condos and fashion plazas and pools and beauty salons, she is definitely a
liberated woman, a gal on the move. And she has always been sexual, even totemic. Before
Barbie, American dolls were flat-footed and breastless, and ineffably dignified. They were
created in the image of little girls or babies. Madame Alexander was the queen of doll makers
in the '50s, and her dollies looked like Elizabeth Taylor in *National Velvet*. They represented Barbie = adult doll not a baby or child
the kind of girls who looked perfect in jodhpurs, whose hair was never out of place, who
grew up to be Jackie Kennedy—before she married Onassis. Her dolls' boyfriends were
figments of the imagination, figments with large portfolios and three piece suits and presi- comparison
dential aspirations, figments who could keep dolly in the style to which little girls of the
40 '50s were programmed to become accustomed, perhaps what accounts for Barbie's vast
popularity in that she was also a '60s woman: into free love and fun colors, anti-class, and
possessed a real, molded boyfriend, Ken, with whom she could chant a mantra.

Ken sexless?
comparison

But there were problems with Ken. <u>I always felt weird about him</u>. He had no genitals, and, even at age ten, I found that ominous. I mean, here was Barbie with these humongous breasts, and that was O.K. with the toy company. And then, there was Ken, with that truncated, unidentifiable lump at his groin. I sensed injustice at work. Why, I wondered, was Barbie de-

questions

signed with such obvious sexual equipment and Ken not? Why was he treated as if it were more mysterious than hers? Did the fact that it was treated as such indicate that somehow his equipment, his essential maleness, was considered more powerful than hers, more worthy of the dignity of concealment? And if the issue in the mind of the toy company was obscenity   50 and its possible damage to children, I still object. How do they think I felt, knowing that no matter how many water beds they slept in, or hot tubs they romped in, or swimming pools they lounged by under the stars, Barbie and Ken could never make love? No matter how much

Barbie's fate

sexuality Barbie possessed, she would never turn Ken on. He would be forever withholding,

conclusion

forever detached. There was a <u>loneliness about Barbie's situation that was always disturbing</u>. And twenty-five years later, movies and videos are still filled with topless women and covered

final observation

men. <u>As if we're all trapped in Barbie's world and can never escape.</u> ■

STUDENT NOTES

First Reading

Barbie as symbol of male domination?
What about GI Joe and boys?
Is Prager really serious about this?
Barbie as paradox—a toy that presents a sexist *Playboy* image of women
   but a toy that is independent and more "liberated" than traditional
   baby dolls.
Tone: witty but serious in spots, raises a lot of issues but doesn't really discuss
   many.

Second Reading

Thesis: The Barbie doll, the creation of a male weapons designer, has
   shaped the way a generation of women defined themselves. (Get other
   opinions)
Body: spins off a number of topics and observations, a list of associations,
   suited for general readers.
Approach: a mix of serious and witty commentary, writer appears to entertain as much as inform or persuade.
Organization: use of modes critical to keeping the essay from becoming a
   rambling list of contradictory ideas. Good use of description, comparison, cause and effect.
Conclusion—"trapped in Barbie's world" good ending.

Prewriting—Possible Topics

Description—childhood toys—models of cars and planes? games—Monopoly (preparing kids for capitalism?)

Comparison/contrast—boy and girl toys and games, playing house vs. playing ball (social roles vs. competition, teamwork)

Cause and effect—we are socialized by our toys and games in childhood, affecting how men and women develop (needs support—Psych class notes)

Example—My daughter's old Beanie Baby?

USING THE READER

The chapters that follow in this Reader portion of *The Trans-Canada Writer* are organized in nine modes focusing on writers' goals. The readings in each section illustrate how writers achieve their purpose in different contexts. Each chapter opens with an explanation of the goal or mode. The opening readings in each chapter are brief, clear-cut examples of the mode and can serve as models for many of your composition assignments. Later readings are longer and more complex and demonstrate writing tasks in a range of disciplines and writing situations.

In addition to the readings assigned by your instructor, try to flip through the Reader and review how different writers state a thesis, support an argument, open an essay, organize ideas, and present a conclusion. Focus on how other writers cope with the problems you encounter in your writing.

■ ■ ■ ■ ■

Strategies for Critical Reading

As you read entries in the Reader, ask yourself these questions:

- What is the writer's purpose?
- What is the thesis?
- What evidence does the writer provide to support the thesis?
- How does the writer organize the essay?
- Who are the intended readers?
- How successful is the writing—in context? Does the writer achieve his or her goals while respecting the needs of the reader and the conventions of the discipline or situation?
- What does the text teach you about writing?

COMPANION WEBSITE

See **http://www.transcanadawriter.nelson.com** for additional information about critical reading.

CHAPTER 12

Description

This chapter focuses on the importance of learning how to use descriptive detail for effective writing. It discusses the difference between subjective and objective description as well as how to blend details. It also offers strategies for reading description in texts.

WHAT IS DESCRIPTION?

Description captures details and impressions of persons, places, objects, or ideas. It records what we see, hear, feel, taste, and smell. Description is probably the most basic task that writers encounter. Whether you are writing a short story or a sales proposal, your success depends on your ability to effectively share details. Good description brings subjects to life through sensory details. Almost all writing requires a skilled use of description to provide a clear picture of your subject.

The way writers select and present details depends on the purpose, readers, and context of a writing task.

Objective and Subjective Description

There are two basic types of description. *Objective* description attempts to create an accurate, factual record, free of personal interpretation or bias. *Subjective* description emphasizes a writer's personal reactions, opinions, and values.

Objective Description

Objective description focuses on facts and observable details. Textbooks, newspaper articles, business reports, and professional journals include objective description. Objective description is effective when the writer's purpose is to present readers with information required to make an evaluation or decision.

- Objective description is best suited for an audience seeking reliable, factual information.
- Objective description avoids figurative language that is subject to interpretation.
- Objective description avoids personalizing a document that must express the views of others.
- Objective description is useful when writing to a critical or hostile audience that demands explanations or justifications of subjective characterizations.

■ Objective description is effective when the evidence you are presenting is compelling and dramatic.

Subjective Description

In contrast to objective description, subjective description creates impressions through sensory details and imagery. Short stories, novels, personal essays, advertising copy, memoirs, and editorials use highly personal sensory details and responses to create an individual's sense of the subject. The writer's perceptual world guides the writing. Instead of photographic realism, subjective description paints scenes, creates moods, or generates emotional responses. Providing accurate information is less important than giving readers a "feel" for the subject. The goal in subjective description is to share a vision, not provide information.

■ Subjective description emphasizes the writer's personal impressions rather than accurate reporting.

■ Subjective description relies on the selection and presentation of details. The choice of words and their connotations is critical in achieving the writer's goal.

■ Subjective description is widely used when the goal is to entertain and persuade readers rather than to provide information.

Blended Description

Most description is not purely objective or subjective. Even when trying to be neutral and unbiased, reporters and historians generally cannot avoid being influenced by their personal values and attitudes. Popular nonfiction writers include subjective touches to humanize their writing and enhance the appeal of their work.

Blended descriptions are useful in strengthening subjective accounts with factual details.

■ Blended descriptions are found in news magazines, literary criticism, and most nonfiction books. The degree and intensity of subjective elements depend on the context and may have to conform to stylistic guidelines established by editors.

■ If you are writing as the agent of others or as part of a larger organization, examine the use of subjective words carefully, and avoid connotations and characterizations that may offend or displease those you represent.

🖵 WRITING **ACTIVITY**

Select sample descriptions from a variety of sources—readings from this chapter, textbooks, magazine articles, brochures, mail-order catalogues, and newspaper advertisements—and review their use of objective and subjective details.

1. Can you detect subjective description in news magazines, such as *Maclean's* or *Time*? Is there a difference between the news stories and personal essays and political commentary pieces?

(Continued)

2. Do you observe different blends of subjective elements in such magazines as *Canadian Living, The Walrus,* and *Reader's Digest?*

3. Circle the subjective details used in ads that describe products.

   Does the writer's stance blend objective and subjective elements?

The Language of Description

Diction—the choice of words—is important in all writing, but it has a special role in description. Whether your description is objective, subjective, or a blend, the words you select should be accurate, precise, appropriate, and effective. In choosing words, consider your purpose, readers, and discipline.

WRITING **ACTIVITIES**

1. Review a number of advertisements in women's magazines. What words and images are used to sell products to women? Would these connotations appeal to men?

2. Analyze several popular television commercials. What connotations are used? Do they have any logical connection to the products or services being sold?

Strategies for *Writing Description*

Critical Thinking and Prewriting

1. **Use brainstorming and lists to generate possible topics.** Choose subjects you are familiar with—people you know, places you have visited, items you work with.

2. **Narrow your list of possible topics and generate details.** Use clustering and freewriting to develop details about your subject.

3. **Use senses other than sight.** Most writers immediately think of description as being visual. But descriptions can be enriched by including impressions of taste, touch, smell, and hearing.

Planning

1. **Determine your purpose.** What is your goal, and what are the most important details needed to support your thesis? A controlling idea or focus is important. Good description is not a random collection of facts or observations.

2. **Define your role.** If you are expressing personal opinion or observations, you are free to add subjective elements to your writing. If you are writing as a representative of a larger body, an objective stance is usually more appropriate.

3. **Consider your reader.** Which type of description best suits your audience—subjective impressions or objective facts? What needs and expectations do your readers have? What details, facts, statistics, or observations will help them appreciate your topic and share your impression?

4. **Review the nature of the audience.** Determine whether you should use technical or specialized terminology.

5. **Select key details.** Having determined the context, choose points that will reflect your purpose and impress your readers. Descriptions should have focus. Eliminate facts that might be interesting in themselves but do not serve your purpose.

6. **Organize details.** Your writing should be logically organized. You may arrange details spatially (for example, describing a house room by room or a city neighbourhood by streets) or in the order of their importance.

Writing the First Draft

1. **Allow details to create a dominant impression.** The description of a room can focus on a single theme.

2. **Describe people and objects in action.** Descriptions of people and objects can become stilted lists of facts. You can bring your subject to life by introducing short narratives or showing people in action.

3. **Use dialogue to add action to descriptions involving people.** Allowing people to speak for themselves is more interesting and effective than simply describing their comments.

4. **Avoid unnecessary detail or static descriptions.** Focus details and avoid writing descriptions that are static and lifeless.

5. **Keep the length of your paper in mind as you write the first draft.**

Revising

1. **Review your plan and read your draft, focusing on its overall impact.** Concentrate on your draft's general effect.
   - Does it capture the core of your topic?
   - Is it too general, too vague?
   - Does it read like a shopping list of facts rather than highlight interesting and important details?

2. **Check the quality of information included.**
   - Are there minor details that should be deleted?
   - Can the description be improved by adding essential or interesting details that you overlooked in the first draft?
   - Do you include impressions from senses other than sight?

3. **Does the paper create a dominant impression?**
   - Does your paper have a clear focus; can you state a thesis?
   - Can ideas be rearranged to add emphasis, suspense, or interest?

4. **Is the description clearly organized?**
   - Does the paper's opening arouse interest?

(Continued)

- Are details logically arranged? Do you use other modes to tell a story, create a pattern, or establish contrasts?
- Does the paper end with a strong image, thought, or question that will leave a lasting impression on readers?

5. **Does your paper maintain a consistent point of view?**
   - Determine whether you should change your role in the description and whether it would be better stated from an objective or subjective viewpoint.

6. **Can action and dialogue be added to enliven the description?**
   - Can you bring facts to life by describing people or things in action or at work?
   - Can speech be included?

7. **Can other modes be blended into the description to make it more interesting or easier to follow?**
   - Could the description be revised by adding narrative elements to tell a story?
   - Would comparison and contrast or cause and effect help present the details?

8. If possible, use peer review to gain an additional perspective.
   - Ask a friend or fellow student to read your draft. Ask your readers whether your paper creates a vivid picture of your subject. Ask what elements could be added to make the essay more effective.

Editing and Proofreading

1. **Read the paper (sometimes reading it aloud helps).** Be sure to revise:
   - Awkward or repetitive phrases
   - Sentence lengths and complexity to avoid redundant, humdrum pattern

2. **Examine your choice of words.** Use:
   - Fresh and inventive words
   - Concrete language
   - Original statements, rather than clichés
   - Accurate and precise words

3. **Use a dictionary and thesaurus to examine word choice.**

General Assignments

Write a description of any of the following topics. Your description may include other modes. Determine whether your description should rely on objective observations and factual detail or subjective impressions. When you select words to describe your topic, be conscious of their connotations. Above all, keep in mind what you are trying to share with your reader.

- The people who gather in a place you frequent—a coffee shop, store, nightclub, library, or student union

- Your best or worst boss or professor

- The most desirable/least desirable place to live in your community
- The most dangerous situation you have faced
- The most serious environmental problem in your region
- The most serious problem you face today
- Student attitudes about a specific subject: terrorism, racism, crime, jobs, television
- Violence in Canada

Writing in Context

1. Imagine that you have been asked to write a description of the campus for a brochure designed to recruit students. Write a three- or four-paragraph description that is easy to read and creates a favourable impression. Consider what would appeal to high school students or adults returning to school.

2. Write an open letter to the graduating class of your high school describing college or university life. You may wish to compare postsecondary education to high school to prepare students for the problems and challenges they will encounter.

Strategies for Reading Description

As you read the descriptions in this chapter, keep these questions in mind:

Context

1. What is the author's goal—to inform, enlighten, share personal observations, or provide information demanded by others? What is the writer's role? Is he or she writing from a personal or professional stance?

2. What is the intended audience—general or specific readers? How much knowledge does the author assume his or her readers have? Are technical terms defined? Does the description appear to have a special focus?

3. What is the nature of the audience? What does the source of the document—news magazine, corporation, personal essay, or book—reveal about the context?

Strategy

1. What details does the writer select? Does he or she appear to be deliberately emphasizing some items while ignoring or minimizing others?

2. Does the description establish a dominant impression? What method does the writer use to create it?

3. How much of the description is objective and how much is subjective?

(Continued)

4. How does the author organize details? Is there any particular method of grouping observations?

5. Does the writer include sensory impressions other than visual details?

Language

1. What level of language does the writer use? Are technical terms explained?

2. What role do connotations have in shaping the description? How do they support the writer's goal?

HUGH MACLENNAN

Hugh MacLennan (1907–1990) was a novelist whose nationalist concerns made him a central figure in the continuing debate about Canada's identity. He was educated at Dalhousie University, at Oxford as a Rhodes scholar, and at Princeton University, where he was awarded a PhD in Classics in 1935. He taught in McGill's Department of English from 1951 to 1981. His first novel, **Barometer Rising**, and collection of essays, **Cross-Country**, established MacLennan as an important interpreter of Canada, a reputation that he was to confirm with subsequent books of essays and such novels of national concern as **Two Solitudes** and **The Precipice.** MacLennan won the Governor General's Award three times for fiction and twice for nonfiction.

The Halifax Explosion*

In the following selection from Barometer Rising, *MacLennan mixes fiction and reportage to re-create the suspense, effects, and sheer pyrotechnical display of a munitions ship explosion, crafting a prose that doesn't compete with the event itself so much as provide a literary medium through which readers can approach the experience.*

The *Mont Blanc* was now in the Narrows and a detail of men went into her chains to unship   1
the anchor. It would be dropped as soon as she reached her appointed station in the Basin.
A hundred yards to port were the Shipyards and another hundred yards off the port bow
was the blunt contour of Richmond Bluff; to starboard the shore sloped gently into a barren
of spruce scrub. During the two minutes it took the *Mont Blanc* to glide through this strait,
most of Bedford Basin and nearly all its flotilla of anchored freighters were hidden from her
behind the rise of Richmond Bluff.

Around the projection of this hill, less than fifty fathoms off the port bow of the in-
coming *Mont Blanc,* another vessel suddenly appeared heading for the open sea. She flew
the Norwegian flag, and to the startled pilot of the munitioner the name *Imo* was plainly   10
visible beside the hawse. She was moving at half-speed and listing gently to port as she
made the sharp turn out of the Basin to strike the channel of the Narrows. And so listing, with white water surging away from her fore-foot, she swept across the path of the
Mont Blanc, exposing a gaunt flank labeled in giant letters BELGIAN RELIEF. Then she
straightened, and pointed the bow directly at the fore-quarter of the munitioner. Only at
that moment did the men on the *Imo's* bridge appear to realize that another vessel stood
directly in their path.

Staccato orders broke from the bridge of the *Mont Blanc* as the two ships moved toward
a single point. Bells jangled, and megaphoned shouts came from both bridges. The ships
sheered in the same direction, then sheered back again. With a violent shock, the bow of the   20
Imo struck the plates of the *Mont Blanc* and went grinding a third of the way through the deck

and forward hold. A shower of sparks splashed out from the screaming metal. The canisters on the deck of the *Mont Blanc* broke loose from their bindings and some of them tumbled and burst open. Then the vessels heeled away with engines reversed and the water boiling out from their screws as the propellers braked them to a standstill. They sprawled sideways across the Narrows, the *Mont Blanc* veering in toward the Halifax shore, the *Imo* spinning about with steerageway lost entirely. Finally she drifted toward the opposite shore.

For a fraction of a second there was intense silence. Then smoke appeared out of the shattered deck of the *Mont Blanc,* followed by a racing film of flame. The men on the bridge
30 looked at each other. Scattered shouts broke from the stern, and the engine-room bells jangled again. Orders were half-drowned by a scream of rusty metal as some sailors amidships followed their own inclination and twisted the davits around to lower a boat. The scurry of feet grew louder as more sailors began to pour out through the hatches onto the deck. An officer ran forward with a hose, but before he could connect it his men were ready to abandon ship.

The film of flame raced and whitened, then it became deeper like an opaque and fulminant liquid, then swept over the canisters of benzol and increased to a roaring tide of heat. Black smoke billowed and rolled and engulfed the ship, which began to drift with the outgoing tide and swing in toward the graving-dock of the Shipyards. The fire trembled and leaped in a body at the bridge, driving the captain and pilot aft, and there they stood
40 helplessly while the tarry smoke surrounded them in greasy folds and the metal of the deck began to glow under their feet. Both men glanced downward. Underneath that metal lay leashed an incalculable energy, and the bonds which checked it were melting with every second the thermometers mounted in the hold. A half-million pounds of trinitrotoluol and twenty-three hundred tons of picric acid lay there in the darkness under the plates, while the fire above and below the deck converted the hollow shell of the vessel into a bake-oven.

If the captain had wished to scuttle the ship at that moment it would have been impossible to do so, for the heat between decks would have roasted alive any man who tried to reach the sea-cocks. By this time the entire crew was in the lifeboat. The officers followed, and the boat was rowed frantically toward the wooded slope opposite Halifax. There, by lying flat among
50 the trees, the sailors hoped they would have a chance when their ship blew up. By the time they had beached the boat, the foredeck of the *Mont Blanc* was a shaking rampart of fire, and black smoke pouring from it screened the Halifax Waterfront from their eyes. The sailors broke and ran for the shelter of the woods.

By this time men were running out of dock sheds and warehouses and offices along the entire waterfront to watch the burning ship. None of them knew she was a gigantic bomb. She had now come so close to the Shipyards that she menaced the graving-dock. Fire launches cut out from a pier farther south and headed for the Narrows. Signal flags fluttered from the Dockyard and the yard-arms of ships lying in the Stream, some of which were already weighing anchor. The captain of the British cruiser piped all hands
60 and called for volunteers to scuttle the *Mont Blanc;* a few minutes later the cruiser's launch was on its way to the Narrows with two officers and a number of ratings. By the time they reached the burning ship her plates were so hot that the seawater lapping the plimsoll line was simmering.

The *Mont Blanc* had become the center of a static tableau. Her plates began to glow red and the swollen air inside her hold heated the cargo rapidly towards the detonation point. Launches from the harbour fire department surrounded her like midges and the water from their hoses arched up with infinite delicacy as they curved into the rolling smoke. The *Imo*, futile and forgotten, was still trying to claw her way off the farther shore.

Twenty minutes after the collision there was no one along the entire waterfront who was unaware that a ship was on fire in the harbor. The jetties and docks near the Narrows were 70 crowded with people watching the show, and yet no warning of danger was given. At that particular moment there was no adequate centralized authority in Halifax to give a warning, and the few people who knew the nature of the *Mont Blanc*'s cargo had no means of notifying the town or spreading the alarm, and no comfort beyond the thought that trinitrotoluol can stand an almost unlimited heat provided there is no fulminate or explosive gas to detonate it.

Bells in the town struck the hour of nine, and by this time nearly all normal activity along the waterfront had been suspended. A tug had managed to grapple the *Mont Blanc* and was towing her with imperceptible movement away from the Shipyards back into the channel of the Narrows. Bluejackets from the cruiser had found the bosun's ladder left by the 80 fleeing crew, and with flesh shrinking from the heat, were going over the side. Fire launches surrounded her. There was a static concentration, and intense expectancy in the faces of the firemen playing the hoses, a rhythmic reverberation in the beat of the flames, a gush from the hose-nozzles and a steady hiss of scalding water. Everything else for miles around seemed motionless and silent.

Then a needle of flaming gas, thin as the mast and of a brilliance unbelievably intense, shot through the deck of the *Mont Blanc* near the funnel and flashed more than two hundred feet toward the sky. The firemen were thrown back and their hoses jumped suddenly out of control and slashed the air with S-shaped designs. There were a few helpless shouts. The all movement and life about the ship were encompassed in a sound beyond hearing as 90 the *Mont Blanc* opened up …

Three forces were simultaneously created by the energy of the exploding ship, an earthquake, an air-concussion, and a tidal wave. These forces rushed away from the Narrows with a velocity varying in accordance with the nature of the medium in which they worked. It took only a few seconds for the earthquake to spend itself and three minutes for the air-expansion to slow down to a gale. The tidal wave traveled for hours before the last traces of it were swallowed in the open Atlantic.

When the shock struck the arch, the rigid ironstone and granite base of Halifax peninsula rocked and reverberated, pavements split and houses swayed as the earth trembled. Sixty miles away in the town of Truro windows broke and fell to the ground, tinkling in 100 the stillness of the streets. But the ironstone was solid and when the shock had passed, it resumed its immobility.

The pressure of the exploding chemicals smashed against the town with the rigidity and force of driving steel. Solid and unbreathable, the forced wall of air struck against Fort Needham and Richmond Bluff and shaved them clean, smashed with one gigantic blow the

North End of Halifax and destroyed it, telescoping houses or lifting them from their foundations, snapping trees and lamp posts, and twisting iron rails into writhing, metal snakes; breaking buildings and sweeping the fragments of their wreckage for hundreds of yards in its course. It advanced two miles southward, shattering every flimsy house in its path, and within thirty seconds encountered the long, shield-like slope of the Citadel which rose before it.

Then, for the first time since it was fortified, the Citadel was able to defend at least a part of the town. The airwall smote it, and was deflected in three directions. Thus some of its violence shot skyward at a twenty-degree angle and spent itself in space. The rest had to pour around the roots of the hill before closing in on the town for another rush forward. A minute after the detonation, the pressure was advancing through the South End. But now its power was diminished, and its velocity was barely twice that of a tornado. Trees tossed and doors broke inward, windows split into driving arrows of glass which buried themselves deep in interior walls. Here the houses, after swaying and cracking, were still on their foundations when the pressure had passed.

Underneath the keel of the *Mont Blanc* the water opened and the harbor bottom was deepened twenty feet along the channel of the Narrows. And then the displaced waters began to drive outward, rising against the town and lifting ships and wreckage over the sides of the docks. It boiled over the shores and climbed the hill as far as the third cross-street, carrying with it the wreckage of small boats, fragments of fish, and somewhere, lost in thousands of tons of hissing brine, the bodies of men. The wave moved in a gigantic bore down the Stream to the sea, rolling some ships under and lifting others high on its crest, while anchor-chains cracked like guns as the violent thrust snapped them. Less than ten minutes after the detonation, it boiled over the breakwater off the park and advanced on McNab's Island, where it burst with a roar greater than a winter storm. And then the central volume of the wave rolled on to sea, high and arching and white at the top, its back glossy like the plumage of a bird. Hours later it lifted under the keel of a steamer far out in the Atlantic and the captain, feeling his vessel heave, thought he had struck a floating mine.

But long before this, the explosion had become manifest in new forms over Halifax. More than two thousand tons of red hot steel, splintered fragments of the *Mont Blanc*, fell like meteors from the sky into which they had been hurled a few seconds before. The ship's anchor soared over the peninsula and descended through a roof on the other side of the Northwest Arm three miles away. For a few seconds the harbor was dotted white with a maze of splashes, and the decks of raddled ships rang with reverberations and clangs as fragments struck them.

Over the North End of Halifax, immediately after the passage of the first pressure, the tormented air was laced with tongues of flame which roared and exploded out of the atmosphere, lashing downwards like a myriad blowtorches as millions of cubic feet of gas took fire and exploded. The atmosphere went white-hot. It grew mottled, then fell to the streets like a crimson curtain. Almost before the last fragments of steel had ceased to fall, the wreckage of the wooden houses in the North End had begun to burn. And if there were any ruins which failed to ignite from falling flames, they began to burn from the fires in their own stoves, onto which they had collapsed.

Over this part of the town, rising in the shape of a typhoon from the Narrows and extending five miles into the sky, was poised a cloud formed by the exhausted gases. It hung still for many minutes, white, glossy as an ermine's back, serenely aloof. It cast its shadow 150 over twenty miles of forest land behind Bedford Basin. ■

UNDERSTANDING CONTEXT

1. After reviewing the difference between subjective and objective language, assess whether MacLennan's description is objective or subjective. How would the choice to be either objective or subjective serve the descriptive purpose in this excerpt?

EVALUATING STRATEGY

1. MacLennan uses a third-person narrator to describe the explosion. Why does MacLennan choose this style of narration?

2. How does MacLennan increase the tension leading up to the explosion?

APPRECIATING LANGUAGE

1. MacLennan uses many nautical terms and archaic words. Create a list of the words that are unfamiliar to you. Find definitions for the words on your list.

2. How does MacLennan's word choice enhance or detract from his description?

3. How much of MacLennan's description is based on fact and how much is based on fiction, do you think? On what basis are you drawing your conclusions?

WRITING SUGGESTIONS

1. Find a description of the explosion in a newspaper or history textbook and compare it with MacLennan's description. What are the similarities? What are the differences? Which of the descriptions is more effective, and why?

2. Write a two-page description of an extraordinary event you have experienced or heard of, and try to capture it as vividly and precisely as possible.

TRUMAN CAPOTE

Truman Capote (1924–1985) was born in New Orleans and first gained prominence as a writer of short stories. At the age of 24 he produced his first novel, **Other Voices, Other Rooms,** which achieved international attention. His other works include **Breakfast at Tiffany's** and **A Tree of Night.** In 1965 he published **In Cold Blood,** which became an immediate bestseller. Based on extensive research and interviews, **In Cold Blood** tells the story of the 1959 mass murder of a Kansas farm family and the fate of the killers. Although nonfiction, Capote's book reads much like a novel. **In Cold Blood** helped shape a new school of journalism that uses the stylistic touches of fiction to relate actual events.

Out There*

The opening pages of In Cold Blood *describe the small town of Holcomb, Kansas, where the murders occurred. Capote spent a great deal of time in Holcomb and describes it almost as if it had been his own hometown. Notice how Capote blends objective facts with subjective impressions.*

1 The village of Holcomb stands on the high wheat plains of western Kansas, a lonesome area that other Kansans call "out there." Some seventy miles east of the Colorado border, the countryside, with its hard blue skies and desert-clear air, has an atmosphere that is rather more Far Western than Middle West. The local accent is barbed with a prairie twang, a ranch-hand nasalness, and the men, many of them, wear narrow frontier trousers, Stetsons, and high-heeled boots with pointed toes. The land is flat, and the views are awesomely extensive; horses, herds of cattle, a white cluster of grain elevators rising as gracefully as Greek temples are visible long before a traveler reaches them.

Holcomb, too, can be seen from great distances. Not that there is much to see—simply
10 an aimless congregation of buildings divided in the center by the main-line tracks of the Santa Fe Railroad, a haphazard hamlet bounded on the south by a brown stretch of the Arkansas (pronounced "Arkan-sas") River, on the north by a highway, Route 50, and on the east and west by prairie lands and wheat fields. After rain, or when snowfalls thaw, the streets, unnamed, unshaded, unpaved, turn from the thickest dust into the direst mud. At one end of the town stands a stark old stucco structure, the roof of which supports an electric sign—Dance—but the dancing has ceased and the advertisement has been dark for several years. Nearby is another building with an irrelevant sign, this one in flaking gold on a dirty window—Holcomb Bank. The bank closed in 1933, and its former counting rooms have been converted into apartments. It is one of the town's two
20 "apartment houses," the second being a ramshackle mansion known, because a good part of the local school's faculty lives there, as the Teacherage. But the majority of Holcomb's homes are one-story frame affairs, with front porches.

Down by the depot, the postmistress, a gaunt woman who wears a rawhide jacket and denims and cowboy boots, presides over a falling-apart post office. The depot itself, with its peeling sulphur-colored paint, is equally melancholy; the Chief, the Super Chief, the El Capitan go by every day, but these celebrated expresses never pause there. No passenger trains do—only an occasional freight. Up on the highway, there are two filling stations, one of which doubles as a meagerly supplied grocery store, while the other does extra duty as a café—Hartman's Café, where Mrs. Hartman, the proprietress, dispenses sandwiches, coffee, soft drinks, and 3.2 beer. (Holcomb, like all the rest of Kansas, is "dry.")   30

And that, really, is all. Unless you include, as one must, the Holcomb School, a good-looking establishment, which reveals a circumstance that the appearance of the community otherwise camouflages: that the parents who send their children to this modern and ably staffed "consolidated" school—the grades go from kindergarten through senior high, and a fleet of buses transport the students, of which there are usually around three hundred and sixty, from as far as sixteen miles away—are, in general, a prosperous people. Farm ranchers, most of them, they are outdoor folk of very varied stock—German, Irish, Norwegian, Mexican, Japanese. They raise cattle and sheep, grow wheat, milo, grass seed, and sugar beets. Farming is always a chancy business, but in western Kansas its practitioners consider themselves "born gamblers," for they must contend with an extremely shallow precipitation (the annual aver-   40
age is eighteen inches) and anguishing irrigation problems. However, the last seven years have been years of droughtless beneficence. The farm ranchers in Finney County, of which Holcomb is a part, have done well; money has been made not from farming alone but also from the exploitation of plentiful natural-gas resources, and its acquisition is reflected in the new school, the comfortable interiors of the farmhouses, the steep and swollen grain elevators.

Until one morning in mid-November of 1959, few Americans—in fact, few Kansans—had ever heard of Holcomb. Like the waters of the river, like the motorists on the highway, and like the yellow trains streaking down the Santa Fe tracks, drama, in the shape of exceptional happenings, had never stopped there. The inhabitants of the village, numbering two hundred and seventy, were satisfied that this should be so, quite content to exist inside   50
ordinary life—to work, to hunt, to watch television, to attend school socials, choir practice, meetings of the 4-H Club. But then, in the earliest hours of that morning in November, a Sunday morning, certain foreign sounds impinged on the normal nightly Holcomb noises—on the keening hysteria of coyotes, the dry scrape of scuttling tumbleweed, the racing, receding wail of locomotive whistles. At the time not a soul in sleeping Holcomb heard them—four shotgun blasts that, all told, ended six human lives. But afterward the townspeople, theretofore sufficiently unfearful of each other to seldom trouble to lock their doors, found fantasy re-creating them over and again—those somber explosions that stimulated fires of mistrust in the glare of which many old neighbors viewed each other strangely, and as strangers. ■   60

UNDERSTANDING CONTEXT

1. How much of Capote's description can be considered objective? How much subjective?

2. Capote includes a great deal of factual detail—names of highways, the number of students in the high school, and Holcomb's population. Why are these facts important in establishing an impression of the town?

3. What does Capote attempt to capture about this town?

EVALUATING STRATEGY

1. *Critical thinking:* A key element in the opening of any book is to get people's attention and motivate them to continue reading. How does Capote generate interest by describing a nondescript town?

2. What is the impact of the closing lines?

APPRECIATING LANGUAGE

1. How does the language of Capote's description differ from that of an encyclopedia or newspaper article?

2. *In Cold Blood* has sold millions of copies. What elements in Capote's style make his story about a crime in a small Kansas town so popular? What phrases strike you as being colourful or interesting?

WRITING SUGGESTIONS

1. Rewrite a recent article from the local newspaper, adding subjective details to arouse human interest for a national audience. Include observations about your community to give readers a feel for the location.

2. Using Capote's description as a resource, write a purely objective one-paragraph description of Holcomb, Kansas.

3. Attempt to write a one-line thesis statement for "Out There."

KEN DRYDEN

Ken Dryden was born in Hamilton, Ontario, in 1947, and made his name as a hockey legend in Canada, playing goaltender for the National Hockey League through six winning teams in the 1970s. He was elected to the Hockey Hall of Fame in 1989. Dryden also has made a name for himself as a politician, businessman, and writer, and has been awarded numerous honorary doctorate degrees.

Dryden's Backyard*

In this excerpt from his book The Game, *Dryden describes a detailed account of his child-hood memories of playing hockey in his family's backyard.*

I get out of bed and pull back the curtains. It has snowed overnight and traces are still gently 1
falling. For several minutes I stand there, my forehead pressed to the window, watching the snow, looking out at the backyards of the houses behind, where the Pritchards, the MacLarens, and the Carpenters lived, and down below at the winter's depth of snow, and at the backyard where I spent my childhood.

    "Dryden's Backyard." That's what it was called in our neighbourhood. It was more than 70 feet long, paved curiously in red asphalt, 45 feet wide at "the big end," gradually narrowing to 35 feet at the flower bed, to 25 feet at the porch—our center line—to 15 feet at "the small end." While Steve Shutt and Guy Lafleur were in Willowdale and Thurso on backyard rinks their fathers built, while Larry Robinson was on a frozen stream in Marvel- 10
ville and Réjean Houle on a road in Rouyn under the only street light that his street had, I was here.

    It was an extraordinary place, like the first swimming pool on the block, except there were no others like it anywhere. Kids would come from many blocks away to play, mostly "the big guys," friends of my brother, a year or two older than him, seven or eight years older than me. But that was never a problem. It was the first rule of the backyard that they had to let me play. To a friend who complained one day, Dave said simply, "If Ken doesn't play, you don't play."

    We played "ball hockey" mostly, with a tennis ball, its bounce deadened by the cold. A few times, we got out a garden hose and flooded the backyard to use skates and pucks, 20
but the big end was slightly lower than the small end, and the water pooled and froze un-evenly. More important, we found that the more literal we tried to make our games, the less lifelike they became. We could move across the asphalt quickly and with great agility in rubber "billy" boots; we could shoot a tennis ball high and hard. But with skates on, with a puck, we were just kids. So after the first few weeks of the first year, we played only ball hockey.

Depending on the day, the time, the weather, there might be any number of kids wanting to play, so we made up games any number could play. With four and less than nine, we played regular games, the first team scoring ten goals the winner. The two best players, who
30 seemed always to know who they were, picked the teams and decided on ends. First choice of players got second choice of ends, and because the size of the big end made it more fun to play in, the small end was the choice to defend. Each team had a goalie—one with goalie pads, a catching glove, and a goalie stick; the other with only a baseball glove and a forward's stick. When we had more than eight players, we divided into three or more teams for a round-robin tournament, each game to five. With fewer than four, it was more difficult. Sometimes we attempted a regular game, often we just played "shots," each player being both shooter and goalie, standing in front of one net, shooting in turn at the other. Most often, however, we played "penalty shots."

But the backyard also meant time alone. It was usually after dinner when the "big
40 guys" had homework to do and I would turn on the floodlights at either end of the house and on the porch, and play. It was a private game. I would stand alone in the middle of the yard, a stick in my hands, a tennis ball in front of me, silent, still, then suddenly dash ahead, stickhandling furiously, dodging invisible obstacles for a shot on net. It was Maple Leaf Gardens filled to wildly cheering capacity, a tie game, seconds remaining. I was Frank Mahovlich, or Gordie Howe, I was anyone I wanted to be, and the voice in my head was that of Leafs broadcaster Foster Hewitt: " . . . . there's ten seconds left, Mahovlich, winding up at his own line, at center, eight seconds, seven, over the blueline, six—he winds up, he shoots, *he scores!*" The mesh that had been tied to the bottoms of our red metal goalposts until frozen in the ice had been ripped away to hang loose from the cross-bars, whipped
50 back like a flag in a stiff breeze. My arms and stick flew into the air, I screamed a scream inside my head, and collected my ball to do it again—many times, for many minutes, the hero of all my own games.

It was a glorious fantasy, and I always heard that voice. It was what made my fantasy seem almost real. For to us, who attended hockey games mostly on TV or radio, an NHL game, a Leafs game, was played with a voice. If I wanted to be Mahovlich or Howe, if I moved my body the way I had seen them move theirs and did nothing else, it would never quite work. But if I heard the voice that said their names while I was playing out that fantasy, I could believe it. Foster Hewitt could make me them.

My friends and I played every day after school, sometimes during lunch and after din-
60 ner, but Saturday was always the big day. I would go to bed Friday night thinking of Saturday, waking up early, with none of the fuzziness I had other days. If it had snowed overnight, Dave and I, with shovels and scrapers, and soon joined by others, would pile the snow into flower beds or high against the back of the garage. Then at 9:00 A.M. the games would begin.

There was one team in the big end, another in the small; third and fourth teams sat like birds on a telephone wire, waiting their turn on the wall that separated the big end from Carpenter's backyard. Each team wore uniforms identical to the other's. It was the Canadian midwinter uniform of the time—long, heavy duffel coats in browns, grays, or blues; tuques in NHL team colors, pulled snug over the ears under the watchful eye of mothers, here rolled up in some distinctive personal style; leather gloves, last year's church gloves, now curling at the wrist and separating between fingers; black rubber "billy" boots over layers of heavy 70 woolen socks for fit, the tops rolled down like "low cuts" for speed and style.

Each game would begin with a faceoff, then wouldn't stop again. Action moved quickly end to end, the ball bouncing and rolling, chased by a hacking, slashing scrum of sticks. We had sticks without tops on their blades—"toothpicks"; sticks with no blades at all— "stubs." They broke piece by heart-breaking piece, often quickly, but still we used them. Only at the start of a season, at Christmas (Dave and I routinely exchanged sticks until one year he gave me a stick and I gave him a pair of socks) and once or twice more, would we get new ones. All except John Stedelbauer. His father owned a car dealership and during the hockey season gave away hockey sticks to his customers as a promotion. Stedelbauer got all the new sticks he needed, fortunately, as they weren't very good. One year he broke 80 nineteen of them.

A goal would be scored, then another, and slowly the game would leapfrog to five. Bodies grew warm from exertion, fingers and toes went numb; noses ran, wiped by unconscious sleeves; coats loosened, tuques fell off; steam puffed from mouths and streamed from tuque-less heads. Sticks hacked and slashed; tennis balls stung. But in the euphoria of the game, the pain disappeared. Sitting on the wall that overlooked his backyard, Rick "Foster" Carpenter, younger and not very athletic, gave the play-by-play, but no one listened. Each of us had his own private game playing in his head. A fourth goal, then a fifth, a cheer and the first game was over. Quickly, four duffel coats, four tuques, four pairs of weathered gloves and rubber "billy" boots would jump from the wall to replace the losers; and the second game 90 would begin. We paused at noon while some went home and others ate the lunch that they had brought with them. At 6:00 P.M., the two or three who remained would leave. Eighteen hours later, after church, the next game would begin.

When I think of the backyard, I think of my childhood; and when I think of my child-hood, I think of the backyard. It is the central image I have of that time, linking as it does all of its parts: father, mother, sister, friends; hockey, baseball, and Dave—big brother, idol, mentor, defender, and best friend. Yet it lasted only a few years. Dave was already twelve when the backyard was built; I was six. He and his friends played for three or four years, then stopped; I played longer but, without them, less often. Yet until moments ago, I had never remembered that. 100

The backyard was not a training ground. In all the time I spent there, I don't remember ever thinking I would be an NHL goalie, or even hoping I could be one. In backyard games, I dreamed I *was* Sawchuk or Hall, Mahovlich or Howe; I never dreamed I would be like them. There seemed no connection between the backyard and Maple Leaf Gardens; there seemed no way to get to there from here. If we ever thought about that, it never concerned us; we just played. It was here in the backyard that we *learned* hockey. It was here we got close to it, we got *inside* it, and it got inside us. It was here that our inextricable bond with the game was made. Many years have now passed, the game has grown up and been complicated by things outside it, yet still the backyard remains—untouched, unchanged, my unseverable link to that time, and that game. ■ 110

UNDERSTANDING CONTEXT

1. How much of Dryden's description can be seen as objective, how much subjective?

2. Dryden includes many references to former NHL players and one former broadcaster. What effect do these specific references have on the description?

EVALUATING STRATEGY

1. What is the piece's purpose? Why does Dryden write about his early childhood experiences playing backyard hockey?

APPRECIATING LANGUAGE

1. What words does Dryden use to evoke the past?

2. Based on his word choices, what year is he describing?

3. How does Dryden's choice of language communicate the piece's era?

WRITING SUGGESTIONS

1. Attempt to write a one-line thesis for "Dryden's Backyard."

2. Write a three-paragraph description of a place from your childhood, like a backyard rink or neighbourhood library, and an activity that happened there.

Blending the Modes   E. B. WHITE

Elwyn Brooks White (1899–1985) was born in Mount Vernon, New York, and attended Cornell University. He was a regular contributor to the **New Yorker** magazine for 50 years. His articles achieved a reputation for their wit and style. White assisted William Strunk in revising his popular book on writing, **The Elements of Style.** White also gained popularity as a writer of children's literature. His books **Stuart Little** and **Charlotte's Web** have become classics.

Once More to the Lake*

First published in Harper's *in 1941, "Once More to the Lake" describes White's nostalgic return to a boyhood vacation spot. As you read the essay, notice how White uses comparison and narration in developing his description.*

August 1941   1

One summer, along about 1904, my father rented a camp on a lake in Maine and took us all there for the month of August. We all got ringworm from some kittens and had to rub Pond's Extract on our arms and legs night and morning, and my father rolled over in a canoe with all his clothes on; but outside of that the vacation was a success and from then on none of us ever thought there was any place in the world like that lake in Maine. We returned summer after summer—always on August 1 for one month. I have since become a salt-water man, but sometimes in summer there are days when the restless-ness of the tides and the fearful cold of the sea water and the incessant wind that blows across the afternoon and into the evening make me wish for the placidity of a lake in the 10 woods. A few weeks ago this feeling got so strong I bought myself a couple of bass hooks and a spinner and returned to the lake where we used to go, for a week's fishing and to revisit old haunts.

I took along my son, who had never had any fresh water up his nose and who had seen lily pads only from train windows. On the journey over to the lake I began to won-der what it would be like. I wondered how time would have marred this unique, this holy spot—the coves and streams, the hills that the sun set behind, the camps and the paths behind the camps. I was sure that the tarred road would have found it out, and I won-dered in what other ways it would be desolate. It is strange how much you can remember about places like that once you allow your mind to return into the grooves that lead back. 20 You remember one thing, and that suddenly reminds you of another thing. I guess I remembered clearest of all the early mornings, when the lake was cool and motionless, remembered how the bedroom smelled of the lumber it was made of and of the wet woods whose scent entered through the screen. The partitions in the camp were thin and did not extend clear to the top of the rooms, and as I was always the first up I would dress

*White, E.B., "Once More to the Lake" from *One Man's Meat,* text copyright © 1941 by E.B. White. Copyright renewed. Reprinted by permission of Tilbury House, Publishers, Gardiner, Maine.

softly so as not to wake the others, and sneak out into the sweet outdoors and start out in the canoe, keeping close along the shore in the long shadows of the pines. I remembered being very careful never to rub my paddle against the gunwale for fear of disturbing the stillness of the cathedral.

30   The lake had never been what you would call a wild lake. There were cottages sprinkled around the shores, and it was in farming country although the shores of the lake were quite heavily wooded. Some of the cottages were owned by nearby farmers, and you would live at the shore and eat your meals at the farmhouse. That's what our family did. But although it wasn't wild, it was a fairly large and undisturbed lake and there were places in it that, to a child at least, seemed infinitely remote and primeval.

I was right about the tar: it led to within half a mile of the shore. But when I got back there, with my boy, and we settled into a camp near a farmhouse and into the kind of summertime I had known, I could tell that it was going to be pretty much the same as it had been before—I knew it, lying in bed the first morning, smelling the bedroom and hearing the boy
40   sneak quietly out and go off along the shore in a boat. I began to sustain the illusion that he was I, and therefore, by simple transposition, that I was my father. This sensation persisted, kept cropping up all the time we were there. It was not an entirely new feeling, but in this setting it grew much stronger. I seemed to be living a dual existence. I would be in the middle of some simple act, I would be picking up a bait box or laying down a table fork, or I would be saying something, and suddenly it would be not I but my father who was saying the words or making the gesture. It gave me a creepy sensation.

We went fishing the first morning. I felt the same damp moss covering the worms in the bait can, and saw the dragonfly alight on the tip of my rod as it hovered a few inches from the surface of the water. It was the arrival of this fly that convinced me beyond any doubt
50   that everything was as it always had been, that the years were a mirage and that there had been no years. The small waves were the same, chucking the rowboat under the chin as we fished at anchor, and the boat was the same boat, the same color green and the ribs broken in the same places, and under the floorboards the same fresh-water leavings and débris—the dead hellgrammite, the wisps of moss, the rusty discarded fish-hook, the dried blood from yesterday's catch. We stared silently at the tips of our rods, at the dragonflies that came and went. I lowered the tip of mine into the water, tentatively, pensively dislodging the fly, which darted two feet away, poised, darted two feet back, and came to rest again a little farther up the rod. There had been no years between the ducking of this dragonfly and the other one—the one that was part of memory. I looked at the boy, who was silently watching his fly,
60   and it was my hands that held his rod, my eyes watching. I felt dizzy and didn't know which rod I was at the end of.

We caught two bass, hauling them in briskly as though they were mackerel, pulling them over the side of the boat in a businesslike manner without any landing net, and stunning them with a blow on the back of the head. When we got back for a swim before lunch, the lake was exactly where we had left it, the same number of inches from the dock, and there was only the merest suggestion of a breeze. This seemed an utterly enchanted sea, this lake you could leave to its own devices for a few hours and come back to, and find it had not stirred, this constant and trustworthy body of water. In the shallows, the dark, water-soaked sticks and twigs, smooth and old, were undulating in clusters on the bottom against the clean ribbed sand, and the track of the mussel was plain. A school of minnows 70 swam by, each minnow with its small individual shadow, doubling the attendance, so clear and sharp in the sunlight. Some of the other campers were in swimming, along the shore, one of them with a cake of soap, and the water felt thin and clear and unsubstantial. Over the years there had been this person with the cake of soap, this cultist, and here he was. There had been no years.

Up to the farmhouse to dinner through the teeming, dusty field, the road under our sneakers was only a two-track road. The middle track was missing, the one with the marks of the hooves and the splotches of dried, flaky manure. There had always been three tracks to choose from in choosing which track to walk in; now the choice was nar- rowed down to two. For a moment I missed terribly the middle alternative. But the way 80 led past the tennis court, and something about the way it lay there in the sun reassured me; the tape had loosened along the backline, the alleys were green with plantains and other weeds, and the net (installed in June and removed in September) sagged in the dry noon, and the whole place steamed with midday heat and hunger and emptiness. There was a choice of pie for dessert, and one was blueberry and one was apple, and the wait- resses were the same country girls, there having been no passage of time, only the illusion of it as in a dropped curtain—the waitresses were still fifteen; their hair had been washed, that was the only difference—they had been to the movies and seen the pretty girls with the clean hair.

Summertime, oh summertime, pattern of life indelible, the fade-proof lake, the woods 90 unshatterable, the pasture with the sweetfern and the juniper forever and ever, summer without end; this was the background, and the life along the shore was the design, their tiny docks with the flagpole and the American flag floating against the white clouds in the blue sky, the little paths over the roots of the trees leading from camp to camp and the paths lead- ing back to the outhouses and the can of lime for sprinkling, and at the souvenir counters at the store the miniature birch-bark canoes and the postcards that showed things looking a little better than they looked. This was the American family at play, escaping the city heat, wondering whether the newcomers in the camp at the head of the cove were "common" or "nice," wondering whether it was true that the people who drove up for Sunday dinner at the farmhouse were turned away because there wasn't enough chicken. 100

It seemed to me, as I kept remembering all this, that those times and those summers had been infinitely precious and worth saving. There had been jollity and peace and goodness. The arriving (at the beginning of August) had been so big a business in itself, at the railway station the farm wagon drawn up, the first smell of the pine-laden air, the first glimpse of the smiling farmer, and the great importance of the trunks and your father's enormous author- ity in such matters, and the feel of the wagon under you for the long ten-mile haul, and at the top of the last long hill catching the first view of the lake after eleven months of not see- ing this cherished body of water. The shouts and cries of the other campers when they saw you, and the trunks to be unpacked, to give up their rich burden. (Arriving was less exciting

110   nowadays, when you sneaked up in your car and parked it under a tree near the camp and took out the bags and in five minutes it was all over, no fuss, no loud wonderful fuss about trunks.)

Peace and goodness and jollity. The only thing that was wrong now, really, was the sound of the place, an unfamiliar nervous sound of the outboard motors. This was the note that jarred, the one thing that would sometimes break the illusion and set the years moving. In those other summertimes all the motors were inboard; and when they were at a little distance, the noise they made was a sedative, an ingredient of summer sleep. They were one-cylinder and two-cylinder engines, and some were make-and-break and some were jump-spark, but they all made a sleepy sound across the lake. The one-lungers

120   throbbed and fluttered, and the twin-cylinder ones purred and purred, and that was a quiet sound, too. But now the campers all had outboards. In the daytime, in the hot mornings, these motors made a petulant, irritable sound; at night, in the still evening when the afterglow lit the water, they whined about one's ears like mosquitoes. My boy loved our rented outboard, and his great desire was to achieve single-handed mastery over it, and authority, and he soon learned the trick of choking it a little (but not too much), and the adjustment of the needle valve. Watching him I would remember the things you could do with the old one-cylinder engine with the heavy flywheel, how you could have it eating out of your hand if you got really close to it spiritually. Motorboats in those days didn't have clutches, and you would make a landing by shutting off the

130   motor at the proper time and coasting in with a dead rudder. But there was a way of reversing them, if you learned the trick, by cutting the switch and putting it on again exactly on the final dying revolution of the flywheel, so that it would kick back against the compression and begin reversing. Approaching a dock in a strong following breeze, it was difficult to slow up sufficiently by the ordinary coasting method, and if a boy felt he had complete mastery over his motor, he was tempted to keep it running beyond its time and then reverse it a few feet from the dock. It took a cool nerve, because if you threw the switch a twentieth of a second too soon you would catch the flywheel when it still had speed enough to go up past center, and the boat would leap ahead, charging bull-fashion at the dock.

140   We had a good week at camp. The bass were biting well and the sun shone endlessly, day after day. We would be tired at night and lie down in the accumulated heat of the little bedrooms after the long hot day and the breeze would stir almost imperceptibly outside and the smell of the swamp drift in through the rusty screens. Sleep would come easily and in the morning the red squirrel would be on the roof, tapping out his gay routine. I kept remembering everything, lying in bed in the mornings—the small steamboat that had a long rounded stem like the lip of a Ubangi, and how quietly she ran on the moonlight sails, when the older boys played their mandolins and the girls sang and we ate doughnuts dipped in sugar, and how sweet the music was on the water in the shining night, and what it had felt like to think about girls then. After breakfast we would go up to the store and

150   the things were in the same place—the minnows in a bottle, the plugs and spinners disarranged and pawed over by the youngsters from the boys' camp, the Fig Newtons and the

Beeman's gum. Outside, the road was tarred and cars stood in front of the store. Inside, all was just as it had always been, except there was more Coca-Cola and not so much Moxie and root beer and birch beer and sarsaparilla. We would walk out with the bottle of pop apiece and sometimes the pop would backfire up our noses and hurt. We explored the streams, quietly, where the turtles slid off the sunny logs and dug their way into the soft bottom; and we lay on the town wharf and fed worms to the tame bass. Everywhere we went I had trouble making out which I was, the one walking at my side, the one walking in my pants.

One afternoon while we were there at that lake a thunderstorm came up. It was like the revival of an old melodrama that I had seen long ago with childish awe. The second-act climax of the drama of the electrical disturbance over a lake in America had not changed in any important respect. This was the big scene, still the big scene. The whole thing was so familiar, the first feeling of oppression and heat and a general air around camp of not wanting to go very far away. In mid-afternoon (it was all the same) a curious darkening of the sky, and a lull in everything that had made life tick; and then the way the boats suddenly swung the other way at their moorings with the coming of a breeze out of the new quarter, and the premonitory rumble. Then the kettle drum, then the snare, then the bass drum and cymbals, then the crackling light against the dark, and the gods grinning and licking their chops in the hills. Afterward the calm, the rain steadily rustling in the calm lake, the return of light and hope and spirits, and the campers running out in joy and relief to go swimming in the rain, their bright cries perpetuating the deathless joke about how they were getting simply drenched, and the children screaming with delight at the new sensation of bathing in the rain, and the joke about getting drenched linking the generations in a strong indestructible chain. And the comedian who waded in carrying an umbrella. 160 170

When the others went swimming, my son said he was going in, too. He pulled his dripping trunks from the line where they had hung all through the shower and wrung them out. Languidly, and with no thought of going in, I watched him, his hard little body, skinny and bare, saw him wince slightly as he pulled up around his vitals the small, soggy, icy garment. As he buckled the swollen belt, suddenly my groin felt the chill of death. ■ 180

UNDERSTANDING CONTEXT

1. What is White's purpose in describing the resort? What lessons or observations does this journey reveal to him?

2. What are the key features of the lake? How much of it had changed in 40 years?

3. White comments in the last line that he "felt the chill of death." How does viewing his son give White a sense of his mortality?

4. *Critical thinking:* What role does time play in this description? What is White saying about the passage of time, the passage of life? How does watching a child grow affect a parent?

EVALUATING STRATEGY

1. How does White use his son as a device for recalling his own youth?

2. Descriptions of places can become tedious lists of geographical details. How does White create action and bring the lake to life?

3. Writers usually rely on visual details to develop a description of a place. Locate places where White uses other sensory impressions. How effective are they?

4. *Other modes:* Locate passages where White uses comparison and narration. How do they develop the essay? Could you classify this essay as narration?

APPRECIATING LANGUAGE

1. White uses figurative language associated with nonnatural objects to describe the lake. For instance, he describes the lake as having the "stillness of a cathedral" and uses references to musical instruments—"the kettle drum, then the snare, then the brass drum and cymbals"—to capture the sound of a storm. What do these word choices suggest about his audience?

2. White uses brand names throughout his essay. What effect do references to Moxie, Fig Newtons, and Coca-Cola have?

WRITING SUGGESTIONS

1. Write an essay describing a place you revisited after a considerable lapse of time. Comment on what has and has not changed. Use as many sensory details as you can.

2. *Collaborative writing:* Work with a group of students who share a common memory of a historical event or recent campus incident. Have each member write a brief narrative. Read each paper aloud to see how people recall and interpret events differently.

Writing beyond the Classroom   TARGET

Target Want Ad

Want ads describe ideal job candidates. This online ad describes openings at a Target facility in Sarasota, Florida.

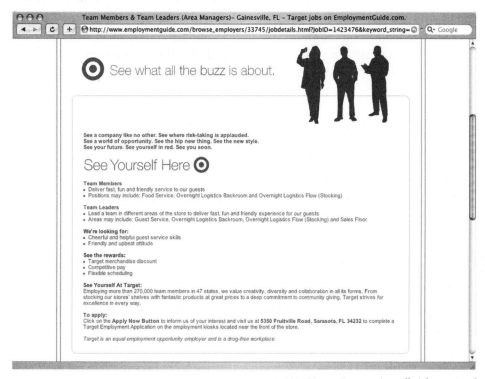

Decoding Want Ads

Want ads describe ideal job candidates. Find an online ad that describes openings at a large company. Use the ad when answering the questions that follow.

UNDERSTANDING CONTEXT

1. What is the goal of a want ad?

2. How else might a corporation advertise its position?

3. What does your ad suggest about the potential reader? Who is the company seeking to attract?

4. If you were interested in this position, what further information would you want? What questions would you want to ask at a job interview?

5. *Critical thinking:* What are the limits of any want ad? Can a job be fully described in a few paragraphs? Why can't employers address all their interests and concerns? Given the cost to print ads, might the Internet give employers more space to describe jobs?

EVALUATING STRATEGY

1. Does the ad first describe the job, then list requirements? Why or why not?

2. Would some potential job seekers be skeptical or suspicious about any job that promises to be "fun"? Might this approach dissuade serious professionals from applying? Why or why not?

APPRECIATING LANGUAGE

1. What words does the ad use to describe the ideal candidate?

2. How would you judge the overall tone of the ad? What kind of language is used in the ad? Are there "trigger" words that might grab job seekers' attention?

3. *Critical thinking:* Study the want ads in a local newspaper. Do you detect differences in wording? Which ads adopt a conservative tone? Which ads use dramatic phrases and emotional appeals?

WRITING SUGGESTIONS

1. Write a want ad for a job you once had. Try to model yours after ones you have seen in the newspaper. Keep your ad as short as possible.

2. Write a résumé responding to this ad. Invent any needed biographical details about education and experience. Review Strategies for Writing Résumés on page 544.

3. *Collaborative writing:* Work with a group of students and write a want ad. Imagine you are hiring a part-time employee to act as secretary for your writing group. Determine the skills needed, the major duties, and how the ad should be worded. If members have differences of opinion, craft more than one ad and ask other students to choose the most effective.

Responding to IMAGES

Seattle Street Youths, 1983   © *Mary Ellen Mark*

1. Describe your first reactions to this picture. Did you feel anger, disgust, fear, concern? What kind of young people are drawn to guns? Describe the problem these boys represent.

2. This photograph was taken in 1983. What do you assume happened to the boys in the picture? Where might they be today? Describe what you think may have happened to them.

3. *Visual analysis:* What do the hats, clothing, and demeanour suggest about these two boys? What do you see in the face of the boy on the left—defiance, resignation, or anger? What does the position of the weapon imply?

4. *Collaborative writing:* Discuss this picture with a group of students and describe how it might be used in an ad about gun control, juvenile programs, tougher laws, or improved social programs. Write the text to accompany the ad. Pay attention to word choice and connotation.

5. Other modes.

   ■ Write a *narrative* to accompany this picture. Invent dialogue for the two boys.

   ■ Write a *cause-and-effect* essay and outline the causes or effects of youth crime.

   ■ Develop a *process* paper detailing the steps it would take for a youth program to intervene in these boys' lives.

   ■ Write a *persuasive* letter to the editor clearly stating your views on gun control. Would handgun bans keep young people from obtaining firearms?

☑ DESCRIPTION **CHECKLIST**

✔ Have you limited your topic?

✔ Does your support suit your context? Should it be objective, subjective, or a blend?

✔ Is your description focused and clearly organized, or is it only a random list of facts and observations?

✔ Have you avoided including unnecessary details and awkward constructions?

✔ Does sensory detail include more than sight? Can you add impressions of taste, touch, sound, or smell?

✔ Do you avoid overly general terms and focus on specific impressions? Have you created dominant impressions?

✔ Do you show rather than tell? Can you add action to your description to keep it from being static?

✔ Do you keep a consistent point of view?

✔ Read your paper aloud. How does it sound? Do any sections need expansion? Are there irrelevant details to delete or awkward expressions to revise?

 COMPANION WEBSITE

See **http://www.transcanadawriter.nelson.com** for additional information on writing description.

CHAPTER 13

Narration: Relating Events

This chapter looks at writing that narrates or relates events. It examines the purpose and role of narration as well as the structure of narration in stories and in report and essay writing.

WHAT IS NARRATION?

A narrative relates an event or tells a story. Even though we tend to think of narrative mainly in the context of short stories and novels, academic and professional writing also relies on narrative to some extent—as in historical scholarship, biographies, quarterly reports, and medical histories. Narratives can be imaginative or factual, fiction or nonfiction. Narrative writing includes most newspaper articles, magazine stories, diaries, and biographies. All narratives seek to answer a simple question: *what happened?*

The Writer's Purpose and Role

Writers tell stories to inform, entertain, enlighten, or persuade. In some instances, the writer's goal is to reconstruct a chain of events as accurately as possible. The purpose of a brief news story or an accident report is to supply readers with an objective statement of facts. In other cases, writers relate a story in order to provide an insight, share an experience, or teach a lesson. The writer will be selective, highlighting key events and describing them in ways to shape readers' perceptions. Some writers prefer to let a story speak for itself, assuming people will understand their point without an actual thesis statement.

Narration can be objective or subjective, depending on the writer's goal and context. Objective narration is generally stated in the third person to give the writer's account a sense of neutrality. In objective narration the author is not a participant but a collector and presenter of facts. An article in *Maclean's* or a chapter in a history book usually consists of objective narration. In assembling the final hours of the *Titanic,* Walter Lord presents an objective catalogue of facts:

> April 15, 1912
> 12:15 a.m. First wireless call for help.
> 12:45 a.m. First rocket fired.
> 12:45 a.m. First boat, No. 7, lowered.
> 01:40 a.m. Last rocket fired.
> 02:05 a.m. Last boat, Collapsible D, lowered.

In contrast, subjective narration highlights the role of the writer, either as an eyewitness to events or as a main participant. James Dillard provides a gripping personal account of trying to resuscitate his victim, focusing not only on the objective appearance of the injured driver but also his own subjective feelings and his role as a participant:

> He was still out cold, limp as a rag doll. His throat was crushed and blood from the jugular vein was running down my arms. He still couldn't breathe. He was deep blue-magenta now, his pulse was rapid and thready. The stench of alcohol turned my stomach, but I positioned his jaw and tried to blow air down into his lungs. It wouldn't go.

Focus

Related closely to the writer's purpose and role is the narrative's focus. A book about World War II can provide an overview of events or a detailed account of the role of women in the defence industry. An article on recycling may provide a survey of national trends or an in-depth history of carpet recycling in a single city. Focus determines the details the writer includes in the narrative and the kind of evidence he or she relies on. A narrative does not have to include each event and every detail:

> For our tenth anniversary my husband and I planned a trip to Hawaii. The seven-hour flight was exhausting, but as soon as I saw the Easter egg blue of the sky and the bright yellows and reds of the flowers I was energized. We rented a car at the airport and drove to our hotel. On the first day we went to the mountains. The scenery was incredible. The following day it rained, so we took the opportunity to visit a local art museum and dine in a Chinese restaurant. The next day we went to the beach.

Attempting to capture a ten-day vacation in a 500-word essay, the student produces only a catalog, a listing of events. The narrative sweeps readers through brief scenes that offer only superficial impressions. It is more effective to concentrate on a single event, as if highlighting a single scene from a movie or chapter in a book.

WRITING **ACTIVITIES**

Select examples of narrative writing from your textbooks, readings from this chapter, news magazine articles, brochures, short stories, or passages from novels.

1. Can you identify the writer's purpose? Are some narratives written solely to inform, while others seek also to persuade or entertain readers?

2. What role does the author play in these narratives? Are some written in the first person? Is the writer the main participant, a minor character, or a witness of the events?

3. How do the various writers focus their narratives? What details do they leave out? How do they introduce background material?

4. Do the writers include dialogue and action to advance the narratives?

Chronology

Chronology or time is a central organizing element in narrative writing. Writers do not always relate events in a straight timeline. A biography, for instance, does not have to open with birth and childhood. Writers often alter time sequences of their stories to dramatize events or limit their topics. Other writers find it more dramatic to open a narrative with a final event and explain what led up to it. The first chapter of a biography about Czar Nicholas II could describe his execution and then flash back to the events leading to his downfall and death.

Each method of organizing a narrative has distinct advantages and disadvantages:

- **Beginning at the beginning** creates an open-ended narrative, providing readers with few hints about later events. Writers who relate complex stories with many possible causes can use a straight chronology to avoid highlighting a single event. Using a direct beginning-to-end approach is the most traditional method of telling a story.

- **Beginning at the middle or turning point** can arouse reader interest by opening with a dramatic scene. This method of organizing plunges the reader directly into the narrative and can give the chain of events a clear focus.

- **Beginning at the end** dramatizes the final event. Organizing a narrative in this way can suggest that the conclusion was inevitable. When everything is presented in flashback, readers see events, actions, and thoughts in hindsight.

WRITING **ACTIVITIES**

Select sample narratives from this chapter or look at one of your favourite books—fiction or nonfiction—and examine how the writers organized the chronology of events.

1. What pattern appears to be the most common?

2. Do any of the authors use flashbacks or flash forwards? If so, what impact do they have? How do they blend these sections into the main narrative without confusing their readers?

3. How do the writers use transitional statements and paragraph breaks to move the narrative and signal changes in time?

4. How do the writers use chronology to establish meaning? Do they use time relationships to indicate cause and effect?

5. How do the writers slow or speed the narrative to emphasize important events or skim through minor ones?

Strategies for Writing Narration

Critical Thinking and Prewriting

1. **List topics suitable to your goal.** Consider the nature of the narrative assignment. What subjects would best suit your purpose?

2. **Determine your purpose.** Does your narrative have a goal beyond telling a story? What details or evidence do readers need to accept your point of view?

3. **Define your role.** Write in the first person, as either the major participant or the witness to events, or write in the third person to establish greater objectivity, inserting personal opinion if desired.

4. **Consider your readers.** How much background information will you have to supply for readers to appreciate the significance of events?

5. **Review the writing situation.** If you are writing a narrative report as an employee, study samples to determine how you should present your story.

6. **Freewrite for a few minutes on the most likely two or three topics to generate ideas.**

7. **Determine whether your narrative would benefit from visuals.**

Planning

1. **Develop a clear thesis.** A narrative usually has a goal to do more than simply list a chain of events.

2. **Identify the beginning and end of your narrative.** You may find it helpful to place background information in a separate foreword or introduction and limit comments on the ending to an afterword. This approach allows the body of the work to focus on a specific chain of events.

3. **Select a chronological pattern.** Determine which pattern would be most effective for your purpose—using a straight chronology, opening with a mid- or turning point, or presenting the final event first.

4. **Select key details that support your thesis.** Focus on those impressions of sight, sound, smell, taste, and touch that will bring your narrative to life.

5. **Draft a timeline, listing main events of the narrative to guide your draft.**

Writing the First Draft

1. **Use your plan as a guide, but be open to new ideas.**

2. **Use dialogue to advance the narrative.** If your narrative contains interactions between people, reconstruct conversations in direct quotations rather than summaries, or allow people to speak for themselves.

3. **Make use of transitional statements.** To prevent readers from becoming confused, make clear transitional statements to move the narrative. Such statements as "two days later" or "later that afternoon" can help readers follow the passage of time. Clear transitions are important if you alter the chronology with flashbacks and flash forwards.

4. **Monitor your length as you write.** If your draft begins to run too long, make notes or list points, and try to complete a full version.

Revising

1. **Review your thesis, plan, and goal.** Examine your prewriting notes and outline to determine if changes are needed.

2. **Read the first draft to get an overall view of your narrative.**
   - Does the opening generate interest and plunge readers into the story?
   - Does the narrative have a thesis, a clear point?
   - Is the narrative easy to follow? Do transitional statements and paragraph breaks help dramatize shifts between main points?
   - Does the narrative end with a memorable impression, thought, or question?

3. **Examine the draft and isolate the narrative's key events.**
   - Can these elements be heightened or expanded?
   - Should these elements be placed in different order?

4. **Decide whether the narrative should be expanded or narrowed.**

5. **Determine whether the narrative can be improved by adding details, including dialogue, or by altering the chronological pattern.**

Editing and Proofreading

1. **Review subsequent drafts for content, style, and tone.** Ensure that your choice of words suits the subject matter, mood, and thesis of the narrative.

2. **Ensure that the narrative does not shift tense without reason.** In relating a narrative, you can write in present or past tense. In some cases, you may shift from past to present to express different actions, but you will otherwise want to remain consistent with your choice of tense.

3. **Avoid shifts in person or stance.** Narratives can be related in first, second, or third person. In most instances, avoid shifts in person, unless there is a clear shift in focus.

General Assignments

Write a narrative on any of the following topics. Your narrative may contain passages making use of other modes, such as description or persuasion. Choose your narrative structure carefully and avoid including minor details that add little to the story line. Use flashbacks and flash forwards carefully. Transitional statements, paragraphing, and line breaks can help clarify changes in chronology.

1. The event or series of events that led you to take some action—quitting a job, ending a relationship, or joining an organization

2. A first date, using dialogue as much as possible to set the tone and advance the narrative

3. An experience that led you to change your opinion about a friend or coworker

4. An accident or medical emergency, focusing on creating a clear, minute-by-minute chronology

5. A telephone call that changed your life, using dialogue as much as possible

Writing in Context

1. Write a letter to a friend relating the events of a typical day in college or university. Select details your friend may find interesting or humorous.

2. Preserve on paper for your children and grandchildren a favourite story told by your grandparents or other relatives. Include necessary background details and identify characters. Consider what you want your descendants to know about their ancestors.

Strategies for Reading Narration

When reading the narratives in this chapter, keep these questions in mind:

Context

1. **What is the author's narrative purpose—to inform, entertain, enlighten, share a personal experience, or provide information required by the reader?** Does the writer have a goal beyond simply telling a story?

2. **Does the writer include a thesis statement?** If so, where does it appear in the essay?

3. **What is the writer's role?** Is the writer a participant or a direct witness? Is he or she writing in a personal context, focusing on internal responses, or in a professional context, concentrating on external events?

4. **What audience is the narrative directed toward—general or specific?** How much knowledge does the author assume readers have?

5. **What is the nature of the discourse community or writing situation?** Is the narration subjective or objective? Does the original source of the narrative—news magazine, book, or professional publication—reveal anything about its context?

Strategy

1. **How does the author open and close the narrative?**

2. **What details does the writer select?** Are some items summarized or ignored? If so, why?

3. **What kind of support does the writer use—personal observation or factual documentation?**

4. **Does the author use dialogue or special effects like flashbacks or flash forwards to advance the narrative?**

5. **What transitional devices does the writer use to prevent confusion?** Does the author use paragraph breaks or time references such as "two hours later" or "later that day"?

Language

1. **What does the level of vocabulary, tone, and style suggest about the writing context?**

2. **How is the author's attitude toward the subject or intended readers reflected by his or her choice of words?**

SAMUEL SCUDDER

Samuel Scudder (1837–1911) attended Williams College. In 1857 he entered Harvard, where he studied under noted scientist Louis Agassiz. Scudder held various positions and helped found the Cambridge Entomological Club. He published hundreds of papers and developed a comprehensive catalogue of 300 years of scientific publications. While working for the United States Geological Survey, he named more than 1,000 species of fossil insects. Much of Scudder's work is still admired for its attention to detail.

Take This Fish and Look at It

Today educators stress critical thinking, which begins with close observation. As you read this essay, consider how effective the professor's teaching method is. Does it rest on the age-old notion that "people learn by doing"?

1   It was more than fifteen years ago that I entered the laboratory of Professor Agassiz, and told   intro sets time
him I had enrolled my name in the Scientific School as a student of natural history. He asked
me a few questions about my object in coming, my antecedents generally, the mode in which   brief summary
I afterwards proposed to use the knowledge I might acquire, and, finally, whether I wished to
study any special branch. To the latter I replied that, while I wished to be well grounded in all
departments of zoology, I purposed to devote myself specially to insects.

"When do you wish to begin?" he asked.   uses dialogue

"Now," I replied.

This seemed to please him, and with an energetic "Very well!" he reached from a shelf a
10   huge jar of specimens in yellow alcohol. "Take this fish," he said, "and look at it; we call it a
haemulon; by and by I will ask what you have seen."

With that he left me, but in a moment returned with explicit instructions as to the care
of the object entrusted to me.

"No man is fit to be a naturalist," said he, "who does not know how to take care of
specimens."

I was to keep the fish before me in a tin tray, and occasionally moisten the surface with   gives direction
alcohol from the jar, always taking care to replace the stopper tightly. Those were not the
days of ground-glass stoppers and elegantly shaped exhibition jars; all the old students will
recall the huge neckless glass bottles with their leaky, wax-besmeared corks, half eaten by
20   insects, and begrimed with cellar dust. Entomology was a cleaner science than ichthyology,
but the example of the Professor, who had unhesitatingly plunged to the bottom of the jar
to produce the fish, was infectious; and though this alcohol had a "very ancient and fishlike
smell," I really dared not show any aversion within these sacred precincts, and treated the
alcohol as though it were pure water. Still I was conscious of a passing feeling of disappointment, for gazing at a fish did not commend itself to an ardent entomologist. My friends at
home, too, were annoyed when they discovered that no amount of eau-de-Cologne would
drown the perfume which haunted me like a shadow.

first impression

In ten minutes I had seen all that could be seen in that fish, and started in search of the Professor—who had, however, left the Museum; and when I returned, after lingering over some of the odd animals stored in the upper apartment, my specimen was dry all over. I dashed the fluid over the fish as if to resuscitate the beast from a fainting fit, and looked with anxiety for a return of the normal sloppy appearance. This little excitement over, nothing was to be done but to return to a steadfast gaze at my mute companion. Half

emphasizes boredom

an hour passed—an hour—another hour; the fish began to look loathsome. I turned it over and around; looked it in the face—ghastly; from behind, beneath, above, sideways, at three-quarters' view—just as ghastly. I was in despair; at an early hour I concluded that lunch was necessary; so, with infinite relief, the fish was carefully replaced in the jar, and for an hour I was free.

On my return, I learned that Professor Agassiz had been at the Museum, but had gone, and would not return for several hours. My fellow-students were too busy to be disturbed by continued conversation. Slowly I drew forth that hideous fish, and with a feeling of desperation again looked at it. I might not use a magnifying-glass; instruments of all kinds were interdicted. My two hands, my two eyes, and the fish: it seemed a most limited field. I pushed my finger down its throat to feel how sharp the teeth were. I began to count the scales in

discovers by drawing

the different rows, until I was convinced that was nonsense. At last a happy thought struck me—I would draw the fish; and now with surprise I began to discover new features in the creature. Just then the Professor returned.

"That is right," said he; "a pencil is one of the best of eyes. I am glad to notice, too, that you keep your specimen wet, and your bottle corked."

With these encouraging words, he added: "Well, what is it like?"

He listened attentively to my brief rehearsal of the structure of parts whose names were still unknown to me: the fringed gill-arches and movable operculum; the pores of the head, fleshy lips and lidless eyes; the compressed and arched body. When I finished, he waited as if expecting more, and then, with an air of disappointment:

"You have not looked very carefully; why," he continued more earnestly, "you haven't even seen one of the most conspicuous features of the animal, which is plainly before your eyes as the fish itself; look again, look again!" and he left me to my misery.

initial reaction

I was piqued; I was mortified. Still more of that wretched fish! But now I set myself to my task with a will, and discovered one new thing after another, until I saw how just the Professor's criticism had been. The afternoon passed quickly; and when, towards its close, the Professor inquired:

"Do you see it yet?"

"No," I replied, "I am certain I do not, but I see how little I saw before."

"That is next best," said he, earnestly, "but I won't hear you now; put away your fish and go home; perhaps you will be ready with a better answer in the morning. I will examine you before you look at the fish."

This was disconcerting. Not only must I think of my fish all night, studying, without the object before me, what this unknown but most visible feature might be; but also,

without reviewing my discoveries, I must give an exact account of them the next day.
I had a bad memory; so I walked home by Charles River in a distracted state, with my two
perplexities.

The cordial greeting from the Professor the next morning was reassuring; here was a
man who seemed to be quite as anxious as I that I should see for myself what he saw.

"Do you perhaps mean," I asked, "that the fish has symmetrical sides with paired
organs?"

His thoroughly pleased "Of course! of course!" repaid the wakeful hours of the previous
night. After he had discoursed most happily and enthusiastically—as he always did—upon
the importance of this point, I ventured to ask what I should do next. asks for help

"Oh, look at your fish!" he said, and left me again to my own devices. In a little more
than an hour he returned, and heard my new catalogue. "That is good, that is good!" he repeated; "but that is not all; go on"; and so for three long days he placed that fish before my
eyes, forbidding me to look at anything else, or to use any artificial aid. <u>"Look, look, look,"</u> repeated
<u>was his repeated injunction.</u> command

<u>This was the best entomological lesson I ever had—a lesson whose influence has</u>
<u>extended to the details of every subsequent study; a legacy the Professor had left to me, as</u> thesis/value
<u>he has left it to so many others, of inestimable value which we could not buy, with which we</u> of lesson
<u>cannot part.</u>

A year afterward, some of us were amusing ourselves with chalking outlandish beasts
on the Museum blackboard. We drew prancing starfishes; frogs in mortal combat; hydra- flash forward
headed worms; stately crawfishes, standing on their tails, bearing aloft umbrellas; and to humorous
grotesque fishes with gaping mouths and staring eyes. The Professor came in shortly after, incident
and was as amused as any at our experiments. He looked at the fishes.

"Haemulons, every one of them," he said; "Mr. —— drew them."

True; and to this day, if I attempt a fish, I can draw nothing but haemulons.

The fourth day, a second fish of the same group was placed beside the first, and I was
bidden to point out the resemblances and differences between the two; another and another
followed, until the entire family lay before me, and a whole legion of jars covered the table
and surrounding shelves; the odor had become a pleasant perfume; and even now, the sight
of an old, six-inch worm-eaten cork brings fragrant memories.

The whole group of haemulons was thus brought in review; and, whether engaged upon
the dissection of the internal organs, the preparation and examination of the bony framework, or the description of the various parts, Agassiz's training in the method of observing
facts and their orderly arrangement was ever accompanied by the urgent exhortation not to
be content with them.

<u>"Facts are stupid things,"</u> he would say, <u>"until brought into connection with some</u> conclusion
<u>general law."</u>

<u>At the end of eight months, it was almost with reluctance that I left these friends and</u>
<u>turned to insects; but what I had gained by this outside experience has been of greater value</u>
<u>than years of later investigation in my favorite groups.</u> ■

UNDERSTANDING CONTEXT

1. What is Scudder's purpose in this narrative? Why is this essay more than a typical "first day at school" story?

2. What did Professor Agassiz mean when he stated that "a pencil is one of the best of eyes"?

3. *Critical thinking:* How effective was Professor Agassiz's teaching method? By directing a new student to simply "look, look again," did he accomplish more than if he had required Scudder to attend a two-hour lecture on the importance of observation? Does this method assume that students have already acquired basic skills? Would this method work for all students? Why or why not?

4. What has this essay taught you about your future career? How can keen observation and attention to detail help you achieve your goals?

EVALUATING STRATEGY

1. How does Scudder give the narrative focus? What details does he omit?

2. Scudder does not bother describing Professor Agassiz. Would that add or detract from the narrative?

3. *Other modes:* How does Scudder use description of the fish, specimen bottles, and smells to provide readers with a clear impression of the laboratory?

APPRECIATING LANGUAGE

1. How much scientific terminology does Scudder use in the narrative? What does this suggest about his intended audience?

2. This essay contains little action. Essentially it is a story about a man interacting with a dead fish. What words add drama and humour to the narrative?

WRITING SUGGESTIONS

1. Apply Professor Agassiz's technique to a common object you might use every day. Take your clock radio or a can of your favourite soft drink and study it for five minutes. Write a description of what you have observed. List the features you never noticed before.

2. Professor Agassiz gave his student little direction other than a simple command. Write a brief account about a time when a parent, teacher, coach, or boss left you to act on your own. What problems or challenges did you encounter? Did you feel frustrated, afraid, angry, or confident? What did you learn?

3. *Collaborative writing:* Working with three or four other students, select an object unfamiliar to the group. Allow each member to study the object and make notes. Compare your findings, and work to create a single description incorporating the findings of the group.

CAROL SHIELDS

Carol Shields is an acclaimed fiction writer and playwright. She is best known for her best-selling and Pulitzer Prize–winning novel, **The Stone Diaries** (1993). **The Stone Diaries** also won Canada's Governor General's Award for Fiction and was nominated for the National Book Critics Circle Award and for the Booker Prize. In addition to her award-winning fiction, Shields has written numerous short-story collections and pieces about the art of writing.

The Same Ticking Clock*

In the following essay, Shields explores the importance of stories—our own and those of others—in helping to liberate us into wider frameworks of reference and perspective.

My friend Sarah was worried about her five-year-old son, Simon. "I hear voices in my head," 1 he told her, "and they're talking all the time."

It took her a few days to figure out that the buzzings in his brain were nothing more than his own thoughts, the beginning of that lifelong monologue that occupies and imprisons the self.

It's here in the private, talky cave of our minds that we spend the greater part of our lives—whether we like it or not. And mostly, it seems, we do like it—"The Soul selects her own Society"—but there are times when the interior tissues thin and when the endless conversation grows unbearably monotonous, when it seems to be going back and forth across the same grooves of experience, the same channels of persuasion, and we long for release. 10 Long, in fact, to become someone else. Even the most fortunate of us lead lives that are sadly limited; we can inhabit only so many places, follow so many lines of work, and can love a finite number of people. We're enclosed not just by the margins of time and by the accident of geography, but by gender and perspective, and by the stubborn resistance of language to certain modes of meditation.

Our own stories, moreover, are not quite enough; why else are our newspapers filled with Dear Abby and Ann Landers, with problem columns for golden-agers, for adolescents, mid-lifers, parents, consumers, patients, and professionals? It's not for the solutions that we devour this often execrable journalese, but for a glimpse of human dilemma, the inaccessible stories of others. Even the smallest narrative fragments have the power to seduce. 20 School children read in their arithmetic books about Mary Brown who buys three pounds of turnips at twenty cents a pound and a kilo and a half of cheese at five dollars a kilo. How much change will she get back from a twenty-dollar bill? The answer arrives easily, or not so easily, but leaves us hungering after the narrative thread—who is this Mary Brown, what will she do with all that cheese, and what of her wider life, her passions and disappointments?

*Shields, Carol, "The Same Ticking Clock" first published in *Language in Her Eye: Views on Writing and Gender by Canadian Women Writing in English*, editors Libby Shier, Sarah Sheard and Eleanor Wachtel (Toronto: Coach House, 1990), is reprinted with the permission of the Carol Shields Literary Trust.

A phrase overheard on a bus or perhaps a single name scratched on a wall has the power to call up the world. We want, need, the stories of others. We need, too, to place our own stories beside theirs, to compare, weigh, judge, forgive, and to find, by becoming something other than ourselves, an angle of vision that renews our image of the world.

30   Writers draw on their own experiences, though only a few draw directly. We want to imbue our fictions with emotional truth; does this require that we stay imprisoned in the tight little outline of our official résumés, that we must write about the Prairies because that's where we live, that we cannot make forays into the swamps of Florida or Mars or Baloneyland, that we must concentrate our steady eyes on the socio-economic class we come from and know best, that we must play it safe—because this is what it amounts to—and write about people of our own generation? A lot of energy has been lost in the name of authenticity; we fear far too much that critical charge—"it doesn't ring true"—and worry too little that it may not ring at all.

"When I write, I am free," Cynthia Ozick argues in one of her essays, collected in her
40 book *Art and Ardor*—and she means utterly free, free to be "a stone, or a raindrop, or a block of wood, or a Tibetan, or the spine of a cactus," Our circumscription is largely of our own making, and at least a portion of it flows from a peculiar reluctance—whether caused by a stance of political purity or a fear of trespassing or "getting it wrong"—to experiment with different points of view, and, in particular, with shifts of gender.

We all know that a fully furnished universe is made up of men and women, and that women writers are often called upon to write about men, and male writers about women. Writers go even further at times, not just writing about the other sex, but speaking through its consciousness, using its voice. The question can be asked, and often is, how successful is this gender-hopping? Does any truth at all seep through? Maybe more than we think. Oscar
50 Wilde had the notion that we can hear more of the author's true voice in her or his fictional impersonations than we can hear in any autobiography. (Not that he bothered with the niceties of gender pronouns.) "Man is least himself," he said, "when he talks in his own person. Give him a mask, and he will tell you the truth." A mask, he said, but he might also have said, a skirt. Or a small pointy beard.

This is not to say that crossing gender lines consists of trickery or sleight of hand; nor is it a masquerade as Anne Robinson Taylor, in her book *Male Novelists and Their Female Voices,* would like us to think; and certainly not an impersonation as Oscar Wilde suggests. To believe this is to deny the writer the powers of observation and imagination and also to resist the true composition of the universe, real or created, in which men and women exist
60 in more or less equal numbers.

Nevertheless it is still considered a rare achievement for a man to have created a believable and significant woman, and a woman a believable and significant man. We point to these gender trips as exceptions, as marvels. Isn't it amazing, we say, that Brian Moore could get inside the head of Judith Hearne and make us believe in her? And Flaubert—how remarkable that he was able to comprehend the temperament of a French housewife, her yearnings and passion! And there must be a couple of others out there—aren't there? Jane Austen gave us a few men who were worth waiting three or four hundred pages for, although there's a chilliness about even the best of them. Charlotte Brontë uses the male voice in her novel *The Professor,* but the tone is painfully awkward. In writing the male character, Brontë says, she was working under a disadvantage; when writing about women she was surer of her ground. Joyce Carol Oates once remarked that she did badly with male narrators because for her the angle of vision was restricted, and too much feeling and self-awareness had to be sacrificed.

A few years ago women could point to their own lack of experience in the world of men, but this situation has been extraordinarily altered by legislation and by a revolution in thinking. What has also been altered is the kind of experience that can legitimately be brought to art—birth, motherhood, the rhythms of the female body, a yearning for love and the domestic component of our lives—which serious literature had previously suppressed. But the news is out: we all, male and female alike, possess a domestic life. The texture of the quotidian is rich with meaning, and the old problem-solution trick is beginning to look like a set-up, a photo opportunity for artificial crisis and faked confrontation. Acknowledgement of that fact leads us to the hypothesis that we are all born with a full range of sympathy toward both men and women—yet something, somewhere, gets in our way and makes us strangers. This is puzzling since, despite the inequities of the power structure, men have always had mothers, sisters, wives, daughters, just as women have had access, albeit limited, to the lives of fathers and brothers, husbands and sons. We have been living under the same roofs all these years and listening to the same ticking clock.

It seems baffling, then, that in this day there should be so few men and women writing well about the other sex and even sadder that they are not writing *for* the other sex. The world we are being offered as readers is only half-realized, a world divided down its middle. As readers we are being misled; as writers we are cheated. I wonder sometimes if the loneliness writers complain about isn't a result of scraping a single personality, our own, down to its last nuance.

What is needed is permission to leave our own skins, worrying less about verisimilitude and trusting the human core we all share. Of course our experiences are necessarily limited—this is part of the human conundrum—but observation and imagination may lead us to what we intuitively know, and have known all along. ∎

UNDERSTANDING CONTEXT

1. What is Shields' goal in the piece?
2. What does the piece have to say about narration?

EVALUATING STRATEGY

1. Shields begins her essay about issues of narration as a narrative about a friend's son. Why does she choose to begin the essay in this manner?

APPRECIATING LANGUAGE

1. Shields uses simple diction in the essay. Does the level of diction undermine or enhance her argument?

WRITING SUGGESTIONS

1. In two or three sentences, summarize Shields' thesis.
2. Create a list of four works of fiction that you have read recently. Note whether the books were written by a man or a woman. Compare and contrast the male and female characters. Relate your findings to Shields' article. Do you agree with her thesis?

JAMES DILLARD

James Dillard is a physician who specializes in rehabilitation medicine. In this narrative, first published in the "My Turn" column in **Newsweek,** he relates an incident that nearly ended his medical career.

A Doctor's Dilemma*

As you read this narrative, keep in mind how most people expect physicians to respond in an emergency.

It was a bright, clear February afternoon in Gettysburg. A strong sun and layers of down did 1
little to ease the biting cold. Our climb to the crest of Little Roundtop wound past somber monuments, barren trees and polished cannon. From the top, we peered down on the wheat field where men had fallen so close together that one could not see the ground. Rifle balls had whined as thick as bee swarms through the trees, and cannon shots had torn limbs from the young men fighting there. A frozen wind whipped tears from our eyes. My friend Amy huddled close, using me as a wind breaker. Despite the cold, it was hard to leave this place.

Driving east out of Gettysburg on a country blacktop, the gray Bronco ahead of us passed through a rural crossroad just as a small pickup truck tried to take a left turn. The Bronco swerved, but slammed into the pickup on the passenger side. We immediately slowed to a 10
crawl as we passed the scene. The Bronco's driver looked fine, but we couldn't see the driver of the pickup. I pulled over on the shoulder and got out to investigate.

The right side of the truck was smashed in, and the side window was shattered. The driver was partly out of the truck. His head hung forward over the edge of the passenger-side window, the front of his neck crushed on the shattered windowsill. He was unconscious and starting to turn a dusky blue. His chest slowly heaved against a blocked windpipe.

A young man ran out of a house at the crossroad. "Get an ambulance out here," I shouted against the wind. "Tell them a man is dying."

I looked down again at the driver hanging from the windowsill. There were six empty beer bottles on the floor of the truck. I could smell the beer through the window. I knew I 20
had to move him, to open his airway. I had no idea what neck injuries he had sustained. He could easily end up a quadriplegic. But I thought: he'll be dead by the time the ambulance gets here if I don't move him and try to do something to help him.

An image flashed before my mind. I could see the courtroom and the driver of the truck sitting in a wheelchair. I could see his attorney pointing at me and thundering at the jury: "This young doctor, with still a year left in his residency training, took it upon himself to play God. He took it upon himself to move this gravely injured man, condemning him forever to this wheelchair …" I imagined the millions of dollars in award money. And all the years of hard work lost. I'd be paying him off for the rest of my life. Amy touched my shoulder. "What are you going to do?" 30

The automatic response from long hours in the emergency room kicked in. I pulled off my overcoat and rolled up my sleeves. The trick would be to keep enough traction straight up on his head while I moved his torso, so that his probable broken neck and spinal-cord injury wouldn't be made worse. Amy came around the driver's side, climbed half in and grabbed his belt and shirt collar. Together we lifted him off the windowsill.

He was still out cold, limp as a rag doll. His throat was crushed and blood from the jugular vein was running down my arms. He still couldn't breathe. He was deep blue-magenta now, his pulse was rapid and thready. The stench of alcohol turned my stomach, but I positioned his jaw and tried to blow air down into his lungs. It wouldn't go.

40 Amy had brought some supplies from my car. I opened an oversize intravenous needle and groped on the man's neck. My hands were numb, covered with freezing blood and bits of broken glass. Hyoid bone—God, I can't even feel the thyroid cartilage, it's gone … OK, the thyroid gland is about there, cricoid rings are here … we'll go in right here …

It was a lucky first shot. Pink air sprayed through the IV needle. I placed a second needle next to the first. The air began whistling through it. Almost immediately, the driver's face turned bright red. After a minute, his pulse slowed down and his eyes moved slightly. I stood up, took a step back and looked down. He was going to make it. He was going to live. A siren wailed in the distance. I turned and saw Amy holding my overcoat. I was shivering and my arms were turning white with cold.

50 The ambulance captain looked around and bellowed, "What the hell … who did this?" as his team scurried over to the man lying in the truck.

"I did," I replied. He took down my name and address for his reports. I had just destroyed my career. I would never be able to finish my residency with a massive lawsuit pending. My life was over.

The truck driver was strapped onto a backboard, his neck in a stiff collar. The ambulance crew had controlled the bleeding and started intravenous fluid. He was slowly waking up. As they loaded him into the ambulance, I saw him move his feet. Maybe my future wasn't lost.

A police sergeant called me from Pennsylvania three weeks later. Six days after successful throat-reconstruction surgery, the driver had signed out, against medical advice,
60 from the hospital because he couldn't get a drink on the ward. He was being arraigned on drunk-driving charges.

A few days later, I went into the office of one of my senior professors, to tell the story. He peered over his half glasses and his eyes narrowed. "Well, you did the right thing medically of course. But, James, do you know what you put at risk by doing that?" he said sternly. "What was I supposed to do?" I asked.

"Drive on," he replied. "There is an army of lawyers out there who would stand in line to get a case like that. If that driver had turned out to be a quadriplegic, you might never have practiced medicine again. You were a very lucky young man."

The day I graduated from medical school, I took an oath to serve the sick and the in-
70 jured. I remember truly believing I would be able to do just that. But I have found out it isn't so simple. I understand now what a foolish thing I did that day. Despite my oath, I know what I would do on that cold roadside near Gettysburg today. I would drive on. ■

UNDERSTANDING CONTEXT

1. What was Dillard's goal in publishing this narrative in a national news magazine?

2. Does this narrative serve to contrast idealism and reality? How does Dillard's oath conflict with his final decision?

3. Does the fact that the victim was drinking have an impact on your reactions to the doctor's actions? Does Dillard seem to show contempt for his patient?

4. *Critical thinking:* Does this essay suggest that there is an undeclared war between doctors and lawyers? Do medical malpractice suits improve or diminish the quality of medicine? Are lawyers to blame for the writer's decision to "drive on"?

EVALUATING STRATEGY

1. *Other modes:* Does this narrative also serve as a persuasive argument? Is the story a better vehicle than a standard argumentative essay that states a thesis and presents factual support?

2. Does this first-person story help place the reader in the doctor's position? Is this a more effective strategy than writing an objective third-person essay about the impact of malpractice suits?

3. Why does Dillard mention that the patient later disobeyed his doctors' orders and left the hospital so he could get a drink?

4. How do you think Dillard wanted his readers to respond to the essay's last line?

APPRECIATING LANGUAGE

1. What words does Dillard use to dramatize his attempts to save the driver's life? How do they reflect the tension he was feeling?

2. What language does Dillard use to demonstrate what he was risking by trying to save a life?

3. What kind of people read *Newsweek?* Do you find this essay's language suitable?

WRITING SUGGESTIONS

1. Relate an emergency situation you experienced or encountered. Using Dillard's essay as a model, write an account capturing what you thought and felt as you acted.

2. Write a letter to the editor of *Newsweek* in response to Dillard's essay. Do you find his position tenable? Are you angry at a doctor who vows not to help accident victims? Or do you blame the legal community for putting a physician in this position?

3. *Collaborative writing:* Discuss Dillard's essay with a number of students and list their reactions to Dillard's final statement. Write a division paper outlining their views.

| Blending the Modes | GEORGE ORWELL |

George Orwell was the pen name of Eric Blair (1903–1950), who was born in India, the son of a British official. Blair attended the prestigious Eton school but joined the Indian Imperial Police instead of attending university. After four years of service in Burma, he left to pursue a writing career. His first book, **Down and Out in Paris and London**, explored the plight of the poor and homeless during the Depression. His later books included **Animal Farm** and **Nineteen Eighty-Four**.

Shooting an Elephant*

As you read the narrative, consider what message about imperialism Orwell was trying to communicate to his British audience. What is his implied thesis? How does he use comparison, description, and persuasion in developing this narrative?

1   In Moulmein, in Lower Burma, I was hated by large numbers of people—the only time in my life that I have been important enough for this to happen to me. I was sub-divisional police officer of the town, and in an aimless, petty kind of way anti-European feeling was very bitter. No one had the guts to raise a riot, but if a European woman went through the bazaars alone somebody would probably spit betel juice over her dress. As a police officer I was an obvious target and was baited whenever it seemed safe to do so. When a nimble Burman tripped me up on the football field and the referee (another Burman) looked the other way, the crowd yelled with hideous laughter. This happened more than once. In the end the sneering yellow faces of young men that met me everywhere, the
10   insults hooted after me when I was at a safe distance, got badly on my nerves. The young Buddhist priests were the worst of all. There were several thousands of them in the town and none of them seemed to have anything to do except stand on street corners and jeer at Europeans.

All this was perplexing and upsetting. For at that time I had already made up my mind that imperialism was an evil thing and the sooner I chucked up my job and got out of it the better. Theoretically—and secretly, of course—I was all for the Burmese and all against their oppressors, the British. As for the job I was doing, I hated it more bitterly than I can perhaps make clear. In a job like that you see the dirty work of Empire at close quarters. The wretched prisoners huddling in the stinking cages of the lock-ups, the grey, cowed faces of the long-
20   term convicts, the scarred buttocks of the men who had been flogged with bamboos—all these oppressed me with an intolerable sense of guilt. But I could get nothing into perspective. I was young and ill-educated and I had had to think out my problems in the utter silence that is imposed on every Englishman in the East. I did not even know that the British

Empire is dying, still less did I know that it is a great deal better than the younger empires that are going to supplant it. All I knew was that I was stuck between my hatred of the empire I served and my rage against the evil-spirited little beasts who tried to make my job impossible. With one part of my mind I thought of the British Raj as an unbreakable tyranny, as something clamped down, in *saecula saeculorum,* upon the will of prostrate peoples; with another part I thought that the greatest joy in the world would be to drive a bayonet into a Buddhist priest's guts. Feelings like these are the normal by-products of imperialism; ask any 30 Anglo-Indian official, if you can catch him off duty.

One day something happened which in a roundabout way was enlightening. It was a tiny incident in itself, but it gave me a better glimpse than I had had before of the real nature of imperialism—the real motives for which despotic governments act. Early one morning the sub-inspector at a police station the other end of the town rang me up on the phone and said that an elephant was ravaging the bazaar. Would I please come and do something about it? I did not know what I could do, but I wanted to see what was happening and I got on to a pony and started out. I took my rifle, an old .44 Winchester and much too small to kill an elephant, but I thought the noise might be useful *in terrorem.* Various Burmans stopped me on the way and told me about the elephant's doings. It was 40 not, of course, a wild elephant, but a tame one which had gone "must." It had been chained up as tame elephants always are when their attack of "must" is due, but on the previous night it had broken its chain and escaped. Its mahout, the only person who could manage it when it was in that state, had set out in pursuit, but he had taken the wrong direction and was now twelve hours' journey away, and in the morning the elephant had suddenly reappeared in the town. The Burmese population had no weapons and were quite helpless against it. It had already destroyed somebody's bamboo hut, killed a cow and raided some fruit-stalls and devoured the stock; also it had met the municipal rubbish van, and, when the driver jumped out and took to his heels, had turned the van over and inflicted violence upon it.   50

The Burmese sub-inspector and some Indian constables were waiting for me in the quarter where the elephant had been seen. It was a very poor quarter, a labyrinth of squalid bamboo huts, thatched with palm-leaf, winding all over a steep hillside. I remember that it was a cloudy stuffy morning at the beginning of the rains. We began questioning the people as to where the elephant had gone, and, as usual, failed to get any definite information. That is invariably the case in the East; a story always sounds clear enough at a distance, but the nearer you get to the scene of events the vaguer it becomes. Some of the people said that the elephant had gone in one direction, some said that he had gone in another, some professed not even to have heard of any elephant. I had almost made up my mind that the whole story was a pack of lies, when we heard yells a little distance 60 away. There was a loud, scandalised cry of "Go away, child! Go away this instant!" and an old woman with a switch in her hand came round the corner of a hut, violently shooing away a crowd of naked children. Some more women followed, clicking their tongues and exclaiming; evidently there was something there that the children ought not to have seen. I rounded the hut and saw a man's dead body sprawling in the mud. He was an Indian,

a black Dravidian coolie, almost naked, and he could not have been dead many minutes. The people said that the elephant had come suddenly upon him round the corner of the hut, caught him with its trunk, put its foot on his back and ground him into the earth. This was the rainy season and the ground was soft, and his face had scored a trench a foot
70 deep and a couple of yards long. He was lying on his belly with arms crucified and head sharply twisted to one side. His face was coated with mud, the eyes wide open, the teeth bared and grinning with an expression of unendurable agony. (Never tell me, by the way, that the dead look peaceful. Most of the corpses I have seen looked devilish.) The friction of the great beast's foot had stripped the skin from his back as neatly as one skins a rabbit. As soon as I saw the dead man I sent an orderly to a friend's house nearby to borrow an elephant rifle. I had already sent back the pony, not wanting it to go mad with fright and throw me if it smelled the elephant.

The orderly came back in a few minutes with a rifle and five cartridges, and meanwhile some Burmans had arrived and told us that the elephant was in the paddy fields below,
80 only a few hundred yards away. As I started forward practically the whole population of the quarter flocked out of their houses and followed me. They had seen the rifle and were all shouting excitedly that I was going to shoot the elephant. They had not shown much interest in the elephant when he was merely ravaging their homes, but it was different now that he was going to be shot. It was a bit of fun to them, as it would be to an English crowd; besides, they wanted the meat. It made me vaguely uneasy. I had no intention of shooting the elephant—I had merely sent for the rifle to defend myself if necessary—and it is always unnerving to have a crowd following you. I marched down the hill, looking and feeling a fool, with the rifle over my shoulder and an ever-growing army of people jostling at my heels. At the bottom, when you got away from the huts, there was a metalled road and beyond that
90 a miry waste of paddy fields a thousand yards across, not yet ploughed but soggy from the first rains and dotted with coarse grass. The elephant was standing eighty yards from the road, his left side towards us. He took not the slightest notice of the crowd's approach. He was tearing up bunches of grass, beating them against his knees to clean them and stuffing them into his mouth.

I had halted on the road. As soon as I saw the elephant I knew with perfect certainty that I ought not to shoot him. It is a serious matter to shoot a working elephant—it is comparable to destroying a huge and costly piece of machinery—and obviously one ought not to do it if it can possibly be avoided. And at that distance, peacefully eating, the elephant looked no more dangerous than a cow. I thought then and I think now that his attack of "must"
100 was already passing off; in which case he would merely wander harmlessly about until the mahout came back and caught him. Moreover, I did not in the least want to shoot him. I decided that I would watch him for a little while to make sure that he did not turn savage again, and then go home.

But at that moment I glanced round at the crowd that had followed me. It was an immense crowd, two thousand at the least and growing every minute. It blocked the road for a long distance on either side. I looked at the sea of yellow faces above the garish clothes—faces all happy and excited over this bit of fun, all certain that the elephant was going to be shot. They were watching me as they would watch a conjuror about to perform a trick. They did not like me, but with the magical rifle in my hands I was momentarily worth watching. And suddenly I realised that I should have to shoot the elephant after all. The people 110 expected it of me and I had got to do it; I could feel their two thousand wills pressing me forward, irresistibly. And it was at this moment, as I stood there with the rifle in my hands, that I first grasped the hollowness, the futility of the white man's dominion in the East. Here was I, the white man with his gun, standing in front of the unarmed native crowd—seemingly the leading actor of the piece; but in reality I was only an absurd puppet pushed to and fro by the will of those yellow faces behind. I perceived in this moment that when the white man turns tyrant it is his own freedom that he destroys. He becomes a sort of hollow, posing dummy, the conventionalised figure of a sahib. For it is the condition of his rule that he shall spend his life in trying to impress the "natives" and so in every crisis he has got to do what the "natives" expect of him. He wears a mask, and his face grows to fit it. I had got to shoot 120 the elephant. I had committed myself to doing it when I sent for the rifle. A sahib has got to act like a sahib; he has got to appear resolute, to know his own mind and do definite things. To come all that way, rifle in hand, with two thousand people marching at my heels, and then to trail feebly away, having done nothing—no, that was impossible. The crowd would laugh at me. And my whole life, every white man's life in the East, was one long struggle not to be laughed at.

But I did not want to shoot the elephant. I watched him beating his bunch of grass against his knees, with that preoccupied grandmotherly air that elephants have. It seemed to me that it would be murder to shoot him. At that age I was not squeamish about killing animals, but I had never shot an elephant and never wanted to. (Somehow it always seems 130 worse to kill a *large* animal.) Besides, there was the beast's owner to be considered. Alive, the elephant was worth at least a hundred pounds; dead, he would only be worth the value of his tusks—five pounds, possibly. But I had got to act quickly. I turned to some experienced-looking Burmans who had been there when we arrived, and asked them how the elephant had been behaving. They all said the same thing: he took no notice of you if you left him alone, but he might charge if you went too close to him.

It was perfectly clear to me what I ought to do. I ought to walk up to within, say, twenty-five yards of the elephant and test his behaviour. If he charged I could shoot, if he took no notice of me it would be safe to leave him until the mahout came back. But also I knew that I was going to do no such thing. I was a poor shot with a rifle and the ground 140 was soft mud into which one would sink at every step. If the elephant charged and I missed him, I should have about as much chance as a toad under a steam-roller. But even then I was not thinking particularly of my own skin, only the watchful yellow faces behind. For at that moment, with the crowd watching me, I was not afraid in the ordinary sense, as I would have been if I had been alone. A white man mustn't be frightened in front of "natives"; and so, in general, he isn't frightened. The sole thought in my mind was that if anything went wrong those two thousand Burmans would see me pursued, caught, trampled on and reduced to a grinning corpse like that Indian up the hill. And if that happened it was quite probable that some of them would laugh. That would never do. There was only

150 one alternative. I shoved the cartridges into the magazine and lay down on the road to get a better aim.

The crowd grew very still, and a deep, low, happy sigh, as of people who see the theatre curtain go up at last, breathed from innumerable throats. They were going to have their bit of fun after all. The rifle was a beautiful German thing with cross-hair sights. I did not then know that in shooting an elephant one should shoot to cut an imaginary bar running from ear-hole to ear-hole. I ought therefore, as the elephant was sideways on, to have aimed straight at his ear-hole; actually I aimed several inches in front of this, thinking the brain would be further forward.

When I pulled the trigger I did not hear the bang or feel the kick—one never does when 160 a shot goes home—but heard the devilish roar of glee that went up from the crowd. In that instant, in too short a time, one would have thought, even for the bullet to get there, a mysterious, terrible change had come over the elephant. He neither stirred nor fell, but every line of his body had altered. He looked suddenly stricken, shrunken, immensely old, as though the frightful impact of the bullet had paralysed him without knocking him down. At last, after what seemed a long time—it might have been five seconds, I dare say—he sagged flabbily to his knees. His mouth slobbered. An enormous senility seemed to have settled upon him. One could have imagined him thousands of years old. I fired again into the same spot. At the second shot he did not collapse but climbed with desperate slowness to his feet and stood weakly upright, with legs sagging and head drooping. I fired a third time. That was the shot 170 that did for him. You could see the agony of it jolt his whole body and knock the last remnant of strength from his legs. But in falling he seemed for a moment to rise, for as his hind legs collapsed beneath him he seemed to tower upwards like a huge rock toppling, his trunk reaching skyward like a tree. He trumpeted, for the first and only time. And then down he came, his belly towards me, with a crash that seemed to shake the ground even where I lay.

I got up. The Burmans were already racing past me across the mud. It was obvious that the elephant would never rise again, but he was not dead. He was breathing very rhythmically with long rattling gasps, his great mound of a side painfully rising and falling. His mouth was wide open—I could see far down into caverns of pale pink throat. I waited a long time for him to die, but his breathing did not weaken. Finally I fired my two remaining 180 shots into the spot where I thought his heart must be. The thick blood welled out of him like red velvet, but still he did not die. His body did not even jerk when the shots hit him, the tortured breathing continued without a pause. He was dying, very slowly and in great agony, but in some world remote from me where not even a bullet could damage him further. I felt that I had got to put an end to that dreadful noise. It seemed dreadful to see the great beast lying there, powerless to move and yet powerless to die, and not even to be able to finish him. I went back for my small rifle and poured shot after shot into his heart and down his throat. They seemed to make no impression. The tortured gasps continued as steadily as the ticking of a clock.

In the end I could not stand it any longer and went away. I heard later that it took him 190 half an hour to die. Burmans were arriving with dahs and baskets even before I left, and I was told they had stripped his body almost to the bones by the afternoon.

Afterwards, of course, there were endless discussions about the shooting of the elephant. The owner was furious, but he was only an Indian and could do nothing. Besides, legally I had done the right thing, for a mad elephant has to be killed, like a mad dog, if its owner fails to control it. Among the Europeans opinion was divided. The older men said I was right, the younger men said it was a damn shame to shoot an elephant for killing a coolie, because an elephant was worth more than any damn Coringhee coolie. And afterwards I was very glad that the coolie had been killed; it put me legally in the right and it gave me a sufficient pretext for shooting the elephant. I often wondered whether any of the others grasped that I had done it solely to avoid looking a fool. ∎

200

UNDERSTANDING CONTEXT

1. What is Orwell's goal in relating this incident? What does this event symbolize?

2. What roles does Orwell play in the narrative? How does his behaviour as a police officer conflict with his personal views?

3. What are Orwell's attitudes toward the Burmese?

4. Orwell's readers were primarily British. What was he trying to impress upon them?

5. *Critical thinking:* Consider Orwell's statement, "With one part of my mind I thought of the British Raj as an unbreakable tyranny . . . with another part I thought that the greatest joy in the world would be to drive a bayonet into a Buddhist priest's guts." What does this admission reveal?

EVALUATING STRATEGY

1. Orwell opens the essay with the statement, "I was hated by large numbers of people." What impact does that have on readers? Does it do more than simply attract attention?

2. How does Orwell balance his role between narrator and participant?

3. *Other modes:* Can this essay also serve as an example? Is the killing of the elephant representative of a larger issue?

APPRECIATING LANGUAGE

1. What metaphors does Orwell use in telling the story?

2. Underline the figurative language Orwell uses to describe the laboured death of the elephant. What images does he use to create a sense of horror?

3. Orwell calls the Burmese "natives," "coolies," and "Burmans." He describes their huts as "squalid" and the rice paddies as a "miry waste." What does this suggest about his view of Asia?

WRITING SUGGESTIONS

1. *Critical thinking:* Orwell relates an incident in which he played a role that conflicted with his personal beliefs. Write a brief narrative about an event that placed you in a similar situation. Have your roles as parent, employee, manager, spouse, student, or friend caused you to act against your values? Select a single event and write a short narrative, clearly outlining how the actions you were compelled to take contrasted with what you really felt at the time. Have you ever been compelled to lie on behalf of others?

2. *Collaborative writing:* Work with other students to create a short statement analyzing Orwell's message about political power and the nature of abusive governments. Have each member write a draft and then work to combine ideas into a single statement. If there are major differences in ideas, develop a comparison or division paper to contrast or list these different views.

Writing beyond the Classroom   JONATHAN SWIFT

Jonathan Swift (1667–1745) was born in Dublin, Ireland; studied at Trinity College, Dublin; and took an MA at Oxford. Ordained an Anglican priest, eventually he was made Dean of St. Patrick's Cathedral in Dublin. He is remembered chiefly for his satires, the most famous of which are ***A Tale of a Tub*** (1704), a vicious satire on government abuses in education and religion, and ***Gulliver's Travels*** (1726). After the death of Queen Anne in 1714, Swift remained almost the rest of his life in Ireland. There he wrote many essays defending the Irish against English oppression. "A Modest Proposal" is one of a series of satirical essays that exposed English cruelties in Ireland. It demonstrates Swift's keen sensitivity to the problems of the poor in his native country as well as his ability to create satire that is both ironic and incisive.

A Modest Proposal

It is a melancholy object to those who walk through this great town or travel in the country, 1 when they see the streets, the roads, and cabin doors, crowded with beggars of the female sex, followed by three, four, or six children, all in rags and importuning every passenger for an alms. These mothers, instead of being able to work for their honest livelihood, are forced to employ all their time in strolling to beg sustenance for their helpless infants: Who as they grow up either turn thieves for want of work, or leave their dear native country to fight for the Pretender in Spain, or sell themselves to the Barbadoes.

I think it is agreed by all parties that this prodigious number of children in the arms, or on the backs, or at the heels of their mothers, and frequently of their fathers, is in the present deplorable state of the kingdom a very great additional grievance; and, therefore, whoever 10 could find out a fair, cheap, and easy method of making these children sound, useful members of the commonwealth, would deserve so well of the public as to have his statue set up for a preserver of the nation.

But my intention is very far from being confined to provide only for the children of professed beggars; it is of a much greater extent, and shall take in the whole number of infants at a certain age who are born of parents in effect as little able to support them as those who demand our charity in the streets.

As to my own part, having turned my thoughts for many years upon this important subject, and maturely weighed the several schemes of our projectors, I have always found them grossly mistaken in their computation. It is true, a child just dropped from its dam may be 20 supported by her milk for a solar year, with little other nourishment; at most not above the value of 2s., which the mother may certainly get, or the value in scraps, by her lawful occupation of begging; and it is exactly at one year old that I propose to provide for them in such a manner as instead of being a charge upon their parents or the parish, or wanting food and raiment for the rest of their lives, they shall on the contrary contribute to the feeding, and partly to the clothing, of many thousands.

There is likewise another great advantage in my scheme, that it will prevent those voluntary abortions, and that horrid practice of women murdering their bastard children,

alas! too frequent among us! sacrificing the poor innocent babes I doubt more to avoid the
30 expense than the shame, which would move tears and pity in the most savage and inhuman breast.

The number of souls in this kingdom being usually reckoned one million and a half, of these I calculate there may be about 200,000 couples whose wives are breeders; from which number I subtract 30,000 couples who are able to maintain their own children (although I apprehend there cannot be so many, under the present distress of the kingdom); but this being granted, there will remain 170,000 breeders. I again subtract 50,000 for those women who miscarry, or whose children die by accident or disease within the year. There only remain 120,000 children of poor parents annually born. The question therefore is, how this number shall be reared and provided for? which, as I have already said, under the present
40 situation of affairs, is utterly impossible by all the methods hitherto proposed. For we can neither employ them in handicraft or agriculture; we neither build houses (I mean live in the country) nor cultivate land; they can very seldom pick up a livelihood by stealing, till they arrive at six years old, except where they are of towardly parts; although I confess they learn the rudiments much earlier; during which time they can, however, be properly looked upon only as probationers; as I have been informed by a principal gentleman in the county of Cavan, who protested to me that he never knew above one or two instances under the age of six, even in a part of the kingdom so renowned for the quickest proficiency in that art.

I am assured by our merchants, that a boy or a girl before twelve years old is no saleable commodity; and even when they come to this age they will not yield above 3l. or 3l.2s. 6d.
50 at most on the exchange; which cannot turn to account either to the parents or kingdom, the charge of nutriment and rags having been at least four times that value.

I shall now therefore humbly propose my own thoughts, which I hope will not be liable to the least objection.

I have been assured by a very knowing American of my acquaintance in London, that a young healthy child well nursed is at a year old a most delicious, nourishing, and wholesome food, whether stewed, roasted, baked, or broiled; and I make no doubt that it will equally serve in a fricassee or a ragout.

I do therefore humbly offer it to public consideration that of the 120,000 children already computed, 20,000 may be reserved for breed, whereof only one-fourth part to be
60 males; which is more than we allow to sheep, black cattle, or swine; and my reason is, that these children are seldom the fruits of marriage, a circumstance not much regarded by our savages; therefore one male will be sufficient to serve four females. That the remaining 100,000 may, at a year old, be offered in sale to the persons of quality and fortune through the kingdom; always advising the mother to let them suck plentifully in the last month, so as to render them plump and fat for a good table. A child will make two dishes at an entertainment for friends; and when the family dines alone, the fore or hind quarter will make a reasonable dish, and seasoned with a little pepper or salt will be very good boiled on the fourth day, especially in winter.

I have reckoned upon a medium that a child just born will weigh 12 pounds, and in a
70 solar year, if tolerably nursed, will increase to 28 pounds.

I grant this food will be somewhat dear, and therefore very proper for landlords, who, as they have already devoured most of the parents, seem to have the best title to the children.

Infant's flesh will be in season throughout the year, but more plentiful in March, and a little before and after; for we are told by a grave author, an eminent French physician, that fish being a prolific diet, there are more children born in Roman Catholic counties about nine months after Lent than at any other season; therefore, reckoning a year after Lent, the markets will be more glutted that usual, because the number of popish infants is at least three to one in this kingdom; and therefore it will have one other collateral advantage, by lessening the number of papists among us.

I have already computed the charge of nursing a beggar's child (in which list I reckon all 80 cottagers, laborers, and four-fifths of the farmers) to be about 2s. per annum, rags included; and I believe no gentleman would repine to give 10s. for the carcass of a good fat child, which, as I have said, will make four dishes of excellent nutritive meat, when he has only some particular friend or his own family to dine with him. Thus the squire will learn to be a good landlord, and grow popular among the tenants; the mother will have 8s. net profit, and be fit for work till she produces another child.

Those who are more thrifty (as I must confess the times require) may flay the carcass; the skin of which artificially dressed will make admirable gloves for ladies, and summer boots for fine gentlemen.

As to our city of Dublin, shambles may be appointed for this purpose in the most conve- 90 nient parts of it, and butchers we may be assured will not be wanting; although I rather recommend buying the children alive, and dressing them hot from the knife as we do roasting pigs.

A very worthy person, a true lover of his country, and whose virtues I highly esteem, was lately pleased in discoursing on this matter to offer a refinement upon my scheme. He said that many gentlemen of this kingdom, having of late destroyed their deer, he conceived that the want of venison might be well supplied by the bodies of young lads and maidens, not exceeding fourteen years of age nor under twelve; so great a number of both sexes in every country being now ready to starve for want of work and service; and these to be disposed of by their parents, if alive, or otherwise by their nearest relations. But with due deference to so excellent a friend and so deserving a patriot, I cannot be altogether in his sentiments; 100 for as to the males, my American acquaintance assured me from frequent experience that their flesh was generally tough and lean, like that of our schoolboys by continual exercise, and their taste disagreeable; and to fatten them would not answer the charge. Then as to the females, it would, I think, with humble submission be a loss to the public, because they soon would become breeders themselves; and besides, it is not improbable that some scrupulous people might be apt to censure such a practice (although indeed very unjustly), as a little bordering upon cruelty; which, I confess, has always been with me the strongest objection against any project, how well so-ever intended.

But in order to justify my friend, he confessed that this expedient was put into his head by the famous Psalmanazar, a native of the island Formosa, who came from thence 110 to London about twenty years ago: And in conversation told my friend, that in his country when any young person happened to be put to death, the executioner sold the carcass to persons of quality as a prime dainty; and that in his time the body of a plump girl of fifteen, who was crucified for an attempt to poison the emperor, was sold to his imperial majesty's prime minister of state, and other great mandarins of the court, in joints from the gibbet, at 400 crowns. Neither indeed can I deny, that if the same use were made of several plump young girls in this town, who without one single groat to their fortunes cannot stir without a chair, and appear at the playhouse and assemblies in foreign fineries which they never will pay for, the kingdom would not be the worse.

120   Some persons of a desponding spirit are in great concern about that vast number of poor people, who are aged, diseased, or maimed, and I have been desired to employ my thoughts what course may be taken to ease the nation of so grievous an encumbrance. But I am not in the least pain upon that matter, because it is very well known that they are every day dying and rotting by cold and famine, and filth and vermin, as fast as can be reasonably expected. And as to the young laborers, they are now in as hopeful a condition: they cannot get work, and consequently pine away for want of nourishment, to a degree that if at any time they are accidentally hired to common labor, they have not strength to perform it; and thus the country and themselves are happily delivered from the evils to come.

I have too long digressed, and therefore shall return to my subject. I think the advantages
130 by the proposal which I have made are obvious and many, as well as of the highest importance.

For first, as I have already observed, it would greatly lessen the number of papists, with whom we are yearly overrun, being the principal breeders of the nation as well as our most dangerous enemies; and who stay at home on purpose to deliver the kingdom to the Pretender, hoping to take their advantage by the absence of so many good Protestants, who have chosen rather to leave their country than stay at home and pay tithes against their conscience to an Episcopal curate.

Secondly, the poor tenants will have something valuable of their own, which by law may be made liable to distress and help to pay their landlord's rent, their corn and cattle being already seized, and money a thing unknown.

140   Thirdly, whereas the maintenance of 100,000 children from two years old and upward, cannot be computed at less than 10s. apiece per annum, the nation's stock will be thereby increased £50,000 per annum, beside the profit of a new dish introduced to the tables of all gentlemen of fortune in the kingdom who have any refinement in taste. And the money will circulate among ourselves, the goods being entirely of our own growth and manufacture.

Fourthly, the constant breeders beside the gain of 8s. sterling per annum by the sale of their children, will be rid of the charge of maintaining them after the first year.

Fifthly, this food would likewise bring great custom to taverns, where the vintners will certainly be so prudent as to procure the best receipts for dressing it to perfection, and con-
150 sequently have their houses frequented by all the fine gentlemen, who justly value themselves upon their knowledge in good eating; and a skilful cook who understands how to oblige his guests, will contrive to make it as expensive as they please.

Sixthly, this would be a great inducement to marriage, which all wise nations have either encouraged by rewards or enforced by laws and penalties. It would increase the care and tenderness of mothers toward their children, when they were sure of a settlement for life to the poor babes, provided in some sort by the public, to their annual profit instead of expense. We should see an honest emulation amount the married women, which of them would bring the fattest child to the market. Men would become as fond of their wives during the time of their pregnancy as they are now of their mares in foal, their cows in calf, their sows when they are ready to farrow; nor offer to beat or kick them (as is too frequent a 160 practice) for fear of a miscarriage.

Many other advantages might be enumerated. For instance, the addition of some thousand carcasses in our exportation of barreled beef, the propagation of swine's flesh, and improvement in the art of making good bacon, so much wanted among us by the great destruction of pigs, too frequent at our table; which are no way comparable in taste or magnificence to a well-grown, fat, yearling child, which roasted whole will make a considerable figure at a lord mayor's feast or any other public entertainment. But this and many others I omit, being studious of brevity.

Supposing that 1,000 families in this city would be constant customers for infants' flesh, besides others who might have it at merry-meetings, particularly at weddings and christen- 170 ings, I compute that Dublin would take off annually about 20,000 carcasses; and the rest of the kingdom (where probably they will be sold somewhat cheaper) the remaining 80,000.

I can think of no one objection that will possibly be raised against this proposal, unless it should be urged that the number of people will be thereby much lessened in the kingdom. This I freely own, and it was indeed one principal design in offering it to the world. I desire the reader will observe, that I calculate my remedy for this one individual kingdom of Ireland and for no other that ever was, is, or I think ever can be upon earth. Therefore let no man talk to me of other expedients: Of taxing our absentees at 5s. a pound: Of using neither clothes nor household furniture except what is of our own growth and manufacture: Of utterly rejecting the materials and instruments that promote foreign luxury: Of curing 180 the expensiveness of pride, vanity, idleness, and gaming in our women: Of introducing a vein of parsimony, prudence, and temperance: Of learning to love our country, in the want of which we differ even from Laplander and the inhabitants of Topinamboo: Of quitting our animosities and factions, nor acting any longer like the Jews, who were murdering one another at the very moment their city was taken: Of being a little cautious not to sell our country and conscience for nothing: Of teaching landlords to have at least one degree of mercy toward their tenants: Lastly, of putting a spirit of honesty, industry, and skill into our shopkeepers; who, if a resolution could now be taken to buy only our native goods, would immediately unite to cheat and exact upon us in the price, the measure, and the goodness, nor could ever yet be brought to make one fair proposal of just dealing, though often and 190 earnestly invited to it.

Therefore I repeat, let no man talk to me of these and the like expedients, till he has at least some glimpse of hope that there will be ever some hearty and sincere attempt to put them in practice.

But as to myself, having been wearied out for many years with offering vain, idle, visionary thoughts, and at length utterly despairing of success, I fortunately fell upon this

proposal; which, as it is wholly new, so it has something solid and real, of no expense and little trouble, full in our own power, and whereby we can incur no danger in disobliging England. For this kind of commodity will not bear exportation, the flesh being of too tender
200 a consistence to admit a long continuance in salt, although perhaps I could name a country which would be glad to eat up our whole nation without it.

After all, I am not so violently bent upon my own opinion as to reject any offer proposed by wise men, which shall be found equally innocent, cheap, easy, and effectual. But before something of that kind shall be advanced in contradiction to my scheme, and offering a better. I desire the author or authors will be pleased maturely to consider two points. First, as things now stand, how they will be able to find food and raiment for 100,000 useless mouths and backs. And secondly, there being a round million of creatures in human figure throughout this kingdom, whose subsistence put into a common stock would leave them in debt 2,000,000 pounds sterling, adding those who are beggars by profession to the bulk
210 of farmers, cottagers, and laborers, with the wives and children who are beggars in effect; I desire those politicians who dislike my overture, and may perhaps be so bold as to attempt an answer, that they will first ask the parents of these mortals, whether they would not at this day think it a great happiness to have been sold for food at a year old in the manner I prescribe, and thereby have avoided such a perpetual scene of misfortunes as they have since gone through by the oppression of landlords, the impossibility of paying rent without money or trade, the want of common sustenance, with neither house nor clothes to cover them from the inclemencies of the weather, and the most inevitable prospect of entailing the like or greater miseries upon their breed for ever.

I profess, in the sincerity of my heart, that I have not the least personal interest in
220 endeavoring to promote this necessary work, having no other motive than the public good of my country, by advancing our trade, providing for infants, relieving the poor, and giving some pleasure to the rich. I have no children by which I can propose to get a single penny; the youngest being nine years old, and my wife past childbearing. ■

UNDERSTANDING CONTEXT

1. Swift uses a conversational tone to present the piece's argument. At what point do you realize that the piece is supposed to be satiric?

2. What is the difference between satire and parody?

3. What is Swift's thesis?

EVALUATING STRATEGY

1. Why does Swift create a narrator or mask for the piece?

2. Is narration an effective method to deliver a satire? Why or why not?

APPRECIATING LANGUAGE

1. Swift uses the language of commerce and numbers to communicate his argument. Why does he choose this type of language?

WRITING SUGGESTIONS

1. Create a list of other works of satire, from either literature or other media. What topic is most frequently satirized?

2. Choose a local issue and present an opinion in three paragraphs. Present the issue in a satiric manner. Share your piece with a classmate to see how effective your piece is in presenting your argument.

Responding to IMAGES

Canadian soldiers on the streets of Montreal during
the October Crisis of 1970.

The Montreal Star

1. Describe your first response to this photograph. What do you know about the FLQ (Front de libération du Québec) or the October Crisis? Prime Minister Trudeau sent in the troops to secure Montreal against a perceived terrorist threat, and stated that it was the provincial government of Bourassa who had requested the imposition of the *War Measures Act*. What is the effect of the *War Measures Act*? Do you think that it was the right decision?

2. Language rights and separation continue to be divisive issues in Quebec. What is your opinion about Quebec separation? The FLQ wanted Quebec sovereignty. They were labelled terrorists at the time because they kidnapped British Trade Minister James Cross and kidnapped and murdered Quebec Labour Minister Pierre Laporte. Is a military response an appropriate action to take against terrorism?

3. Visual analysis: Why do you think that the photographer took this photograph? What is the effect of the row of children in front of the soldiers? What is your response to seeing the Canadian flag on the helicopter?

4. *Collaborative writing:* Work with a group of students and develop a caption for this photograph to be used in a high school history book. Create a caption that is accurate and objective. Pay attention to the use of words and the impact of connotations. If members of your group disagree, develop opposing captions.

5. *Other modes*

   ■ Write a *description* essay that analyzes the images present in this photograph, such as the flag and the people's gestures.

   ■ Write a *cause-and-effect* essay that outlines the impact this image has on the public. Does an image like this remind Canadians about the negative aspects of separation? Does it explain why there has never been a terrorist attack on Canadian soil since?

   ■ Write a *classification* paper that establishes how you think politicians should respond in a crisis. What actions are appropriate? What actions should never be taken?

   ■ Write a *persuasive* essay in favour of deploying troops to quell a perceived terrorist attack in a major Canadian city.

☑ NARRATION **CHECKLIST**

Before submitting your paper, review these points:

✓ Does your narrative have a clear focus?

✓ Can your readers clearly follow the chronology of events?

✓ Do you write in a consistent tense? Does your narrative contain illogical shifts from past to present?

✓ Does the narrative flow evenly, or is it cluttered with unnecessary detail?

✓ Does your narrative maintain a consistent point of view? Do you switch from first to third person without reason?

✓ Does your narrative suit your purpose, reader, and discourse community?

COMPANION WEBSITE

See **http://www.transcanadawriter.nelson.com** for additional information on writing narration.

CHAPTER 14

Example: Presenting Illustrations

This chapter examines the importance of example in writing. It looks at example as ways to illustrate, define, provide evidence for, and support a perspective.

WHAT IS AN EXAMPLE?

Examples serve to illustrate an idea, issue, problem, situation, theory, or trait. They also often serve to establish a definition or support a point of view. Writers also use examples to support an argument. Attorneys filing claims of sexual harassment may present specific violations to substantiate a client's case. Students demanding greater campus security might list recent thefts in a letter to the dean to substantiate the need for increased protection.

An example supplies information about a type. An example essay might relate the story of a marathon winner to illustrate how people can overcome challenges, or provide details about an entrepreneur turning an abandoned church into a bookstore as an illustration of recycling abandoned buildings.

Purpose: To Inform or Persuade

Examples clarify abstract or complex ideas that are difficult to comprehend or are easily misinterpreted. Because readers have differing perceptual worlds and personal or cultural definitions of general terms, examples offer concrete details:

> *Dorm residents may use small electrical devices*—hair dryers, curling irons, clock radios, or electric shavers—*but are prohibited from operating major appliances*—televisions, microwaves, toaster ovens, or refrigerators.
>
> —STUDENT MANUAL

- Informative examples should be accurate, concrete, and readily understandable.
- The language used in informative examples should be crafted carefully to suit the topic and audience.
- Persuasive examples should be ones readers will identify and accept.
- Because examples are often isolated incidents, they should be supported by evidence demonstrating a general trend—statistics, surveys, and expert testimony.

Extended Examples

Writers may use a single extended example to explain an idea or support an argument. Extended examples allow writers to tell a story, create human interest, and provide a context for evidence such as quotations and statistics.

Advantages

- Extended examples clarify concepts by telling a story that can arouse interest, build suspense, and dramatize factual detail.
- Extended examples allow writers to explore an issue in depth, so that readers can appreciate the complexity of the larger issue it represents.

Disadvantages

- Readers may dismiss a single example as a random event that has no wider significance. The use of other evidence, such as facts and statistics, can bolster the importance of the example.
- Extended examples may not be representative. Because no two people, objects, or events are exactly alike, no individual example is likely to fully illustrate a subject. Extended examples require accurate commentary to prevent confusion.

Enumerated Examples

To overcome problems that can occur with a single example, writers often present more than one illustration. By listing a number of examples, they hope that readers will find it easier to identify their subject.

Advantages

- Using a number of examples demonstrates a range or spectrum of possibilities.
- Readers who might ignore or misinterpret a single example are more likely to gain a balanced view of the subject if more than one illustration is given.

Disadvantages

- Enumerated examples can be too brief to fully explain or represent an issue, so writers often vary the length of examples, listing some while describing others in depth.
- A list of isolated examples can appear to be simply a collection of random events that provides weak support for an argument. The inclusion of facts, testimony, and statistics can provide additional evidence.
- Although a series of brief examples can create a fast-paced essay, they can lack focus. Lists of examples should be carefully organized in a logical pattern.

WRITING **ACTIVITY**

List examples that would support the following general statements:

1. People will try almost anything to lose weight.
2. Consumer decisions affect the environment.
3. Technology is robbing people of personal privacy.
4. Today's job market demands computer literacy.
5. The Internet has influenced journalism.

Hypothetical Examples

Writers often use hypothetical examples to explain or dramatize a point:

> *Make sure you report all injuries—even superficial wounds—to your supervisor be-fore leaving the plant.* For example, *if you fall and hurt your knee but fail to inform your supervisor, you may be unable to prove the injury was work related and be un-able to receive full benefits if you later discover surgery is required.*

Thesis

Hypothetical example

Advantages

■ Hypothetical examples are useful when no factual example exists or if actual situations are too complicated to serve as explanations.

■ Hypothetical examples allow writers to speculate about possible events. Typically, factual examples of future events don't exist.

■ Fictional examples are useful when writers wish to avoid bias and subjective judgments. Factual examples may stir controversy or personal interpretations.

Disadvantages

■ Hypothetical examples are not based in fact, and they often provide weak evidence for arguments. Hypothetical examples require support from other forms of evidence to support a thesis.

■ Hypothetical examples can seem distant and unrealistic. They can be made effective if they include facts and provide realistic scenarios readers will identify with.

Factual Examples

Factual examples use actual events and people to explain an idea or illustrate a point:

> *Make sure you report all injuries—even superficial wounds—to your supervi-sor before leaving the plant. Last spring a shipping clerk injured her knee on the loading dock. Thinking she had suffered only a minor bruise, she completed her*

Thesis

Factual example

shift and went home without informing her supervisor. During the night she awoke in great pain and went to the emergency room where doctors discovered a fracture requiring surgery. Because she could not prove the injury occurred at work, she had to pay over $2,500 in insurance co-payments.

Advantages

- Factual examples command attention because they are based in actual events, involving people readers may know or at least identify with.

- Factual illustrations can be documented, dramatizing the reality of the issue or problem.

Disadvantages

- Factual examples may contain specific details that are not generally representative.

- Because factual examples usually describe past events, some readers may infer that they are irrelevant to current circumstances.

WRITING **ACTIVITY**

Provide a hypothetical or factual example to support or illustrate the following thesis statements:

1. Peer pressure drives many adolescents to engage in self-destructive behaviour.
2. Credit cards lead some consumers to spend recklessly.
3. Public schools are failing to prepare students for university.
4. Many undergraduates find it almost impossible to complete a bachelor's degree in four years.
5. A false allegation, even if proved untrue, can ruin a person's reputation.

Strategies for Writing Examples

Critical Thinking and Prewriting

1. **You can begin writing an example essay in two ways:** First, think of a specific person, place, situation, event, or object and determine whether it represents something greater.
   - Second, select a general concept, idea, or subject and develop a factual or hypothetical example or examples to explain or support your thesis.
2. **Consider your readers' perceptual world.** The attitudes, education, values, and experiences of your readers will determine how they will respond to examples you use to inform or persuade your audience.

3. **Engage critical thinking.** Examples, like statistics, can be both persuasive and misleading. Examples, no matter how interesting or compelling, are individual events, persons, or situations and may not be representative of the whole. Examples are anecdotal accounts and rarely provide convincing support for an argument unless supplemented with other forms of evidence.

4. **Begin listing examples.** Use brainstorming, listing, and asking questions to generate as many examples as you can. Freewrite to explore longer or extended examples.

Planning

1. **Clearly define the general principle, rule, situation, or fact the example will illustrate.** Examples can become simply narratives unless they support a clearly defined subject. Make sure your statement clearly expresses what you are trying to illustrate.

2. **Determine whether your essay would benefit from a single extended example or a series of examples.**

3. **Organize examples using a chronological, spatial, or emphatic pattern.**

4. **Determine the best placement for the thesis and definitions.**

5. **Review the clarity of your thesis before writing.** Check to see if your thesis expresses a general idea or principle that can be illustrated or proven by examples.

6. **Review your examples.**
   - Do the examples clearly support or illustrate the thesis?
   - Are the examples ones readers will understand and appreciate? Do they take the readers' perceptual world into account?
   - Are the examples arranged in a logical pattern?

Writing the First Draft

1. **Use the plan as a guide but be open to additional examples.**

2. **Distinguish between relevant and incidental events.**

3. **Use introductory and transitional statements to link examples and the thesis:**

   Crime is increasing on this campus. *For example*, two assaults have occurred . . .
   Kai Long lost ten pounds in two weeks on this diet, *illustrating* that . . .

Revising

1. **Review the plan and clarity of the thesis.**

2. **Review new ideas developed in the first draft and whether they support the thesis or general point.**

3. **Do the examples make a clear point?**

4. **Is other evidence needed to support the main point or make a stronger argument?**
   - Can facts, quotations, or statistics be blended into the essay to offer additional proof?

5. **Can the thesis be refined to more sharply delineate what these examples are supposed to illustrate?**
   - The more clearly stated the thesis, the more effective its supporting examples will be.

(Continued)

6. **Decide whether your point is better supported by hypothetical or factual examples.**
   - You may wish to mix factual and hypothetical examples to provide both actual details and unbiased illustrations.

7. **Assess the quantity and value of your examples.**

8. **Are examples clearly organized or do they form a random pattern?**

Editing and Proofreading

1. **Examine examples for consistency in voice, tone, style, and tense.**
   - Keep the examples in the same tense and voice. Avoid shifting from first to third person or from past to present unless there are logical transitions.
   - Maintain a common tone and style. The examples, though separate items, should form a seamless narrative.

2. **Review diction for unintended connotations.** Because examples are supposed to illustrate and explain an idea, careful word choice is essential to avoid misleading readers.

3. **Examine paragraph breaks and transitions for clarity.** Readers will rely on structure to follow examples and relate them to a general principle.

4. **Make the opening and final examples memorable.** First and last impressions are most likely to influence readers and give them illustrations they can recall and repeat to others.

General Assignments

Write an example paper on any of the following topics. Your example may inform or persuade. You may use both factual and hypothetical examples.

Begin with a point of view. State your opinion on one of the following issues and use examples as illustrations:

1. Materialism in Canada

2. Television violence

3. The prevailing attitude on your campus about rising tuition costs, or any other current topic

4. Courage

Begin with a specific person, place, item, or event and explain its greater significance, demonstrating how it illustrates or symbolizes a general trend or concept:

1. Describe a common behaviour you have observed. What does this action represent? You might see road rage as an example of growing selfishness, or littering as a sign of disrespect for public property.

2. Write about an incident that taught you a lesson. What does this episode reveal about society, human nature, your family, or friends?

3. Describe a television program, concert, or movie that represents what you consider to be good or bad in popular culture.

Writing in Context

1. Write a letter to the editor of a magazine to praise or criticize its coverage of a specific event. Support your views with examples.

2. Write a response to an essay question that asks for historical examples of movements that changed Canadian society.

3. Write a hypothetical example illustrating the proper course of action in an emergency.

Strategies for Reading Examples

When reading the example essays in this chapter, keep the following questions in mind:

Context

1. What is the author's purpose—to inform or persuade? What does the example illustrate?

2. What is the thesis or general point? Is it clearly defined? Can you restate it in your own words?

3. What can you tell about the intended audience? Are the examples targeted to a specific group of readers? Are the illustrations ones that general readers can recognize and appreciate?

Strategy

1. Does the writer use a single extended example or a series of illustrations?

2. Does the author use other forms of support—facts, testimony, statistics?

3. Are the examples convincing? Do they truly represent a general condition, or are they drawn out of context?

4. How is the essay organized?

5. Where is the thesis or general principle placed in the essay? Would it be more effective if located elsewhere?

6. What transitional devices are used to organize the examples?

Language

1. Do the tone, style, and diction used to relate the example suit the writer's purpose?

2. What role do connotations play in relating examples? How do they shape the reader's perception?

PICO IYER

Pico Iyer (b. 1957) was born in England of Indian parents and educated at Oxford and Harvard. He joined **Time** in 1982 and has published travel books as well as many essays and reviews in such magazines as **Partisan Review, Village Voice,** and **The Times Literary Supplement.** In a recent collection of essays, **The Global Soul: Jet Lag, Shopping Malls, and the Search for Home,** as well as in **Imagining Canada: An Outsider's Hope for a Global Future,** he explores the theme of multiculturalism.

In Praise of the Humble Comma*

In the following essay, Iyer reflects on the power of punctuation to create order in meaning, enacting his points through example as he proceeds.

1   The gods, they say, give breath, and they take it away. But the same could be said—could it not?—of the humble comma. Add it to the present clause, and, all of a sudden, the mind is, quite literally, given pause to think; take it out if you wish or forget it and the mind is deprived of a resting place. Yet still the comma gets no respect. It seems just a slip of a thing, a pedant's tick, a blip on the edge of our consciousness, a kind of printer's smudge almost. Small, we claim, is beautiful (especially in the age of the microchip). Yet what is so often used, and so rarely recalled, as the comma—unless it be breath itself?

Punctuation, one is taught, has a point: to keep up law and order. Punctuation marks are the road signs placed along the highway of our communication—to control speeds,
10   provide directions, and prevent head-on collisions. A period has the unblinking finality of a red light; the comma is a flashing yellow light that asks us only to slow down; and the semicolon is a stop sign that tells us to ease gradually to a halt, before gradually starting up again. By establishing the relations between words, punctuation establishes the relations between the people using words. That may be one reason why schoolteachers exalt it and lovers defy it ('We love each other and belong to each other let's don't ever hurt each other Nicole let's don't ever hurt each other,' wrote Gary Gilmore to his girlfriend). A comma, he must have known, 'separates inseparables', in the clinching words of H.W. Fowler, King of English Usage.

Punctuation, then, is a civic prop, a pillar that holds society upright. (A run-on sentence,
20   its phrases piling up without division, is as unsightly as a sink piled high with dirty dishes.) Small wonder, then, that punctuation was one of the first proprieties of the Victorian age, the age of the corset, that the modernists threw off: the sexual revolution might be said to have begun when Joyce's Molly Bloom spilled out all her private thoughts in 36 pages of unbridled, almost unperioded and officially censored prose; and another rebellion was surely marked when e.e. cummings first felt free to commit 'God' to the lower case.

*Iyer, Pico, "In Praise of the Humble Comma" copyright © 2001, Time Inc. All rights reserved. Reprinted by permission.

Punctuation thus becomes the signature of cultures. The hot-blooded Spaniard seems to be revealed in the passion and urgency of his doubled exclamation points and question marks ('¡Caramba! ¿Quien sabe?'), while the impassive Chinese traditionally added to his so-called inscrutability by omitting directions from his ideograms. The anarchy and commotion of the '60s were given voice in the exploding exclamation marks, riotous capital 30 letters, and Day-Glo italics of Tom Wolfe's spray-paint prose; and in Communist societies, where the State is absolute, the dignity—and divinity—of capital letters is reserved for Ministries, Sub-Committees and Secretariats.

Yet punctuation is something more than a culture's birthmark; it scores the music in our minds, gets our thoughts moving to the rhythm of our hearts. Punctuation is the notation in the sheet music of our words, telling us when to rest, or when to raise our voices; it acknowledges that the meaning of our discourse, as of any symphonic composition, lies not in the units but in the pauses, the pacing and the phrasing. Punctuation is the way one bats one's eyes, lowers one's voice, or blushes demurely. Punctuation adjusts the tone and colour and volume till the feeling comes into perfect focus: not disgust exactly, but distaste; not lust, or like, but love. 40

Punctuation, in short, gives us the human voice, and all the meanings that lie between the words. 'You aren't young, are you?' loses its innocence when it loses the question mark. Every child knows the menace of a dropped apostrophe (the parent's 'Don't do that' shifting into the more slowly enunciated 'Do not do that'), and every believer, the ignominy of having his faith reduced to 'faith'. Add an exclamation point to 'To be or not to be . . .' and the gloomy Dane has all the resolve he needs; add a comma, and the noble sobriety of 'God save the Queen' becomes a cry of desperation bordering on double sacrilege.

Sometimes, of course, our markings may be simply a matter of aesthetics. Popping in a comma can be like slipping on the necklace that gives an outfit quiet elegance, or like catching the sound of running water that complements, as it completes, the silence of a Japanese 50 landscape. When V. S. Naipaul, in his latest novel, writes, 'He was a middle-aged man, with glasses,' the first comma can seem a little precious. Yet it gives the description a spin, as well as a subtlety, that it otherwise lacks, and it shows that the glasses are not part of the middle-agedness, but something else.

Thus all these tiny scratches give us breadth and heft and depth. A world that has only periods is a world without inflections. It is a world without shade. It has a music without sharps and flats. It is martial music. It has a jackboot rhythm. Words cannot bend and curve. A comma, by comparison, catches the gentle drift of the mind in thought, turning in on itself and back on itself, reversing, redoubling, and returning along the course of its own sweet river music; while the semicolon brings clauses and thoughts together with all the 60 silent discretion of a hostess arranging guests around her dinner table.

Punctuation, then, is a matter of care. Care for words, yes, but also, and more important, for what the words imply. Only a lover notices the small things: the way the afternoon light catches the nape of a neck, or how a strand of hair slips out from behind an ear, or the way a finger curls around a cup. And no one scans a letter so closely as a lover, searching for its small print, straining to hear its nuances, its gasps, its sighs and hesitations, poring over the secret messages that lie in every cadence. The difference between 'Jane (whom I adore)' and 'Jane, whom I adore,' and

the difference between them both and 'Jane—whom I adore—' marks all the distance between ecstasy and heartache. 'No iron can pierce the heart with such force as a period put at just the
70 right place,' in Isaac Babel's lovely words; a comma can let us hear a voice break, or a heart. Punctuation, in fact, is a labour of love. Which brings us back, in a way, to gods. ■

UNDERSTANDING CONTEXT

1. Iyer uses a variety of methods to support his argument. Create a list of the methods that he employs.

2. Iyer uses several quotes in the essay. Why does he provide the quotes?

EVALUATING STRATEGY

1. Iyer uses analogies throughout the essay. Create a list of the analogies that he employs.

2. Briefly summarize Iyer's thesis.

3. Iyer's essay is about a particular piece of punctuation. Describe the effect of the way that he punctuates the essay.

APPRECIATING LANGUAGE

1. Describe the tone of Iyer's essay.

2. Does the tone undermine or enhance his argument?

WRITING SUGGESTION

1. Choose a divisive issue affecting your campus currently. Write an essay that supports one side of the issue. Present your argument by using an analogy.

JOE RODRIGUEZ

Joe Rodriguez served as an editorial writer for the *San Jose Mercury News* before becoming one of the newspaper's staff columnists. He has written extensively about life in Southern California, commenting on Mexican-American identity, bilingual education, gun control, drugs, and city planning. He published several articles about the price of urban renewal, stating, "There's more humanity in one block of real neighborhood than in a square mile of a subdivision."

Mexicans Deserve More Than La Mordida*

As you read Rodriguez's essay, notice how he uses a minor incident to represent a complex social problem. Consider if this bribery incident illustrates a problem greater than the corruption found in other countries.

"I wouldn't give you a dime for Mexico!"   1

My father used to tell us that every time Mexico broke his heart. He was *muy indio,* with dark reddish brown skin, huge calloused hands and a handsomely hooked nose. On our occasional trips to Tijuana to visit relatives, he'd see Indian women begging on the streets, Indian kids selling Chiclets chewing gum, and white-skinned Mexicans owning and running everything.

"Not a dime for Mexico!"

He was more Mexican than I'll ever be, more Mexican than any Harvard educated technocrat, any Spanish-looking *gachupin,* any middle-class Zapatista guerrilla-intellectual, or any bald-headed ex-president crook from Mexico City's ritzy Polanco district. My father 10 wasn't referring to the nation's people, but to a political and social system that still fosters extreme poverty, discrimination and injustice, and to the privileged and the ruthless who benefit by it.

I should have remembered my Dad's dime recently when two Mexico City policemen pulled me over for making an illegal left-hand turn at the Monument of Cuauhtemoc on the famous Paseo de la Reforma boulevard.

I was driving back into the giant city after three days in the countryside.

I had escaped a traffic accident only minutes earlier. I was hot, tired, grumpy and jumpy. I was driving a rental car. These conditions made me the perfect *pollo* for these two uniformed coyotes.   20

Both cops got out. The older one checked out the rental plates. The younger one wanted to see my driver's license.

"Where's your hotel?" he asked.

Right over there, I said, the Maria Cristina Hotel on Rio Lerma Street.

"I don't know any hotel by that name," he said. "Prove it. Show me something from the hotel."

I fumbled through my wallet, finally producing a card-key from the hotel. The dance between the cops and me had begun.

"I see," the young policeman said. "What are you doing in Mexico?"

30   I'm a journalist, I said. I'd been reporting in Queretaro state.

"You know," he said, "for making that illegal turn, we're going to have to take away your driver's license and the plates from the car."

I said, What? Why can't you just give me a ticket?

He then walked away and asked the other, older, policeman, "How do you want to take care of this?"

The veteran officer then took over.

"The violation brings a fine of 471 pesos," he told me. "But we still have to take your plates and license. You can pick them up at police headquarters when you pay the fine. Or, I can deliver them to you tomorrow at your hotel, but only after you pay."

40   By now, I figured this was all B.S., but I wasn't absolutely sure. Who ever heard of license plate confiscation for minor traffic violations? Still, I didn't know what my rights were as a motorist. Why didn't I prepare myself for something like this?

"So, since you say you need the car," the cop said, "*¿Nos podemos arreglar esto de otra manera?* (Can we take care of this another way?)."

I would prefer a ticket, I said.

The veteran cop stretched his arms upward, relaxed a bit, and then rested his forearms on my door. He leaned in and stuck his face inches from mine, and smiled.

"*Lo que tenemos aqui, se llama la corrupción*," he said. "What we have here is called corruption."

50   So there it was—*la mordida*—the bite, the bribe, a complex government system based not on civil service, but on bribery, political patronage, personal favoritism and individual gain.

Everybody in Mexico knows that corruption is rampant among the local, state and federal police forces and the military. A national agency has even taken out full-page newspaper ads asking people not to pay off corrupt cops, saying "*la mordida* spreads as easily as rabies."

Just last month, Mexico's national drug czar, a well-respected general, was arrested for protecting a northern drug lord. Corruption at the top only emboldens the small-fries like these two brown-shirted Mexico City cops.

60   Mexico's people deserve so much better. It is their personal integrity and family strength that carry the nation, despite the incompetence and dishonesty of the ruling party and corrupt officials big and small. And it's well within the United States' ability to step up the few binational efforts that exist to train Mexican police officers—the honest and sharp ones—in modern methods and ethics.

I wish I had thought about that and my father's dime and refused to play the game as I sat parked on Mexico City's most prominent boulevard, but I didn't.

"What do you say you help us out with 500 pesos?" the veteran cop said.

What do you mean, I said. The violation is worth less than that.

"400 pesos."

I don't have that much, I said, lying through my teeth.

"300 pesos."

We got stuck on 300 pesos for a while until he came down to 250 pesos, or about $31.25 in American dollars. I thumbed through my wallet for the bills, trying to keep him from seeing that I had much more money.

"Listen," he said. "You're a journalist from the United States. *Tu ganas pura lana.* You make lots of money. You can give me 300 pesos easy."

I don't make a lot of money, I said. My newspaper does, not me. I'm not rich. I'm just another Mexican like you trying to get by.

He wasn't moved.

Once I had the 250 pesos out of my wallet, he handed me a notebook through the window.

"Put the money in this so people don't see it pass hands."

I put the money in the notebook and gave it to him. He asked me once again for more.

"*Andale, hombre,*" he said. "You can give me another 50 pesos. Consider it my tip." ■

UNDERSTANDING CONTEXT

1. How would you describe *la mordida* in your own words?

2. What attitude toward *la mordida* does the statement "Not a dime for Mexico" reflect?

3. Does this minor request for a bribe—which could occur in any country—illustrate something unique to Mexico?

4. *Critical thinking:* Why is bribery wrong? How does corruption, even in trivial matters, affect people's faith in their government and institutions?

EVALUATING STRATEGY

1. Rodriguez selects a minor incident to reveal the nature of *la mordida.* Would a major bribery scandal involving national elections be a better example?

2. Would a series of shorter examples better represent the extent of *la mordida* in Mexican society?

3. Why is dialogue important in relating this example?

4. What role does the writer play in this example? Why are his reactions important?

APPRECIATING LANGUAGE

1. What does the writer's choice of words reveal about his attitude toward *la mordida*?

2. *La mordida* means "the bite" in Spanish. What connotations does "the bite" have?

WRITING SUGGESTIONS

1. Illustrate a common social problem or incident with a personal experience. You might provide an example of online dating, road rage, recycling, sexual harassment, sports gambling, or binge drinking.

2. *Collaborative writing:* Work with a group of students and develop a list of social problems—discrimination, corruption, alcoholism, and so forth—and then select one and provide one or more examples revealing the nature and extent of the problem.

BRONWEN WALLACE

Bronwen Wallace was born in 1945 in Kingston, Ontario, and educated at Queen's University. After receiving her MA, she moved to Windsor where she founded a women's bookstore and started working with women's groups. In the 1970s, she returned to Kingston, continued to work with women's groups, and began to teach creative writing and Women's Studies. Her poetry collections are a testimony to her social activism, involving her commitment to women's rights, civil rights, and social policy. A primary focus of Wallace's work centres on violence against women and children.

An Auction at Mother's Childhood Home*

In this essay, Wallace recounts a trip to an auction at her mother's former home. The essay highlights the differences in the way that society treats family history. Wallace uses her experience as an example of how women's history is not privileged by society.

Last week, my mother and I went to an auction sale in Enterprise, Ontario. It was one of 1
many such sales I will attend this summer, though I seldom buy anything. I just like to look
at the jumble of things—and I like to watch the auctioneers in action, their singsong patter
one of the sounds that mean summer to me.

Last week's sale was no different than any other. There was the usual collection of everything from canning jars to double beds, a wonderful set of wicker lawn furniture, some
beautiful old tools—you know, the sort of stuff that just seems to grow from 40-odd years of
living in one place. And there was that strangely familiar silence in the empty house, as if the
house itself were wondering what—or rather, who—would happen to it next.

This sale did have one major difference, though. The house we were visiting was the 10
house my mother had lived in as a girl, the house where my father had courted her and
where their wedding luncheon had been served after the ceremony. She took me through all
the rooms, telling me how they had looked back then—my grandfather had sold the place
40 years ago—describing the views out the various windows, as she remembered them. We
ran into old school chums of hers and the talk drifted, as it does among women, until various members of various families, their antecedents and connections, their current states of
health, their children and grandchildren, were all satisfactorily accounted for.

It was strange to stand in that house, where I had never stood before, and to realize how
little I knew of my mother's early life. My father's boyhood home is very familiar to me, as is
his family. My mother's is not. Some of this, in my case, is simply a result of circumstance— 20
my maternal grandmother died before I was born, whereas my father's mother lived until I
was in my 20s. Both my grandfathers died when I was a child.

But there is a cultural factor here as well. In a patriarchy, the primacy of the father is
taken for granted. And what this often means, in everyday life, is the loss of our mothers'

*Wallace, Bronwen, "An Auction at Mother's Childhood Home" from *Arguments with the World: Essays by Bronwen Wallace*, ed. Joanne Page (Kingston: Quarry Press, 1992). Reprint by permission of Quarry Press.

families and our mothers' childhoods. It is a loss—or rather, a renunciation—that is symbolized when a married woman takes her husband's name, a situation that, until recently, was assumed as a matter of course. It is also a loss that every woman I know speaks of—sometimes with bitterness and pain.

30 My first book of poems, *Marrying into the Family,* explored this loss in many ways. I began to write the poems in the first place because I was struck by how little I knew about any of my female ancestors. I was struck, too, by how many had died young, either in childbirth or from TB, and how quickly they had been succeeded by second wives, stepmothers. And since contact was not always maintained with the first wife's family, the natural, hereditary links seemed doubly lost to me.

"As a woman," writes poet Lorna Crozier in an essay, "I cannot take my mother's name, my mother has no name; as a woman, I cannot take my mother's country, my mother has no country. As a woman, my country has no name, my name is no one's country."

Often this loss includes the loss of material links as well. Many, many women I know, whose mothers have died, complain of losing precious reminders of her—dishes, furniture, 40 jewelry—when their fathers remarry and these are taken over by his new wife. Under this grief is also a current of anger, too. Anger that the mother can be so easily replaced and all trace of her existence lost to her children.

This loss is compounded by the lack of information available to us about past women's lives. If I want to get a sense of my father's life, for example, I have lots of easily available books, movies, television programs. Not so my mother's. One of the advantages of Women's Studies programs, and other sorts of feminist research, is that they act as reclamation projects, returning to us at least some of what has been lost.

We all begin with a mother. We all begin with a mother who is the center of our world, the most powerful person we know. It is amazing that so much power and importance can 50 be lost so quickly or that it can come to be perceived only as negative, as when mothers alone are blamed for the failings of their children or when we speak disparagingly of someone who is "too close" to his or her mother.

Indeed, our culture has spent a lot of time finding ways to curtail the power of the mother. The increasing intervention of more and more technology in the birthing process is one example. The fate that many mothers meet in the courts is another. Phyllis Chesler's book *Mothers on Trial* provides excellent documentation for the numerous situations in which women lose custody disputes, often to abusive men, because they are seen to be "unfit" by patriarchal standards. Another way of "blaming mother." Or think of mother-in-law jokes, culturally accepted ways of diminishing her power.

60 And yet that power can never be entirely diminished. Even when men's lives and men's doings are the center of our culture, there are thousands of oblique, often subversive, references to the power of the mother. Indeed, it is almost as if these references have to be oblique in order not to be censored. Some feminist scholars argue that they are all that is left of a rich and complex matriarchal literature which we have lost.

Take *Cinderella,* for example, one of the oldest fairy tales known. Like many of these tales, it comes from an ancient oral tradition and this particular story is known in many languages, including Chinese. In all versions, the presence of Cinderella's dead mother's spirit is remarkable. In the familiar Grimm version she is a little bird who lives in the tree which grows on her grave, and it is she who provides Cinderella with the clothes that she wears to the ball. In one sense, she is far more powerful than the prince, and it is by her 70 power that Cinderella is delivered to a life of wealth and safety. It is interesting to note, too, that the stepmother, the usurper, is seen as "evil" in this tale because she shows no affection for another woman's child. The fact that all this power gets diminished, in the Walt Disney version, to a silly fairy godmother says a great deal.

This reading of Cinderella is only one, of course, but it's one to think about. Many feminists dismiss Cinderella as being only about how girls should grow up to marry princes. We must remember, first of all, that most of these tales have peasant origins and that, from this point of view, marrying a prince might be just fine. We might also reread this tale—and others—to find out what it says about mothers and their power. Some scholars argue that earlier versions of these tales give even more power to the mother, power that has been 80 curtailed in later, patriarchal versions.

Or think of stories like *Anne of Green Gables* and *Jane Eyre* in the light of what they say about the sorrow and dislocation of motherless children. And in the great southern black spiritual, "Sometimes I Feel Like a Motherless Child," the loss of the mother becomes a metaphor for the loss of a country, for being sold into slavery in an alien and hostile place.

In modern literature by women, the search for the mother and what she means is a constant theme. Grace Paley comes to mind, as does Jamaica Kincaid, Margaret Laurence, Adrienne Rich, and many, many others. I'll end with one of my favorite quotes from "The Ottawa Valley," a story by Alice Munro in which a woman remembers a journey she made, 90 as a young girl with her mother, to her mother's birthplace. A story in which she tries to come to terms with everything her mother means to her and with her own conflicting feelings about her mother, feelings which, until recently, we have not been given the language to explore:

> *The problem, the only problem, is my mother. And she is the one of course that I am trying to get; it is to reach her that this whole journey has been undertaken. With what purpose? To mark her off, to describe, to illuminate, to celebrate, to get rid of her, and it did not work, for she looms too close, just as she always did. She is heavy as always, she weighs everything down, and yet she is indistinct, her edges melt and flow. Which means she has stuck to me as close as ever and refused to fall away, and* 100 *could go on and on, applying what skills I have, using what tricks I know, and it would always be the same.* ■

UNDERSTANDING CONTEXT

1. In three sentences, summarize Wallace's thesis.

2. Wallace uses many examples to support her thesis. List the types of examples.

EVALUATING STRATEGY

1. Is the use of examples an effective strategy to support her thesis?

2. Choose one of her examples. Explain how it supports her thesis.

3. Do you agree with her thesis?

APPRECIATING LANGUAGE

1. Wallace uses a colloquial style of language, interspersed with literary references. Does her language undermine or enhance her argument?

2. Compare her language with the literary references she uses. Which is more effective in communicating its central idea?

WRITING SUGGESTION

1. Choose an issue about which you feel strongly or that affects you personally. Use a personal experience as an example to support your argument in support of the issue.

Blending the Modes   TONY BROWN

Tony Brown is best known as host of **Tony Brown's Journal,** a public television program that first aired in 1976. Born in Charleston, West Virginia, Brown attended Wayne State University. Active in civil rights, Brown worked as a social worker and drama critic for the **Detroit Courier.** In 1971 he founded the School of Communications at Howard University in Washington, D.C. In 1995 he published **Black Lies, White Lies: The Truth According to Tony Brown.**

Death of a Dream*

As you read Brown's essay, notice how he uses a single illustration to persuade readers to share his views. Highlight places where Brown uses narration, description, and comparison in his essay.

Up! Up! You mighty race. You can accomplish what you will.

—*Marcus Garvey*

It was a day of celebration when Rick Singletary opened the largest Black-owned super-   1
market in the country in Columbus, Ohio—a spectacular $4.4 million operation. He had worked for a major grocery chain for fourteen years and started his own store with his life savings, those of his mother, and a government-insured loan from the Reagan administration. He located Singletary Plaza Mart in the Black community because he knew there was a need for a grocery store there, and because he wanted to create jobs for Blacks.

The entrepreneur needed only a $200,000-a-week volume to keep 130 Black people working. And yet, in a tragedy that exemplifies the real reason why Black America has never been able to compete with White America, Singletary's store failed. Although his research had shown that Blacks in Columbus spent $2.5 million per week on groceries, he could   10
not get them to spend even $200,000 of it in the store he had built for them in their own neighborhood.

I am familiar with the details because I tried to help Singletary, and I tried to help the Blacks in his community realize what was happening. For three days, I joined others in the Buy Freedom campaign of Black economic empowerment in Columbus. But, sadly, we failed to save his store.

This is not simply a neighborhood issue, it is a national disgrace. Rick Singletary, a good man who banked on his community, went bankrupt. He lost his life savings and his mother's savings, and 130 Black people lost their jobs. *This story is repeated somewhere in the Black community every day.* This gives credence to my theory that the most   20
successful economic boycott ever conducted in America is the boycott by Blacks of their own businesses.

*Brown, Tony, "Death of a Dream" excerpts from pp. 266–7, 271–3 from *Black Lies, White Lies* by Tony Brown, Copyright © 1995 by Tony Brown. Reprinted by permission of HarperCollins Publishers, William Morrow.

Making Blacks Competitive

The key to making Black America competitive with White America is really quite simple. Black Americans now earn nearly $500 billion annually, according to economist Andrew F. Brommer. This is roughly equivalent to the gross domestic product of Canada or Australia. And yet Blacks spend only 3 percent of their income with a Black business or Black professional. By spending 97 percent of their money outside of their racial community, they exacerbate their own social and economic problems.

30   This is the reason that Blacks do not keep pace economically or socially with the rest of the country. Since 80 percent of Americans are employed in small businesses, it is common sense that if businesses in the Black neighborhoods do not flourish, job opportunities will be greatly reduced.

    To succeed as a people, Blacks have to invest in and build their community. Other ethnic groups turn their money over multiple times within their communities. If money turns over ten times, it means that for every $100 spent by an individual, nine other individuals or businesses will have access to that same $100. This investment increases the community's economic strength by $1,000 instead of just $100.

    It works this way. You earn $100 a week and I earn $100 a week. You give me ninety-seven of your dollars. I'm living on $197 and you're living on $3. How can your house be

40 as big as mine? How can your car be as new as mine? How, even, can your IQ be as high as mine? Income affects nearly all aspects of life. A higher paycheck means you can afford to live in a better neighborhood with better schools and more opportunities for intellectual development. Studies have found that the group in America with the highest income is the group with the highest IQ. The group with the second-highest income is the group with the second-highest IQ. The overall IQ of Blacks is low in part because the income retained by Blacks is at the bottom.

Take Back Your Mind

Rick Singletary knows this all too well. The problem is not that Blacks don't have money. The problem is what we do with it, or don't do with it. Just as we waste our votes by not demanding anything in return, we don't spend our money where it pays off.

50   Over the last twenty-five years, the Black community has had a major thrust in politics and civil rights. We have staged Freedom Marches, but we have never stopped to think about what really buys freedom. It isn't worn-out shoes, and it isn't even civil rights legislation. True freedom springs from economic parity with other Americans.

    Money is not everything, but I rate it right up there with oxygen. After almost one hundred years of social engineering, Blacks can sit next to White people in classrooms and restaurants and on airplanes, but can they afford it? *The bottom line is that the only color of freedom is green.* Pride, education, and economic self-sufficiency were the message of Marcus Garvey and Booker T. Washington. But those two great Black men were vilified by the self-serving, self-hating elitists among their own people, and their vital message of self-reliance was blocked. Instead Blacks have spent decades with their arms extended 60 and their hands out, doing the economic death dance to the tune of integration. ■

UNDERSTANDING CONTEXT

1. What does the failure of Singletary's supermarket represent to Brown? Why does he see it as representing a "national disgrace"?

2. Why do African Americans, in Brown's opinion, "boycott" black businesses?

3. How can blacks achieve economic parity with other Americans in Brown's view?

4. *Critical thinking:* Does Brown's argument reveal the misguided goals of the civil rights movement or does it appear to "blame the victim"? Does an argument for self-reliance necessarily suggest that government action is not needed or that existing programs could be cut?

EVALUATING STRATEGY

1. How effective is the example of Rick Singletary? Does it bring Brown's point to life?

2. Would a hypothetical example be as effective as an actual one?

3. Brown introduces facts and numbers; why are these important?

4. Where does Brown place his thesis? Could it be located elsewhere?

5. *Other modes:* How does Brown use argument in this essay?

APPRECIATING LANGUAGE

1. How does Brown describe Singletary? Do Brown's words depict him as a hero or role model?

2. How effective are phrases such as "the color of freedom is green" and "economic death dance"? Do you find them striking or too dramatic?

WRITING SUGGESTIONS

1. Select a person you consider a role model and describe how his or her actions represent a trend that should be supported or followed by others.

2. *Collaborative writing:* Discuss the actions of Singletary and Brown's analysis with other students. Brainstorm within the group and provide a local example of someone whose efforts failed or succeeded to help his or her community.

Writing beyond the Classroom   COVENANT HOUSE

Covenant House is the nation's largest shelter program for homeless youth. Begun in 1969 by a priest who took in six runaways during a blizzard, the program has grown to serve thousands each year. The agency is supported almost entirely by donations from individuals.

Covenant House Needs Your Help

As you read this web page soliciting support, notice how examples are used to dramatize the plight of homeless youth and illustrate the program's services.

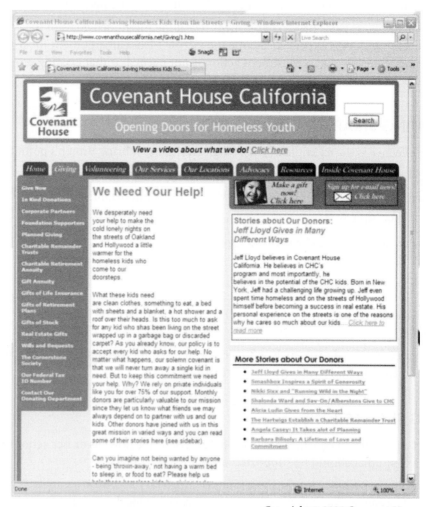

Copyright © 2005 Covenant House

UNDERSTANDING CONTEXT

1. What services does Covenant House provide?

2. Why does Covenant House need financial support?

3. Why do homeless youths face greater challenges today?

4. What is the mission of Covenant House?

EVALUATING STRATEGY

1. What purpose do examples serve? Is it important to provide names of those served? Why or why not?

2. What role do statistics play? Is it important to balance examples with factual detail?

3. How effective is the visual impact of this web page? Do you find it easy to read? Does it communicate at a glance? Does the photograph grab attention and demonstrate the severity of the problem of homeless young people?

APPRECIATING LANGUAGE

1. Does this level of diction seem appropriate for a mass audience?

2. Do you think using the word "kid" is effective? Why or why not? Might some readers object to this term?

WRITING SUGGESTIONS

1. Develop the text for a fundraising brochure or web page using examples for support. Determine the best examples that would both dramatize a social problem and demonstrate how the organization works to solve it.

2. *Collaborative writing:* Discuss this web page with a group of students then develop a process essay that explains step by step how you would conduct a national fundraising campaign to draw attention to the problem of homeless youth and encourage donations.

Responding to IMAGES

Patient in mental asylum, Turin, Italy

© *Magnum*

1. *Visual analysis:* What is your immediate reaction to this image? Does the man's pose suggest humour, wit, defiance, or desperation? How does the caption influence your response?

2. What does this photograph represent to you in terms of mental illness? Do most people understand how disabling mental disease can be for both patients and their loved ones?

3. Would you consider using this photograph in a fundraising brochure for a mental health campaign? Why or why not?

4. Write a fictional narrative to accompany this photograph. Write the patient's diary entry, a consoling letter by a friend, or a doctor's patient history.

5. *Collaborative writing:* Discuss this photograph with a group of students and measure reactions. Do any of them know someone who has suffered from a severe mental illness? Work together to write a brief statement about how the public should be educated about mental illness. Do people consider mental disorders true disabilities?

6. *Other modes*
   - Develop a *comparison* essay contrasting the way people view physical and mental illnesses. Do people suffering from a mental disorder receive less support, sympathy, and acceptance than those with physical disabilities? Why or why not?
   - Create a *definition* paper that establishes the severity of mental illness required for a patient to receive disability payments.

☑ EXAMPLE **CHECKLIST**

Before submitting your paper, review these points:

✔ Is your thesis clearly stated?

✔ Is the example clearly stated, logically organized, and supported by details?

✔ Are conflicting interpretations disproven or acknowledged?

✔ Do you avoid sweeping generalizations and unsupported conclusions?

✔ Do you anticipate future changes that might alter predictions?

✔ Do you avoid making errors in critical thinking, especially hasty generalization and confusing a time relationship for cause and effect?

✔ Have you tested your ideas through peer review?

 COMPANION WEBSITE

See **http://www.transcanadawriter.nelson.com** for additional information on writing example essays.

CHAPTER 15

Definition: Establishing Meaning

This chapter explores the nature and role of definition in effective communication. It looks at how to create accurate and precise definitions to anchor meaning for specific discourse communities.

WHAT IS DEFINITION?

To communicate effectively, writers must share a common understanding with readers of how language is used. Words and ideas must be *defined* to eliminate confusion and misinterpretation. Definitions explain and limit the meaning of a word or concept. Fields such as chemistry, literature, and anatomy have technical words that must be learned in order to communicate within the discipline.

Clearly stated definitions play a critical role in academic, professional, government, and business writing. To prevent confusion and conflict—even litigation, in some cases—many union contracts, insurance policies, or sales agreements include definitions so all parties will share a common interpretation of important terms.

The word *definition* leads most students to think of a dictionary. But defining involves more than simply looking up the meaning of a word. Definitions are not always precise or universally accepted. To be an effective writer, it is important to appreciate the range of definitions:

- **Standard definitions** are universally accepted and rarely subject to change. Such words as *tibia, dolphin, uranium, felony,* and *turbine* have exact meanings that are understood and shared by scholars, professionals, and the general public.

- **Regulatory definitions** are officially designated terms that are subject to change. Most organizations and groups issue definitions to guide policy, control operations, inform the public, and make decisions. Canada Revenue Agency's definition of a *deductible tax credit,* for example, can change yearly. Regulatory definitions may be universally accepted, but they can change or be limited to a specific region, organization, or discipline.

- **Evolving definitions** reflect changes in community attitudes, social values, government policies, and scientific research. In the 19th century, striking children was a widely accepted method of discipline called *corporal punishment.* Today, the same behaviour would be defined as *child abuse.* Evolving definitions track social change but rarely shift as abruptly as regulatory definitions.

- **Qualifying definitions** limit meanings of words or concepts that are abstract or subject to interpretation. Some definitions are hotly debated. Researchers, politicians, and social commentators continually argue over whether drug addiction, for example, should be defined as a *disability* that entitles people to receive benefits.

- **Cultural definitions** are shaped by the history, values, and attitudes of a national, ethnic, or religious group. Just as evolving definitions change over time, cultural differences differ from group to group. People the world over embrace *freedom* but define it differently. For most Canadians, *freedom* is defined in personal terms, meaning freedom of movement and expression for individual citizens. In other countries, people may define *freedom* in national terms, as protecting the independence and security of their homeland even if it is maintained by censorship and restricted personal liberties.

- **Personal definitions** are used by writers to express individual interpretations of words or ideas. Personal definitions are based on the writer's perceptual world and his or her sense of values.

WRITING **ACTIVITY**

Determine what type of definition would best suit each of the following topics. In some instances, there may be more than one possible definition.

1. Internal combustion engine
2. Cyberspace
3. Stalking
4. Road rage
5. Pornography

The Purpose of Definition

Definitions serve to establish meaning and to provide a common or shared understanding. But they can also be persuasive. Definitions can be used to express an opinion, influence perceptions, or shape the debate over a problem or issue. To transform public attitudes and change their perceptions, writers frequently urge readers to redefine something—for example, to change their perceptions to see striking a child as *abuse* instead of *spanking* or to accept *graffiti* as *street art.*

WRITING **ACTIVITY**

Provide persuasive definitions for the following terms. Your definition can reflect your personal opinions and values.

1. Family values
2. Domestic violence
3. Racism
4. Gun control
5. Poverty

Methods of Definition

Writers create definitions using a number of strategies:

1. **Defining through synonyms** is the simplest method of providing meaning for a word or concept. Glossaries and dictionaries customarily define technical terms or foreign words with synonyms. For example, a *casement* can be explained as a *window*.

■ Because no two words are exact equivalents, be cautious about using a single word in a definition. Connotations can distort meanings.

2. **Defining by description** provides details about a subject and gives readers a sense of what it might look, feel, taste, smell, or sound like. Defining *costrel* as "a small flask with a loop or loops that is suspended from a belt" provides readers with a clear picture of the object.

■ Describing objects in action creates a clear picture. Because some items may have many functions, indicate exceptions or alternative actions to prevent oversimplification.

3. **Defining by example** provides specific illustrations to establish meaning. Examples establish meaning through identification. Telling a Grade 4 class that "a verb is a word that expresses action" is not as effective as providing examples children can easily recognize—*run, buy, talk, sell, build, think.*

■ Complex or abstract concepts are easier to comprehend if defined by example.

4. **Defining by comparison** uses analogies; this strategy is particularly useful for less familiar terms and concepts. To explain the NASA term *power down*, a television reporter remarks that the astronauts are "conserving power by turning off nonessential electrical devices, much like switching off the radio and windshield wipers on a car." Comparative definitions must be used carefully to avoid oversimplification.

5. **Extended definitions** qualify or limit the meaning of abstract, disputed, or highly complex words or concepts. Such words as *sin, love,* and *racism* cannot be adequately defined through synonyms, brief descriptions, or a few examples. A complete definition might require several paragraphs or pages.

Strategies for Writing Definition

Critical Thinking and Prewriting

1. **Determine the goal of your definition—to inform or persuade.** Decide whether your purpose is to provide information about a topic, guiding readers to understand a concept or object, or to influence their opinion about a subject or issue.

2. **Write a list of ideas, people, items, concepts, theories, and places.** One way of starting is simply to begin isolating possible topics. At first, list as many ideas as possible.

3. **Review the list and note the best ways of defining selective topics.** Some topics may be challenging to define because they are complex, controversial, or elusive. If you discover a particular subject difficult, explore another idea.

Planning

1. **Write a clearly stated one-sentence definition of your subject if possible.** Try to focus your thoughts by stating a working thesis to target your planning.

2. **Define your role.** Your definition can be based on personal observation and opinion or standard principles and methods followed in a specific discipline or profession.

3. **Consider your audience.** Your definition should offer recognizable examples in language they will understand. Determine what uses your audience has for the definition.

4. **Use a balance of defining methods.** Each method of defining has advantages and disadvantages. It is usually effective to blend descriptions, synonyms, examples, and comparisons.

5. **Organize your essay.** Arrange your material in a logical pattern—spatial, chronological, or emphatic.

Writing the First Draft

1. **Keep extended definitions on target.** Refer to your plan and thesis as you write. Extended examples are designed to illustrate a point.

2. **Use or refer to existing definitions.** Instead of creating your own definition, you can often adopt or make use of an existing one. When you use existing definitions, acknowledge their sources. If you disagree with an existing official definition, restate it and then demonstrate how your interpretation differs.

3. **Clearly summarize the definition in a sentence or two.** Readers are not likely to recall ideas scattered throughout an essay. If possible, distill your main points into one or two clearly stated sentences that readers can underline for easy reference.

4. **Define abstract or elusive topics by setting boundaries.**
   - Openly state what your subject is *not* to set firm boundaries and reduce reader confusion.
   - Provide examples in a pro and con fashion, illustrating what does and does not fall within the boundaries of your definition.
   - Lists of examples or comparisons are effective in providing a personal definition of an abstract concept open to varied interpretations.

Revising

1. **Review your plan; then examine the content of your draft.** Does your paper *define* the topic or merely *describe* it? A definition supplies specific limitations to a subject, giving readers an understanding so they can recognize the subject or condition when they encounter it. Your paper must provide more than impressions—it must distinguish what separates this topic from similar ones.

2. **Review your thesis or summary.** Do you provide a clearly stated definition that readers can remember or highlight for future reference?

3. **Analyze extended definitions for irrelevant or missing details.** Does the narrative simply tell a story or does it *define* the subject by supplying facts, observations, and details needed to inform or persuade readers?

4. **Review informative definitions for clarity.** Are the limits of the definition clearly stated and supported by facts and details?

5. **Review persuasive definitions for critical thinking.**
   - In shaping opinion, do you take your readers' existing knowledge and attitudes into account? Do you address their existing conceptions?
   - Do you show how your definition differs from others?
   - Do you demonstrate why your definition is superior to others?
   - Have you avoided logical fallacies?

6. **Review the introduction and conclusion.**
   - Does the opening introduce the subject and arouse interest?
   - Does the conclusion create a strong impression readers will remember?

7. **Review the overall structure of the body.**
   - Is the supporting material clearly organized and joined by transitional statements? Do the separate paragraphs serve to advance the definition?

Editing and Proofreading

1. **Review your choice of words.**
   - Does your paper contain words that require further definition to prevent confusion?
   - Are there any connotations that may alienate or mislead readers?

2. **Read your paper (aloud).**
   - Are there awkward, wordy, or repetitive phrases that can be deleted or revised?

3. **Review the thesis statement.**
   - Is your definition clearly stated so readers can grasp a general sense of your thesis without having to read the entire essay?

4. **Use peer editing.**
   - Ask readers whether they can restate your definition in their own words. If they cannot, revise your thesis or add more details and examples.

General Assignments

Write a definition on any of the following topics. Your definition will probably use other modes—narration, description, example, comparison, or persuasion. Choose your terminology carefully and avoid words with misleading connotations. Remember, your main goal is to define, not describe or tell a story. Give your readers ways of recognizing your subject on their own.

- A good relationship
- An educated person
- A healthy lifestyle
- Self-respect
- Racism

Writing in Context

1. Imagine you have been asked to write a brief brochure about college or university life to be distributed to disadvantaged high school students. Define the characteristics of a good postsecondary student, stressing hard work and study habits.

2. You have been asked to participate in a panel on sexual harassment. In preparation, provide two definitions of sexual harassment—one expressing the perspective of men on campus, the other that of women. Try to be objective and state differences fairly.

Strategies for Reading Definition

As you read the definition essays in this chapter, keep these questions in mind:

Context

1. Which type of definition is the author developing—standard, regulatory, evolving, qualifying, cultural, or personal?

2. What is the author's purpose—to inform or persuade?

3. What is the nature of the context, the audience, discipline, or writing situation? Is the writer addressing a general or specific reader?

Strategy

1. What methods of definition does the writer use—synonyms, examples, comparisons, or descriptions?

2. Is the definition limited to a specific incident or context, or can it be applied generally? Is the writer defining a particular person or personality trait that could be shared by millions?

3. Does the writer provide personal examples, or does he or she rely on official sources to establish the definition?

Language

1. What roles do word choice and connotation play in establishing the definition?

2. What do the tone and level of language reveal about the writer's purpose and intended audience?

EILEEN SIMPSON

Eileen Simpson is a psychotherapist who struggled for years to overcome dyslexia, a reading disorder that affects approximately 4 out of every 100 people. She is the author of several books, including **Poets in Their Youth**, a memoir of her marriage to poet John Berryman. Other books based on her personal experiences explored problems of children growing up without parents. This selection comes from her 1979 book **Reversals: A Personal Account of Victory over Dyslexia.**

Dyslexia*

Simpson provides a standard definition of an existing term by examining its Greek and Latin roots and then demonstrates the effects dyslexia has on its victims. Notice that she supplies examples to help readers fully appreciate the implications of a widely misunderstood disorder.

1   Dyslexia (from the Greek, *dys,* faulty + *lexis,* speech, cognate with the Latin *legere,* to read), developmental or specific dyslexia as it's technically called, the disorder I suffered from, is the inability of otherwise normal children to read. Children whose intelligence is below average, whose vision or hearing is defective, who have not had proper schooling, or who are too emotionally disturbed or brain-damaged to profit from it belong in other diagnostic categories. They, too, may be unable to learn to read, but they cannot properly be called dyslexics.

For more than seventy years the essential nature of the affliction has been hotly disputed by psychologists, neurologists, and educators. It is generally agreed, however, that it is the result of a neurophysiological flaw in the brain's ability to process language. It is prob-
10 ably inherited, although some experts are reluctant to say this because they fear people will equate "inherited" with "untreatable." Treatable it certainly is: not a disease to be cured, but a malfunction that requires retraining.

Reading is the most complex skill a child entering school is asked to develop. What makes it complex, in part, is that letters are less constant than objects. A car seen from a distance, close to, from above, or below, or in a mirror still looks like a car even though the optical image changes. The letters of the alphabet are more whimsical. Take the letter *b.* Turned upside down it becomes a *p.* Looked at in a mirror, it becomes a *d.* Capitalized, it becomes something quite different, a *B.* The *M* upside down is a *W.* The *E* flipped over becomes Ǝ. This reversed *E* is familiar to mothers of normal children who have just begun to go to school. The
20 earliest examples of art work they bring home often have I LOVƎ YOU written on them.

Dyslexics differ from other children in that they read, spell, and write letters upside down and turned around far more frequently and for a much longer time. In what seems like a capricious manner, they also add letters, syllables, and words, or, just as capriciously, delete them. With palindromic words (was-saw, on-no), it is the order of the letters rather than the orientation they change. The new word makes sense, but not the sense intended. Then there are other words where the changed order—"sorty" for story— does not make sense at all.

The inability to recognize that g, *g*, and *G* are the same letter, the inability to maintain the orientation of the letters, to retain the order in which they appear, and to follow a line of text without jumping above or below it—all the results of the flaw—can make of an orderly page of words a dish of alphabet soup.   30

Also essential for reading is the ability to store words in memory and to retrieve them. This very particular kind of memory dyslexics lack. So, too, do they lack the ability to hear what the eye sees, and to see what they hear. If the eye sees "off," the ear must hear "off" and not "of," or "for." If the ear hears "saw," the eye must see that it looks like "saw" on the page and not "was." Lacking these skills, a sentence or paragraph becomes a coded message to which the dyslexic can't find the key.

It is only a slight exaggeration to say that those who learned to read without difficulty can best understand the labor reading is for a dyslexic by turning a page of text upside down and trying to decipher it.

While the literature is replete with illustrations of the way these children write and spell,   40 there are surprisingly few examples of how they read. One, used for propaganda purposes to alert the public to the vulnerability of dyslexics in a literate society, is a sign warning that behind it are guard dogs trained to kill. The dyslexic reads:

a Wurring

Guard God

Patoly

for

Warning

Guard Dog

Patrol   50

and, of course, remains ignorant of the danger.

Looking for a more commonplace example, and hoping to recapture the way I must have read in fourth grade, I recently observed dyslexic children at the Educational Therapy Clinic in Princeton, through the courtesy of Elizabeth Travers, the director. The first child I saw, eight-year-old Anna (whose red hair and brown eyes reminded me of myself at that age), had just come to the Clinic and was learning the alphabet. Given the story of "Little Red Riding Hood," which is at the second grade level, she began confidently enough, repeating the title from memory, then came to a dead stop. With much coaxing throughout, she read as follows:

Grandma you a top. Grandma [looks over at picture of Red Riding Hood]. Red Riding   60
Hood [long pause, presses index finger into the paper. Looks at me for help. I urge: Go
ahead] the a [puts head close to the page, nose almost touching] on Grandma

for

Once upon a time there was a little girl who had a red coat with a red hood. Etc.

"Grandma" was obviously a memory from having heard the story read aloud. Had I needed a reminder of how maddening my silences must have been to Miss Henderson, and how much patience is required to teach these children, Anna, who took almost ten minutes to read these few lines, furnished it. The main difference between Anna and me at that age is that Anna clearly felt no need to invent. She was perplexed, but not anxious, and seemed to
70   have infinite tolerance for her long silences.

Toby, a nine-year-old boy with superior intelligence, had a year of tutoring behind him and could have managed "Little Red Riding Hood" with ease. His text was taken from the *Reader's Digest's Reading Skill Builder*, Grade IV. He read:

> *A kangaroo likes as if he had but truck together warm. His saw neck and head do not . . . [Here Toby sighed with fatigue] seem to feel happy back. They and tried and so every a tiger Moses and shoots from lonesome day and shouts and long shore animals. And each farm play with five friends . . .*

He broke off with the complaint, "This is too hard. Do I have to read any more?"
His text was:

80   > *A kangaroo looks as if he had been put together wrong. His small neck and head do not seem to fit with his heavy back legs and thick tail. Soft eyes, a twinkly little nose and short front legs seem strange on such a large strong animal. And each front paw has five fingers, like a man's hand.*

An English expert gives the following bizarre example of an adult dyslexic's performance:

> *An the bee-what in the tel mother of the biothodoodoo to the majoram or that emidrate eni eni Krastrei, mestriet to Ketra lotombreidi to ra from treido as that.*

His text, taken from a college catalogue the examiner happened to have close at hand, was:

> *It shall be in the power of the college to examine or not every licentiate, previous to his admission to the fellowship, as they shall think fit.*

90   That evening when I read aloud to Auntie for the first time, I probably began as Toby did, my memory of the classroom lesson keeping me close to the text. When memory ran out, and Auntie did not correct my errors, I began to invent. When she still didn't stop me, I may well have begun to improvise in the manner of this patient—anything to keep going and keep up the myth that I was reading—until Auntie brought the "gibberish" to a halt. ■

UNDERSTANDING CONTEXT

1. What basic definition does Simpson provide? What misinterpretation does she note can occur if a condition is considered "inherited"?

2. How does Simpson summarize controversies in the field of research? What do scientists from different disciplines agree on?

3. What is the implication to dyslexics and their parents that dyslexia is "not a disease to be cured, but a malfunction that requires retraining"?

4. *Critical thinking:* How can this disorder affect a child's development if it is not detected?

EVALUATING STRATEGY

1. Why is it effective to provide an etymology of the word *dyslexia* at the opening? Does this help satisfy reader curiosity about a term many people have heard but do not fully understand?

2. How does Simpson's introduction of personal experience affect the definition? Does this add a human dimension to her definition, or does it detract from its objectivity? Would the inclusion of personal experience be appropriate in a textbook?

3. Do the examples of dyslexic reading dramatize the effects of this disorder? Would an explanation alone suffice to impress readers with the crippling effects of a reading disorder?

4. *Other modes:* How does Simpson use *description* and *narration* to develop her definition? What role can stories or case studies provide readers seeking to understand a complex subject?

APPRECIATING LANGUAGE

1. Simpson is defining a complex disorder. How does her language indicate that she is seeking to address a general audience? Would the vocabulary differ in a definition written for psychology students?

2. Simpson cites an example of a dyslexic reading a warning sign as "propaganda." Does the use of this word weaken her argument that dyslexia is a serious condition? Why or why not?

3. How does Simpson define the term "palindromic"?

WRITING SUGGESTIONS

1. Write a concisely worded definition of dyslexia in your own words.

2. *Critical writing:* Write an essay expressing your view on how dyslexics should be graded in college or university. Should students with dyslexia be allowed more time on essay tests, be offered special tutorial services, or be given alternative assignments and examinations? Can students with disabilities be accommodated while maintaining academic standards?

3. *Collaborative writing:* Working with several other students, craft a brief explanation of dyslexia to be incorporated into a brochure for parents of children with learning disabilities. Keep your audience in mind, and avoid making negative comments that might upset parents.

JANE JACOBS

Jane Jacobs (1916–2006) was one of the 20th century's most important urban planners, emigrating from New York City to Toronto in 1968. Following the publication of her highly regarded **The Death and Life of Great American Cities**, she published a number of other books, including **The Economy of Cities, The Question of Separatism: Quebec and the Struggle Over Sovereignty, Cities and the Wealth of Nations**, and **The Nature of Economies**.

Streets that Work*

In her essay, Jacobs argues for a more socially responsible approach to urban planning. While tackling a complex topic, Jacobs presents a clear argument by providing the reader with clear definitions of unfamiliar terms. Jacob also presents her argument in clearly defined steps to show how easily the process can be achieved.

1   Twenty years ago it was commonly believed that to benefit cities a plan must be sweeping and comprehensive. Small improvements and non-disruptive plans were sneered at as 'the band-aid approach'. Slums were bulldozed to make way for monolithic public housing projects. Neighbourhoods were bisected, trisected, and sometimes vivisected for links in city-wide expressway systems. Historic and humanely scaled landscapes were demolished to make way for high-rise apartment or office buildings. Zoning was aimed at segregating the different components of city life from one another.

Reality finally caught up with us: not only was the destruction expensive, the results were disappointing socially, functionally, and aesthetically.

10   Even so, old ways of thinking die hard. Once people have taken it for granted that little worthwhile can be accomplished without the guidance of sweeping schemes—masterminding big change far into the future—they tend to be at a loss in finding constructive alternatives.

Since we think with words even more than with diagrams, sometimes a single change of phrase helps open our minds to possibilities and alternatives. Just so, nowadays a new term, 'retrofitting', has begun to enter the planning vocabulary. Retrofitting means accepting what exists as a base, a given, and deliberately improving it with varied small changes. These little alterations, thought of and undertaken as opportunity offers, incrementally add up to very significant improvement. By its very nature, this approach is economic, conserving, efficient, flexible, and responsive.

20   What it requires, in place of comprehensive and dictatorial plans, is a shared set of perceptions and values, so that the incremental changes, as they add up, are coherent rather than chaotic and at cross-purposes.

The most requisite 'shared value' is a simple belief that the city is a good place, not something to be hated, not something to be accepted as a necessary evil, certainly not something to try to destroy. This may seem self-evident, but apparently is not. The very genesis of so-called

*Jacobs, Jane, "Streets that Work" from *Canadian Heritage,* 13, 2 (May/June 1987). Copyright © 1987 Jane Jacobs.

modern city planning was hatred of the city, and especially of its most important visual and functional artifacts, its streets. The great men of planning and its philosophy—Ebenezer Howard, Corbusier, Lewis Mumford, and the others—deplored cities, were disgusted by their streets, and even sought to erase them as far as possible.

A second necessary shared value has already been alluded to: belief that small improve- 30 ments are worthwhile, faith that they add up, and recognition that they are all the more effective because they are not disruptive and all the more congenial because they can occur as opportunity offers and circumstance permits.

We must also recognize that small—in itself—isn't necessarily beautiful. Thus, besides that fundamental belief in the value of the city and the value of incremental improvement, we need general guidelines for retrofitting city streets, rules of thumb that can be kept in mind in the trenches by embattled local block groups, neighbourhood associations, home-owners and tenants, and—yes—even professional city planners. The seven guides that fol-low, many of them aptly illustrated in my own city of Toronto, are proposed not as the last word, but as a start. They too can be augmented incrementally, as experience suggests addi- 40 tions or refinements:

1. Avoid monotony. When retrofitting a street, try to insert what isn't there already, and with respect to what is inserted, avoid monotony too. The worst possible insertion is a long, blank wall. This would hardly seem necessary to mention except that it is transgressed so often by shopping malls, arenas, buildings of all kinds that should be improved with the use of imagination, sensitive design, and inclusion of varied functions at street level.

Fountains can be wonderful insertions. One of the things we all like when we visit old cities in Europe—I'm thinking of Zurich—is the many fountains dotted about the city. In the old days, every district had to have its fountain for households to get their water. Europe has since been retrofitted with indoor plumbing but its fountains still serve a social pur- 50 pose—they're hangouts, places to meet, and they're nice, visual exclamation points.

In Canada, we seem to have only the great monumental fountain or the little drinking fountain in the park. There's nothing in between. A lot could be done here with fountains.

When inserting something different, aesthetics can help, even cosmetics can, but it will count for a lot more if you can also add something functionally different. Putting stores into the ground floor of a parking garage, for example, could enliven what is usually a dead stretch. But a word of caution: there's no use putting in stores where they'd go out of busi-ness or remain empty. You have to think whether they're practical.

2. Go with what's natural to the circumstances. For instance, a lot of horizontal green-ery is not natural to most city streets. *Vertical* greenery is. Streets are natural places for trees, 60 for vines, for greenery taking little ground area. A city can't support many trees.

Vines unfortunately have a bad name, partly because architects don't like to have their buildings covered up and partly because the probing roots of some vine species can damage mortar. But it would be nice to see certain kinds of vines planned as an element of design. Used properly on the right type of surface, deciduous plants like Virginia Creeper can shield masonry from acid rain, and vines on a south wall can work wonders keeping a building cool in summer.

3. *Be aware, and open to discovery.* This applies even to things that seem invisible. Take the bicycle. A cyclist tells me some of the best bike routes are on streets where there
70 is just a little more room in the curb lane. Say there's a parking lane, then lanes of traffic, and there's a little more room in each lane than necessary. If the excess of, say, three feet is consolidated into the lane next to the parking, you create an invisible bike path. I'd never analyzed this before, but when I used to ride my bike to work in New York, I too had certain paths I'd chosen because they felt spacious. I wonder that I'd never noticed just why. This is the kind of thing we must notice. And we all can't notice everything—so listen to other people.

4. *Don't try to be comprehensive.* That's how you get into the worst trouble, trying to coordinate everything desirable at once, which is cumbersome, frustrating, and unpractical. Many of our cities' worst problems stem from overly zealous, comprehensive planning
80 and policy making. There are many tales, but here's one of the more incredible: Once, when I lived in New York, I was looking through the Urban Renewal Administration files to find out how a really very decent neighbourhood had gotten designated for urban renewal, and had been knocked down, to the great hardship of many people. And what do you think? It began with a letter—from some innocent in the neighbourhood—to the Planning Commission, asking if they could have trees planted on the street. This is a fact. From the Planning Commission, the letter was sent to various civil servant specialists, and everybody it went to latched onto it as a chance to do something his department wanted. When the Urban Renewal people saw the letter, they got so comprehensive they doomed the neighbourhood.

90 **5. *Start with what's easiest.*** This is a good general principle in life. Don't begin where everything is stacked against you, where you'll need the most specialists, and especially not where the people involved are going to oppose what you contemplate.

If the plan works, you can build on that success. People can actually see what you're talking about. You have a successful precedent, making it easier to overcome objections and red tape where similar changes would be harder to initiate.

6. *Work incrementally.* Little drops of water, little grains of sand, they do add up. But more than that, they point the way to still further things. I'm thinking of Toronto's experience with infill housing, which started when there was a citizen revolt at Dundas and Sherbourne Streets about knocking down old buildings to make way for another one of
100 those massive high-rise developments.

The people in that neighbourhood were fed up with the city's fabric being comprehensively torn apart, and at the last minute their protests succeeded in stopping the wreckers. That gave time to develop a counter-proposal—one that was economically feasible and wouldn't require demolition of existing buildings. It took real genius at cutting red tape to get over the hurdles and permit the construction of infill housing (new construction in vacant lots that blends with the style and character of the existing architecture around it). In the process the city began to learn a whole new way of working. The Department of Housing was reincarnated, and went on to develop all kinds of lots, mostly small, as infill sites. In the past, they'd have been written off as too small or

awkward to fool with. There was some opposition, but the city was sensible. It began 110
with the easiest places. This showed people that the new way of working wasn't like the
old assisted housing that ruins the area all around it. The more infill was done, the more
acceptable it became.

Because planners were learning a different way of working, the City Planning Department was equipped in a way it hadn't been before to work on Toronto's St. Lawrence neighbourhood. This was a different problem, a large clean-sweep area that would have been made
a project in the past. It's called a neighbourhood because it's not a project. The department
had so much expertise at knitting up the city's fabric—where it was torn, or tattered—that it
could work on this large swatch of land as if it was an extension of that fabric. Even with the
best intentions—to make nice streetscapes, human-scaled and for people—I'm sure the St. 120
Lawrence planning couldn't have been done without that prior experience of infill planning.
I watched the change in the planners' and architects' perceptions of city fabric as they went
through this experience. They couldn't even have thought of how to plan St. Lawrence previously. This is an example of how working incrementally, in itself, leads to new techniques and
design ideas if you build on experience.

After watching this, I became optimistic about the next possible incremental change
in Toronto, since there were planners with experience in a new way of seeing the city and
dealing with it. I hoped the city would take some of the monotonous and monolithic
housing projects—beginning with the easiest ones—and start knitting these back into the
city: for instance, by making reasons for people outside the projects to go into them by liv- 130
ening them up, inserting new and interesting and convenient things—in short, retrofitting
them both for their own residents and for others. We can't afford to blow up our many
dismal projects, as was done in the case of St. Louis' infamous Puritt-Igoe project, and it
is outrageous to make people endure their faults interminably. The practical approach is
to retrofit them.

Several years ago I heard this was being thought of for St Jamestown in Toronto, which
seems a good choice as it's probably one of the easiest with which to begin. However, I'm
pessimistic. The old, besetting sin of planners seems again taking command: trying to be
comprehensive instead of getting started with something—one street, one part of a street,
whatever can be begun easily, then building on that. 140

Perhaps if Toronto fails to begin incrementally improving its sterile housing projects,
some other city will. I hope it starts happening someplace, because literally every city in the
world, from Toronto to Beijing, Amsterdam to Zagreb, is waiting for practical examples of
how to incorporate wretchedly-designed projects functionally and socially into the fabrics
of cities.

7. Remember who the real jurors are. They aren't the architectural and planning magazines. They aren't the private or public clients who pay for street changes. They aren't the
schools of architecture. They aren't the jurors of design competitions.

The real jurors of street success are the people who use and enjoy them. If you heed their
responses as indicated by the use they make of what you do—or by their lack of use and 150
appreciation—they'll show very quickly what success you've had. ■

UNDERSTANDING CONTEXT

1. Who is Jacobs' audience?

2. Jacobs presents her solution in clear steps. Briefly summarize her steps.

3. What is Jacobs' thesis? Briefly summarize it in your own words.

EVALUATING STRATEGY

1. Jacobs chooses to present her argument directly and clearly. In presenting her argument, she offers examples for evidence. Is it an effective strategy?

APPRECIATING LANGUAGE

1. Jacobs states that "sometimes a single change of phrase helps open our minds to possibilities and alternatives." Think of examples of simple changes in phrasing that open up new ways of seeing and thinking about life.

2. Jacobs employs clear language. With the exception of "retrofit," she does not employ jargon. How does her level of diction help to communicate her argument?

WRITING SUGGESTION

1. Look at your campus. Write an essay explaining how your college or university could improve its appearance by following Jacobs' suggestions.

HEATHER PRINGLE

Born in Edmonton in 1952, Heather Pringle is an award-winning author and popular science writer for magazines such as **Science, Discover, Canadian Geographic, National Geographic Traveler,** and **Saturday Night.** Pringle writes primarily in the field of archeology but also in anthropology and history. She has travelled extensively, often journeying into remote regions, such as the islands of Tonga and the back country of Peru. Currently, she lives in British Columbia.

The Way We Woo*

In her essay, Pringle explores the similarities between mating rituals in the wild and in the singles bars. By comparing the activity in the singles bars to that in the natural world, Pringle sheds new light on human mating rituals and argues for a broader understanding of these rituals.

Helen Fisher slips into a ringside seat, amusement stirring in her dark eyes. It's just after eight 1 on a steamy Friday night at the Mad Hatter Restaurant and Pub, one of dozens of softly lit singles bars on Manhattan's prosperous Upper East Side. A bevy of young businessmen, ties loosened and beer glasses in hand, lean against the railings, sizing up each female who walks in the door. On the street outside, barhoppers stream by the plate-glass windows like tropical fish. "There's constant motion here," says Fisher. "It looks like a real good pickup bar."

Elegantly dressed in a black skirt and sweater set, Fisher looks more like a society columnist than someone about to settle down for an evening in a singles bar. But the 48-year-old anthropologist has spent the past decade deciphering the mysteries of human mating behaviour, and she still relishes the odd evening in the field. "Men and women have no idea 10 the amount of sexual signals they are sending out to each other," she says, angling her chair for a better view. "They'd be amazed."

Fisher, a research associate in the department of anthropology at the American Museum of Natural History in New York, is one of a new scientific breed seeking out the biological and genetic roots of our love lives. Unwilling to accept traditional views, she and her colleagues have begun taking a fresh look at human romance—from the first twinges of physical attraction to the heady flush of courtship and the bitter acrimony of divorce. Taking clues from the animal kingdom and anthropology, they are turning up answers to some of the most enduring mysteries of romance: why men fall for pretty faces and women pine for men of means; why males roam from bed to bed, while females dream of Mr. Right; and why 20 love is so intoxicating and divorce so commonplace.

As she glances across the room, Fisher begins pointing out some of the subtleties of human courtship, patterns of behaviour that seem to stem from a distant past. Those men by

*Pringle, Heather, "The Way We Woo" reprinted by permission of Heather Pringle.

the railing, for example? Fisher grins. Singles bars, she explains, work much like the mating grounds of sage grouse and other birds. After staking out individual territories in the most prominent area in the bar, the men are now attempting to attract females with simple courtship displays: stretching, exaggerating simple movements, and laughing heartily. "One of them is even swinging from side to side, which is a real gesture of approachability," she says.

Fisher points out a miniskirted woman deep in conversation with a man at the bar. "See
30 how she's gesturing and swaying and preening?" Fisher asks. "She keeps on touching her eyes, her nose, and her mouth." Stroking her face as if stroking that of her companion, she is flashing a series of intention cues—messages that she wants to touch him. But he remains strangely impassive, refusing to turn even his shoulders toward her. The conversation may be flowing, says Fisher, but the courtship ritual is rapidly stalling. As we watch, shameless voyeurs, the animated discussion slowly sputters and dies. "The pickup runs on messages," concludes Fisher, shaking her head, "and every one of them has to be returned." Turning to the bartender, the woman asks for her bill, then hurries out into the night.

What is ultimately going on here? Beyond the rejected advances and the private humiliations, Fisher sees the workings of an age-old ritual. After years of study and debate, she and
40 other evolutionary anthropologists now suggest that human romance has been shaped by biology and the forces of natural selection. According to this controversial line of thought, humans conduct their love lives in much the same manner around the world. From the singles bars of North America to the marriage brokers of Asia, we attract, court, and discard mates in ways that subtly but surely promote the survival of our species.

It's a theory that challenges decades of entrenched thinking. Historians have long insisted that love itself was a cultural invention, an emotion first conceived by the courtly poets of Europe some eight hundred years ago and subsequently passed on to Europe's idle rich. In time, went this thinking, the idea of romantic love percolated to the lower classes, who in turn carried it to colonies far and wide. Such views dovetailed nicely with modern anthropological
50 thought. Since the 1920s, when American scientist Margaret Mead returned from fieldwork on the South Seas islands of Samoa, most anthropologists believed that human behaviour was shaped largely by culture. Children, they noted, were as impressionable as clay. "It's a view that there is basically no human nature," says David Buss, a professor of psychology at the University of Michigan in Ann Arbor, "that humans are simply a product of their environment."

Over the past two decades, however, serious cracks have appeared in those theoretical walls. Influenced by Charles Darwin, a small but vocal group of social scientists now suggest that natural selection, not culture, has shaped certain key human behaviours. Over hundreds of thousands of years, they theorize, evolution has moulded not only anatomy but the human psyche itself, favouring certain social behaviours, certain states of mind, that promote sur-
60 vival and reproductive success. In other words, biology lies just beneath the surface of much human psychology. Could our romances, they ask, be guided by certain evolved mechanisms? Could the human heart be unconsciously governed by the ancient encodings of our genes?

Psychologists Martin Daly and Margo Wilson think the answers are in little doubt. After fifteen years of research, the husband-and-wife team at McMaster University in Hamilton, Ontario, conclude that love runs a remarkably similar course around the world.

Wilson smiles as she observes that men tend to be attracted to the same qualities in women everywhere—even in traditional Islamic cultures, where females are veiled from head to shoulder. "The fact that you have these flirtatious eyes looking out from a whole black garb must just stimulate the imagination far beyond what is beneath the veil," she laughs. "Mystery is sexually exciting."   70

Wilson's interest in human romance first arose in the mid-1970s, when she and Daly came across the writings of those investigating the evolutionary basis of social behaviour in animals. After examining the life histories of animals as diverse as the dung fly, the Jamaican lizard, and the elephant seal, researchers had noted that males and females often approached the mating game very differently as a result of basic reproductive biology. Among most mammal species, for instance, females slave away much of their adult lives caring for their young—nurturing embryos, nursing infants, and often protecting litters alone. Absorbed by maternal duties, they are physically incapable of producing as many young as their male counterparts are. With a greater investment in their young, females tend to pick mates carefully, selecting those best able to help their brood survive. Most males, on the other hand, are spared such intensive pa- 80
rental labour. Serving largely as sperm donors, they take a different tactic, favouring quantity over quality in mating and inseminating as many fertile females as possible.

Intrigued, Daly and Wilson wondered how the behaviour of *Homo sapiens* fit into this pattern. Like other mammalian females, women invest long months in pregnancy, breast-feeding, and early childcare, keeping their families small. Men, however, are less burdened. (One eighteenth-century Moroccan emperor reputedly fathered seven hundred sons and more than three hundred daughters before celebrating his fiftieth birthday.) Could such radical biological differences shape human romance? Would men the world over, for ex-ample, be more promiscuous than women?

While comprehensive statistics were scarce, the team soon began piecing together an aston- 90
ishing case. In an American study of middle-aged couples published in 1970, one social scien-tist reported that twice as many males as females had committed adultery. In a German study of young working-class singles, 46 percent of the males, compared with only 6 percent of the females, were interested in casual sex with an attractive stranger. All around the world, from the Amazonian rainforest to the Kalahari Desert, field accounts of anthropologists lined up on this point: men of all ages craved far more sexual variety than women. Quips Wilson, "Male sexual psychology seems to be that you're willing to do it with, you know, chickens or anything."

Daly and Wilson found one other sweeping pattern in the anthropological literature: in every society, men and women entered into marriages—formal, long-standing unions that gave legitimacy to the resulting children. Had basic biology also shaped wedlock? If the biol- 100
ogists were right, women would marry men most capable of contributing to their children's well-being, while men would marry the most fertile females they could find.

In fact, the psychologists discovered, men generally wed younger women—a finding that squared well with evolution-minded predictions. As Wilson points out, women in their early twenties are much more fertile than those in their thirties; older men are far more likely to have acquired the kind of wealth and social status that could shelter their children from harm. And, notes Wilson, research shows that the attractiveness of a male in most cultures is judged more by his maturity, skills, and status than by a square-cut jaw and fine features. "Like Henry Kissinger," says Wilson of the former US Secretary of State. "People used to say 110 he was really handsome. He was in a high-status position, a very powerful position."

Passion Play: A Step-by-Step Script

After spending long, smoky evenings observing couples in North American singles bars, researchers have discerned several steps in human courtship:

Approach: As a rule, it is the female who begins the mating ritual, walking up to a male or taking a seat beside him. If he reciprocates her interest by turning and looking, a conversation ensues.

Talk: As the two chat, accents and manner of speech are highly revealing. "Talking is an enormous escalation point," notes Helen Fisher. "How many people have opened their mouth and had a horrible accent, and you just realized, no way? A lot of pickups end there." But if a man and a woman successfully negotiate that hurdle, they slowly turn to face each other, moving first their heads, then their shoulders and, finally, their entire bodies.

Touch: Generally, the woman will touch first, brushing her hand briefly along a man's arm or shoulder. If the man responds in kind, touching becomes more frequent.

Gaze: As the conversation becomes more intense and pleasurable, the couple begin glancing into each other's eyes, until they are finally unable to look away. Researchers call this the "copulatory gaze."

Body Synchrony: Mesmerized by talk and touch, the couple begin moving in harmony. If the female lifts her glass for a sip, the mate does too. If he slouches in his chair to the right, she mirrors his movement. "I would like to speculate," writes Timothy Perper in his book *Sex Signals: The Biology of Love*," that by the time they are fully synchronized, each person is physiologically prepared for intercourse."

To study human tastes in mates in more detail, David Buss drew up a list of thirty-one attributes and arranged for men and women in Africa, Asia, Europe, and South America to grade them by importance. "The results amazed me in that they basically confirmed the evolutionary predictions that others had speculated about," he notes. In the thirty-seven cultures polled, responses were strongly consistent, suggesting a universal, biological truth honed over millennia of evolution. While both sexes graded traits such as intelligence and kindness highly, they diverged sharply in two areas. "Women place a premium on status, older age and maturity, and resources," says Buss. "Men place a premium on youth and physical attractiveness."

120 Buss suggests that the male predilection for beauty is informed by sound biological logic. How else could a man judge the potential fertility of his mate? "The capacity of a woman to bear children is not stamped on her forehead," he writes in a recent paper. "It is not part of her social reputation, so no one is in a position to know. Even the woman herself lacks direct knowledge of her fertility and reproductive value." But certain visual cues, he explains, could serve as rough measures. Shapely legs, shiny hair, lustrous eyes, and a clear, unblemished

complexion in a female all signal health and youth. And some researchers have suggested that symmetrical facial features—particularly eyes of well-matched colour and alignment—could indicate mutation-free genes. Ancestral males drawn to such qualities, notes Buss, would have likely fathered more children than men attracted to other physical traits.

The differing biological goals of the sexes also have profound effects on human rela-   130
tions and courtship behaviour. While women need time to size up a man's finances and social status, men can measure beauty and youth with a mere flicker of an eye. Consider the recently published results of a study at the Florida State University at Tallahassee. Psychologists Russell Clark and Elaine Hatfield dispatched young men to different corners of the campus, instructing each to pitch one of three questions to female strangers: "Would you go out with me tonight?" "Would you come over to my apartment tonight?" or "Would you go to bed with me tonight?" While 56 percent of the females consented to a date, only 6 percent agreed to visit the male's apartment—and none consented to sex. But when a female approached male strangers with the same questions, 50 percent of the men agreed to a date, 69 percent consented to an apartment visit—and 75 percent offered to go to bed   140
with her that night.

As Buss and other psychologists slowly piece together the evolution of physical attrac-tion, other researchers examine the biological and genetic origins of the emotion of love itself. At the University of Nevada, Las Vegas, just a short stroll away from the rotund cu-pids and neon hearts adorning the city's all-night wedding chapels, anthropologist William Jankowiak is sweeping aside earlier cultural theories. Passionate attachments, he suggests, "must have evolved for some sense of adaptation. [They] must have helped *Homo sapiens* survive in the battle against the cockroach."

A soft-spoken but intense scholar, Jankowiak became interested in the evolution of love some six years ago while conducting fieldwork in Inner Mongolia. During casual reading   150
of ancient Chinese folktales, he was amazed to discover descriptions of passionate love that could have been penned today. "I said, 'My God, I wonder if this has been universal in Chi-nese history,' and it was. And then I started wondering if this was universal all over."

Turning to the scientific literature, Jankowiak unearthed two studies published in the 1960s by American psychologist Paul Rosenblatt. Interested in the emergence of love as a basis for marriage, Rosenblatt had pored over anthropological reports for dozens of human cultures, concluding that less than two-thirds had any concept of the emotion of love. As Jankowiak read the studies, however, he could see that Rosenblatt had missed a key source of information—the folklore of tribal peoples. Troubled by the omission, Jankowiak decided to start from scratch, eager to see whether love was an emotion present in all cultures.   160

With graduate student Edward Fischer, Jankowiak settled into the work, searching for love songs, tales of elopement, and other signs of romantic entanglements. In cultures where no trace of passion could be found in the literature, Jankowiak called up the anthropologists themselves to enquire whether any relevant evidence had been left out. In the end, the two researchers recorded romantic love in a resounding 88.5 percent of the 166 cultures they studied. For Jankowiak, the results strongly suggested that love is a common part of the hu-man condition, an experience owing more to biology than to culture.

Still, some scholars puzzled over the small number of societies where no sign of romantic love had been uncovered. If love was a universal condition, how had inhabitants of these cultures mustered such resistance? At the University of California, Santa Barbara, doctoral candidate Helen Harris decided to take a closer look at one such society—the Mangaians of the South Pacific. According to anthropological reports, the inhabitants of Mangaia had developed a highly sexual culture. At the age of thirteen or so, boys on the island were trained by older women to bring female partners to orgasm several times before reaching climaxes of their own. The craft perfected, the young men began courting the favours of island women— averaging three orgasms a night, seven nights a week. But according to an anthropologist who lived among the Mangaians in the 1950s, neither sex ever experienced the emotion of love. "He said that when he talked about it, the Mangaians didn't understand," notes Harris.

Harlequin's Lock on Our Hearts

Every month, Harlequin Enterprises Limited ships its purple prose around the globe— from Abu Dhabi to Zimbabwe and from Iceland to Tonga. Selling more than two hundred million books a year, the Canadian firm claims to have made "the language of love universal, crossing social, cultural, and geographical borders with an ease unrivalled by any other publisher." What is its secret of success?

As it turns out, Harlequin editors understand human desire pretty well. According to company guidelines for the Harlequin Regency line of novels, for example, heroines must be attractive and quick-witted and range in age between eighteen and twenty-eight years old. The objects of their affections, on the other hand, must be virile and prosperous, possess high societal positions—"we prefer peers," say the editors—and range in age from twenty-four to thirty-five years old.

Such matches are made in heaven, according to mate-preference studies conducted by Douglas Kenrick and an associate at Arizona State University in Tempe. As Kenrick notes, females are strongly drawn to men who possess leadership skills and occupy the top rungs of a hierarchy. Moreover, they crave mates up to eight or nine years older than themselves. Men, on the other hand, are not particularly charmed by leadership. Instead, they hanker after beautiful females in their twenties—something that Harlequin editors seem to have known all along.

Perplexed, Harris began her own fieldwork, interviewing males and females who had been adolescents during the 1950s. As her research proceeded, she could see that the sensational tales of sexual prowess had obscured the rich emotional life of Mangaia. Now middle-aged, the men and women recounted tales of deep passion, even love at first sight. "One of the women said she was in one of the stores on the island, she turned around, and she saw this man," recalls Harris. "She did not know him, but feelings just came over her that she had never felt before. . . . She analyzed it and said, 'I think it was just God's way of getting two people together. It's natural for people to feel this way.' And she and this man finally married after some years."

While it seems likely that romantic love arose in all human cultures, from the lean rein- deer herders of Lapland to the now silent scholars of the Sung Dynasty, it is less clear just when and why this emotional state evolved. Researchers have yet to discern any convincing 190 evidence of such strong emotions in the animal kingdom, for instance. And surveys have shown that intimate, long-lasting associations between a male and a female are strikingly rare even among our close primate relatives. "Yet the hallmark of the human animal is that we form these pair bonds," says Helen Fisher, sitting down with a glass of iced tea in her small Manhattan apartment. "So how come?"

In search of clues, Fisher turned to the zoological literature, studying several species that form such intimate bonds. In foxes, she found a clear biological imperative. Bearing some five helpless kits at a time, female red foxes become virtual prisoners of their broods. Equipped with only thin, low-fat milk, mothers must nurse each of their young every two to three hours. Without a male to help feed her, a female would soon starve to death. "But when 200 the kits begin to wander off," says Fisher, "the pair bond breaks up. It lasts only long enough to raise those kits through infancy."

As Fisher sees it, hominid females may have become similarly vulnerable some four million years ago. With climatic change, our simian ancestors were forced from the receding forests of Africa onto vast grassy plains, where stealthy predators stalked. "What I think," says Fisher, who has just published her theories in a new book, *Anatomy of Love: The Natural History of Monogamy, Adultery, and Divorce,* "is that we came down from the trees and we were forced onto two legs instead of four. Females suddenly needed to carry their babies in their arms instead of on their backs. What a huge reproductive burden," she says with a wince. "They also had to start carrying sticks and stones for tools and weapons in this dangerous 210 place. So women needed a mate to help rear their young."

As they roamed farther onto the grasslands, early human males also found compelling reasons to pair off with females. Along the vast savannas, food sources such as cashew trees, berry patches, and the occasional meaty carcass were widely scattered. Constantly roaming, males were unable to feed or defend large harems. "Polygyny was almost impossible for men," says Fisher, "and pair bonding was critical for women." So males who fell in love and formed pairs with females were more successful in passing on their genes, thus perpetuating the penchant for intimacy.

Setting down her iced tea, Fisher points out that science has yet to prove her theories conclusively. No one, for instance, has located specific genes capable of turning love on or 220 off in the human psyche. Even so, some medical research supports her contention. At the New York State Psychiatric Institute in New York City, researcher Michael Liebowitz suggests that the powerful emotion of love is created by a tidal wave of certain naturally produced chemicals in the brain. And others have suggested that the taps for these chemicals might be directly controlled by our genes.

A psychiatrist who specializes in the treatment of anxiety and depression, Liebowitz first began to suspect the chemical basis of love in the early 1980s after noticing the pro- found effects of particular antidepressants on patients who were addicted to the thrill of new relationships. After researching the matter carefully, he now suggests that the sheer

230 intoxication of love—the warm, reckless euphoria that sweeps over us and drives away all other thoughts—may be caused by certain chemical excitants flooding into brain structures thought to control love and emotional arousal.

One of the most likely chemical candidates, he says, is phenylethylamine, a natural amphetamine-like substance that has been found by other researchers to have some powerful effects on the behaviour of certain laboratory animals. Mice injected with the substance squeal exuberantly and leap into the air like popcorn, and rhesus monkeys given a closely related compound make kissing sounds. And there is evidence that humans are highly susceptible too. When Liebowitz and colleague Donald Klein treated romance junkies with antidepressants that raise the levels of phenylethylamine in the brain, the patients gradually
240 gave up their hungry search for new mates. "They could settle down and accept life with more stable and appropriate partners," explains Liebowitz.

The Universal Seven-Year Itch

While North Americans vow at the altar to forsake all others, less than 50 percent make good on their promise. But Canadians and Americans are not alone in their adulteries; infidelity is the rule rather than the exception around the world.

The Kuikuru of the Amazonian rainforest, for example, often seek out lovers just a few months after marriage. Kuikuru men and women have been known to juggle as many as twelve extra partners at a time, and their affairs are discussed with great openness and delight in the Amazonian society.

Among traditional Hindu communities in India, adultery is strongly discouraged. But infidelity clearly flourishes anyway. Notes one Sanskrit proverb: "Only when fire will cool, the moon burn, or the ocean fill with tasty water will a woman be pure."

In Japan, specially designated love hotels cater to adulterous couples. Furnished with such exotica as wall-to-wall mirrors, video recorders, whips, and handcuffs, rooms are rented by the hour and enjoy a brisk trade during the day and early evening.

Impressed by such evidence, Liebowitz suggests that neural chemicals play a key part in sparking the giddy excitement of attraction. But the effects of such chemicals are temporary. As time passes, Liebowitz theorizes, nerve endings in the brain may cease to respond to phenylethylamine and a second chemical system kicks into place. Based on such natural narcotics as endorphins, it can endow lovers with the warm, comfortable feelings of a secure attachment. "Unfortunately, that leads people to take dependable partners too much for granted," says Liebowitz. "They think, oh well, somebody else is very attractive, and my long-term relationship is not as exciting as that." Thirsting for the amphetamine high again, many
250 will eventually abandon their partners for someone new.

Even here, in betrayal and divorce, evolutionary theorists such as Fisher see a form of natural logic. Research has shown, she notes, that the powerful attraction phase of love generally lasts from two to three years. And statistics suggest that divorce rates peak in and around the fourth year of marriage. In Fisher's view, the timing is significant. As it happens, women in traditional hunting and gathering societies—which resemble those in which humans first evolved—frequently nurse infants for as long as four years. During that period, they depend on their mates to supply some food and protection. But once a child is weaned and can be cared for by others, the mother may consider switching mates.

"I think four million years ago, there would have been advantages to primitive divorce," says Fisher. "If a male and a female raised a child through infancy and then broke up and 260 formed new pair bonds, what they would actually be doing is creating genetic variety. And that's really critical to evolution."

But, as Fisher concedes, such biologically based codes of conduct may have served as far better in the grasslands of Africa than they do today in a world of divorce lawyers, property settlements, and child-custody battles. As she sets her empty glass on the table, the anthropologist shakes her head at the irony of it all. "Look at the incredible problem we're in. A drive to make a commitment, to love, to remain together. A drive to break up and pair again. And a drive to be adulterous on the side. No wonder we all struggle in every culture in the world." She pauses and smiles. "We are built to struggle." ■

UNDERSTANDING CONTEXT

1. Who, specifically, is Pringle targeting as her audience?

2. Pringle makes many references across time and space, covering a vast range of historical periods and geographical distances. Why? How does this range assist her in explaining and supporting her main point?

EVALUATING STRATEGY

1. What is the purpose of Pringle's essay?

2. Restate the thesis of this essay in your own words.

3. How does Pringle choose to introduce the essay? Does she begin deductively or inductively, and how does this choice influence the effectiveness of the essay opening?

APPRECIATING LANGUAGE

1. Look up the word *woo* in a dictionary. What other terms do you know, both formal and informal, defining the same activity?

2. Locate instances of direct quotation in the essay. How do the quoted passages contribute to the essay's subject?

3. Does Pringle's essay strike you as academic or journalistic in approach? Why?

WRITING SUGGESTIONS

1. Write a well-constructed summary of Pringle's entire essay.

2. Summarize the main distinctions between the nature/nurture (culture) debate to which this essay refers.

3. *Critical thinking:* Are you convinced that human mating behaviour is biological in origin, as the anthropologists in Pringle's essay argue, or do you think human sexual signals are the result of learned behaviour, influenced largely by cultural, political, and economic factors? Write an essay explaining your position, with clear reasons and examples to support your claims.

4. *Reflective writing:* a) Write a two-page description of your own patterns of behaviour concerning human courtship. What dress codes, facial expressions, physical movements, and verbal communication do you rely on for providing sexual signals in situations conducive to "mating" behaviour. b) Now describe the wooing. Patterns of behaviour of a male or female friend. What differences and similarities do you discern?

Blending the Modes   MARIE WINN

Marie Winn was born in Czechoslovakia (now the Czech Republic) and grew up in New York. After completing her education at Radcliffe College, Winn began a career in publishing, writing and editing a number of children's books. While working with children's literature, she explored the effects television has on childhood development. She has written extensively on children and television, publishing articles in **The New York Times** and **The Village Voice.** In 1977 she published an influential study, **The Plug-In Drug: Television, Children and Family,** which was revised in 1985. Her other books include **Children without Childhood** (1983), **Unplugging the Plug-In Drug** (1987), **The Secret Life of Central Park** (1997), and **Red-Tails in Love: A Wildlife Drama in Central Park** (1998). In 2002 Winn published a 25th anniversary edition of **The Plug-In Drug,** subtitled **Television, Computers, and Family Life.**

TV Addiction*

In building her case that television has negative effects, Winn first defines the term "addiction," then argues that television, like drugs and alcohol, damages those who allow it to consume their lives.

Cookies or Heroin?

The word "addiction" is often used loosely and wryly in conversation. People will refer to 1
themselves as "mystery-book addicts" or "cookie addicts." E. B. White wrote of his annual surge of interest in gardening: "We are hooked and are making an attempt to kick the habit." Yet nobody really believes that reading mysteries or ordering seeds by catalogue is serious enough to be compared with addictions to heroin or alcohol. In these cases the word "addiction" is used jokingly to denote a tendency to overindulge in some pleasurable activity.

People often refer to being "hooked on TV." Does this, too, fall into the lighthearted category of cookie eating and other pleasures that people pursue with unusual intensity? Or is there a kind of television viewing that falls into the more serious category of destructive addiction?   10

Not unlike drugs or alcohol, the television experience allows the participant to blot out the real world and enter into a pleasurable and passive mental state. To be sure, other experiences, notably reading, also provide a temporary respite from reality. But it's much easier to stop reading and return to reality than to stop watching television. The entry into another world offered by reading includes an easily accessible return ticket. The entry via television

---

does not. In this way television viewing, for those vulnerable to addiction, is more like drinking or taking drugs—once you start it's hard to stop.

Just as alcoholics are only vaguely aware of their addiction, feeling that they control their drinking more than they really do ("I can cut it out any time I want—I just like to have three or four drinks before dinner"), many people overestimate their control over television watching. Even as they put off other activities to spend hour after hour watching television, they feel they could easily resume living in a different, less passive style. But somehow or other while the television set is present in their homes, it just stays on. With television's easy gratifications available, those other activities seem to take too much effort.

A heavy viewer (a college English instructor) observes:

> *I find television almost irresistible. When the set is on, I cannot ignore it. I can't turn it off. I feel sapped, will-less, enervated. As I reach out to turn off the set, the strength goes out of my arms. So I sit there for hours and hours.*

Self-confessed television addicts often feel they "ought" to do other things—but the fact that they don't read and don't plant their garden or sew or crochet or play games or have conversations means that those activities are no longer as desirable as television viewing. In a way, the lives of heavy viewers are as unbalanced by their television "habit" as drug addicts' or alcoholics' lives. They are living in a holding pattern, as it were, passing up the activities that lead to growth or development or a sense of accomplishment. This is one reason people talk about their television viewing so ruefully, so apologetically. They are aware that it is an unproductive experience, that by any human measure almost any other endeavor is more worthwhile.

It is the adverse effect of television viewing on the lives of so many people that makes it feel like a serious addiction. The television habit distorts the sense of time. It renders other experiences vague and curiously unreal while taking on a greater reality for itself. It weakens relationships by reducing and sometimes eliminating normal opportunities for talking, for communicating.

And yet television does not satisfy, else why would the viewer continue to watch hour after hour, day after day? "The measure of health," wrote the psychiatrist Lawrence Kubie, "is flexibility . . . and especially the freedom to cease when sated." But heavy television viewers can never be sated with their television experiences. These do not provide the true nourishment that satiation requires, and thus they find that they cannot stop watching.

A former heavy watcher, a filmmaker, describes a debilitating television habit:

> *I remember when we first got the set I'd watch for hours and hours, whenever I could, and I remember that feeling of tiredness and anxiety that always followed those orgies, a sense of time terribly wasted. It was like eating cotton candy; television promised so much richness, I couldn't wait for it, and then it just evaporated into air. I remember feeling terribly drained after watching for a long time.*

Similarly a nursery-school teacher remembers her own childhood television experience:

> *I remember bingeing on television when I was a child and having that vapid feeling after watching hours of TV. I'd look forward to watching whenever I could, but*

it just didn't give back a real feeling of pleasure. It was like no orgasm, no catharsis, very frustrating. Television just wasn't giving me the promised satisfaction, and yet I kept on watching. It filled some sort of need, or had to do with an inability to get something started.

The testimonies of ex-television addicts often have the evangelistic overtones of stories   **60**
heard at Alcoholics Anonymous meetings.

A handbag repair-shop owner says:

I'd get on the subway home from work with the newspaper and immediately turn to the TV page to plan out my evening's watching. I'd come home and then we'd watch TV for the rest of the evening. We'd eat our dinner in the living room while watching, and we'd only talk every once in a while, during the ads, if at all. I'd watch anything, good, bad, or indifferent.

All the while we were watching I'd feel terribly angry at myself for wasting all that time watching junk. I could never go to sleep until at least the eleven o'clock news, and then sometimes I'd still stay up for the late-night talk show. I had a feel-   **70**
ing that I had to watch the news programs, even though most of the time nothing much was happening and I could easily find out what by reading the paper the next morning. Usually my wife would fall asleep on the couch while I was watching. I'd get angry at her for doing that. Actually, I was angry at myself.

I had a collection of three years of back issues of different magazines, but I never got around to reading them. I never got around to sorting or labeling my collection of slides I had made when traveling. I only had time for television. We'd take the telephone off the hook while watching so we wouldn't be interrupted! We like classical music, but we never listened to any, never!

Then one day the set broke. I said to my wife, "Let's not fix it. Let's just see what   **80**
happens." Well, that was the smartest thing we ever did. We haven't had a TV in the house since then.

Now I look back and I can hardly believe we could have lived like that. I feel that my mind was completely mummified for all those years. I was glued to that machine and couldn't get loose, somehow. It really frightens me to think of it. Yes, I'm frightened of TV now. I don't think I could control it if we had a set in the house again. I think it would take over no matter what I did.

Heavy television viewers often make comparisons between their viewing habits and substance addictions. Several decades ago, a lawyer reported:

I watch TV the way an alcoholic drinks. If I come home and sit in front of the TV,   **90**
I'll watch any program at all, even if there's nothing on that especially appeals to me. Then the next thing I know it's eleven o'clock and I'm watching the Johnny Carson show, and I'll realize I've spent the whole evening watching TV. What's more, I can't stand Johnny Carson! But I'll still sit there watching him. I'm addicted to TV, when it's there, and I'm not happy about the addiction. I'll sit there getting madder and madder at myself for watching, but still I'll sit there. I can't turn it off.

Nor is the television addict always blind to the dysfunctional aspects of his addiction. A homemaker says:

> *Sometimes a friend will come over while I'm watching TV. I'll say, "Wait a second.*
> 100 *Just let me finish watching this," and then I'll feel bad about that, letting the machine*
> *take precedence over people. And I'll do that for the stupidest programs, just because*
> *I* have *to watch, somehow.*

In spite of the potentially destructive nature of television addiction, it is rarely taken seriously in American society. Critics mockingly refer to television as a "cultural barbiturate" and joke about "mainlining the tube." A spectacle called *Media Burn* perfectly illustrates the feeling of good fun that often surrounds the issue of television addiction. The event, which took place in San Francisco when television was still a young medium, involved the piling up of forty-four old television sets in the parking lot of the Cow Palace, soaking them with kerosene, and applying a torch. According to the programs distributed before the event, 110 everybody was supposed to experience "a cathartic explosion" and "be free at last from the addiction to television."

The issue of television addiction takes on a more serious air when the addicts are our own children. A mother reports:

> *My ten-year-old is as hooked on TV as an alcoholic is hooked on drink. He tries to*
> *strike desperate bargains: "If you let me watch just ten more minutes, I won't watch*
> *at all tomorrow," he says. It's pathetic. It scares me.*

A number of years ago a mother described her six-year-old son's need to watch:

> *We were in Israel last summer where the TV stations sign off for the night at about ten.*
> *Well, my son would turn on the set and watch the Arabic stations that were still on,*
> 120 *even though he couldn't understand a word, just because he had to watch something.*

Other signs of serious addiction come out in parents' descriptions of their children's viewing behavior:

> *We used to have very bad reception before we got on Cable TV. I'd come into the*
> *room and see my eight-year-old watching this terrible, blurry picture and I'd say,*
> *"Heavens, how can you see? Let me try to fix it," and he'd get frantic and scream,*
> *"Don't touch it!" It really worried me, that he wanted to watch so badly that he was*
> *even willing to watch a completely blurred image.*

Another mother tells of her eight-year-old son's behavior when deprived of television:

> *There was a time when both TV sets were out for about two weeks, and Jerry reached a*
> 130 *point where I felt that if he didn't watch something, he was really going to start climbing*
> *the walls. He was fidgety and nervous. He'd crawl all over the furniture. He just didn't*
> *know what to do with himself, and it seemed to get worse every day. I said to my hus-*
> *band, "He's having withdrawal symptoms," and I really think that's what it was. Finally*
> *I asked one of my friends if he could go and watch the Saturday cartoons at their house.*

In the early 1980s Robin Smith, a graduate student at the University of Massachusetts in Amherst, conducted a research study on television addiction as part of a doctoral dissertation. Setting out to discover whether television viewing can truly be classified as an addiction according to a particular, narrow definition she had constructed from the work of various social scientists, Smith sent out a questionnaire to 984 adults in Springfield, Massachusetts, in which they were asked to rate their own behavior in regard to television viewing. Using a number of statistical tests to analyze the responses, the author concluded that the results failed to confirm that television addiction exists. "Television addiction does not appear to be a robust phenomenon," Smith wrote in that poetic yet obscure way academics sometimes have of expressing things.

Striving to understand why television is so widely considered an addiction, in the conclusion of her research paper Smith noted:

> . . . the popularity of television as "plug-in drug" is enduring. One possible source of this image lies in the nature of viewing experience. The only study to date that examines the nature of the viewing experience in adults found that television watching, of all life activities measured in the course of one week, was the least challenging, involved the least amount of skill, and was most relaxing.

If television viewing is so bereft of value by most measures of well-being, and yet takes up the greatest part of people's leisure hours, it becomes moot whether it is defined as an addiction or simply a powerful habit. As psychologists Robert Kubey and Mihaly Csikszentmihalyi concluded in their book about the television experience: "A long-held habit becomes so ingrained that it borders on addiction. A person may no longer be watching television because of simple want, but because he or she virtually has to. Other alternatives may seem to become progressively more remote. What might have been a choice years earlier is now a necessity."

Robert Kubey explains further: "While television can provide relaxation and entertainment . . . it still rarely delivers any lasting fulfillment. Only through active engagement with the worlds we inhabit and the people in them can we attain for ourselves the rewards and meaning that lead to psychological well-being." ∎

UNDERSTANDING CONTEXT

1. How does Winn define "addiction"? How does addiction, in her view, differ from overindulgence in something pleasurable?

2. Describe the negative effects Winn sees in habitual television viewing.

3. How does the simple ease and accessibility of watching television versus going out to a movie contribute to making television so addictive?

4. One viewer Winn quotes states, "I had the feeling that I *had* to watch the news programs, that I *had* to know what was happening." Today are more people likely to feel almost obligated to watch television to be informed, to be a good citizen? Can the news be as dangerously addicting as entertainment shows?

5. *Critical thinking:* Do you think that many of Winn's observations about television addiction describe people who feel compelled to spend hours on the Internet? Can cyberspace be just as addictive and just as harmful?

EVALUATING STRATEGY

1. Why is it important for Winn to first define "addiction" before moving to her argument about television?

2. How effective is her use of interviews or case studies of television viewers? Is it important to hear from the "addicts" in their own words?

3. *Other modes:* How much of this definition essay can be considered a *persuasive argument?* What role do *description* and *narration* play in developing the definition?

APPRECIATING LANGUAGE

1. Winn quotes one viewer who reports that television leaves him "sapped, will-less, enervated." How important are words like these to argue that television is addictive?

2. Winn uses the word *sated* twice over the course of two lines. Look this up in a dictionary. Why is it a key word in defining an addiction?

3. *Critical thinking:* Would some people object to applying the word *addiction* to an activity that is not life threatening? Drugs and alcohol, after all, lead to disease and early death. Does using the term in other contexts weaken its impact?

WRITING SUGGESTIONS

1. Write a short analysis of your own childhood experiences with television. How many hours did you watch a day? What were your favourite programs? Did television add to or detract from your development? Did you forgo studying, playing with other children, reading, or spending time with your family to watch television?

2. *Collaborative writing:* Working with a group of other students, write a paper instructing parents step by step how to monitor their children's viewing habits. How can parents prevent their children from becoming television addicts?

Writing beyond the Classroom   DON ROSENBERG

Don Rosenberg is a psychologist and therapist in Milwaukee. He wrote the following definition of depression for a brochure to be distributed in a mental health clinic.

What Is Depression?*

As you read this definition, notice that it is directed to people who may suffer from depression. How does it differ from a definition of depression you might find in a psychology textbook?

Depression is an internal state—a feeling of sadness, loss, "the blues," deep disappointment. 1 *When it is more severe, you may have feelings of irritability, touchiness, guilt, self-reproach, loss of self-esteem, worthlessness, hopelessness, helplessness, and even thoughts of death and suicide.* It may include such other feelings as tearfulness, being sensitive and easily hurt, loss of interests, loss of sexual drive, loss of control in life, feeling drained and depleted, anger at yourself, and loss of the ability to feel pleasure.

It may be accompanied by *physical symptoms* similar to the sense of profound loss, including:

- *loss of appetite*, often with weight loss, but sometimes we find increased eating
- *insomnia or early-morning waking*, often 2–4 times per night, nearly every day, but some-   10 times we see a need to sleep excessively
- moving and speaking slows down, but sometimes we see *agitation*
- *fatigue or loss of energy* nearly every day
- *loss of concentration*, foggy and indecisive
- sometimes includes anxious and headachy feelings and also *frequent crying*

Besides the physical sensations and emotions of depression, depressed people may *withdraw, may brood or ruminate about problems,* have trouble remembering things, wonder if they would be better off dead, and become very concerned about bodily symptoms and pains. They may be grouchy, sulking, restless, and unwilling to interact with family and friends. ■   20

UNDERSTANDING CONTEXT

1. What role does definition play in the treatment of any disorder? Do people need to find a name or label for what troubles them? Is that the first step to coping with or resolving a problem?

---

*Rosenberg, Don, "What Is Depression?" reprinted by permission of the author.

2. Can you define *depression* in your own words?

3. What are the physical symptoms of depression?

EVALUATING STRATEGY

1. How effective are the techniques used for emphasis—italics, bulleted points?

2. How is the message directed to its readers? Do you sense that only those experiencing these symptoms are likely to read this document?

APPRECIATING LANGUAGE

1. How does Rosenberg describe depression? Do the words create impressions people are likely to recognize?

2. There are few technical or professional terms in this definition. Does this sacrifice accuracy? Why or why not?

WRITING SUGGESTIONS

1. Take a definition from the glossary section of a textbook and write a general version for an audience of clients, consumers, or students.

2. *Collaborative writing:* Discuss a common problem or issue with fellow students: job insecurity, lack of sleep, stressful family relationships, stalking, or child care. Select a term you often overhear and provide a clear definition for it. Have each member of the group list features of this term. Try to incorporate objective elements. Have the group prepare two versions—one designed for an "official" publication, such as a college or university textbook, the other for an informal handout.

Responding to IMAGES

© *Tom Stewart/CORBIS*

1. How do you define patriotism? Do you think people who display the flag are patriotic? Can people disagree with the government and their leaders and still be patriots?

2. Do many people in your neighbourhood display a flag? Do they have anything in common? Do Canadians have the same response to their flag as Americans do to theirs?

3. *Critical thinking:* Do you think some people misuse the idea of patriotism to camouflage ideas and attitudes that run counter to the *Charter of Rights and Freedoms?* Why or why not?

4. *Visual analysis:* What does the composition of this photograph suggest to you? Would the image have different meaning if the person flying the flag was a firefighter, a woman in a business suit, an African American, a student with long hair, a biker, or a Muslim woman wearing a scarf? Would the image be different if the structure in the background was a school, a police station, a mobile home, or a yacht? Why or why not?

5. *Collaborative writing:* Discuss this photograph with a group of students. Ask them to write down their immediate reaction to the image. Share the responses and discuss differences of opinions. What does this image reveal about people's perceptual worlds? Work together to create one or more captions that express the view or views of your group.

☑ DEFINITION **CHECKLIST**

Before submitting your paper, review these points:

✔ Is your purpose clear—to inform or persuade?

✔ Do you avoid defining a word with the same word, such as "a diffusion pump diffuses"?

✔ Is your level of technical or professional language suited to your audience?

✔ Does your definition provide enough information and examples so that readers can restate your thesis in their own words?

✔ Are there existing definitions you can use for reference or contrast?

✔ Do extended definitions contain illustrations, narratives, or comparisons readers may misinterpret or not recognize?

✔ Do you state the essence of your definition in a short summary statement readers can remember or highlight for future reference?

COMPANION WEBSITE

See **http://www.transcanadawriter.nelson.com** for additional information on writing definitions.

CHAPTER 16

Comparison and Contrast: Analyzing Similarities and Differences

This chapter examines the analytical method of comparison and contrast. It offers guidance in investigating commonalities and differences between things, and it offers strategies for developing writing that is structured through comparison and contrast.

WHAT IS COMPARISON AND CONTRAST?

Comparison and contrast is an analytical mode that answers the question, *How are things alike or different?* What distinguishes a gasoline engine from a diesel engine? What is the difference between Sunni and Shia Muslims? What do Quebec's Parti Quebecois and Bloc Quebecois hold in common? All of these questions can be addressed by analyzing similarities and differences.

You have probably encountered questions on essay examinations that require comparison-and-contrast responses:

Which arrangement offers business owners greater protection of personal assets—full or limited partnerships?

Contrast Freud's dream theory with Jung's concept of the unconscious.

At the end of *The Great Gatsby,* Nick Carraway decides to return to the West because he is too "squeamish" for the East. What differences did Fitzgerald see between the East and West?

Outline the principal differences between warm- and cold-blooded animals.

Comparison-and-contrast writing is commonly used to organize research papers. You might compare two short stories by Timothy Findley in an English course, explain the differences between methods of depreciation in accounting, or contrast conflicting theories of childhood development in psychology.

The Purposes of Comparison and Contrast

Writers use comparison and contrast for two basic purposes:

1. **To *explain* by drawing distinctions between related subjects.** When writers draw distinctions, they explain differences between similar subjects but do not choose one over the other. Comparison can pair extended definitions to show readers the difference, for example, between air-cooled and water-cooled engines, or African and Indian elephants.

2. **To *persuade* readers to make a choice.** Comparison also is used to outline advantages and disadvantages to demonstrate the superiority or desirability of one subject over another. For example, television commercials compare competing products.

SELECTING TOPICS FOR COMPARISON-AND-CONTRAST PAPERS

When developing a paper using comparison and contrast, you must be sure your subjects share enough common points for meaningful discussion. Comparing a sports car to a pickup truck or an adventure film to a romantic comedy is not likely to generate more than superficial observations. Comparisons have to be carefully limited, especially for comparisons of broad or complex subjects.

▉ WRITING **ACTIVITY**

Use exploratory techniques to develop ideas on the following pairs. If you are unfamiliar with one topic, select another one that stimulates your thoughts. List similarities and note differences. Consider how you might limit the scope of your comparison. Your goal may be to inform or recommend.

1. Two people you know well: your parents, two bosses, or two close friends
2. Canadian versus Asian attitudes toward family, career, marriage, or government
3. Your generation's attitudes or values versus those of your parents' generation
4. Liberal versus conservative views of government, justice, poverty, or national defense
5. Two popular bands, filmmakers, fashion designers, or political candidates
6. Print versus online journalism

ORGANIZING COMPARISON-AND-CONTRAST PAPERS

Perhaps the greatest challenge writers face in writing comparison and contrast is organizing ideas. Without careful planning, you may find yourself shifting awkwardly back and forth between subjects. Your reader may have difficulty following your train of thought and may confuse one subject with another. Whether drawing distinctions or making recommendations, writers use two basic methods of organizing comparison-and-contrast writing.

Subject by Subject

The *subject-by-subject* method divides the paper into two sections. Writers state all the information about topic A and then discuss topic B. Usually, the actual comparisons are drawn in the second part of the paper, where B is discussed in relation to A.

Advantages

- The subject-by-subject method is a simple, straightforward method of organizing your essay and thus is useful if you have limited time.
- The subject-by-subject method is suited for short, highly readable papers.
- Abstract topics, such as economic theories, religious beliefs, and scientific principles, are often easier to organize in a subject-by-subject method because few individual features are shared by both subjects.

Disadvantages

- Long papers organized subject by subject can be difficult to follow. It can be difficult for readers to recall enough details from the first subject to appreciate how it differs from the second.
- Because subjects are discussed separately, it can be difficult to present specific facts side by side. Readers are forced to page back and forth to compare details, such as prices and statistics.

Point by Point

The *point-by-point* method organizes the comparison of A and B on a series of specific subtopics. Following an introduction, A and B are discussed in a number of comparisons. Hotels, for example, have common features—location, appearance, atmosphere, number of rooms, banquet facilities, and rates—so, a writer could organize information about two hotels in each paragraph and state her clear preference for one of the hotels in both the introduction and conclusion.

Advantages

- The point-by-point method is useful in organizing long papers that can be broken into units. Instead of splitting a 20-page report into two 10-page sections, you can create a series of related comparisons.
- This method allows writers to place specific details side by side so that readers can easily compare prices, dimensions, and figures without having to search through the entire document.

■ A point-by-point approach is useful in preparing a document for multiple readers. Because it is organized in sections, a reader can easily isolate the information most relevant to his or her purpose.

Disadvantages

■ The point-by-point method can be difficult to use if the subjects are abstract and lack detail. Comparing two philosophies or two films may be easier to organize by discussing each separately.

■ The point-by-point method can distort a topic if the specific points of comparison are poorly chosen. Major issues can be overlooked or minimized and minor details overemphasized unless the categories are carefully planned.

Blending the Methods

Writers often blend elements of both methods in a single essay. As you read the comparison-and-contrast entries in this chapter you will notice that few exactly fit either method. But as with all writing, clear organization is essential to avoid confusion, especially when your essay addresses more than one topic.

WRITING **ACTIVITY**

Select ideas from the previous exercise or develop ones from the following topics and create an outline using the subject-by-subject method, point-by-point method, or a blend of methods.

1. The sense of privacy in a small town versus a large city
2. Media images of P.E.I. and Newfoundland
3. The quality of a football team's offence and defence
4. Reality TV's heroes and villains
5. Male and female attitudes about sex, dating, or relationships

Strategies for Writing Comparison and Contrast

Critical Thinking and Prewriting

1. **List topics in a tandem fashion.** You can start by developing a series of possible topics by listing pairs of items:

Personal digital assistant (PDA) & paper day planner	U.S. & Canadian health care
English only & bilingual schools	VHS & DVD

2. **Choose related topics.** The subjects you select must have enough in common to establish meaningful similarities and enough in contrast to distinguish them to establish more than trivial differences.

3. **Select a single topic that has changed.** Instead of comparing two people, two jobs, or two neighbourhoods, you might write a before-and-after essay that shows how a subject has changed over time.

4. **Avoid superficial comparisons.**

5. **Determine your purpose.** Is your goal to explain differences between two topics or to recommend one subject over another? Do you wish to inform readers, or do you wish to persuade them to make a choice?

5. **Examine categories for balance.** Ensure that you avoid weighting your essay to favour one subject over another by stressing the advantages of one while emphasizing the disadvantages of another.

6. **Consider the appropriateness of using visuals.** Can you present contrasting photographs or images to dramatize similarities and differences? Can you create graphs or charts to demonstrate differences in facts, number, or statistics?

7. **Test ideas through peer review.** You may gain new insights on your subject by asking fellow students and friends for their thoughts and reactions.

Planning

1. **Consider your audience.** Before you can compare two items, you may have to explain background information.

2. **Review the scope of the assignment and your thesis.** Because you are discussing more than a single topic, it is important to focus your subject.

3. **Determine which method suits your purpose.** A short, nontechnical paper might be best organized using the subject-by-subject method. Longer works with details that should be placed side by side are better developed using the point-by-point method.

4. **Clearly state your thesis.** Whether your goal is to inform or persuade, your comparison needs a well-stated thesis.

5. **Prioritize points.** Determine the most important points of comparison. You may develop many ideas that you may not have space or time to fully develop.

6. **Develop an outline.** Because you are handling two topics, you may find that you need a more detailed outline to write a comparison than to write a narrative or description.

Writing the First Draft

1. **Focus on the goal of your comparison to guide the draft.** Because you are addressing two subjects, you can easily get distracted. Use your thesis to direct your writing.

2. **Get your ideas on paper by writing separate descriptions.** If you find it difficult to get started or follow a detailed outline, it may be easier to describe each subject separately.

3. **Most comparisons consist of paired descriptions.** Make your descriptions effective by creating dominant impressions, describing people and objects in action, and including dialogue to give voice to people.

(Continued)

4. **Use parallel structures to organize comparisons.** Readers will find your ideas easier to follow and easier to evaluate if you place ideas in a consistent pattern.

5. **Be aware of the impact of connotations.** The words you select in describing your topics will influence your readers' interpretations.

6. **Keep the length of your paper in mind as you write.** It is always difficult to measure how many ideas and details you will develop as you write. When you discuss two topics, you may find your essay lengthening.

Revising

1. **Review your plan and read your draft for its overall impact.**
   - Is the thesis clear? Does your paper accurately establish differences or effectively state a recommendation?
   - Is each subject fully developed and fairly described with enough detail?
   - Is the draft focused? Or is it too long, too confused?
   - Does the draft fulfill the needs of the assignment?

2. **Evaluate the way you describe or define each subject.**
   - Do you accurately and precisely define what you are comparing?
   - Have you limited the topics?
   - Are there misconceptions or vague statements that require greater clarity?

3. **Review the organization.**
   - Is the paper logically organized? Should you consider rewriting the paper using a different method?

4. **Examine the information you have included.**
   - Does the essay present enough facts, observations, and details about both subjects?

5. **Evaluate transitions between ideas.**
   - Can readers follow your train of thought? Are there clear shifts from one topic to another?
   - Can paragraph breaks and other devices help readers follow your ideas?

6. **Review the emphasis of main points.**
   - Are the main points of the comparison clearly highlighted and easy to remember?

7. **Study the impact of the introduction and conclusion.**
   - Does the introduction set up the comparison and introduce your purpose and thesis?
   - Does the conclusion make a final impression, restate the significant differences, or reinforce your recommendations?

8. **Evaluate the use of any visuals.** If you included visual aids, examine them carefully. Do they clearly illustrate similarities and differences in your subjects? Do the images add value to your writing, or are they unrelated or distracting? Are graphs or charts based on accurate data? Are the visual aids easy to understand?

Editing and Proofreading

1. **Read the paper (aloud).** Listen to your sentences.
   - Are there awkward or repetitive phrases?
   - Do any passages require streamlining or greater detail?
2. **Review your choice of words.**
   - Do you accurately define each subject and main points?
   - Do the connotations of your words reflect your meaning?
3. **Use peer editing to identify problems you may have overlooked.**

SUGGESTED TOPICS FOR WRITING COMPARISON AND CONTRAST

General Assignments

Write a comparison paper on one of the following topics. You may use either subject-by-subject or point-by-point methods of organization. Your paper will likely blend both of these approaches. *Clearly determine your purpose—to inform or persuade.*

- High school and college or university
- The two most influential teachers/coaches/supervisors you have known
- Two popular sitcoms/newsmagazines/soap operas/talk shows/reality shows
- Your best and worst college or university courses
- Your parents' values and your own
- A subject that has changed over time, such as a friend's attitude, a job's appeal, a band's popularity

Writing in Context

1. Write the text for a brief pamphlet directed to high school seniors comparing high school and college or university.

2. Write an e-mail to a friend comparing the best and worst aspects of your college or university, dorm, neighbourhood, or job.

3. Examine a magazine article on cars, computers, or entertainment. Write an e-mail to the editor commenting on the magazine's best and worst features.

4. Compare two popular restaurants for a review in the campus newspaper. Direct your comments to students who are interested in inexpensive but healthy and delicious food.

Strategies for Reading Comparison and Contrast

In reading the comparison-and-contrast essays in this chapter, keep these questions in mind:

Context

1. What is the writer's goal—to draw distinctions or to recommend a choice?

2. What details does the writer present about each subject?

3. Who is the intended audience? Is the essay directed to a general or a specific reader?

4. Is the comparison valid? Is the writer comparing two subjects in a fair manner? Have any points been overlooked?

5. Does the author have an apparent bias?

6. If the comparison makes a recommendation, does the selection seem valid? What makes the chosen subject superior to others? What evidence is presented?

Strategy

1. What is the basic pattern of the comparison—subject by subject, point by point, or a blend?

2. Does the author use a device to narrow the topic or to advance the comparison?

3. Does the writer use visual aids, such as graphs, charts, or highlighted text?

4. Is the essay easy to follow? Are transitions between subjects clearly established by paragraph breaks and other devices?

Language

1. Does the writer use words with connotations that ascribe positive or negative qualities to one or both of the subjects? How does the author characterize the topics?

2. What does the diction, level of language, and use of technical terms reveal about the intended audience?

3. If the writer is suggesting a choice, how does the language demonstrate his or her preference?

BRUCE CATTON

Bruce Catton (1899–1978) grew up listening to stories of Civil War veterans. His own college career was interrupted by service in the First World War. Catton went to work as a reporter for the **Cleveland Plain Dealer** and later served as information director for several government agencies. In 1953 his book **A Stillness at Appomattox** became a bestseller, and Catton received a Pulitzer Prize. He wrote several other books about the Civil War and edited **American Heritage** magazine for two decades.

Grant and Lee*

Perhaps no other essay is as widely anthologized as a sample of comparison writing than Catton's "Grant and Lee," which first appeared in a collection, The American Story. *Directed to a general audience, the essay seeks to contrast the two most famous generals of the Civil War.*

When Ulysses S. Grant and Robert E. Lee met in the parlor of a modest house at Appomattox   1
Court House, Virginia, on April 9, 1865, to work out the terms for the surrender of Lee's Army of Northern Virginia, a great chapter in American life came to a close, and a great new chapter began.

These men were bringing the Civil War to its virtual finish. To be sure, other armies had yet to surrender, and for a few days the fugitive Confederate government would struggle desperately and vainly, trying to find some way to go on living now that its chief support was gone. But in effect it was all over when Grant and Lee signed the papers. And the little room where they wrote out the terms was the scene of one of the poignant, dramatic contrasts in American history.   10

They were two strong men, these oddly different generals, and they represented the strengths of two conflicting currents that, through them, had come into final collision.

Back of Robert E. Lee was the notion that the old aristocratic concept might somehow survive and be dominant in American life.

Lee was tidewater Virginia, and in his background were family, culture, and tradition . . . the age of chivalry transplanted to a New World which was making its own legends and its own myths. He embodied a way of life that had come down through the age of knighthood and the English country squire. America was a land that was beginning all over again, dedicated to nothing much more complicated than the rather hazy belief that all men had equal rights and should have an equal chance in the world. In such a land Lee stood for the feeling   20
that it was somehow of advantage to human society to have a pronounced inequality in the social structure. There should be a leisure class, backed by ownership of land; in turn, society

---

*Catton, Bruce, "Grant and Lee" from *The American Story* by Earll Schenk Miers. Reprinted by permission of the U.S. Capital Historical Society.

itself should be keyed to the land as the chief source of wealth and influence. It would bring forth (according to this ideal) a class of men with a strong sense of obligation to the community; men who lived not to gain advantage for themselves, but to meet the solemn obligations which had been laid on them by the very fact that they were privileged. From them the country would get its leadership; to them it could look for the higher values—of thought, of conduct, of personal deportment—to give it strength and virtue.

30   Lee embodied the noblest elements of this aristocratic ideal. Through him, the landed nobility justified itself. For four years, the Southern states had fought a desperate war to uphold the ideals for which Lee stood. In the end, it almost seemed as if the Confederacy fought for Lee; as if he himself was the Confederacy . . . the best thing that the way of life for which the Confederacy stood could ever have to offer. He had passed into legend before Appomattox. Thousands of tired, underfed, poorly clothed Confederate soldiers, long since past the simple enthusiasm of the early days of the struggle, somehow considered Lee the symbol of everything for which they had been willing to die. But they could not quite put this feeling into words. If the Lost Cause, sanctified by so much heroism and so many deaths, had a living justification, its justification was General Lee.

40   Grant, the son of a tanner on the Western frontier, was everything Lee was not. He had come up the hard way and embodied nothing in particular except the eternal toughness and sinewy fiber of the men who grew up beyond the mountains. He was one of a body of men who owed reverence and obeisance to no one, who were self-reliant to a fault, who cared hardly anything for the past but who had a sharp eye for the future.

These frontier men were the precise opposite of the tidewater aristocrats. Back of them, in the great surge that had taken people over the Alleghenies and into the opening Western country, there was a deep, implicit dissatisfaction with a past that had settled into grooves. They stood for democracy, not from any reasoned conclusion about the proper ordering of human society, but simply because they had grown up in the middle

50   of democracy and knew how it worked. Their society might have privileges, but they would be privileges each man had won for himself. Forms and patterns meant nothing. No man was born to anything, except perhaps to a chance to show how far he could rise. Life was competition.

Yet along with this feeling had come a deep sense of belonging to a national community. The Westerner who developed a farm, opened a shop, or set up in business as a trader, could hope to prosper only as his own community prospered—and his community ran from the Atlantic to the Pacific and from Canada down to Mexico. If the land was settled, with towns and highways and accessible markets, he could better himself. He saw his fate in terms of the nation's own destiny. As its horizons expanded, so did his. He had, in other words, an acute

60   dollars-and-cents stake in the continued growth and development of his country.

And that, perhaps, is where the contrast between Grant and Lee becomes most striking. The Virginia aristocrat, inevitably, saw himself in relation to his own region. He lived in a static society which could endure almost anything except change. Instinctively, his first loyalty would go to the locality in which that society existed. He would fight to the limit of endurance to defend it, because in defending it he was defending everything that gave his own life its deepest meaning.

The Westerner, on the other hand, would fight with an equal tenacity for the broader concept of society. He fought so because everything he lived by was tied to growth, expansion, and a constantly widening horizon. What he lived by would survive or fall with the nation itself. He could not possibly stand by unmoved in the face of an attempt to destroy 70 the Union. He would combat it with everything he had, because he could only see it as an effort to cut the ground out from under his feet.

So Grant and Lee were in complete contrast, representing two diametrically opposed elements in American life. Grant was the modern man emerging; beyond him, ready to come on the stage, was the great age of steel and machinery, of crowded cities and a restless burgeoning vitality. Lee might have ridden down from the old age of chivalry, lance in hand, silken banner fluttering over his head. Each man was the perfect champion of his cause, drawing both his strengths and his weaknesses from the people he led.

Yet it was not all contrast, after all. Different as they were—in background, in personality, in underlying aspiration—these two great soldiers had much in common. Under every- 80 thing else, they were marvelous fighters. Furthermore, their fighting qualities were really very much alike.

Each man had, to begin with, the great virtue of utter tenacity and fidelity. Grant fought his way down the Mississippi Valley in spite of acute personal discouragement and profound military handicaps. Lee hung on in the trenches at Petersburg after hope itself had died. In each man there was an indomitable quality. . . . the born fighter's refusal to give up as long as he can still remain on his feet and lift his two fists.

Daring and resourcefulness they had, too; the ability to think faster and move faster than the enemy. These were the qualities which gave Lee the dazzling campaigns of Second Manassas and Chancellorsville and won Vicksburg for Grant. 90

Lastly, and perhaps greatest of all, there was the ability, at the end, to turn quickly from war to peace once the fighting was over. Out of the way these two men behaved at Appomattox came the possibility of a peace of reconciliation. It was a possibility not wholly realized, in the years to come, but which did, in the end, help the two sections to become one nation again . . . after a war whose bitterness might have seemed to make such a reunion wholly impossible. No part of either man's life became him more than the part he played in their brief meeting in the McLean house at Appomattox. Their behavior there put all succeeding generations of Americans in their debt. Two great Americans, Grant and Lee— very different, yet under everything very much alike. Their encounter at Appomattox was one of the great moments of American history. ■ 100

UNDERSTANDING CONTEXT

1. What does Catton see as the most striking difference between the generals?

2. How did Grant and Lee differ in background and sense of allegiance?

3. What were the historical forces that shaped the two men?

4. *Critical thinking:* Essentially, Catton is telling the story of a confrontation between victor and vanquished, yet his account does not seem to depict the men as winner and loser. Catton does not dwell on what made Grant victorious or on the causes for Lee's defeat. What does this reveal about his purpose?

EVALUATING STRATEGY

1. How does Catton organize the essay?

2. *Critical thinking:* The Civil War was, in part, a battle over slavery. Catton does not mention this issue. Does his account appear to be ethically neutral, suggesting that neither side was morally superior in its war aims?

APPRECIATING LANGUAGE

1. Does Catton appear to be neutral or biased in his description of the two men?

2. What does the tone, level of language, and word choice suggest about Catton's intended audience?

WRITING SUGGESTIONS

1. Write an essay comparing two people in the same profession. Compare two teachers, coaches, landlords, attorneys, ministers, or coworkers. Try to focus on their personalities and philosophies rather than on their appearance. You may wish to limit your paper to a specific attitude, situation, or behaviour.

2. *Collaborative writing:* Work with a group of students to write a short dramatic scene based on Catton's essay. Use set descriptions to establish the locale, and invent dialogue. Discuss with members of the group how Lee and Grant might have sounded. What words might they have chosen? How would their vocabulary indicate their different backgrounds?

RACHEL CARSON

Rachel Carson (1907–1964) was a marine biologist known for the literary quality of her writing. She won critical acclaim with her first two books, **The Sea Around Us** (1951) and **The Edge of the Sea** (1955). Then, in 1962, she hit the bestseller list with **Silent Spring**, a frightening exposé of the hazards that insecticides and weed killers were posing to both wildlife and human beings. As much as anything else, this one book can be said to have launched the modern environmental movement.

A Fable for Tomorrow*

Rapid industrialization both in manufacturing and agriculture brought unprecedented material advantages to the developed world throughout the first half of the 20th century. At the same time, insufficient notice was being taken of the damages such industrialization was inflicting on the natural environment. Although Silent Spring is a well-researched book by a reputable scientist, it is intended for a general audience. The following preface to that book is an imaginative rendering of the eventual consequences of continued indifference to the environment.

There was once a town in the heart of America where all life seemed to live in harmony 1
with its surroundings. The town lay in the midst of a checkerboard of prosperous farms, with fields of grain and hillsides of orchards where, in spring, white clouds of bloom drifted above the green fields. In autumn, oak and maple and birch set up a blaze of color that flamed and flickered across a backdrop of pines. Then foxes barked in the hills and deer silently crossed the fields, half hidden in the mists of the fall mornings.

Along the roads, laurel, viburnum and alder, great ferns and wildflowers delighted the traveler's eye through much of the year. Even in winter the roadsides were places of beauty, where countless birds came to feed on the berries and on the seed heads of the dried weeds rising above the snow. The countryside was, in fact, famous for the abundance and variety of 10
its bird life, and when the flood of migrants was pouring through in spring and fall people traveled from great distances to observe them. Others came to fish the streams, which flowed clear and cold out of the hills and contained shady pools where trout lay. So it had been from the days many years ago when the first settlers raised their houses, sank their wells, and built their barns.

Then a strange blight crept over the area and everything began to change. Some evil spell had settled on the community: mysterious maladies swept the flocks of chickens; the cattle and sheep sickened and died. Everywhere was a shadow of death. The farmers spoke of much illness among their families. In the town the doctors had become more and more puzzled by new kinds of sickness appearing among their patients. There had been several sudden and 20
unexplained deaths, not only among adults but even among children, who would be stricken suddenly while at play and die within a few hours.

There was a strange stillness. The birds, for example—where had they gone? Many people spoke of them, puzzled and disturbed. The feeding stations in the backyards were deserted. The few birds seen anywhere were moribund; they trembled violently and could not fly. It was a spring without voices. On the mornings that had once throbbed with the dawn chorus of robins, catbirds, doves, jays, wrens, and scores of other bird voices there was now no sound; only silence lay over the fields and woods and marsh.

On the farms the hens brooded, but no chicks hatched. The farmers complained that 30 they were unable to raise any pigs—the litters were small and the young survived only a few days. The apple trees were coming into bloom but no bees droned among the blossoms, so there was no pollination and there would be no fruit.

The roadsides, once so attractive, were now lined with browned and withered vegetation as though swept by fire. These, too, were silent, deserted by all living things. Even the streams were now lifeless. Anglers no longer visited them, for all the fish had died.

In the gutters under the eaves and between the shingles of the roofs, a white granular powder still showed a few patches; some weeks before it had fallen like snow upon the roofs and the lawns, the fields and streams.

No witchcraft, no enemy action had silenced the rebirth of new life in this stricken 40 world. The people had done it themselves.

This town does not actually exist, but it might easily have a thousand counterparts in America or elsewhere in the world. I know of no community that has experienced all the misfortunes I describe. Yet every one of these disasters has actually happened somewhere, and many real communities have already suffered a substantial number of them. A grim specter has crept upon us almost unnoticed, and this imagined tragedy may easily become a stark reality we all shall know.

What has already silenced the voices of spring in countless towns in America? This book is an attempt to explain. ◼

UNDERSTANDING CONTEXT

1. What sort of a world does Carson describe in the first two paragraphs of the essay?

2. Can you tell exactly what it is that causes the change between the world of the first two paragraphs and the world described next? What do you know about what caused the devastation?

3. What does Carson mean when she says the people had done it themselves?

4. What is Carson's purpose in providing this fictional account of destruction?

EVALUATING STRATEGY

1. Note each reference to silence. How do all of those references relate to the title of the book Carson is introducing, *Silent Spring?*

2. How does Carson use a "before and after" comparison to make her point?

APPRECIATING LANGUAGE

1. The first two paragraphs describe the town in almost fairy-tale language. In the remainder of the essay, which specific words help capture the negative atmosphere that Carson is trying to create?

2. Although Carson is a scientist, she chose to use in this introduction language that would be easily understood by the layperson. Why do you think she might have made that choice?

WRITING SUGGESTIONS

1. You may have seen specific places go through a transformation on a smaller scale of the sort Carson describes. Write two paragraphs in which you first describe a place as you once knew it and then as it exists now.

2. People also go through transformations. Write two paragraphs in which you first describe a person as he or she once was, then describe that person as he or she is now.

NORA EPHRON

Nora Ephron, born in New York City in 1941, is a well-known American journalist, publishing essays in magazines such as **The New York Times Magazine, Esquire,** and **New York Magazine.** She has written two best-selling collections of essays and the novel **Heartburn.**

The New Porn*

In her essay Ephron explores society's growing fascination with haute cuisine and the high costs of these meals. She presents her argument by using expensive meals as an example of a current decadent trend in society. She compares this trend to a form of pornography.

1 Every so often, I manage to get through the day without reading the *New York Times*. This is an extremely risky thing to do—you never know whether the day you skip the *Times* will turn out to be the one day when some fascinating article will appear and leave you to spend the rest of your life explaining to friends who bring it up that you missed it. Fortunately, this rarely happens. But on Friday, November 14, 1975, I managed to miss the *New York Times*, and I learned my lesson.

That, as it happens, was the day the *Times* ran a page-one story by its food writer Craig Claiborne about a four-thousand-dollar meal he and his friend Pierre Franey ate at a Paris restaurant, and I think it is safe to say that no article the *Times* has printed in the last year
10 has generated as much response. (The only recent exception that comes to mind is one that Charlotte Curtis wrote about cottage cheese.) In any case, a few days later, in desperation, I went back and read it. As you undoubtedly know, Claiborne had bid three hundred dollars in an auction for dinner for two at any restaurant in the world; because American Express was footing the bill, there was a stipulation that the restaurant be on the American Express card. Claiborne chose to dine at a chic spot on the Right Bank called Chez Denis, and there he and Franey managed to get through thirty-one courses and nine wines. Two things were immediately clear to me when I read the article: first, that the meal had been a real disappointment, though Craig only hinted at that with a few cutting remarks about the blandness of the sorrel soup and the nothingness of the sweetbread parfait; and second,
20 that the *Times* had managed to give front-page play to a story that was essentially a gigantic publicity stunt for American Express. What good sports the people at American Express were about the entire episode! How jolly they were about paying the bill! 'We were mildly astonished at first but now we're cheerful about it,' a spokesman for the company said—and well he might have been. Four thousand dollars is a small price to pay for the amount of corporate good will the article generated—and that outraged me; I have dealt with the people at American Express about money on several occasions, and they have never been cheerful with *me*.

*Ephron, Nora, "The New Porn" reprinted by permission of International Creative Management, Inc. Copyright © 1978 by Nora Ephron.

Because my outrage was confined to such a narrow part of the event, I was quite surprised a few days later when I began to read some of the letters the *Times* received about the dinner. There were eventually some five hundred in all, four to one against Claiborne, and the general tenor of them related to the total vulgarity of spending four thousand dollars on a dinner when millions were starving. Knee-jerk liberalism is apparently alive and well after all. There were references to Nero and Marie Antoinette, and there were also a few media-wise letter writers who chose to object not to the article itself but to the *Times*'s decision to run it on the front page. The *Times* printed a short and rather plaintive reply from Claiborne, who said that he could not see how anyone could claim that the meal had 'deprived one human being of one mouthful of food'.

All of this raised some interesting questions. For openers, how much money did Claiborne have to spend to cross the line into wretched excess? Would five hundred dollars have done it? A thousand dollars? Had he spent two thousand dollars, would the *Times* have received only three hundred letters? Would the objections have been even more intense if he had spent the four thousand dollars but put the tab on his expense account? Then, too, there is the question of editorial play: how much difference would it have made if the *Times* had run the article inside the newspaper? These are obviously unanswerable, almost existential questions, and a bit frivolous to boot—but there is something more serious underlying this whole tempest.

Claiborne was clearly puzzled by the reaction to his piece. He had managed to commit a modern atrocity—even if he did rip off American Express, for which he is to be commended—and there is a good reason why it never crossed his mind that he was doing so: except for the price tag, what he did was no more vulgar and tasteless than what he and hundreds of other journalists do every day. Newspapers and magazines are glutted with recipes for truffle soufflés and nit-picking restaurant reviews and paeans to the joys of arugula. Which of us will ever forget the thrilling night that Gael Greene blew five hundred dollars on dinner at the Palace, or that spine-tingling afternoon when Craig and Pierre jumped into the car and drove all the way from East Hampton to Southampton just in time to find the only butcher on eastern Long Island with a pig's ear? Or was it pork fat for pâté? God knows what it was, but the point is that it should not have taken a four-thousand-dollar dinner at Chez Denis to remind the readers of the *Times* that Nero fiddled while Rome burned. All of this—let's face it—is pretty vulgar stuff. It's also fun to read. But when it's accompanied by a four-thousand-dollar price tag, it reminds people of something they should have known all along: it's not about food, it's about money. Craig Claiborne writes about consuming—which should not be confused with consumerism, or Ralph Nader, or anything of the sort. And in his way, he is representative of one of the major trends in publishing today, he is a purveyor of what I tend to think of as the new porn.

Before going further, I should define what I mean by porn in this context: it's anything people are ashamed of getting a kick out of. If you want to sell porn to a mass audience, you have to begin by packaging it in a way that's acceptable; you have to give people an excuse to buy it. *Playboy's* Hugh Hefner was the first person in publishing to understand this; if he has done nothing else for American culture, he has given it two of the great lies of the twentieth

70 century: 'I buy it for the fiction' and 'I buy it for the interview'. Of late, Hefner has been hoist with his own petard. He has spent twenty years making the world safe for split beaver, and now he is surprised that magazines that print it are taking circulation away from his own.

The new porn has nothing to do with dirty pictures. It's simply about money. The new porn is the editorial basis for the rash of city and local magazines that have popped up around the country in the past ten years. Some of these magazines are first-rate—I am particularly partial to *Texas Monthly*—but generally they are to the traditional shelter magazines what *Playboy* is to *Hustler*: they have taken food and home furnishings and plant care and surrounded them up with just enough political and sociological reporting to give their readers an excuse to buy them. People who would not be caught dead
80 subscribing to *House & Garden* subscribe to *New York* magazine. But whatever the quality, the serious articles in *New York* have nothing whatever to do with what that magazine is about. That magazine is about buying plants, and buying chairs, and buying pastrami sandwiches, and buying wine, and buying ice cream. It is, in short, about buying. And let's give credit where credit is due: with the possible exception of the Neiman-Marcus catalogue, which is probably the granddaddy of this entire trend, no one does buying better than *New York* magazine.

In fact, all the objections the *Times* readers made to Claiborne's article can be applied to any one of the city and local magazines. How can you write about the perfect ice cream cone or the perfect diet cola or the perfect philodendron when millions of people have never seen
90 a freezer, suffer from sugar deficiencies, and have no home to put potted plants in? How can you publish a magazine whose motto is essentially 'Let them eat cheesecake'? Well, you can. And thousands of people will buy it. But don't make the mistake of giving the game away by going too far. Five extra pages on how to survive in a thirty-thousand-dollar living room, one extra price tag on a true nonessential, and your readers will write in to accuse you of terminal decadence. And when this happens, what will be truly shocking will not be the accusation—which will be dead on—but the fact that it took them so long to get the point.

Terminal decadence.

Exactly. ■

UNDERSTANDING CONTEXT

1. What is the central comparison that Ephron is making?

2. How does she make the comparison?

EVALUATING STRATEGY

1. Briefly summarize Ephron's thesis.

2. Why does she use a comparison to present her argument?

3. Ephron refers frequently to specific locations and items (for example, *Chez Denis* on *Paris's Right Bank* and *American Express*); how do these concrete cultural references contribute to the effectiveness of her discussion?

APPRECIATING LANGUAGE

1. What is your reaction to the title of the piece?

2. Why do you think she puts "porn" in the title?

3. Ephron chooses to use informal language at times (for example, *Gael Greene blew five hundred dollars on dinner at the Palace*). Find other instances of informal language in the essay and consider how more formal terminology would alter the effectiveness of her discussion.

WRITING SUGGESTIONS

1. Write a well-constructed summary of Ephron's essay.

2. Do you agree with Ephron's definition of porn as "anything people are ashamed of getting a kick out of"? Construct your own definition of porn. In a comparative essay, explain the similarities and differences between your definition of porn and Ephron's, explaining the reasons for your choice.

3. Choose a controversial issue about which you feel strongly. Present an argument in support of the issue, using a comparison to support your position.

BARBARA EHRENREICH

Barbara Ehrenreich was born in Butte, Montana, and attended Reed College in Oregon, where she received a bachelor's degree in chemical physics. In 1968 she completed a doctorate in cell biology at Rockefeller University in New York. While in graduate school, she became active in political and social issues, such as education, low-income housing, and the war in Vietnam. She has published numerous articles in **Time, Ms., Mother Jones, The New Republic,** and **The Nation.**

Food Worship*

In the following essay, Barbara Ehrenreich offers a humorous appraisal of gluttony, links it with fanatical exercising, and reaches some provocative conclusions about our values.

1 Ethiopia reminds us that there are still people for whom food is primarily a means to biological survival. Here, to judge from the rapid conversion of real estate into takeout shops for gourmets and the sudden prominence of vegetables that begin with the letter *a*, food has come to mean much more: status, authority, entertainment, style, possibly religion. Among the upscale, trend-setting people who are held up for our admiration in commercials for credit cards and wine coolers, food appears to be more fascinating than either sex or trivia games. An evening on the town, which used to mean dinner and a show, now means a showy dinner, followed perhaps by a chaste gelato.

In fact, in anticipation of the time when food will have surpassed all other ingredients of
10 high culture and when upward mobility will hinge on a mastery of puff pastry rather than a familiarity with computers or great books, I am thinking of substituting food emporiums for museums on my children's Sunday outings. Already, food has gained an equal footing with fashion and skin care in the men's magazines, driven diet books to the remainder shelves, and—as food history, food criticism, etc.—gained a foothold in academia. Those areas of artistic and intellectual endeavor that wish to survive may have to take up food themes or be content to make the same kind of accommodation to the restaurant that music has made to the piano bar.

As a longtime admirer of foods that outrank me in social status, I am not complaining. Thanks to the food fixation of the upwardly mobile, pita bread and salad bars have
20 sedimented down to Burger King, suggesting that cold poached salmon may not be far behind. And I will admit to having occasionally dined—on other people's expense accounts— at establishments so tony that the dishes are reportedly rinsed in Perrier and the beef has graduated from stress-free, organic grazing environments. So it is without envy or ingratitude that I have been wondering, why food? Why food of all the obsessions—sex, astrology, real estate, tropical bird feeding—available to those in the Gold Card bracket?

The first explanation I have come up with is a straightforward biological one. Upscale people are fixated with food simply because they are now able to eat so much of it without getting fat, and the reason they don't get fat is that they maintain a profligate level of calorie expenditure. The very same people whose evenings begin with melted goat cheese and wind up, hours later, with raspberries cushioned on a lascivious créme à l'anglaise get up at dawn 30 to run, break for a midmorning aerobics class, and watch the evening news while racing on a stationary bicycle.

This explanation assumes that past generations of dieters—the mothers and grand-mothers of today's big-time eaters—left a large proportion of our contemporaries geneti-cally imprinted with a hunger of deep and savage proportions. After having been teased for so long with grapefruit halves and celery sticks, this vast hunger quite justifiably demands plates heaping with Tex-Mex, three-course lunches and between-meal pasta primavera pick-me-ups. Paradoxically, of course, the very occupations that pay well enough to finance gastronomic intake on such a scale—corporate law, international banking, cocaine retail-ing—involve almost zero energy expenditures in the course of a day's work. Hence the wild 40 aerobic flailings and desperate five-mile runs required to maintain a fast-track metabolism. Exercise is the yuppie version of bulimia.

Not to push this theory too far, you might say that exercise is to eating in the eighties as contraception was to sex in the sixties. The pill, IUDs and eventually legalized abortion freed sex from its ancient biological consequences and helped usher in the sexual revolution. In the same way, jogging, jazzercise, and Jane Fonda's videotape have uncoupled gluttony from obe-sity and thus made possible what may someday be called the gastrointestinal revolution.

But hunger, revived hourly by workouts and runs, only explains why people eat, not what they eat. People who are merely hungry have been known to eat almost anything—bologna sandwiches, bowls of millet, unripe Brie. Something larger than hunger sends 50 young account executives rushing out of their condos after dark to pick up an extra bottle of walnut oil or raspberry vinegar. And that can only be the drive to impress, intimidate, and inspire insecurity in one's dinner guests.

As a way of establishing one's own status or gauging another's, food has obvious advan-tages over our former cultural obsession, sex. A sexual encounter can only give you insight into your partner's personal warmth, generosity, capacity for whimsy, and so forth. But a bout of competitive eating, as it is now called, gives you fairly precise information about your dining partner's current and anticipated income, social class or origin, and probable taste in home furnishings. Does your date think sushi is still stylish? Then he has probably been passed over for promotion and squeezed out when his apartment went co-op. If, on 60 the other hand, he goes unhesitatingly for the baby bass en croute, he may have a Harvard MBA and a flair for currency speculation, just the kind of things that should, in the world of culinary high-rollers, make you want to eat out with him more often.

The fact that physical exercise—at least when performed with no thought of wages or other compensation and preferably at some expense to the exerciser—is itself a high-status activity only heightens the necessity of conspicuous eating. Whereas a decade or so ago, the woman who ordered an abstemious chef's salad for lunch placed herself on a moral plane above her sister diners, today she would only be suspected of sloth. Clearly, one would have to be a dancercise dropout or a marathon reject to get by on less than two thousand calories 70 at midday. In fact, when has anyone last seen chef's salad on a menu of any importance? Nor is it fashionable any longer to claim to require only coffee for breakfast: friends would suspect you of failing to jog to work and wonder where you even got the strength to grind the beans. Conversely, of course, anyone who makes a point of getting about town without running shoes risks being suspected of secret abstentions from béarnaise sauce and mousse. No one stays on the fast track these days without developing the metabolic capacity of the shrew, that tiny mammal that consumes three times its weight in food each day.

I hesitate to moralize about how this upscale metabolic speedup might look to a resident of a sub-Saharan refugee camp, for I remember all too well how I responded, as a child, to any dinnertable reference to children so unfortunate that they would feel blessed to encoun- 80 ter my plate of fried Spam and potatoes. (So wrap it up and send it to India then.) Yet our parents' point sunk in: we all know that there is a connection between waste in one location and simultaneous starvation in another, between the gluttony of a few and the chronic hunger of the world's many. Perhaps if we could get our minds off the next meal and the caloric residue of the last one, we might figure out what to do about it. ■

UNDERSTANDING CONTEXT

1. Ehrenreich compares what people eat to their social mobility. How does she make this comparison?

2. What other comparisons does she make in the piece?

EVALUATING STRATEGY

1. Briefly summarize Ehrenreich's thesis.

2. Consider the metaphor within the title of this essay. How effective is the comparison it suggests for Ephron's thesis?

3. How does Ehrenreich use comparisons throughout this essay to support her purpose?

4. Ehrenreich uses humour in the piece. Using an example from the piece, explain how humour helps to support her thesis.

APPRECIATING LANGUAGE

1. Ehrenreich uses many words that are associated with the culinary arts. Make a list of these words.

2. Why does she use these words? Does her choice of vocabulary undermine or enhance her argument?

WRITING SUGGESTIONS

1. Write a well-constructed summary of Ehrenreich's essay.

2. *Reflective writing:* Consider the role of food in your social circle. How important is it? Is Ehrenreich's claim that food is becoming "more fascinating than either sex or trivia games" relevant to your group? Write a two-page comparison of your relationship to food within your family circle and your relationship to food within your social circle.

3. Ephron targets a universal interest (food) and proceeds to argue for a larger meaning behind the activity of eating. Analyze a common student activity and argue for a larger meaning behind it. Be sure to use a comparison to support your thesis.

SEAN WAISGLASS

Sean Waisglass is a Toronto-based writer and photographer whose subjects range from sports to street life in urban spaces.

The New City Is an Old Photoblog*

In their 1960s book on Toronto, The New City: A Prejudiced View of Toronto, *Henri Rossier and Pierre Berton remind readers of the power of street photography. In his article, Waisglass compares the older book with the modern idea of the photoblog.*

1 When it comes to photographing cities, there's something wonderful about pictures taken in the personal documentary style, or street photography, that middle ground between the snapshot of the non-photographer and the purposeful shot of the pro.

Personal documentary-style photos are a different beast than snapshots, which are equally spontaneous but lack artifice and craft. And they have a different feel than the purposeful shot, those photos taken by pros for spot news or touristy-type books that have style, but lack the vitality of something taken on the spur of the moment for the simple pleasure of it. They are visual hidden treasures retrieved in a rectangular frame: photos that are earned by getting out on the pavement and cruising, or that come about as by-products of day-to-day
10 travel like taking a shortcut home from work, or walking to the corner store to buy coffee filters.

Wonderful is no doubt the right word to use, because that is what photographs of a city that hit the high-notes inspire: you wonder where the photo was taken, or wonder how you could have missed this subtle gem existing right under your nose, or wonder how many of these eyebrow-raising ephemeral moments you miss every day in the habitual rush of city living.

You can find stellar examples of this style in both Toronto's champion photoblog, Daily Dose of Imagery (found online at wvs.topleftpixel.com), and in that website's long lost relative, *The New City: A Prejudiced View of Toronto,* a tragically out-of-print book of photos taken circa 1958–61.
20 Sam Javanrouh's popular Daily Dose of Imagery website, started in mid-2003, features daily posts of mostly digital photographs of the city; excellent pixelated snaps such as the peeling paint sandwiching the storefront windows of an aging furniture store, a spinning Esso sign in front of a criss-cross of streetcar wires, heads poking up from behind a white patio side-wall as a cyclist in pink passes by, or the comfortable-looking Q and A session after a documentary screening at the Bloor Cinema.

Javanrouh turns the "forest for the trees" idiom on its head and comes to know the larger whole by looking at its smaller parts. He also knows that mundane is in the eye of the beholder, and that what might turn out as a pedestrian shot in other hands can be made sublime.

*Waisglass, Sean, "*The New City* is an Old Photoblog" reprinted by permission of the author, Sean Waisglass.

The New City, published in 1961 by MacMillan, features the black and white pho-   30
tography of Henri Rossier capturing similar moments from another time, and is one of
the great documents of Toronto (well worth scouring used bookstores or shelling out
online for).

It's a testament to the quality of the photos in the book that Rossier gets top billing over
the book's author, Canadian literary icon Pierre Berton. As explained by Berton in the intro,
Rossier was a young amateur shooter from Switzerland who walked into his office with a
portfolio of photos taken during the two years he had been in the city, and asked for help
creating a book. Described as "a newcomer who has been here long enough to know his way
around but not too long to grow blasé," Rossier's photos won Berton over with their depiction of a new Toronto blossoming.   40

It was the beginning of an immigration boom (in the next 30 years, non-Caucasians
would rise from 3 to 30 percent of the population), and during an expansion period that
would create new neighbourhoods and boroughs. It was the last days of Old Toronto, and
the rise of said New City. And like any phase in life (even the awkward years of adolescence),
it was worth snapping some shots of for posterity's sake.

Berton's penchant for writing stuffy-sounding historical epics has often overshadowed the fact that he was a nimble scribe in the mold of journalism greats like Liebling
or Mencken—keen, witty, and aware that a good yarn is as important as presenting the
facts. Discussed by Berton are the different sects and castes of the city and where they dwell
(see "Italian Town" or "The Guilded Ghetto"), as is Toronto's changing shape and size, its   50
collective character, and the looming spectre of public transit.

But the star of the show is Rossier, whose photos were inspired by the style of that era, when
photojournalism had hit its high watermark in *Life* magazine's photo essays and in the work of
the legendary Magnum photography agency. Using his rangefinder Lieca (still the sharpest and
quietest 35mm film cameras to date) to keep an eye on things, he is in the park when the local
kids get a hockey game going, riding the Ferris Wheel at the Ex, peeking through the window
of a Chinatown barbershop, or watching as folks ogle new-model cars shining in a lot.

And craftily, Rossier also documents the changeover process and its fallout—the fad-
ing of the old and the fertilizing and reaping of the new. His lens captures what he deems
in the informative photo index as "the last of the organ grinders" at Rosedale Station. He   60
ends a series of motor vehicle-related shots with that of a forlorn-looking horse and car-
riage on Spadina. There's the full-wall advertisement for televisions painted over an older
one for a tool and die company on Queen Street East (possibly now covered by a billboard
for computers?), and in another photo, what we now call urban sprawl creeps towards an
orchard near O'Connor Drive in the east end.

Often grainy, and sometimes slightly out of focus, Rossier's shots are more about
capturing the zeitgeist of the city than making pretty pictures—they're about people and
spaces, the little things. These are the kinds of photos that stand as unofficial time capsules
for future generations, frozen moments that often say more than filmed ones.

Flipping through the pages of Rossier's evocative journal of the past only rein-   70
forces the relevance of Javanrouh's photoblog of the present. It can't be coincidence

that Rossier's worthy successor is correspondingly both a recent immigrant to Toronto (Javanrouh moved here from Iran in 1999), and not a photographer by profession. There is a kinship, a direct lineage of photo-junkies making a personal project out of their burgeoning relationship with their new home—our city. With cameras in hand, they've paced Toronto with eyes wide open and noticed those little things that amalgamate to make the whole, prodding those of us who have grown too familiar to pause and take notice too. ■

UNDERSTANDING CONTEXT

1. Waisglass gives privilege to the personal photograph over the professional. Do you agree with the attributes Waisglass assigns to the personal photograph?

2. What is Waisglass' purpose in writing the piece?

EVALUATING STRATEGY

1. Briefly summarize Waisglass' thesis.

2. Waisglass compares the two photographers. What are the similarities? Why does he compare them?

APPRECIATING LANGUAGE

1. Define zeitgeist.

2. Why does Waisglass think that it is important to capture it?

WRITING SUGGESTION

1. Take a series of photographs of where you live. Next, write an essay that explains the photographs' importance as part of the story of the place photographed.

| Blending the Modes | ASADEH MOAVENI |

Azadeh Moaveni, whose parents left Iran following the fall of Shah in 1979, was born in Palo Alto, California. She describes the complex identity she developed as someone growing up in a community of exiles trying to make lives in a new country in her book *Lipstick Jihad: A Memoir of Growing Up Iranian in America and American in Iran.*

Maman and America*

In this passage from Lipstick Jihad, *Moaveni uses comparison to dramatize the differences between her divorced parents, her teenage conflicts with her mother, whom she calls Maman, and her mother's conflicting opinions of American culture.*

When it served her purposes, Maman embraced America and lovingly recited all the quali- 1
ties that made it superior to our backward-looking Iranian culture. That Americans were
honest, never made promises they didn't intend to keep, were open to therapy, believed a
divorced woman was still a whole person worthy of respect and a place in society—all this
earned them vast respect in Maman's book. It seemed never to occur to her that values
do not exist in a cultural vacuum but are knit into a society's fabric; they earn their place,
derived from other related beliefs. Maman thought values were like groceries; you'd cruise
through the aisles, toss the ones you fancied into your cart, and leave the unappealing ones
on the shelf. When I was a teenager we constantly fought over her pilfering through Iranian
and American values at random, assigning a particular behavior or habit she felt like pro- 10
moting to the culture she could peg it to most convincingly.

Our earliest battle on this territory was over Madonna. Maman called her *jendeh,* a
prostitute, which I considered an offensive way to describe the singer of "La Isla Bonita." On
what grounds, I argued, was she being condemned? Was it because she flaunted her sexuality, and if so, did that make out-of-wedlock sexuality a bad thing? My defense of Madonna
seemed to infuriate Maman; her eyes flashed, and her bearing radiated a grave, ominous
disappointment. It was the same disproportionate reaction she'd show when I would forget
which elder in a room full of aging relatives I should have served tea to first, or when I'd
refuse to interrupt an afternoon with a friend to take vitamins to an elderly Iranian lady
who couldn't drive. Certain conversations or requests, unbeknownst to me, would become 20
symbolic tests of my allegiance to that Iranian world, and the wrong response would plunge
Maman into dark feelings of failure and regret.

At the prescient age of thirteen, I realized our Madonna arguments signaled far more
serious confrontations to come. Maman's contempt for Madonna seemed like sheer
hypocrisy to me. Was this the same woman who thought it regressive and awful that
Iranian culture valued women through their marital status, and rated their respectability
according to the success or failure of their marriage? The woman who denounced a culture

that considered divorced women criminals? She believed it was only modern to consider women fully equal to men, independent beings with a sacred right to everything men were 30 entitled. Somehow, it became clear through her designation of Madonna as whore, that she also thought it fully consistent to believe premarital sex (for women) was wrong, and that women who practiced it were morally compromised. The men she forgave, offering an explanation worthy of an Iranian villager: "They can't help themselves." Women, it seemed, were physiologically better equipped for deprivation. Often our fights would end with me collapsing in tears, her bitterly condemning my unquestioning acceptance of "this decadent culture's corrupt ways," and my usual finale: "It's all your fault for raising me here; what did you expect?"

In Maman's view, America was responsible for most that had gone wrong in the world. *Een gavhah,* these cows, was her synonym for Americans. She'd established her 40 criticisms early on, and repeated them so often that to this day they are seared on my brain: "Americans have no social skills. . . . They prefer their pets to people. . . . Shopping and sex, sex and shopping; that's all Americans think about. . . . They've figured out how corrupt they are, and rather than fix themselves, they want to force their sick culture on the rest of the world." Since she mostly wheeled out these attitudes to justify why I couldn't be friends with Adam-the-long-haired-guitarist or why I couldn't go to the movies twice in one week, or why I couldn't wear short skirts, I wondered whether they were sincere, or tactical.

Her restrictions were futile, and only turned me into a highly skilled liar with a suspiciously heavy backpack. Every morning she would drop me off at a friend's house, 50 ostensibly so we could walk to school together. Once inside I traded the Maman-approved outfit for something tighter, smeared some cherry gloss on my lips, and headed off to class. Knowing I could secretly evade her restrictions helped me endure the sermons, but sometimes the injustice of her moralizing would provoke me, and I would fling jingoistic clichés designed to infuriate her: "Love it or leave it. . . . These colors don't run. . . . No one's keeping you here." At hearing these words come out of my mouth she'd hurl a piece of fruit at me, dissolve into angry tears, and suddenly the fact that I was torturing my poor, exiled single mother filled me with terrible grief, and I would apologize profusely, begging forgiveness in the formal, filial Farsi I knew she craved to hear. In the style of a traditional Iranian mother, she would pretend, for five days, that I did not exist; thaw on 60 the sixth; and by the seventh have forgotten the episode entirely, privately convinced that my rude friends, who didn't even say *salaam* to her when they came over, were responsible for ruining my manners.

When we encountered other second-generation Iranians at Persian parties, I was struck by how much less conflicted they seemed over their dueling cultural identities. I decided my own neurotic messiness in this area was the fault of my divorced parents. The only thing they agreed on was the safety record of the Volvo, and how they should both drive one until I finished junior high. But when it came to anything that mattered, for instance how I should be raised, they didn't even bother to carve out an agreement, so vast was the gulf that separated their beliefs. My father was an atheist (Marx said God was dead) who called the Prophet Mohammad a pedophile for marrying a nine-year-old girl. He thought the de- **70** fining characteristics of Iranian culture—fatalism, political paranoia, social obligations, an enthusiasm for guilt—were responsible for the failures of modern Iran. He wouldn't even condescend to use the term "Iranian culture," preferring to refer, to this day, to "that stinking culture"; he refused to return to Iran, even for his mother's funeral, and wouldn't help me with my Persian homework, a language, he pronounced direly "you will *never* use." When I announced my decision to move to Iran, his greatest fear, I think, was that something sufficiently awful would happen to me that it would require his going back. That he had married Maman, a hyper-ideologue, a reactionary as high-strung as they come, was baffling; little wonder they divorced when I was an infant. Daddy was the benevolent father personified; he couldn't have cared less about curfews, dating, a fifth ear piercing, or whether my hair **80** was purple or not. ■

UNDERSTANDING CONTEXT

1. How does Moaveni explain her mother's conflicted attitude toward America?

2. Why did Moaveni and her mother fight over Madonna? What did Madonna represent?

3. How does Moaveni describe the differences between her parents? How did her father's attitudes toward Iran differ from her mother's?

4. How did Moaveni's mother view differences between men and women?

5. *Critical thinking:* Do all immigrant parents and their American-born children face a similar clash over cultural values and identity? Could similar mother and daughter arguments occur in Korean, Mexican, or Vietnamese families?

EVALUATING STRATEGY

1. How does Moaveni use an argument over Madonna to highlight her conflict with her mother?

2. Moaveni states that her mother thought of values as being products on a shelf. Is this an effective comparison? Why or why not?

3. How did Moaveni use her parents' attitudes about Farsi, the Iranian language, to dramatize their differences?

4. *Other modes:* How does Moaveni use *description, definition,* and *narration* to develop her comparisons?

APPRECIATING LANGUAGE

1. What words does Moaveni use to describe her parents?

2. What terms does Maman use to praise and condemn Americans? What connotations do these terms have? Do you think they reflect the positive and negative views many people from other countries have about the United States? Why or why not?

WRITING SUGGESTIONS

1. Write a comparison essay that describes one or more of your own adolescent conflicts with one or both of your parents. What were the points of contention? What did they symbolize?

2. *Collaborative writing:* Discuss Moaveni's essay with a group of students. Work together to develop a brief essay that outlines the problems immigrant families face living in Canada or the United States. Do some people, like Moaveni's father, seek to forget their old country and assimilate, while others, like Moaveni's mother, seek to maintain cultural values and traditions?

Writing beyond the Classroom   PEGGY KENNA AND SONDRA LACY

Peggy Kenna and Sondra Lacy are communications specialists based in Arizona who work with foreign-born employees. In addition, they provide cross-cultural training to executives conducting international business. Kenna is a speech and language pathologist who specializes in accent modification. Kenna and Lacy have collaborated on a series of 50-page booklets that compare American and foreign business organizations, habits, behaviours, and negotiating styles. Widely sold in airports, these booklets give Americans tips on doing business overseas.

Communication Styles: United States and Taiwan*

This section from Business Taiwan *contrasts American and Taiwanese styles of communicating. Designing their booklets for quick skimming, Kenna and Lacy use charts to highlight cultural differences.*

UNITED STATES

■ *Frank*

Americans tend to be very straightforward and unreserved. The people of Taiwan often find them abrupt and not interested enough in human relationships.

■ *Face saving less important*

To Americans accuracy is important but errors are tolerated. Admitting mistakes is seen as a sign of maturity. They believe you learn from failure and therefore encourage some risk taking.

Americans believe criticism can be objective and not personal; however, all criticism should be done with tact.

■ *Direct eye contact*

Direct eye contact is very important to Americans since they need to see the non-verbal cues the speaker is giving. Nonverbal cues are a very important part of the American English language. Americans use intermittent eye contact when they are speaking but fairly steady eye contact when they are listening.

TAIWAN

■ *Subtle*

Frankness is not appreciated by the people of Taiwan. They particularly dislike unqualified negative statements.

■ *Face saving important*

The Chinese do not like to be put in the position of having to admit a mistake or failure. They also do not like to tell you when they don't understand your point.

You also should not admit too readily when you don't know something as it can cause you to lose face.

■ *Avoid direct eye contact*

Holding the gaze of another person is considered rude.

*Kenna, Peggy and Lacy, Sondra, "Communication Styles: United States and Taiwan" from *Business Taiwan* by Peggy Kenna and Sondra Lacy. Copyright © 1994. Used with permission of The McGraw-Hill Companies, Inc.

UNITED STATES

■ *Direct and to the point*

Americans prefer people to say what they mean. Because of this they tend to sometimes miss subtle nonverbal cues. Americans are uncomfortable with ambiguousness and don't like to have to "fill in the blanks." They also tend to discuss problems directly.

■ *"Yes" means agreement*

Americans look for clues such as nodding of the head, a verbal "yes" or "uh huh" in order to determine if their arguments are succeeding.

TAIWAN

■ *Indirect and ambiguous*

People in Taiwan dislike saying "no." They may not tell you when they don't understand. They often hedge their answers if they know you won't like the answer. If they say something like, "We'll think about it," they may mean they aren't interested.

They dislike discussing problems directly and will often go around the issue, which can be frustrating for Americans.

The Chinese language (Mandarin) is so concise that the listener needs to use much imagination to "fill in the gaps."

■ *"Yes" means "I hear"*

People in Taiwan do not judge information given to them so they do not indicate agreement or disagreement; they only nod or say "yes" to indicate they are listening to you.

The people of Taiwan believe politeness is more important than frankness, so they will not directly tell you "no." The closest they will come to "no" is "maybe." ■

UNDERSTANDING CONTEXT

1. What appear to be the major differences between American and Taiwanese methods of communicating?

2. Why is it important for Americans to be sensitive about making direct eye contact with Taiwanese?

3. How do Americans and Taiwanese accept failure?

4. *Critical thinking:* Why would this booklet be valuable to Americans visiting Taiwan on business? Does such a brief, to-the-point guide risk relying on stereotypes?

EVALUATING STRATEGY

1. How easy is this document to read and review? How accessible would the information be if it were written in standard paragraphs?

2. What does the directness of the document reveal about the intended audience? Would it be suitable for a college or university classroom?

APPRECIATING LANGUAGE

1. What language do the writers use in describing the Taiwanese? Do they attempt to be neutral, or does their word choice favour one nationality over another?

2. Kenna and Lacy suggest that many Taiwanese find Americans to be "abrupt." Is this a good word choice? Does the guide express common prejudices?

WRITING SUGGESTIONS

1. Using Kenna and Lacy's entry as a source, write a short process paper instructing how an American should present an idea or product in Taiwan. Assume you are writing to sales representatives travelling to Taiwan for the first time. Provide step-by-step suggestions for how they should conduct themselves from the moment they enter a seminar room to make a presentation.

2. *Collaborative writing:* Working with a group of students, discuss the differences between high school teachers and college or university instructors, then develop a chart contrasting their attitudes toward absenteeism, late homework, tests, and research papers.

Responding to IMAGES

Statues commemorating North America's first saints at The Martyrs' Shrine near Roberval, Lac Saint-Jean County, Quebec

Gabor Szilasi, Seven Canadian Martyrs, Roberval, Lac Saint Jean County, 1976 © SODART 2007. Photo © National Gallery of Canada. Purchased 1977

1. What is your first reaction to seeing these two photographs together? Do they strike you as racist, silly, or curious?

2. Do you find it ironic that the cross is in the foreground of both photographs? Why or why not?

3. *Collaborative writing:* Discuss these photographs with a group of students. Are any of the students Christian? Are any of them from families of colour? Are any of them of First Nations heritage? Is there a link between religion and racism? Be sure to explain your response fully.

4. *Visual analysis:* Study the composition of the two photographs. Describe the visual similarities and differences. Why is the cross centred in both photos?

A meeting of the Ku Klux Klan in Vancouver in 1930

Vancouver Public Library, Special Collections, VPL 8956D

5. *Other modes*
   ■ Write a description to accompany these photographs in a high school history book or a museum display. Try to objectively explain why they are juxtaposed.
   ■ Develop a division essay that details different reasons that many people use religion to defend seemingly unethical opinions or actions.
   ■ Write a persuasive essay clearly stating your position on religion's social function.

☑ COMPARISON AND CONTRAST **CHECKLIST**

✔ Are your subjects closely related enough to make a valid comparison?

✔ Have you identified the key points of both subjects?

✔ Have you selected the best method of organizing your paper?

✔ Is the comparison easy to follow? Are transitions clear?

✔ Does the comparison meet reader needs and expectations?

✔ Have you defined terms or provided background information needed by readers to fully appreciate the comparison?

✔ Is your thesis clearly stated and located where it will have the greatest impact?

COMPANION WEBSITE

See **http://www.transcanadawriter.nelson.com** for additional information on writing comparison.

CHAPTER 17

Process: Explaining How Things Work and Giving Directions

This chapter examines writing that analyzes how a procedure, event, or operation takes place. It first looks at writing that *explains* how things work; it then turns to writing that *gives directions for*, or *instructs*, how things work.

WHAT IS PROCESS?

Process writing shows how things work or how specific tasks are accomplished. The first type of process writing demonstrates how a complex procedure or event occurs. Biology textbooks describe how the heart operates by separating its actions into a series of steps. Process writing is a directed form of narration that explains how an operation takes place.

The second type of process writing gives directions for completing a specific task. Recipes, owners' manuals, textbooks, and home repair articles provide readers with step-by-step directions. These instructions are challenging to create because writers may be unable to determine how much background information to provide and may easily forget a critical piece of information.

Explaining How Things Work

Just as an analysis through classification and division seeks to explain an abstract or complex subject by separating it into smaller categories, process writing separates the workings of complicated operations into steps or stages.

When you write explanations, it is important to consider your readers' existing knowledge. You may need to define technical terms, use illustrative analogies, such as comparing the heart to a pump or a computer virus to an human infection, and relate brief narratives so that readers will understand the process. Some writers will use an extended analogy, comparing a nuclear power plant to a tea kettle or terrorism to a brush fire.

◼ WRITING **ACTIVITY**

Develop an outline listing ideas for a paper explaining one of the following topics:

1. The admissions procedure at your college or university
2. The way you perform a task at home, at school, or in your job

(Continued)

---

3. The formation of a hurricane or tornado

4. The process determining which teams will play in the World Series or Grey Cup

5. The way couples resolve conflicts

Strategies for Writing Explanations

Critical Thinking and Prewriting

1. **List possible topics.** Choose subjects you are familiar with and that can be fully explained given the scope of the assignment.

2. **Prewrite to explore the most promising topics.** Use freewriting and brainstorming to identify topics best suited to the assignment. Avoid overly complex subjects that require extensive background explanation or are subject to numerous interpretations.

3. **Study your topic carefully.** Note the principal features that need emphasis. Highlight features that are commonly confused or might be difficult for readers to understand.

Planning

1. **Determine how much background information is needed.** Your readers may require, for example, a basic knowledge of how normal cells divide before being able to comprehend the way cancer cells develop. In some instances, you have to address widely believed misconceptions.

2. **Define clear starting and ending points.** In some cases the process may have an obvious beginning and end. If you were to write a paper about the process of getting a divorce, would you stop when final papers are signed or continue to discuss alimony and child visitation rights? When does a divorce end?

3. **Separate the process into logical stages.** Readers will naturally assume all the stages are equally significant unless you indicate their value or importance. Minor points should not be overemphasized by being divided into distinct steps.

4. **Develop an outline listing steps and major points to guide the first draft.** Keep your readers in mind—you are teaching when you write process. Your goal is to transfer your knowledge or experience to your readers so they will share your understanding of a particular operation or event.

5. **Determine whether visual aids such as photographs, diagrams, or charts would be appropriate to illustrate the process.**

Writing the First Draft

1. **Keep your audience in mind as you write.** The key problem in explaining something you are familiar with is assuming that your readers share your knowledge base.

2. **Use transitional phrases and paragraph breaks to separate stages.** Statements such as "at the same time" or "two days later" can help readers follow the chronology and direction of events.

3. **Stress the importance of time relationships.** Process writing creates a slow-motion explanation that can be misleading if the chain of events naturally occurs in a short period. You can avoid this confusion by opening with a "real-time" description of the process. The rest of the paper might repeat this process in four or five pages, slowly relating each stage in great detail.

4. **Use images, details, narratives, and examples to enrich the description of each stage.** Give readers a full appreciation of each stage by describing it in details they can grasp. Avoid long strings of nonessential, technical language. Use comparisons and narratives to provide readers with clear pictures of events and situations.

5. **Alert readers to possible variations.** If the process is subject to change or alternative forms, present readers with the most common type. Indicate, either in the introduction or in each stage, that exceptions or variations can occur.

Revising

1. **Review your plan and goals; then read your paper aloud with your reader in mind.**
   - Determine whether your paper provides enough information to explain the process.
   - Examine your paper for terms or concepts that need definition or further explanation.

2. **Review transitions and paragraph breaks for clarity.** Essentially, an explanation paper describes a process in slow motion, breaking a complex chain of events into separate steps.
   - Do not cluster too many important ideas into a single step.
   - Avoid exaggerating the significance of a minor point by isolating it as a single step.

3. **Review the use of visual aids for accuracy.**

4. **Use peer review to test your paper.**
   - Ask others how easy it is for them to understand the process. What improvements could be made?

Editing and Proofreading

1. **Read the paper aloud to test for clarity.**
   - Make sure that you define technical or widely misunderstood terms.
   - Examine the level of diction to determine whether it is suited to your readers' existing knowledge.

2. **Use peer editing to locate errors you may have missed.**

GIVING DIRECTIONS

Directions are step-by-step instructions guiding readers through a specific goal or task. Recipes and repair manuals show readers how to prepare a meal or change a tire. Negative instructions work best when you are trying to get readers to change their habits or avoid common errors. For giving instructions, you may find it useful to number steps. Highlighting, bold type, and underlining can dramatize text and make the document easy to read in an emergency.

WRITING **ACTIVITY**

Select one of the topics below and use prewriting techniques to develop a plan for a short set of directions. Remember to consider each target audience.

1. Provide directions to the campus for out-of-town visitors arriving at the local airport. Give readers visual references, such as landmarks, to identify key intersections.

2. Inform new students how to check out books from the campus library.

3. Instruct students how to balance work and school.

4. Use your own experience to create a list of suggestions to help students study for exams, save money on books, lose weight, read faster, save time, or exercise.

5. Offer tips to parents concerned about their children's use of the Internet. Alert them to potential hazards and suggest remedies.

Strategies for Writing Directions

Critical Thinking and Prewriting

1. **List possible topics under the phrase "How to . . ."**
   - Select subjects you are familiar with and can fully explain in a page or two of directions.

2. **Explore the most promising topics.**
   - Freewriting and brainstorming can help identify topics best suited to the assignment.
   - Limit the subject to a single task or problem—how to change a tire instead of how to maintain your car.

3. **Consider your audience carefully.** Remember that giving directions requires you to ask people to not only *read* but also *act* on your ideas.
   - Determine how much knowledge your readers have.
   - Consider any safety precautions, misconceptions, or confusion that must be addressed before proceeding.

Planning

1. **Define the scope of your directions.** Clearly define the task or goal—you should be directing readers to accomplish something specific. Directions must be goal centred.

2. **Define clear starting and ending points.** Give readers clear instructions about when to start the process and when to end it.

3. **Make sure directions are self-contained.** A recipe, for example, should list *all* the ingredients, appliances, and instructions required to accomplish the task.

4. **Break the process into even steps.** Avoid placing too much information or too many actions in a single step.

5. **Consider using numbered steps.** Readers find it easier to follow numbered steps and can mark their places if interrupted.

6. **Consider using visual aids such as charts, graphs, diagrams, maps, or photographs to illustrate the process.**

7. **Prepare a clearly organized outline.**

Writing the First Draft

1. **Using your outline as a guide, write a draft, keeping your goal and your readers in mind.** Consider your readers strangers to your process who need exact details, such as dates, times, and room numbers.

2. **Provide complete instructions.** Remember, readers are doing this process for the first time and must rely on your directions; give full details about each step.

3. **Give negative instructions.** Tell people what not to do, especially if you know that people are prone to make errors, skip steps, substitute cheaper materials, or ignore potential problems.

4. **Warn readers of possible events that they may misinterpret as mistakes.** If a person assembling a desk discovers that the legs are wobbly, he or she may think the product is defective. If this is normal—if the legs tighten up when the drawers are installed—let readers know.

5. **Consider using visual aids.** Large print, capital letters, bold or italic type, and underlining can highlight text for easy reading.

6. **Warn readers of any potential hazards to their safety, health, property, or the environment.**

Revising

1. **Review your outline and then read your draft for completeness, organization, and readability.**
   - Directions should be stated in short, precise sentences. Delete wordy or unnecessary phrases.
   - Each step should be well defined, with a clear goal.

2. **Review the overall organization and transitions.** Have you broken the process into workable steps?

3. **Examine any visual aids for accuracy and relevance.**

4. **Test your writing through peer review.**
   - Ask people to read your paper; then quiz them on important points.
   - Readers unfamiliar with the process may spot missing critical information that you have overlooked.

Editing and Proofreading

1. **Read the paper aloud to test for clarity.**
   - Make sure you define technical or widely misunderstood terms.
   - Examine the level of diction to determine whether it is suited to your readers' existing knowledge.

2. **Use peer editing to locate errors that you may have missed.**

SUGGESTED TOPICS FOR WRITING PROCESS

General Assignments

Explaining How Things Work

Write a process paper on any of the following topics. Assume you are writing to a general, university-educated audience. You may develop your explanation using narratives, comparisons, and definitions. Explain the process as a clearly stated chain of events. Draw from your own experiences.

- How students register for courses
- The operation of an appliance, such as a microwave, washing machine, or refrigerator
- The process of a disease or disability
- The way the body loses fat through diet or exercise
- How restaurants prevent food poisoning

Giving Directions

Write a process paper giving specific directions to complete a specific task. You may wish to place your instructions in numbered steps rather than standard paragraphs. Remember to highlight potential hazards.

- How to purchase a new or used car
- How to quit smoking
- How to find a job
- How to avoid identity theft
- How to treat a second-degree burn

Writing in Context

1. Imagine that you have been selected to write a section for a student handbook instructing first-year students how to register for classes. Write a step-by-step paper giving complete instructions. Give exact room numbers, times, and locations. You may wish to refer to a campus map. When you complete a draft of your paper, review it carefully to see whether you have left out any essential information.

2. Select a process that you have learned on a job and write instructions suitable for training a new employee. Consider how your job may have changed. Give trainees the benefit of your experience and add tips that might not be included in the standard job descriptions. Warn readers, for instance, of common problems that arise.

Strategies for Reading Process

As you read the process entries in this chapter, keep these questions in mind:

Context

1. What is the writer's goal—to explain or instruct?
2. Is the goal clearly stated?
3. What are the critical stages or steps in the process?
4. What errors should readers avoid?

Strategy

1. What is the nature of the intended audience? How much existing knowledge does the writer assume that readers have?
2. How are steps or stages separated? Are transitions clearly established?
3. Are the instructions easy to follow?
4. Are any special effects, such as highlighting, numbered steps, and visual aids, skillfully used?

Language

1. Are technical terms clearly defined and illustrated?
2. Does the writer use concrete words to create clear images of what is being explained?

MORTIMER ADLER

Mortimer Adler (1902–2001) was born in New York City. He taught psychology at Columbia University, then moved to Chicago, where he taught the philosophy of law for more than twenty years. He resigned from the University of Chicago in 1952 to head the Institute for Philosophical Research in San Francisco. His books include **How to Read a Book** and **Philosopher at Large: An Intellectual Autobiography.** Adler became famous as an editor of the **Encyclopedia Britannica** and leader of the Great Books Program of the University of Chicago. This program encouraged adults from all careers to read and discuss classic works. This essay first appeared in the **Saturday Review of Literature** in 1940.

How to Mark a Book*

Before reading Adler's essay, consider your own reading habits. Do you read with a pen in your hand? Do you scan a work first or simply begin with the first line? Do you take notes? Do you have problems remembering what you read?

introduction   You know you have to read "between the lines" to get the most out of anything. I want to   1
persuade you to do something equally important in the course of your reading. I want to
persuade you to "write between the lines." Unless you do, you are not likely to do the most
efficient kind of reading. <u>I contend, quite bluntly, that marking up a book is not an act of</u>
thesis <u>mutilation but of love.</u>

You shouldn't mark up a book which isn't yours. Librarians (or your friends) who lend
you books expect you to keep them clean, and you should. If you decide that I am right
disclaimer about the usefulness of marking books, you will have to buy them. Most of the world's great
books are available today, in reprint editions, at less than a dollar.

<u>There are two ways in which one can own a book. The first is the property right you</u>   10
<u>establish by paying for it, just as you pay for clothes and furniture. But this act of purchase</u>
defines "full <u>is only the prelude to possession. Full ownership comes only when you have made it a part</u>
ownership" <u>of yourself, and the best way to make yourself a part of it is by writing in it.</u> An illustration
may make the point clear. You buy a beefsteak and transfer it from the butcher's icebox to
your own. But you do not own the beefsteak in the most important sense until you consume
it and get it into your bloodstream. I am arguing that books, too, must be absorbed in your
bloodstream to do you any good.

describe "false <u>Confusion about what it means to own a book leads people to a false reverence for</u>
reverence for <u>paper, binding, and type—a respect for the physical thing—the craft of the printer rather</u>
paper" <u>than the genius of the author.</u> They forget that it is possible for a man to acquire the idea,   20
to possess the beauty, which a great book contains, without staking his claim by pasting his
bookplate inside the cover. Having a fine library doesn't prove that its owner has a mind

enriched by books; it proves nothing more than that he, his father, or his wife, was rich enough to buy them.

There are three kinds of book owners. The first has all the standard sets and best-sellers—unread, untouched. (This deluded individual owns woodpulp and ink, not books.) The second has a great many books—a few of them read through, most of them dipped into, but all of them as clean and shiny as the day they were bought. (This person would probably like to make books his own, but is restrained by a false respect for their physical appearance.) The third has
30 a few books or many—every one of them dogeared and dilapidated, shaken and loosened by continual use, marked and scribbled in from front to back. (This man owns books.)

classifies three types of book owners

Is it false respect, you may ask, to preserve intact and unblemished a beautifully printed book, an elegantly bound edition? Of course not. I'd no more scribble all over a first edition of *Paradise Lost* than I'd give my baby a set of crayons and an original Rembrandt! I wouldn't mark up a painting or a statue. Its soul, so to speak, is inseparable from its body. And the beauty of a rare edition or of a richly manufactured volume is like that of a painting or a statue.

But the soul of a book *can* be separated from its body. A book is more like the score of a piece of music than it is like a painting. No great musician confuses a symphony with the printed sheets of music. Arturo Toscanini reveres Brahms, but Toscanini's score of the
40 C-minor Symphony is so thoroughly marked up that no one but the maestro himself can read it. The reason why a great conductor makes notations on his musical scores—marks them up again and again each time he returns to study them—is the reason why you should mark your books. If your respect for magnificent binding or typography gets in the way, buy yourself a cheap edition and pay your respects to the author.

Why is marking up a book indispensable to reading? First, it keeps you awake. (And I don't mean merely conscious; I mean wide awake.) In the second place, reading, if it is active, is thinking, and thinking tends to express itself in words, spoken or written. The marked book is usually the thought-through book. Finally, writing helps you remember the thoughts you had, or the thoughts the author expressed. Let me develop these three points.

explains need to write as you read

50 If reading is to accomplish anything more than passing time, it must be active. You can't let your eyes glide across the lines of a book and come up with an understanding of what you have read. Now an ordinary piece of light fiction, like say, *Gone with the Wind*, doesn't require the most active kind of reading. The books you read for pleasure can be read in a state of relaxation, and nothing is lost. But a great book, rich in ideas and beauty, a book that raises and tries to answer great fundamental questions, demands the most active reading of which you are capable. You don't absorb the ideas of John Dewey the way you absorb the crooning of Mr. Vallee. You have to reach for them. That you cannot do while you're asleep.

defines "active reading"

If, when you've finished reading a book, the pages are filled with your notes, you know that you read actively. The most famous active reader of great books I know is President
60 Hutchins, of the University of Chicago. He also has the hardest schedule of business activities of any man I know. He invariably reads with a pencil, and sometimes, when he picks up a book and pencil in the evening, he finds himself, instead of making intelligent notes, drawing what he calls "caviar factories" on the margins. When that happens, he puts the book down. He knows he's too tired to read, and he's just wasting time.

why write?   But, you may ask, why is writing necessary? Well, the physical act of writing, with your own hand, brings words and sentences more sharply before your mind and preserves them better in your memory. To set down your reaction to important words and sentences you have read, and the questions they have raised in your mind, is to preserve those reactions and sharpen those questions.

Even if you wrote on a scratch pad, and threw the paper away when you had finished 70 writing, your grasp of the book would be surer. But you don't have to throw the paper away. The margins (top and bottom, as well as side), the end-papers, the very space between the lines, are all available. They aren't sacred. And, best of all, your marks and notes become an integral part of the book and stay there forever. You can pick up the book the following week or year, and there are all your points of agreement, disagreement, doubt, and inquiry. It's like resuming an interrupted conversation with the advantage of being able to pick up where you left off.

reading as conversation   <u>And that is exactly what reading a book should be: a conversation between you and the author.</u> Presumably he knows more about the subject than you do; naturally, you'll have the proper humility as you approach him. But don't let anybody tell you that a reader is 80 supposed to be solely on the receiving end. Understanding is a two-way operation; learning doesn't consist in being an empty receptacle. The learner has to question himself and question the teacher. He even has to argue with the teacher, once he understands what the teacher is saying. And marking a book is literally an expression of your differences, or agreements of opinion, with the author.

There are all kinds of devices for marking a book intelligently and fruitfully. Here's the way I do it:

uses numbered steps and italics for easy reading

1. *Underlining:* of major points, of important or forceful statements.

2. *Vertical lines at the margin:* to emphasize a statement already underlined.

3. *Star, asterisk, or other doo-dad at the margin:* to be used sparingly, to emphasize the ten 90 or twenty most important statements in the book. (You may want to fold the bottom corner of each page on which you use such marks. It won't hurt the sturdy paper on which most modern books are printed, and you will be able to take the book off the shelf at any time and, by opening it at the folded-corner page, refresh your recollection of the book.)

4. *Numbers in the margin:* to indicate the sequence of points the author makes in developing a single argument.

5. *Numbers of other pages in the margin:* to indicate where else in the book the author made points relevant to the point marked; to tie up the ideas in a book, which, though they may be separated by many pages, belong together. 100

6. *Circling of key words or phrases.*

7. *Writing in the margin, or at the top or bottom of the page, for the sake of:* recording questions (and perhaps answers) which a passage raised in your mind; reducing a complicated discussion to a simple statement; recording the sequence of major

points right through the book. I use the end-papers at the back of the book to make a personal index of the author's points in the order of their appearance.

The front end-papers are, to me, the most important. Some people reserve them for a fancy bookplate. I reserve them for fancy thinking. After I have finished reading the book and making my personal index on the back end-papers, I turn to the front and try to outline the book, not page by page, or point by point (I've already done that at the back), but as an integrated structure, with a basic unity and an order of parts. This outline is, to me, the measure of my understanding of the work.

If you're a die-hard anti-book-marker, you may object that the margins, the space between the lines, and the end-papers don't give you room enough. All right. How about using a scratch pad slightly smaller than the page-size of the book—so that the edges of the sheets won't protrude? Make your index, outlines, and even your notes on the pad, and then insert these sheets permanently inside the front and back covers of the book.

Or, you may say that this business of marking books is going to slow up your reading. It probably will. That's one of the reasons for doing it. Most of us have been taken in by the notion that speed of reading is a measure of our intelligence. There is no such thing as the right speed for intelligent reading. Some things should be read quickly and effortlessly, and some should be read slowly and even laboriously. The sign of intelligence in reading is the ability to read different things according to their worth. In the case of good books, the point is not to see how many of them you can get through, but rather how many can get through you—how many you can make your own. A few friends are better than a thousand acquaintances. If this be your aim, as it should be, you will not be impatient if it takes more time and effort to read a great book than it does a newspaper.

goal of reading good books

You may have one final objection to marking books. You can't lend them to your friends because nobody else can read them without being distracted by your notes. Furthermore, you won't want to lend them because a marked copy is a kind of intellectual diary, and lending it is almost like giving your mind away.

If your friend wishes to read your *Plutarch's Lives, Shakespeare,* or *The Federalist Papers,* tell him gently but firmly to buy a copy. You will lend him your car or your coat—but your books are as much a part of you as your head or your heart. ∎

conclusion

UNDERSTANDING CONTEXT

1. In Adler's view, when do you really *own* a book? What makes a book truly yours? What makes a book like a steak?

2. What does Adler mean by the "soul" of a book? How does respecting it differ from respecting its "body"?

3. Why is it important, in Adler's view, to write as you read?

4. *Critical thinking:* This essay was first published more than sixty years ago. Are Adler's suggestions any different from the study skills you may have learned in high school or college?

EVALUATING STRATEGY

1. What audience is Adler addressing?

2. *Other modes:* Where does Adler use *comparison, description,* and *classification* in developing this essay?

3. Adler provides seven suggestions that are stated in italics and numbered. If this advice were written in a standard paragraph, would it be as effective? Why or why not?

APPRECIATING LANGUAGE

1. The *Saturday Review of Literature* had a general but highly literate readership, much like that of today's *New Yorker* or *Vanity Fair.* Does the tone and style of the article seem suited to this audience?

2. Are there any words, phrases, references, or expressions in this sixty-year-old article that need updating?

WRITING SUGGESTIONS

1. Using Adler's seven suggestions, write a brief one-page guide on active reading directed to high school students.

2. *Collaborative writing:* Adler presents tips for active reading. Work with a group of students and discuss their experiences in studying for examinations. Record your ideas and suggestions, and then write a well-organized list of tips to help new students develop successful study skills.

ARMOND D. BUDISH

Armond D. Budish is an attorney and consumer-law reporter. He practises law in Ohio, where he writes columns on consumer issues for the **Cleveland Plain Dealer.** He has also published articles for **Family Circle** magazine. His book **How to Beat the Catastrophic Costs of Nursing Home Care** was published in 1989.

Fender Benders: Do's and Don't's*

As you read this article, notice how Budish makes use of numbered steps and bold type to make this Family Circle *article easy to skim.*

The car ahead of you stops suddenly. You hit the brakes, but you just can't stop in time. Your front bumper meets the rear end of the other car. Ouch! 1

There doesn't seem to be any damage, and it must be your lucky day because the driver you hit agrees that it's not worth hassling with insurance claims and risking a premium increase. So after exchanging addresses, you go your separate ways.

Imagine your surprise when you open the mail a few weeks later only to discover a letter from your "victim's" lawyer demanding $10,000 to cover car repairs, pain and suffering. Apparently the agreeable gentleman decided to disagree, then went ahead and filed a police report blaming you for the incident and for his damages.

When automobiles meet by accident, do you know how to respond? 10

Here are 10 practical tips that can help you avoid costly legal and insurance hassles.

1. **Stop! It's the Law.**

   No matter how serious or minor the accident, stop immediately. If possible, don't move your car—especially if someone has been injured. Leaving the cars as they were when the accident occurred helps the police determine what happened. Of course, if your car is blocking traffic or will cause another accident where it is, then move it to the nearest safe location.

   For every rule there are exceptions, though. If, for example, you are rear-ended at night in an unsafe area, it's wisest to keep on going and notify the police later. There have been cases in which people were robbed or assaulted when they got out of their cars. 20

2. **Zip Loose Lips.**

   Watch what you say after an accident. Although this may sound harsh, even an innocent "I'm sorry" could later be construed as an admission of fault. Also be sure not to accuse the other driver of causing the accident. Since you don't know how a stranger will react to your remarks, you run the risk of making a bad situation worse.

Remember, you are not the judge or jury; it's not up to you to decide who is or is not at fault. Even if you think you caused the accident, you might be wrong. For example: Assume you were driving 15 miles over the speed limit. What you probably were not aware of is that the other driver's blood-alcohol level exceeded the legal limits, so he was at least equally at fault.

3. **Provide Required Information.**

If you are involved in an accident, you are required in most states to give your name, address and car registration number to: any person injured in the accident; the owner, driver or passenger in any car that was damaged in the accident; a police officer on the scene. If you don't own the car (say it belongs to a friend or your parents), you should provide the name and address of the owner.

You must produce this information even if there are no apparent injuries or damages and even if you didn't cause the accident. Most states don't require you to provide the name of your insurance company, although it's usually a good idea to do so. However, *don't* discuss the amount of your coverage—that might inspire the other person to "realize" his injuries are more serious than he originally thought.

What should you do if you hit a parked car and the owner is not around? The law requires you to leave a note with your name, and the other identifying information previously mentioned, in a secure place on the car (such as under the windshield wiper).

4. **Get Required Information.**

You should obtain from the others involved in the accident the same information that you provide them with. However, if the other driver refuses to cooperate, at least get the license number and the make and model of the car to help police track down the owner.

5. **Call the Police.**

It's obvious that if it's a serious accident in which someone is injured, the police should be called immediately. That's both the law and common sense. But what if the accident seems minor? Say you're stopped, another car taps you in the rear. If it's absolutely clear to both drivers that there is no damage or injury, you each can go your merry way. But that's the exception.

Normally, you should call the police to substantiate what occurred. In most cities police officers will come to the scene, even for minor accidents, but if they won't, you and the other driver should go to the station (of the city where the accident occurred) to file a report. Ask to have an officer check out both cars.

If you are not at fault, be wary of accepting the other driver's suggestion that you leave the police out of it and arrange a private settlement. When you submit your $500 car-repair estimate several weeks later, you could discover that the other driver has developed "amnesia" and denies being anywhere near the accident. If the police weren't present on the scene, you may not have a legal leg to stand on.

Even if you *are* at fault, it's a good idea to involve the police. Why? Because a police officer will note the extent of the other driver's damages in his or her report, limiting your liability. Without police presence the other driver can easily inflate the amount of the damages.

6. **Identify Witnesses.**

Get the names and addresses of any witnesses, in case there's a legal battle some time in the future. Ask bystanders or other motorists who stop whether they saw the accident; if they answer "yes," get their identifying information. It is also helpful to note the names and badge numbers of all police officers on the scene.

7. **Go to the Hospital.**

If there's a chance that you've been injured, go directly to a hospital emergency room or to your doctor. The longer you wait, the more you may jeopardize your health and the more difficult it may be to get reimbursed for your injuries if they turn out to be serious.

8. **File a Report.**

Every driver who is involved in an automobile incident in which injuries occur must fill out an accident report. Even if the property damage is only in the range of $200 to $1,000, most states require that an accident report be filed. You must do this fairly quickly, usually in 1 to 30 days. Forms may be obtained and filed with the local motor vehicle department or police station in the city where the accident occurred.

9. **Consider Filing an Insurance Claim.**

Talk with your insurance agent as soon as possible after an accident. He or she can help you decide if you should file an insurance claim or pay out of your own pocket.

For example, let's say you caused an accident and the damages totaled $800. You carry a $250 deductible, leaving you with a possible $550 insurance claim. If you do submit a claim, your insurance rates are likely to go up, an increase that will probably continue for about three years. You should compare that figure to the $550 claim to determine whether to file a claim or to pay the cost yourself. (Also keep in mind that multiple claims sometimes make it harder to renew your coverage.)

10. **Don't Be Too Quick to Accept a Settlement.**

If the other driver is at fault and there's any chance you've been injured, don't rush to accept a settlement from that person's insurance company. You may not know the extent of your injuries for some time, and once you accept a settlement, it's difficult to get an "upgrade." Before settling, consult with a lawyer who handles personal injury cases.

When you *haven't* been injured and you receive a fair offer to cover the damage to your car, you can go ahead and accept it. ■

70

80

90

100

UNDERSTANDING CONTEXT

1. What problems can motorists have if they are careless about handling even minor accidents?

2. What are some of the most important things you should do if involved in a fender bender?

3. Why should you go to the hospital even if you have what appears to be a minor injury?

4. *Critical thinking:* Should this article be printed as a pamphlet and distributed to drivers' education classes? Have you known anyone who has gotten into difficulties that could have been avoided if he or she had followed the writer's advice?

EVALUATING STRATEGY

1. How does Budish arouse reader attention in the opening?

2. How effective are the numbered steps? Would the article lose impact if printed in standard paragraphs?

3. How easy is this article to remember? Can you put it down and recall the main points?

APPRECIATING LANGUAGE

1. This article was written for *Family Circle*. Does the language appear to be targeted to a female audience?

2. Why does Budish, who is an attorney, avoid legal terminology?

3. Does Budish's language create concrete images that make strong impressions to dramatize his subject?

WRITING SUGGESTIONS

1. Using this article as a model, provide the general public with a similar list of tips to prevent heart disease, deter muggers, prepare their children for school, or save money for retirement.

2. *Collaborative writing:* Work with a group of students to provide tips for new students on campus. Use peer review to make sure you do not overlook details in guiding students to accomplish a specific goal.

WILLIAM K. ZINSSER

William Zinsser is an American writer, editor, and teacher who began his career as a journalist and shifted to teaching writing and journalism at such institutions as Yale University, the New School in New York City, and the Graduate School of Journalism at Columbia University. He has written numerous books, including **Writing to Learn**, and **Writing About Your Life**.

Simplicity*

In his essay, "Simplicity," William Zinsser argues that the way to ensure clear, responsible communication in writing is to eliminate every sign of cluttered thinking, from vague language to unnecessary words (echoing George Orwell's insistence on clarity in "Politics and the English Language").

Clutter is the disease of American writing. We are a society strangling in unnecessary words, 1
circular constructions, pompous frills and meaningless jargon.

Who can understand the clotted language of everyday American commerce: the memo, the corporation report, the business letter, the notice from the bank explaining its latest "simplified" statement? What member of an insurance or medical plan can decipher the brochure explaining his costs and benefits? What father or mother can put together a child's toy from the instructions on the box? Our national tendency is to inflate and thereby sound important. The airline pilot who announces that he is presently anticipating experiencing considerable precipitation wouldn't think of saying it may rain. The sentence is too simple— there must be something wrong with it. 10

But the secret of good writing is to strip every sentence to its cleanest components. Every word that serves no function, every long word that could be a short word, every adverb that carries the same meaning that's already in the verb, every passive construction that leaves the reader unsure of who is doing what—these are the thousand and one adulterants that weaken the strength of a sentence. And they usually occur in proportion to education and rank.

During the 1960s the president of my university wrote a letter to mollify the alumni after a spell of campus unrest. "You are probably aware," he began, "that we have been experiencing very considerable potentially explosive expressions of dissatisfaction on issues only partially related." He meant that the students had been hassling them about different things. 20
I was far more upset by the president's English than by the students' potentially explosive expressions of dissatisfaction. I would have preferred the presidential approach taken by

Franklin D. Roosevelt when he tried to convert into English his own government's memos, such as this blackout order of 1942:

> *Such preparations shall be made as will completely obscure all Federal buildings and non-Federal buildings occupied by the Federal government during an air raid for any period of time from visibility by reason of internal or external illumination.*

"Tell them," Roosevelt said, "that in buildings where they have to keep the work going to put something across the windows."

30   Simplify, simplify. Thoreau said it, as we are so often reminded, and no American writer more consistently practiced what he preached. Open *Walden* to any page and you will find a man saying in a plain and orderly way what is on his mind:

> *I went to the woods because I wished to live deliberately, to front only the essential facts of life, and see if I could not learn what it had to teach, and not, when I came to die, discover that I had not lived.*

How can the rest of us achieve such enviable freedom from clutter? The answer is to clear our heads of clutter. Clear thinking becomes clear writing; one can't exist without the other. It's impossible for a muddy thinker to write good English. He may get away with it for a paragraph or two, but soon the reader will be lost, and there's no sin so grave, for
40   the reader will not easily be lured back.

Who is this elusive creature, the reader? The reader is someone with an attention span of about 30 seconds—a person assailed by many forces competing for attention. At one time those forces were relatively few: newspapers, magazines, radio, spouse, children, pets. Today they also include a galaxy of electronic devices for receiving entertainment and information—television, VCRs, DVDs, CDs, video games, the Internet, e-mail, cell phones, BlackBerries, iPods—as well as a fitness program, a pool, a lawn and that most potent of competitors, sleep. The man or woman snoozing in a chair with a magazine or a book is a person who was being given too much unnecessary trouble by the writer.

It won't do to say that the reader is too dumb or too lazy to keep pace with the train of
50   thought. If the reader is lost, it's usually because the writer hasn't been careful enough. That carelessness can take any number of forms. Perhaps a sentence is so excessively cluttered that the reader, hacking through the verbiage, simply doesn't know what it means. Perhaps a sentence has been so shoddily constructed that the reader could read it in several ways. Perhaps the writer has switched pronouns in midsentence, or has switched tenses, so the reader loses track of who is talking or when the action took place. Perhaps Sentence B is not a logical sequel to Sentence A; the writer, in whose head the connection is clear, hasn't bothered to provide the missing link. Perhaps the writer has used a word incorrectly by not taking the trouble to look it up.

Faced with such obstacles, readers are at first tenacious. They blame themselves—they
60   obviously missed something, and they go back over the mystifying sentence, or over the whole paragraph, piecing it out like an ancient rune, making guesses and moving on. But they won't do that for long. The writer is making them work too hard, and they will look for one who is better at the craft.

Writers must therefore constantly ask: what am I trying to say? Surprisingly often they don't know. Then they must look at what they have written and ask: have I said it? Is it clear to someone encountering the subject for the first time? If it's not, some fuzz has worked its way into the machinery. The clear writer is someone clearheaded enough to see this stuff for what it is: fuzz.

I don't mean that some people are born clearheaded and are therefore natural writers, whereas others are naturally fuzzy and will never write well. Thinking clearly is a conscious act that writers must force on themselves, as if they were working on any other project that requires logic: making a shopping list or doing an algebra problem. Good writing doesn't come naturally, though most people seem to think it does. Professional writers are constantly bearded by people who say they'd like to "try a little writing sometime"—meaning when they retire from their real profession, like insurance or real estate, which is hard. Or they say, "I could write a book about that." I doubt it.

Writing is hard work. A clear sentence is no accident. Very few sentences come out right the first time, or even the third time. Remember this in moments of despair. If you find that writing is hard, it's because it *is* hard. ∎

---

5 --

is too dumb or too lazy to keep pace with the ~~writer's~~ train of thought. My sympathies are ~~entirely~~ with him. ~~He's not so dumb.~~ If the reader is lost, it is generally because the writer ~~of the article~~ has not been careful enough to keep him on the ~~proper~~ path.

This carelessness can take any number of ~~different~~ forms. Perhaps a sentence is so excessively ~~long and~~ cluttered that the reader, hacking his way through ~~all~~ the verbiage, simply doesn't know what _it_ ~~the writer~~ means. Perhaps a sentence has been so shoddily constructed that the reader could read it in any of _several_ ~~two or three different~~ ways. ~~He thinks he knows what the writer is trying to say, but he's not sure.~~ Perhaps the writer has switched pronouns in mid-sentence, or ~~perhaps he~~ has switched tenses, so the reader loses track of who is talking ~~to whom~~ or ~~exactly~~ when the action took place. Perhaps Sentence B is not a logical sequel to Sentence A — the

writer, in whose head the connection is ~~perfectly~~ clear, has
not ^bothered to provide^ ~~given enough thought to providing~~ the missing link. Perhaps the writer has used an important word incorrectly by not
taking the trouble to look it up ~~and make sure.~~ He may think
that "sanguine" and "sanguinary" mean the same thing, but
~~I can assure you that~~ the difference is a bloody big one ~~to the~~
~~reader.~~ ^The reader^ ~~He~~ can only ~~try to~~ infer ~~about~~ (speaking of big differences) what the writer is trying to imply.

Faced with ^these^ ~~such a variety of~~ obstacles, the reader
is at first a remarkably tenacious bird. He ~~tends to~~ blame ^s^
himself ~~.~~ ^H^e obviously missed something, ~~he thinks,~~ and he goes
back over the mystifying sentence, or over the whole paragraph,
6 --
piecing it out like an ancient runs, making guesses and moving
on. But he won't do this for long. ~~He will soon run out of~~
~~patience.~~ The writer is making him work too hard, ~~harder~~
~~than he should have to work~~ and the reader will look for
~~a writer~~ ^one^ who is better at his craft.

The writer must therefore constantly ask himself: What am
I trying to say? ~~in this sentence?~~ (Surprisingly often, he
doesn't know. ~~And~~ Then he must look at what he has ~~just~~
written and ask: Have I said it? Is it clear to someone
^encountering^ ~~who is coming upon~~ the subject for the first time? If it's
not, ~~clear,~~ it is because some fuzz has worked its way into the
machinery. The clear writer is a person ~~who is~~ clear-headed
enough to see this stuff for what it is: fuzz.

I don't mean ~~to suggest~~ that some people are born
clear-headed and are therefore natural writers, whereas
^others^ ~~other people~~ are naturally fuzzy and will ~~therefore~~ never write
well. Thinking clearly is ^a^ ~~an entirely~~ conscious act that the

writer must ~~keep forcing~~ force upon himself, just as if he were
~~starting out~~ embarking on any other ~~kind of~~ project that ~~calls for~~ requiring logic:
adding up a laundry list or doing an algebra problem ~~or playing~~
~~chess.~~ Good writing doesn't ~~just~~ come naturally, though most
people obviously think it does ~~it's as easy as walking.~~ The professional

Two pages of the final manuscript of this chapter from the First Edition of *On Writing Well*. Although they look like a first draft, they had already been rewritten and retyped—like almost every other page—four or five times. With each rewrite I try to make what I have written tighter, stronger and more precise, eliminating every element that's not doing useful work. Then I go over it once more, reading it aloud, and am always amazed at how much clutter can still be cut. (In later editions I eliminated the sexist pronoun "he" denoting "the writer" and "the reader.")

UNDERSTANDING CONTEXT

1. What does Zinsser argue about the relationship between two processes: thinking and writing?

2. One of the myths about effective writing is that good writers are born, not made. How does Zinsser address this belief?

EVALUATING STRATEGY

1. Analyze and explain the process by which Zinsser unfolds his argument about the need for clarity and simplicity in writing.

2. Explain the process Zinsser advocates for eliminating clutter in writing.

APPRECIATING LANGUAGE

1. Zinsser writes that clutter in writing is a "disease," and that it is "strangling" society. What are the implications of such metaphors? Can you find other uses of metaphor to describe unclear writing in the essay?

WRITING SUGGESTIONS

1. Write a one-paragraph summary of Zinsser's essay.

2. Write a two-page essay reflecting on your own relationship to clutter in your writing and how you eliminate it.

3. *Critical thinking:* Write an essay considering the validity of Zinsser's insistence on uncluttered writing. Is the goal of clarity always admirable and appropriate? Could his emphasis on stripped-down language be seen as partly a personality, or even cultural, trait than an absolute guideline for effective writing?

4. Write an essay that compares and contrasts Zinsser's "Simplicity" with George Orwell's "Politics and the English Language."

Blending the Modes   MALCOLM X

Malcolm X (1925–1965) was born Malcolm Little in Omaha, Nebraska, where his father worked as a preacher. While in prison for robbery, Malcolm converted to the Black Muslim faith. He changed his last name to X to reject his "slave name" and dramatize African Americans' loss of heritage. He became a rising force in the Nation of Islam and in 1963 was named its first "national minister." After a trip to Mecca, he converted to orthodox Islam and rejected the racial views advocated by Black Muslims. He founded the Muslim Mosque, Inc., in 1964. A year later, he was shot and killed at a Harlem rally.

My First Conk*

In this section from his autobiography, Malcolm X explains the process of "conking," or straightening hair, popular with some African Americans in the 1940s and 1950s. As you read this essay, note how Malcolm X explains the process, then uses it as an example in an argument about black identity.

Shorty soon decided that my hair was finally long enough to be conked. He had promised 1 to school me in how to beat the barbershops' three- and four-dollar price by making up congolene, and then conking ourselves.

I took the little list of ingredients he had printed out for me, and went to a grocery store, where I got a can of Red Devil lye, two eggs, and two medium-sized white potatoes. Then at a drugstore near the poolroom, I asked for a large jar of Vaseline, a large bar of soap, a large-toothed comb and a fine-toothed comb, one of those rubber hoses with a metal spray-head, a rubber apron and a pair of gloves.

"Going to lay on that first conk?" the drugstore man asked me. I proudly told him, grinning, "Right!"   10

Shorty paid six dollars a week for a room in his cousin's shabby apartment. His cousin wasn't at home. "It's like the pad's mine, he spends so much time with his woman," Shorty said. "Now, you watch me—"

He peeled the potatoes and thin-sliced them into a quart-sized Mason fruit jar, then started stirring them with a wooden spoon as he gradually poured in a little over half the can of lye. "Never use a metal spoon; the lye will turn it black," he told me.

A jelly-like, starchy-looking glop resulted from the lye and potatoes, and Shorty broke in the two eggs, stirring real fast—his own conk and dark face bent down close. The congolene turned pale-yellowish. "Feel the jar," Shorty said. I cupped my hand against the outside, and snatched it away. "Damn right, it's hot, that's the lye," he said. "So you know 20 it's going to burn when I comb it in—it burns bad. But the longer you can stand it, the straighter the hair."

*Malcolm X, "My First Conk" from *The Autobiography of Malcolm X* by Malcolm X and Alex Haley, copyright © 1964 by Alex Haley and Malcolm X. Copyright © 1965 by Alex Haley and Betty Shabazz. Used by permission of Random House, Inc.

He made me sit down, and he tied the string of the new rubber apron tightly around my neck, and combed up my bush of hair. Then, from the big Vaseline jar, he took a handful and massaged it hard all through my hair and into the scalp. He also thickly Vaselined my neck, ears and forehead. "When I get to washing out your head, be sure to tell me anywhere you feel any little stinging," Shorty warned me, washing his hands, then pulling on the rubber gloves, and tying on his own rubber apron. "You always got to remember that any congolene left in burns a sore into your head."

30   The congolene just felt warm when Shorty started combing it in. But then my head caught fire.

I gritted my teeth and tried to pull the sides of the kitchen table together. The comb felt as if it was raking my skin off.

My eyes watered, my nose was running. I couldn't stand it any longer; I bolted to the washbasin. I was cursing Shorty with every name I could think of when he got the spray going and started soap-lathering my head.

He lathered and spray-rinsed, lathered and spray-rinsed, maybe ten or twelve times, each time gradually closing the hot-water faucet, until the rinse was cold, and that helped some.

40   "You feel any stinging spots?"

"No," I managed to say. My knees were trembling.

"Sit back down, then. I think we got it all out okay."

The flame came back as Shorty, with a thick towel, started drying my head, rubbing hard. *"Easy, man, easy!"* I kept shouting.

"The first time's always worst. You get used to it better before long. You took it real good, homeboy. You got a good conk."

When Shorty let me stand up and see in the mirror, my hair hung down in limp, damp strings. My scalp still flamed, but not as badly; I could bear it. He draped the towel around my shoulders, over my rubber apron, and began again Vaselining my hair.

50   I could feel him combing, straight back, first the big comb, then the fine-tooth one.

Then, he was using a razor, very delicately, on the back of my neck. Then finally, shaping the sideburns.

My first view in the mirror blotted out the hurting. I'd seen some pretty conks, but when it's the first time, on your own head, the transformation, after the lifetime of kinks, is staggering.

The mirror reflected Shorty behind me. We both were grinning and on top of my head was this thick, smooth sheen of shining red hair—real red— as straight as any white man's.

How ridiculous I was! Stupid enough to stand there simply lost in admiration of my hair 60 now looking "white," reflected in the mirror in Shorty's room. I vowed that I'd never again be without a conk, and I never was for many years.

This was my first really big step toward self-degradation: when I endured all of that pain, literally burning my flesh to have it look like a white man's hair. I had joined that multitude of Negro men and women in America who are brainwashed into believing that the black people are "inferior"—and white people "superior"—that they will even violate and mutilate their God-created bodies to try to look "pretty" by white standards.

Look around today, in every small town and big city, from two-bit catfish and soda-pop joints into the "integrated" lobby of the Waldorf-Astoria, and you'll see conks on black men. And you'll see black women wearing these green and pink and purple and red and platinum-blonde wigs. They're all more ridiculous than a slapstick comedy. It makes you wonder if the 70 Negro has completely lost his sense of identity, lost touch with himself.

You'll see the conk worn by many, many so-called "upper class" Negroes, and, as much as I hate to say it about them, on all too many Negro entertainers. One of the reasons that I've especially admired some of them, like Lionel Hampton and Sidney Poitier, among others, is that they have kept their natural hair and fought to the top. I admire any Negro man who has never had himself conked, or who has had the sense to get rid of it—as I finally did.

I don't know which kind of self-defacing conk is the greater shame—the one you'll see on the heads of the black so-called "middle class" and "upper class," who ought to know better, or the one you'll see on the heads of the poorest, most downtrodden, ignorant black men. I mean the legal minimum-wage ghetto-dwelling kind of Negro, as I was when I got 80 my first one. It's generally among these poor fools that you'll see a black kerchief over the man's head, like Aunt Jemima; he's trying to make his conk last longer, between trips to the barbershop. Only for special occasions is this kerchief-protected conk exposed—to show off how "sharp" and "hip" its owner is. The ironic thing is that I have never heard any woman, white or black, express any admiration for a conk. Of course, any white woman with a black man isn't thinking about his hair. But I don't see how on earth a black woman with any race pride could walk down the street with any black man wearing a conk—the emblem of his shame that he is black.

To my own shame, when I say all of this I'm talking first of all about myself—because you can't show me any Negro who ever conked more faithfully than I did. I'm speaking from 90 personal experience when I say of any black man who conks today, or any white-wigged black woman, that if they gave the brains in their heads just half as much attention as they do their hair, they would be a thousand times better off. ■

UNDERSTANDING CONTEXT

1. What motivated black people to endure the painful "conking" process?

2. Why does Malcolm X see the conk as an "emblem of shame"?

3. Why is Malcolm X especially disturbed by the sight of conks worn by middle-class and professional African Americans?

4. *Critical thinking:* A century ago, Jewish immigrants were urged, often by American Jews, to shave their beards and discard traditional garments in order to succeed in the New World. Are these changes harmless adaptations to a new culture or do they represent a form of self-loathing? Do you see current examples of men and women altering their identity?

EVALUATING STRATEGY

1. Malcolm X begins the essay with a story, told without any commentary. Do you find it effective to explain the process, then discuss its social significance?

2. How does Malcolm X use dialogue to bring the narrative to life?

3. *Other modes:* Can you consider this essay a blend of process, example, and argument? What parts do these elements play in the essay?

4. *Critical thinking:* Social critics generally comment on social behaviour from a distance. How does the story of his own conking give Malcolm X greater insight into black self-degradation? Without introducing his own experiences, what effect would the last four paragraphs have?

APPRECIATING LANGUAGE

1. What language does Malcolm X use to dramatize the pain of being conked?

2. At one point, Malcolm X states he was "brainwashed." Why is this a key term? How did popular culture "brainwash" generations of African Americans to admire "whiteness" and despise black identity?

3. Malcolm X uses the word *shame* repeatedly. How do you define *shame*?

WRITING SUGGESTIONS

1. Write a short essay about a process you have experienced—getting your ears pierced, applying for a loan, trying out for a team, auditioning for a part. First describe the process; then comment on what you learned about yourself and society.

2. *Collaborative writing:* Discuss the last sentence of the essay with a number of students. Do many people—of all races—devote more attention to their hair than their brains? Write a list of examples showing how people seek to alter their appearance to achieve a new identity.

Writing beyond the Classroom   eHOW

How to Lease a Car with the Option to Buy

As you read these instructions about leasing a car, determine whether you would find them easy to follow. Are they clearly organized and do they provide enough detail?

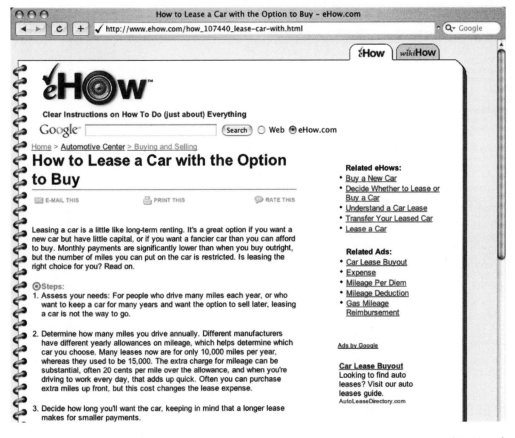

(Continued)

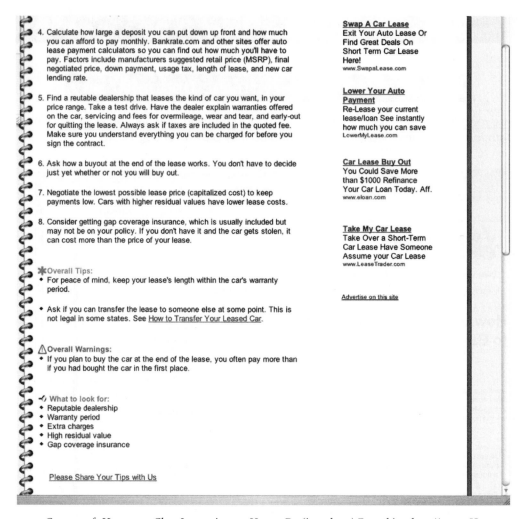

4. Calculate how large a deposit you can put down up front and how much you can afford to pay monthly. Bankrate.com and other sites offer auto lease payment calculators so you can find out how much you'll have to pay. Factors include manufacturers suggested retail price (MSRP), final negotiated price, down payment, usage tax, length of lease, and new car lending rate.

5. Find a reutable dealership that leases the kind of car you want, in your price range. Take a test drive. Have the dealer explain warranties offered on the car, servicing and fees for overmileage, wear and tear, and early-out for quitting the lease. Always ask if taxes are included in the quoted fee. Make sure you understand everything you can be charged for before you sign the contract.

6. Ask how a buyout at the end of the lease works. You don't have to decide just yet whether or not you will buy out.

7. Negotiate the lowest possible lease price (capitalized cost) to keep payments low. Cars with higher residual values have lower lease costs.

8. Consider getting gap coverage insurance, which is usually included but may not be on your policy. If you don't have it and the car gets stolen, it can cost more than the price of your lease.

❊ Overall Tips:
- For peace of mind, keep your lease's length within the car's warranty period.

- Ask if you can transfer the lease to someone else at some point. This is not legal in some states. See How to Transfer Your Leased Car.

⚠ Overall Warnings:
- If you plan to buy the car at the end of the lease, you often pay more than if you had bought the car in the first place.

↻ What to look for:
- Reputable dealership
- Warranty period
- Extra charges
- High residual value
- Gap coverage insurance

Please Share Your Tips with Us

Swap A Car Lease
Exit Your Auto Lease Or Find Great Deals On Short Term Car Lease Here!
www.SwapaLease.com

Lower Your Auto Payment
Re-Lease your current lease/loan See instantly how much you can save
LowerMyLease.com

Car Lease Buy Out
You Could Save More than $1000 Refinance Your Car Loan Today. Aff.
www.eloan.com

Take My Car Lease
Take Over a Short-Term Car Lease Have Someone Assume your Car Lease
www.LeaseTrader.com

Advertise on this site

Courtesy of eHow.com - Clear Instructions on How to Do (just about) Everything. http://www.eHow.com

UNDERSTANDING CONTEXT

1. How is leasing a car different from buying a car? What are the major advantages and disadvantages?

2. Who should *not* lease a car? Why?

3. What questions should consumers ask car dealers before they lease a vehicle?

4. What is a buyout? How does it work?

5. How can consumers reduce their monthly payments?

6. *Critical thinking:* Do you think it is advisable for all consumers to consider their long-term needs and driving habits before buying a vehicle as well? Do many people buy cars based on style or performance alone?

EVALUATING STRATEGY

1. Why are numbered points useful in giving these directions?
2. What role do visuals play in making a web page easy to read and navigate?
3. How do bold fonts emphasize key points? Would two pages of text in standard paragraphs communicate as well? Why or why not?

APPRECIATING LANGUAGE

1. What does the level of diction and word choice reveal about the intended audience?
2. Do the authors successfully avoid overly technical language that some readers would find difficult?

WRITING SUGGESTIONS

1. Write a short set of directions to accomplish a task in an emergency. Give numbered steps to alert dorm residents what to do if they discover a fire, tell parents how to respond if their child is lost, or direct consumers how to protect their identity if their credit cards are stolen.
2. *Collaborative writing:* Work with a group of students and write a short persuasive essay urging car buyers to avoid common mistakes in selecting, financing, or insuring a new or used car.

Responding to IMAGES

In 1966, civil rights activist Malcolm X appeared as the mystery guest on CBC's *Front Page Challenge,* a popular current events program.

CBC Still Photo Collection

1. What is your first impression of this photograph?

2. How does the photograph signal the differences between the United States and Canada in the 1960s?

3. Looking at the photograph, what are your assumptions about the four panel members? Are they representative of Canadian culture? Describe the makeup of the panel.

4. *Front Page Challenge* was hugely popular, and it ran on the CBC for 38 seasons, from 1957 to 1995. Why do you think that a current events quiz show was so popular? Would it be popular now? Why or why not?

5. *Visual analysis:* Malcolm X was usually depicted as a serious and angry man. He promoted equality by any means necessary, including violence. What is the effect of seeing him smile in this photograph? In contrast, describe your response to the panel's facial expressions.

6. *Collaborative writing:* On *Front Page Challenge*, the identity of the guest was determined by the panel through the guest's responses to the panel's questions. The panel would receive a hint at the start of the question period. In a group, have one member find a person from a current newspaper article. The rest of the group will create and ask a series of questions to determine the guest's identity. Try expanding the game by bringing in a prominent person on campus as the mystery guest.

7. *Other modes*

   ■ Write an essay *comparing* a current quiz show to *Front Page Challenge*. Is the current quiz show popular? Compare the new show's subject with *Front Page Challenge*'s focus on current events. Why do you think that the new program is popular?

   ■ Develop a *cause-and-effect* paper showing how the lack of current events programming has led to students being less informed about current events. Are students better informed about current events? Is it important that they are aware of current events?

☑ PROCESS **CHECKLIST**

Before submitting your paper, review these points:

✔ Is the process clearly defined?

✔ Do you supply background information readers need?

✔ Is the information easy to follow? Is the chain of events or the sequence of steps logically arranged?

✔ Could the text be enhanced by large print, bold or italic type, figures, or tables?

✔ Are your instructions complete? Do readers know when one step is over and another begins?

✔ Do your instructions alert readers to normal changes that they might mistake for errors?

✔ Are hazards clearly stated?

✔ Did you use peer review to test your document?

COMPANION WEBSITE

See **http://www.transcanadawriter.nelson.com** for additional information about writing process.

CHAPTER 18

Division and Classification: Separating into Parts and Rating Categories

This chapter examines how analysis is informed by the processes of division and classification. It looks at how to separate wholes into categorized parts, and how to inquire into an organized relationship of parts, both to each other and to the whole.

WHAT ARE DIVISION AND CLASSIFICATION?

Division and classification are two important forms of analysis that help readers to understand complex subjects. Division refers to separating subjects into parts. Classification, which often guides decision making, rates subjects by placing them on a scale of differing categories.

DIVISION

Division makes complicated subjects easier to comprehend and work with. In order to understand how the human body works, for example, medical disciplines divide it into systems: digestive, respiratory, nervous, muscular-skeletal, reproductive, and so on. Another example is the psychological term *depression*, which often is used to express everything from minor disappointment to suicidal despair. A mental health brochure, however, divides the disorder into specific types to inform patients about the variety of depressive illnesses:

Bereavement   *A two- to nine-week process of grieving with sad and empty feelings after the death of someone important to you. May linger for much longer after the loss of a parent, child, or partner, but tends to gradually improve over time. You should observe steady readjustment to your changed world and resumption of social activities and pleasures.*

Adjustment reaction   *A period of up to six months after a major stressful event during which depressed mood or hopeless feelings are more intense than normal and interfere with daily social and school or work activities. Like bereavement, it is often helped by brief crisis therapy or family therapy.*

Major depression   *Depressed mood or loss of interests with a variety of symptoms and feelings of depression, discussed earlier, lasting at least two weeks. Major depression ranges from mild cases with few symptoms to severe cases (known as "clinical depression") marked by a persistent bleak outlook, which may lead to thoughts of escape through suicide. Depression may begin to lift after several weeks or may become chronic, lasting two years or more.*

In this case division presents readers with a series of definitions. Division can be used to organize a set of narratives, descriptions, processes, or persuasive arguments.

WRITING **ACTIVITY**

Select one of the topics and divide it into subtopics. You can use an existing division or invent one of your own.

1. Tests students face in college or university
2. Student housing on or off campus
3. Blind dates
4. Current movies
5. Popular night spots

Strategies for Writing Division

Critical Thinking and Prewriting

1. **Begin by listing possible topics for division.** Not all subjects are suitable for division. Interesting topics can resist easy separation into distinct parts. Begin by listing as many possibilities as you can, using prewriting techniques to discard difficult topics and identify promising ones.

2. **Clearly limit your subject.** If you do not initially limit the overall topic, you will find it difficult to break it down into parts.

3. **Avoid oversimplifying your subject.** You have no doubt seen magazine articles announcing three kinds of bosses, four types of marriages, or five methods of child rearing. Although these divisions can be amusing and insightful, they can trivialize or oversimplify a subject. Not all people or situations can neatly fit into three or four types.

4. **Use methods of division suitable to your subject, task, readers, and assignment to create meaningful distinctions.** There are many methods of making divisions. In a history or political science class you could divide Canadian prime ministers into liberals, conservatives, and centrists or those sympathetic, hostile, or indifferent toward a particular issue. Few professors or fellow students, however, would be interested in reading a paper dividing prime minister into groups according to their astrological sign or their pets.

5. **Remember, the goal of division is to make a subject easier to understand and work with.** Your division should have a purpose beyond simply breaking it into parts.

Planning

1. **Write a clear thesis statement or definition at the top of the page to guide planning.**
2. **Select a division method that includes all parts of the whole.** If you divide university students into three types, for example, ensure everyone on campus can be included in one group. Eliminate potential gaps. Every member of the whole must be addressed, even if only in an introduction acknowledging exceptions to general categories.
3. **Ensure individual parts fit only one category.**
4. **Avoid creating categories that include too many differences.** Not all items within a category will be identical, but to make sense a division should have a focus.
5. **Determine what other modes you will use.** A division essay is actually a collection of related narratives, definitions, arguments, examples, processes, or descriptions. Study your subject and select the best method of addressing each subtopic.
6. **Develop an outline that clearly divides your topic to guide the first draft.**

Writing the First Draft

1. **Focus your writing by clearly envisioning your purpose.** Divisions should help explain a subject and make it easier to work with.
2. **Follow guidelines for writing other modes—definition, narrative, example, process, and so forth—in developing each category.**
3. **Use parallel structures to develop categories.** Readers will find your categories easier to follow if you provide a common pattern of development.
4. **Monitor the length of your draft.** Because of their complexity, division papers can become lengthy. If you realize that your subject is too ambitious, that it would take 10 pages to fully address a topic selected for a 500-word essay, you may wish to return to prewriting to narrow your topic or select a different subject.
5. **Be open to new ideas but remain focused.** A division paper has a clear purpose— not every interesting idea or observation you develop belongs in this assignment.

Revising

1. **Examine your thesis and overall draft.**
   - Is the thesis clearly stated? Is your purpose clear?
   - Does your method of division make sense? Does it draw meaningful or only arbitrary distinctions between items?
   - Does the essay help readers understand a complex subject or only confuse the issue?
2. **Review the essay for balance and thoroughness.**
   - Do you describe some categories superficially, whereas others contain extensive examples, narratives, and details?
   - Do some sections need expansion and others trimming?
3. **Analyze the essay for parallel development.**
   - Do you follow a general pattern to discuss each item so that readers can easily compare them, or are the subtopics presented in a jumbled manner that mixes narratives, definitions, and examples without a common thread?

(Continued)

4. **Are the divisions clearly defined?**
   - Can some items be placed in more than one division?

5. **Do the divisions account for every part of the whole?**
   - Are there any items that remain undiscussed or unqualified, leaving readers wondering where to place them?

6. **Do you qualify your observations and account for possible exceptions?**
   - Can there be exceptions to your division? You may wish to state in an introduction or conclusion that not every item may fit your pattern of division or that your division may not be operative at all times or in all conditions.
   - Acknowledge any limitations to your thesis.

7. **Use peer review.**
   - Ask others to review your essay for clarity and completeness.

Editing and Proofreading

1. **Review word choice for accuracy and connotations.**
   - Are your subheadings meaningful and easy to remember?
   - Do some words have connotations that may mislead readers?
   - Do technical terms require definition or qualification?

2. **Read your paper aloud to identify errors.**

3. **Use peer editing to locate errors you may have missed.**

CLASSIFICATION

Like division, classification breaks a complex subject into parts. However, in classification, the categories are rated according to a standard. Teachers grade tests according to the number of correct answers. Geologists classify rocks by their hardness. Motion pictures are rated G, PG, 14A, 18A, or R, based on their depictions of sex and violence. Classification can reflect personal preferences. A food critic may grant a new restaurant one or five stars depending solely on his or her experience. Classification assists people to make decisions and direct actions. Classification can set prices, establish salaries, and in some instances save lives.

■ WRITING **ACTIVITY**

Select one of the following topics and develop at least three classifications. Remember to use a single standard to rate the topic—price, quality, size, performance, severity, and so forth.

1. Professional athletes or teams
2. Local restaurants
3. University professors
4. Friendships
5. Courses in your major

Strategies for Writing Classification

Critical Thinking and Prewriting

1. **Understand the difference between division and classification.** Remember that in classification you not only divide a subject into parts but also rate the parts on a scale.

2. **List topics that you might be able to classify.** Consider subjects that you customarily rate on a scale.

3. **To focus prewriting, start with a scale.** Because classification rates subjects on a standard, you can easily identify workable subjects and discard unusable ones if you work with a scale. You might develop a generic chart to explore topics, using 1–5 stars, an A–F grading system, or a 1–10 scale to rate your topics.

Planning

1. **Establish a clearly defined standard of measurement.** If you plan to classify cars by price, determine whether you will use wholesale or dealer prices. Establish the methods used to obtain your figures.

2. **Do not mix standards.** The most common mistake writers make in classification is mixing standards.

3. **Define each category clearly.** Each category should be clearly defined so readers can understand what separates each classification.

4. **Arrange categories in order.** Organize the categories so they follow a ladder-like progression, such as judging items from the best to the worst.

5. **Provide enough categories or classes to include all parts of the whole.**

6. **Ensure all topics fit only one class.** Every unit should fit only a single category. Ensure you have no leftover items that either can fit in more than one class or cannot be accounted for.

7. **Note any exceptions or variations to the classification.**

Writing the First Draft

1. **As you write, keep your thesis in mind—to rate items on a scale.**

2. **Use concrete language and details to distinguish each class and describe each item.** Avoid vague or general descriptions. Be as accurate as you can in defining standards.

3. **Illustrate each class with examples readers can identify.** Consider your audience carefully to select items they will understand.

4. **Use parallel structures to develop categories.** Develop common reference points so that readers can distinguish between categories and compare examples.

5. **Monitor the length of your draft.** As with division, a classification paper can easily balloon into a much longer essay. If you realize that to fully classify your subject, your essay will expand beyond the scope of the assignment, consider narrowing your topic or selecting a new subject.

6. **Note new ideas, but remember your goal—to rate items on a common scale.**

(Continued)

Revising

1. **Analyze your thesis.**
   - Is your overall subject clearly defined?

2. **Review your method of classification.**
   - Does your classification make meaningful or only arbitrary distinctions between items? Will your scale help people understand the subject and make decisions?
   - Are your categories clearly defined?
   - Are there any gaps between categories? Do categories overlap?
   - Are the categories arranged in a progressive order?

3. **Examine the categories for balance and completeness.**
   - Are some categories sharply defined and others vaguely worded?
   - Are some categories illustrated with four examples and others with just one?

4. **Can all items or parts be placed on your scale? Do you account for variations or exceptions?**

5. **Use peer review to identify areas needing improvement.**

Editing and Proofreading

1. **Reread your paper aloud.**
   - Is your paper stated in concrete, accurate language?
   - Do any terms require further clarification or definition?
   - Do some words have connotations that may confuse readers?

2. **Consider using visual aids.**
   - Would visual aids be appropriate?
   - Would your classification be easier to understand and recall if the text were supported by a figure or table?

3. **Use peer editing to locate errors you may have missed.**

SUGGESTED TOPICS FOR WRITING DIVISION AND CLASSIFICATION

General Assignments

Separating into Parts

Write a division essay on any of the following topics. Your division may make use of standard categories or ones you invent. Remember to clearly state the way you are dividing your subject. Each subject or example should be supported with definitions, brief narratives, or descriptions.

- Dates you have had
- Basketball, football, or baseball teams

- Popular music
- Student housing
- Local restaurants

Rating Categories

Write a classification essay on any of the following topics. Use a single method rating the subtopics, from best to worst or easiest to hardest.

- Diets
- Current movies
- Professors, coaches, or bosses you have known
- Cars
- Personal computers

Writing in Context

1. Assume you have been asked by a national magazine to write about students' political attitudes. You may develop your essay by division or classification. You can discuss politics in general terms of liberal and conservative attitudes or concentrate on a single issue, such as capital punishment or legalizing marijuana.

2. Write a humorous paper about campus fashion by dividing students into types. Invent titles or labels for each group and supply enough details so that readers can readily fit the people they meet into one of your categories.

■·□·■·□·■

Strategies for Reading Division and Classification

As you read the division and classification entries in this chapter, keep these questions in mind:

Context

1. What is the writer trying to explain by dividing or classifying the subject? Does the writer have another goal—to inform, entertain, or persuade?

2. Do the divisions risk oversimplifying the subject?

3. Do the classification essays have a clearly defined scale or standard?   ut they

4. Do the standards seem fair or adequate? Do they accurately meaclaim to evaluate?

(Continued)

Strategy

1. How does the writer introduce or establish the divisions or classes?

2. How does the author illustrate each type with other modes such as example, definition, or narrative?

3. Does the writer use an existing, long-established standard or one he or she invented?

4. Is the goal of the paper to explain items or recommend one over others?

Language

1. What does the level of language reveal about the intended audience?

2. What words does the author use to describe or define categories? Do the connotations of any of these words reveal positive or negative attitudes toward specific items? Do you detect a bias?

DREW HAYDEN TAYLOR

Born in 1962, Drew Hayden Taylor is one of Canada's leading Native playwrights and humourists. As a journalist, he contributed to magazines and newspapers before turning to screenwriting, producing scripts for the television shows **Street Legal, The Beachcombers,** and **North of Sixty.** Learning the craft of playwriting from his involvement in a theatre company on Manitoulin Island, Ontario, he began to write plays, including **Toronto at Dreamer's Rock, Girl Who Loved Her Horses, The Bootlegger Blues,** and **Someday.**

Pretty Like a White Boy*

Hayden Taylor uses humour in the following essay to expose the serious limitations and consequences of viewing the world through the rigid grids of racial categories.

In this big, huge world, with all its billions and billions of people, it's safe to say that everybody will eventually come across personalities and individuals that will touch them in some peculiar yet poignant way. Individuals that in some way represent and help define who you are. I'm no different, mine was Kermit the Frog. Not just because Natives have a long tradition of savouring Frogs' legs, but because of his music. If you all may remember, Kermit is quite famous for his rendition of "It's Not Easy Being Green." I can relate. If I could sing, my song would be "It's Not Easy Having Blue Eyes in a Brown Eyed Village."   1

Yes, I'm afraid it's true. The author happens to be a card-carrying Indian. Once you get past the aforementioned eyes, the fair skin, light brown hair, and noticeable lack of cheekbones, there lies the heart and spirit of an Ojibway storyteller. Honest Injun, or as the more politically correct term may be, honest aboriginal.   10

You see, I'm the product of a white father I never knew, and an Ojibway woman who evidently couldn't run fast enough. As a kid I knew I looked a bit different. But, then again, all kids are paranoid when it comes to their peers. I had a fairly happy childhood, frolicking through the bullrushes. But there were certain things that, even then, made me notice my unusual appearance. Whenever we played cowboys and Indians, guess who had to be the bad guy, the cowboy.

It wasn't until I left the Reserve for the big bad city that I became more aware of the role people expected me to play, and the fact that physically I didn't fit in. Everybody seemed to have this preconceived idea of how every Indian looked and acted. One guy, on my first day of college, asked me what kind of horse I preferred. I didn't have the heart to tell him "hobby."   20

I've often tried to be philosophical about the whole thing. I have both white and red blood in me, I guess that makes me pink. I am a "Pink" man. Try to imagine this, I'm walking around on any typical Reserve in Canada, my head held high, proudly announcing to everyone "I am a Pink Man." It's a good thing I ran track in school.

*Taylor, Drew Hayden, "Pretty Like a White Boy" from *An Anthology of Canadian Native Literature in English,* ed. Daniel David Moses and Terry Goldie (Toronto: Oxford University Press, 1992). Reproduced by permission of Drew Hayden Taylor.

My pinkness is constantly being pointed out to me over and over and over again. "You don't look Indian?" "You're not Indian, are you?" "Really?!?" I got questions like that from both white and Native people, for a while I debated having my status card tattooed on my forehead.

And like most insecure people and specially a blue eyed Native writer, I went through a particularly severe identity crisis at one point. In fact, I admit it, one depressing spring evening, I dyed my hair black. Pitch black.

The reason for such a dramatic act, you may ask? Show Business. You see, for the last eight years or so, I've worked in various capacities in the performing arts, and as a result I'd always get calls to be an extra or even try out for an important role in some Native oriented movie. This anonymous voice would phone, having been given my number, and ask if I would be interested in trying out for a movie. Being a naturally ambitious, curious, and greedy young man, I would always readily agree, stardom flashing in my eyes and hunger pains from my wallet.

A few days later I would show up for the audition, and that was always an experience. What kind of experience you may ask? Picture this, the picture calls for the casting of seventeenth-century Mohawk warriors living in a traditional longhouse. The casting director calls the name "Drew Hayden Taylor" and I enter.

The casting director, the producer, and the film's director look up from the table and see my face, blue eyes flashing in anticipation. I once was described as a slightly chubby beachboy. But even beachboys have tans. Anyway, there would be a quick flush of confusion, a recheck of the papers, and a hesitant "Mr. Taylor?" Then they would ask if I was at the right audition. It was always the same. By the way, I never got any of the parts I tried for, except for a few anonymous crowd shots. Politics tells me it's because of the way I look, reality tells me it's probably because I can't act. I'm not sure which is better.

It's not just film people either. Recently I've become quite involved in Theatre, Native theatre to be exact. And one cold October day I was happily attending the Toronto leg of a province-wide tour of my first play, *Toronto at Dreamer's Rock*. The place was sold out, the audience very receptive and the performance was wonderful. Ironically one of the actors was also half white.

The director later told me he had been talking with the actor's father, an older Non-Native type chap. Evidently he had asked a few questions about me, and how I did my research. This made the director curious and he asked about his interest. He replied, "He's got an amazing grasp of the Native situation for a white person."

Not all these incidents are work related either. One time a friend and I were coming out of a rather upscale bar (we were out YUPPIE watching) and managed to catch a cab. We thanked the cab driver for being so comfortably close on such a cold night, he shrugged and nonchalantly talked about knowing what bars to drive around. "if you're not careful, all you'll get is drunk Indians." I hiccuped.

Another time this cab driver droned on and on about the government. He started out by criticizing Mulroney, and eventually to his handling of the Oka crisis. This perked up my ears, until he said, "If it were me, I'd have tear-gassed the place by the second day. No more problem." He got a dime tip. A few incidents like this and I'm convinced I'd make a great undercover agent for one of the Native political organizations.

But then again, even Native people have been known to look at me with a fair amount of suspicion. Many years ago when I was a young man, I was working on a documentary on Native culture up in the wilds of Northern Ontario. We were at an isolated cabin filming a   70 trapper woman and her kids. This one particular nine-year-old girl seemed to take a shine to me. She followed me around for two days both annoying me and endearing herself to me. but she absolutely refused to believe that I was Indian. The whole film crew tried to tell her but to no avail. She was certain I was white.

Then one day as I was loading up the car with film equipment, she asked me if I wanted some tea. Being in a hurry I declined the tea. She immediately smiled with victory crying out, "See, you're not Indian, all Indians drink tea!"

Frustrated and a little hurt I whipped out my Status card and thrust it at her. Now there I was, standing in a Northern Ontario winter, showing my Status card to a nine-year-old non-status Indian girl who had no idea what one was. Looking back, this may not have been   80 one of my brighter moves.

But I must admit, it was a Native woman that boiled everything down in one simple sentence. You may know that woman, Marianne Jones from *The Beachcombers* television series. We were working on a film together out west and we got to gossiping. Eventually we got around to talking about our respective villages. Hers on the Queen Charlotte Islands, or Haida Gwaii as the Haida call them, and mine in central Ontario.

Eventually childhood on the Reserve was being discussed and I made a comment about the way I look. She studied me for a moment, smiled, and said, "Do you know what the old women in my village would call you?" Hesitant but curious, I shook my head. "They'd say you were pretty like a white boy." To this day I'm still not sure if I like that.   90

Now some may argue that I am simply a Métis with a Status card. I disagree, I failed French in grade 11. And the Métis as everyone knows have their own separate and honourable culture, particularly in western Canada. And of course I am well aware that I am not the only person with my physical characteristics.

I remember once looking at a video tape of a drum group, shot on a Reserve up near Manitoulin Island. I noticed one of the drummers seemed quite fairhaired, almost blond. I mentioned this to my girlfriend at the time and she shrugged saying, "Well, that's to be expected. The highway runs right through the Reserve."

Perhaps I'm being too critical. There's a lot to be said for both cultures. For example, on the left hand, you have the Native respect for Elders. They understand the concept of wis-   100 dom and insight coming with age.

On the white hand, there's Italian food. I mean I really love my mother and family but seriously, does anything really beat good Veal Scallopini? Most of my aboriginal friends share my fondness for this particular brand of food. Wasn't there a warrior at Oka named Lasagna? I found it ironic, though curiously logical, that Columbus was Italian. A connection I wonder?

Also Native people have this wonderful respect and love for the land. They believe they are part of it, a mere chain in the cycle of existence. Now, as many of you know, this conflicts with the accepted Judeo-Christian i.e. western view of land management. I even believe

110 somewhere in the first chapters of the Bible it says something about God giving man dominion over Nature. Check it out, Genesis 4:?, "Thou shalt clear cut." So I grew up understanding
that everything around me is important and alive. My Native heritage gave me that.

And again, on the white hand, there's breast implants. Darn clever them white people.
that's something Indians would never have invented, seriously. We're not ambitious enough.
We just take what the Creator decides to give us, but no, not the white man. Just imagine it,
some serious looking white man, and let's face it people, we know it was a man who invented
them, don't we? So just imagine some serious looking white doctor sitting around in his
laboratory muttering to himself, "Big tits, big tits, hmm, how do I make big tits?" If it was an
Indian, it would be "Big tits, big tits, white women sure got big tits" and leave it at that.

120 So where does that leave me on the big philosophical score-board, what exactly are my
choices again; Indians—respect for elders, love of the land. White people—food and big tits.
In order to live in both cultures I guess I'd have to find an Indian woman with big tits who
lives with her grandmother in a cabin out in the woods and can make Fettucini Alfredo on
a wood stove.

Now let me make this clear, I'm not writing this for sympathy, or out of anger, or even
some need for self-glorification. I am just setting the facts straight. For as you read this, a new
Nation is born. This is a declaration of independence, my declaration of independence.

I've spent too many years explaining who and what I am repeatedly, so as of this moment, I officially secede from both races. I plan to start my own separate nation. Because I
130 am half Ojibway, and half Caucasian, we will be called the Occasions. And I of course, since
I'm founding the new nation, will be a Special Occasion. ∎

UNDERSTANDING CONTEXT

1. Who is Taylor's audience?

2. How does Taylor communicate across cultural differences for readers who do not
   share his background?

EVALUATING STRATEGY

1. Briefly summarize Taylor's thesis.

2. Taylor's organizational strategy is to divide and classify what he terms as the distinguishing characteristics of his two heritages. What are those characteristics?

3. Is his organizational strategy effective? Why or why not?

APPRECIATING LANGUAGE

1. Taylor uses a variety of terms to describe his Native heritage. Create a list of the terms
   that he uses.

2. Which terms on your list are viewed as positive and which are viewed as negative?
   Explain your classifications fully.

3. Look up the definition of *stereotype.* Create a list of stereotypes that Taylor targets in this essay.

WRITING SUGGESTIONS

1. Write a well-constructed summary of Taylor's essay.

2. *Reflective writing:* Have you ever been the target of stereotypes or targeted others with them? Write an essay explaining how stereotypes have affected your life.

3. *Critical thinking:* Analyze Taylor's use of humour in this essay. Do you think it enhances his purpose or detracts from it? Write an essay explaining your analysis and position.

NAOMI KLEIN

Naomi Klein is an award-winning journalist who has been at the forefront of the global justice movement. Her internationally syndicated column appears in **The Nation, The Guardian,** and **The Globe and Mail.** In 2004, she released **The Take,** a film about Argentina's occupied factories, co-produced with director Avi Lewis.

The Beginning of the Brand*

Think of the number of ads you encounter every day on television, on the Internet, or on the way to class. If you're like most consumers, chances are you hardly notice the vast majority of them. As the advertising industry expands exponentially, the public is becoming indifferent or immune to the messages it sends out. To counter this, marketers are forced to dream up newer, more elaborate and intrusive techniques. In this excerpt from her international best-seller, No Logo: Taking Aim at the Brand Bullies (2000), *Naomi Klein briefly reviews the history of "branding" and discusses some of the marketing world's strategies to reach consumers hardened by a greater and greater onslaught of daily advertising.*

1   It's helpful to go back briefly and look at where the idea of branding first began. Though the words are often used interchangeably, branding and advertising are not the same process. Advertising any given product is only one part of branding's grand plan, as are sponsorship and logo licensing. Think of the brand as the core meaning of the modem corporation, and of the advertisement as one vehicle used to convey that meaning to the world.

The first mass-marketing campaigns, starting in the second half of the nineteenth century, had more to do with advertising than with branding as we understand it today. Faced with a range of recently invented products—the radio, phonograph, car, light bulb and so on—advertisers had more pressing tasks than creating a brand identity for any given corpo-
10 ration; first, they had to change the way people lived their lives. Ads had to inform consumers about the existence of some new invention, then convince them that their lives would be better if they used, for example, cars instead of wagons, telephones instead of mail and electric light instead of oil lamps. Many of these new products bore brand names—some of which are still around today—but these were almost incidental. These products were themselves news; that was almost advertisement enough.

The first brand-based products appeared at around the same time as the invention-based ads, largely because of another relatively recent innovation: the factory. When goods began to be produced in factories, not only were entirely new products being introduced but old products—even basic staples—were appearing in strikingly new forms. What made early
20 branding efforts different from more straightforward salesmanship was that the market was now being flooded with uniform mass-produced products that were virtually indistinguishable from one another. Competitive branding became a necessity of the machine

age—within a context of manufactured sameness, image-based difference had to be manufactured along with the product.

So the role of advertising changed from delivering product news bulletins to building an image around a particular brand-name version of a product. The first task of branding was to bestow proper names on generic goods such as sugar, flour, soap and cereal, which had previously been scooped out of barrels by local shopkeepers. In the 1880s, corporate logos were introduced to mass-produced products like Campbell's Soup, H.J. Heinz pickles and Quaker Oats cereal. As design historians and theorists Ellen Lupton and J. Abbott Miller note, logos were tailored to evoke familiarity and folksiness . . . in an effort to counteract the new and unsettling anonymity of packaged goods. "Familiar personalities such as Dr. Brown, Uncle Ben, Aunt Jemima, and Old Grand-Dad came to replace the shopkeeper, who was traditionally responsible for measuring bulk foods for customers and acting as an advocate for products . . . a nationwide vocabulary of brand names replaced the small local shopkeeper as the interface between consumer and product."[1] After the product names and characters had been established, advertising gave them a venue to speak directly to would-be consumers. The corporate "personality," uniquely named, packaged and advertised, had arrived.

For the most part, the ad campaigns at the end of the nineteenth century and the start of the twentieth used a set of rigid, pseudoscientific formulas: rivals were never mentioned, ad copy used declarative statements only and headlines had to be large, with lots of white space—according to one turn-of-the-century adman, "an advertisement should be big enough to make an impression but not any bigger than the thing advertised."

But there were those in the industry who understood that advertising wasn't just scientific; it was also spiritual. Brands could conjure a feeling—think of Aunt Jemima's comforting presence—but not only that, entire corporations could themselves embody a meaning of their own. In the early twenties, legendary adman Bruce Barton turned General Motors into a metaphor for the American family, "something personal, warm and human," while GE was not so much the name of the faceless General Electric Company as, in Barton's words, "the initials of a friend." In 1923 Barton said that the role of advertising was to help corporations find their soul. The son of a preacher, he drew on his religious upbringing for uplifting messages: "I like to think of advertising as something big, something splendid, something which goes deep down into an institution and gets hold of the soul of it. . . . Institutions have souls, just as men and nations have souls," he told GM president Pierre du Pont.[2] General Motors ads began to tell stories about the people who drove its cars—the preacher, the pharmacist or the country doctor who, thanks to his trusty GM, arrived "at the bedside of a dying child" just in time "to bring it back to life."

By the end of the 1940s, there was a burgeoning awareness that a brand wasn't just a mascot or a catchphrase or a picture printed on the label of a company's product; the company as a whole could have a brand identity or a "corporate consciousness," as this ephemeral quality was termed at the time. As this idea evolved, the adman ceased to see himself as a pitchman and instead saw himself as "the philosopher-king of commercial culture,"[3] in the words of ad critic Randall Rothberg. The search for the true meaning of brands-or the "brand essence," as it is often called—gradually took the agencies away from individual products and their attributes and toward a psychological/anthropological examination of what brands mean to the culture and to people's lives. This was seen to be of crucial importance, since corporations may manufacture products, but what consumers buy are brands.

It took several decades for the manufacturing world to adjust to this shift. It clung to the idea that its core business was still production and that branding was an important add-on. Then came the brand equity mania of the eighties, the defining moment of which arrived in 1988 when Philip Morris purchased Kraft for $12.6 billion—six times what the company was worth on paper. The price difference, apparently, was the cost of the word "Kraft." Of course Wall Street was aware that decades of marketing and brand bolstering added value to a company over and above its assets and total annual sales. But with the Kraft purchase, a huge dollar value had been assigned to something that had previously been abstract and unquantifiable—a brand name. This was spectacular news for the ad world, which was now able to make the claim that advertising spending was more than just a sales strategy: it was an investment in cold hard equity. The more you spend, the more your company is worth. Not surprisingly, this led to a considerable increase in spending on advertising. More important, it sparked a renewed interest in puffing up brand identities, a project that involved far more than a few billboards and TV spots. It was about pushing the envelope in sponsorship deals, dreaming up new areas in which to "extend" the brand, as well as perpetually probing the zeitgeist to ensure that the "essence" selected for one's brand would resonate karmically with its target market. For reasons that will be explored in the rest of this chapter, this radical shift in corporate philosophy has sent manufacturers on a cultural feeding frenzy as they seize upon every comer of unmarketed landscape in search of the oxygen needed to inflate their brands. In the process, virtually nothing has been left unbranded. That's quite an impressive feat, considering that as recently as 1993 Wall Street had pronounced the brand dead, or as good as dead. . . .

The marketing world is always reaching a new zenith, breaking through last year's world record and planning to do it again next year with increasing numbers of ads and aggressive new formulae for reaching consumers. The advertising industry's astronomical rate of growth is neatly reflected in year-to-year figures measuring total ad spending in the U.S. . . . , which have gone up so steadily that by 1998 the figure was set to reach $196.5 billion, while global ad spending is estimated at $435 billion.[4] According to the 1998 United Nations Human Development Report, the growth in global ad spending "now outpaces the growth of the world economy by one-third."

This pattern is a by-product of the firmly held belief that brands need continuous and constantly increasing advertising in order to stay in the same place. According to this law of diminishing returns, the more advertising there is out there (and there always is more, because of this law), the more aggressively brands must market to stand out. And of course, no one is more keenly aware of advertising's ubiquity than the advertisers themselves, who view commercial inundation as a clear and persuasive call for more—and more intrusive—advertising. With so much competition, the agencies argue, clients must spend more than ever to make sure their pitch screeches so loud it can be heard over all the others. David Lubars, a senior ad executive in the Omnicom Group, explains the industry's guiding principle with more candor than most. Consumers, he says, "are like roaches—you spray them and spray them and they get immune after a while."[5]

So, if consumers are like roaches, then marketers must forever be dreaming up new concoctions for industrial-strength Raid. And nineties marketers, being on a more advanced rung of the sponsorship spiral, have dutifully come up with clever and intrusive new selling techniques to do just that. Recent highlights include these innovations: Gordon's gin experimented   110 with filling British movie theaters with the scent of juniper berries; Calvin Klein stuck "CK Be" perfume strips on the backs of Ticketmaster concert envelopes; and in some Scandinavian countries you can get "free" long-distance calls with ads cutting into your telephone conversations. And there's plenty more, stretching across ever more expansive surfaces and cramming into the smallest of crevices: sticker ads on pieces of fruit promoting ABC sitcoms, Levi's ads in public washrooms, corporate logos on boxes of Girl Guide cookies, ads for pop albums on takeout food containers, and ads for Batman movies projected on sidewalks or into the night sky. There are already ads on benches in national parks as well as on library cards in public libraries, and in December 1998 NASA announced plans to solicit ads on its space stations. Pepsi's ongoing threat to project its logo onto the moon's surface hasn't yet materialized, but   120 Mattel did paint an entire street in Salford, England, "a shriekingly bright bubblegum hue" of pink—houses, porches, trees, road, sidewalk, dogs and cars were all accessories in the televised celebrations of Barbie Pink Month.[6] Barbie is but one small part of the ballooning $30 billion "experiential communication" industry, the phrase now used to encompass the staging of such branded pieces of corporate performance art and other "happenings."

That we live a sponsored life is now a truism and it's a pretty safe bet that as spending on advertising continues to rise, we roaches will be treated to even more of these ingenious gimmicks, making it ever more difficult and more seemingly pointless to muster even an ounce of outrage. ■

Notes

1. Ellen Lupton and J. Abbott Miller, *Design Writing Research: Writing on Graphic Design* (New York: Kiosk, 1996), p. 177.

2. Roland Marchand, "The Corporation Nobody Knew: Bruce Barton, Alfred Sloan, and the Founding of the General Motors' Family," *Business History Review,* December 22, 1991, p. 825.

3. Randall Rothberg, *Where the Suckers Moon* (New York: Vintage, 1995), p. 137.

4. Stats are from McCann-Erikson's ad spending forecast appearing in *Advertising Age* and the *United Nations Human Development Report,* 1998. Most industry watchers estimate that U.S. spending from global brands represents 40 percent of the total ad spending in the rest of the world. Canadian ad spending, which is less rigorously tracked by the industry, follows the same growth, but with smaller figures. Between 1978 and 1994, for instance, it grew from a $2.7 billion industry to a $9.2 billion industry (source: "A Report Card on Advertising Revenues in Canada," 1995).

5. Yumiko Ono, "Marketers Seek the 'Naked' Truth in Consumer Psyches," *Wall Street Journal,* May 30, 1997, B1.

6. *Daily Mail* (London), November 17, 1997.

UNDERSTANDING CONTEXT

1. Who is Klein's audience?

2. Klein argues that branding is different from advertising. Explain the difference.

EVALUATING STRATEGY

1. What is the excerpt's purpose?

2. Summarize Klein's thesis.

3. Do you agree with her thesis?

4. At the end of this excerpt, Klein uses the metaphor of consumers as roaches. Do you think the metaphor is a good one? Explain.

APPRECIATING LANGUAGE

1. Describe the tone of Klein's piece.

2. How is the tone created? Explore word choice.

WRITING SUGGESTIONS

1. Write a well-constructed summary of Klein's essay.

2. *Reflective writing:* Consider Klein's final point in this excerpt—that the "ingenious gimmicks" of branding and advertising are making it difficult for consumers to "muster even an ounce of outrage." What do you think of her assumption that consumers ought to feel outrage? Do you agree that consumers are victimized by advertising? Write a three-page persuasive essay exploring this question.

3. Is it impossible for advertising to be responsible? Explore various Web sites that address advertising standards, such as www.responsible-advertising.org, www.adstandards.com, www.cca-kids.ca, and www.media-awareness.ca. How do such organizations attempt to empower citizens in relation to advertising? Write a well-constructed argument, with evidence to support your position.

WILLIAM LUTZ

William Lutz is a fierce and funny critic of "Doublespeak," inflated and misleading language. For years he edited the **Quarterly Review of Doublespeak,** and has authored several books that expose Orwellian language, including **Doublespeak, Doublespeak Defined,** and **The New Doublespeak.** This excerpt looks at the ways advertisers manipulate language to deceive consumers.

With These Words I Can Sell You Anything*

In his essay, Lutz explores the various techniques that advertisers use to deceive consumers. Specifically, Lutz focuses on how advertisers have developed a series of terms that hold double meanings.

One problem advertisers have when they try to convince you that the product they are 1 pushing is really different from other, similar products is that their claims are subject to some laws. Not a lot of laws, but there are some designed to prevent fraudulent or untruthful claims in advertising. Even during the happy years of non-regulation under President Ronald Reagan, the FTC did crack down on the more blatant abuses in advertising claims. Generally speaking, advertisers have to be careful in what they say in their ads, in the claims they make for the products they advertise. Parity claims are safe because they are legal and supported by a number of court decisions. But beyond parity claims there are weasel words.

Advertisers use weasel words to appear to be making a claim for a product when in fact they are making no claim at all. Weasel words get their name from the way weasels eat the 10 eggs they find in the nests of other animals. A weasel will make a small hole in the egg, suck out the insides, then place the egg back in the nest. Only when the egg is examined closely is it found to be hollow. That's the way it is with weasel words in advertising: Examine weasel words closely and you'll find that they're as hollow as any egg sucked by a weasel. Weasel words appear to say one thing when in fact they say the opposite, or nothing at all.

"Help"—The Number One Weasel Word

The biggest weasel word used in advertising doublespeak is "help." Now "help" only means to aid or assist, nothing more. It does not mean to conquer, stop, eliminate, solve, heal, cure, or anything else. But once the ad says "help," it can say just about anything after that because "help" qualifies everything coming after it. The trick is that the claim that comes after the weasel word is usually so strong and so dramatic that you forget the word "help" and 20 concentrate only on the dramatic claim. You read into the ad a message that the ad does not contain. More importantly, the advertiser is not responsible for the claim that you read into the ad, even though the advertiser wrote the ad so you would read that claim into it.

*Lutz, William, "With These Words I Can Sell You Anything" reprinted by permission of the Jean V. Naggar Literary Agency.

The next time you see an ad for a cold medicine that promises that it "helps relieve cold symptoms fast," don't rush out to buy it. Ask yourself what this claim is really saying. Remember, "helps" means only that the medicine will aid or assist. What will it aid or assist in doing? Why, "relieve" your cold "symptoms." "Relieve" only means to ease, alleviate, or mitigate, not to stop, end, or cure. Nor does the claim say how much relieving this medicine will do. Nowhere does this ad claim it will cure anything. In fact, the ad doesn't even claim it

30 will *do* anything at all. The ad only claims that it will aid in relieving (not curing) your cold symptoms, which are probably a runny nose, watery eyes, and a headache. In other words, this medicine probably contains a standard decongestant and some aspirin. By the way, what does "fast" mean? Ten minutes, one hour, one day? What is fast to one person can be very slow to another. Fast is another weasel word.

Ad claims using "help" are among the most popular ads. One says, "Helps keep you young looking," but then a lot of things will help keep you young looking, including exercise, rest, good nutrition, and a facelift. More importantly, this ad doesn't say the product will keep you young, only "young *looking*." Someone may look young to one person and old to another.

40 A toothpaste ad says, "Helps prevent cavities," but it doesn't say it will actually prevent cavities. Brushing your teeth regularly, avoiding sugars in foods, and flossing daily will also help prevent cavities. A liquid cleaner ad says, "Helps keep your home germ free," but it doesn't say it actually kills germs, nor does it even specify which germs it might kill.

"Help" is such a useful weasel word that it is often combined with other action-verb weasel words such as "fight" and "control." Consider the claim, "Helps control dandruff symptoms with regular use." What does it really say? It will assist in controlling (not eliminating, stopping, ending, or curing) the *symptoms* of dandruff, not the cause of dandruff nor the dandruff itself. What are the symptoms of dandruff? The ad deliberately leaves that undefined, but assume that the symptoms referred to in the ad are the flaking and itching

50 commonly associated with dandruff. But just shampooing with *any* shampoo will temporarily eliminate these symptoms, so this shampoo isn't any different from any other. Finally, in order to benefit from this product, you must use it regularly. What is "regular use"—daily, weekly, hourly? Using another shampoo "regularly" will have the same effect. Nowhere does this advertising claim say this particular shampoo stops, eliminates, or cures dandruff. In fact, this claim says nothing at all, thanks to all the weasel words.

Look at ads in magazines and newspapers, listen to ads on radio and television, and you'll find the word "help" in ads for all kinds of products. How often do you read or hear such phrases as "helps stop . . . ," "helps overcome . . . ," "helps eliminate . . . ," "helps you feel . . . ," or "helps you look . . ."? If you start looking for this weasel word in advertising,

60 you'll be amazed at how often it occurs. Analyze the claims in the ads using "help," and you will discover that these ads are really saying nothing.

There are plenty of other weasel words used in advertising. In fact, there are so many that to list them all would fill the rest of this book. But, in order to identify the doublespeak of advertising and understand the real meaning of an ad, you have to be aware of the most popular weasel words in advertising today.

Virtually Spotless

One of the most powerful weasel words is "virtually," a word so innocent that most people don't pay any attention to it when it is used in an advertising claim. But watch out. "Virtually" is used in advertising claims that appear to make specific, definite promises when there is no promise. After all, what does "virtually" mean? It means "in essence of effect, although not in fact." Look at that definition again. "Virtually" means *not in fact*. It does *not* mean "almost" or "just about the same as," or anything else. And before you dismiss all this concern over such a small word, remember that small words can have big consequences.

In 1971 a federal court rendered its decision on a case brought by a woman who became pregnant while taking birth control pills. She sued the manufacturer, Eli Lilly and Company, for breach of warranty. The woman lost her case. Basing its ruling on a statement in the pamphlet accompanying the pills, which stated that, "When taken as directed, the tables offer virtually 100 percent protection," the court ruled that there was no warranty, expressed or implied, that the pills were absolutely effective. In its ruling, the court pointed out that, according to the *Webster's Third New International Dictionary*, "virtually" means "almost entirely" and clearly does not mean "absolute" (*Whittington v. Eli Lilly and Company*, 333 F. Supp. 98). In other words, the Eli Lilly Company was really saying that its birth control pill, even when taken as directed, *did not in fact* provide 100 percent protection against pregnancy. But Eli Lilly didn't want to put it that way because then many women might not have bought Lilly's birth control pills.

The next time you see the ad that says that this dishwasher detergent "leaves dishes virtually spotless," just remember how advertisers twist the meaning of the weasel word "virtually." You can have lots of spots on your dishes after using this detergent and the ad claim will still be true, because what this claim really means is that this detergent does not *in fact* leave your dishes spotless. Whenever you see or hear an ad claim that uses the word "virtually," just translate that claim into its real meaning. So the television set that is "virtually trouble free" becomes the television set that is not in fact trouble free, the "virtually foolproof operation" of any appliance becomes an operation that is in fact not foolproof, and the product that "virtually never needs service" becomes the product that is not in fact service free.

New and Improved

If "new" is the most frequently used word on a product package "improved" is the second most frequent. In fact, the two words are almost always used together. It seems just about everything sold these days is "new and improved." The next time you're in the supermarket, try counting the number of times you see these words on products. But you'd better do it while you're walking down just one aisle, otherwise you'll need a calculator to keep track of your counting.

Just what do these words mean? The use of the word "new" is restricted by regulations, so an advertiser can't just use the word on a product or in an ad without meeting certain requirements. For example, a product is considered new for about six months during a national advertising campaign. If the product is being advertised only in a limited test market area, the word can be used longer, and in some instances has been used for as long as two years.

What makes a product "new"? Some products have been around for a long time, yet every once in a while you discover that they are being advertised as "new." Well, an advertiser can call a product new if there has been "a material functional change" in the product. What is "a material functional change," you ask? Good question. In fact it's such a good question it's being asked all the time. It's up to the manufacturer to prove that the product has undergone such a change. And if the manufacturer isn't challenged on the claim, then there's no one to stop it. 110 Moreover, the change does not have to be an improvement in the product. One manufacturer added an artificial lemon scent to a cleaning product and called it "new and improved," even though the product did not clean any better than without the lemon scent. The manufacturer defended the use of the word "new" on the grounds that the artificial scent changed the chemical formula of the product and therefore constituted "a material functional change."

Which brings up the word "improved." When used in advertising, "improved" does not mean "made better." It only means "changed" or "different from before." So, if the detergent maker puts a plastic pour spout on the box of detergent, the product has been "improved," and away we go with a whole new advertising campaign. Or, if the cereal maker adds more fruit or a different kind of fruit to the cereal, there's an improved product. Now you know 120 why manufacturers are constantly making little changes in their products. Whole new advertising campaigns, designed to convince you that the product has been changed for the better, are based on small changes in superficial aspects of a product. The next time you see an ad for an "improved" product, ask yourself what was wrong with the old one. Ask yourself just how "improved" the product is. Finally, you might check to see whether the "improved" version costs more than the unimproved one. After all, someone has to pay for the millions of dollars spent advertising the improved product.

Of course, advertisers really like to run ads that claim a product is "new and improved." While what constitutes a "new" product may be subject to some regulation, "improved" is a subjective judgment. A manufacturer changes the shape of its stick deodorant, but the shape 130 doesn't improve the function of the deodorant. That is, changing the shape doesn't affect the deodorizing ability of the deodorant, so the manufacturer calls it "improved." Another manufacturer adds ammonia to its liquid cleaner and calls it "new and improved." Since adding ammonia does affect the cleaning ability of the product, there has been a "material functional change" in the product, and the manufacturer can now call its cleaner "new," and "improved" as well. Now the weasel words "new and improved" are plastered all over the package and are the basis for a multimillion-dollar ad campaign. But after six months the word "new" will have to go, until someone can dream up another change in the product. Perhaps it will be adding color to the liquid, or changing the shape of the package, or maybe adding a new dripless pour spout, or perhaps a ———. The "improvements" are endless, 140 and so are the new advertising claims and campaigns.

"New" is just too useful and powerful a word in advertising for advertisers to pass it up easily. So they use weasel words that say "new" without really saying it. One of their favorites is "introducing," as in, "Introducing improved Tide," or "Introducing the stain remover." The first is simply saying, here's our improved soap; the second, here's our new advertising campaign for our detergent. Another favorite is "now," as in, "Now there's Sinex," which simply means that Sinex is available. Then there are phrases like "today's Chevrolet," "Presenting Dristan," and "A fresh way to start the day." The list is really endless because advertisers are always finding new ways to say "new" without really saying it. If there is a second edition of this book, I'll just call it the "new and improved" edition. Wouldn't you really rather have a "new and improved" edition of this book rather than a "second" edition?   150

Acts Fast

"Acts" and "works" are two popular weasel words in advertising because they bring action to the product and to the advertising claim. When you see the ad for the cough syrup that "Acts on the cough control center," ask yourself what this cough syrup is claiming to do. Well, it's just claiming to "act," to do something, to perform an action. What is it that the cough syrup does? The ad doesn't say. It only claims to perform an action or do something on your "cough control center." By the way, what and where is your "cough control center"? I don't remember learning about that part of the body in human biology class.

Ads that use such phrases as "acts fast," "acts against," "acts to prevent," and the like are saying essentially nothing, because "act" is a word empty of any specific meaning. The ads are always careful not to specify exactly what "act" the product performs. Just because a   160 brand of aspirin claims to "act fast" for headache relief doesn't mean this aspirin is any better than any other aspirin. What is the "act" that this aspirin performs? You're never told. Maybe it just dissolves quickly. Since aspirin is a parity product, all aspirin is the same and therefore functions the same.

Works Like Anything Else

If you don't find the word "acts" in an ad, you will probably find the weasel word "works." In fact, the two words are almost interchangeable in advertising. Watch out for ads that say a product "works against," "works like," "works for," or "works longer." As with "acts," "works" is the same meaningless verb used to make you think that this product really does something, and maybe even something special or unique. But "works," like "acts," is basically a word empty of any specific meaning.   170

Like Magic

Whenever advertisers want you to stop thinking about the product and to start thinking about something bigger, better, or more attractive than the product, they use that very popular weasel word, "like." The word "like" is the advertiser's equivalent of a magician's use of misdirection.

"Like" gets you to ignore the product and concentrate on the claim the advertiser is making about it. "For skin like peaches and cream" claims the ad for a skin cream. What is this ad really claiming? It doesn't say this cream will give you peaches-and-cream skin. There is no verb in this claim, so it doesn't even mention using the product. How is skin ever like "peaches and cream"? Remember, ads must be read literally and exactly, according to the dictionary definition of words. (Remember "virtually" in the Eli Lilly case.) The ad is making absolutely
180   no promise or claim whatsoever for this skin cream. If you think this cream will give you soft, smooth, youthful-looking skin, you are the one who has read that meaning into the ad.

The wine that claims "It's like taking a trip to France" wants you to think about a romantic evening in Paris as you walk along the boulevard after a wonderful meal in an intimate little bistro. Of course, you don't really believe that a wine can take you to France, but the goal of the ad is to get you to think pleasant, romantic thoughts about France and not about how the wine tastes or how expensive it may be. That little word "like" has taken you away from crushed grapes into a world of your own imaginative making. Who knows, maybe the next time you buy wine, you'll think those pleasant thoughts when you see this brand of wine, and you'll buy it. Or, maybe you weren't even thinking about buying wine at all, but now you just
190   might pick up a bottle the next time you're shopping. Ah, the power of "like" in advertising.

How about the most famous "like" claim of all, "Winston tastes good like a cigarette should"? Ignoring the grammatical error here, you might want to know what this claim is saying. Whether a cigarette tastes good or bad is a subjective judgment because what tastes good to one person may well taste horrible to another. Not everyone likes fried snails, even if they are called escargots. (*De gustibus non est disputandum*, which was probably the Roman rule for advertising as well as for defending the games in the Colosseum.) There are many people who say all cigarettes taste terrible, other people who say only some cigarettes taste all right, and still others who say all cigarettes taste good. Who's right? Everyone, because taste is a matter of personal judgment.

Moreover, note the use of the conditional, "should." The complete claim is, "Winston
200   tastes good like a cigarette should taste." But should cigarettes taste good? Again, this is a matter of personal judgment and probably depends most on one's experiences with smoking. So, the Winston ad is simply saying that Winston cigarettes are just like any other cigarette: Some people like them and some people don't. On that statement, R.J. Reynolds conducted a very successful multimillion-dollar advertising campaign that helped keep Winston the number-two-selling cigarette in the United States, close behind number one, Marlboro.

Can't It Be up to the Claim?

Analyzing ads for doublespeak requires that you pay attention to every word in the ad and determine what each word really means. Advertisers try to wrap their claims in language that sounds concrete, specific, and objective, when in fact the language of advertising is anything but. Your job is to read carefully and listen critically so that when the announcer
210   says that "Crest can be of significant value . . . ," you know immediately that this claim says absolutely nothing. Where is the doublespeak in this ad? Start with the second word.

Once again, you have to look at what words really mean, not what you think they mean or what the advertiser wants you to think they mean. The ad for Crest only says that using Crest "can be" of "significant value." What really throws you off in this ad is the brilliant use of "significant." It draws your attention to the word "value" and makes you forget that the ad only claims that Crest "can be." The ad doesn't say that Crest *is* of value, only that it is "able" or "possible" to be of value, because that's all that "can" means.

It's so easy to miss the importance of those little words, "can be." Almost as easy as missing the importance of the words "up to" in an ad. These words are very popular in sales ads. You know, the ones that say, "Up to 50 percent Off!" Now, what does that claim mean? 220 Not much, because the store or manufacturer has to reduce the price of only a few items by 50 percent. Everything else can be reduced a lot less, or not even reduced. Moreover, don't you want to know 50 percent off of what? Is it 50 percent off the "manufacturer's suggested list price," which is the highest possible price? Was the price artificially inflated and then reduced? In other ads, "up to" expresses an ideal situation. The medicine that works "up to ten times faster," the battery that lasts "up to twice as long," and the soap that gets you "up to twice as clean" all are based on ideal situations for using those products, situations in which you can be sure you will never find yourself.

Unfinished Words

Unfinished words are a kind of "up to" claim in advertising. The claim that a battery lasts "up to twice as long" usually doesn't finish the comparison—twice as long as what? A birthday 230 candle? A tank of gas? A cheap battery made in a country not noted for its technological achievements? The implication is that the battery last twice as long as batteries made by other battery makers, or twice as long as earlier model batteries made by the advertiser, but the ad doesn't really make these claims. You read these claims into the ad, aided by the visual images the advertiser so carefully provides.

Unfinished words depend on you to finish them, to provide the words the advertisers so thoughtfully left out of the ad. Pall Mall cigarettes were once advertised as "A longer finer and milder smoke." The question is, longer, finer, and milder than what? The aspirin that claims it contains "Twice as much of the pain reliever doctors recommend most" doesn't tell you what pain reliever it contains twice as much of. (By the way, it's aspirin. That's right; 240 it just contains twice the amount of aspirin. And how much is twice the amount? Twice of what amount?) Panadol boasts that "nobody reduces fever faster," but, since Panadol is a parity product, this claim simply means that Panadol isn't any better than any other product in its parity class. "You can be sure if it's Westinghouse," you're told, but just exactly what it is you can be sure of is never mentioned. "Magnavox gives you more" doesn't tell you what you get more of. More value? More television? More than they gave you before? It sounds nice, but it means nothing, until you fill in the claim with your own words, the words the advertisers didn't use. Since each of us fills in the claim differently, the ad and the product can become all things to all people, and not promise a single thing.

250   Unfinished words abound in advertising because they appear to promise so much. More importantly, they can be joined with powerful visual images on television to appear to be making significant promises about a product's effectiveness without really making any promises. In a television ad, the aspirin product that claims fast relief can show a person with a headache taking the product and then, in what appears to be a matter of minutes, claiming complete relief. This visual image is far more powerful than any claim made in unfinished words. Indeed, the visual image completes the unfinished words for you, filling in with pictures what the words leave out. And you thought that ads didn't affect you. What brand of aspirin do you use?

    Some years ago, Ford's advertisements proclaimed "Ford LTD—700 percent quieter."
260 Now, what do you think Ford was claiming with these unfinished words? What was the Ford LTD quieter than? A Cadillac? A Mercedes Benz? A BMW? Well, when the FTC asked Ford to substantiate this unfinished claim, Ford replied that it meant that the inside of the LTD was 700 percent quieter than the outside. How did you finish those unfinished words when you first read them? Did you even come close to Ford's meaning?

Combining Weasel Words

A lot of ads don't fall neatly into one category or another because they use a variety of different devices and words. Different weasel words are often combined to make an ad claim. The claim, "Coffee-Mate gives coffee more body, more flavor," uses Unfinished Words ("more" than what?) and also uses words that have no specific meaning ("body" and "flavor"). Along with "taste" (remember the Winston ad and its claim to taste good) "body" and "flavor"
270 mean nothing because their meaning is entirely subjective. To you, "body" in coffee might mean thick, black, almost bitter coffee, while I might take it to mean a light brown, delicate coffee. Now, if you think you understood that last sentence, read it again, because it said nothing of objective value; it was filled with weasel words of no specific meaning: "thick," "black," "bitter," "light brown," and "delicate." Each of those words has no specific, objective meaning, because each of us can interpret them differently.

    Try this slogan: "Looks, smells, tastes like ground-roast coffee." So, are you now going to buy Taster's Choice instant coffee because of this ad? "Looks," "smells," and "tastes" are all words with no specific meaning and depend on your interpretation of them for any meaning. Then there's that great weasel word "like," which simply suggests a comparison but does not
280 make the actual connection between the product and the quality. Besides, do you know what "ground-roast" coffee is? I don't, but it sure sounds good. So, out of seven words in this ad, four are definite weasel words, two are quite meaningless, and only one has any clear meaning.

    Remember the Anacin ad—"Twice as much of the pain reliever doctors recommend most"? There's a whole lot of weaseling going on in this ad. First, what's the pain reliever they're talking about in this ad? Aspirin, of course. In fact, any time you see or hear an ad using those words "pain reliever," you can automatically substitute the word "aspirin" for them. (Makers of acetaminophen and ibuprofen pain relievers are careful in their advertising to identify their products as nonaspirin products.) So, now we know that Anacin has aspirin in it. Moreover, we know that Anacin has twice as much aspirin in it, but we don't know twice as much as what. Does it have twice as much aspirin as an ordinary aspirin tablet? 290 If so, what is an ordinary aspirin tablet, and how much aspirin does it contain? Twice as much as Excedrin or Bufferin? Twice as much as a chocolate chip cookie? Remember those Unfinished Words and how they lead you on without saying anything.

Finally, what about those doctors who are doing all that recommending? Who are they? How many of them are there? What kind of doctors are they? What are their qualifications? Who asked them about recommending pain relievers? What other pain relievers did they recommend? And there are a whole lot more questions about this "poll" of doctors to which I'd like to know the answers, but you get the point. Sometimes, when I call my doctor, she tells me to take two aspirin and call her office in the morning. Is that where Anacin got this ad?

Read the Label, or the Brochure

Weasel words aren't just found on television, on the radio, or in newspaper and magazine 300 ads. Just about any language associated with a product will contain the doublespeak of advertising. Remember the Eli Lilly case and the doublespeak on the information sheet that came with the birth control pills. Here's another example.

In 1983, the Estée Lauder cosmetics company announced a new product called "Night Repair." A small brochure distributed with the product stated that "Night Repair was scientifically formulated in Estée Lauder's U.S. laboratories as part of the Swiss Age-Controlling Skincare Program. Although only nature controls the aging process, this program helps control the signs of aging and encourages skin to look and feel younger." You might want to read these two sentences again, because they sound great but say nothing.

First, note that the product was "scientifically formulated" in the company's laboratories. 310 What does that mean? What constitutes a scientific formulation? You wouldn't expect the company to say that the product was casually, mechanically, or carelessly formulated, or just thrown together one day when the people in the white coats didn't have anything better to do. But the word "scientifically" lends an air of precision and promise that just isn't there.

It is the second sentence, however, that's really weasely, both syntactically and semantically. The only factual part of this sentence is the introductory dependent clause—"only nature controls the aging process." Thus, the only fact in the ad is relegated to a dependent clause, a clause dependent on the main clause, which contains no factual or definite information at all and indeed purports to contradict the independent clause. The new "skincare program" (notice it's not a skin cream but a "program") does not claim to stop or even retard 320 the aging process. What, then, does Night Repair, at a price of over $35 (in 1983 dollars) for a .87-ounce bottle do? According to this brochure, nothing. It only "helps," and the brochure does not say how much it helps. Moreover, it only "helps control," and then it only helps control the "*signs* of aging," the aging itself. Also, it "encourages" skin not to *be* younger but only to "look and feel" younger. The brochure does not say younger than what. Of the sixteen words in the main clause of this second sentence, none are weasel words. So, before you spend all that money for Night Repair, or any other cosmetic product, read the words carefully, and then decide if you're getting what you think you're paying for.

Other Tricks of the Trade

Advertisers' use of doublespeak is endless. The best way advertisers can make something out
330 of nothing is through words. Although there are a lot of visual images used on television and in magazines and newspapers, every advertiser wants to create that memorable line that will stick in the public consciousness. I am sure pure joy reigned in one advertising agency when a study found that children who were asked to spell the work "relief" promptly and proudly responded "r-o-l-a-i-d-s."

The variations, combinations, and permutations of double-speak used in advertising go on and on, running from the use of rhetorical questions ("Wouldn't you really rather have a Buick?" "If you can't trust Prestone, who can you trust?") to flattering you with compliments ("The lady has taste." "We think a cigar smoker is someone special." "You've come a long way baby."). You know, of course, how you're *supposed* to answer those questions, and you know
340 that those compliments are just leading up to the sales pitches for the products. Before you dismiss such tricks of the trade as obvious, however, just remember that all of these statements and questions were part of very successful advertising campaigns.

A more subtle approach is the ad that proclaims a supposedly unique quality for a product, a quality that really isn't unique. "If it doesn't say Goodyear, it can't be Polyglas." Sounds good, doesn't it? Polyglas is available only from Goodyear because Goodyear copy-righted that trade name. Any other tire manufacturer could make exactly the same tire but could not call it "Polyglas," because that would be copyright infringement. "Polyglas" is simply Goodyear's name for its fiberglass-reinforced tire.

Since we like to think of ourselves as living in a technologically advanced country, sci-
350 ence and technology have a great appeal in selling products. Advertisers are quick to use scientific doublespeak to push their products. There are all kinds of elixirs, additives, scientific potions, and mysterious mixtures added to all kinds of products. Gasoline contains "HTA," "F-130," "Platformate," and other chemical-sounding additives, but nowhere does an advertisement give any real information about the additive.

Shampoo, deodorant, mouthwash, cold medicine, sleeping pills, and any number of other products all seem to contain some special chemical ingredient that allows them to work wonders. "Certs contains a sparkling drop of Retsyn." So what? What's "Retsyn"? What's it do? What's so special about it? When they don't have a secret ingredient in their product, advertisers still find a way to claim scientific validity. There's "Sinarest. Created
360 by a research scientist who actually gets sinus headaches." Sounds nice, but what kind of research does this scientist do? How do you know if she is any kind of expert on sinus medicine? Besides, this ad doesn't tell you a thing about the medicine itself and what it does.

Advertising Doublespeak Quick Quiz

Now it's time to test your awareness of advertising doublespeak. (You didn't think I would just let you read this and forget it, did you?) The following is a list of statements from some recent ads. Your job is to figure out what each of these ads really says.

DOMINO'S PIZZA: "Because nobody delivers better."

SINUTAB: "It can stop the pain."

TUMS: "The stronger acid neutralizer."

MAXIMUM STRENGTH DRISTAN: "Strong medicine for tough sinus colds."   **370**

LISTERMINT: "Making your mouth a cleaner place."

CASCADE: "For virtually spotless dishes nothing beats Cascade."

NUPRIN: "Little. Yellow. Different. Better."

ANACIN: "Better relief."

SUDAFED: "Fast sinus relief that won't put you fast asleep."

ADVIL: "Better relief."

PONDS COLD CREAM: "Ponds cleans like no soap can."

MILLER LITE BEER: "Tastes great. Less filling."

PHILIPS MILK OF MAGNESIA: "Nobody treats you better than MOM (Philips Milk of Magnesia)."   **380**

BAYER: "The wonder drug that works wonders."

CRACKER BARREL: "Judged to be the best."

KNORR: "Where taste is everything."

ANUSOL: "Anusol is the word to remember for relief."

DIMETAPP: "It relieves kids as well as colds."

LIQUID DRANO: "The liquid strong enough to be called Drano."

JOHNSON & JOHNSON BABY POWDER: "Like magic for your skin."

PURITAN: "Make it your oil for life."

PAM: "Pam, because how you cook is as important as what you cook."

IVORY SHAMPOO AND CONDITIONER: "Leave your hair feeling Ivory clean."   **390**

TYLENOL GEL-CAPS: "It's not a capsule. It's better."

ALKA-SELTZER PLUS: "Fast, effective relief for winter colds." ■

THE WORD OF ADVERTISING

In the world of advertising, people wear "dentures," not false teeth; they suffer from "occasional irregularity," not constipation; they need deodorants for their "nervous wetness," not for sweat; they use "bathroom tissue," not toilet paper; and they don't dye their hair, they "tint" or "rinse" it. Advertisements offer "real counterfeit diamonds" without the slightest hint of embarrassment, or boast of goods made out of "genuine imitation leather" or "virgin vinyl."

In the world of advertising, the girdle becomes a "body shaper," "form persuader," "control garment," "controller," "outerwear enhancer," "body garment," or "anti-gravity panties," and is sold with such trade names as "The Instead," "The Free Spirit," and "The Body Briefer."

A study some years ago found the following words to be among the most popular used in U.S. television advertisements: "new," "improved," "better," "extra," "fresh," "clean," "beautiful," "free," "good," "great," and "light." At the same time, the following words were found to be among the most frequent on British television: "new," "good-better-best," "free," "fresh," "delicious," "full," "sure," "clean," "wonderful," and "special." While these words may occur most frequently in ads, and while ads may be filled with weasel words, you have to watch out for all the words used in advertising, not just the words mentioned here.

Every word in an ad is there for a reason; no word is wasted. Your job is to figure out exactly what each word is doing in an ad—what each word really means, not what the advertiser wants you to think it means. Remember, the ad is trying to get you to buy a product, so it will put the product in the best possible light, using any device, trick, or means legally allowed. Your own defense against advertising (besides taking up permanent residence on the moon) is to develop and use a strong critical reading, listening, and looking ability. Always ask yourself what the ad is *really* saying. When you see ads on television, don't be misled by the pictures, the visual images. What does the ad say about the product? What does the ad *not* say? What information is missing from the ad? Only by becoming an active, critical consumer of the doublespeak of advertising will you ever be able to cut through the doublespeak and discover what the ad is really saying.

Professor Del Kehl of Arizona State University has updated the Twenty-third Psalm to reflect the power of advertising to meet our needs and solve our problems. It seems fitting that this chapter close with this new Psalm.

The Adman's 23rd

———————————————————

The Adman is my shepherd;
I shall ever want.
He maketh me to walk a mile for a Camel;
He leadeth me beside Crystal Waters
In the High Country of Coors;
He restoreth my soul with Perrier.
He guideth me in Marlboro Country
For Mammon's sake.

Yea, though I walk through the Valley of the Jolly Green Giant,
In the shadow of B.O., halitosis, indigestion,
headache pain, and hemorrhoidal tissue,
I will fear no evil
For I am in Good Hands with Allstate;
Thy Arid, Scope, Tums, Tylenol, and Preparation H —
They comfort me.
Stouffer's preparest a table before the TV
In the presence of all my appetites;
Thou anointest my head with Brylcream;
My Decaffeinated Cup runneth over.
Surely surfeit and security shall follow me
All the days of Metropolitan Life,
And I shall dwell in a Continental Home
With a mortgage forever and ever.
Amen ■

UNDERSTANDING CONTEXT

1. What is Lutz's purpose in this essay?
2. Who is the audience for this essay? Why?

EVALUATING STRATEGY

1. Briefly summarize Lutz's thesis.
2. What strategy does he use to support his thesis? Is it an effective strategy?

APPRECIATING LANGUAGE

1. Lutz's article focuses on the proper definition of words. What is the difference between connotation and denotation?
2. Create a list of words in which the connotation is more widely used than the word's original meaning.
3. Create a list of words that you use regularly that could be considered "weasel" words.

WRITING SUGGESTIONS

1. Write a well-constructed summary of Lutz's essay.
2. Collect three print advertisements from one magazine or newspaper. Explain why all three were placed in the same magazine or newspaper. Compare the language in the ads. Explain which of the three ads is the most effective.

STEPHANIE ERICSSON

Stephanie Ericsson grew up in California and became a screenwriter and advertising copywriter. She has written books based on her own experiences, including two books about addiction: ***Shamefaced: The Road to Recovery*** (1985) and ***Women of AA: Recovering Together*** (1985). She also wrote about the unexpected death of her husband in ***Companion Through the Darkness: Inner Dialogues on Grief*** (1993). The following year she published ***Companion into the Dawn: Inner Dialogues on Loving***, a collection of essays.

The Ways We Lie*

Before reading this essay, consider your own views about lying. Do you always tell the truth? Are lies always immoral or deceitful or do they sometimes shield people from unpleasant facts or spare people's feelings? Do you consider failing to inform someone or allowing someone to believe an untruth a lie? Is honesty always the best policy?

1 The bank called today and I told them my deposit was in the mail, even though I hadn't written a check yet. It'd been a rough day. The baby I'm pregnant with decided to do aerobics on my lungs for two hours, our three-year-old daughter painted the living-room couch with lipstick, the IRS put me on hold for an hour, and I was late to a business meeting because I was tired.

I told my client the traffic had been bad. When my partner came home, his haggard face told me his day hadn't gone any better than mine, so when he asked, "How was your day?" I said, "Oh, fine," knowing that one more straw might break his back. A friend called and wanted to take me to lunch. I said I was busy. Four lies in the course of a day, none of which I felt the least bit guilty about.

10 We lie. We all do. We exaggerate, we minimize, we avoid confrontation, we spare people's feelings, we conveniently forget, we keep secrets, we justify lying to the big-guy institutions. Like most people, I indulge in small falsehoods and still think of myself as an honest person. Sure I lie, but it doesn't hurt anything. Or does it?

I once tried going a whole week without telling a lie, and it was paralyzing. I discovered that telling the truth all the time is nearly impossible. It means living with some serious consequences: The bank charges me $60 in overdraft fees, my partner keels over when I tell him about my travails, my client fires me for telling her I didn't feel like being on time, and my friend takes it personally when I say I'm not hungry. There must be some merit to lying.

But if I justify lying, what makes me any different from slick politicians or the corporate
20 robbers who raided the S&L industry? Saying it's okay to lie one way and not another is hedging. I cannot seem to escape the voice deep inside me that tells me: When someone lies, someone loses.

What far-reaching consequences will I, or others, pay as a result of my lie? Will someone's trust be destroyed? Will someone else pay my penance because I ducked out? We must consider the *meaning of our actions*. Deception, lies, capital crimes, and misdemeanors all carry meanings. Webster's definition of *lie* is specific:

1. a false statement or action especially made with the intent to deceive;

2. anything that gives or is meant to give a false impression.

A definition like this implies that there are many, many ways to tell a lie. Here are just a few.

The White Lie

A man who won't lie to a woman has very little consideration for her feelings.
—Bergen Evans

The white lie assumes that the truth will cause more damage than a simple, harmless untruth.   30
Telling a friend he looks great when he looks like hell can be based on a decision that the friend needs a compliment more than a frank opinion. But, in effect, it is the liar deciding what is best for the lied to. Ultimately, it is a vote of no confidence. It is an act of subtle arrogance for anyone to decide what is best for someone else.

Yet not all circumstances are quite so cut-and-dried. Take, for instance, the sergeant in Vietnam who knew one of his men was killed in action but listed him as missing so that the man's family would receive indefinite compensation instead of the lump-sum pittance the military gives widows and children. His intent was honorable. Yet for twenty years this family kept their hopes alive, unable to move on to a new life.

Facades

Et tu, Brute?

—Caesar*

We all put up facades to one degree or another. When I put on a suit to go to see a client,   40
I feel as though I am putting on another face, obeying the expectation that serious business-people wear suits rather than sweatpants. But I'm a writer. Normally, I get up, get the kid off to school, and sit at my computer in my pajamas until four in the afternoon. When I answer the phone, the caller thinks I'm wearing a suit (though the UPS man knows better).

But facades can be destructive because they are used to seduce others into an illusion. For instance, I recently realized that a former friend was a liar. He presented himself with all the right looks and the right words and offered lots of new consciousness theories, fabulous books to read, and fascinating insights. Then I did some business with him, and the time came for him to pay me. He turned out to be all talk and no walk. I heard a plethora of reasonable excuses, including in-depth descriptions of the big break around the corner. In six months   50

*Eds. NOTE—"And you, Brutus? (Latin). In Shakespeare's play *Julius Caesar,* Caesar asks this question when he sees Brutus, whom he has believed to be his friend, among the conspirators who are stabbing him.

of work, I saw less than a hundred bucks. When I confronted him, he raised both eyebrows and tried to convince me that I'd heard him wrong, that he'd made no commitment to me. A simple investigation into his past revealed a crowded graveyard of disenchanted former friends.

Ignoring the Plain Facts

Well, you must understand that Father Porter is only human. . . .
—*A Massachusetts priest*

In the '60s, the Catholic Church in Massachusetts began hearing complaints that Father James Porter was sexually molesting children. Rather than relieving him of his duties, the ecclesiastical authorities simply moved him from one parish to another between 1960 and 1967, actually providing him with a fresh supply of unsuspecting families and innocent children to abuse. After treatment in 1967 for pedophilia, he went back to work, this time in Minnesota. The new diocese was aware of Father Porter's obsession with children, but they needed priests and recklessly believed treatment had cured him. More children were abused until he was relieved of his duties a year later. By his own admission, Porter may have abused as many as a hundred children.

Ignoring the facts may not in and of itself be a form of lying, but consider the context of this situation. If a lie is *a false action done with the intent to deceive,* then the Catholic Church's conscious covering for Porter created irreparable consequences. The church became a co-perpetrator with Porter.

Deflecting

When you have no basis for an argument, abuse the plaintiff.
—*Cicero*

I've discovered that I can keep anyone from seeing the true me by being selectively blatant. I set a precedent of being up-front about intimate issues, but I never bring up the things I truly want to hide; I just let people assume I'm revealing everything. It's an effective way of hiding.

Any good liar knows that the way to perpetuate an untruth is to deflect attention from it. When Clarence Thomas exploded with accusations that the Senate hearings were a "high-tech lynching," he simply switched the focus from a highly charged subject to a radioactive subject. Rather than defending himself, he took the offensive and accused the country of racism. It was a brilliant maneuver. Racism is now politically incorrect in official circles—unlike sexual harassment, which still rewards those who can get away with it.

Some of the most skillful deflectors are passive-aggressive people who when accused of inappropriate behavior, refuse to respond to the accusations. This you-don't-exist stance infuriates the accuser, who, understandably, screams something obscene out of frustration.

The trap is sprung and the act of deflection successful, because now the passive-aggressive person can indignantly say, "Who can talk to someone as unreasonable as you?" The real issue is forgotten and the sins of the original victim become the focus. Feeling guilty of name-calling, the victim is fully tamed and crawls into a hole, ashamed. I have watched this fighting technique work thousands of times in disputes between men and women, and what I've learned is that the real culprit is not necessarily the one who swears the loudest.

Omission

The cruelest lies are often told in silence.

—*R. L. Stevenson*

Omission involves telling most of the truth minus one or two key facts whose absence changes the story completely. You break a pair of glasses that are guaranteed under normal use and get a new pair, without mentioning that the first pair broke during a rowdy game of basketball. Who hasn't tried something like that? But what about omission of information that could make a difference in how a person lives his or her life?

For instance, one day I found out that rabbinical legends tell of another woman in the Garden of Eden before Eve. I was stunned. The omission of the Sumerian goddess Lilith from Genesis—as well as her demonization by ancient misogynists as an embodiment of female evil—felt like spiritual robbery. I felt like I'd just found out my mother was really my stepmother. To take seriously the tradition that Adam was created out of the same mud as his equal counterpart, Lilith, redefines all of Judeo-Christian history.

Some renegade Catholic feminists introduced me to a view of Lilith that had been suppressed during the many centuries when this strong goddess was seen only as a spirit of evil. Lilith was a proud goddess who defied Adam's need to control her, attempted negotiations, and when this failed, said adios and left the Garden of Eden.

This omission of Lilith from the Bible was a patriarchal strategy to keep women weak. Omitting the strong-woman archetype of Lilith from Western religions and starting the story with Eve the Rib has helped keep Christian and Jewish women believing they were the lesser sex for thousands of years.

Stereotypes and Clichés

Where opinion does not exist, the status quo becomes stereotyped and all originality is discouraged.

—*Bertrand Russell*

Stereotype and cliché serve a purpose as a form of shorthand. Our need for vast amounts of information in nanoseconds has made the stereotype vital to modern communication. Unfortunately, it often shuts down original thinking, giving those hungry for the truth a candy bar of misinformation instead of a balanced meal. The stereotype explains a situation with just enough truth to seem unquestionable.

110   All the "isms"—racism, sexism, ageism, et al.—are founded on and fueled by the stereotype and the cliché, which are lies of exaggeration, omission, and ignorance. They are always dangerous. They take a single tree and make it a landscape. They destroy curiosity. They close minds and separate people. The single mother on welfare is assumed to be cheating. Any black male could tell you how much of his identity is obliterated daily by stereotypes. Fat people, ugly people, beautiful people, old people, large-breasted women, short men, the mentally ill, and the homeless all could tell you how much more they are like us than we want to think. I once admitted to a group of people that I had a mouth like a truck driver. Much to my surprise, a man stood up and said, "I'm a truck driver, and I never cuss." Needless to say, I was humbled.

Groupthink

Who is more foolish, the child afraid of the dark, or the man afraid of the light?

—*Maurice Freehill*

Irving Janis, in *Victims of Group Think*, defines this sort of lie as a psychological phenomenon
120   within decision-making groups in which loyalty to the group has become more important than any other value, with the result that dissent and the appraisal of alternatives are suppressed. If you've ever worked on a committee or in a corporation, you've encountered groupthink. It requires a combination of other forms of lying—ignoring facts, selective memory, omission, and denial, to name a few.

        The textbook example of groupthink came on December 7, 1941. From as early as the fall of 1941, the warnings came in, one after another, that Japan was preparing for a massive military operation. The Navy command in Hawaii assumed Pearl Harbor was invulnerable— the Japanese weren't stupid enough to attack the United States' most important base. On the other hand, racist stereotypes said the Japanese weren't smart enough to invent a torpedo
130   effective in less than 60 feet of water (the fleet was docked in 30 feet); after all, U.S. technology hadn't been able to do it.

        On Friday, December 5, normal weekend leave was granted to all the commanders at Pearl Harbor, even though the Japanese consulate in Hawaii was busy burning papers. Within the tight, good-ole-boy cohesiveness of the U.S. command in Hawaii, the myth of invulnerability stayed well entrenched. No one in the group considered the alternatives. The rest is history.

Out-and-Out Lies

The only form of lying that is beyond reproach is lying for its own sake.

—*Oscar Wilde*

Of all the ways to lie, I like this one the best, probably because I get tired of trying to figure out the real meanings behind things. At least I can trust the bald-faced lie. I once asked my five-year-old nephew, "Who broke the fence?" (I had seen him do it.) He answered, "The murderers." Who could argue?

At least when this sort of lie is told it can be easily confronted. As the person who is 140 lied to, I know where I stand. The bald-faced lie doesn't toy with my perceptions—it argues with them. It doesn't try to refashion reality, it tries to refute it. *Read my lips.* . . . No sleight of hand. No guessing. If this were the only form of lying, there would be no such thing as floating anxiety or the adult-children of alcoholics movement.

Dismissal

Pay no attention to that man behind the curtain! I am the Great Oz!
                                                                    —*The Wizard of Oz*

Dismissal is perhaps the slipperiest of all lies. Dismissing feelings, perceptions, or even the raw facts of a situation ranks as a kind of lie that can do as much damage to a person as any other kind of lie.

The roots of many mental disorders can be traced back to the dismissal of reality. Imagine that a person is told from the time she is a tot that her perceptions are inaccurate. *"Mommy, I'm scared."* "No, you're not, darling." *"I don't like that man next door, he makes* 150 *me feel icky."* "Johnny, that's a terrible thing to say, of course you like him. You go over there right now and be nice to him."

I've often mused over the idea that madness is actually a sane reaction to an insane world. Psychologist R. D. Laing supports this hypothesis in *Sanity, Madness & the Family,* an account of his investigations into families of schizophrenics. The common thread that ran through all of the families he studied was a deliberate, staunch dismissal of the patient's perceptions from a very early age. Each of the patients started out with an accurate grasp of reality, which, through meticulous and methodical dismissal, was demolished until the only reality the patient could trust was catatonia.

Dismissal runs the gamut. Mild dismissal can be quite handy for forgiving the foibles of 160 others in our day-to-day lives. Toddlers who have just learned to manipulate their parents' attention sometimes are dismissed out of necessity. Absolute attention from the parents would require so much energy that no one would get to eat dinner. But we must be careful and attentive about how far we take our "necessary" dismissals. Dismissal is a dangerous tool, because it's nothing less than a lie.

Delusion

We lie loudest when we lie to ourselves.

                                                                    —*Eric Hoffer*

I could write the book on this one. Delusion, a cousin of dismissal, is the tendency to see excuses as facts. It's a powerful lying tool because it filters out information that contradicts what we want to believe. Alcoholics who believe that the problems in their lives are legitimate reasons for drinking rather than results of the drinking offer the classic example of deluded thinking. Delusion uses the mind's ability to see things in myriad ways to support what it wants to be the truth.

But delusion is also a survival mechanism we all use. If we were to fully contemplate the consequences of our stockpiles of nuclear weapons or global warming, we could hardly function on a day-to-day level. We don't want to incorporate that much reality into our lives because to do so would be paralyzing.

Delusion acts as an adhesive to keep the status quo intact. It shamelessly employs dismissal, omission, and amnesia, among other sorts of lies. Its most cunning defense is that it cannot see itself.

> The liar's punishment . . . is that he cannot believe anyone else.
> —*George Bernard Shaw*

These are only a few of the ways we lie. Or are lied to. As I said earlier it's not easy to entirely eliminate lies from our lives. No matter how pious we may try to be, we will still embellish, hedge, and omit to lubricate the daily machinery of living. But there is a world of difference between telling functional lies and living a lie. Martin Buber* once said, "The lie is the spirit committing treason against itself." Our acceptance of lies becomes a cultural cancer that eventually shrouds and reorders reality until moral garbage becomes as invisible to us as water is to a fish.

How much do we tolerate before we become sick and tired of being sick and tired? When will we stand up and declare our *right* to trust? When do we stop accepting that the real truth is in the fine print? Whose lips do we read this year when we vote for president? When will we stop being so reticent about making judgments? When do we stop turning over our personal power and responsibility to liars?

Maybe if I don't tell the bank the check's in the mail I'll be less tolerant of the lies told me every day. A country song I once heard said it all for me: "You've got to stand for something or you'll fall for anything." ■

UNDERSTANDING CONTEXT

1. Why do people lie?

2. Does Ericsson see a difference in the severity of lies? Are some lies more harmful than others?

3. Can people cause unintended harm even when believe they are lying for a valid reason? Consider Ericsson's example of the army sergeant who listed a dead man as missing in action so his family could receive continued benefits.

4. How do people lie by omission?

*Eds. Note—Austrian-born Judaic philosopher (1878–1965).

5. *Critical thinking:* Ericsson includes "groupthink" and "stereotypes" in her list of lies. Are these really "lies" or merely mistakes in judgment? If people wrongly believe something to be true is that the same thing as consciously stating something they know is untrue?

EVALUATING STRATEGY

1. How important are the labels Ericsson gives each type of lie?

2. How does Ericsson use examples to illustrate each lie?

3. Ericsson includes brief quotations for each example. Are these effective? Do they add authority to her argument?

4. Ericsson uses both historical and hypothetical examples. Are they both effective? Can historical examples appear biased? Are hypothetical examples weak because they are imaginary?

5. Ericsson uses first-person examples of her own lying. What does this admission suggest? What effect does it have on readers?

APPRECIATING LANGUAGE

1. What does the style and level of diction suggest about Ericsson's intended audience?

2. *Critical thinking:* Consider the language used to describe lying. What do such terms as *misspoke, fibbed, misstated, gave the wrong impression*, and *white lie* suggest? How do connotations shape our view of lying?

WRITING SUGGESTIONS

1. Write an essay that provides your personal classification of lies, ranking them from the most to least harmful. Provide examples of each type.

2. Describe a situation in which someone you know told a lie. Did one deception lead to another? Did the lie cause harm unanticipated harm?

3. *Collaborative writing:* Discuss Ericsson's essay with a group of students and record their responses to this question: If they observed a coworker stealing from their employer, would they say nothing, talk to the employee, or tell a supervisor? If asked by a superior whether they had seen anyone take anything, would they inform on their colleague or lie? Would their decision be influenced by the value of the theft? Record your group's statements and develop a classification or division essay detailing their responses.

Blending the Modes MARTIN LUTHER KING JR.

Martin Luther King Jr. (1929–1968) was a leading figure in the civil rights movement in the 1950s and 1960s. A noted minister, King blended his deeply felt religious values and his sense of social justice. He created the Southern Christian Leadership Conference, organized many demonstrations, and lobbied for voting rights. In 1964 he received the Nobel Peace Prize. He was assassinated in 1968.

Ways of Meeting Oppression*

In this section from his 1958 book Stride Toward Freedom, *King classifies three ways that oppressed people have responded to their condition. King uses classification as a method to make a persuasive argument urging readers to accept his recommended choice of action.*

1   Oppressed people deal with their oppression in three characteristic ways. One way is acquiescence: The oppressed resign themselves to their doom. They tacitly adjust themselves to oppression, and thereby become conditioned to it. In every movement toward freedom some of the oppressed prefer to remain oppressed. Almost 2,800 years ago Moses set out to lead the children of Israel from the slavery of Egypt to the freedom of the promised land. He soon discovered that slaves do not always welcome their deliverers. They become accustomed to being slaves. They would rather bear those ills they have, as Shakespeare pointed out, than flee to others that they know not of. They prefer the "fleshpots of Egypt" to the ordeals of emancipation.

10   There is such a thing as the freedom of exhaustion. Some people are so worn down by the yoke of oppression that they give up. A few years ago in the slum areas of Atlanta, a Negro guitarist used to sing almost daily: "Been down so long that down don't bother me." This is the type of negative freedom and resignation that often engulfs the life of the oppressed.

But this is not the way out. To accept passively an unjust system is to cooperate with that system; thereby the oppressed become as evil as the oppressor. Noncooperation with evil is as much a moral obligation as is cooperation with good. The oppressed must never allow the conscience of the oppressor to slumber. Religion reminds every man that he is his brother's keeper. To accept injustice or segregation passively is to say to the oppressor that his actions are morally right. It is a way of allowing his conscience to fall asleep. At this moment the
20   oppressed fails to be his brother's keeper. So acquiescence—while often the easier way—is not the moral way. It is the way of the coward. The Negro cannot win the respect of his oppressor by acquiescing; he merely increases the oppressor's arrogance and contempt. Acquiescence is interpreted as proof of the Negro's inferiority. The Negro cannot win the respect of the white people of the South or the peoples of the world if he is willing to sell the future of his children for his personal and immediate comfort and safety.

A second way that oppressed people sometimes deal with oppression is to resort to physical violence and corroding hatred. Violence often brings about momentary results. Nations have frequently won their independence in battle. But in spite of temporary victories, violence never brings permanent peace. It solves no social problem; it merely creates new and more complicated ones.

Violence as a way of achieving racial injustice is both impractical and immoral. It is impractical because it is a descending spiral ending in destruction for all. The old law of an eye for an eye leaves everybody blind. It is immoral because it seeks to humiliate the opponent rather than win his understanding; it seeks to annihilate rather than to convert. Violence is immoral because it thrives on hatred rather than love. It destroys community and makes brotherhood impossible. It leaves society in monologue rather than dialogue. Violence ends by defeating itself. It creates bitterness in the survivors and brutality in the destroyers. A voice echoes through time saying to every potential Peter, "Put up your sword."* History is cluttered with the wreckage of nations that failed to follow this command.

If the American Negro and other victims of oppression succumb to the temptation of using violence in the struggle for freedom, future generations will be the recipients of a desolate night of bitterness, and our chief legacy to them will be an endless reign of meaningless chaos. Violence is not the way.

The third way open to oppressed people in their quest for freedom is the way of nonviolent resistance. Like the synthesis in Hegelian philosophy, the principle of nonviolent resistance seeks to reconcile the truths of two opposites—the acquiescence and violence—while avoiding the extremes and immoralities of both. The nonviolent resister agrees with the person who acquiesces that one should not be physically aggressive toward his opponent; but he balances the equation by agreeing with the person of violence that evil must be resisted. He avoids the nonresistance of the former and the violent resistance of the latter. With nonviolent resistance, no individual or group need submit to any wrong, nor need anyone resort to violence in order to right a wrong.

It seems to me that this is the method that must guide the actions of the Negro in the present crisis in race relations. Through nonviolent resistance the Negro will be able to rise to the noble height of opposing the unjust system while loving the perpetrators of the system. The Negro must work passionately and unrelentingly for full stature as a citizen, but he must not use inferior methods to gain it. He must never come to terms with falsehood, malice, hate, or destruction.

Nonviolent resistance makes it possible for the Negro to remain in the South and struggle for his rights. The Negro's problem will not be solved by running away. He cannot listen to the glib suggestion of those who would urge him to migrate en masse to other sections of the country. By grasping his great opportunity in the South he can make a lasting contribution to the moral strength of the nation and set a sublime example of courage for generations yet unborn.

*The apostle Peter had drawn his sword to defend Christ from arrest. The voice was Christ's, who surrendered himself for trial and crucifixion (John 18:11).

By nonviolent resistance, the Negro can also enlist all men of good will in his struggle for equality. The problem is not a purely racial one, with Negroes set against whites. In the end, it is not a struggle between people at all, but a tension between justice and injustice. Nonviolent resistance is not aimed against oppressors but against oppression. Under its banner
70 consciences, not racial groups, are enlisted. ■

UNDERSTANDING CONTEXT

1. Briefly describe the three ways people respond to oppression, according to King. Do you know of other ways? Do some people respond to oppression by blaming each other?

2. Humility is a Christian value. How does King, a minister, argue that humble acceptance of injustice is immoral?

3. King admits that nations have achieved freedom through violence, but why does he reject violence for African Americans?

EVALUATING STRATEGY

1. Why does King use classification to suggest a solution instead of writing a simple persuasive argument?

2. What transitional statements does King use to direct his readers?

3. How does King use religious values to advance his argument?

APPRECIATING LANGUAGE

1. How does King define the difference between "acquiescence" and "nonviolent resistance"?

2. What do King's use of biblical analogies and reference to Hegelian philosophy reveal about his intended audience?

WRITING SUGGESTIONS

1. Use this essay as a model to write your own classification paper persuading people to accept one method over others to respond to a common problem—the end of a relationship, the loss of a loved one, being victimized, or discovering a partner's infidelity. Discuss why other responses are less desirable than the one you recommend.

2. *Collaborative writing:* Discuss King's classifications with a group of students. How many people suffering oppression in the world today appear to be following the "third way"? Have a member take notes; then work together to draft a short paper dividing or classifying, if possible, your group's observations.

Black's Law Dictionary is a standard reference used by attorneys, paralegals, administrators, and law enforcement personnel. Like any dictionary, it serves to define terms.

Homicide*

In reading this entry, pay attention to the special use of language. Note how the legal definition of homicide differs from the common assumption that homicide is synonymous with murder.

Homicide. The killing of one human being by the act, procurement, or omission of another. A person is guilty of criminal homicide if he purposely, knowingly, recklessly or negligently causes the death of another human being. Criminal homicide is murder, manslaughter or negligent homicide. Model Penal Code, §210.1; 18 U.S.C.A. §1111 et seq. *See* Manslaughter; Murder.

Homicide is not necessarily a crime. It is a necessary ingredient of the crimes of murder and manslaughter, but there are other cases in which homicide may be committed without criminal intent and without criminal consequences, as, where it is done in the lawful execution of a judicial sentence, in self-defense, or as the only possible means of arresting an escaping felon. The term "homicide" is neutral; while it describes the act, it pronounces no judgment on its moral or legal quality. People v. Mahon, 77 Ill.App.3d 413, 395 N.E.2d 950, 958. *See Excusable homicide; Justifiable homicide, below.*

Classification

Homicide is ordinarily classified as "justifiable," "excusable," and "felonious." For the definitions of these terms, and of some other compound terms, see *below.*

Culpable homicide. Described as a crime varying from the very lowest culpability, up to the very verge of murder.

Excusable homicide. The killing of a human being, either by misadventure or in self-defense. Such homicide consists of a perpetrator's acting in a manner which the law does not prohibit, such as self-defense or accidental homicide. Law v. State, 21 Md.App. 13, 318 A.2d 859, 869. The name itself imports some fault, error, or omission, so trivial, however, that the law excuses it from guilt of felony, though in strictness it judges it deserving of some little degree of punishment. It is of two sorts,— either *per infortunium,* by misadventure, or se *defendendo,* upon a sudden affray. Homicide *per infortunium* is where a man, doing a lawful act, without any intention of hurt, unfortunately kills another; but, if death ensues from any unlawful act, the offense is manslaughter, and not misadventure. Homicide *se defendendo* is where a man kills another upon a sudden affray, merely in his own defense,

*"Homicide" definition reprinted from *Black's Law Dictionary, 6th ed.,* 1990 with permission of Thomson West.

or in defense of his wife, child, parent, or servant, and not from any vindictive feeling. *See* Self-defense; also *Justifiable homicide, below.*

Felonious homicide. The wrongful killing of a human being, of any age or either sex, without justification or excuse in law; of which offense there are two degrees, manslaughter
30 and murder.

Homicide by misadventure. The accidental killing of another, where the slayer is doing a lawful act, unaccompanied by any criminally careless or reckless conduct. The same as "homicide *per infortunium.*" See Manslaughter.

Homicide by necessity. A species of justifiable homicide, because it arises from some unavoidable necessity, without any will, intention, or desire, and without any inadvertence or negligence in the party killing, and therefore without any shadow of blame. *See* Self-defense.

Homicide per infortunium. Homicide by misfortune, or accidental homicide; as where a man doing a lawful act without any intention of hurt, accidentally kills another; a species of
40 excusable homicide. *See* Negligent homicide.

Homicide se defendendo. Homicide in self-defense; the killing of a person in self-defense upon a sudden affray, where the slayer had no other possible (or, at least, probable) means of escaping from his assailant. A species of excusable homicide. *See* Self-defense.

Justifiable homicide. Such as is committed intentionally, but without any evil design, and under such circumstances of necessity or duty as render the act proper, and relieve the party from any shadow of blame; as where a sheriff lawfully executes a sentence of death upon a malefactor, or where the killing takes place in the endeavor to prevent the commission of felony which could not be otherwise avoided, or, as a matter of right, such as self-defense or other causes provided for by statute. See Self-defense; also *Excusable*
50 *homicide, above.*

Negligent homicide. Criminal homicide constitutes negligent homicide when it is committed negligently. Model Penal Code, §210.4. *See* Negligent homicide; also *Vehicular homicide, below.*

Reckless homicide. See that title.

Vehicular homicide. The killing of a human being by the operation of an automobile, airplane, motorboat or other motor vehicle in a manner which creates an unreasonable risk of injury to the person or property of another and which constitutes a material deviation from the standard of care which a reasonable person would observe under the same circumstances. ■

UNDERSTANDING CONTEXT

1. Does it surprise you to learn that homicide may not be a crime? What does this teach you about the differences between common and specialized uses of words?

2. What does the law regard as the most serious, most criminal forms of homicide?

3. *Critical thinking:* What values seem to play a role in determining what is excusable and what is criminal homicide?

EVALUATING STRATEGY

1. How well organized is this entry? Is it easy to follow?
2. How important are the examples used to support the definitions?

APPRECIATING LANGUAGE

1. What do the tone, style, and word choice reveal about the intended audience?
2. How might you reword this passage for a general audience?

WRITING SUGGESTIONS

1. Select one of the types of homicide and illustrate it with a hypothetical narrative. Make sure your example follows the definition.
2. *Collaborative writing:* Working with a group of students, rework this passage, restating it in plain English for a creative writing class interested in writing detective stories.

Responding to IMAGES

Prime Minister Pierre Trudeau meets with John Lennon and Yoko Ono, in 1969, to discuss their peace initiative

John Lennon and Yoko Ono with Prime Minister P.E. Trudeau, Ottawa, Ont. December 22, 1969 © Library and Archives Canada. Reproduced with the permission of Library and Archives Canada. Source: Library and Archives Canada/Credit: Duncan Cameron/ Duncan Cameron fonds/R3506-1-1-E/PA-110804

1. Describe your immediate reaction to these photographs. How does the image of Prime Minister Trudeau contrast with that of Prime Minister Martin? What differences do you see?

2. *Visual analysis:* Based on the two photographs, describe the atmosphere or mood of the two meetings.

3. Is there a significance to either of the photographs? How do the photographs comment on the power of celebrity to affect social change? Can celebrity affect social change?

4. While Lennon and Bono used these meetings to push their activist agendas, could the politicians use the meetings for different reasons? Explain what some of the reasons might be.

5. What role have celebrities played in affecting social or political change? Are they still able to affect change?

Prime Minister Paul Martin meets with Bono in 2004, just prior to the beginning of the federal election, to discuss AIDS funding to Africa

AP

6. *Critical thinking:* What do these photographs say about the changes in Canada from 1969 to 2004? What do the photographs suggest about differences between politicians from the past and the present? What do the photographs suggest about the differences between rock stars?

7. *Collaborative writing:* Work with a group of students to draft a short essay to accompany these photographs. Explain the changing role of celebrity in the political arena.

8. *Other modes*

   ■ *Compare* how the two prime ministers are different. Do we expect less from politicians now? Given the constant media glare, is it important for our prime ministers to be seen as in touch with the celebrity world? Have politicians become another type of celebrity?

   ■ Use these photographs as *examples* of how well-intentioned celebrities can be co-opted by politicians for their personal agendas. Has the relationship between politicians and celebrity changed?

DIVISION AND CLASSIFICATION **CHECKLIST**

Before submitting your paper, review these points:

✔ Have you clearly defined your goal—to write a division or classification paper?

✔ Do you make meaningful divisions or classifications? Does your paper oversimplify a complex subject?

✔ Are your categories clearly defined?

✔ Do you avoid overlapping categories?

✔ Do you use parallel patterns to develop categories and items?

✔ In classification, do you use a single standard of evaluation?

✔ Do all the parts of your subject clearly fit into a single category? Are there any items left over?

 COMPANION WEBSITE

See **http://www.transcanadawriter.nelson.com** for additional information on division and classification.

CHAPTER 19

Cause and Effect: Determining Reasons and Measuring Results

This chapter explores the role of cause and effect in analysis. It offers guidance on how to perceive and establish cause-and-effect relationships, while also cautioning against the construction of false causal relationships.

WHAT IS CAUSE AND EFFECT?

Another important form of analysis for complex subjects is *cause and effect*. What led to the stock market crash of 1929? What motivated terrorists to attack the World Trade Center? What caused the Soviet Union to collapse? Would a handgun ban lower street crime? Would legalizing drugs reduce crime or create more problems? Analysis relying on cause and effect seeks to determine why something occurred or to measure and predict results.

Historians devote much of their work to analyzing the causes of events. Did Lenin cause the Russian Revolution or did the revolution create Lenin? What led to the women's movement of the 1970s? Historians also consider the ramifications of current events and speculate about the future. What role will China play in the 21st century? Will a global economy diminish national sovereignty?

Nearly all professions and disciplines engage in cause-and-effect reasoning. Many of the papers you will be assigned in college or university, and much of the writing you will do in your careers, will be developed using cause and effect. Identifying the reasons that something occurred can be formidable. Determining future outcomes, no matter how much evidence you may have to work with, can remain largely guesswork. Critical thinking skills are essential to successfully produce cause-and-effect writing.

Determining Causes

In some instances causes can be established through investigation and research. Doctors can diagnose an infection as the cause of a fever. Accountants can study financial records to discover why a company lost money. But many controversial issues remain subject to debate.

◼ WRITING **ACTIVITY**

Select one of the following topics and develop ideas using a variety of prewriting strategies.

1. The reasons you or your parents selected this college or university

(Continued)

2. Causes of domestic violence, poverty, racism, or other social problem

3. Reasons that many Canadians do not vote

4. The major causes of conflict between parents and children

5. Why people gamble

Measuring and Predicting Effects

Writers use cause and effect to measure and predict effects. By gathering evidence, evaluating data, and considering alternative interpretations, experts attempt to determine the effect of a new drug, a change in social policy, or technological innovation.

As with determining causes, measuring effects can be challenging. How can a company measure the effects of an advertising campaign? If sales increase, can this be attributed to the new commercials, a competitor's price increase, or a drop in interest rates?

Predicting future outcomes can be challenging because evidence can be difficult to collect or may be subject to various interpretations. In addition, numerous unforeseen factors can take place to alter expected events. A school board that decides to close schools because of a declining birthrate may fail to account for an influx of immigrants or the closure of private schools that would place more students into the public system.

WRITING **ACTIVITY**

Select one of the following topics and develop ideas using a variety of prewriting strategies.

1. The effect of cable television on popular culture

2. Effects you have experienced from exercising or changing your diet

3. The effects losing a job can have on a person's self-worth

4. The impact of graffiti on a neighbourhood

5. The effects of television advertising on children

Strategies for Writing Cause and Effect

Critical Thinking and Prewriting

1. **Review critical thinking.** Before beginning to write, review Strategies for Increasing Critical Thinking (see page 30) and Common Errors in Critical Thinking (see pages 31–35).
   - Read about deduction and induction.

- ■ Appreciate the importance of close observation and objective evaluation.
- ■ Remind yourself to distinguish between fact and opinion in developing topics.
- ■ Avoid jumping to conclusions, making sweeping generalizations, and mistaking time relationships for cause and effect.

2. **Develop potential topics** using the following devices.
   - ■ List events, situations, actions, and decisions, then explore their causes.

   Examples:

Changing your major	Causes:
Addiction	Causes:
Teen obesity	Causes:

   - ■ List events, situations, actions, and decisions; then explore their effects.

   Examples:

Your parents' divorce	Effects:
Antismoking, antidrug campaign	Effects:
Moving into your own apartment	Effects:

3. **Determine the goal of your paper—to establish causes, measure results, or predict future outcomes.**

4. **Select topics suitable to your purpose.** Consider the scope of the assignment and the amount of time you can devote to research and writing.
   - ■ Writing about the causes or effects of social, political, environmental, and technological issues may require extensive research. Without factual evidence, your paper can simply become a list of unsupported assumptions and generalizations.
   - ■ Consider writing cause-and-effect papers based on personal experience and observation.
   - ■ Keep the length of your paper and the due date in mind as you develop your topic.

5. **Talk with your instructor about possible topics.** Ensure the subjects you are considering meet the instructor's expectations.

6. **List as many causes or effects as you can.**
   - ■ Use clustering or freewriting to develop a list of causes or effects.
   - ■ Do not edit this list; jot down ideas that may seem irrelevant. Because your topic may change, don't discard ideas that might stimulate further thought.

7. **Search for supporting material.**
   - ■ Evaluate sources carefully. Look for signs of bias, unproven assumptions, or mistakes in logic.

8. **Determine whether visuals can enhance your paper.** If appropriate to the discipline or writing context, photographs, figures, and tables can illustrate or document causes and effects.

(Continued)

Planning

1. **Write a clear thesis statement listing the main causes or effects at the top of the page to guide planning.**

2. **Qualify your approach.** It can be difficult to discuss all the causes or effects of a complex subject. Limit your discussion, stating in the introduction how you intend to establish causes or measure results.

3. **Evaluate your reader's needs.** What evidence does your reader require to accept your conclusions? Are government statistics more impressive than expert testimony? Does any background information have to be presented? Are there misconceptions that must be addressed or terms needing definition?

4. **Offer logical, acceptable evidence.** Present support from reliable sources your readers will respect. Use brief narratives and examples to dramatize data.

5. **Revise your list of causes and effects.**
   - Delete minor, repetitive, or marginal ideas.
   - Highlight those points needing further development and use prewriting techniques to explore these issues further.
   - Examine each item on your list. Can some be separated into two causes or three separate effects? Can closely related points be combined?

6. **Write a new list, ranking points by order of importance.** Examine the number of points you have developed in light of the scope of the document. Would it be better to discuss one or two causes in depth or provide a list of eight reasons with only light support and explanation?

7. **Organize causes and effects by order of importance, moving from most to least or least to most significant.**

Writing the First Draft

1. **Keep your goal or thesis in mind as you write.** Writing cause-and-effect papers can raise numerous issues, and it is easy to write off topic, to explore interesting but unrelated ideas.

2. **Keep the scope of the paper in mind as you write and consider limiting the topic if the draft becomes too lengthy.** If your 500-word essay begins to expand so that it would require 2,000 or 3,000 words to fully discuss each item on your list, consider focusing on the principal causes or effects.

3. **Qualify remarks, noting possible exceptions or alternative interpretations.** Avoid making absolute statements that can be easily refuted by readers recognizing a single exception.

4. **Use other modes to organize your discussion of cause and effects.** You can use comparison to discuss alternative interpretations, classification to present a spectrum of causes or effects, and example to illustrate ideas.

5. **Use transitional statements and paragraph breaks to signal shifts between separate causes or effects.**

6. **Make notes as you write.** As you write, new ideas may occur to you, ideas you thought significant may become harder to explain than you thought, or minor points

may expand in importance. Note changes in your chain of thought to signal further revisions, taking care to mark these notes clearly so that you'll remember to come back to them. The order of your paragraphs may change because new ideas take priority.

Revising

1. **Review the entire essay.**
   - Does your paper meet the needs of the writing assignment?
   - Did your topic prove suitable for the scope of the assignment?
2. **Examine your thesis and list of causes or effects.**
   - Is the thesis clearly stated? Can it be further refined?
   - Have you supplied enough supporting evidence?
3. **Review your discussion of causes and effects.**
   - Does your paper devote too much space to minor points? Do more causes and effects need to be presented?
   - Does your paper offer only a superficial list of ideas? Should you narrow the thesis and discuss fewer causes or effects in greater detail?
4. **Examine your critical thinking.**
   - Review your use of induction and deduction. Do you jump to conclusions or ignore alternative interpretations? Do you base your reasoning on untested assumptions?
   - Have you avoided making errors in logic (see pages 31–35)?
5. **Review your introduction and conclusion.**
   - Does the first paragraph clearly announce your purpose, limit the topic, and qualify your approach?
   - Does the conclusion end the paper on a strong point by emphasizing the significance of your causes and effects?
6. **Review the use of visual aids.**
   - Are they appropriate for this paper?
   - Do they accurately and effectively illustrate or document the causes or effects you discuss?
7. **Use peer review to identify areas needing improvement.**

Editing and Proofreading

1. **Read your paper aloud.**
   - Are ideas stated in concrete language readers can understand?
   - Do some terms require further clarification or definition?
   - Do the tone and style of your words reflect your purpose?
2. **Review the structure of your paper.**
   - Are transitions clear? Could changes in paragraphing or revised transitional statements make the essay easier to follow?
3. **Use peer editing to locate errors you may have missed.**

SUGGESTED TOPICS FOR WRITING CAUSE AND EFFECT
General Assignments

Write a cause-and-effect paper on any of the following topics. Your paper can focus on determining causes, measuring effects, or explaining both causes and effects. Cause-and-effect papers often require research to present evidence. It is possible to use cause and effect in less formal papers, in which you offer personal experience and observations as support. Review Strategies for Increasing Critical Thinking (see page 30).

Write a paper explaining the causes of the following topics:

- Teenage pregnancy
- Domestic violence
- Your choice of major or career goal
- A recent campus or local scandal, incident, or controversy
- Apathy toward poor people

Write a paper measuring the effects of the following topics:

- The Internet
- Immigration
- Harsher drunk-driving laws
- Mobile phones
- Welfare reform
- Living in a dorm

Writing in Context

1. Analyze in a short essay a recent event on your campus, in your community, or at your place of work. Examine what caused this event. If several causes exist, you may use division to explain them or classification to rank them from the most to least important.

2. Write a letter to the editor of the college or university newspaper predicting the effects of a current policy change, incident, or trend in student behaviour.

3. Imagine a job application asks you to write a 250-word essay presenting your reasons for choosing your career. Write a one-page essay that lists your most important reasons. As you write, consider how an employer would evaluate your response.

Strategies for Reading Cause and Effect

As you read the cause-and-effect entries in this chapter, keep the following questions in mind.

Context

1. What is the writer's purpose—to establish causes, measure results, or predict outcomes? Does the writer use cause and effect to simply report a change or to support a persuasive argument?

2. Subject the essay to critical reading. Does the writer avoid logical fallacies? Are causes and effects clearly linked—or can they simply be time relationships or the results of coincidence?

3. Does the writer qualify his or her conclusions? Does he or she acknowledge alternative interpretations?

Strategy

1. Is the thesis effectively placed?

2. What evidence does the author present—personal observations, statistics, scientific studies, or the testimony of experts? Is the evidence sufficient? Is it accurate and fair?

3. How does the author organize the essay?

4. Does the writer practice critical thinking? Does the writer mistake symptoms for causes, assume past trends will continue, or rest conclusions on unproven assumptions?

5. What other modes does the writer use—narration, comparison, definition?

Language

1. Does the author's choice of words indicate bias?

2. What role does diction and connotation play in stating causes and results?

3. What do the tone and style suggest about the writer's intended audience? Are technical terms defined?

ANGELA OREND

Angela Orend is a Visiting Professor in the Department of Sociology at the University of Louisville, where she received both her graduate and undergraduate degrees. Her research and theoretical interests focus on issues of commodification with respect to the sociology of consumption, the body, and popular culture. Other recent works include **"Commodification and Popular Imagery of the Biker in American Culture"** and **"The Sub-Culture of a Skate-Park: A Socio-Visual Analysis."**

Corporate Logo Tattoos: Literal Corporate Branding?*

In her essay, Orend explores the recent trend of getting corporate logo tattoos. She examines some of the possible reasons for this trend and connects the trend to a larger social statement about personal identity.

1 Want to get free lunches for the rest of your life? All you have to do is get the Casa Sanchez corporate logo tattooed anywhere on your body and you can get free lunches forever! Casa Sanchez, a Mexican restaurant in San Francisco, is not the only company offering this kind of deal (Wells 1999). The Great Northern Brewing Company, which brews Black Star Beer, recently held its second annual Black Star Beer Tattoo Contest, giving away a Harley Davidson to who ever showed up with the biggest tattoo of the "yahoo-in cowboy" company logo (Wells 1999). More recently, the Daytona Cubs baseball team has recently announced that they will give free season tickets for life to anyone who will tattoo the Cubs logo on their body (NPR 2001).

The list of companies offering free products or discounts for people who get their cor-
10 porate logo tattoos are endless and have been increasing in number over the last few years. I should mention that these are NOT temporary tattoos—they are permanent. The temporary logo tattoo phenomena, used by NASCAR, Ford, Reebok, Dunkin Donuts, and many other companies, has been a fairly widespread marketing strategy used over the last few years.

The idea of corporations offering free merchandise or discounts to people who perma-
nently tattoo themselves with a corporate logo seems to have started with an April Fool's Day joke. In 1994 NPR's "All Things Considered" program reported that companies such as Pepsi, KFC, Apple Computer, and the GAP were offering discounts to teenagers who would tattoo their ears with corporate logos (NPR 1994). In exchange for branding themselves with the corporate symbol, consumers were told they would receive a lifetime 10% discount
20 on that company's products. As a result of the program, "Tattooed Ears Cause New Teen Craze," teenagers were said to be calling in masses only to be disappointed to find out the campaign was a hoax.

Well, corporate logo tattoos are no longer a joke. I have been researching this topic for a few years now and have been surprised at the number of people getting them and the various forms that the tattoos take. Even more interesting than consumers who are paid in exchange for becoming human billboards are those who are paying to have it done to them.

*Orend, Angela, "Corporate Logo Tattoos: Literal Corporate Branding?" reprinted by permission of Angela Orend.

For a few decades now, fans of Harley Davidson have been tattooing themselves with various versions of that motorcycle company's logo. According to the International Trademark Association, the Harley tattoo is still the most widespread corporate logo tattoo in North America (Sheldon et al. 2001). In recent years, however, logo tattoos have spread out into other corporate brands: Nike, Adidas, Budweiser, Corona, Apple computers, Ford, Chevy, Volkswagen, just to mention a few. In *No Logo* (1999), Naomi Klein argues that the Nike swoosh tattoo was reported as the most requested tattoo in North America (56). While it seems this statement was based upon personal observations and not empirical research, the fact still remains that the Nike swoosh, among other corporate logo tattoos, are on the rise (Magill 2002). Indeed, in 1997 Grace Bradberry stated in *The Times* of London that "having a designer logo tattooed onto one's ankle or wrist has become the ultimate in chic (Bradberry 1997: F1).

What is going on here? Why do people feel so connected to a brand that they will literally become human billboards and permanently tattoo themselves with a corporate logo? Is this brand loyalty, brand fetishism, an extreme example of the Culture Industry, human commodification, postmodern consumer tribes, or just a new postmodern play on self-expression? Or, is it a mix of all of these?

Before answering this question, it is important to understand the socio-historical aspects of tattoos. Throughout most of human history, tattoos were used to signify one's status within the social structure. As Bryan Turner argues, "body marks in pre-literate societies were permanent, collective, and largely obligatory" because "they were set within a shared culture of collective meanings" (1999: 39). In modern times, the meaning and motivations behind tattoos began to shift from representations of collective self-identity to individualistic representations of self-expression and individuality. Many modern tattoo consumers indicate that they see their tattoos as an attack on social conformity and argue that their tattoos evoke feelings of self-empowerment and individual self-expression and often express social resistance through bodily deviance (Polhemus and Proctor 1978; Sanders 1989; Velliquette et. al 1998). In this sense, modern tattoo consumers are said to be resisting dominant cultural ideology. Clinton Sanders sums up the modern argument for tattoos this way: "the power of (the) tattoo, like that of street graffiti is primarily derived from its ability to outrage member of conventional society" (1989: 162).

While the notion that tattoos are an attempt to resist mainstream culture should not be wholly discounted, its basic argument has become highly questionable when we try to apply it to corporate logo tattoos in the sense that major corporations are a part of dominant mainstream culture. Additionally, tattoos in general have proliferated in mainstream culture as they have become more socially acceptable and commonplace. While complete documentation of the number of people with tattoos is not available, it is estimated that between 12 to 20 million Americans have tattoos and that the numbers are rising daily (Velliquette et al. 1997). Additionally, tattoo establishments are currently among the top six growing businesses in America (Velliquette et al. 1997).

The postmodern explanation of tattoos tends to agree that they are expressions of identity, protest, and cultural defiance, while also accepting that they have become part of the "supermarket of style" for many tattoo consumers (Polhemus 1995). For example, Paul

Sweetman argues that even though tattoos have become a pop cultural trend, they can be more
70 than "mere accessories" and "are employed by some as a form of anti-fashion and as a way of
fixing or anchoring the reflexively constructed self" (1999: 52–53). Others, like Bryan Turner,
disagree and takes the argument one step further, adding that within postmodern society,
tattoos have become "optional, decorative, impermanent, and narcissistic" (1999: 42).

The sociological perspectives on the historical meanings and motivations behind tattoos
lead to several theoretical explanations concerning corporate logo tattoos. Such markings
may be expressions of personal brand loyalty to a corporation. As one Apple tattoo recipient
states, "I'm a Mac freak—I identify strongly with Apple and Mac computers—I got it done
to convince myself I would always be true to Apple, not for religious or political reasons, but
to convince myself that Macs are the way ahead" (Kahney 2002).

80 In postmodern consumer culture brands have become more than just products. Corporations present products as being representative of certain personalities and lifestyles,
consumers fetishize the brand, not the product itself. With brand fetishism, brands represent and become equated with lifestyles as brand awareness and advertising become more
important than the product itself (Vanderbilt 1997). In applying the notion of brand fetishism to corporate logo tattoos, the tattoo is an expression of what the brand represents, not
necessarily a loyalty to the superiority of the product. Advertising expert Colette Henry
argues that logo tattoos represent a way for consumers to proclaim one's philosophy of life
(Henry 2000). She explains, "young Americans with Nike swoosh tattoos have adopted the
advertising slogan 'Just Do It!' as their personal philosophy of life" (2000).

90 According to Jean Baudrillard, social meanings in postmodern times are created
through commodified signs that have imploded the social world (1998). The implosion
of the commodity-sign in the social world is caused by the mass reproduction of signs in
advertising (and other media) that has turned the social world into a simulated "carnival
of signs" where a self-referential system of signifiers makes it difficult to tell the real from
the simulated real (1998). Baudrillard insists that we are consuming not the object of the
sign, but rather the system of implicit meanings that the object of the sign represents, but
the meanings are simulated and meaningless. Within the logic of consumer capitalism, the
collective "carnival of signs" prevails as everything becomes a commodified product embedded with meaningless social symbols. If Baudrillard is correct and postmodern consump-
100 tion is the "active manipulation of signs" where the commodity-sign proliferates, corporate
logo tattoos are nothing more than a fashion accessory in the hyperreality of postmodern
consumer culture. The human body becomes a multi-dimensional billboard representing
another simulated hyperreality. Corporate logo tattoo consumers are not interested in the
product or duped by capitalism, they are simply expressing various simulations of reality
and have fetishized the social meanings of the brand and commodity-sign logo.

Consumers of corporate logo tattoos might also be internalizing the powerful ideology of
the Culture Industry, a concept developed by Theodor Adorno and Max Horkheimer in the
Dialectic of Enlightenment (1947). The Culture Industry is said to create, market, and maintain
dominant cultural ideology through mass standardization and powerful marketing strategies.
110 Adorno and Horkheimer argue that under capitalism, all of culture will eventually be subsumed

by the Culture Industry (2002). Hence, the dominant ideology in consumer capitalism is individuality and self-expression through consumption. People attempt to represent themselves and their individuality through the commodities they consume. For example, one Nike tattoo consumer proclaimed that he got his Nike swoosh tattoo because, "I wanted to be different, and I thought that [my Nike tattoo] would be" (Stouder 2003). Undoubtedly, Adorno and Horkheimer would argue that his tattoo was just another example of the commercialization of art (the logo as a form of pop art) and an expression of pseudo-individuality, not true individuality. The very idea that corporate logos are everywhere within consumer culture negates the notion that their logo consumption is an individual self-expression of individuality.

While the postmodernist arguments do not have too much in common with Adorno   120 and Horkheimer, they do seem to agree that everything in society, including the human body, has become commodified. So, it should come as no surprise that corporate logo tattoos have become a popular trend. Michel Foucault argues that the "body is the prisoner of the culture" and maintains that the body is inherently a social creation that is shaped by ideology; however, he also argues that the body can at the same time express resistance to dominant ideology (1979). For Foucault, power is not in the hands of only a few, but is instead exercised through the power relations of ideological discourse. Power is diffused in society through complex social networks. Within this argument, corporate logo tattoo consumers are not passively manipulated (as the Culture Industry thesis would have us believe) into internalizing a dominant ideology, but are instead actively engaged in an exercise of power,   130 albeit within the context of hegemonic discourse. Corporate logo tattoo consumers may have commodified the human body into capitalistic discourse just as they would any other product. In this respect, it is simply an aspect of human commodification where the consumer is engaging in a conversation with society. On the other hand, because power is not a zero sum game, it appears that getting a logo tattoo can also be an expression of resistance or a cultural exercise of power.

Within similar ideas of human commodification, corporate logo tattoos could be an end to individualism itself and a celebration of mass conformity through multiple loyalties within transferable postmodern consumer tribes. In *The Time of the Tribes* (1996), Michel Maffesoli argues that postmodern society has "gone beyond individualism" and towards   140 collective neotribalistic cultures that are "organized around the catchwords, brand names and sound-bites of consumer culture" (1996: 9). In this argument, corporate logo tattoo consumers are engaged in a "Dionysian celebration" of consumer culture. Consumer tribes are not bound to any particular place or tradition, their loyalties are voluntary and optional. In an attempt to form personal and social identities, consumers begin to identify with the dominant discourse of consumer culture. Corporate logo tattoo consumers are thus expressing collective representations of consumer culture, not individual representations of individuality.

So, which of these explanations is it? Are corporate logo tattoo consumers duped into the hegemonic discourse, showing resistance to it, internalizing it, or just reacting to the   150 fragmentation of postmodern times by commodifying the body and aesthetic art forms? Unfortunately, at this time sociology cannot answer these questions since there has not been sufficient research done focusing specifically on corporate logo tattoos. More sociological research is necessary to uncover the meanings and motivations that the recipients of corporate logo tattoos give to the situation. This is exactly what I am proposing to do. If you, or someone you know has a corporate logo tattoo, please contact me at logotattoos@yahoo.com. ∎

Notes

Adorno, Theodor W. and Max Horkheimer. 2002. *Dialectic of Enlightenment* translated by Edmund Jephcott. California: Stanford University Press.

Baudrillard, Jean. 1998. *The Consumer Society*. London: Sage.

Bradberry, Grace. 1997. "Branded for Life," *The Times*. November 20: F1.

Foucault, Michel. 1979. *Discipline and Punish: The Birth of the Prison* translated by Alan Sheridan. New York: Vintage Books.

Henry, Colette. 2001. "Making Ads Their Own," *Marketing: Ireland's Marketing Monthly*. November.

Kahney, Leander. 2002. "Tat's the Way Mac Heads Like It," online at http://www.wired.com/news/mac/0,2125,54202,00.html. August 5.

Magill, Christina. 2002. Personal email correspondence. February 20.

NPR. 1994. "Tattooed Ears Cause New Teen Craze," *All Things Considered*. April 1.

———. 2001. "Baseball Tattoos," *All Things Considered*. Dec. 5.

Polhemus, Ted. 1995. *Streetstyle: From Sidewalk to Catwalk*. London: Thames and Hudson.

Polhemus, Ted and Larry Proctor. 1978. *Fashion and Anti-Fashion*. London: Thames and Hudson.

Sanders, Clinton. 1989. *Customizing the Body: The Art and Culture of Tattooing*. Philadelphia, PA: Temple University Press.

Sheldon, Jamie, Cooley Godward LLP, and Mary DeLongis. 2001. "Tattoo You—With a Trademark," *International Trademark Association Bulletin Archive*. July.

Stouder, Amy. 2003. "Body Rage Fascination With Body Piercing and Tattooing."

Sweetman, Paul. 1999. "Anchoring the (Postmodern) Self? Body Modification, Fashion, and Identity," *Body & Society*. Vol. 5(2-3): 51–76.

Turner, Bryan. 1999. "The Possibility of Primitiveness: Towards a Sociology of Body Marks in Cool Societies," *Body & Society*. Vol. 5(2-3): 39–50.

Vanderbilt, Tom. 1997. "The Advertised Life," pp. 127–142 in *Commodify Your Dissent* edited by Thomas Frank and Matt Weiland. New York: W.W. Norton & Company.

Velliquette, Anne M., Jeff B. Murray, and Elizabeth H. Creyer. 1998. "The Tattoo Renaissance: An Ethnographic Account of Symbolic Consumer Behavior," *Advances in Consumer Research*. Vol. 25: 461–467.

Wells, Melanie. 1999. "Hey, is that an advertisement on your arm? From tattoos to ATMs, ads pop up in new places," *USA TODAY*. July 23: 12B.

UNDERSTANDING CONTEXT

1. List the number of meanings Orend offers behind the acquisition of corporate logo tattoos.

2. Why does she offer so many different meanings? Explain which one you believe presents the strongest reason.

EVALUATING STRATEGY

1. Briefly summarize Orend's thesis.

2. How does she support her thesis?

3. What methods does she use to support her thesis?

APPRECIATING LANGUAGE

1. Who is Orend's audience? Why?

WRITING SUGGESTIONS

1. Write a well-constructed summary of Orend's essay.

2. Write an essay on a popular trend that you have seen or experienced. What is the effect on those who follow the trend? Does their adherence to the trend represent a larger social issue?

LESTER B. PEARSON

Lester Bowles Pearson (1897–1972) was, successively, a teacher of history at the University of Toronto, a brilliant civil servant in Canada's Department of External Affairs, and Liberal prime minister of Canada from 1963 to 1968. He was also twice president of the United Nations Assembly, the only Canadian ever to hold this prestigious position. Because of his role in bringing about a resolution to the Suez Crisis in 1956, he was awarded the Nobel Prize for Peace.

The Implications of a Free Society*

In his essay, Pearson offers a summary of his political philosophy. He uses description and metaphor to persuade his reader of the importance for Canada of the values of tolerance and cooperation. He goes on to show how adopting these values will make Canada a better country.

1   The essential lubricant for a free society is tolerance. This, however, does not necessarily apply to *all* societies. There are obvious examples of states which are held together without the least regard for tolerance. It does apply, however, to all states where there is government by consent. Canada, where various groups live and work together within the boundaries of a national state, is a good example of this principle in operation. This country exists on the assumption that, as far as is humanly possible, the interests of no group—racial, geographic, economic, religious, or political—will prevail at the expense of any other group. We have committed ourselves to the principle that by compromise and adjustment we can work out some sort of balance of interests which will make it possible for the members of
10   all groups to live side by side without any one of them arbitrarily imposing its will on any other. It is my belief that this is the only basis upon which Canada can possibly exist as a nation, and that any attempt to govern the country on any other basis would destroy it. In these circumstances, the basic quality of tolerance in our national character is of the first importance.

     Of almost equal importance for our national welfare, and indeed arising out of the practice of tolerance, is the avoidance of extreme policies. This is often called walking in the middle of the road. This of course is not so easy as people usually think. It imposes both self-restraint and discipline, even when we assume that the traffic is all going in the one direction. Anyone who chooses to travel in the middle of the road must not deny the use of either
20   side of it to persons who prefer to walk there. He condemns himself, therefore, to accept during the journey the constant jostling of companions on either side. This middle ground is, I think, becoming more and more difficult to maintain, and the temptation to abandon it is constantly increasing, especially in the face of the road blocks thrown up by unfriendly

*Pearson, Lester B., "The Implications of a Free Society" from *Words and Occasions* by Lester B. Pearson (Toronto: University of Toronto Press, 1970). Reprinted by permission of University of Toronto Press.

fellow travellers. I do not wish here to criticize those who choose other ground upon which to walk, or to question the basis of their choice. I wish only to make a strong plea for the preservation of this middle position in our national life. Paradoxically, it is only in this way that the existence of many of those on each side can also be preserved. If the middle group is eliminated, less tolerant elements fall under the irresistible temptation to try to capture the whole roadway. When the middle of the road is no longer occupied firmly by stable and progressive groups in the community, it is turned into a parade ground for those extremist   30
forces who would substitute goose-stepping for walking. All others are driven to hide, disconsolate and powerless, in the hedges, ditches, and culverts.

How can the meaning of the middle way in our free society be described in a few words? What principle does it stand for? Where does it lead in practice? Is it merely the political line of least resistance along which drift those without the courage of their convictions, or simply without convictions? It is, or should be, far more than that. The central quality of this approach is the stress which it always lays on human values, the integrity and worth of the individual in society. It stands for the emancipation of the mind as well as for personal freedom and well-being. It is irrevocably opposed to the shackling limitations of rigid political dogma, to political oppression of, and to economic exploitation by, any part   40
of the community. It detests the abuse of power either by the state or by private individuals and groups. It respects first of all a person for what he is, not who he is. It stands for his right to manage his own affairs, when they *are* his own; to hold his own convictions and speak his own mind. It aims at equality of opportunity. It maintains that effort and reward should not be separated and it values highly initiative and originality. It does not believe in lopping off the tallest ears of corn in the interests of comfortable conformity.

The middle way presents no panacea for the easy attainment of general welfare, but it accepts the responsibility of government to assist in protecting and raising the living standards of all, and, if necessary, to take bold and well-planned action to help maintain economic activity for that purpose.   50

The middle way, unlike extremism in political doctrine, has positive faith in the good will and common sense of most people in most circumstances. It relies on their intelligence, their will to co-operate, and their sense of justice. From its practitioners, it requires determination and patience, tolerance and restraint, the discipline of the mind rather than the jackboot, and the underlying belief that human problems, vast and complicated though they may be, are capable of solution. ∎

UNDERSTANDING CONTEXT

1. Who is Pearson's audience? Why?

2. How does Pearson's argument in this essay relate to the Canadian image of a multicultural mosaic?

EVALUATING STRATEGY

1. Briefly summarize Pearson's thesis.

2. Pearson uses a central metaphor to present his argument. What is the metaphor? How is the metaphor used to present the argument?

3. Explain the cause-and-effect structure by which Pearson structures his argument in this essay.

APPRECIATING LANGUAGE

1. How does Pearson's use of diction distinguish desirable from undesirable Canadian traits?

2. What does "free society" mean to you?

3. *Critical thinking:* What words would you use to describe your approach to tolerance?

WRITING SUGGESTIONS

1. Write a one-paragraph summary of Pearson's essay.

2. Write a cause-and-effect essay explaining how the practice of tolerance, in Pearson's view, will create a particularly Canadian society.

3. *Critical thinking:* Is "walking in the middle of the road," as Pearson describes tolerance, always admirable and desirable? Does the "middle way" preclude a passionate existence? Is the "middle way" that Pearson advocates a path that you would follow? Discuss your response in an essay that integrates subjective and objective elements.

4. *Critical thinking:* If "the basic quality of tolerance" constitutes the Canadian character, as Pearson argues, what is the basic quality that defines the American character? Write a cause-and-effect essay comparing Canadian and American approaches to tolerance.

JOHN TAYLOR GATTO

John Taylor Gatto taught in New York City public schools for 25 years and was named the city's Teacher of the Year three times. He has published several books about public education, including **Dumbing Us Down, The Exhausted School,** and **The Empty Child.** Since leaving teaching, Gatto has become a public speaker, addressing audiences at the White House and NASA's Goddard Space Flight Center.

Why Schools Don't Educate*

In this section from a speech Gatto presented after receiving an award, he outlines the effects schools and television have had on children. As you read his list, consider if there could be other causes for the symptoms he observes.

Two institutions at present control our children's lives—television and schooling, in that 1
order. Both of these reduce the real world of wisdom, fortitude, temperance, and justice to a never-ending, nonstop abstraction. In centuries past, the time of a child and adolescent would be occupied in real work, real charity, real adventures, and the real search for mentors who might teach what one really wanted to learn. A great deal of time was spent in community pursuits, practicing affection, meeting and studying every level of the community, learning how to make a home, and dozens of other tasks necessary to becoming a whole man or woman.

But here is the calculus of time the children I teach must deal with:

Out of the 168 hours in each week, my children must sleep fifty-six. That leaves them 10
112 hours a week out of which to fashion a self.

My children watch fifty-five hours of television a week, according to recent reports. That leaves them fifty-seven hours a week in which to grow up.

My children attend school thirty hours a week; use about eight hours getting ready, going, and coming home; and spend an average of seven hours a week in homework—a total of forty-five hours. During that time they are under constant surveillance, have no private time or private space, and are disciplined if they try to assert individuality in the use of time or space. That leaves twelve hours a week out of which to create a unique consciousness. Of course my kids eat, too, and that takes some time—not much, because we've lost the tradition of family dining. If we allot three hours a week to evening meals we arrive at a net 20
amount of private time for each child of nine hours.

It's not enough. It's not enough, is it? The richer the kid, of course, the less television he watches, but the rich kid's time is just as narrowly proscribed by a broader catalogue of commercial entertainments and his inevitable assignment to a series of private lessons in areas seldom of his choice.

And these things are, oddly enough, just a more cosmetic way to create dependent human beings, unable to fill their own hours, unable to initiate lines of meaning to give substance and pleasure to their existence. It's a national disease, this dependency and aimlessness, and I think schooling and television and lessons—the entire Chatauqua idea—have
30 a lot to do with it.

Think of the things that are killing us as a nation: drugs, brainless competition, recreational sex, the pornography of violence, gambling, alcohol, and the worst pornography of all—lives devoted to buying things—accumulation as a philosophy. All are addictions of dependent personalities and that is what our brand of schooling must inevitably produce.

I want to tell you what the effect is on children of taking all their time— time they need to grow up—and forcing them to spend it on abstractions. No reform that doesn't attack these specific pathologies will be anything more than a facade.

1. The children I teach are indifferent to the adult world. This defies the experience of
40   thousands of years. A close study of what big people were up to was always the most
     exciting occupation of youth, but nobody wants to grow up these days, and who can
     blame them. Toys are us.

2. The children I teach have almost no curiosity, and what little they do have is transitory;
   they cannot concentrate for very long, even on things they choose to do. Can you see a
   connection between the bells ringing again and again to change classes, and this phenomenon of evanescent attention?

3. The children I teach have a poor sense of the future, of how tomorrow is inextricably
   linked to today. They live in a continuous present; the exact moment they are in is the
   boundary of their consciousness.

50 4. The children I teach are ahistorical; they have no sense of how the past has predestined
     their own present, limiting their choices, shaping their values and lives.

5. The children I teach are cruel to each other; they lack compassion for misfortune,
   they laugh at weakness, they have contempt for people whose need for help shows too
   plainly.

6. The children I teach are uneasy with intimacy or candor. They cannot deal with genuine
   intimacy because of a lifelong habit of preserving a secret self inside an outer personality made up of artificial bits and pieces, of behavior borrowed from television or acquired to manipulate teachers. Because they are not who they represent themselves to be,
   the disguise wears thin in the presence of intimacy, so intimate relationships have to be
60   avoided.

7. The children I teach are materialistic, following the lead of schoolteachers who materialistically "grade" everything—and television mentors who offer everything in the world for sale.

8. The children I teach are dependent, passive, and timid in the presence of new challenges. This timidity is frequently masked by surface bravado or by anger or aggressiveness, but underneath is a vacuum without fortitude.

I could name a few other conditions that school reform will have to tackle if our national decline is to be arrested, but by now you will have grasped my thesis, whether you agree with it or not. Either schools, television, or both have caused these pathologies. It's a simple matter of arithmetic. Between schooling and television, all the time children have is eaten 70 up. That's what has destroyed the American family; it no longer is a factor in the education of its own children. ■

UNDERSTANDING CONTEXT

1. How, in Gatto's opinion, are education and television linked in children's lives?

2. How has television affected children's views of the world and their attitudes toward others?

3. Gatto states that schoolchildren are "cruel" and "passive." Can one be both cruel and passive?

4. *Critical thinking:* Gatto states that "children live in a continuous present" without a sense of past and future. Is this a natural attribute of childhood or something induced by television? Doesn't television at least portray popular history?

EVALUATING STRATEGY

1. How effective are Gatto's use of numbered steps?

2. All of Gatto's eight points open with the statement, "The children I teach . . ." Does this repetition become redundant or build emphasis?

3. What risk does a writer run in criticizing children? How might parents respond?

APPRECIATING LANGUAGE

1. Gatto uses the word *ahistorical.* How would you define this word?

2. Gatto calls "being devoted to buying things" the "worst pornography of all." Is *pornography* an effective word choice?

WRITING SUGGESTIONS

1. Write your own essay detailing the effects television has had on your generation or children you observe. Do your observations parallel those of Gatto?

2. *Collaborative writing:* Discuss Gatto's article with a group of students. Record their observations on school reform. Select the major ideas and use them to draft a letter to a local school board suggesting ways of improving education.

Blending the Modes | DAVID SUZUKI

Born in Vancouver, BC, in 1936, David Suzuki is a world-renowned geneticist and science educator who has brought global attention to environmental problems through his innovative writings and use of media. A prolific author of essays and several books, he also has created popular science shows, such as the television series **The Nature of Things** and the radio program **Quirks and Quarks.** He has earned ACTRA and GEMINI awards as well as the Governor General's Award for Conservation and the Order of Canada.

Living with Nature*

In his essay, Suzuki explores the effects of letting children engage with the natural world, despite society's misgivings. He argues that children will be more sympathetic to environmental issues if they are not afraid of bugs and other creatures.

In spite of the vast expanse of wilderness in this country, most Canadian children grow up 1 in urban settings. In other words, they live in a world conceived, shaped and dominated by people. Even the farms located around cities and towns are carefully groomed and landscaped for human convenience. There's nothing wrong with that, of course, but in such an environment, it's very easy to lose any sense of connection with nature.

In city apartments and dwellings, the presence of cockroaches, fleas, ants, mosquitoes or houseflies is guaranteed to elicit the spraying of insecticides. Mice and rats are poisoned or trapped, while the gardener wages a never-ending struggle with ragweed, dandelions, slugs and root-rot. We have a modern arsenal of chemical weapons to fight off these invaders and we use them lavishly. 10

We worry when kids roll in the mud or wade through a puddle because they'll get "dirty." Children learn attitudes and values very quickly and the lesson in cities is very clear—nature is an enemy, it's dirty, dangerous or a nuisance. So youngsters learn to distance themselves from nature and to try to control it. I am astonished at the number of adults who loathe or are terrified by snakes, spiders, butterflies, worms, birds—the list seems endless.

If you reflect on the history of humankind, you realize that for 99 per cent of our species' existence on the planet, we were deeply embedded in and dependent on nature. When plants and animals were plentiful, we flourished. When famine and drought struck, our numbers fell accordingly. We remain every bit as dependent on nature today—we need plants to fix photons of energy into sugar molecules and to cleanse the air and replenish the oxygen. It 20 is folly to forget our dependence on an intact ecosystem. But we do whenever we teach our offspring to fear or detest the natural world. The urban message kids get runs completely counter to what they are born with, a natural interest in other life forms. Just watch a child in a first encounter with a flower or an ant—there is instant interest and fascination. We condition them out of it.

*Suzuki, David, "Living with Nature" reprinted by permission of David Suzuki.

The result is that when my 7-year-old daughter brings home new friends, they invariably recoil in fear or disgust when she tries to show them her favorite pets—three beautiful salamanders that her grandfather got for her in Vancouver. And when my 3-year-old comes wandering in with her treasures—millipedes, spiders, slugs and sowbugs that she catches under rocks lining the front lawn—children and adults alike usually respond by saying "yuk."

I can't overemphasize the tragedy of that attitude. For, inherent in this view is the assumption that human beings are special and different and that we lie outside nature. Yet it is this belief that is creating many of our environmental problems today.

Does it matter whether we sense our place in nature so long as we have cities and technology? Yes, for many reasons, not the least of which is that virtually all scientists were fascinated with nature as children and retained that curiosity throughout their lives. But a far more important reason is that if we retain a spiritual sense of connection with all other life forms, it can't help but profoundly affect the way we act. Whenever my daughter sees a picture of an animal dead or dying, she asks me fearfully, "Daddy, are there any more?" At 7 years, she already knows about extinction and it frightens her.

The yodel of a loon at sunset, the vast flocks of migrating waterfowl in the fall, the indomitable salmon returning thousands of kilometres—these images of nature have inspired us to create music, poetry and art. And when we struggle to retain a handful of California condors or whooping cranes, it's clearly not from a fear of ecological collapse, it's because there is something obscene and frightening about the disappearance of another species at our hands.

If children grow up understanding that we are animals, they will look at other species with a sense of fellowship and community. If they understand their ecological place—the biosphere—then when children see the great virgin forests of the Queen Charlotte Islands being clearcut, they will feel physical pain, because they will understand that those trees are an extension of themselves.

When children who know their place in the ecosystem see factories spewing poison into the air, water and soil, they will feel ill because someone has violated their home. This is not mystical mumbo-jumbo. We have poisoned the life support systems that sustain all organisms because we have lost a sense of ecological place. Those of us who are parents have to realize the unspoken, negative lessons we are conveying to our children. Otherwise, they will continue to desecrate this planet as we have.

It's not easy to avoid giving these hidden lessons. I have struggled to cover my dismay and queasiness when Severn and Sarika come running in with a large wolf spider or when we've emerged from a ditch covered with leeches or when they have been stung accidentally by yellow jackets feeding on our leftovers. But that's nature. I believe efforts to teach children to love and respect other life forms are priceless. ■

UNDERSTANDING CONTEXT

1. What does Suzuki see as the principal effects of urban living on children?

2. *Critical thinking:* Does Suzuki offer a credible solution to urban children's alienation from nature?

EVALUATING STRATEGY

1. Describe the process by which children in cities, according Suzuki's argument, become alienated from nature.

2. *Critical thinking:* Is Suzuki's use of personal anecdote effective for arguing cause and effect? How does the blending of cause and effect with process writing enhance his case?

APPRECIATING LANGUAGE

1. How does Suzuki use technical terms to give authority to his discussion without losing a general audience?

2. Find three examples of Suzuki's shift between abstract language for general concepts and concrete language for examples and details.

WRITING SUGGESTIONS

1. Write a one-sentence thesis for "Living with Nature."

2. Write a well-constructed, one-paragraph summary of Suzuki's essay.

3. *Critical thinking:* Does Suzuki's focus on cities unfairly target urbanization as a central cause of alienation from nature? Write a 250-word essay explaining one other major cause of environmental neglect.

4. *Critical thinking:* Write an essay on how your own childhood conditioning caused you to become alienated from nature in ways you would like to alter.

BRENT STAPLES

Brent Staples was born in Chester, Pennsylvania, and graduated from Widener University in 1973. He received a doctorate in psychology from the University of Chicago in 1982. After writing for several Chicago publications, he joined **The New York Times** in 1985 and became a member of its editorial board in 1990. He has also contributed articles to **Ms.** and **Harper's.** In 1994 he published a memoir, **Parallel Time: Growing Up in Black and White**, recalling a childhood of violence and poverty.

Black Men and Public Space*

In this Harper's article, Staples recounts the effects he has had on white pedestrians. As a black male, he realized he had the power to cause fellow citizens to alter their behaviour by simply walking in their direction.

1 My first victim was a woman—white, well-dressed, probably in her early twenties. I came upon her late one evening on a deserted street in Hyde Park, a relatively affluent neighborhood in an otherwise mean, impoverished section of Chicago. As I swung onto the avenue behind her, there seemed to be a discreet, uninflammatory distance between us. Not so. She cast back a worried glance. To her, the youngish black man—a broad 6 feet 2 inches with a beard and billowing hair, both hands shoved into the pockets of a bulky military jacket—seemed menacingly close. After a few more quick glimpses, she picked up her pace and was soon running in earnest. Within seconds she disappeared into a cross street.

10   That was more than a decade ago. I was 22 years old, a graduate student newly arrived at the University of Chicago. It was in the echo of that terrified woman's footfalls that I first began to know the unwieldy inheritance I'd come into—the ability to alter public space in ugly ways. It was clear that she thought herself the quarry of a mugger, a rapist, or worse. Suffering a bout of insomnia, however, I was stalking sleep, not defenseless wayfarers. As a softy who is scarcely able to take a knife to a raw chicken—let alone hold one to a person's throat—I was surprised, embarrassed, and dismayed all at once. Her flight made me feel like an accomplice in tyranny. It also made it clear that I was indistinguishable from the muggers who occasionally seeped into the area from the surrounding ghetto. That first encounter, and those that followed, signified that a vast, unnerving gulf lay between nighttime
20 pedestrians—particularly women—and me. And I soon gathered that being perceived as dangerous is a hazard in itself. I only needed to turn a corner into a dicey situation, or crowd some frightened, armed person in a foyer somewhere, or make an errant move after being pulled over by a policeman. Where fear and weapons meet—and they often do in urban America—there is always the possibility of death.

*Staples, Brent, "Black Men and Public Space" originally titled "Just Walk on By: A Black Man Ponders His Power to Alter Public Space" in *Harper's Magazine*, 1986. Reprinted by permission of the author.

In that first year, my first away from my hometown, I was to become thoroughly familiar with the language of fear. At dark, shadowy intersections, I could cross in front of a car stopped at a traffic light and elicit the *thunk, thunk, thunk, thunk* of the driver—black, white, male, or female—hammering down the door locks. On less traveled streets after dark, I grew accustomed to but never comfortable with people crossing to the other side of the street rather than pass me. Then there were the standard unpleasantries with policemen, doormen, 30 bouncers, cabdrivers, and others whose business it is to screen out troublesome individuals *before* there is any nastiness.

I moved to New York nearly two years ago and I have remained an avid night walker. In central Manhattan, the near-constant crowd cover minimizes tense one-on-one street encounters. Elsewhere—in SoHo, for example, where sidewalks are narrow and tightly spaced buildings shut out the sky—things can get very taut indeed.

After dark, on the warrenlike streets of Brooklyn where I live, I often see women who fear the worst from me. They seem to have set their faces on neutral, and with their purse straps strung across their chests bandolierstyle, they forge ahead as though bracing themselves against being tackled. I understand, of course, that the danger they perceive is not a 40 hallucination. Women are particularly vulnerable to street violence, and young black males are drastically overrepresented among the perpetrators of that violence. Yet these truths are no solace against the kind of alienation that comes of being ever the suspect, a fearsome entity with whom pedestrians avoid making eye contact.

It is not altogether clear to me how I reached the ripe old age of 22 without being conscious of the lethality nighttime pedestrians attributed to me. Perhaps it was because in Chester, Pennsylvania, the small, angry industrial town where I came of age in the 1960s, I was scarcely noticeable against a backdrop of gang warfare, street knifings, and murders. I grew up one of the good boys, had perhaps a half-dozen fistfights. In retrospect, my shyness of combat has clear sources. 50

As a boy, I saw countless tough guys locked away; I have since buried several, too. They were babies, really—a teenage cousin, a brother of 22, a childhood friend in his mid-twenties—all gone down in episodes of bravado played out in the streets. I came to doubt the virtues of intimidation early on. I chose, perhaps unconsciously, to remain a shadow—timid, but a survivor.

The fearsomeness mistakenly attributed to me in public places often has a perilous flavor. The most frightening of these confusions occurred in the late 1970s and early 1980s, when I worked as a journalist in Chicago. One day, rushing into the office of a magazine I was writing for with a deadline story in hand, I was mistaken for a burglar. The office manager called security and, with an ad hoc posse, pursued me through the labyrinthine halls, 60 nearly to my editor's door. I had no way of proving who I was. I could only move briskly toward the company of someone who knew me.

Another time I was on assignment for a local paper and killing time before an interview. I entered a jewelry store on the city's affluent Near North Side. The proprietor excused herself and returned with an enormous red Doberman pinscher straining at the end of a leash. She stood, the dog extended toward me, silent to my questions, her eyes bulging nearly out of her head. I took a cursory look around, nodded, and bade her good night.

Relatively speaking, however, I never fared as badly as another black male journal-
70 ist. He went to nearby Waukegan, Illinois, a couple of summers ago to work on a story about a murderer who was born there. Mistaking the reporter for the killer, police offic-ers hauled him from his car at gunpoint and but for his press credentials would probably have tried to book him. Such episodes are not uncommon. Black men trade tales like this all the time.

Over the years, I learned to smother the rage I felt at so often being taken for a criminal. Not to do so would surely have led to madness. I now take precautions to make myself less threatening. I move about with care, particularly late in the evening. I give a wide berth to nervous people on subway platforms during the wee hours, particularly when I have exchanged business clothes for jeans. If I happen to be entering a building behind some
80 people who appear skittish, I may walk by, letting them clear the lobby before I return, so as not to seem to be following them. I have been calm and extremely congenial on those rare occasions when I've been pulled over by the police.

And on late-evening constitutionals I employ what has proved to be an excellent tension-reducing measure: I whistle melodies from Beethoven and Vivaldi and the more popular classical composers. Even steely New Yorkers hunching toward nighttime destinations seem to relax, and occasionally they even join in the tune. Virtually everybody seems to sense that a mugger wouldn't be warbling bright, sunny selections from Vivaldi's Four Seasons. It is my equivalent of the cowbell that hikers wear when they know they are in bear country. ■

UNDERSTANDING CONTEXT

1. What is Staples's thesis? What is Staples saying about race, class, crime, prejudice, and fear in our society?

2. What attitudes does the writer have to the way women respond to him? What causes their reactions?

3. Staples reports that both black and white drivers lock their doors when they encounter him. What is he saying about racial perceptions and fear?

4. How do you interpret the conclusion? Why would people be reassured by a black man whistling classical music? What does this say about prejudice, stereotyping, and class? What else would make a black man less threatening—singing spirituals, carrying the *Wall Street Journal,* walking a poodle? Why?

EVALUATING STRATEGY

1. What is the impact of the first sentence?

2. Staples shifts the chronology several times. How does he prevent readers from being confused? How important are transitional statements and paragraph breaks?

3. *Other modes:* How does Staples use narration, comparison, and example in developing his essay?

APPRECIATING LANGUAGE

1. Staples avoids using such words as *racist, prejudice,* and *stereotypes* in his essay. Do words like these tend to be inflammatory and politically charged? Would it detract from his message?

2. What do the tone and style of the essay suggest about the response Staples hoped to achieve from his readers?

WRITING SUGGESTIONS

1. Write an essay narrating your own experiences in public space. You can explore how you cause others to react to your presence or how location affects your behaviour. What happens when you cross the campus late at night, drive alone, or enter a high-crime neighbourhood?

2. *Collaborative writing:* Discuss this essay with a group of students. Consider if a white man in shabby clothing or a black man in a business suit would provoke the same or different responses in white pedestrians. Is class or race the defining factor in provoking fear? Develop an outline for a sociological experiment measuring people's reactions to a variety of test figures engaged in the same actions. Write a process paper explaining how the experiment might be set up and the results evaluated.

| Writing beyond the Classroom | THOMAS JEFFERSON ET AL. |

During the hot summer of 1776, the Second Continental Congress met in Philadelphia. Following a call for a resolution of independence from Great Britain, John Adams, Thomas Jefferson, Benjamin Franklin, Robert Livingston, and Roger Sherman were charged with drafting a declaration. Jefferson wrote the original draft, which was revised by Adams and Franklin before being presented to the entire Congress. After further changes, the Declaration of Independence was adopted and signed.

The Declaration of Independence

The Declaration of Independence presents a theory of government greatly influenced by the concept of natural rights espoused by Locke and Rousseau, and then provides evidence that the British have failed to respect these rights. Notice that most of the declaration is a list of causes for the colonies to seek independence.

1   In Congress, July 4, 1776. The unanimous Declaration of the thirteen united States of America,

When in the Course of human events, it becomes necessary for one people to dissolve the political bands which have connected them with another, and to assume among the powers of the earth, the separate and equal station to which the Laws of Nature and of Nature's God entitle them, a decent respect to the opinions of mankind requires that they should declare the causes which impel them to the separation.

We hold these truths to be self-evident, that all men are created equal, that they are en-dowed by their Creator with certain unalienable Rights, that among these are Life, Liberty
10 and the pursuit of Happiness.

That to secure these rights, Governments are instituted among Men, deriving their just powers from the consent of the governed.

That whenever any Form of Government becomes destructive of these ends, it is the Right of the People to alter or to abolish it, and to institute new Government, laying its foun-dation on such principles and organizing its powers in such form, as to them shall seem most likely to effect their Safety and Happiness. Prudence, indeed, will dictate that Governments long established should not be changed for light and transient causes; and accordingly all experience hath shown, that mankind are more disposed to suffer, while evils are sufferable, than to right themselves by abolishing the forms to which they are accustomed. But when a
20 long train of abuses and usurpations, pursuing invariably the same Object evinces a design to reduce them under absolute Despotism, it is their right, it is their duty, to throw off such Government, and to provide new Guards for their future security.

Such has been the patient sufferance of these Colonies; and such is now the necessity which constrains them to alter their former Systems of Government. The history of the present King of Great Britain is a history of repeated injuries and usurpations, all having in direct object the establishment of an absolute Tyranny over these States. To prove this, let Facts be submitted to a candid world.

He has refused his Assent to Laws, the most wholesome and necessary for the public good.

He has forbidden his Governors to pass Laws of immediate and pressing importance, 30 unless suspended in their operation till his Assent should be obtained; and when so suspended, he has utterly neglected to attend to them.

He has refused to pass other Laws for the accommodation of large districts of people, unless those people would relinquish the right of Representation in the Legislature, a right inestimable to them and formidable to tyrants only.

He has called together legislative bodies at places unusual, uncomfortable, and distant from the depository of their public Records, for the sole purpose of fatiguing them into compliance with his measures.

He has dissolved Representative Houses repeatedly, for opposing with manly firmness his invasions on the rights of the people. 40

He has refused for a long time, after such dissolutions, to cause others to be elected; whereby the Legislative powers, incapable of Annihilation, have returned to the People at large for their exercise; the State remaining in the mean time exposed to all the dangers of invasion from without, and convulsions within.

He has endeavoured to prevent the population of these States; for that purpose obstructing the Laws for Naturalization of Foreigners; refusing to pass others to encourage their migrations hither, and raising the conditions of new Appropriations of Lands.

He has obstructed the Administration of Justice, by refusing his Assent to Laws for establishing Judiciary powers.

He has made Judges dependent on his Will alone, for the tenure of their offices, and the 50 amount and payment of their salaries.

He has erected a multitude of New Offices, and sent hither swarms of Officers to harrass our people, and eat out their substance.

He has kept among us in times of peace, Standing Armies without the Consent of our legislatures.

He has affected to render the Military independent of and superior to the Civil power.

He has combined with others to subject us to a jurisdiction foreign to our constitution, and unacknowledged by our laws; giving his Assent to their Acts of pretended Legislation:

For quartering large bodies of armed troops among us:

For protecting them, by a mock Trial, from punishment for any Murders which they 60 should commit on the Inhabitants of these States:

For cutting off our Trade with all parts of the world:

For imposing Taxes on us without our Consent:

For depriving us in many cases, of the benefits of Trial by Jury:

For transporting us beyond Seas to be tried for pretended offences:

For abolishing the free System of English Laws in a neighbouring Province, establishing therein an Arbitrary government, and enlarging its Boundaries so as to render it at once an example and fit instrument for introducing the same absolute rule in these Colonies:

70   For taking away our Charters, abolishing our most valuable Laws, and altering fundamentally the Forms of our Governments:

For suspending our own Legislatures, and declaring themselves invested with power to legislate for us in all cases whatsoever.

He has abdicated Government here, by declaring us out of his Protection and waging War against us.

He has plundered our seas, ravaged our Coasts, burnt our towns, and destroyed the lives of our people.

He is at this time transporting large Armies of foreign Mercenaries to compleat the works of death, desolation and tyranny, already begun with circumstances of Cruelty &

80 perfidy scarcely paralleled in the most barbarous ages, and totally unworthy the Head of a civilized nation.

He has constrained our fellow Citizens taken Captive on high Seas to bear Arms against their Country, to become the executioners of their friends and Brethren, or to fall themselves by their Hands.

He has excited domestic insurrections amongst us, and has endeavoured to bring on the inhabitants of our frontiers, the merciless Indian Savages, whose known rule of warfare, is an undistinguished destruction of all ages, sexes and conditions.

In every stage of these Oppressions We have Petitioned for Redress in the most humble terms: Our repeated Petitions have been answered only by repeated injury. A Prince, whose

90 character is thus marked by every act which may define a Tyrant, is unfit to be the ruler of a free people.

Nor have We been wanting in attentions to our British brethren. We have warned them from time to time of attempts by their legislature to extend an unwarrantable jurisdiction over us. We have reminded them of the circumstances of our emigration and settlement here. We have appealed to their native justice and magnanimity, and we have conjured them by the ties of our common kindred to disavow these usurpations, which, would inevitably interrupt our connections and correspondence. They too have been deaf to the voice of justice and consanguinity. We must, therefore, acquiesce in the necessity, which denounces our Separation, and hold them, as we hold the rest of mankind, Enemies in War, in Peace

100 Friends.

We, therefore, the Representatives of the united States of America, in General Congress, Assembled, appealing to the Supreme Judge of the world for the rectitude of our intentions, do, in the Name, and by Authority of the good People of these Colonies, solemnly publish and declare, That these United Colonies are, and of Right ought to be, Free and Independent States; that they are Absolved from all Allegiance to the British Crown, and that all political connection between them and the State of Great Britain, is and ought to be totally dissolved; and that as Free and Independent States, they have full Power to levy War, conclude Peace, contract Alliances, establish Commerce, and to do all other Acts and Things which Independent States may of right do.

And for the support of this Declaration, with a firm reliance on the protection of 110
divine Providence, we mutually pledge to each other our Lives, our Fortunes and our sacred
Honor. ■

UNDERSTANDING CONTEXT

1. What were the principal causes for the Congress to declare independence?

2. Why do Jefferson and the other authors argue that these grievances cannot be resolved
   in any other fashion?

3. Do some items in the Declaration of Independence strike you as relevant to current
   conditions? Should Americans be more familiar with a document that helped create
   their country and establish its values?

EVALUATING STRATEGY

1. How does the Declaration of Independence use induction and deduction?

2. How much of the document is devoted to listing causes? Is enough evidence presented
   to provide support for the decision to sever ties with Britain?

APPRECIATING LANGUAGE

1. How does this document refer to the king?

2. This document was drafted in 1776. How has the language changed in 200 years?

WRITING SUGGESTIONS

1. The Declaration of Independence states that the "pursuit of Happiness" is an unalienable right. Write an essay discussing the effects this pursuit of happiness has had on
   generations of Americans. How has the guarantee for the search for happiness shaped
   American culture and society?

2. *Collaborative writing:* Discuss the Declaration of Independence with a group of
   students. Does the current government reflect Jefferson's ideals? Work together
   and record your observations. What has been the long-term impact of Jefferson's
   document?

■ ■ ■ ■ ■

Responding to IMAGES

Jackie Robinson broke professional baseball's colour barrier in 1947.
Before playing with the Brooklyn Dodgers, Robinson played with the
team's minor league affiliate, the Montreal Royals.

Hulton Archive/Getty Images

1. *Visual analysis:* What is your immediate reaction to this image? How does the caption influence your response?

2. How does this photograph differ from your current opinion of professional sports? In your opinion, what was the significance of Robinson's accomplishment? Was it important that he played baseball? Why or why not? Why do you think he played in Montreal first?

3. What has been the effect of Robinson breaking the colour barrier? Is race or colour still an issue in professional sport? In the larger society?

4. Jackie Robinson's accomplishment predates Dr. Martin Luther King's and Malcolm X's activities and accomplishments. How do you think Robinson's accomplishment affected the civil rights agendas of King and Malcolm X?

5. *Collaborative writing:* Discuss this photograph with a group of students and measure reactions. Do any of them know someone who has suffered from racial discrimination? Work together to write a brief statement about how the public should be educated about racial discrimination. Do people still consider racial discrimination a serious social issue?

6. *Other modes*

   ■ Develop a comparison essay contrasting Robinson with a modern athlete. Robinson was noted for his stoic demeanor. He rarely railed against the unfair treatment he received. Compare this brief description of Robinson's behaviour with the modern athlete. How are the two different? Whose conduct is more beneficial in creating a better understanding between different races or cultures? Which athlete presents a better role model?

   ■ Create a *definition* paper that establishes the effect of breaking the colour barrier on North American society.

☑ | CAUSE-AND-EFFECT **CHECKLIST**

Before submitting your paper, review these points:

✔ Is your thesis clearly stated?

✔ Are causes clearly stated, logically organized, and supported by details?

✔ Are conflicting interpretations disproven or acknowledged?

✔ Are effects supported by observation and evidence? Do you avoid sweeping generalizations and unsupported conclusions?

✔ Do you anticipate future changes that might alter predictions?

✔ Do you avoid making errors in critical thinking, especially hasty generalization and confusing a time relationship for cause and effect?

✔ Have you tested your ideas through peer review?

COMPANION WEBSITE

See **http://www.transcanadawriter.nelson.com** for additional information on writing cause and effect.

CHAPTER 20

Argument and Persuasion: Influencing Readers

WHAT IS ARGUMENT AND PERSUASION?

One of the most important analytical modes in writing is that of *argument:* writing to persuade. Argument and persuasion pervade our daily lives: billboards, e-mails, magazine ads, and television commercials urge us to buy computers, automobiles, perfumes, and soft drinks. Political candidates solicit our votes. Public service announcements warn us against the dangers of cigarette smoking and drunk driving. As a student you have to develop persuasive arguments in essays and research papers to demonstrate your thinking skills and knowledge. After graduation you will need a persuasive résumé and cover letter to enter the job market. In your career you will have to impress clients, motivate employees, justify decisions, defend actions, and propose new ideas with well-stated arguments and persuasive appeals.

Arguments are assertions designed to convince readers to accept an idea, adopt a solution, or change their opinions. Writers use reason and facts to support their arguments, often disproving or disputing conflicting theories or alternative proposals in the process.

Persuasive Appeals

Aristotle and other philosophers in ancient times established three classic persuasive appeals to convince people to accept ideas or take action: *logos, pathos,* and *ethos.* Today these appeals appear in television commercials, political campaign speeches, business proposals, and ordinary e-mail. Because each appeal has advantages and disadvantages, writers often use more than one.

Logos

Logos (**logic**) supports a point of view or proposed action with critical thinking, reasoned arguments, and evidence:

Test results—Findings established by experiments or research

Statistics—Data represented as numbers and percentages

Documents—Materials such as diaries, letters, reports, photographs, and videos generated by participants or witnesses of specific events or situations

Expert testimony—Opinions by respected authorities

Eyewitness testimony—Statements by those who observed or experienced an event or situation

Interpretation—Critical reading and analysis of accepted laws, principles, contracts, and other documents, such as the Canadian *Charter of Rights and Freedoms*

Examples—Specific instances, events, or cases

Hypothetical examples—Fictional examples used to illustrate ideas

Surveys—Polls of public opinion or interviews with sample audiences

Logic is widely used in academic, business, and government writing.

Advantages

Logical appeals provide evidence needed for major decisions, especially group decisions. In addition, the facts used to support an argument can be verified by readers.

Disadvantages

Logical appeals demand a high degree of reader attention and specialized knowledge. Readers may not be motivated to follow a complex train of thought or study statistics.

Pathos

Pathos (**emotion**) uses images, sensations, or shock techniques to lead people to react in a desired manner. Emotional appeals call on people's deeply felt needs and desires:

Creativity—The desire for recognition and self-expression

Achievement—The desire to attain money, fame, or professional accomplishments

Independence—The drive to be unique, to stand out, to be an individual

Conformity—The need to be part of a group, to have friends, to be one of the "in" group

Endurance—The desire to be recognized for bearing burdens others have avoided or could not bear; feeling successful by simply surviving

Fear—The need to resist, avoid, or defeat threats to self, family, or the community; to fight crime, cancer, or terrorism

Popularity—The desire to be accepted, respected, admired by friends, coworkers, or the opposite sex

Emotional appeals are widely used in public relations, marketing, advertising, and political campaigns. Sex appeal is used to sell products ranging from cars to shampoo. Images of starving children will provoke pity and empathy, encouraging people to donate money or lobby politicians for government action. Fear of crime, terrorism, disease, or job loss can be used to motivate audiences to vote for a candidate or support a change in policy.

Advantages

Emotional appeals produce immediate, often powerful, responses.

Disadvantages

Emotional appeals tend to be short lived, can easily backfire, and provide limited factual support for readers to share with others.

Ethos

Ethos (**ethics**) uses shared values to influence readers. Appeals based on ethics may call upon reasoning but do not rest wholly on the logical analysis of evidence. Like emotional appeals, those based on ethics reflect deeply held convictions rather than personal motivations:

  Religion—The desire to follow the rules and behaviour espoused by one's faith

  Patriotism—The drive to place one's country above personal needs

  Standards—The desire to be a good citizen, a good lawyer, or a good parent; to express the higher ideals of a community, profession, or social role

  Humanitarianism—A secular appeal to help others, save the environment, protect the weak, or be "a citizen of the world"

  Ethical appeals form the basis of many sermons, editorials, and political speeches that emphasize shared values and beliefs.

Advantages

Ethical appeals call upon people's core values and can be powerful motivators.

Disadvantages

Ethical appeals work only on audiences with common moral philosophies.

Blending Appeals

To create effective persuasive messages, writers frequently blend factual details with emotionally charged human interest stories.

WRITING **ACTIVITY**

Select one or more of the following writing situations and give examples of the best appeal or appeals. Note advantages and disadvantages of each appeal.

1. An announcement encouraging students to avoid binge drinking

2. The text of a public service announcement reminding people to vote

3. A scientist's statement to the House of Commons urging further funds for genetic research

4. An automobile manufacturer's letter to car owners explaining the need for a recall to repair an engine defect

5. An environmental group's letter requesting that the city cease using lawn chemicals in public parks

UNDERSTANDING LOGIC

Of the three persuasive appeals, logic is the probably the most important one you will use in academic and professional writing. You can take entire courses devoted to logic, reasoning, statistics, and probability. However, even a brief overview of logic can sharpen your critical thinking and writing skills.

Two of the basic terms in logic—*deduction* and *induction*—are commonly misunderstood and worth reviewing in some detail. Many of the problems we encounter as students, consumers, employees, family members, and citizens involve deductive and inductive thinking. Whether you are constructing an argument using deduction or induction, it is important to avoid *logical fallacies*—errors in critical thinking.

Deduction

Deduction is a logical argument stated in a formula or syllogism. A major premise presents a statement of what is true or assumed to be true. Then a minor premise—a sample case or specific example—is measured against it. A conclusion is then drawn from the comparison.

Major Premise:	All cows are mammals.
Minor Premise:	Bessie is a cow.
Conclusion:	*Bessie is a mammal.*

Deduction based on major premises is a common form of logic in daily living. For example, you confront deduction every time you enter a liquor store and see a sign reading "You must be 19 to buy beer." In checking a young person's ID, the sales clerk practises an exercise in simple deduction:

Major Premise:	Customers must be 19 to buy beer.
Minor Premise:	Sharon Smith is 17.
Conclusion:	*Sharon Smith cannot buy beer.*

It's important to realize, however, that if the major premise in deductive reasoning is incorrect or vaguely worded, problems can emerge. Apartment leases, for example, usually include bans against making "excess noise," but what actually constitutes "excess noise"? Do the standards differ between an apartment building housing the elderly and one filled with university students? Can you argue against eviction if the police were never called and no neighbour filed a complaint? If landlords and tenants have different interpretations of the terms of a lease, conflicts can occur.

By developing an understanding of deduction, you can prevent potential disputes in business and personal relationships by clearly defining the major premise and ensuring that all parties accept a common definition.

Questions

1. Can you think of instances where you have encountered problems in deduction? Have you had disputes based on conflicting interpretations of a lease, warranty, tax regulation, or school policy?

2. Do you see any potential problems with the following rules or major premises? Could different interpretations create confusion or conflicts?
   - Disadvantaged students have priority for on-campus jobs.
   - Students must have completed a substantial amount of work to be eligible for a course extension.
   - Family members of employees can receive a 20 percent discount.

Induction

Unlike deduction, induction does not begin with a premise or assertion of what is true. Instead, an inductive argument starts with evidence, detailed information. From these specifics, a conclusion is drawn.

A criminal trial best illustrates the inductive process. In a murder case, the crown prosecutor presents evidence of the defendant's guilt—eyewitness testimony, fingerprints, expert witnesses, and so forth—and tells the jury that all the evidence adds up to a clear guilty verdict. The defence attorney may introduce contradictory evidence or question the interpretation of the prosecution's evidence to argue that there is not enough proof to conclude that the defendant is guilty. Lawyers don't use the term *inductive leap*—but the legal concept of *reasonable doubt* is very close.

As with deduction, problems occur with inductive logic. Evidence may be overlooked or misinterpreted. A political survey conducted through the Internet, for example, cannot provide an accurate survey of public opinion because it fails to consider those who either do not have computers or did not visit the particular website.

Questions

1. How often have you used induction in solving problems or making decisions? What problems have you encountered?

2. Have you observed the use of inductive reasoning during televised trials? How effective have cross-examinations been in raising reasonable doubt?

3. Do your textbooks in other courses offer methods of collecting and evaluating evidence? Do separate disciplines place different values on types of evidence?

PERSUASION AND AUDIENCE

Whenever you write, you should consider your audience—the people who will read your papers, e-mails, reports, and letters. A narrative or description will be effective only if readers understand the definitions, examples, and details you present to support your thesis. In writing persuasion, however, you have to consider your readers even more carefully. Unlike a narrative or a description, an argument seeks not to simply tell a story or share information but influence people to change their minds or take action. Readers of persuasive writing are more likely to be critical, even hostile to your viewpoints. To win support, you may have to refute alternative arguments, dismiss competing interpretations of evidence, or admit the value of opposing ideas. Psychologist Carl R. Rogers studied problems in communications and emphasized the importance of building trust by addressing audience concerns and objections. Rogerian arguments work to build consensus by showing respect to people holding opposing viewpoints.

Appealing to Hostile Readers

Perhaps the most challenging problem writers face is attempting to persuade a hostile audience—readers you know or expect will have negative attitudes about you, the organization you represent, or the ideas you advocate. Although no technique will magically convert opponents into supporters, you can overcome a measure of hostility and influence those who may be undecided with a few strategies:

1. **Openly admit differences.** Instead of attempting to pretend that no conflict exists, frankly state that your view may differ from that of your readers. This honest admission can achieve a measure of objectivity and respect.

2. **Responsibly summarize opposing viewpoints.** By fairly restating your opponents' views, you are more likely to lead readers to agree with you and demonstrate impartiality.

3. **Avoid making judgmental statements.** Don't label people with differing views with hostile or negative language. Use neutral terms to make distinctions. Demeaning language will only alienate your audience.

4. **Stress shared values, experiences, and problems.** Build bridges with your readers by emphasizing past cooperation and common concerns.

5. **Ask readers to maintain an open mind.** Don't demand or expect to convert readers, but keep in mind that almost everyone will agree to try to be open-minded and receptive to new ideas.

6. **Overcome negative stereotypes.** Play the devil's advocate to determine what negative stereotypes your readers might have about you, the organization you represent, or your thesis. Include examples, references, evidence, and stories in your paper to counter these negative impressions.

WRITING **ACTIVITY**

Select one of the following writing contexts and list some strategies to overcome hostile reactions. What facts, narratives, appeals, or approaches would help advance the writer's thesis? What issues does the writer have to address? How can he or she counter objections? What information would the writer have to include?

1. A member of First Nations writing a letter to the editor of a conservative business magazine arguing for stronger employment equity policies

2. A real estate developer writing to a community group opposing the building of a new shopping mall in its neighbourhood

3. A student group writing to alumni to suggest that funds being raised for a new athletic facility be spent on computer labs

4. A tenant writing to a landlord urging him or her to add security features, such as deadbolts, to apartments

5. A university administrator developing an open letter to students to defend a campus organization's decision to invite a controversial public speaker

Strategies for Writing Argument and Persuasion

Critical Thinking and Prewriting

1. **List as many topics, problems, issues, controversies, debates, and decisions you can think of.** Brainstorm, freewrite briefly, and list questions to isolate promising topics.

2. **Review the scope of the assignment.** Effective argument-and-persuasion papers require substantial evidence and reasoning.

3. **Determine the goal of your essay**—to persuade readers to accept your opinion or to motivate readers to take action or alter behaviour. Unlike a description or narrative, an argumentative paper has a specific goal.

4. **Consider your audience.** To craft an effective argument, it is important to consider your audience.
   - Define your readers and their perceptual world. List the past experiences, social roles, values, norms, attitudes, and reference groups that may influence their thinking.

(Continued)

- Consider their immediate attitude toward your topic.
- List questions and concerns your readers may have.
- List appeals readers will relate to and respond to.

5. **Develop a thesis statement and a list of principal appeals with your readers in mind.**

6. **List evidence needed to support your thesis.** Conduct a computer search using key words to locate current sources about your topic. Evaluate sources carefully for accuracy and bias.

Planning

1. **Review critical thinking.** Before writing a plan, review Strategies for Increasing Critical Thinking (see page 30) and Common Errors in Critical Thinking (see pages 31–35).

2. **Write your thesis statement at the top of the page to guide planning.** Qualify your thesis, avoiding generalizations, absolute statements, and unsupported assumptions.

3. **Develop an introduction that arouses attention, establishes your approach, and uses persuasive appeals to create a favourable relationship with readers.** You may wish to open your essay with a question, a narrative, a quote, or a statistic that illustrates or dramatizes the issue.

4. **Do not mistake propaganda for persuasion.** Do not assume that hurling accusations, using inflated statistics, employing shock tactics, or demonizing your opponents will make your argument successful.

5. **Organize ideas in order of importance.** Place the most convincing appeal or argument at the beginning or end of your paper, where reader attention is strongest.

6. **Consider using visuals.** If visuals are appropriate to the writing context, photographs, figures, and tables can add effective support to a persuasive message—provided they are carefully selected and properly presented. Avoid using images that may alienate readers.

7. **Conclude the paper with a thought-provoking impression or a clear call to action.** End the paper with a final fact, example, or quotation that will influence readers to consider your thesis, perhaps even read more to fully understand your point of view. If your goal is to direct people to alter their behaviour, present explicit instructions so that motivated readers can take immediate action.

Writing the First Draft

1. **Keep your thesis and audience in mind as you write.** Effective persuasive arguments are directed to a specific audience. As you write, concentrate on your readers.

2. **Qualify remarks, noting possible alternative views.** Avoid making absolute statements that can be easily refuted by citing a single exception.

3. **Recognize the strength and weakness of each appeal.** Balance emotional appeals with facts. Dramatize statistics with human interest. Tailor ethical appeals to your readers' perceptual world.

4. **Present factual detail in ways readers can understand.** To present facts, use methods such as example, analogy, and narrative to illustrate and dramatize facts.

5. **Use transitional phrases and paragraph breaks to signal shifts between the main points of your argument.**

6. **Keep the scope of the assignment in mind as you write, and consider limiting the topic if the draft becomes too lengthy.** If your draft begins to expand so that it will require ten pages rather than the thousand words you intended to fully address the topic, limit the scope of your paper.

7. **Anticipate reader objections as you write.** Play the devil's advocate as you write. Consider how you can overcome or counter readers' negative assumptions about your thesis.

Revising

1. **Review the needs of the writing assignment; then examine your entire essay.**
   - On first reading, does your essay meet the needs of the assignment?
   - Is the topic suitable?
   - Is the thesis clearly stated?
   - If you are motivating readers to take action, are they given a clearly defined course of action?

2. **Examine your use of appeals.**
   - Are logical appeals clear, accurate, and suitable to your task?
   - Do you present clear, convincing evidence your readers will accept?
   - Do emotional appeals avoid bias or propaganda that may offend or backfire?
   - Are ethical appeals suited to your audience? Do your readers share the values you call upon?

3. **Review critical thinking.** Do you avoid Common Errors in Critical Thinking (see pages 31–35)?

4. **Review your introduction and conclusion.**
   - Does the first paragraph clearly announce your purpose, limit the topic, and qualify your approach? Does it grab attention and prepare readers to accept your message?
   - Does the conclusion urge readers to consider your thesis or direct them to take action?

5. **Examine the paper's structure.**
   - Are there clear transitions between main points?
   - Could paragraph breaks be altered to demonstrate shifts and emphasize ideas?

6. **Review your use of visuals.** Do they support your message? Are they appropriate, effective, and clearly presented?

7. **Use peer review to identify areas needing improvement.**

Editing and Proofreading

1. **Reread your paper aloud.**
   - Are ideas stated in concrete language readers can understand?
   - Do any words have connotations unsuited to your purpose or audience?
   - Do the tone and style suit your topic, audience, and message?

2. **Use peer editing to locate errors you may have missed.**

SUGGESTED TOPICS FOR WRITING ARGUMENT AND PERSUASION

General Assignments

Write a persuasive argument to a general audience on one of the following topics. You may use one or more appeals. You can frame your paper in the form of an essay, letter, flyer, advertisement, or other document.

- The way the public school system fails to prepare students for university
- Environmentally friendly living
- The drinking age
- Family values
- The insanity defence

Select one of the following issues and craft a persuasive essay targeted to one of the audiences listed.

ISSUES	AUDIENCES
Distribution of condoms in public schools	Suburban residents
	Minority police officers
Gun control	Senior citizens
Recycling	Public health workers
Legalization of marijuana for medical purposes	Retired school teachers
	Small business owners
Bilingual education	Urban teenagers
	Young parents

Writing in Context

Write a letter to the editor of the campus newspaper about a problem or situation you have observed but no one seems willing to address. Urge the university community to take notice and possible action.

Strategies for Reading Argument and Persuasion

As you read the argument and persuasion entries in this chapter, keep these questions in mind.

Context

1. What is the author's thesis? What does he or she want readers to accept? Is the writer persuading readers to accept an opinion or motivate them to take action?

2. How credible is the thesis? Does it make sense? Are alternative views discussed?

3. How does the author characterize those who advocate differing views?

4. Does the writer appear to have an unfair bias?

Strategy

1. Which appeals does the writer use? Does he or she blend logic and emotion, evidence with ethics?

2. Do the appeals seem effective, given the intended audience?

3. Where does the author place the thesis?

4. Are emotional appeals suitable or do they reflect bias?

5. Are errors in critical thinking avoided?

6. Does the reader appear to anticipate a sympathetic, neutral, or hostile audience?

Language

1. What role does connotation play in shaping arguments using logical, emotional, or ethical appeals?

2. What does the author's choice of words reveal about the intended audience?

3. Does word choice indicate bias?

GEORGE ORWELL

George Orwell was the pen name of Eric Blair (1903–1950), who was born in India, the son of a British official. Blair attended the prestigious Eton school but joined the Indian Imperial Police instead of attending university. After four years of service in Burma, he left to pursue a writing career. His first book, **Down and Out in Paris and London,** explored the plight of the poor and homeless during the Depression. His later books included **Animal Farm** and **Nineteen Eighty-Four.**

Politics and the English Language*

In this classic essay, written in 1946, Orwell makes a direct link between threats to democracy and linguistic decay. Orwell explores the link between a sloppy vocabulary and a sloppy mind. He argues that to guard against political deception, the public must arm itself with a strong vocabulary and precise writing.

1 Most people who bother with the matter at all would admit that the English language is in a bad way, but it is generally assumed that we cannot by conscious action do anything about it. Our civilization is decadent and our language—so the argument runs—must inevitably share in the general collapse. It follows that any struggle against the abuse of language is a sentimental archaism, like preferring candles to electric light or hansom cabs to aeroplanes. Underneath this lies the half-conscious belief that language is a natural growth and not an instrument which we shape for our own purposes.

Now, it is clear that the decline of a language must ultimately have political and economic causes: it is not due simply to the bad influence of this or that individual writer. But
10 an effect can become a cause, reinforcing the original cause and producing the same effect in an intensified form, and so on indefinitely. A man may take to drink because he feels himself to be a failure, and then fail all the more completely because he drinks. It is rather the same thing that is happening to the English language. It becomes ugly and inaccurate because our thoughts are foolish, but the slovenliness of our language makes it easier for us to have foolish thoughts. The point is that the process is reversible. Modern English, especially written English, is full of bad habits which spread by imitation and which can be avoided if one is willing to take the necessary trouble. If one gets rid of these habits one can think more clearly, and to think clearly is a necessary first step toward political regeneration: so that the fight against bad English is not frivolous and is not the exclusive concern of professional
20 writers. I will come back to this presently, and I hope that by that time the meaning of what I have said here will have become clearer. Meanwhile, here are five specimens of the English language as it is now habitually written.

These five passages have not been picked out because they are especially bad—I could have quoted far worse if I had chosen—but because they illustrate various of the mental vices from which we now suffer. They are a little below the average, but are fairly representative examples. I number them so that I can refer back to them when necessary:

1. *I am not, indeed, sure whether it is not true to say that the Milton who once seemed not unlike a seventeenth-century Shelley had not become, out of an experience ever more bitter in each year, more alien [sic] to the founder of that Jesuit sect which nothing could induce him to tolerate.*   30
   —PROFESSOR HAROLD LASKI (Essay in *Freedom of Expression*)

2. *Above all, we cannot play ducks and drakes with a native battery of idioms which prescribes egregious collocations of vocables as the Basic* put up with *for* tolerate, *or* put at a loss *for* bewilder.
   —PROFESSOR LANCELOT HOGBEN (*Interglossia*)

3. *On the one side we have the free personality: by definition it is not neurotic, for it has neither conflict nor dream. Its desires, such as they are, are transparent, for they are just what institutional approval keeps in the forefront of consciousness; another institutional pattern would alter their number and intensity; there is little in them that is natural, irreducible, or culturally dangerous. But* on the   40 other side, *the social bond itself is nothing but the mutual reflection of these self-secure integrities. Recall the definition of love. Is not this the very picture of a small academic? Where is there a place in this hall of mirrors for either personality or fraternity?*
   —ESSAY ON PSYCHOLOGY IN *POLITICS* (New York)

4. *All the "best people" from the gentlemen's clubs, and all the frantic fascist captains, united in common hatred of Socialism and bestial horror at the rising tide of the mass revolutionary movement, have turned to acts of provocation, to foul incendiarism, to medieval legends of poisoned wells, to legalize their own destruction of proletarian organizations, and rouse the agitated petty-bourgeoise   50 to chauvinistic fervor on behalf of the fight against the revolutionary way out of the crisis.*
   —COMMUNIST PAMPHLET

5. *If a new spirit is to be infused into this old country, there is one thorny and contentious reform which must be tackled, and that is the humanization and galvanization of the B.B.C. Timidity here will bespeak canker and atrophy of the soul. The heart of Britain may be sound and of strong beat, for instance, but the British lion's roar at present is like that of Bottom in Shakespeare's* A Midsummer Night's Dream—*as gentle as any sucking dove. A virile new Britain cannot continue indefinitely to be traduced in the eyes or rather ears,*   60 *of the world by the effet languors of Langham Place, brazenly masquerading as "standard English." When the Voice of Britain is heard at nine o'clock, better far*

and infinitely less ludicrous to hear aitches honestly dropped than the present priggish, inflated, inhibited, school-ma'amish arch braying of blameless bashful mewing maidens!

—LETTER IN *TRIBUNE*

Each of these passages has faults of its own, but, quite apart from avoidable ugliness, two qualities are common to all of them. The first is staleness of imagery; the other is lack of precision. The writer either has a meaning and cannot express it, or he inadvertently 70 says something else, or he is almost indifferent as to whether his words mean anything or not. This mixture of vagueness and sheer incompetence is the most marked characteristic of modern English prose, and especially of any kind of political writing. As soon as certain topics are raised, the concrete melts into the abstract and no one seems able to think of turns of speech that are not hackneyed: prose consists less and less of *words* chosen for the sake of their meaning, and more and more of *phrases* tacked together like the sections of a prefabricated henhouse. I list below, with notes and examples, various of the tricks by means of which the work of prose construction is habitually dodged:

Dying metaphors. A newly invented metaphor assists thought by evoking a visual image, while on the other hand a metaphor which is technically "dead" (e.g. *iron resolution*) 80 has in effect reverted to being an ordinary word and can generally be used without loss of vividness. But in between these two classes there is a huge dump of worn-out metaphors which have lost all evocative power and are merely used because they save people the trouble of inventing phrases for themselves. Examples are: *Ring the changes on, take up the cudgel for, toe the line, ride roughshod over, stand shoulder to shoulder with, play into the hands of, no axe to grind, grist to the mill, fishing in troubled waters, on the order of the day, Achilles' heel, swan song, hotbed.* Many of these are used without knowledge of their meaning (what is a "rift," for instance?), and incompatible metaphors are frequently mixed, a sure sign that the writer is not interested in what he is saying. Some metaphors now current have been twisted out of their original meaning without those who use them even 90 being aware of the fact. For example, *toe the line* is sometimes written as *tow the line*. Another example is *the hammer and the anvil,* now always used with the implication that the anvil gets the worst of it. In real life it is always the anvil that breaks the hammer, never the other way about: a writer who stopped to think what he was saying would avoid perverting the original phrase.

Operators or verbal false limbs. These save the trouble of picking out appropriate verbs and nouns, and at the same time pad each sentence with extra syllables which give it an appearance of symmetry. Characteristic phrases are *render inoperative, militate against, make contact with, be subjected to, give rise to, give grounds for, have the effect, of, play a leading part (role) in, make itself felt, take effect, exhibit a tendency to, serve the purpose of, etc., etc.* The 100 keynote is the elimination of simple verbs. Instead of being a single word, such as *break, stop, spoil, mend, kill,* a verb becomes a *phrase,* made up of a noun or adjective tacked on to some general-purpose verb such as *prove, serve, form, play, render.* In addition, the passive voice is wherever possible used in preference to the active, and noun constructions are used instead of gerunds (*by examination of* instead of *by examining*). The range of verbs is further cut down by means of the *–ize* and *de-* formations, and the banal statements are given an appearance of profundity by means of the *not un-* formation. Simple conjunctions and prepositions are replaced by such phrases as *with respect to, having regard to, the fact that, by dint of, in view of, in the interests of, on the hypothesis that;* and the ends of sentences are saved by anticlimax by such resounding commonplaces as *greatly to be desired, cannot be left out of account, a development to be expected in the near future, deserving of serious consideration,* 110 *brought to a satisfactory conclusion,* and so on and so forth.

Pretentious diction. Words like *phenomenon, element, individual (as noun), objective, categorical, effective, virtual, basic, primary, promote, constitute, exhibit, exploit, utilize, eliminate, liquidate,* are used to dress up a simple statement and give an aire of scientific impartiality to biased judgements. Adjectives like *epoch-making, epic, historic, unforgettable, triumphant, age-old, inevitable, inexorable, veritable,* are used to dignify the sordid process of international politics, while writing that aims at glorifying war usually takes on an archaic color, its characteristic words being; *realm, throne, chariot, mailed fist, trident, sword, shield, buckler, banner, jackboot, clarion.* Foreign words and expressions such *as cul de sac, ancien régime, deus ex machina, mutatis mutandis, status quo, gleichschaltung, welt-* 120 *anschauung,* are used to give an air of culture and elegance. Except for the useful abbreviations i.e., e.g., and etc., there is no real need for any of the hundreds of foreign phrases now current in the English language. Bad writers, and especially scientific, political, and sociological writers, are nearly always haunted by the notion that Latin or Greek words are grander than Saxon ones, and unnecessary words like *expedite, ameliorate, predict, extraneous, deracinated, clandestine, subaqueous,* and hundreds of others constantly gain ground from their Anglo-Saxon numbers[1]. The jargon peculiar to Marxist writing (*hyena, hangman, cannibal, petty bourgeois, these gentry, lackey, flunkey, mad dog, White Guard,* etc.) consists largely of words translated from Russian, German, or French; but the normal way of coining a new word is to use Latin or Greek root with the appropriate affix and, 130 where necessary, the *–ize* formation. It is often easier to make up words of this kind (*deregionalize, impermissible, extramarital, non-fragmentary* and so forth) than to think up the English words that will cover one's meaning. The result, in general, is an increase in slovenliness and vagueness.

Meaningless words. In certain kinds of writing, particularly in art criticism and literary criticism, it is normal to come across long passages which are almost completely lacking in meaning[2]. Words like *romantic, plastic, values, human, dead, sentimental, natural, vitality,* as used in art criticism, are strictly meaningless, in the sense that they not only do not point to any discoverable object, but are hardly ever expected to do so by the reader. When one critic writes, "The outstanding feature of Mr. X's work is its living quality," while another writes, 140 "The immediately striking thing about Mr. X's work is its peculiar deadness," the reader accepts this as a simple difference of opinion. If words like *black* and *white* were involved, instead of the jargon words *dead* and *living,* he would see at once that language was being used in an improper way. Many political words are similarly abused. The word *Fascism* has now no meaning except in so far as it signifies "something not desirable." The words *democracy,*

socialism, freedom, patriotic, realistic, justice have each of them several different meanings which cannot be reconciled with one another. In the case of a word like *democracy,* not only is there no agreed definition, but the attempt to make one is resisted from all sides. It is al-most universally felt that when we call a country democratic we are praising it: consequently
150 the defenders of every kind of regime claim that it is a democracy, and fear that they might have to stop using that word if it were tied down to any one meaning. Words of this kind are often used in a consciously dishonest way. That is, the person who uses them has his own private definition, but allows his hearer to think he means something quite different. Statements like *Marshal Petain was a true patriot, The Soviet press is the freest in the world, The Catholic Church is opposed to persecution,* are almost always made with intent to deceive. Other words used in variable meanings, in most cases more or less dishonestly, are: *class, totalitarian, science, progressive, reactionary, bourgeois, equality.*

Now that I have made this catalogue of swindles and perversions, let me give another example of the kind of writing that they lead to. This time it must of its nature be an imagi-
160 nary one. I am going to translate a passage of good English into modern English of the worst sort. Here is a well-known verse from *Ecclesiastes:*

> *I returned and saw under the sun, that the race is not to the swift, nor the battle to the strong, neither yet bread to the wise, nor yet riches to men of understanding, nor yet favour to men of skill; but time and chance happeneth to them all.*

Here it is in modern English:

> *Objective considerations of contemporary phenomena compel the conclusion that success or failure in competitive activities exhibits no tendency to commensurate with innate capacity, but that a considerable element of the unpredictable must invariably be taken into account.*

170 This is a parody, but not a very gross one. Exhibit (3) above, for instance, contains several patches of the same kind of English. It will be seen that I have not made a full translation. The beginning and ending of the sentence follow the original meaning fairly closely, but in the middle the concrete illustrations—race, battle, bread—dissolve into the vague phrases "success or failure in competitive activities." This had to be so, because no modern writer of the kind I am discussing—no one capable of using phrases like "objective considerations of contemporary phenomena"—would ever tabulate his thoughts in that precise and de-tailed way. The whole tendency of modern prose is away from concreteness. Now analyze these two sentences a little more closely. The first contains forty-nine words but only sixty syllables; and all its words are those of everyday life. The second contains thirty-eight words
180 of ninety syllables: eighteen of those words are from Latin roots, and one from Greek. The first sentence contains six vivid images, and only one phrase ("time and chance") that could be called vague. The second contains not a single fresh, arresting phrase, and in spite of its ninety syllables it gives only a shortened version of the meaning contained in the first. Yet without a doubt it is the second kind of sentence that is gaining ground in modern English.

I do not want to exaggerate. This kind of writing is not yet universal, and outcrops of simplicity will occur here and there in the worst-written page. Still, if you or I were told to write a few lines on the uncertainty of human fortunes, we should probably come much nearer to my imaginary sentence than to the one from *Ecclesiastes.* As I have tried to show, modern writing at its worst does not consist in picking out words for the sake of their meaning and inventing images in order to make the meaning clearer. It consists in gumming together long strips of words which have already been set in order by someone else, and making the results presentable by sheer humbug. The attraction of this way of writing is that it is easy. It is easier—even quicker, once you have the habit—to say *In my opinion it is not an unjustifiable assumption that* than to say *I think,* If you use ready-made phrases, you not only don't have to hunt about for the words; you also don't have to bother with the rhythms of your sentences since these phrases are generally so arranged as to be more or less euphonious, When you are composing in a hurry—when you are dictating to a stenographer, for instance, or making a public speech—it is natural to fall into a pretentious, Latinized style. Tags like *a consideration which we should do well to bear in mind* or *a conclusion to which all of us would really assent* will save many a sentence from coming down with a bump. By using stale metaphors, similes, and idioms, you save much mental effort, at the cost of leaving your meaning vague, not only for your reader but for yourself. This is the significance of mixed metaphors. The sole aim of a metaphor is to call up a visual image. When these images clash—as in *The Fascist octopus has sung its swan song, the jackboot is thrown into the melting pot*—it can be taken as certain that the writer is not seeing a mental image of the objects he is naming; in other words he is not really thinking. Look again at the examples I gave at the beginning of this essay. Professor Laski (1) uses five negatives in fifty three words. One of these is superfluous, making nonsense of the whole passage, and in addition there is the slip—*alien* for akin—making further nonsense, and several avoidable pieces of clumsiness which increase the general vagueness. Professor Hogben (2) plays ducks and drakes with a battery which is able to write prescriptions, and, while disapproving of the everyday phrase *put up with,* is unwilling to look *egregious* up in the dictionary and see what it means; (3), if one takes an uncharitable attitude towards it, is simply meaningless: probably one could work out its intended meaning by reading the whole of the article in which it occurs. In (4), the writer knows more or less what he wants to say, but an accumulation of stale phrases chokes him like tea leaves blocking a sink. In (5), words and meaning have almost parted company. People who write in this manner usually have a general emotional meaning—they dislike one thing and want to express solidarity with another—but they are not interested in the detail of what they are saying. A scrupulous writer, in every sentence that he writes, will ask himself at least four questions, thus:

1. What am I trying to say?

2. What words will express it?

3. What image or idiom will make it clearer?

4. Is this image fresh enough to have an effect?

And he will probably ask himself two more:

1. Could I put it more shortly?

2. Have I said anything that is avoidably ugly?

But you are not obliged to go to all this trouble. You can shirk it by simply throwing your mind open and letting the ready-made phrases come crowding in. They will construct your sentences for you—even think your thoughts for you, to a certain extent—and at need they will perform the important service of partially concealing your meaning even from yourself. It is at this point that the special connection between politics and the debasement of language becomes clear.

In our time it is broadly true that political writing is bad writing. Where it is not true, it will generally be found that the writer is some kind of rebel, expressing his private opinions and not a "party line." Orthodoxy, of whatever color, seems to demand a lifeless, imitative style. The political dialects to be found in pamphlets, leading articles, manifestoes, White papers and the speeches of undersecretaries do, of course, vary from party to party, but they are all alike in that one almost never finds in them a fresh, vivid, homemade turn of speech. When one watches some tired hack on the platform mechanically repeating the familiar phrases—*bestial, atrocities, iron heel, bloodstained tyranny, free peoples of the world, stand shoulder to shoulder*—one often has a curious feeling that one is not watching a live human being but some kind of dummy: a feeling which suddenly becomes stronger at moments when the light catches the speaker's spectacles and turns them into blank discs which seem to have no eyes behind them. And this is not altogether fanciful. A speaker who uses that kind of phraseology has gone some distance toward turning himself into a machine. The appropriate noises are coming out of his larynx, but his brain is not involved as it would be if he were choosing his words for himself. If the speech he is making is one that he is accustomed to make over and over again, he may be almost unconscious of what he is saying, as one is when one utters the responses in church. And this reduced state of consciousness, if not indispensable, is at any rate favorable to political conformity.

In our time, political speech and writing are largely the defense of the indefensible. Things like the continuance of British rule in India, the Russian purges and deportations, the dropping of the atom bombs on Japan, can indeed be defended, but only by arguments which are too brutal for most people to face, and which do not square with the professed aims of the political parties. Thus political language has to consist largely of euphemism, question-begging and sheer cloudy vagueness. Defenseless villages are bombarded from the air, the inhabitants driven out into the countryside, the cattle machine-gunned, the huts set on fire with incendiary bullets: this is called *pacification*. Millions of peasants are robbed of their farms and sent trudging along the roads with no more than they can carry: this is called *transfer of population* or *rectification of frontiers*. People are imprisoned for years without trial, or shot in the back of the neck or sent to die of scurvy in Arctic lumber camps: this is called *elimination of unreliable elements*. Such phraseology is needed if one wants to name things without calling up mental pictures of them. Consider for instance some comfortable

English professor defending Russian totalitarianism. He cannot say outright, "I believe in killing off your opponents when you can get good results by doing so." Probably, therefore, he will say something like this:

> *While freely conceding that the Soviet regime exhibits certain features which the humanitarian may be inclined to deplore, we must, I think, agree that a certain curtailment of the right to political opposition is an unavoidable concomitant of transitional periods, and that the rigors which the Russian people have been called upon to undergo have been amply justified in the sphere of concrete achievement.* 270

The inflated style itself is a kind of euphemism. A mass of Latin words falls upon the facts like soft snow, blurring the outline and covering up all the details. The great enemy of clear language is insincerity. When there is a gap between one's real and one's declared aims, one turns as it were instinctively to long words and exhausted idioms, like a cuttlefish spurting out ink. In our age there is no such thing as "keeping out of politics." All issues are political issues, and politics itself is a mass of lies, evasions, folly, hatred, and schizophrenia. When the general atmosphere is bad, language must suffer. I should expect to find—this is a 280 guess which I have not sufficient knowledge to verify—that the German, Russian and Italian languages have all deteriorated in the last ten or fifteen years, as a result of dictatorship.

But if thought corrupts language, language can also corrupt thought. A bad usage can spread by tradition and imitation even among people who should and do know better. The debased language that I have been discussing is in some ways very convenient. Phrases like *a not unjustifiable assumption, leaves much to be desired, would serve no good purpose, a consideration which we should do well to bear in mind*, are a continuous temptation, a packet of aspirins always at one's elbow. Look back through this essay, and for certain you will find that I have again and again committed the very faults I am protesting against. By this morning's post I have received a pamphlet dealing with conditions in Germany. The author 290 tells me that he "felt impelled" to write it. I open it at random, and here is almost the first sentence I see: "[The Allies] have an opportunity not only of achieving a radical transformation of Germany's social and political structure in such a way as to avoid a nationalistic reaction in Germany itself, but at the same time of laying the foundations of a co-operative and unified Europe." You see, he "feels impelled" to write—feels, presumably, that he has something new to say—and yet his words, like cavalry horses answering the bugle, group themselves automatically into the familiar dreary pattern. This invasion of one's mind by ready-made phrases (*lay the foundations, achieve a radical transformation*) can only be prevented if one is constantly on guard against them, and every such phrase anaesthetizes a portion of one's brain. 300

I said earlier that the decadence of our language is probably curable. Those who deny this would argue, if they produced an argument at all, that language merely reflects existing social conditions, and that we cannot influence its development by any direct tinkering with words and constructions. So far as the general tone or spirit of a language goes, this may be true, but it is not true in detail. Silly words and expressions have often disappeared, not through any evolutionary process but owing to the conscious action of a minority. Two recent examples were *explore every avenue* and *leave no stone unturned*, which were killed by the jeers of a few journalists. There is a long list of flyblown metaphors which could similarly be got rid of if enough people would interest themselves in the job; and it should also be possible to laugh the *not un-* formation out of existence[3], to reduce the amount of Latin and Greek in the average sentence, to drive out foreign phrases and strayed scientific words, and, in general, to make pretentiousness unfashionable. But all these are minor points. The defense of the English language implies more than this, and perhaps it is best to start by saying what it does *not* imply.

To begin with it has nothing to do with archaism, with the salvaging of obsolete words and turns of speech, or with the setting up of a "standard English" which must never be departed from. On the contrary, it is especially concerned with the scrapping of every word or idiom which has outworn its usefulness. It has nothing to do with correct grammar and syntax, which are of no importance so long as one makes one's meaning clear, or with the avoidance of Americanisms, or with having what is called a "good prose style." On the other hand, it is not concerned with fake simplicity and the attempt to make written English colloquial. Nor does it even imply in every case preferring the Saxon word to the Latin one, though it does imply using the fewest and shortest words that will cover one's meaning. What is above all needed is to let the meaning choose the word, and not the other way around. In prose, the worst thing one can do with words is surrender to them. When you think of a concrete object, you think wordlessly, and then, if you want to describe the thing you have been visualizing you probably hunt about until you find the exact words that seem to fit it. When you think of something abstract you are more inclined to use words from the start, and unless you make a conscious effort to prevent it, the existing dialect will come rushing in and do the job for you, at the expense of blurring or even changing your meaning. Probably it is better to put off using words as long as possible and get one's meaning as clear as one can through pictures and sensations. Afterward one can choose—not simply *accept*—the phrases that will best cover the meaning, and then switch round and decide what impressions one's words are likely to make on another person. This last effort of the mind cuts out all stale or mixed images, all prefabricated phrases, needless repetitions, and humbug and vagueness generally. But one can often be in doubt about the effect of a word or a phrase, and one needs rules that one can rely on when instinct fails. I think the following rules will cover most cases:

(i) Never use a metaphor, simile or other figure of speech which you are used to seeing in print.

(ii) Never use a long word where a short one will do.

(iii) If it is possible to cut a word out, always cut it out.

(iv) Never use the passive where you can use the active.

(v) Never use a foreign phrase, a scientific word or a jargon word if you can think of an everyday English equivalent.

(vi) Break any of these rules sooner than say anything outright barbarous.

These rules sound elementary, and so they are, but they demand a deep change of attitude in anyone who has grown used to writing in the style now fashionable. One could keep all of them and still write bad English, but one could not write the kind of stuff that I quoted in those five specimens at the beginning of this article.   350

I have not here been considering the literary use of language, but merely language as an instrument for expressing and not for concealing or preventing thought. Stuart Chase and others have come near to claiming that all abstract words are meaningless, and have used this as a pretext for advocating a kind of political quietism. Since you don't know what Fascism is, how can you struggle against Fascism? One need not swallow such absurdities as this, but one ought to recognize that the present political chaos is connected with the decay of language, and that one can probably bring about some improvement by starting at the verbal end. If you simplify your English, you are freed from the worst follies of ortho- doxy. You cannot speak any of the necessary dialects, and when you make a stupid remark its stupidity will be obvious, even to yourself. Political language—and with variations this 360 is true of all political parties, from Conservatives to Anarchists— is designed to make lies sound truthful and murder respectable, and to give an appearance of solidity to pure wind. One cannot change this all in a moment, but one can at least change one's own habits, and from time to time one can even, if one jeers loudly enough, send some worn-out and useless phrase some *jackboot, Achilles' heel, hotbed, melting pot, acid test, veritable inferno,* or other lump of verbal refuse—into the dustbin where it belongs.

Notes:

1. "An interesting illustration of this is the way in which the English flower names which were in use till very recently are being ousted by Greek ones, *snapdragon* becoming *antirrhinum, forget-me-not* becoming *myosotis,* etc. It is hard to see any practical reason 370 for this change of fashion: it is probably due to an instinctive turning-away from the more homely word and a vague feeling that the Greek word is scientific" (Orwell's note).

2. "Example: 'Comfort's catholicity of perception and image, strangely Whitmanesque in range, almost the exact opposite in aesthetic compulsion, continues to evoke that trem- bling atmospheric accumulative hinting at a cruel, an inexorably serene timelessness. . . . Wrey Gardiner scores by aiming at simple bullseyes with precision. Only they are not so simple, and through this contented sadness runs more than the surface bitter-sweet of resignation' *(Poetry Quarterly)*" (Orwell's note).

3. "One can cure oneself of the *not un-* formation by memorizing this sentence: *A not unblack dog was chasing a not unsmall rabbit across a not ungreen field*" (Orwell's note). ■ 380

UNDERSTANDING CONTEXT

1. Orwell is best known for writing novels that explore themes of totalitarianism. How does this essay, which criticizes imprecise and unclear writing, fit into that context?

EVALUATING STRATEGY

1. Briefly summarize Orwell's thesis.

2. Explain Orwell's organizational structure. Is it clear and precise? How does his organization influence the substance of his argument?

APPRECIATING LANGUAGE

1. Orwell often uses heightened diction. Create a list of unfamiliar words from the essay and look up their definitions.

2. How does Orwell's use of language affect his argument? Does his use of language follow, or enact, the guidelines he espouses in the essay?

3. Describe Orwell's tone and attitude throughout the essay. How does his tone and attitude influence the effectiveness of his argument?

WRITING SUGGESTIONS

1. Create a well-constructed summary of Orwell's essay in one paragraph.

2. Create five new and fresh metaphors to replace dead ones. Remember Orwell's advice that a good metaphor should invoke a visual image and that it causes the reader to think.

3. *Critical thinking:* Do you agree with Orwell's thesis? Are his expectations for effective communication in writing reasonable? Do you think that his guidelines for good writing allow for time constraints and other realistic conditions exerted on the choices made by politicians and professional writers? Write a well-constructed persuasive essay in response.

4. Find an interview with a politician (it can be in print or another form of media). After closely examining the politician's use of language, "translate" the interview into language that follows Orwell's guidelines. Compare your version with the original. Are there discrepancies? Write a persuasive essay discussing your observations.

BRIAN FAWCETT

Brian Fawcett, born in Prince George, BC, in 1944, is a writer, former columnist for **The Globe and Mail**, past editor of **Books in Canada**, and former Chair of the Writers Union of Canada Charter 94 Committee. He has written numerous articles and reviews, and among his many book publications are **Permanent Relationships: Poems; Creatures of State; Aggressive Transport: Two Narrative Revisions, 1975–1982; The Secret Journal of Alexander Mackenzie; Capital Tales; The Compact Garden;** and **Gender Wars: A Novel.**

Politics and the English Language (1991)*

Fawcett's essay was written to offer guidance to students writing for their college or university newspapers. Using George Orwell's 1946 essay "Politics and the English Language," he discusses how Orwell's fundamental principles of clear thinking and honest expression are still relevant even though the political scene has changed. While Fawcett's essay uses more humour than Orwell's, Fawcett argues that Orwell's principles can still be applied in contemporary society.

Almost a half century has passed since George Orwell wrote "Politics and the English Language." For most English-speaking writers who have had a strong desire to discover and tell the truth, the essay has been a basic text. In it, Orwell argued that clear thinking and good writing are integral to the health of democracy, and that bad language can and does corrupt thought. Those ideas are almost self-evident truths today, and the detailed arguments Orwell made in the essay remain remarkably current. My renovation of the essay's contents will therefore be—as my title suggests—a bracketed and respectful addendum.

Since 1946, when Orwell published his essay, there have been profound changes in the way human beings speak, write, and use knowledge. Radio, television, and a number of less public but powerful cybernetic technologies now occupy our days, often filling our heads with information we either haven't asked for or don't have the right equipment or the wealth to make use of. We "communicate" or "process information" through immensely powerful and fast electronic systems, but we write less, and, I suspect, think less. Certainly the critical thought going on these days concerning the crucial subjects of politics and culture is in a state of conceptual disarray. Contemporary electronic communications are a matter of fewer and fewer people speaking to (and for) more and more people.

Despite this, the English language itself has taken only one major turn Orwell didn't foresee. In 1946, he feared that the undefeated totalitarianisms of World War II would breed Newspeak, the official language of his novel *1984*. Newspeak made understanding impossible by truncating or outlawing all the textures and nuances of language. But instead of Newspeak, the 1990s are filled with technogibberish dialects that glamourize the obvious

1

10

20

*Fawcett, Brian, "Politics and the English Language (1991)" from *Unusual Circumstances, Interesting Times* by Brian Fawcett, published by New Star Books 1991. Reprint by permission of the publisher.

and the trivial, and obscure (or sever) connections to other fields of meaning. The intent of these dialects is to make it difficult for anyone to communicate beyond their "lifestyle" enclave. The dialects serve the same purpose as Newspeak—creating political silence—by conning us into thinking that we're somehow more fashionable and smarter than the next enclave, and by getting us to fiddle endlessly with an assortment of disposable commodities, fake threats to our well-being, and obsessive notions of correct behaviour that border on fanaticism.

What that means is that politics—or maybe it is just authority—has changed. Some
30 changes have been for the better, and some haven't. Within the industrialized nations, violent authority can no longer successfully operate indefinitely, and police states have demonstrated that they simply aren't efficient enough to compete with cybernetic economies—as witnessed by the recent economic and political collapse of the Soviet bloc. Violent authority is still the rule outside the industrialized part of the world, where, if anything, life has become more violent and arbitrary. In the privileged societies like ours, authority has merely gotten itself out of our faces and into our lowest appetites. Universal social justice, it should be noted, is as distant as it has ever been.

For an individual trying to think and write accurately in the intellectual and informational environments of the 1990s, politics are no longer a matter of complaining about the
40 stupidity or corruption of the government. Politics—and they are a plural now—are the things we do to one another, or allow to be done to us by others through indifference or lust or whatever we've decided is self-interest. As the millennium nears, and as the referent ideologies that have guided and/or deluded us through the century collapse around us, politics have more to do with how we allow ourselves to be lied to and deceived than how we are imprisoned or liberated. In the industrialized democracies, most of us are free as the birds. We just happen to be turkeys and chickens, with a few aggressive but deluded raptors tossed into the mix to make the peaceful cower and to give the brainlessly ambitious something to aspire to.

Communists, capitalists, fascists, and all the permutations in between have become
50 meaningless epithets. Orwell himself saw that coming. Everything he wrote from *Homage to Catalonia* to his death argues against the structuring of politics by ideological claim. For us, his essay "Second Thoughts on James Burnham" (1946) ought to be read as the companion piece to "Politics and the English Language" because it reveals his characteristic skill at eluding the seductive ideological nets of his time. In that essay he summarizes Burnham's future scenario in *The Managerial Revolution* (1940) in terms that will be chillingly familiar to us: "Capitalism is disappearing, but socialism is not replacing it. What is now arising is a new kind of planned, centralized society which will be neither capitalist nor, in any accepted sense of the word, democratic. The rulers of this new society will be the people who effectively control the means of production: that is, business executives, technicians, bureau-
60 crats and soldiers, lumped together by Burnham under the name of 'managers.'" That's a fair description of the corporate oligarchy that controls the world today—an oligarchy that operates on eighteen-month financial horizons and proudly promises an end to the excesses of ideological politics. That Orwell was able to foresee and critique the weaknesses of a

vast political change that contemporary analysts are just now learning to bend their minds around is typical of just how brilliant his intellectual method was.

Understanding how the new politics work will require a few conceptual simplifications. One of them is recognizing that there are only three kinds of political beings in the world. First, there are people who will try to see and tell the truth, and try to act on it in the interests of everyone. Second, there are—let me put this as succinctly as possible—assholes. Third, there are people who are too weakened by poverty, disease, and violence to care about being 70 either of the first two. Good politics consists of behaviours that enlarge the numbers of type A and reduce, without violence or arrogance, the numbers of types B and C. I'm pretty sure that George Orwell would agree with this simplification.

In the new environment, clear political writing and thinking is perhaps more urgently needed than ever. It remains an essential component of democracy—which is, after all, not a political state but a social, intellectual, and moral activity. For that activity to regain the alertness it requires to be effective, the toolbox a political writer needs to deal with the 1990s needs some additions.

I'm going to suggest a few tools. For the sake of convenience, I'll divide them into two categories, practical and conceptual. Most of the practical ones have to do with keeping 80 writing direct and simple and personal, which is the only antidote I know for the poison of technogibberish. The conceptual tools I use are generally attitudinal tactics aimed at inducing and nourishing the habitual skepticism Orwell taught me. What follows isn't meant to be either an exclusive or exhaustive toolbox on its own, merely an addition to Orwell's. Intellectual tools don't work the same way for everyone, but I can at least testify that the ones I offer help me to keep my eyes open in the cyclone of lies daily life has become. And sometimes, they help me to close them with laughter. ■

PRACTICAL WRITING TOOLS

1. George Orwell's "Politics and the English Language" ought to be reread about every six months. Nearly everything he said remains relevant. His examples should be periodically updated with your own.

2. Write simple sentences whenever you can, and let your musicianship take care of the need for melody. If you've got a tin ear, get into another line of work.

3. Fill your writing with nouns and verbs. Naming things accurately makes them palpable, and making them move in specific ways enables them to be tested. Beware of adjectives and adverbs because they are linguistic grease. Using more than two successive adjectives in a single sentence is a reliable signal that a Mazola party is going on in the writer's head.

4. Never use a semicolon. I know I'm repeating Orwell, but this is so important it bears repeating. Semicolons are absolutely reliable signals that a sentence should be rewritten, generally to make it more direct. And incidentally, you should only use a colon if you're wearing a tuxedo or sitting on white porcelain.

5. Contemporary writers should learn how to use a word processor, and how to manipulate data systems. If you're a working writer, it is more important to own a word processor than a car. Word processors are necessary to keep up to the current speeds of information transmission and production, and because having other people decipher your lousy hand-writing is vile and exploitive political behaviour.

CONCEPTUAL TOOLS

1. Beware of sacred cattle. They are stupid, filled with inflated ideas about their importance and the unimportance of everything in their projected path, and if you let them run around inside your head they will eat or trample everything, including your intelligence. On the other hand, do not attempt to run anyone else's sacred cattle over a cliff unless you're certain you can succeed. Today's sacred cattle are a new and much more dangerous breed than the ones that emerged in the 1950s and are now dying out. The new breed are very aggressive, they're used to living in information-overloaded cities, and if you wave a red flag at them they'll pin you to the nearest concrete abutment without a qualm.

2. Good political writing always recognizes when it is running in a stampede and attempts to get out of it as quickly as possible, preferably without trying to work the herd. This is a fancy way of saying that the job of a political writer is to ask the questions that aren't being addressed by the visible agendas of authority or exclusive interest. Generally speaking, figuring out or making up answers is someone else's job—someone you probably won't trust or like. Never trust anyone with an answer to a question you haven't asked.

3. Recognize that everyone is sincere and that sincerity has no relationship to anything but righteousness, which is an enemy of good political writing, and usually, death to clear thinking. Accusing anyone of insincerity precludes the possibility of further political debate, and you're supposed to be writing in order to start and keep people talking to one another.

4. The language of political speeches and official communiques is never meaningless. Most of the time, speeches, press releases and official communiques are cybernetic devices meant to occupy a vital political moment or space without committing the originating speaker, institution or agency to action. They require full translation, which involves an analysis of what they both say and don't say. This is also true of commercial language, which is becoming indistinguishable from political language.

5. If you don't believe in God, don't quote Her. By this I mean that writers must try to be personal, and should not make their voices out to be more than they are—the words and gestures of a single person who has thought through and researched a subject matter. Practising this successfully involves a number of mental habits, some of which are as follows:

   (a) never using the word "we" unless you know who you're collectivizing and are willing to kiss them all on the mouth—and mean it.

(b) never using the word "reality" without putting quotes around it.

(c) recognizing that there is no such thing as a rhetorical question.

(d) never dismissing a dead or older writer for not knowing what is currently fashionable around the office or inside your dopey head.

(e) remembering that the surface of any important truth will more resemble the skin of a toad than an alabaster statue or brochure materials that promise to make you into a human bullet. Warts are not something that will disappear from writing and thinking just because we don't approve of bumps and lesions. They're what used to be called texture, and without texture there is no such thing as meaning. Bullets, whatever form they come in, are the opposite of meaning, and they are signals of the collapse of human intelligence.

6. Try not to contribute to the cacophony of disinformation and nonsense. In a democracy the only opinion anyone is entitled to is an informed and preferably detailed one. If all you're hearing is the sound of your own voice, silence is the right option.

7. Finally, make people laugh with your writing. Laughter disrupts narrow logic, which is the operating system for authority, cattle stampedes, and ill-conceived judgments of all sorts. People who are laughing find it hard to start wars, molest children, and are unlikely to discover that the person or persons in their immediate vicinity are in league with the devil. Orthodoxy most easily breeds where laughter is absent.

UNDERSTANDING CONTEXT

1. What advantages arise from Fawcett's choice to use Orwell's title for his essay?

2. Orwell published his *Politics and the English Language* in 1946, the year after the end the Second World War. What motives might Fawcett have nearly 50 years later for writing an essay that heavily echoes Orwell's?

EVALUATING STRATEGY

1. Briefly summarize Fawcett's thesis.

2. Fawcett uses humour throughout his essay. Is it an effective strategy? Why or why not?

3. Why does Fawcett present both practical and conceptual tools for writing?

APPRECIATING LANGUAGE

1. What is a *sacred cow*? Create a list of as many sacred cows as you can.

2. What is your reaction to Fawcett referring to God as *Her*? Why does he do it?

WRITING SUGGESTIONS

1. Write a careful, one-paragraph summary of Fawcett's essay.

2. Do you think an updated version of Orwell's essay makes good sense? Write a two-page argument considering this question.

3. *Critical thinking.* Compare Fawcett's essay with Orwell's. Write a persuasive essay explaining which of the two essays is more effective and why.

4. Write your own "manifesto" on good principles of writing.

MARGARET ATWOOD

Margaret Atwood was born in 1939 in Ottawa and grew up in northern Ontario and Quebec, and Toronto. She received her undergraduate degree from Victoria College at the University of Toronto and her master's degree from Radcliffe College. Throughout her 30 years of writing, She has received numerous awards and several honorary degrees. She is the author of more than 25 volumes of poetry, fiction, and nonfiction and is perhaps best known for her novels, which include The **Edible Woman, The Handmaid's Tale**, and **The Blind Assassin**, which won the prestigious Booker Prize in 2000. Along with her creative work, Atwood writes widely on the art and craft of writing.

The Writer's Responsibility*

In this piece, which was given as an address to a group of writers, Atwood argues that writers must be engaged in the political and social issues of their times. She argues that it is the writers' duty to address the problematic issues facing their societies.

The subject we have come together to address is one which increases in importance as the   1
giants of this world move closer and closer to violent and fatal confrontation. Broadly put, it is: what is the writer's responsibility, if any, to the society in which he or she lives? The question is not a new one; it's been with us at least since the time of Plato; but more and more the answers of the world's governments have taken the form of amputation: of the tongue, of the soul, of the head.

We in Canada are ill-equipped to come to grips even with the problem, let alone the solution. We live in a society in which the main consensus seems to be that the artist's duty is to entertain and divert, nothing more. Occasionally our critics get a little heavy and start talking about the human condition, but on the whole the audience prefers art not to be a   10
mirror held up to life but a Disneyland of the soul, containing Romanceland, Spyland, Pornoland, and all the other Escapelands which are so much more agreeable than the complex truth. When we take an author seriously, we prefer to believe that her vision derives from her individual and subjective and neurotic tortured soul—we like artists to have tortured souls—not from the world she is looking at. Sometimes our artists believe this version too, and the ego takes over. *I, me* and *mine* are our favourite pronouns; *we, us* and *ours* are low on the list. The artist is not seen as a lens for focusing the world but as a solipsism. We are good at measuring an author's production in terms of his craft. We are not good at analyzing it in terms of his politics, and by and large we do not do so.

By "politics" I do not mean how you voted in the last election, although that is included.   20
I mean who is entitled to do what to whom, with impunity; who profits by it; and who therefore eats what. Such material enters a writer's work not because the writer is or is not

consciously political but because a writer is an observer, a witness, and such observations are the air he breathes. They are the air all of us breathe; the only difference is that the author looks, and then writes down what he sees. What he sees will depend on how closely he looks and at what, but look he must.

In some countries, an author is censored not only for what he says but how he says it, and an unconventional style is therefore a declaration of artistic freedom. Here we are eclectic; we don't mind experimental styles, in fact we devote learned journals to their analysis; but our
30 critics sneer somewhat at anything they consider "heavy social commentary" or—a worse word—"message." Stylistic heavy-guns are dandy, as long as they aren't pointed anywhere in particular. We like the human condition as long as it is seen as personal and individual. Placing politics and poetics in two watertight compartments is a luxury, just as specialization of any kind is a luxury, and it is possible only in a society where luxuries abound. Most countries in the world cannot afford such luxuries, and this North American way of thinking is alien to them. It was even alien in North America, not long ago. We've already forgotten that in the 1950s many artists, both in the United States and here, were persecuted solely on the grounds of their presumed politics. Which leads us to another mistaken Canadian belief: the belief that it can't happen here.

40 It has happened here, many times. Although our country is one of the most peaceful and prosperous on earth, although we do not shoot artists here, although we do not execute political opponents and although this is one of the few remaining countries in which we can have a gathering like this without expecting to be arrested or blown up, we should not overlook the fact that Canada's record on civil rights issues is less than pristine. Our treatment of our native peoples has been shameful. This is the country in which citizens of Japanese origin were interned during the Second World War and had their property stolen (when a government steals property it is called "confiscation"); it is also the country in which thousands of citizens were arrested, jailed and held without warrant or explanation, during the time of the War Measures Act, a scant eleven years ago. There was no general outcry
50 in either case. Worse things have not happened not because we are genetically exempt but because we lead pampered lives.

Our methods of controlling artists are not violent, but they do exist. We control through the marketplace and through critical opinion. We are also controlled by the economics of culture, which in Canada still happen to be those of a colonial branch-plant. In 1960 the number of Canadian books published here was minute, and the numbers sold pathetic. Things have changed very much in twenty years, but Canadian books still account for a mere 25 percent of the overall book trade and paperback books for under 5 percent. Talking about this situation is still considered nationalistic chauvinism. Nevertheless, looked at in the context of the wider picture, I suppose we are lucky to have any percent at all; they haven't yet
60 sent in the Marines and if they do it won't be over books, but over oil.

We in this country should use our privileged position not as a shelter from the world's realities but as a platform from which to speak. Many are denied their voices; we are not. A voice is a gift; it should be cherished and used, to utter fully human speech if possible.

Powerlessness and silence go together; one of the first efforts made in any totalitarian takeover is to suppress the writers, the singers, the journalists, those who are the collective voice. Get rid of the union leaders and pervert the legal system and what you are left with is a reign of terror.

As we read the newspapers, we learn we are existing right now in a state of war. The individual wars may not be large and they are being fought far from here, but there is really only one war, that between those who would like the future to be, in the words of George Orwell, 70 a boot grinding forever into a human face, and those who would like it to be a state of something we still dream of as freedom. The battle shifts according to the ground occupied by the enemy. Greek myth tells of a man called Procrustes, who was a great equalizer. He had a system for making all human beings the same size: if they were too small he stretched them, if they were too tall he cut off their feet or their heads. The Procrustes today are international operators, not confined to any one ideology or religion. The world is full of perversions of the notion of equality, just as it is full of perversions of the notion of freedom. True freedom is not being able to do whatever you like to whomever you want to do it to. Freedom that exists as a result of the servitude of others is not true freedom.

The most lethal weapon in the world's arsenals is not the neutron bomb or chemical 80 warfare, but the human mind that devises such things and puts them to use. But it is the human mind also that can summon up the power to resist, that can imagine a better world than the one before it, that can retain memory and courage in the face of unspeakable suffering. Oppression involves a failure of the imagination: the failure to imagine the full humanity of other human beings. If the imagination were a negligible thing and the act of writing a mere frill, as many in this society would like to believe, regimes all over the world would not be at such pains to exterminate them. The ultimate desire of Procrustes is a population of lobotomized zombies. The writer, unless he is a mere word processor, retains three attributes that power-mad regimes cannot tolerate: a human imagination, in the many forms it may take; the power to communicate; and hope. It may seem odd for 90 me to speak of hope in the midst of what many of my fellow Canadians will call a bleak vision, but as the American writer Flannery O'Connor once said, people without hope do not write novels. ■

UNDERSTANDING CONTEXT

1. Who is Atwood's audience?
2. Atwood argues that writing is a political act. Explain how it is a political act.

EVALUATING STRATEGY

1. What is the piece's purpose?
2. Briefly summarize Atwood's thesis.
3. Do you agree with her thesis?

APPRECIATING LANGUAGE

1. Describe the tone of Atwood's piece.

2. How does she create the tone? Explore her choice of words.

WRITING SUGGESTIONS

1. Write a well-constructed summary of Atwood's essay.

2. *Reflective writing:* What do you think is a writer's primary responsibility? To whom, or what, should a writer be responsible? Write a two-page persuasive essay exploring this question.

3. Can you think of writers whom you believe are irresponsible? In what ways have they been irresponsible? Write a well-constructed argument, with evidence to support your position.

JOHN FRASER

Born in 1941, John Fraser is an award-winning Canadian journalist who serves as the fourth Master of Massey College at the University of Toronto. Fraser also is Chair of the Canadian Journalism Foundation (CJF) and teaches a course in Canadian newspaper history at St. Michael's College, University of Toronto.

Universities Need Money, Yes, But a Social Mission, Too*

In the following article, Fraser examines the role of today's "multiversities" and what a responsive and responsible education should comprise for contemporary democratic cultures.

One of the best of the many submissions to last February's Rae Report on Post-Secondary 1 Education in Ontario was largely ignored by the writers of that important study. But the paper's slow-burning fuse is still active—a compelling indictment of the failure of university culture to deal with the growing cynicism about democracy and citizenship.

This is not exactly a problem most observers park at the front door of post-secondary institutions of higher learning. And that, according to the paper's eminent author, is a large part of the reason there is so much malaise in today's university culture. "The Mission of the University" was written by a former dean of arts at York University, George Fallis, now happily returned to teaching in York's departments of economics and social science.

When he orchestrated his massive report, former Ontario premier Bob Rae was 10 understandably focused on pragmatic approaches to the economic quagmire in which many Canadian universities find themselves. This paper, however, forcefully implies that many woes are only a part of the problem. Until universities and the government and private-sector institutions that sponsor them understand a larger dilemma, all the loot in the world isn't going to fix the systemic malaise.

Although Prof. Fallis accepts that all the principal objectives of the Rae Report are urgent ("accessibility, quality, funding"—the mantra is familiar even if it remains unaddressed), he clearly feels universities need a higher mission than merely fine-tuning existing conditions.

"We live in tumultuous times," he writes, "unpredictable and perplexing. The ideas of 20 our age are changing society. The ideas of our age may transform the university. The new relationship between citizen, market and state limits government expenditure, forcing higher tuition fees and increased reliance on external fundraising. Governments are shifting from supporting basic research toward supporting applied research and are asking that commercialization of research become a fundamental responsibility of the multiversity.

"The university is a long-lived institution. We risk squandering our inheritance, partly through inattention, partly through intransigence, and partly through the prodigal adaptation to the ideas of the age."

*Fraser, John, "Universities Need Money, Yes, But a Social Mission, Too" *The Globe and Mail,* March 26, 2005. Reprinted by permission of the author.

Liberal democratic theory, Prof. Fallis argues, has focused on equality, liberty, power and
30 representation, yet much of the new politics—on all levels of endeavour—has to deal with
profound disagreements and, often enough, hardened cynicism. The route map according
to the Fallis argument appears to be through new concepts such as "deliberative democracy,"
whereby "deliberation should occur not just in the explicit political process, but in many
dispersed forums of civil society."

This, according to Prof. Fallis, is the precise meeting place between society and university: "The deliberation of democracy will surely draw upon existing knowledge and call
for new knowledge. It will require the adjudication of competing knowledge claims. It will
require the involvement of public intellectuals and engaged, informed citizens. All these are
the stuff and substance of the university."

40 Prof. Fallis argues that universities must accept this new mission and they should be held
accountable for how well they do it: "The university is the ideal forum—in the classroom
and through its graduates and its professors as public intellectuals—for such deliberation
in a civil society."

Great universities should not be judged just by the quality of their research, or the learning of their students or the accomplishments of their graduates, "but also by their service to
democratic society as critic, conscience and public intellectual and by their preparation of
students for citizenship."

This idea is new, in a field where new ideas are rare.

The argument in Prof. Fallis' paper is complex and might have struck those intent on im-
50 mediate concrete solutions as abstruse or marginal. But it is finding a resonance and life beyond
the appendices of the Rae Report. The Council of Ontario Universities has recently posted it on
its website [http://www.cou.on.ca] and universities themselves have started to pick it up.

When I talked to him earlier this week, I asked Prof. Fallis if the paper—which I heard
about in excited terms during a discussion with graduate students—had had any influence
on the Rae Report. "Not that I could see," he said, "but then I'm not sure it could have.

"Mr. Rae was very clear and open about what he saw as his mandate and how he would
interpret it. He was fighting for immediate concerns and more money. . . .

"Yet something was lost in not recognizing the most important aspects of the university's mission. The university has to think in new ways, and it must recognize that it has a
60 responsibility to democracy." ■

UNDERSTANDING CONTEXT

1. Fraser's essay originally appeared in a weekend edition of *The Globe and Mail*. What
   does this information suggest about Fraser's purpose and audience?

EVALUATING STRATEGY

1. State Fraser's argument in one clear, specific sentence.

2. Consider the introduction to Fraser's essay. Does it open deductively or inductively?
   Is his choice effective?

3. How does Fraser structure his argument? Explain the process of thinking that organizes and builds the argument.

APPRECIATING LANGUAGE

1. Look up definitions for the following words: *intransigence, malaise, mandate.*

2. What do the following concepts mean to you: *citizenship, civil society, deliberative democracy?*

3. Is Fraser's use of language effective for making his argument within the context of his particular audience?

WRITING SUGGESTIONS

1. Write a well-constructed, one-paragraph summary of Fraser's essay.

2. Research the term *multiversity* and write a short, persuasive essay comparing your university to the concept of a multiversity.

3. Search the Internet for the main article to which Fraser refers in his article: George Fallis's "The Mission of the University." Write a summary of the article.

4. Write a persuasive essay on what you think the "higher mission" of universities should be today.

5. Write a persuasive essay explaining how your university is or is not preparing you to be a participant in society.

| Blending the Modes | ALICE MUNRO |

Alice Munro is one of Canada's most prolific and highly regarded writers of fiction. Born in 1931 in Wingham, Ontario, she won the Governor General's Award for her first collection of stories, **Dance of the Happy Shades** (1968). In 1971 she published a collection of interlinked stories published as a novel, **Lives of Girls and Women,** followed by many more award-winning book collections, including **Something I've been Meaning to Tell You; Who Do You Think You Are?; The Moons of Jupiter; The Progress of Love; Friend of My Youth; The Love of a Good Woman; Hateship, Friendship, Courtship, Loveship, Marriage; Vintage Munro;** and **Runaway.** She also has published scores of stories in magazines such as **The New Yorker, The Atlantic Monthly,** and **The Paris Review.**

A Walk on the Wild Side*

In her essay Munro makes a compelling argument for a more sensible and ecological use of space that has outlived its intended purpose. She uses the abandoned regional railway line to argue for a more creative approach to adapting to changing environmental conditions.

1 Where I grew up, on the rural west side of the town of Wingham in southern Ontario, the Maitland River was at the foot of our property. The river flats and the bottomlands were generally too stony for crops, but made good pasture. There were scattered trees where the cattle could shelter from the sun, and the river provided drinking water. From the rough natural vegetation of the bottomlands and river flats, the grazing cattle produced a grassy parkland that reached to the foot of our property in a grove of elm trees within sight of the house.

Downstream to the west, and visible from our place, a wide curve of the river had broad-ened the flats, and to the north, it had undercut a high steep bank covered with trees—the
10 whole being, in effect, a great amphitheater half a mile or more in width, floored with elm and maple parkland. On the high, distant skyline back from the amphitheater was Roly Grain's farmstead—house, barn, and silo. To the south, where Roly Grain's sideroad joined Highway 86 just at the bridge where the river completes its curve, the village of Zetland once thrived—remembered by my father, but in my time utterly vanished. When I was young, the skyline with Roly Grain's farmstead seemed to me the end of the world, and the vanished village whose time had ended somehow filled out that idea.

This scene—an amphitheater floored with parkland and reaching to the end of the world and joined to us by the river—was my first access to the countryside of southern Ontario, which was and has remained magical. When I was very young, I dreamt I saw a pure white
20 horse with a jeweled bridle come down to drink at the river—but I didn't think that was a dream. When I lived in British Columbia, I longed for the sight of Ontario landscape—the

big solitary oaks and beeches and maples looming in a summer haze in the open fields, the carpet of leeks and trilliums and bloodroot in the sunny woods before the leaves come out, the unexpected little rough hills with their hawthorns and tough daisies, the creeks and bogs and the long smooth grassy slopes. On a motor trip home via the state of Washington, we came out of the splendid mountains and forest onto the great rolling country of the Palouse-Big Bend wheatlands, and I felt as if I had retrieved a lost part of myself, because it was something "like home."

Some 15 or so years ago, I returned to Ontario to live, not to the place where I grew up but to a small town nearby and to essentially the same landscape. But things have 30 changed. The elm trees are gone—the last one of our flats, a seeming survivor of the Dutch elm disease, fell in a storm in 1977. The bottomlands are no longer pastured, for reasons I have not investigated, and have grown up in coarse vegetation—tall grasses, stinging nettle, joe-pye weed, wild parsnip, thistles, goldenrod, hawthorn, and scrub willow, to name only a part of it—and the walkable land is gone. The local rivers and streams are not poisonously polluted but are often choked with various kinds of algae and water plants overstimulated by fertilizer runoff from cultivated fields. Even if I were to hack my way through the jungle of vegetation, the river doesn't have the swimmable water I once knew.

The amphitheater in the curve of the river belonged to our neighbors, but I regarded it 40 as mine, or ours, or not anyone's—accessible to everyone not afraid of cows. This was generally the rule—you could walk the countryside on private property without fear of being hauled up for trespass. Now, more and more rural land is posted against trespass, and when I walk in the country, I would seldom think of cutting across a piece of private land, posted or unposted, unless I had the owner's permission. The countryside of Ontario was once an unofficial recreation area for local people. For a variety of reasons—too many people, larger cultivated fields, the unpastured bottomlands—that day is gone. There has been no adequate replacement.

Two years ago my husband and I discovered the walking and bicycling trails in Wisconsin that have been converted from abandoned railways. Near Blue Mounds, a little west of 50 Madison, on a fine summer morning, we came upon the Military Road Trail. When we are traveling, we find that our staying power is improved if we get about an hour's walk a day, and the trail was exactly what we were looking for. We walked from Blue Mounds to Barneveld, had lunch there in a pub right beside the trail, and walked back to Blue Mounds. We were so elated by this walk that we decided to change the itinerary of our trip to visit the other Wisconsin trails, and we were not disappointed. We talked about the reasons for our exhilaration and came up with something like this: "One of life's great pleasures is to feel possessive of your homeland, and one way to get that feeling is to see the country as a landscape that belongs to you and to which you belong, and to see it close up and at not too great a speed." 60

But Wisconsin is not our homeland. It was good to know that there was a government there that had taken this trouble to provide for its people—to recognize that the need to walk is as important as the need to drive on a highway. But it wasn't our government. So we came home with the hope that this sort of program could be started in southern Ontario, where at this very time so many railways are being abandoned. Recently one Sunday, we toured along the abandoned sections of the CPR from Credit Forks to Wingham, which has a branch to Fergus. Near Credit Forks, where the line crosses a secondary highway, we found 12 cars parked. They belonged to people who were walking the line, having clambered over the ridge of earth the company has bulldozed up to block passage to vehicles.

70 At another crossing, we saw cyclists throwing their bikes over the barrier. All along the line from Wingham to Credit Forks, we encountered people walking and cycling, including a farmer who owned adjoining land. He said he would like to see the abandoned line become a trail. When you see valiant cyclists pumping along the thin edge of paved highways with the traffic roaring by, you can appreciate the appeal a controlled trail has for them, and you can also appreciate that the Ontario government, despite its advocacy of outdoor exercise, is doing nothing to facilitate cycling as an activity that large numbers of people could enjoy.

If the line west out of Credit Forks follows the same history as other abandoned railway lines in Ontario, there will be a brief period during which people will walk and bike along it,
80 and then the adjoining landowners will close it down, whether by legal purchase or not. One fence across the line effectively closes the whole section between road crossings. All across the province, bits and pieces of abandoned lines can be found, fragmented by closure by adjoining landowners. These potential trails are being lost. And they are not just trails but existing corridors of vegetation. Along the Guelph to Goderich line, we saw banks of wild strawberries, thimbleberry and wild raspberry bushes, tame cherry trees and lilac bushes gone wild, and many, many young elm trees—enough, perhaps, to form a reservoir within which an immunity could be developed to the Dutch elm disease. Wouldn't it be worth preserving our vegetation, our nurseries of elm trees? (And trees growing up along the tracks would provide privacy for the landowners.)

90 I've turned my celebration of southern Ontario countryside into a plea, because I really believe that access to the land is a right and a necessity, just as paved roads and schools and hospitals are. I believe that it's important to our well-being. I think that people who see the landscape in this way will give thought to protecting and preserving it. The railways have been heavily subsidized, so surely we all have some claim on the lines when they are abandoned. If the provincial government would just accept custody of these lines, it would make possible a period in which interested parties could lobby for various plans, and the corridors wouldn't be immediately fragmented and lost. I hope they won't be. ■

UNDERSTANDING CONTEXT

1. Who is Munro's audience?

2. Why does Munro tell the readers about her childhood? How does her reflection on the past avoid sentimentality?

3. How does Munro's sense of place in the essay affect the power of her argument?

EVALUATING STRATEGY

1. Briefly summarize Munro's thesis and find three different statements in which she makes her main point.

2. Why does Munro devote the majority of her argument to descriptions of landscape?

3. How does Munro create a sense of human fragmentation as a consequence of environmental fragmentation and decay?

APPRECIATING LANGUAGE

1. Study the adjectives that Munro uses to describe the forces she believes are working toward the appreciation and advantage of the environment and those working against it.

2. How does Munro balance subjective and objective language in her argument?

WRITING SUGGESTIONS

1. Summarize Munro's essay in one paragraph.

2. *Reflective writing:* Have you ever walked "on the wild side," either along trails that were converted from railway lines or some other version of reclaimed nature? Write a two-page essay in which you describe your experience while constructing an argument that urges sustained development of environmentally sound reclamation projects.

3. *Critical thinking:* Is technology the culprit in Munro's essay, or is there a more profound source prompting what she calls her "plea"? Write a persuasive essay exploring the underlying factor you think is most responsible for the destruction and loss she observes.

■ ■ ■ ■ ■

Responding to IMAGES

In 1991, the RCMP decided to allow Sikh officers to wear their turbans as part of their uniforms

CP/Toronto Sun(Paul Henry)

1. What is your first reaction to this image? Write a brief autobiographical narrative about how Canada's policy of multiculturalism has affected your life.

2. How do you think history will recall this event? What is the larger significance of this moment? Does it make an important statement about Canadian culture? Be sure to explain your answer fully.

3. What does this photograph reveal about Canadian society? Is it significant that the officer is part of the RCMP? Is the RCMP symbolic of Canada? Be sure to explain your answer fully.

4. Does this photograph serve as a Rorschach test of Canadian's attitudes about multiculturalism or racism? How might people around the world respond differently to this image?

5. *Critical thinking:* How would you define "multiculturalism" or "cultural mosaic? Does the freedom of cultural expression diminish the larger Canadian identity? Is Canadian society enhanced by multiculturalism? Write a clear definition of "multiculturalism" and provide examples to illustrate your thesis.

6. *Visual analysis:* Describe the other officer's expression as he looks at the Sikh officer. What assumptions about the Caucasian officer do you make, based on this photograph?

7. *Collaborative writing:* Discuss this image with a group of students and craft a short essay explaining why multiculturalism is an important element of Canadian society. If members of your groups have differing opinions, write a comparison or division essay.

8. *Other modes*

   ■ Write an essay that details the *effects* of multiculturalism on the Canadian public.

   ■ Write a *division* paper that outlines the different opinions about multiculturalism. Provide examples of multiculturalism's effect on Canadian society.

☑ ARGUMENT AND PERSUASION **CHECKLIST**

Before submitting your paper, review these points:

✔ Is your message clearly defined?

✔ Does your paper meet readers' needs? Do you provide the support they need to accept your thesis?

✔ Do you support your views with adequate evidence?

✔ Do you anticipate reader objections and alternative points of view?

✔ Do you balance the strengths and weaknesses of logical, ethical, and emotional appeals?

✔ Do you avoid overstated, sentimental, or propagandist appeals?

✔ Do you avoid preaching to the converted? Will only those who already agree with you accept your arguments?

✔ Do you make it easy for undecided readers to accept your position without feeling manipulated or patronized?

✔ Have you tested your argument with peer review?

 ## COMPANION WEBSITE

See **http://www.transcanadawriter.nelson.com** for additional information about argument and persuasion.

PART THREE

Research and Writing

CHAPTER 21

Conducting Research

This chapter examines the role of research and offers an overview of the research process. It also provides guidance in formulating effective research topics and overcoming research problems.

The research paper is, in the fullest sense, a discovery and an education that leads you beyond texts, beyond a library, and encourages you to investigate on your own.

—AUDREY J. ROTH

WHAT IS RESEARCH?

Most students expect to encounter research assignments throughout their academic experience, but few reflect on the nature of research and why it is essential to academic writing. In fact, the words *research paper* on a syllabus can instill anxiety and dread. Perhaps you found writing term papers in high school a frustrating and time-consuming chore. For many students research papers imply endless hours spent locating sources, photocopying articles, downloading databases, taking notes, selecting facts, organizing quotations, writing, and rewriting. To obtain a more meaningful relationship to research, it is important to consider why students are required to learn research methods and to write research papers. In other words, what is the purpose of research—and the research paper?

Conducting research can have many academic rewards. It allows you to investigate a subject that interests you; compare your own views on the subject with those of experts; examine the views of different established authorities on the subject; give your views more authoritative weight and credibility by supporting them in a context of established authorities; narrow a subject to a topic; and narrow a topic to a working thesis. Above all, a research paper will allow you to *position* your views more thoroughly, by enabling you to (1) explore and learn more about a subject; (2) discover how a subject is understood by experts in the field; and (3) bring your own views into relation with established authorities.

Your ability to write effective research papers will greatly determine your success at college or university. Instructors assign research papers because, unlike objective tests, they measure your ability to solve problems, apply knowledge, gather evidence, and interpret data.

Learning how to write a good research paper will not only improve your academic performance but also sharpen the critical thinking skills needed for most careers. Although few people write traditional research papers once they leave university, almost every professional uses the same methods to produce annual reports, market studies, product evaluations, proposals, and letters. Executives, administrators, attorneys, entrepreneurs, and scientists must base their decisions and recommendations on information. The ability to locate accurate sources, evaluate evidence, and interpret findings is essential for success in any field.

Common Misconceptions

Many students work very hard collecting material and writing pages of text only to receive low grades because the paper they produce fails to meet the instructor's requirements. Even students who do well on research papers often make the project more burdensome and time consuming than necessary.

What a research paper is *not:*

- **A research paper is not a summary of everything you can find about your topic.** The goal in writing a research paper is not to present a collection of facts and quotations "about" a topic but to state a clear thesis supported by evidence. Although it is important to survey information, using 20 sources instead of 10 will not necessarily improve the quality of your paper. The goal of a research paper is to present carefully selected evidence that supports your thesis.

- **A research paper does not simply repeat what others have written.** A research paper is more than a string of related quotations and summaries. The focus of a research paper is your thesis and commentary—not pages of text you have cut and pasted from the Internet.

- **A research paper does not merely support a preconceived point of view.** Honest research begins with a topic or question. You should reach a conclusion and develop a thesis only after carefully examining the evidence. Taking the ideas of others out of context to support your position on abortion or the death penalty is not research.

- **A research paper does not include the ideas of others without documentation.** Including the ideas and words of others in your text without attribution is plagiarism. Whenever you add ideas, facts, quotations, and summaries of outside sources, you must identify them.

CONDUCTING RESEARCH: AN OVERVIEW

Writing a research paper can be made less intimidating and less arduous if you break the process into key steps:

- Understand the scope of the assignment.
- Select an appropriate topic.
- Conduct preliminary research.

- Limit the topic and develop a working thesis.
- Create a timeline.
- Collect and evaluate relevant evidence.

Understand the Scope of the Assignment

Even when instructors allow students to select topics themselves, most still provide directions or guidelines that outline the scope of the assignment. Students may be required to use a certain number of sources, present evidence in a specific manner, or address a particular issue:

> Write an eight- to ten-page research paper using APA documentation that compares past and present treatments of a common psychological disorder. Your sources must include at least two professional interviews.

- **It is important to fully understand all the requirements of an assignment and refer to them throughout the process.** Perhaps the most common mistake students make is failing to address the needs of the assignment. Once you begin looking up sources and examining data, you can be easily led astray and write a paper that is interesting but fails to meet the instructor's requirements. The psychology student writing about schizophrenia may be impressed by some recent medical articles and write a thorough research paper outlining genetic factors. Although it may be well written and properly documented, if it fails to draw a comparison between past and present treatments and does not include interviews, the paper may be wholly unacceptable.

- **Ask your instructor for clarification of any points you find confusing.** If your instructor does not supply handouts, take careful notes to record specific requirements and directions. If your instructor does not assign topics, you may wish to ask for suggestions. Ask your instructor which topics to avoid.

- **Make copies of any instructor handouts or notes and keep them next to your computer or in your backpack or briefcase for quick reference.** Refer to these guidelines when visiting the library or searching the Internet. Ensure your research remains focused on sources that address the needs of the assignment.

Select an Appropriate Topic

The first step in writing a research paper is selecting a topic or topics. Until you begin collecting evidence, you may not be sure if the subjects you start with are workable. Often, subjects that you might find interesting at first become unmanageable because sources are lacking or too numerous to handle.

Strategies for Selecting a Topic

1. **Select a topic that matches the assignment.** If your instructor requires you to include personal interviews, you may find it difficult to locate people who can provide insights on highly specialized issues; therefore, keep your topic broad.

2. **Select a topic that interests you.** If you don't really care about your subject, you may find it difficult to sustain a long research effort. If you choose a topic that you have little knowledge about, you will have to conduct extensive background research. Brainstorm to discover whether your existing knowledge and experiences apply to the assignment. Discuss possible topics with your instructor or friends, and ask for suggestions.

3. **Select a topic that is flexible.** Until you begin researching, you cannot tell how much information is readily available. Think of your topic as an accordion, something that may have to be compressed or expanded.

4. **Be willing to alter or reject topics.** Your first topic is only a starting point. If you find it difficult to work with, drop it and select another. Do not feel obligated to stick with something unless required by your instructor. Use clustering, brainstorming, and asking questions to develop new approaches to your topic.

Topics to Avoid

Difficulties commonly arise from the following kinds of topics, which are often best avoided altogether.

- **Topics that rely on a single source.** Research papers coordinate information from several sources. If you select an event covered in one news story or a process explained by a single set of instructions, you will not be able to achieve a major goal of a research paper. Check with your instructor if you are interested in a topic with only a single source.

- **Highly controversial topics—unless you can develop a new approach.** It is unlikely you can write anything about capital punishment or abortion that has not already been stated—unless you look at the issue from a unique perspective. You might research murder rates or examine Islamic views on abortion. Controversial subjects may be difficult to research because many of the sources are biased. Discuss your topic with your instructor and ask for recommended approaches or alternative subjects.

- **New topics.** Issues raised by events that have just happened may be difficult to research because little has been published except news reports and fragmentary comments. A quick Internet search might locate the amount of reliable material currently available.

- **Topics lacking credible sources.** Conducting research about UFOs, psychic phenomena, and Bigfoot sightings can be difficult because sources may be anecdotal and unscientific. Avoid "conspiracy"-related issues. By their nature, these topics resist objective investigation. A reference librarian can suggest sources or a new topic.

Courtesy of Bartleby.com, Inc.

- **Popular topics.** As with writing about a controversial topic, it may be difficult to find something new to say about an issue many students have written about. Popular issues may be hard to research because many of the books may already be checked out of the library.

- **Topics difficult to narrow or expand.** Until you begin discovering sources, you will not know how complex your task will be. If you select a topic that resists alterations, you may be forced to reject it in favour of a more manageable subject.

Conduct Preliminary Research

Once you have selected a topic or topics, you are ready to explore your subject. Your goal at this point is not to locate specific sources for your research paper but to survey the field of knowledge; to get a sense of the discipline; to identify schools of thought; and to research trends, areas of conflict, and new discoveries.

Strategies for Conducting Preliminary Research

1. **Review textbooks and lecture notes.** Textbooks often include endnotes, bibliographies, and footnotes that can direct you to books, articles, and websites about specific issues. In addition, textbooks and your notes can help you create a list of people, events, ideas, and places to use as search terms.

2. **Search online encyclopedias and reference works.** Online reference sources, such as Answers.com (http://www.answers.com) and Bartleby.com (http://www.Bartleby.com), offer online dictionaries, cross-referenced encyclopedias, and lists of websites that can provide a broad overview of your subject and links to specific sources.

3. **Search the Internet.** There are a variety of popular search engines you can use to survey information available on your subject:

AllTheWeb	http://www.alltheweb.com
AltaVista	http://www.altavista.com
Excite	http://www.excite.com
Google	http://www.google.com
HotBot	http://www.hotbot.com
Lycos	http://www.lycos.com
Yahoo!	http://www.yahoo.com

   Each of these search engines accesses millions of sites on the Internet. Students unfamiliar with searching the Internet are often frustrated by the overwhelming list of unrelated "hits" they receive; search engines provide tools to narrow your search. To use these tools efficiently, keep the following suggestions in mind:

- Check the spelling of search terms, especially names.
- Make search terms as specific as possible.
- Put quotation marks around search words or phrases. Entering "Leopold and Loeb" will locate only documents containing this phrase, eliminating documents about King Leopold or Loeb Realty. See page 462 for a sample Internet search using "Leopold and Loeb."
- Use Boolean Search Operators AND, OR, NOT.

  Entering *Orwell* AND *Nature* locates sites containing both terms.

  Entering *Orwell* NOT *Nature* excludes sites containing the second term.

  Entering *Orwell* OR *Nature* locates sites containing either term.

- Check to be sure information is up to date by entering *javascript:alert (document.lastModified)* in the address bar of your web browser from the page you want to check. A dialog box will pop up that indicates the date and time of the latest update for that page.
- Take advantage of subject directories, offered by many search engines, such as AltaVista and Yahoo!. Surveying the subject categories related to your preliminary topic may help you search more efficiently.

4. **Review specialized encyclopedias, dictionaries, and directories.** A general encyclopedia, such as the *Encyclopedia Britannica,* can offer only brief commentaries on subjects and will not include minor people, events, or subjects. The reference room of your library is likely to have specialized encyclopedias that may offer substantial entries:

Art

Encyclopedia of World Art

The Oxford Companion to Art

Biography

Who's Who in the World

Contemporary Authors

Business/Economics

Dictionary of Banking and Finance

Encyclopedia of Economics

Education

Encyclopedia of Education

The International Encyclopedia of Education

Engineering

The Engineering Index

Information Sources in Engineering

(Continued)

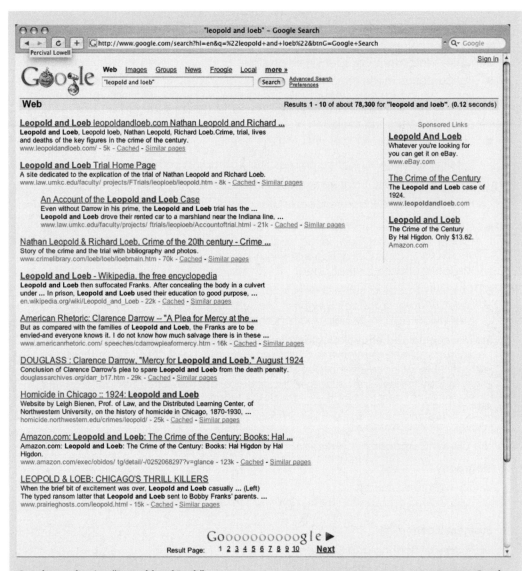

Google search using "Leopold and Loeb"

© 2008 Google

History

Dictionary of American History

Dictionary of Historical Terms

An Encyclopedia of World History

Literature/Film

Cassell's Encyclopedia of World Literature

The Oxford Companion to American Literature

Sample website from "Leopold and Loeb" search

Scott A. Newman, The Leopold and Loeb Case of 1924, http://chicago.urban-history. org/evt/evt02/evt0200.shtml, Jazz Age Chicago. Copyright © 2007 Scott A. Newman

Music

Dictionary of Musical Technology

The New Oxford History of Music

Philosophy

The Concise Encyclopedia of Western Philosophy and Philosophers

Encyclopedia of Philosophy

Political Science

The Blackwell Encyclopedia of Political Thought

Encyclopedia of American Political History

Psychology

Dictionary of Psychology

Encyclopedia of Human Behavior

Religion

The New Catholic Encyclopedia

The Encyclopedia of American Religions

(Continued)

Science/Technology

Dictionary of Mathematics

Encyclopedia of Medical History

Social Sciences

Dictionary of Anthropology

Encyclopedia of Crime and Justice

5. **Review indexes, databases, and abstracts.** Available in print, online, or on CD-ROM, these are valuable tools in conducting research. Databases list articles. Many provide abstracts that briefly summarize articles, usually in a single paragraph. Still other databases are especially useful because they include the entire article in addition to abstracts. If the complete text is available, you may download and save the file for later reading and note taking. Skimming abstracts allows you to quickly review a dozen articles in the time it would take to locate a magazine and find a single article. Abstracts not only list the source of the full article but also indicate its length and special features, such as photographs or tables. Such sources as *Chemical Abstracts, Psychological Abstracts,* and *Criminal Justice Abstracts* provide summaries in specific disciplines.

Sample Abstract from **Expanded Academic Index**

	Database: Expanded Academic Index
	Subject: AIDS (disease) in motion pictures
Title	*TV Movies of the first decade of AIDS (American Values and Images)*
Magazine	*Journal of Popular Film and Television, Spring 1993 v 21 n 1 p19 (8)*
	[indicates this is an eight-page article]
Authors	*Author: Frank Pilipp and Charles Shull*
Summary	*Abstract: The decade of 1983–1993 has produced several full-length feature films which respond to the AIDS epidemic. Three of them, 'As Is,' 'Andre's Mother,' and 'An Early Frost' undoubtedly portray the virus as non-partisan when it comes to gender, color, or sexual orientation, although they fail to destroy the image of AIDS as being a purely homosexual disease. The disease instead is viewed as punishment inflicted on the main characters and their families for their violation of middle-class norms and values.*
Listings for related articles	*Subjects: Homosexuals—portrayals, depictions, etc.*
	Motion pictures—criticism, interpretation, etc.
	AIDS (disease) in motion pictures—criticism, interpretation, etc.
	Features: illustration; photograph
	AN: 14558418

Some common online indexes and databases include:

ABC Political Science

ABI/Inform

Academic Search

Art Index

Associations Unlimited

Biography & Genealogy Master Index

Business Abstracts

Business Newsbank

CARL UnCover

Contemporary Authors

Dissertation Abstracts

Education Index

ERIC

General Science Index

Historical Abstracts

Humanities Index

Masterplots

Medline

MLA Bibliography

National Criminal Justice Reference Service

Newspaper Abstracts

Psychological Literature

Reader's Guide Abstracts

Sociological Abstracts

Women's Resources International

Limit the Topic and Develop a Working Thesis

After surveying the field of knowledge, consider whether your topic is worth pursuing. If you cannot find enough material or if the sources are too diverse or scattered, you may wish to consider a new subject. In most instances, the preliminary material you have located may help you further limit your topic:

Orwell's *Nineteen Eighty-Four*
Loss of Freedom Predicted by Orwell in *Nineteen Eighty-Four*
Role of Technology in Orwell's *Nineteen Eighty-Four*
Orwell and the Loss of Nature in *Nineteen Eighty-Four*

Famous Trials
Role of Media in High-Profile Trials
Leopold and Loeb Case
Role of the Press in the Leopold and Loeb Case

Asking questions can help target your paper and prevent you from simply summarizing the work or the ideas of others:

What effect does the loss of nature have on humanity in *Nineteen Eighty-Four?*
Did media coverage affect the outcome of the Leopold and Loeb case?

At this point you may be able to develop a working thesis, a starting point for your research paper. Although it may be general and subject to change, the working thesis moves beyond a narrowed topic or question to make a tentative statement:

Orwell considered contact with nature essential to individual liberty.
Excessive media coverage influenced the outcome of the Leopold and Loeb case.

A working thesis is a tentative statement subject to change. A working thesis is a tool to guide your research; keep an open mind and be willing to alter your opinion.

Create a Timeline

When you begin a long research project, it is important to carefully budget your time and resources. In developing a long paper, ensure you devote enough time for each stage in the writing process. Don't spend six weeks gathering materials and try to write, revise, edit, and proofread a ten-page paper over a weekend.

■ **Note the due date and work backward to create a schedule that allows sufficient time for each stage in the writing process.**

May 10   Paper due

May 5   Target date for completion

May 1	Final draft prepared for final editing and proofreading
April 25	Second draft completed
April 15	First draft completed for revision and rewriting
April 10	Final outline completed, final thesis
April 5	Research completed and sources selected
March 15	Topic narrowed, working thesis, and research initiated
March 10	Topic selected and preliminary research started
March 5	Research project assigned

- **Chart your progress on a calendar to keep on track.**

- **Establish cutoff dates for major stages in the process. If you cannot find enough material by a fixed date, talk with your instructor and consider changing topics.** If you find too much material, narrow your topic.

- **Don't allow the research stage to expand past a specific date.** Keep the scope of the assignment and the length of the paper in mind to guide the quantity of material you collect. The advent of the photocopier and the Internet have made it too easy to copy and print more articles than you may need.

Collect and Evaluate Relevant Evidence

The type of evidence you will need to support your thesis will depend on the discipline, the topic, and the scope of the assignment. There are two kinds of sources: primary and secondary. Primary sources are original documents and observations and include works of art, such as novels, poems, and plays; historical documents; letters; diaries; autobiographies; speeches; interviews; raw data, such as polls or observations of experiments; eyewitness testimony; and photographs of events. Secondary sources are interpretations of primary sources and include literary criticism, commentaries, biographies, analytical studies, reviews, and editorials. You may use only primary or secondary sources or a combination. A literary paper might focus on a novel (primary source) and include biographical material about the author and critical interpretations (secondary sources). An economics paper on a recent market trend may examine stock market statistics (primary sources) and comments by experts (secondary sources).

How to Locate Library Sources

Large university libraries may have their collections separated by discipline or department. Look for maps or guides to locate materials. Though the books may be arranged on different floors or even in different buildings on your campus, all libraries will use either the Library of Congress or Dewey Decimal system. Libraries organize books, magazines, videos, and other sources by *call numbers*. Call numbers are standard. *The Ecstasy of Rita Joe*, for example, will have the same Library of Congress call number in the Robarts Library at the University of Toronto as it does at Robertson Library at the University of Prince Edward Island.

Library of Congress System

A	General Works
B	Philosophy/Religion
C	History/Auxiliary Sciences
D	History/Topography (except America)
E–F	America
G	Geography
H	Social Sciences (Psychology, Sociology, etc.)
J	Political Science
K	Law
L	Education
M	Music
N	Fine Arts
P	Language and Literature
Q	Science
R	Medicine
S	Agriculture
T	Technology
U	Military Science
V	Naval Science
Z	Bibliography and Library Science

Dewey Decimal System

000–099	General Works
100–199	Philosophy and Psychology
200–299	Religion
300–399	Social Science
400–499	Language
500–599	Pure Science
600–699	Technology/Applied Sciences
700–799	The Arts
800–899	Literature
900–999	History

Computerized Catalogues

Online catalogues list a library's holdings of books, magazines, videos, and other sources. The exact instructions for searching a catalogue will vary slightly. Most systems provide onscreen directions to locate specific works by subject, author, or title.

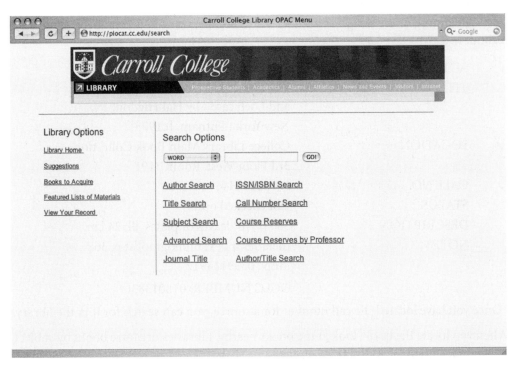

Copyright © 2007 Carroll College, Waukesha, Wisconsin

If you do not have a particular source in mind, you can enter a subject or topic:

Leopold and Loeb

LIST OF ITEMS   12 ITEMS MATCH YOUR SEARCH

ITEM	-AUTHOR-	TITLE	
1	Bellak, Leopold, 1916–	The schizophrenic syndrome, Leo	1967
2	Busch, Francis X	Prisoners at the bar: an accou	1952
3		Compulsion [videorecording]	1995
4	Darrow, Clarence, 1857–	Clarence Darrow pleas in defen	1926
5	Darrow, Clarence, 1857–	The plea of Clarence Darrow in	1924
6	DeFord, Miriam Allen 18	Murderers sane and mad	1965
7	Geis, Gilbert	Crimes of the century: from Leo	1998
8	Higdon, Hal	The crime of the century	1975
9	Levin, Meyer, 1905–	Compulsion—New York, Simon	1956
10	Loeb, Leo, 1869–	The venom of Heloderma	1913
11	McKernan, Maureen	The amazing crime and trial	1924
12	Vaughn, Betty Ann Erick	The forensic speaking in the	1948

By highlighting or entering the number of the source, you can access specific information about it:

AUTHOR	Higdon, Hal.
TITLE	The crime of the century: the Leopold and Loeb case / by Hal Higdon.
	New York : Putnam, [c1975]
LOCATION	College Library Main Book Collection 3rd Floor West, Room 3191
CALL NO.	HV6245 H46
STATUS	Not checked out
DESCRIPTION	380 p., [8] leaves of plates: ill; 24 cm.
NOTES	Includes index. Bibliography: p. 368
	ISBN: 0399114912
	OCLC NUMBER: 01801383

Once you have located the call number for a source, you can search for it in the library.

- When you locate the book, look at the books nearby. Libraries organize books by subject, so you may find other useful titles on the same shelf.

Computerized catalogues are often linked to other libraries so you can search for sources located at other campuses or in local public libraries. Computerized catalogues also list databases of abstracts and articles. Ask a librarian if you can access the library's databases from a remote site (for example, at home, in your dorm room, or from a laptop with Internet connection).

Locating Periodicals

Libraries refer to magazines and journals as *periodicals* or *serials*. You can locate a magazine or a newspaper in the catalogue or *periodical holding list*. However, this will simply explain where *Newsweek* or *The Globe and Mail* is located in the building, in bound volumes, microfilm, or online. To find which articles and issues to search for, you have to consult specific databases (see pages 464–465). Databases list articles under key words. The *MLA Bibliography,* for instance, lists articles about literature and authors:

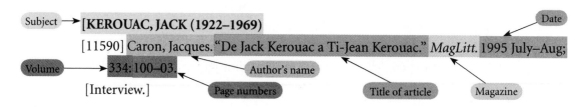

Fiction

[11590] Oates, Joyce Carol; Dauzat, Pierre-Emmanuel, translator. "Au bout de la route." *MagLitt.* 1995 July–Aug; 334: 96–99.

Letters

[11591] "Letters from Jack Kerouac to Ed White, 1947–68." *MissR.* 1994; 17(3): 107–60 [Includes letters (1947–1968) to White, Ed.]

Prose/Some of the Dharma

[11592] Sampas, John, foreword; Stanford, David, ed. and introd. *Some of the Dharma.* New York, NY: Viking; 1997. 420pp. ISBN 0-670-84877-8 [And poetry. Edition.]

Other Secondary Sources

In addition to books and periodicals, secondary sources include government documents, statistics, microfilms, audio and video recordings, photographs, and film. Your library may have special collections of artifacts not included in most databases. Depending on your topic, you may be able to obtain valuable information from corporations, organizations, federal agencies, provincial and local governments, or historical and professional societies.

SELECTING AND EVALUATING SOURCES

Database and Internet searches may provide you with hundreds, even thousands, of sources. Before you begin printing or photocopying, consider the type and number of sources needed. Without planning a list, you may waste a great deal of time collecting sources that may be interesting but unsuited to your paper.

Strategies for Selecting and Evaluating Sources

1. **List the types of sources needed to support your working thesis.** Review the assignment, instructor's directions, your preliminary research, and your working thesis to develop a list of needed sources:

   Working Thesis:

   Orwell considered contact with nature essential to individual liberty.

   Sources needed:

   Orwell's attitudes toward nature

   Orwell's view of technology

   Biographical commentary on Orwell's views

   Letters, essays, journals showing Orwell's views of nature and human liberty

   (Continued)

For a ten-page paper, you may need only one or two biographical sources—not five or six. Ensure you select enough sources for each item on your list.

2. **Collect a variety of evidence.** If you are writing a paper about the homeless, you may wish to balance personal accounts with statistics and expert opinions.

3. **Avoid collecting needless or repetitive data.** The Internet has made it possible to access billions of documents. Although it is important to grasp the sweep and range of material about your subject, avoid printing more items than you need for your paper.

   - Select the most useful sources, briefly noting similar articles for confirmation.
   - Refer to the assignment and your working thesis to keep your research focused.
   - Skim books and long documents by examining tables of contents and indexes to measure their usefulness before checking them out.

4. **Select reliable sources.** Recognized publishers, magazines, and established databases such as MLA, West Law, and Psychological Abstracts are edited by professionals who follow established standards. Articles appearing in *The New England Journal of Medicine*, *The Harvard Law Review*, or *Nursing* have been reviewed by physicians, attorneys, and nurses. Small-press publications and individual websites, however, may produce material based solely on rumour, anecdotal observation, and facts taken out of context. Do not assume that all the books in the library or sites found on the Internet are of equal value.

   - Books can be evaluated by checking reviews, many of which are available online. You can also examine the author's use of sources. Does the book include a bibliography? Does the author provide endnotes and support his or her conclusions with facts, quotations, or statistics? Is the author's biography available in *Who's Who* or other databases? Does the author seem biased?
   - You can get a sense of the quality of a magazine by reviewing other issues and examining the editorial staff. Determine the audience for the magazine. Publications designed for general readers, such as *Reader's Digest* or *People*, are less rigorous about checking specific facts than professional journals in law or medicine.
   - Verify information you may find on the web by seeking confirming articles on established databases. Examine the server or producer of the website. Is it a professional organization, university, or government agency? Or is it a small, amateur, or personal site? Does the information seem biased or objective?

5. **Verify controversial conclusions.** A book or website might offer a striking piece of evidence or make a dramatic conclusion. Before using this material, consider the source. Was the book published by a recognized publisher? Did the article come from a biased publication? Did you find this website using an established database, such as InfoTrac or Medline, or by searching the web with a general search engine, such as AltaVista or Yahoo!?

   - Review other books, articles, or material presented by this source.
   - Read a periodical's editorial page for signs of obvious bias. Even the tone of a publication's advertising can indicate whether the source is biased or objective.
   - Select key words from the material and search established databases for confirmation.
   - Ask a reference librarian or your instructor to assist you in evaluating sources.

6. **Distinguish between fact and opinion.** In evaluating sources it is important to separate factual data from interpretation and analysis. The author of a book, magazine article, or website might accurately report a change in oil prices but present a highly personal and subjective interpretation or prediction.

7. **Examine sources for lapses in critical thinking.** Remember that all the books, articles, and studies you discover were created by human beings who, despite their degrees or expertise, may be biased or mistaken.

   ■ Do not assume that everything you read is accurate or true.

☑ EVALUATING INTERNET SOURCES **CHECKLIST**

As you search for sources online, determine their value and reliability:

✔ **Source:** What is the domain name of the source? The URL—the site's Internet address—can help you evaluate an online source.

DOMAIN	SOURCE
.com	company or for-profit organization
.edu	college or university
.gov	federal government
.mil	military
.net	Internet provider or individual
.org	nonprofit organization or individual

Does a reputable organization sponsor the site? Is this organization likely to be impartial in its examination of the information? Does the organization benefit from persuading you to accept its position? Do you detect inflammatory language that reveals bias or prejudice?

✔ **Authorship:** Does the site mention the author or webmaster? This information is often noted at the bottom of the site's home page, but does not always appear on internal pages. Does the author or webmaster include an e-mail address? An e-mail to the author or webmaster can yield valuable insights.

✔ **Credibility:** If you are able to identify the site's author, can you also determine whether he or she has significant knowledge about the topic? Does the site present objective information or express personal views? Does the author include his or her résumé?

   ■ To check if the author has also published books, check your library's online catalog or Amazon.com (http://www.amazon.com), which lists books and often includes reader reviews.

   ■ Place the author's full name in quotation marks and use it as a search term using a search engine like AltaVista, Google, or Yahoo! to locate biographical information.

✔ **Purpose:** Can you determine the site's intended purposes? Is the site designed to present all available evidence? Does it seem to take a side? Is the site intended to inform readers or to sell a product or service?

(Continued)

✔ **Audience:** Does the site expect its readers to have an opinion before visiting the site? Does the site encourage its readers to form an opinion based solely on the information presented? Or does the site invite further investigation by providing links to related sites?

✔ **Language:** Is the information presented in a manner that allows virtually any reader to understand it? Is specialized terminology included? Does its presence have a negative effect on the presentation or the general reader's comprehension?

✔ **Presentation:** Has the site been planned and designed well? Is it easy to navigate? Are the links active, current, and relevant? Does the text reflect that careful planning has been devoted to it, including thorough proofreading? Don't allow impressive graphics, sound, and video to substitute for accuracy in the information.

✔ **Timeliness:** Many sites are not dated, making it difficult to determine the currency of the information. If dates do not appear, test links to see if they are still active. Place key terms and phrases in quotations and use them as search terms using search engines, such as AltaVista, Google, or Yahoo!, to determine dates and perhaps locate more recent sources.

✔ **Critical Thinking:** Do you detect errors in critical thinking, such as hasty generalizations, dependence on anecdotal evidence, faulty comparisons, false authorities, or attacking personalities? (See pages 31–35.)

Strategies for Overcoming Problems with Research

Students frequently encounter common problems in conducting library research.

1. **There are no sources on the topic.** If your library and Internet search fails to yield sufficient results, review the subject and search words you are using.

   ■ Check the spelling of your key words.
   ■ Check a thesaurus for synonyms.
   ■ Review the Library of Congress Subject Headings for alternative search terms.
   ■ Review textbooks, encyclopedias, and other reference sources for search terms.
   ■ Ask a reference librarian or your instructor for suggestions.

2. **There are sources about the subject but none are related to the specific topic or working thesis.** You do not have to find articles that exactly match your topic or thesis. Because one of the goals of a research paper is originality, your thesis may address unexplored territory. You can still use related or background sources.

   ■ Pointing out the lack of sources can be crucial in demonstrating the value of your paper and the uniqueness of your approach.

3. **Sources present conflicting findings or opinions.** Experts often disagree. Biographers and historians evaluate people and events differently. Scientists dispute theories and present different interpretations of data.

- As a student you are not expected to resolve conflicts among experts, but you should report what you find.
- On the basis of your evaluation of the evidence, you may side with one group or alter your thesis to conclude that at present it is impossible to make a definitive statement.

4. **There are several books and articles, but they present the same information or refer to a common original source.** If you discover that the five books you have selected about teenage suicide or a person's life present virtually the same material, select the most representative, relevant, or best-written book.
   - Although you may select only a single source, it is important to comment on the consistency of expert opinion.

5. **The only available sources are fragmentary, biased, outdated, inaccurate, or unprofessional.** In some instances the only available sources will lack substance or quality. A controversial historical incident may have produced a rash of inflammatory editorials, biased newspaper accounts, or subjective memoirs by adversaries.
   - Ask your instructor whether you should consider changing your topic.
   - Consult a reference librarian for alternative sources.
   - As a researcher you are not responsible for the lack of evidence or the quality of sources you can locate—but you should comment on the limited value of existing evidence.

TAKING NOTES

Traditional textbooks suggest students record notes on index cards. Placing single facts or quotations on separate cards makes it easy to shuffle and reorder them after developing an outline. Today most students photocopy or print pages and highlight selected passages. Others will scan text directly onto a computer disk. Yet another option is to download and save full-text articles from databases. Useful passages can be highlighted in bold or other colours for later incorporation into a research paper.

Whatever method you use to record information from outside sources, it is essential to accomplish three tasks:

1. Accurately record information you will need to cite the source.

   Books: author's full name, full title (including any subtitle), publisher, place of publication, and year.
   - If a publisher lists several cities, choose the first location listed.
   - Note editions, translators, editors, or forewords.

   Articles: author's full name, full title (including any subtitle), full title of the magazine or newspaper, edition, volume, pages, and date.
   - If you photocopy pages from a book or magazine, write the information directly on the copies for future reference.

Motion pictures: title, director, studio, city, year of release.

Videotape or DVD: title, director, production company, city, date of production or original broadcast.

Electronic sources: author's (or editor's) full name, title of website or document, sponsoring organization, date you accessed the source, the full Internet address or URL— http://www.cnn.com/2005/US/12/01/new.orleans.open.ap/index.html, not simply www.cnn.com.

■ Ensure that website addresses appear on the printed version. If they do not, record the information.

2. **Double-check your notes for accuracy.** If you take notes rather than photocopy a source, ensure that you have properly copied facts, numbers, and names. Understand the difference between quoting and paraphrasing sources:

Original text:

> *When Robert Moses began building playgrounds in New York City, there were 119. When he stopped, there were 777. Under his direction, an army of men that at times during the Depression included 84,000 laborers reshaped every park in the city and then filled the parks with zoos and skating rinks, boathouses and tennis houses, bridle paths and golf courses, 288 tennis courts and 673 baseball diamonds.*
>
> THE POWER BROKER *BY ROBERT A. CARO*

Student notecard, full direct quotation:

Robert A. Caro, The Power Broker. *New York: Vintage, 1975.*

> *"When Robert Moses began building playgrounds in New York City, there were 119. When he stopped, there were 777. Under his direction, an army of men that at times during the Depression included 84,000 laborers reshaped every park in the city and then filled the parks with zoos and skating rinks, boathouses and tennis houses, bridle paths and golf courses, 288 tennis courts and 673 baseball diamonds." Pg. 7*

Student notecard, partial direct quotation using ellipsis (. . .) to show omitted text:

Robert A. Caro, The Power Broker. *New York: Vintage, 1975.*

> *"When Robert Moses began building playgrounds in New York City, there were 119. When he stopped, there were 777. Under his direction, an army of men . . . reshaped every park in the city. . . ." Pg. 7*

■ In deleting details, ensure that your notes accurately reflect the meaning of the original text. Do not take quotations out of context that alter the author's point of view.

Student notecard, paraphrase, putting text into your own words:

Robert A. Caro, The Power Broker. *New York: Vintage, 1975.*

Robert Moses increased the number of New York City playgrounds from 119 to 777. During the Depression over 80,000 workers restored every city park, embellishing them with zoos, playgrounds, and hundreds of tennis courts and baseball diamonds. Pg. 7

Even though the student is not copying Robert Caro word for word, he or she will have to cite Caro in the research paper to acknowledge the source of the statistics.

3. **Label research materials.**
   - Ensure that you print or photocopy all the material needed. Your copies should be complete.
   - Clip or staple articles to prevent pages from becoming mixed up.
   - Label, number, or letter your sources for easy reference. You may find it useful to write notecards for some or all of your sources so that they can be easily arranged on your desk.

4. **Organize database files.**
   - For files you've downloaded from databases, consolidate them and make a backup disk.
   - As a quick and easy reference, consolidate abstracts of the articles to form a single file that provides an overview of the items that you've identified as potentially useful.

PRIMARY RESEARCH

Conducting Interviews

Interviews allow you to collect information from professionals, eyewitnesses, and others with direct experience about your topic. Interviews, however, can be challenging to conduct and analyze.

1. **Determine whether interviews will provide useful information.** Not all subjects are conducive to interviews. You may be unable to identify a local expert on your topic. Print and electronic sources may be more useful.
   - Many print articles serve as interviews because they are written by experts and eyewitnesses. In addition, in writing an article a person has the opportunity to check facts, verify recollections, and evaluate responses more carefully than in an interview.

2. **Locate backup sources if possible.** Because interviews can be difficult to arrange and subjects may have to cancel a meeting at the last moment, avoid basing your whole paper on interviews.
   - Search for print or electronic sources that can provide information needed to support your working thesis.

3. **Identify possible subjects.** You may ask your instructor or network with local organizations, corporations, and government agencies to locate people who may be willing to provide interviews.
   - Because scheduling meetings may be difficult, locate several prospects.

4. **Determine the information or insights you wish to obtain from an interview.** There is no reason to use an interview to gather background information that you can easily obtain from other sources. Conducting an interview gives you an opportunity to ask questions, to interact with a source, to ask an expert or witness to comment on other sources, or to help you locate resources you may have overlooked.

5. **Schedule interviews in advance.** Because it may be difficult to find a time and place to meet people and last-minute changes can occur, schedule interviews well in advance. If you can, offer the subject additional dates and times in case the first appointment · you arrange must be postponed.

6. **Provide subjects with questions in advance.** Reporters and television interviewers usually prefer not to give people questions in advance because they seek spontaneous reactions. As a researcher, however, you are seeking information. Giving subjects a few days or a week to consider the topic of your interview may help them focus their thoughts or locate information.

7. **Ask specific questions.** An interview is not a conversation or an endless monologue. You should ask specific questions to produce comments that you can use in your paper:

   As a director of a program for the homeless, could you say how many of the homeless suffer from mental illness?
   What is the biggest obstacle preventing the homeless from gaining independence?

8. **Ask consistent questions.** If you are interviewing more than one subject, don't ask one person, "How many of the homeless are mentally ill?" and then ask another, "How many of the homeless are schizophrenic?" If you use conflicting terms, you will not be able to compare results.

9. **Do not tape-record the interview without permission.** For professional or legal reasons, many subjects will not allow you to tape an interview. Ask in advance whether they will permit recording.

10. **Ask how the subject wishes to be credited.** An attorney working for the Crown may not wish to be viewed as speaking for the federal government. A physician may prefer not to have his or her hospital mentioned in your paper.

11. **Review the interview material with your subject to ensure accuracy.**

12. **Ensure you have accurately recorded names, facts, and statistics.** Take careful notes during the interview and verify that you have accurately represented the subject's thoughts.

13. **Use the interview to verify print evidence or seek new sources.** If you have the opportunity to interview a practscing psychiatrist, you can ask him or her whether he or she is familiar with a book you have read or a new study found on the Internet.

You might also ask the physician for suggested readings or other interview subjects.

- Although you do not want a single source to heavily influence how you shape your final paper, you may wish to ask an expert to review your sources and thesis.

14. **Recognize the limits of interviews.** Interviews can be compelling because they bring you face to face with your topic. But remember, an interview presents a single person's experiences or point of view. The observations of one person may be highly individualistic and not representative of others. His or her views should be given no more weight than a book or article.

LOCATING AND EVALUATING VISUALS

In some assignments, graphs, charts, tables, and photographs are essential sources that should be included in your paper. In other instances, you may develop your own graphics to highlight data, or include your own photographs. In other courses, assignments focus primarily on text and visuals can be of limited value.

Strategies for Locating and Evaluating Visuals

1. **Determine the importance of visuals.** Incorporate visuals only if they provide essential information. Scan, download, or photocopy tables, photographs, graphs, and charts you find in print or online documents for future use.
   - Ensure you note the complete source of the visual.
2. **Search online library galleries, educational websites, and stock photo services for images.** Libraries, educational websites, and stock photo services offer millions of commercial, historical, and news photographs; illustrations; and graphics.
   - Study the site's search engines to narrow your search. Most sites list links and allow you to search for images in specific categories, such as historical, commercial, art, news, people, or graphics.
3. **Before selecting visuals, examine them for relevance, distortion, or bias.**
   - See Analyzing Visuals (pages 519–525).
   - See Graphics (pages 526–530).
4. **If you take your own photographs, document the subject, location, and date for each image.**

RESEARCH ACTIVITIES

1. **Use library or online sources to answer the following questions:**
   - Where is the headquarters for B.F. Goodrich?
   - When and where was Jack Nicholson born?

(Continued)

- Who is the current mayor of Vancouver?
- When did Ford produce the Edsel?
- Who developed methadone?

2. **Create a list of sources for one of the following topics:**
   - The construction of the Confederation Bridge
   - The role of the green monkey in AIDS
   - The 1919 World Series scandal
   - Protecting elephant herds from ivory poachers
   - Reviews of a new movie

3. **Review selections in the reader section of this book to develop topics and identify sources.**
   - Use databases or the Internet to search for information about an author.
   - Use one of the questions following a selection to develop a topic.
   - Examine an article you have read for key words to guide a database or online search.

☑ RESEARCH **CHECKLIST**

As you conduct your research, consider these questions:

✔ Do you fully understand the needs of the assignment? Do you know what your instructor expects in terms of topic, content, sources, and documentation?

✔ Have you narrowed your topic sufficiently to target a search for sources?

✔ Has your preliminary research given you a global view of the field? Can you detect trends or patterns in the research, prevailing theories, or conflicts?

✔ Have you developed a flexible working thesis to guide your research?

✔ Have you explored database and online sources as well as books and articles?

✔ Are you keeping the final paper in mind as you conduct research? If you sense your paper expanding beyond its target length, narrow your topic.

✔ Does the material you select accurately and fairly represent the wider spectrum of research material, or are you taking material out of context to support a preconceived thesis?

✔ Are you recording the data needed to document your sources in the final paper?

   If you have difficulties locating material, ask your instructor or reference librarian for assistance.

FOR FURTHER READING

Badke, William. *The Survivor's Guide to Library Research.*

Berdie, Douglas R., et al. *Questionnaires: Design and Use.*

Converse, Jean M. *Survey Questions: Handcrafting the Standardized Questionnaire.*

Dillman, Don A. *Mail and Telephone Surveys: The Total Design Method.*

Harmon, Charles. *Using the Internet, Online Services, and CD-ROMs for Writing Research and Term Papers.*

Harnack, Andrew, and Eugene Kleppinger. *Online! A Reference Guide to Using Internet Resources.*

Roth, Audrey J. *The Research Paper: Process, Form, and Content.*

Rubin, Herbert J., and Irene S. Rubin. *Qualitative Interviewing: The Art of Hearing Data.*

Shepherd, Robert D. *Writing Research Papers: Your Complete Guide to the Process of Writing a Research Paper, from Finding a Topic to Preparing the Final Draft.*

Woodward, Jeannette A. *Writing Research Papers: Investigating Resources in Cyberspace.*

E-SOURCES

The Library of Congress
http://www.loc.gov

Reference Desk
http://www.utoronto.ca/writing/advise.html
http://www.acts.twu.ca/lbr/research_essays.htm
http://www.ashland.edu/library/internet/refres.html

A Student's Guide to Research with the WWW
http://www.utm.utoronto.ca/library/instruction/researchinternet.html
http://www.slu.edu/departments/english/research/

Critically Analyzing Information Sources
http://www.library.cornell.edu/olinuris/ref/research/skill26.htm

COMPANION WEBSITE

See **http://www.transcanadawriter.nelson.com** for additional information on conducting research.

Writing the Research Paper

WHAT IS A RESEARCH PAPER?

Research is critical to any kind of writing that seeks to show valid, verifiable evidence for the views that are asserted. Collecting data, assembling quotations, finding evidence, and developing a thesis are essential to laying the groundwork for your research papers in university. Before you plunge into working with sources and making citations, however, it is important to take three preliminary steps:

1. **Review the needs of the assignment.** If you have not examined the instructor's requirements recently, refresh your memory. Study any handouts or notes you may have made.

   ■ Do you fully understand what is expected in terms of topic, content, sources, and format? If you are unsure, talk with your instructor.

   ■ Do your working thesis, sources, and notes fit the scope of the assignment? Should some sources be discarded? Should other avenues of research be pursued?

2. **Take a global look at your sources and notes.** Review the full scope of what your research has revealed. Consider the whole body of evidence you have discovered, including those items you examined but did not select.

   ■ What have you learned about the subject? Have you uncovered information that leads you to further narrow your topic or refine the thesis?

   ■ Do sources contradict or disprove your assumptions? Should you rethink your point of view?

   ■ What do the sources reveal about the state of knowledge about your topic? Is there consensus or conflict? Are there patterns in the evidence?

   ■ How reliable are the sources? Are they based on a careful reading of the subject, thorough research, and controlled experiments, or are they biased and/or do they rely on anecdotal data?

   ■ Are there sources that can be grouped together, such as articles by experts who share the same opinion or similar statistics? Can some sources be considered duplicates?

   ■ Can you prioritize sources? Which are the most important?

3. **Reshape your paper by reviewing your topic, examining the evidence, and refining the working thesis.**

REFINE YOUR THESIS AND DEVELOP AN OUTLINE

After examining your sources, refine the thesis. If you have limited the original topic, you may need to develop a thesis that addresses the new focus of your paper. In writing shorter papers, you may have needed only a brief plan or list of ideas to guide the first draft. But in writing a research paper, it is useful to develop a full outline to organize your ideas and sources.

Working Thesis

Orwell considered contact with nature essential to individual liberty.

Revised Thesis

Winston Smith's humanity and individual autonomy are stunted not only by the brutality of Oceania and the ever-present Thought Police, but by his lack of contact with nature.

Working Outline

A working outline is a rough guide to direct your first draft. Because it is not likely to be read by anyone other than yourself, it does not have to follow any particular format. Use it as a blueprint to organize your main points and sources.

I INTRO—Conventional readings of *1984*
   A Simes quote
   B Wolzheck quote
   C Janeson quote
   D Goodman quote

II Transition/Thesis—Important Role of Nature Overlooked

III Unnatural/Artificial Life in Oceania
   A "Golden Country Dream" quote (*1984* pg. 29)
   B Smith and Julia in nature
   C Nature and sexual passion—(*1984* quote pg. 105)

IV Nature as Orwell's Moral Gold Standard
   A Sandison quote
   B Letter to Henry Miller quote (*Collected Essays* 4:80)

V Orwell's Lack of Faith in Technology
   A Electricity quote (*Road* pg. 84)
   B Bugs quote (*Road* pg. 71)

VI Orwell's Doubts about Progress
   A Pleasure Spots quote (*Collected Essays* 4:80)
   B Radio quote (*Collected Essays* 4:80)

VII Conclusion
   A Sandison quote (pg. 10)
   B Final Point—*1984* relevant for 21st century

Along with an outline, develop a timeline to chart your progress. Make sure you budget enough time for each stage of the writing process, including revising and editing.

Strategies for Developing an Outline

1. **Write a clear thesis statement.** The thesis is the mission statement of your paper. It should provide a clear focus for the paper and direct your first draft.

2. **Write an outline in light of your thesis and the needs of the assignment.** Ensure that your outline addresses the goals of the paper and the instructor's requirements.

3. **Don't expect that your sources will neatly fall into place like pieces of a puzzle.** In many instances, the evidence you find may be fragmentary and lead in different directions. Outline your ideas and observations, weaving into the text those sources that confirm your point of view.

4. **Use sources to support your views; don't simply summarize them.** An outline forms a skeleton or framework for the first draft. Indicate where you will place source material such as quotations, facts, or statistics.

5. **In writing an outline, leave ample space for alterations.** Do not feel obligated to include all the sources you have located.

6. **Label your sources for easy reference.** You may wish to develop a shorthand reference for each source, labelling sources A, B, C, or giving them descriptive names to guide your outline.

7. **Separate longer sources for use in multiple places.** If you have located a long quotation, do not feel obligated to place it in a single block of text. Instead, you may select two or three sections and distribute them throughout the paper.

8. **Design an introduction that announces the topic, sets up the thesis, and prepares readers for the direction of the paper.** Because research papers can be long and complex, it is important to give readers a road map, an explanation of what will follow.

9. **Organize the body by using the modes of organization.** Clear structure plays an important role in making your paper readable and convincing. Without a clear pattern of organization, your paper may become a confusing list of quotations and statistics.

10. **Craft a conclusion that ends the paper on a strong point rather than a simple summary of points.** Although it may be useful to review critical points at the end of a long paper, the conclusion should leave the reader with a memorable fact, quotation, or restatement of the thesis.

WRITING THE RESEARCH PAPER

Your goal in writing the first draft, as in any paper, is to get your ideas on paper. Using outside sources, however, complicates the writing process. Students often make common errors in approaching the evidence they have collected.

Strategies for Using Sources

1. **Avoid simply reporting on what you found.** The quotations, facts, and statistics you have selected should support your point of view. Avoid patching together outside sources with little original commentary or analysis:

   When it first opened on Broadway, Death of a Salesman had a great impact on audiences (Stein, 19). According to Sally Lyman, "The play captured the hidden anxiety coursing through postwar America" (17). Another critic, Timothy Baldwin, stated, "This play made the audience face its greatest fear—growing old" (98). Fred Carlson said that he walked out of the theater shaken and deeply moved (23).

   ■ Although outside sources may be interesting and worth quoting or paraphrasing, your ideas, interpretations, and arguments should form the basis of the paper.

2. **Summarize conflicting opinions.** One of the responsibilities of a researcher is to fairly represent the available body of evidence. If respected authorities disagree, you should explain the nature of the controversy:

   Scientists debate whether this disorder is hereditary. Yale researchers Brown and Smith cite the British twin study as evidence of a genetic link (35–41). However, both the American Medical Association and the National Institutes of Health insist the small numbers of subjects in the twin study do not provide sufficient evidence to support any conclusions (Kendrick 19–24).

3. **Indicate whether sources represent widely held views.** Often you will find that sources present similar views or interpretations. If you find four or five sources that present the same information, you may wish to select the source that is the most thorough, most recent, or best written. You can emphasize the significance of this source by mentioning that its ideas are shared by others:

   Nearly all experts on teenage suicide support Jane Diaz's observation that low self-esteem, stress, and substance abuse are the principal contributing factors to the current rise in adolescent suicide (Smith 28; Johnson 10–15; King 89–92).

4. **Comment on the quality as well as quantity of your sources.** Not all sources have equivalent value. Sources may be inaccurate, biased, or based on limited evidence. If you conduct research on controversial issues or events, you may find little reliable

   (Continued)

material. If you are unable to determine which source is closest to the truth or which study is accurate, inform your readers of the problem you face:

Although the 1908 railroad strike received national attention, few major newspapers offered more than superficial reports. Sensational accounts of lynching, rape, and murder appeared in New York and Chicago tabloids. The radical Torch of Labor *blamed the deaths of two strikers on a plot engineered by Wall Street bankers. The conservative* Daily World *insisted union organizers were bent on overthrowing the government. Most sources, however, do agree that Red Williams played a critical role in organizing a labor protest that ultimately weakened the emerging Transport Workers Union.*

GUIDELINES FOR USING DIRECT QUOTATIONS

Direct quotations give power and authority to your research paper by introducing the words of others just as they were written or stated. But to be effective, direct quotations have to be carefully chosen, accurately presented, and skillfully woven into the text of your paper.

1. **Limit use of direct quotations.** Avoid reproducing long blocks of text, unless direct evidence is essential for accuracy or emphasis. In many instances, you can summarize and paraphrase information.

   - Use direct quotations when they are brief, memorable, and so well stated that that a paraphrase would reduce their impact. Avoid using direct quotations when you can accurately restate the information in a documented paraphrase.
   - Remember, the focus of a research paper is your ideas, observations, and conclusions, not a collection of direct quotations.

2. **Link direct quotations into your commentary.** Avoid isolating quotations:

Faulty:
Television advertising exploded in the Fifties. "Advertising agencies increased spending on television commercials from $10 million in 1948 to $2 billion in 1952" (Smith 16). These revenues financed the rapid development of a new industry.

Revised:
Television advertising exploded in the Fifties. According to Kai Smith, "Advertising agencies increased spending on television commercials from $10 million in 1948 to $2 billion in 1952" (16). These revenues financed the rapid development of a new industry.

3. **Introduce block quotes with a complete sentence followed by colon:**

The Quiz Show Scandal of the 1950s shook public confidence in the new medium. The idea that the highly popular shows were rigged to ensure ratings infuriated and disillusioned the public:

> NBC received thousands of letters and telephone calls from irate viewers who felt cheated. Although the public readily accepted that Westerns and soap operas were fictional, they believed that the teachers and housewives who appeared on shows like "Twenty-One" were "real people" like themselves. Having followed their favorite contestants week after week, loyal viewers strongly identified with people they considered genuine. Learning that all the furrowed brows and lip biting were choreographed, they felt duped. (Brown 23)

4. **Provide background information to establish the value of direct quotations.** Bibliographical entries at the end of your paper may explain a source but do not help readers understand its significance:

Faulty:
President Roosevelt showed signs of declining health as early as 1942. Sheridan noted, "His hands trembled when writing, he complained of headaches, and he often seemed unable to follow the flow of conversation around him" (34–35).

Revised:
President Roosevelt showed signs of declining health as early as 1942. George Sheridan, a young naval aide who briefed the White House during the Battle of Midway, was shocked by the President's condition. Sheridan noted, "His hands trembled when writing, he complained of headaches, and he often seemed unable to follow the flow of conversation around him" (34–35).

5. **Indicate quotations within quotations.** Although most writers try to avoid using direct quotations that appear in another source, sometimes it cannot be avoided. You can easily indicate a quote within a quote with "(qtd. in . . .)."

Original Source:
From Sandra Bert's *The Plague* (page 23)
The medical community of San Francisco was overwhelmed by the sudden increase in AIDS cases in the early 1980s. Tim Watson, a resident at the time, said, "It was like being hit by a tidal wave. We went home every night absolutely stunned by the influx of dying young men."

Research Paper quoting Tim Watson:
Within a few years the number of AIDS cases, especially in the Bay Area, exploded. Physicians were shocked by the rising numbers of patients with untreatable infections. "It was like being hit by a tidal wave," Watson remembered (qtd. in Bert, 23).

6. **Accurately delete unneeded material from quotations.** You can abbreviate long quotations, deleting irrelevant or unimportant details by using ellipsis points (. . .). Three evenly spaced periods indicate words have been deleted from a direct quotation.

Original:
The governor vetoed the education bill, which had been backed by a coalition of taxpayers and unions, because it cut aid to inner city schools.
— JAMES KIRKLAND

Shortened quotation using ellipsis points:

Kirkland reported that "the governor vetoed the education bill . . . because it cut aid to inner city schools."

- Use a period and three ellipsis points (four dots. . . .) to indicate deletion of one or more full sentences.
- Avoid making deletions that distort the original meaning. Do not eliminate qualifying statements.

Original:
Given the gang wars, the failure of treatment programs, the rising number of addicts, I regretfully think we should legalize drugs until we can find better solutions to the problem.
— MAYOR WELLS

Improper use of ellipsis points:

At a recent press conference, Mayor Wells stated, "I . . . think we should legalize drugs . . ."

7. **Use square brackets to insert words or indicate alterations.** In some instances, you may have to insert a word to prevent confusion or a grammatical error.

Original:
Poe, Whitman, and Ginsburg are among some of America's greatest poets.
— JOHN DEMMER

Brackets enclose altered verb:

> Demmer states that "Poe . . . [is] among some of America's greatest poets."

Strategies for Citing Sources

Many students find citing sources one of the challenging aspects of writing a research paper. Mastering the details of accounting for each source can be frustrating. It is important to understand that documenting where you obtained information for your paper serves three key purposes:

1. **Citations prevent allegations of plagiarism.** Plagiarism occurs when you present the facts, words, or ideas of someone else as your own. Students often find it difficult to believe that copying something out of *The World Book* for a term paper can be considered a crime, but plagiarism has serious consequences. In many universities students who submit a plagiarized paper will automatically fail the course. In some schools, students will be expelled. Outside academics, plagiarism (often called "copyright infringement") has ruined the careers of politicians, artists, and executives. Prominent columnists and reporters have been fired from newspapers and magazines for using the ideas of others without acknowledging their original source. Hollywood studios have been sued by artists who claim ideas from their rejected screenplays were used in other films.

   - Accurate documentation protects you from plagiarism by clearly labelling borrowed ideas.

2. **Citations support your thesis.** Attorneys arguing a case before a judge or jury present labelled exhibits to prove their theory of a case. As a researcher, you support your thesis by introducing expert testimony, facts, case histories, and eyewitness accounts. Like an attorney, you have to clearly identify the source for evidence for it to be credible. A paper about crime that draws upon statistics from the RCMP and studies from the attorney general will be more credible than one relying only on personal websites, blogs, and opinions.

   - The more controversial your thesis, the more readers will demand supporting evidence.

3. **Citations refer readers to other sources.** Citations not only illustrate which ideas originated with the writer and which were drawn from other sources, but also alert readers where they can find more information. Through your citations, readers may learn of a biography or a website offering additional evidence.

Exceptions to Citing Sources

You do not need to use citations for every fact, quotation, or idea you present in your paper:

1. **Common expressions or famous quotations.** Famous sayings by such people as Shakespeare, Jesus, or Benjamin Franklin (for example, "To err is human" or "I am the

resurrection") do not have to be cited, even when presented as direct quotations. If you are unsure, ask your instructor.

2. **Facts considered in the "realm of common knowledge."** You do not have to provide a citation if you referred to a source to check a fact that is readily available in numerous sources. No one will accuse you of stealing facts that are commonly known and not subject to change or interpretation.

In almost every other instance, however, you have to acknowledge the use of outside material:

1. **Direct quotations.** Whenever you quote a source word for word, you must place it in quotation marks and cite its source.

2. **Indirect quotations or paraphrases.** Even if you do not copy a source but state the author's ideas in your own words, you must cite the source. Changing a few words or condensing a page of text into a few sentences does not alter the fact that you are using someone else's ideas.

3. **Specific facts, statistics, and numbers.** Data will be credible and acceptable only if you present the source. If you state, "Last year 54,450 drunk drivers were arrested in California," readers will naturally wonder where you obtained that number. Statistics make credible evidence only if readers trust their source.

4. **Figures, tables, and other visual aids.** Indicate the source of any graphic you reproduce.

You must also cite the source for information you use to create a visual display.

Strategies for Revising and Editing Research Papers

1. **Review the assignment, thesis, and working outline.**
2. **Examine your draft for use of sources.**
   - Does the draft fulfill the needs of the assignment?
   - Does the text support the thesis?
   - Is the thesis properly placed?
   - Are enough sources presented?
   - Is there any evidence that should be included or deleted?
   - Do you provide enough original commentary, or is your paper merely a collection of facts and quotations?
3. **Read the draft.**
   - Does the paper have an even style and tone? Are there awkward transitions between sources and your commentary?
4. **Revise the introduction and conclusion.**
5. **Edit for mechanical and spelling errors.** Ensure your paper follows the appropriate style for documenting sources.

DOCUMENTATION STYLES

Writers document their use of outside sources with one of several methods. The MLA and APA formats are commonly used in the humanities and social sciences. Both methods provide guidelines for placing parenthetical notes after quoting or paraphrasing outside sources and listing them at the end of the paper. Many textbooks suggest recording each source on a note card so they can be easily shuffled and placed in alphabetical order. If you are writing on a computer, you may find it easier to scroll down and enter each source as you refer to it.

The MLA Style

The MLA style, created by the Modern Language Association, is used in language and literature courses. Parenthetical notes listing the author or title and page numbers are inserted after quotations and paraphrases. At the end of the paper all the sources are alphabetized on a "Works Cited" page. For full details about using the MLA style, consult Joseph Gibaldi's *MLA Style Manual and Guide to Scholarly Publishing*, second edition; *MLA Handbook for Writers of Research Papers*, sixth edition; or the MLA website (http://www.mla.org/style).

Strategies for Writing Parenthetical Notes

Parenthetical notes usually include an author's last name and a page number. If no author is listed, titles—sometimes abbreviated—are used. To keep the notes as brief as possible, the MLA format does not precede page numbers with *p.*, *pp.*, or commas. The parenthetical note is considered part of the sentence and comes before the final mark of punctuation. Notes should be placed as close to the source as possible without interrupting the flow of the text.

1. **Parenthetical notes include author and page number.** A direct quotation from Ralph Ellison's novel *Invisible Man* is indicated with a parenthetical note placed after it:

   The novel's unnamed character calls himself invisible because society does not recognize him as a human being. He defends his retreat from society, realizing that many would view his decision as a sign of irresponsibility. "Responsibility," he argues, "rests on recognition, and recognition is a form of agreement" (Ellison 14).

2. **Parenthetical notes include only page numbers if the author is clearly identified in the text:**

   Sheila Smitherin praised Ellison's novel, stating that modern black literature "was born on the pages of Invisible Man" (32).

(Continued)

3. **If two or more sources are cited within a sentence, notes are inserted after the material that is quoted or paraphrased:**

Smith stated that the novel "exposed the deep-rooted racism society was unwilling to confront" (34), leading one columnist to argue that the book should be taught in every high school (Wilson 12–13).

4. **Long quotations are indented ten spaces without quotation marks, and double-spaced:**

The Group Theater revolutionized American drama. According to Frank Kozol, the members tried to create something then unseen on the New York stage:

> *Clurmanans and his followers wanted to develop a new kind of theater. They not only wanted to produce new, socially relevant plays, but create a new relationship between playwright and cast. It would be a collective effort. Designed to be a theater without stars, actors lived together and shared living expenses. They were infused with the revolutionary spirit of the times. The Group Theater soon launched the career of Clifford Odets, whose plays were among the most poignant depictions of life during the Great Depression. (Taylor 34–35)*

Notice that the parenthetical note appears outside the final punctuation of the last sentence.

Strategies for Writing a Works Cited Page

List all sources you have cited on a separate sheet at the end of your paper, titled "Works Cited." If you include works you have read for background but have not actually cited, title the page "Works Consulted."

NOTE: MLA style underlines titles of books and periodicals rather than placing them in italics (<u>Time</u> magazine not Time magazine) and places carets around website URLs (<www.cnn.com>).

■ Arrange the list of works alphabetically by the author's last name or first significant word of the title if no author is listed:

Jones, Wilson. <u>Chicago Today</u>. New York: Putnam, 2002.

"A New Look for Toronto." <u>Toronto Magazine</u> Fall 2003: 21.

- For sources with more than one author, alphabetize by the first author's last name:

  Zinter, Mary, and Jan Ames. <u>First Aid</u>. New York: Dial, 2002.

- Begin each citation even with the left margin, and indent subsequent lines five spaces. Double-space the entire page. Do not separate entries with additional spaces:

  Abrams, Jane. "Rebuilding America's Cities." <u>Plain Dealer</u> [Cleveland] 21 Jan.

     2002: 12.

  Brown, Gerald. The Death of the Central City: The Malling of America. New York:

     Macmillan, 2003.

- If more than one source is used for an author, alphabetize the works but list the author's last name only once, substituting three hyphens for the name in subsequent citations:

  Keller, Joseph. <u>Assessing Blame</u>. New York: Columbia UP, 2003.

  ---. <u>Quality Control</u>. New York: Miller, 2000.

GUIDELINES FOR LISTING SOURCES IN WORKS CITED AND PARENTHETICAL NOTES

Books

1. Write the author's last name, first name, then any initial. Copy the name as written on the title page. "C. W. Brown" would appear as:

   Brown, C. W.

   Omit any degrees or titles such as Ph.D. or Dr.

2. State the full title of the book. Place a colon between the main heading and any sub-title. Underline all the words and punctuation in the title, except for the final period.

   Brown, C. W. <u>Sharks and Lambs: Wall Street in the Nineties</u>.

3. Record the city of publication, publisher, and date of publication. If the book lists several cities, use only the first. If the city is outside Canada or the United States, add an abbreviation for the country. If a city is unfamiliar, include an abbreviation for the province or state. Record the main words of the publisher, deleting words like "publishing" or "press" (Monroe for Monroe Publishing Company). Use the initials "UP" for "University Press." End the citation with the last year of publication.

Works Cited Entry:

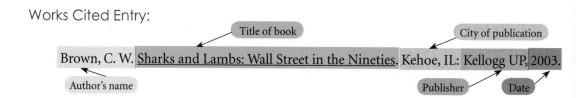

Brown, C. W. Sharks and Lambs: Wall Street in the Nineties. Kehoe, IL: Kellogg UP, 2003.

Book with Two or Three Authors

Works Cited Entry:

> Smith, David, John Adams, and Chris Cook. <u>Writing On-line</u>. New York: Macmillan,
>
> 2000.

Parenthetical Note:

> (Smith, Adams, and Cook 23–24)

Book with Four or More Authors

Works Cited Entry:

> Chavez, Nancy, et al. <u>Mexico Today</u>. New York: Putnam, 2003.

Parenthetical Note:

> (Chavez et al. 87)

Book with Corporate Author

Works Cited Entry:

> National Broadcasting Company. <u>Programming Standards</u>. New York: National
>
> Broadcasting Company, 2002.

Parenthetical Note:

> (National Broadcasting Company 112)

To avoid a cumbersome parenthetical note, you can mention the author or title in the text:

> According to the National Broadcasting Company's <u>Programming Standards</u>,
>
> "No single executive should be able to cancel a program" (214).

Book with Unnamed Authors

Works Cited Entry:

New Yale Atlas. New York: Random House, 2003.

Parenthetical Note:

(New Yale 106)

Book with Multiple Volumes

Works Cited Entry:

Eisenhower, Dwight. Presidential Correspondence. Vol. 2. New York: Dutton, 1960.

6 vols.

Parenthetical Note:

(Eisenhower 77)

If you cite more than one volume in your paper, indicate the number:

(Eisenhower 2: 77)

Book in Second or Later Edition

Works Cited Entry:

Franklin, Marcia. Modern France. 3rd ed. Philadelphia: Comstock, 1987.

Parenthetical Note:

(Franklin 12)

Work in an Anthology

Works Cited Entry:

Ford, John M. "Preflash." The Year's Best Fantasy. Ed. Ellen Datlow and Terri

Windling. New York: St. Martin's, 1989. 65–82.

Parenthetical Note:

(Ford 65–66)

Note: If you include more than one work from the same anthology, list the anthology in the Works Cited section separately under the editors' names and list individual entries in a shortened form:

Ford, John M. "Preflash." Datlow and Windling 265–82.

Book in Translation

Works Cited Entry:

Verne, Jules. <u>Twenty Thousand Leagues Under the Sea</u>. Trans. Michel Michot.

Boston: Pitman, 1992.

Parenthetical Note:

(Verne 65)

Book with Editor or Editors

Works Cited Entry:

Benson, Nancy, ed. <u>Ten Great American Plays</u>. New York: Columbia UP, 2002.

Parenthetical Note:

(Benson 23)

The preceding parenthetical note would be used to cite Benson's comments.

Book with Author and Editor

Works Cited Entry:

Gissing, George. <u>Workers in the Dawn</u>. Ed. Jason Day. London: Oxford UP, 1982.

Parenthetical Note:

(Gissing 78)

Book in a Series

Works Cited Entry:

Swessel, Karyn, ed. <u>Northern Ireland Today</u>. Modern Europe Ser. 3. New York:

Wilson, 2003.

Parenthetical Note:

(Swessel 34)

Republished Book

Works Cited Entry:

Smith, Jane. <u>The Jersey Devil</u>. 1922. New York: Warner, 2002.

Parenthetical Note:

(Smith 23–25)

Periodicals

Newspaper Article

Works Cited Entry:

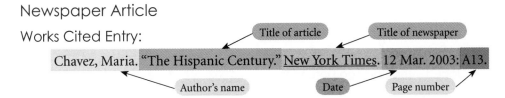

Parenthetical Note:

(Chavez)

Note: If an article has only one page, page numbers are not included in parenthetical notes.

Magazine Article

Works Cited Entry:

Janssen, Mary. "Iran Today." <u>Time</u> 25 Mar. 2003: 341.

Note: If an article appears on nonconsecutive pages, list the first page followed by a "+" sign.

Parenthetical Note:

(Janssen 38)

Scholarly Article

Works Cited Entry:

Grant, Edward. "The Hollywood Ten: Fighting the Blacklist." <u>California Film</u>

<u>Quarterly</u> 92.2 (2002): 14–32.

Parenthetical Note:

(Grant 21–23)

Newspaper or Magazine Article with Unnamed Author

Works Cited Entry:

"The Legacy of the Gulf War." <u>American History</u> 12 Mar. 2003: 23–41.

Parenthetical Note:

("Legacy" 25)

Letter to the Editor

Works Cited Entry:

Roper, Jack. Letter. <u>Chicago Defender</u> 12 Jan. 2002, sec. B: 12.

Parenthetical Note:

(Roper)

Other Print Sources

Encyclopedia Article with Author

Works Cited Entry:

Keller, Christopher. "Lisbon." <u>World Book Encyclopedia</u>. 2003.

Entry · *Title of encyclopedia* · *Date* · *Author's name*

Note: Provide edition number if given.

Parenthetical Note:

(Keller)

Note: Page numbers are not used with works in which articles are arranged alphabetically.

Encyclopedia Article with Unnamed Author

Works Cited Entry:

"Lisbon." *Columbia Illustrated Encyclopedia*. 2002.

Parenthetical Note:

("Lisbon")

Pamphlet with Author

Works Cited Entry:

Tindall, Gordon, ed. <u>Guide to New York Churches</u>. New York: Chamber of

Commerce, 1998.

Parenthetical Note:

> (Tindall 76–78)

Pamphlet with Unnamed Author

Works Cited Entry:

> <u>Guide to New York Museums</u>. New York: Columbia University, 2003.

Parenthetical Note:

> (<u>Guide</u> 176–82)

The Bible

Works Cited Entry:

> <u>Holy Bible</u>. New International Version. Grand Rapids, MI: Zondervan, 1988.

Note: Titles of sacred texts are not underlined, unless they are specific editions.

Parenthetical Note:

> (Mark 2: 4–9)

Nonprint Sources

Motion Picture

Works Cited Entry:

Note: You may wish to include names of performers, directors, or screenwriters if they are of special interest to readers. These names should be inserted between the title and the distributor.

Television Program

Works Cited Entry:

> "The Long Goodbye." <u>Law and Order</u>. Dir. Jane Hong. Writ. Peter Wren. Perf. Rita
>
>   Colletti, Diane Nezgod, and Vicki Shimi. NBC. WTMJ, Milwaukee. 12 May 2005.

Videotape or DVD

Works Cited Entry:

> <u>Colonial Williamsburg</u>. Compiled by Janet Freud. American Home Video, 1996.

Live Performance of a Play

Works Cited Entry:

<u>All My Sons</u>. By Arthur Miller. Dir. Anita Dayin. Lyric Theater, New York. 10 May 2006.

Speech

Works Cited Entry:

Goode, Wilmont. "America in the Next Century." Chicago Press Club. 12 Oct.

2003.

Personal or Telephone Interview

Works Cited Entry:

Weston, Thomas. Personal interview. 21 May 2006.

In the preceding citation, you would substitute "Telephone" for "Personal" if the interview was conducted by telephone.

Parenthetical Notes for Nonprint Sources

Because nonprint sources do not have page numbers and often have long titles, parenthetical notes can be cumbersome. Most writers avoid inserting citations by mentioning the source within the text:

Multiple personality disorder was featured in a recent episode of <u>Law and Order</u>.

In <u>Gone With the Wind</u> special effects were used to re-create the burning of

Atlanta.

Interviewed in the fall of 2003, Laura Dornan suggested that many critics failed

to see the feminist theme in her play.

Electronic Sources

Web Pages

Web pages vary greatly. In general, include the name of the person or organization that created the site, author (if listed), the title (if there is not a title, you can use a description, such as the one used in the next entry), the date of creation or most recent update, the date of access, and the URL. For a website with a particularly long URL, you may specify the URL of the site's search page, if available, or the sequence of links that took you to the page you cite.

Works Cited Entry:

> Chicago Irish Center. Home page. 5 Apr. 2003. 10 May 2006 <http://www.chi.irish
>
> .cent.org>.

Electronic Journal Article

Works Cited Entry:

> Smith, Perry. "Truman Capote and Kansas." <u>Phoenix</u> 2.7 (2003). 15 Mar. 2006
>
> <http:// www.englishlit.com/hts/phoenix/index>.

Online Newspaper Article

Works Cited Entry:

> "<u>Long Day's Journey into Night</u> Production Disappointing." <u>New York Times on</u>
>
> <u>the Web</u> 17 Mar. 2003. 22 Apr. 2005 <http://www.nytimes.com/aponline/
>
> a/ap-play.html>.

Reference Database

Works Cited Entry:

> <u>The Emerald Project: Irish Literature from 1500–2000</u>. 2000 Boston University.
>
> 21 Oct. 2005 <http://www/bostonuniv/emerald/>.

Electronic Texts

Many books are available online. Because they lack page numbers, mention the title within the text to avoid long parenthetical notes.

Works Cited Entry:

> Gissing, George. <u>Demos</u>. London, 1892. <u>The Online Books Page</u>. Ed. Charles
>
> Aldarondo. Jan. 2002. Project Gutenberg Literary Archive Foundation.
>
> 5 Mar. 2006 <http://www.gutenberg.org/dirs/etext03/demos10.txt>

CD-ROM

Works Cited Entry:

> "Understanding <u>Macbeth</u>." <u>Master Dramas</u>. CD-ROM. New York: Educational
>
> Media, 2002.

E-mail

Works Cited Entry:

Ballard, Morton D. "Rental Cars." E-mail to Germaine Reinhardt. 21 May 2005.

Discussion Group Posting

Works Cited Entry:

Humphrey, Doug. "US Radar Coverage." Online posting. 1 Nov. 2005.

Coldwarcomms. 15 Mar. 2006 <http://groups.yahoo.com/group/

coldwarcomms/message/9306>.

Synchronous Communication

To cite a posting from forums such as MOO, MUD, or IRC, include names of speakers, a description of the event, the date, the name of the forum, date of access, and telnet address.

Works Cited Entry:

Gladkin, Dorcas. Melville discussion of "Biblical Symbolism in Moby Dick." 19 Oct.

2004. MediaMOO. 1 Nov. 2005 <telnet://www.litcafe/homepages/smith/

melville.html>.

Linked Sources

MLA does not provide a method of citing hypertext links, but the following format allows readers to follow your search:

Works Cited Entry:

Laskowski, Edward. "BMI: Is It Accurate for Weightlifters?" Nov. 15, 2005. Mayo

Foundation for Medical Education and Research. 14 Dec. 2005 <http://www

.mayoclinic.com>. Path: Ask a Specialist; Fitness.

Visuals

Table, Graph, Chart, or Map

Works Cited Entry:

Carlino's Sales. Table. "From Hoboken to Hollywood." The New Yorker 25 May

2006: 21.

Parenthetical Notes:

Visuals are numbered and captioned:

George Carlino was one of many writers in the Nineties who abandoned writing

highly acclaimed but little-read novels to writing lucrative screenplays (see Table 1).

Year	Novel	Publisher's Advance	Movie Rights
1992	Jersey Angel	$10,000	$25,000
1995	Bronxman	$15,000	$100,000
1997	Talk Radio	$18,000	$750,000
1999	Screenplay for Walker's Point		$1.2 million

Table 1. Carlino's Sales. "From Hoboken to Hollywood." The New Yorker 25 May

2006: 21.

Advertisement

General Motors. Advertisement. Time 15 Dec. 2005: 12.

Photograph

Include the photographer or original source, title or description, and year, and information about the book, newspaper, or online source of the image. Avoid long parenthetical notes by referring to the image within the text and its number:

The most famous photograph of World War II was Joe Rosenthal's shot of the flag

raising on Iwo Jima (see Figure 10).

Works Cited Entry:

Joe Rosenthal. Marines Raising American Flag on Iwo Jima. 1945. Corbis. 12 Feb.

2006. <http://pro.corbis.com/>.

APA STYLE

Most courses in the social sciences, including anthropology, education, political science, psychology, and sociology, follow the rules for documentation created by the American Psychological Association. For full details, consult the American Psychological Association's *Publication Manual of the American Psychological Association, Fifth Edition.*

Strategies for Writing Parenthetical Notes

In APA documentation parenthetical notes are placed after material requiring documentation, and all sources are recorded in a reference list at the end of the paper.

1. **Parenthetical notes include author, year of publication, and, for direct quotes, page numbers.** Most sources are identified by the author's name and the year of publication. Page numbers are usually omitted from paraphrases but are always included in direct quotations. The information may be placed in a single note or distributed throughout the text:

   Smith (2003) suggested that multiple personality disorder was more common

   than previously reported.

   It has been suggested that multiple personality disorder is more common than

   previously believed (Smith, 2003).

   Based on recent studies, Smith (2003) asserts that "multiple personality disorder

   is more common than previously reported" (p. 321).

2. **Multiple parenthetical notes indicate more than one source.** If two or more sources are cited within a sentence, notes are inserted after the material quoted or paraphrased:

   Johnson (2002) stated that the study "revealed that Chicago schools were

   adequately staffed" (p. 43), leading Renfro (2003) to reject the teachers' union

   proposal.

3. **For the first text reference, list up to five authors' names:**

   Johnson, Hyman, Torque, and Kaiser (2003) observed that computers enhance

   student performance.

   Note: With multiple authors in a parenthetical citation, use an ampersand (&):

   (Johnson, Hyman, Torque, & Kaiser, 2003)

4. **For the first reference of a citation with six or more authors, list the first author's name and "et al." (and others):**

   Johnson et al. (2003) examined computer education in Chicago, New York,

   El Paso, and Philadelphia.

5. **List corporate and group authors in full initially; then abbreviate:**

   Computers are valuable in teaching higher mathematics (Modern Education Council [MEC], 2002). Textbook publishers now include online support for individual tutoring (MEC, 2002).

6. **Assign letters (a, b, c) to indicate use of more than one work by an author with same year of publication:**

   Kozik studied students in Chicago bilingual classes (2002a) and later reviewed the performance of an English immersion program in San Diego (2002b).

7. **Alphabetize multiple sources and separate with a semicolon:**

   Several reports suggest that noise pollution can directly contribute to hypertension (Jones, 1997; Smith, 2002).

8. **Websites can be mentioned within the text:**

   Chinese educators have attempted to expand Internet access for university students, particularly in the fields of engineering and medicine. Their efforts can be documented by examining Peking University's website at http://www.upkng.eng.edu.

Strategies for Writing a References Page

List all the sources you have cited on a separate sheet at the end of your paper titled "References" (centre the word References and do not italicize it or place it in quotation marks). If you include works you have read for background but not actually cited, title the page "Bibliography."

1. **Arrange the list of works alphabetically by authors' or editors' last names, followed by initials.** If no authors are listed, alphabetize by the first significant word of the title:

   Jones, W. (2002). *Chicago today*. New York: Putnam.

   A new look for Toronto. (2003, Fall). *Toronto Magazine*, 21.

2. **For sources with more than one author, alphabetize by the first author's last name and list subsequent authors by last names and initials:**

   Zinter, M., & Ames, J. (2002). *First aid*. New York: Dial.

(Continued)

3. **Begin each citation even with the left margin, then indent subsequent lines five spaces. Double-space the entire page. Do not separate entries with additional spaces:**

Abrams, J. (2002, January 21). Rebuilding America's cities. *Cleveland Plain Dealer*,

pp. 1, 7, 8.

Brown, G. (2003). *The death of the central city: The malling of America*. New

York: Macmillan.

4. **If more than one source from a given author is used, list the works in chronological order and repeat the author's name:**

Brown, G. (2000). *Hope for renewal*. New York: Putnam.

Brown, G. (2003). *The death of the central city: The malling of America*. New

York: Macmillan.

GUIDELINES FOR LISTING SOURCES IN REFERENCES AND PARENTHETICAL NOTES

Books

1. Write the author's last name, first and subsequent initials:

   Brown, C. W.

2. Place the year of publication in parentheses, followed by a period and one space:

   Brown, C. W. (2003).

3. Italicize the full title of the book. Place a colon between the main heading and any subtitle. Capitalize only the first word in the title and any subtitle and any proper nouns or adjectives within the title:

   Brown, C. W. (2003). *Sharks and lambs: Wall Street in the nineties.*

4. Record the city of publication and publisher.

   Brown, C. W. (2003). *Sharks and lambs: Wall Street in the nineties.* New York:

   Kellogg Press.

Note: Do not shorten or abbreviate words like "University" or "Press."

Parenthetical Notes:

> Brown (2003) stated . . .
>
> (Brown, 2003)
>
> (Brown, 2003, pp. 23–25)

Book with Two or Three Authors

References Entry:

> Hutcheon, Linda, and Michael Hutcheon. Bodily Charm: Living Opera. Lincoln:
>
> U of Nebraska P, 2000.

Parenthetical Notes:

> First note:
>
> Smith, Johnson, and Cook (1989) stated . . .
>
> Subsequent notes:
>
> Smith et al. (1989) revealed . . .
>
> First note:
>
> (Smith, Johnson, & Cook, 1989)
>
> Subsequent notes:
>
> (Smith et al., 1989)

Book with Corporate Author

References Entry:

> National Broadcasting Company. (2002). *Programming standards.* New York:
>
> National Broadcasting Company.

Parenthetical Notes:

> According to the National Broadcasting Company's *Programming Standards*
>
> (2002), "No single executive should be able to cancel a program" (p. 214).
>
> (National Broadcasting Company [NBC], 2002, p. 214)

Book with Unnamed Author

References Entry:

> *New Yale atlas.* (2003). New York: Random House.

Parenthetical Notes:

> According to the *New Yale atlas* (2003) . . . (p. 106).
>
> (*New Yale atlas,* 2003, p. 106)

Book with Multiple Volumes

References Entry:

> Eisenhower, D. (1960). *Presidential correspondence.* (Vol. 2). New York: Dutton Books.

Parenthetical Notes:

> Eisenhower (1960) predicted . . . (p. 77).
>
> (Eisenhower, 1960, p. 77)

Book in Second or Later Edition

References Entry:

> Franklin, M. (1987). *Modern France* (3rd ed.). Philadelphia: Comstock Press.

Parenthetical Notes:

> Franklin (1987) stated . . . (p. 12).
>
> (Franklin, 1987, p. 12)

Book in Translation

References Entry:

> Verne, J. (1992). *Twenty thousand leagues under the sea* (M. Michot, Trans.).
>
> Boston: Pitman Press.

Parenthetical Notes:

> Verne (1992) . . . (p. 65)
>
> (Verne, 1992, p. 65)

Book with Editor or Editors

References Entry:

> Benson, N. (Ed.). (2002). *The absent parent.* New York: Columbia House.

Parenthetical Notes:

> According to Benson (2002) . . . (p. 212).
>
> (Benson, 2002, p. 212)

Book with Author and Editor

References Entry:

> Gissing, G. (1982). *Workers in the dawn* (J. Day, Ed.). London: Oxford University Press.

Parenthetical Note:

> (Gissing, 1982, p. 78)

Republished Book

References Entry:

> Smith, J. (2002). *The Jersey devil*. New York: Warner Books. (Original work published
>
> 1922).

Parenthetical Notes:

> Smith (2002) observes . . . (pp.12–13).
>
> (Smith, 2002, pp. 12–13)

Periodicals

Newspaper Article

References Entry:

> Chavez, M. (2002, August 15). The Hispanic century. *New York Times,* pp. 2A, 8–9A.
>
> Note: List all page numbers, separated by commas.

Parenthetical Notes:

> Chavez (2002) states . . . (p. 8A)
>
> (Chavez, 2002, p. 8A)

Magazine Article

References Entry:

> Janssen, M. (1997, January/February). Iran today. *Foreign Affairs, 64,* 78–88.

Parenthetical Notes:

> Janssen (1997) notes . . . (pp. 80–82)
>
> (Janssen, 1997, pp. 80–82)

Scholarly Article

References Entry:

> Grant, E. (2002). The Hollywood ten: Fighting the blacklist. *California Film*
>
>   Quarterly, 92, 112–25.

Parenthetical Notes:

> Grant (2002) observes . . . (pp. 121–23).
>
> (Grant, 2002, pp. 121–23)

Newspaper or Magazine Article with Unnamed Author

References Entry:

> The legacy of the Gulf War. (2000, October). *American History, 48,* 23–41.

Parenthetical Notes:

> In "The Legacy of the Gulf War" (2000) . . .
>
> ("Legacy," 2000, pp. 22–24)
>
> Note: For parenthetical notes, use shortened titles in quotation marks.

Letter to the Editor

References Entry:

> Roper, J. (1997, June 12). [Letter to the editor]. *Chicago Defender,* p. B12.

Parenthetical Notes:

> According to Roper (1997) . . . (p. B12).
>
> (Roper, 1997, p. B12)

Other Print Sources

Encyclopedia Article

References Entry:

> Keller, C. (2003). Lisbon. *In Encyclopedia of Europe.* New York: Wiley.

Parenthetical Notes:

> Keller (2003) reports . . . (p. 232).
>
> (Keller, 2003, p. 232)

Encyclopedia Article with Unnamed Author

References Entry:

Lisbon. (2002). In *Columbia illustrated encyclopedia.* New York: Columbia.

Parenthetical Notes:

In "Lisbon" (2002) . . . (p. 156).

("Lisbon," 2002, p. 156)

Pamphlet

References Entry:

Tindall, G. (Ed.). (2002). *Guide to New York churches.* New York: New York Chamber of Commerce.

Parenthetical Notes:

Tindall (2002) noted . . . (pp. 34–36).

(Tindall, 2002, pp. 34–36)

Nonprint Sources

Motion Picture

References Entry:

Scorsese, M. (Director). (1995). *Casino* [Motion picture]. United States: Universal.

Parenthetical Notes:

Scorsese (1995) depicts . . .

(Scorsese, 1995)

Television Program

References Entry:

Hong, J. (Producer). (1997, May 12). *Women at work.* [Television broadcast]. New York: Public Broadcasting System.

Parenthetical Notes:

According to Hong (1997) . . .

(Hong, 1997)

Videotape

References Entry:

> Freud, J. (Producer), & Johnson, K. (Director). (1996). [Video]. *Colonial Williamsburg.*
>
> New York: American Home Video.

Parenthetical Notes:

> Freud and Johnson (1996) . . .
>
> (Freud & Johnson, 1996)

Speech

References Entry:

> Goode, W. (2003, October 12). *America in the next century.* Address before the
>
> Chicago Press Club, Chicago, IL.

Parenthetical Notes:

> According to Goode (2003) . . .
>
> (Goode, 2003)

Electronic Sources

Web Pages

References Entry:

> Regis, T. (2003, January 5). Developing distance learning. [Electronic version]. *Regis.*
>
> Retrieved October 27, 2005, from http://regis.devel/home/distlearng/toc.html.

Parenthetical Notes:

> Regis (2003) suggests . . .
>
> (Regis, 2003)

Electronic Journal Article

References Entry:

> Smith, P. (2002, March 2). Help for homeless promised. *Psychology Journal* [Online
>
> serial]. Retrieved January 25, 2006, from http://www.psychojourn./hts/index.

Note: Because the content of websites can change, it is important to list the date you retrieved the information.

Parenthetical Notes:

According to Smith (2002) . . .

(Smith, 2002)

Online Newspaper Article

References Entry:

Gulf war syndrome: Diagnostic survey reveals dangerous trend. (2003, March 11).

New York Times. Retrieved December 15, 2005, from http://www.nytimes

.com/aponline/ap-gulf.html.

Parenthetical Notes:

In "Gulf War" (2003) . . .

("Gulf War," 2003)

Database

References Entry:

Criminal Justice Network. (2002). *Capital cases and defense funding.* Retrieved

June 23, 2005, from freenet.crimjus.ca. login as guest, go index (2005,

June 23).

Parenthetical Notes:

According to Capital Cases (2002) . . .

("Capital Cases," 2002)

Electronic Texts

References Entry:

Weston, T. (1989). *The electronic teacher.* The Education Server at Columbia

University. Retrieved May 25, 2005, from http://www.edserv.edu/index.html.

Parenthetical Notes:

Weston (1989) points out . . .

(Weston, 1989)

CD-ROM

References Entry:

MedNet, Inc. (2002). *Directory of mental disorders* [CD-ROM]. New York: MedNet.

Parenthetical Notes:

MedNet (2002) states . . .

(MedNet, 2002)

E-mail

Because e-mail is not recorded in archives and not available to other researchers, it is mentioned in the text but often not included in the list of references. It can be listed if the contents are of scholarly interest:

References Entry:

Medhin, L. <lmedhin@tat.interport.net>. (2006, March 1).

Budget request [Office e-mail]. (2006, April 2).

Parenthetical Notes:

Medhin (2006) suggests . . .

(Medhin, 2006)

If you do not list an e-mail source in the References, treat it as a personal communication— mentioned in the text only, as follows.

Parenthetical Notes:

Medhin (personal communication, March 1, 2006) suggested . . .

Medhin (personal communication, March 1, 2006).

Synchronous Communication

To cite a posting from forums such as MOO, MUD, or IRC, include names of speakers, a description of the event, the date, the name of the forum, date of retrieval and telnet address:

References Entry:

Goring, D. (2003, May 12). Seminar discussion on alcoholism. Retrieved June 5,

2005, from telnet://www.drugabuse.parc.edu:8888.

Parenthetical Notes:

Goring (2003) indicates . . .

(Goring, 2003)

Linked Sources

References Entry:

> Trainer, L. The education of women. Lkd. *Education Today,* at Columbia Network.
>
> > Retrieved May 10, 2005, from http://www.colwork.net/.

Parenthetical Notes:

> Trainer (2002) . . .
>
> (Trainer, 2002)

Visuals

Table, Map, or Chart

References Entry:

> *New Jersey* [Map]. (2006) Trenton, NJ: Garden State Tourism.

Photograph

References Entry:

> Jane Mathers. *Fire sweeps downtown.* [Photograph]. Retrieved March 21, 2006,
>
> > from http://www.suntimes.com/images/fire/Mar06/index/html

Number visuals and add caption crediting the original author or source and copyright holder:

> *Figure 1.* Fire Sweeps Downtown.
>
> *Note:* Retrieved from http://www.suntimes.com/images/fire/Mar06/index/html

---

✔ RESEARCH PAPER **CHECKLIST**

Before submitting your research paper, review these questions:

- ✔ Does your research paper have a clearly stated thesis?
- ✔ Do you provide sufficient evidence to support your thesis?
- ✔ Does the paper focus on your ideas and commentary or does it only summarize other sources?
- ✔ Do you comment on the quantity and quality of the evidence you have found?
- ✔ Does the opening introduce the subject, present the thesis, or explain your research method?
- ✔ Does the conclusion end the paper on a strong point?

(Continued)

✔ Does the paper follow the appropriate style for citing sources?

✔ Questions for your instructor:

- Is my topic acceptable?
- How many sources do I need?
- Does my paper need an outline?
- Which documentation style is required?

FOR FURTHER READING

American Chemical Society. *The ACS Style Guide: A Manual for Authors and Editors.*

American Institute of Physics. *AIP Manual of Style.*

American Medical Association. *American Medical Association Manual of Style.*

American Psychological Association. *Publication Manual of the American Psychological Association.*

University of Chicago Press. *The Chicago Manual of Style.*

Council of Science Editors. *Scientific Style and Format: The CBE Manual for Authors, Editors, and Publishers* (note: A 7th edition will be published soon).

Gibaldi, Joseph. *MLA Style Manual.*

Hacker, Diana. *Research and Documentation in the Electronic Age.*

Harvard Law Review. *The Bluebook: A Uniform System of Citation.*

Lester, James D. *Writing Research Papers: A Complete Guide.*

Meyer, Michael. *The Little, Brown Guide to Writing Research Papers.*

Turabian, Kate. *A Manual for Writers of Term Papers, Theses, and Dissertations.*

Veit, Richard. *Research: The Student's Guide to Writing Research Papers.*

Walker, Melissa. *Writing Research Papers: A Norton Guide.*

E-SOURCES

MLA Style Frequently Asked Questions
http://www.utoronto.ca/writing/advise.html#style
http://www.mla.org/style_faq

Using Modern Language Association (MLA) Format
http://owl.english.purdue.edu/handouts/research/r_mla.html

APA Style Frequently Asked Questions
http://www.apastyle.org/faqs.html

Using American Psychological Association (APA) Format
http://owl.english.purdue.edu/handouts/research/r_apa.html

COMPANION WEBSITE

See **http://www.transcanadawriter.nelson.com** for additional information on writing research papers.

PART FOUR

Special Writing Situations

CHAPTER 23

Writing with Visuals

This chapter explores the importance of images in communication today and how to integrate writing and visuals. It begins with guidance in analyzing and interpreting visuals—photographs, graphics, charts—examining them for perspective, context, and social implications. It then focuses on visuals in the writing context and how to use visuals to support writing goals.

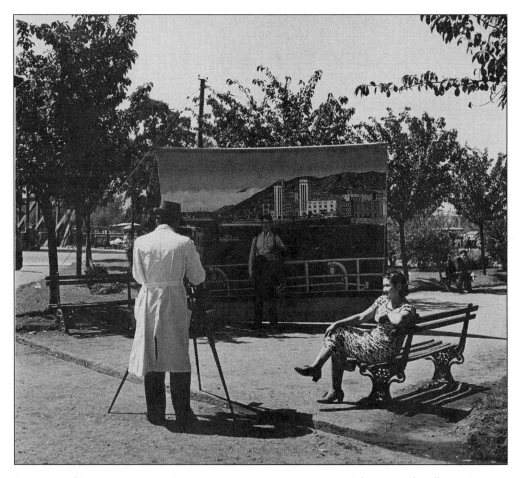

Image vs. reality

© *Hulton-Deutsch Collection/CORBIS*

ANALYZING VISUALS

Communication relies increasingly on images today. We are bombarded with advertisements, graphs, and photographs. Websites include streaming video, and digital cameras can instantly transmit photos and video worldwide. Cable news networks project images of breaking events 24 hours a day. Personal computers and desktop publishing enable students and small-business owners to develop sophisticated multimedia presentations that rival those created by major corporations. Images can be used to grab attention, evoke an emotional response, record events, document conditions, display evidence, illustrate an idea or condition, establish a mood, or develop a context for discussion. Visual images command attention. They can be presented without comment or woven into the text of a written message.

PHOTOGRAPHS, FILM, AND VIDEO

Photographs, film, and video are compelling. There is an impression that "the camera does not lie." People writing reports about a car accident can exaggerate or minimize the damage, but a photograph, we believe, provides us with irrefutable evidence. But visuals can be highly subjective and often misleading. They require careful analysis to determine their meaning and reliability.

The impression a photograph or video makes is shaped by a number of factors: perspective and contrast, context, timing and duplication, manipulation, and captions.

PERSPECTIVE AND CONTRAST

The impression we get of events, objects, and people depends on perspective, the angle and distance of the camera, and the subject. A hundred protesters photographed in close-up will look like an overwhelming force. Fists raised, faces twisted in emotion, lunging toward the camera, they can appear all-powerful and unstoppable. Photographed from a distance, the crowd can seem small against a landscape of multistory buildings or acres of empty pavement. A luxury car photographed in front of

James Dean in Times Square, 1955

© Dennis Stock, 1955/MAGNUM

The image as icon. Elvis Presley performs at Maple Leaf Gardens in Toronto

York University Libraries, Clara Thomas Archives & Special Collections, ASC00832

a stately country home appears as a symbol of elegance, whereas parked next to a migrant farmworker's shack, the same car appears oppressive, a symbol of tasteless greed and injustice.

The photograph of James Dean in Times Square (page 519) is shot at some distance. Dean is shown not in isolation but within an environment. Though he is at the centre of the photograph, his stature is diminished by the urban landscape. Tall buildings rise above him. The iron fence on the right restricts

A photograph from the Elvis Festival in Collingwood, Ontario

Peter Bregg/HELLO!

his freedom of movement. In addition, the environment is hostile—dark, cold, and wet. Dean is hunched forward, his collar turned up against the wind, his hands buried in his pockets against the cold. The picture creates an image of brooding loneliness and alienation, suited to Dean's Hollywood image as a loner and troubled rebel.

CONTEXT

Photographs and video images are isolated glimpses of larger events. A camera captures a split second of reality, but it does not reveal what happened before or after the image was taken. A photograph of a baseball player hitting a home run shows a moment of athletic triumph, but it does not reveal the player's batting average or who won the game. A single striking image may distort our impressions of a larger event.

Karla Homolka leaving her family home in St. Catharine's, Ontario, in 1993, the year she went on trial for her involvement with Paul Bernardo in the murders of Kristen French and Leslie Mahaffy. Notice the sinister expression in Homolka's eyes suggested by the camera, as well as the inclusion of Homolka's sister, Lori, in the foreground. Lori had slept upstairs while Homolka and Bernardo drugged and raped a third Homolka sister, Tammy, who choked and died during the assault.

Peter Power/Toronto Star

Motion picture and video cameras bring world events into our homes—but it is a narrow window on the world. Television cameras can be trained on a violent demonstration, suggesting a wave of widespread protest, while only a block away people walk without incident through crowded streets.

Cable network news creates the illusion that you are being informed about world events, but it is highly limited to covering visual stories. More complicated stories may

Osama bin Laden replaces
Uncle Sam in political ad

*© TomPaine.com (A Project
of The Institute for
America's Future)*

not provide gripping visuals or may require too much explanation to make good television.

Visual Connotations

Images, like words, have connotations. They create emotional responses. Campaign commercials show political candidates with their families, visiting the elderly, shaking hands with firefighters to link themselves with positive images. Book covers and movie posters only vaguely associated with World War II often feature a large swastika because it is a symbol bound to attract attention.

Certain images become icons, symbols of an event, culture, attitude, or value. Reproduced in books and films, on murals and T-shirts, they serve to communicate a message with a single image. Marilyn Monroe's upswept skirt symbolizes sex. The World Trade Center attack has become an international symbol of terrorism. Often the icon takes on a meaning of its own.

TIMING AND DUPLICATION

Timing and duplication can enhance an image's impact and distort perceptions. If two celebrities meet briefly at a crowded special event and photographs of them shaking hands are widely reproduced over several months, it can create the impression they are close friends. Few recognize that they are simply seeing the same moment from different angles. Stalin, Roosevelt, and Churchill met on only a few occasions during the Second World War, but the continual reproduction of photographs of them together helped create the image of the Big Three as a solid alliance against Hitler.

MANIPULATING IMAGES

Photographers and filmmakers can use lighting, perspective, and contrast to alter perceptions of reality. Short actors can be made to seem taller on screen by lowering cameras or placing taller people in the background. Make-up and lighting can magnify or diminish facial features. Kaiser Wilhelm and Joseph Stalin, wanting to project images of power and authority, had portraits and photographs of themselves camouflage the fact that each had one arm noticeably shorter than the other.

Photographs and film can be edited, revised, cut, and altered after the fact. Leon Trotsky was once a powerful Soviet leader, often photographed standing next to Lenin. Under Stalin's rule, by contrast, thousands of pictures were retouched to remove Trotsky from group photographs in the attempt to obliterate the latter's role in the Russian Revolution.

Prime Minister Robert Borden (left) and Winston Churchill, then First Lord of the Admiralty, in London, 1912. Notice how Borden is placed in the prominent position (left side), where he appears larger than Churchill, signalling his superior political position to Churchill at the time.

Library and Archives Canada/C-002082

With computer technology, images can be easily digitally removed and inserted. Photographs, movies, and videos now have an increasing power to create their own reality, which may exaggerate, minimize, or distort actual events.

GENDER AND CULTURAL ISSUES

Images, like language, affect our perceptions and often reflect prevailing attitudes and biases. Historically, photographs focused on male activities, actions, and behaviours, with women generally appearing as family members, sex objects, or in secondary roles to men.

Social change reflected by a clash of traditional gender images. Makeup and jewelry are decidedly feminine, in stark contrast to the masculine hard hat.   © SuperStock

Automobile ads still frequently show men standing next to or driving a car, while women are draped across the hood as a kind of ornament. Similarly, photographs taken of visible minorities often historically reflected and generated stereotyped views. As cultural attitudes and gender roles change, popular culture and advertising alter our perceptions of men and women.

Perception and Analysis

Our analysis of images is shaped by our perceptions, both personal and cultural. A photograph taken in Iran depicts a male professor lecturing female seminary students from behind a screen. To Western eyes, this image can seem a shocking example of oppression and exclusion. To many Iranians, however, the image of women studying Islam represents inclusion and empowerment.

In Iran, a male professor lectures female students from behind a screen.   © MAGNUM

Strategies for Analyzing Visual Images

1. **Examine the image holistically.** What does it represent? What is your initial reaction? Does it convey a message?

2. **Consider the nature of the image.** Is this a professional portrait or a candid press shot? Was this video taken at a prepared ceremony or a spontaneous event? Were people, images, or objects deliberately posed to make a statement?

3. **Examine perspective.** Is the subject depicted in close-up or at a distance? Does the subject appear in control of the environment, or does the background dominate the frame?

4. **Analyze contrasts and contexts.** Is the background supportive, neutral, or hostile to the subject? Does the image depict conflict or harmony?

5. **Examine poses and body language of human figures.** How are human figures depicted? What emotions do they seem to express?

6. **Look for bias.** Do you sense that the photographers were trying to manipulate the people or events depicted, casting them in either a favourable or negative light?

7. **Consider the larger context.** Does the image offer a fair representation of a larger event, or is it an isolated exception?

8. **Review the image for possible manipulation.** Could camera angles or retouching have altered what appears to be a record of actual events?

9. **Consider the story the image seems to tell.** What is the thesis of this image? What visual details or symbols help tell the story?

CAPTIONS

Images are frequently accompanied by captions that can shape the way people interpret them. Descriptive or narrative captions place an image in a context, often using verbal connotations to shape perceptions.

For example, the news photograph of a riot in India following the assassination of Indira Gandhi in 1984 could be accompanied by a range of captions:

> New Delhi, India, 1984
> Police attack demonstrators
> Police quell riot
> Protestors clash with police following Gandhi assassination
> Violence erupts in India following Gandhi assassination
> Police restore order following Gandhi assassination

Each caption would prompt readers of a magazine or newspaper to view the image in a different light. Captions, in many cases, can be as powerful as the image they describe, turning photojournalism into propaganda or revealing personal and social biases.

A range of captions could accompany this photograph of the aftermath of the assassination of Indira Gandhi in 1984, each prompting the viewer to interpret the image in a different light.

© Jacques Langevin/
CORBIS SYGMA

Strategies for Analyzing Captions

1. **Examine the photograph before reading the caption.** How do you interpret the image? What can you tell from the setting, perspective, contrast, and visual connotations?

2. **Read the caption carefully.** What does it contain—objective information about time, date, and location, or a subjective description or commentary?

3. **Consider the connotations of the caption.** Does the caption suggest positive or negative interpretations of the image depicted? Is a bulldozer "destroying" or "clearing" a forest? Is a politician waving off journalists "leaving a press conference" or "ducking reporters"?

4. **Read the accompanying text.** If the photograph appears in a book, article, or e-mail, read the text to determine whether the author reveals any bias.

5. **Reconsider the validity of the image.** Consider whether the image has been taken out of context and does not fairly represent what it claims.

GRAPHICS

Graphics are a visual representation of numbers and facts. Like photographs, they are compelling because they communicate a fact in an instant. But like photographs, they can alter perceptions by perspective.

For instance, if a company's sales increase to 11 percent in a year, that fact can be accurately demonstrated in a graph:

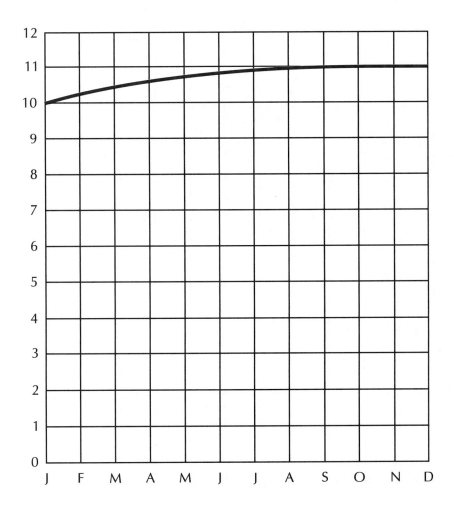

The same increase can look larger by truncating the graph, cutting off the bottom to exaggerate the increase:

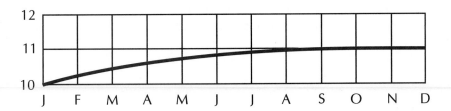

Altering the graph by adding a decimal point can make a small increase seem like a dramatic surge:

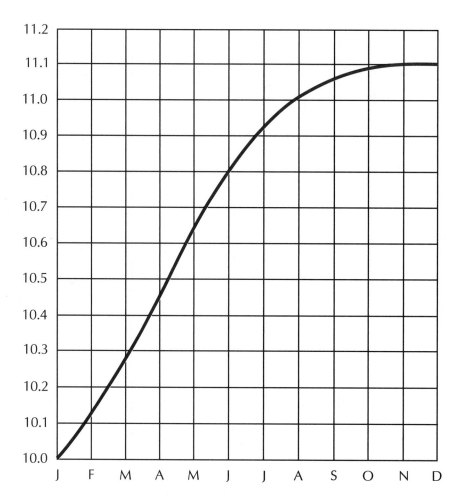

None of these graphs is inaccurate or dishonest, but each alters perceptions for the casual viewer.

An illustration can use a visual illusion to make things seem larger or smaller than they actually are. Suppose a corporation wants to impress investors with the fact that it doubled profits last year from $30 million to $60 million. A simple bar chart demonstrates the difference quite dramatically:

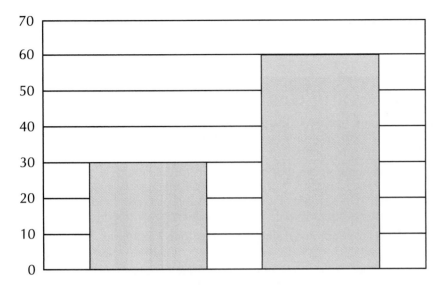

The bar on the right fills twice the space as the bar on the left, accurately showing the relationship between 30 and 60. If the bar, however, is replaced with an image like a money bag, the visual depiction makes a more dramatic impact:

Unlike the first bag, the second bag of money is enlarged in two directions. The first bag, the second bag of money representing $60 million is both twice as high and twice as wide as the $30 million bag. If you take the time to look at the numbers on the left side of the chart, you realize the difference is that between 30 and 60. But because the big money bag takes four times, not two times, as much space as the smaller one, it looks four times the size. It would take $240 million to fill this bag. The chart does not lie, the numbers are accurate, but again the visual impression distorts perceptions.

Just as a snapshot captures a brief moment of reality, a visual aid can distort reality by presenting carefully selected data that are accurate but misleading.

Strategies for Analyzing Graphics

1. **Realize that graphs, charts, and other visual aids are not facts but representations of facts.** Detailed graphics can appear accurate, but their visuals are based on facts and statistics that require verification.

2. **Examine how facts and numbers are displayed.** Visual aids can magnify or minimize facts. How much is $7 million in sales? Placed on a chart that runs from $1 million to $10 million, $7 million will fill 70 percent of the frame. Placed on a chart that runs from $1 to $100 million, the same amount will fill only 7 percent of the frame.

3. **Determine the source of the visual aid and the numbers or facts it represents.** Visual aids, like statistics, can be objectively evaluated only when you understand their source.

4. **Realize that visual aids, though they communicate at glance, require a dual analysis.** First, you must verify whether the numbers depicted are current, accurate, and meaningful. Second, you must determine if the visual aid distorts the facts, presenting them in such a way to prove a preconceived point of view.

WRITING WITH VISUALS

Visuals—photographs, diagrams, charts, maps, drawings, and graphs—can enhance written documents. Visually oriented people are more likely to remember what they see than what they read. Pictures can bring a description to life, dramatize a situation, and document an event. Graphs and tables help readers visualize and comprehend data and statistics. Images create immediate impressions that can attract attention, establish a context, and shape reader expectations.

Visuals, however, have to be used carefully. Like the words you choose, any visual image must suit the writing context and not detract from the goal of the document. Visuals that are effective in one document may be inappropriate in another.

VISUALS AND THE WRITING CONTEXT

Photo software and digital cameras make it very easy to download images or incorporate your own photographs into documents. Effective visuals can add depth and rigor to a document. Inappropriate visuals, however, weaken a document by making it appear amateurish and unprofessional. Before including visuals in any document, it is important to consider the writing context or genre.

1. **What is your goal—to inform, persuade, refute an argument, or motivate people to take action?** What visuals, if any, will support your purpose?

2. **Who are your readers—what are their needs, attitudes, values, and concerns?** Will readers respond favourably to your visuals? Images may be amusing to some but offensive to others. Will readers understand how the images, graphs, or tables support your text?

3. **What is the discipline or situation?** Engineers or architects will demand far more precise plans of a proposed building than the general public. Historians will scrutinize photographs of historical events for signs of bias. Professors of philosophy or literature likely will find images in essays inappropriate.

4. **What is the nature of the document?** An ad for a sports car needs a striking and memorable image to communicate at a glance. A formal business report will have specific guidelines and standards for presenting visuals. Review sample documents to determine how visuals will be considered appropriate.

THE ROLE OF VISUALS

Visuals serve specific purposes. **Design features,** such as photographs, decorative borders, stylistic lettering, logos, and symbols, can identify a subject, idea, or organization; set a tone or mood; and prepare readers to view information in a specific context. A brochure about homelessness, containing pictures of volunteers distributing food baskets, immediately states a different purpose and approach than one showing activists marching on City Hall.

- Design features are essential in web pages, posters, brochures, ads, newsletters, promotional material, and product packaging.

- Design features in college or university papers and formal business reports, which are expected to communicate through substance rather than image, are generally limited to text decisions, such as fonts, spacing, and margins. Such visual elements as decorative borders and elaborate logos are avoided.

- Design features should match the tone and style of the document's level of diction and connotation.

  General illustrations and attention-getters, such as a striking image, graph, or photograph, can serve to attract attention and illustrate an idea. They often appear without captions in popular magazines, promotional literature, and websites.

- Illustrations and attention-getters have to be chosen carefully to elicit the response you want. Avoid images that may be controversial, offensive, or confusing.

- If you present illustrations without a caption, ensure that they create the impression you intend. Captions can guide how readers see the image.

- Attention-getters are rarely used in formal academic papers or business reports. Often they are used only as cover art for major documents and are generally conservative in nature. A 100-page proposal to rehabilitate a stadium might display a photograph of the existing building or an architect's drawing of the completed restoration on its cover.

  Specific illustrations document a specific event or illustrate a particular example. A homeowner filing a flood insurance claim could include a photograph to document the extent of the damage. A city engineering report might use an aerial photograph of a neighbourhood to demonstrate the extent of flood damage.

Graphs can highlight important facts and numbers that may be hard to appreciate when expressed in text alone.

■ Specific illustrations are generally consecutively numbered and captioned. Formal reports may only number exhibits or label images with factual details, such as time, place, and location. Informal documents, such as promotional brochures, might use subjective captions to create positive or negative impressions.

■ Specific illustrations are referred to by number or caption to connect them to the text:

> Last year sales fell dramatically in all sectors (fig. 6).
> Kuwait's oil exports increased greatly last year (see World Oil Exports, 2005).

■ Specific illustrations should clearly represent what is stated in the text. Avoid images that may be controversial, distracting, or subject to varying interpretations. Graphs and tables should be suited to the audience.

■ Specific illustrations may require exact details about the time, date, and location of a photograph. A medical journal showing a series of CAT scans documenting a patient's recovery would have to include dates and information about the imaging equipment used to provide accurate data.

Explain the source of images to establish credibility. A report about UFOs that includes images of strange objects flying over a city would gain authority if the pictures come from the Canadian Space Agency.

New Orleans Superdome, ©
September 1, 2005

*Michael Ainsworth/ Dallas
Morning News/Corbis*

■ Documents using specific illustrations often have to follow professional formats of captioning, lettering, or documentation. Many disciplines have style manuals dictating how illustrations should appear in documents. If no manuals exist, follow examples found in professional journals and official reports.

Your choice of visuals will depend on the purpose of your document or presentation. An ad, website, or newsletter might contain only visual elements to create eye appeal and establish a style or tone for the message. A biology research paper may contain only specific visuals, such as tables and microscopic photographs of cells. A sales brochure for a luxury car, however, might use a striking general illustration on the cover to grab attention, and specific illustrations of leather seats, wood panelling, and a high-performance engine to emphasize particular features.

TYPES OF VISUALS

Photographs

Photographs can be compelling support provided they suit the document's context. The picture of the hurricane victims at the Superdome (see page 532) captures the human drama of an actual event. It would make a powerful image for a fundraising brochure, a Red Cross website, or a book cover. It would not be suited for a report arguing that the government responded appropriately to the disaster or some kinds of academic papers. Photographs can highlight a specific person, object, or location or provide readers with a "big picture" view. Photographs can capture events as they happen or preserve images carefully posed for the camera.

For all their power, photographs have limitations. They can overemphasize minor events. A dramatic news photo of a demonstration that results in a dozen arrests and a few injuries may be splashed across the front pages of newspapers, while a riot that killed hundreds goes unnoticed because no cameras recorded the events. And as we saw earlier in this chapter, photos can be misleading in other ways.

Strategies for Using Photographs

1. **Select photographs from reliable sources.** Books, news magazines, newspapers, news services, and stock photo websites provide visuals suited for academic and professional writing. Stock photo services often include specific details about photographs, including date, location, and event. Avoid using visuals that cannot be verified.

2. **Include photographs that serve specific purposes.** Avoid including images that do not serve to set a tone, illustrate a general idea, attract attention, or document a particular point.

3. **Let the context of the document guide your selection.** Keep your goal, readers, and discipline in mind when you include images.

(Continued)

4. **Avoid cluttering a document with too many images.** Images should support the text, not overwhelm or distract from it. You can integrate specific illustrations within the text and supply additional images in an appendix, CD, or supporting website.

5. **Link specific illustrations to text.** To prevent confusion, direct readers to look at specific images by referring to them in the text by figure number, caption, or page number.

6. **Include sources of photographs.** Photographs require sources for validity as well as impact. Include sources, dates, and locations in captions or a reference page. Readers may suspect plagiarism or question the validity of images if the latter are presented without sources.

Tables and Graphs

Tables and graphs express numbers, facts, or statistics in visual form. They can be used to dramatize facts or simply help people comprehend and remember data. **Tables** present numbers in columns for easy reading and reference. Important tables, such as delivery schedules or price lists, can be placed on a separate page in large type so that they can be detached, scanned, or copied for readers to use as reference tools.

QUARTERLY SALES FIGURES
(IN MILLIONS)

	VHS	DVD
New York	2.5	1.3
Chicago	1.2	1.2
Los Angeles	3.0	2.5

Line graphs show changing numbers over time. They can help readers review and appreciate the rise and fall of sales, prices, cases of flu, homicides, or the earth's temperature over days, weeks, months, or years. Timelines should be clearly presented. Line graphs that include anomalies might need explanations or a footnote to explain a dramatic change that might be misunderstood.

Bar charts represent data visually by using bars or columns to show differences in values with different heights of bars. Like line graphs, they can show changes over time or comparisons between different topics. A bar chart about high school graduation rates could reflect a 10-year period of a single city or last year's statistics for 10 different cities. Bars or columns can be coded to show subdivisions.

Pie charts show percentages of a whole by slicing a circle into shaded or coloured sections. A pie chart could classify immigrants by their nation of origin, a company's sales by product, or an investor's portfolio by stock type. Because pie charts break down a single subject at one time, more than one chart has to be used to compare different subjects or demonstrate a change over time.

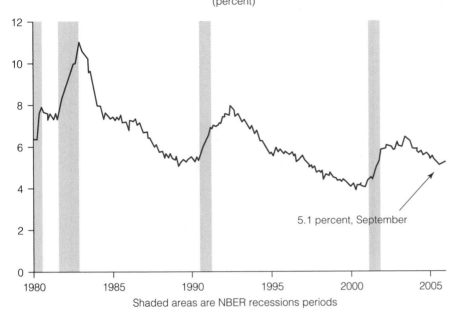

Unemployment Rate at Low Level
(percent)

Shaded areas are NBER recessions periods

5.1 percent, September

Line Graph   *http://www.house.gov/budget/chartsgraphs.htm*

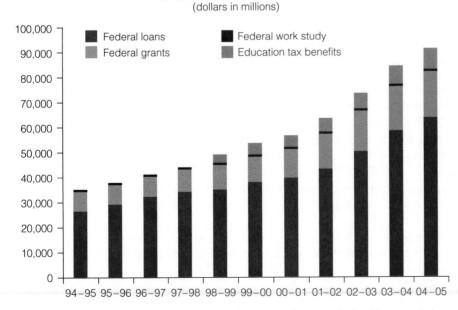

Increases in Federal Student Aid
(dollars in millions)

Federal loans   Federal work study

Federal grants   Education tax benefits

Bar Chart   *http://www.house.gov/budget/chartsgraphs.htm*

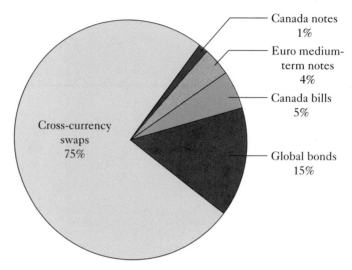

Forecast Composition of Foreign Currency Liabilities
As at March 31, 2007

Pie Chart   http://www.budget.gc.ca/2007/bp/bpa3e.html

Source: Chart A3.4, Annex 3, Budget 2007, Department of Finance Canada, http://www.budget.gc.ca/2007/bp/bpa3e
.html. Reproduced with the permission of the Minister of Public Works and Government Services Canada, 2007.

Strategies for Using Tables, Graphs, and Charts

1. **Select tables, graphs, and charts from reliable sources.** Statistics can be taken out of context, poorly collected, misinterpreted, or distorted. Use visuals from major news services, government agencies, and nonpartisan organizations.

2. **Use visuals your readers will be able to understand and refer to.** Avoid including overly detailed or complex charts or graphs that require specialized knowledge or training. You may use simplified visuals in the main document for general readers and present more complex visuals in an appendix or supporting website for readers requiring greater detail.

3. **Present tables, charts, and graphs in a readable format.** Avoid shrinking visuals to a size that makes them difficult to see. To prevent large-scale charts and graphs from interrupting text, consider placing them in an appendix.

4. **Include sources.** Readers will accept visuals as accurate only if they know where they came from. You can note a graph's source, date, and other important information in a caption or source list.

5. **Link specific illustrations to text.** To prevent confusion, direct readers to look at specific images by referring to them in the text by number, caption, or page number.

6. **Analyze visuals for bias.** Truncated and two-dimensional graphs (see pages 526–529) can be used to distort, inflate, and dramatize numbers. Avoid using or creating graphs and charts that try to maximize or minimize numbers.

WRITING CAPTIONS

Captions that accompany visuals can present objective identifications or make subjective statements, guiding reader interpretations.

The photograph of the hurricane victims outside the Superdome (see page 532) could be accompanied by an objective description that simply labels the image:

Superdome, New Orleans, September 1, 2005
Hurricane Katrina victims outside New Orleans Superdome

Subjective captions present readers with an implication of the photograph's meaning:

Five days after Hurricane Katrina, victims await rescue
Minority victims crowd outside Superdome

Captions like these contain descriptive or narrative elements suggesting a delayed or racially biased response to the disaster.

A chart showing a 9 percent increase in a company's sales can be labelled with an objective caption:

Research in Motion's sales, 2006
Research in Motion's sales rise 9 percent in 2006

Subjective captions use connotations to maximize or minimize numbers:

Research in Motion's sales soar 9 percent in 2006
Research in Motion's sales rise less than 10 percent in 2006

Strategies for Writing Captions

1. Use captions for specific illustrations to connect images to the text.
2. Ensure that captions connect to the text. Avoid mentioning names, places, or events in the caption that are not explained in the text.
3. Identify people in photographs from left to right.
4. Ensure that the tone, style, and wording of captions suit the writing context.

UNDERSTANDING FAIR USE

Nearly all visual aids you may find in print or online are probably copyrighted and cannot be reproduced or distributed without permission. The concept of fair use allows college or university students to include a photograph or chart in a research paper as long as the source is identified. However, the same image cannot be used in a website, brochure, ad, packaging, mass e-mail, T-shirt, or poster without permission.

Stock photo and clip art services offer images in the public domain and are therefore available for wider use.

Strategies for Using Visuals in Academic Writing

1. **Review the assignment to see whether visuals will enhance your paper.** A research paper in biology, engineering, business, or economics might demand extensive use of visual aids. In other courses, visuals may be nonessential but helpful. In a literature or political science course, visuals may be irrelevant.

2. **Select visuals that support specific points in your paper.** Limit use of attention-getters and general illustrations.

3. **Let your thesis guide your use of visuals.** Visuals should provide illustrations that explain or provide evidence for important points in your paper. Do not include photographs just because they are striking or interesting. Like quotations, visuals should directly support your thesis.

4. **Consider your method of development.** A narrative paper may benefit from a timeline or line graph. Comparisons can be illustrated with tables and bar charts. Diagrams, photographs, and maps can explain a process.

5. **Use objective captions and references to link visuals to your text.** Freestanding images can be distracting or confusing. Consecutively number each image and use parenthetical notes to link them to your text:

   Between 1986 and 2005 the price of oil fluctuated greatly (fig. 12).

6. **Select appropriate sizes.** Simple charts and photographs may be shrunk to the size of an oversized postage stamp and wrapped with text to create a readable text. Detailed photographs, maps, and intricate charts may require a full page to be readable.

7. **Don't allow visuals to overwhelm the text.** If you have a large number of images, especially ones requiring a full page, consider placing some or all of them in an appendix.

8. **Document sources of visuals or information you use to create visuals.** Like quotations, visuals from other sources should be documented. If you create your own graphs or charts, indicate the source for the numbers or statistics they represent. Captions should list sources (see photographs in this chapter).

9. **Budget your time carefully.** Locating or creating visuals can be time consuming. Determine whether your time would be better spent revising and editing your paper.

E-SOURCES

Basic Strategies in Reading Photographs
http://nuovo.com/southern-images/analyses.html

Making Sense of Documentary Photography
http://historymatters.gmu.edu/mse/Photos

Faking Images in Photojournalism
http://commfaculty.fullerton.edu/lester/writings/faking.html

Stock Photo Services
http://www.FotoSearch.com
http://www.corbis.com
http://www.indexstock.com

Some Tips for Writing Captions
http://www.nyu.edu/classes/copyXediting/captions.html

CHAPTER 24

Writing for Professional, Collaborative, and Oral Purposes

This chapter provides an overview of writing for professional and collaborative environments, including writing for oral and multimedia presentations. It examines the main characteristics of professional writing and offers strategies for producing e-mails, résumés, and cover letters. It offers strategies for collaborative writing processes and explains how to apply collaborative writing strategies to online writing groups. It also looks at the difference between writing and public speaking, offering guidelines for preparing and performing oral presentations and using visuals to enhance presentations.

WHAT IS PROFESSIONAL WRITING?

Once you enter the workforce, you will communicate with others through a variety of documents, ranging from brief e-mail notes to lengthy reports and proposals. Although executives, managers, scientists, and professionals follow the basic rules of standard written English, significant differences exist between academic and professional writing.

Professional writing occurs in a specific context. The tone, style, diction, and format of professional documents are shaped by the history of the organization, the discipline, the reader, the audience, and the topic. The writing style suited for an ad agency or interior decorator might be considered unprofessional in a law or accounting firm.

When you write, consider the nature of your career, the image and history of the organization, your superiors' concerns, and the needs and expectations of your readers.

Professional writing focuses on specific readers. You may find yourself addressing people with limited knowledge of your particular field. You also may encounter readers hostile to your ideas or the organization you represent. Readers may not be objective. They may have fixed views and resist your recommendations.

Professional writing is practical and emphasizes results. In business and industry, ideas and answers mean money. You may have to urge readers to accept your recommendations, purchase your products, or accept your proposals. You may be asking people to invest large sums of money or make commitments involving substantial resources.

Professional writing is sensitive to legal implications. Letters, e-mails, reports, and contracts can become legal documents. Writers must be careful to avoid making statements they cannot support. A poorly worded phrase, even a grammar or typographical error, can place writers in legal jeopardy, exposing them and their employers to litigation.

Professional writing is carefully designed. Writers must consider how professional documents will look. Business documents are carefully designed to follow professional standards and match an organization's image. Law firms, banks, government agencies, and accounting firms will use traditional letterheads, margins, and fonts. Ad agencies, rock radio stations, and hair salons may use colourful designs to attract attention and project a unique image. In addition, business writers use bold headings, white space, and bulleted points to highlight important ideas and help readers follow their train of thought.

Professional writing represents the views of others. In your career, you likely will work as a representative of a corporation, organization, partnership, or agency.

- Never write anything that would be unacceptable to your employer.

- Avoid making promises or commitments unless you know that your organization or employer will honour them.

- Never use official stationery for personal letters.

E-MAIL

Today almost every job uses e-mail to communicate. Some people confuse e-mail with "instant messages" or chat room conversations. These people write and answer e-mail without thinking, producing a stream of tangled ideas, missing details, grammatical errors, and inappropriate comments. E-mail, like any kind of writing, takes thought and planning to be effective.

Strategies for Writing E-mail

1. **Realize that e-mail is *real mail*.** E-mail can be stored, distributed, and printed. Unlike a note or memo that can be retrieved or corrected, e-mail, once sent, becomes permanent. *Never send e-mail when you are tired or angry. Avoid sending messages you will later regret.*

2. **Follow the prewriting, drafting, revising, and editing strategies you would use in writing a paper document.** Don't let an e-mail message simply record whatever comes into your head. E-mail should have a clear purpose and an easy-to-follow organization. Plan before you write.

3. **Understand what messages *should not* be expressed in e-mail.** E-mail is considered appropriate for short, informative messages. Do not attempt to send a 15-page report by e-mail, although it might be sent as an attachment. Do not send personal

(Continued)

or sensitive information by e-mail. E-mail is seen as too informal and too public for confidential correspondence.

4. **Respond to e-mail carefully.** Often e-mail messages will list multiple readers. Before sending a reply, determine whether you want everyone or just a few people to see your response.

5. **Make sure you use the correct e-mail address.** E-mail addresses can be complicated and oddly spelled. Often names are shortened or reversed. Donald Peterson might appear as "donald.peterson," "dpeterson," or "petersond." Double-check addresses.

6. **Clearly label your e-mail in the subject line.** Spam—unwanted e-mail messages—uses misleading headings such as "Following your request" or "next week's conference" to grab attention. To prevent your e-mail from being overlooked or deleted before it is read, use specific identifying details in the subject such as "RE: April 19th dental benefits reminder" or "Smithkin Supplies Annual Audit."

7. **Include your reader's full name and the date in your inside address.**

8. **Keep e-mail direct and concise.** People expect e-mail to be brief and easy to read. Avoid complicated sentences and long paragraphs. Use short paragraphs and bulleted or numbered points to increase readability.

9. **End the e-mail with a clear summary, request, or direction.**
   - Summarize important points.
   - If you are asking for information or help, clearly state what you need, when you need it, and how you can be reached.
   - If you want readers to take action, provide clear directions.

10. **Ask readers for an acknowledgment if you want to ensure that they received your message.**

11. **Review, edit, and double-check e-mail before sending.** Check your spelling, addresses, names, prices, or figures for accuracy. Read your e-mail aloud to catch missing words, illogical statements, confusing sentences, or awkward phrases.

12. **Print hard copies of important e-mail for future reference.**

Sample E-mail

From: John MacLaine
To: Sales Staff
Date: January 30, 2008
RE: Expense Account Reports

To all sales staff:

As of March 1, 2006, Atlantic Mutual will no longer provide sales representatives with company cars or expense accounts. Instead, sales representatives will be given a flat monthly grant to cover office, travel, and vehicle expenses:

Inside Sales Reps $250 per month

District Sales Reps $500 per month

Regional Sales Reps $750 per month

This policy affects only regular monthly expenses. Atlantic Mutual will continue to pay all expenses for those attending regional and national sales conventions.

If you have any questions about the new policy, please contact me at Ext. 7689.

John MacLaine

RÉSUMÉS AND COVER LETTERS

The first business documents you likely will have to produce are a résumé and cover or application letter. To facilitate this important task, you need to understand what a résumé is:

1. **A résumé is a 10-second advertisement.** Research has revealed that the average executive spends about 10 seconds skimming a résumé before rejecting it or setting it aside for further review. A résumé is not a list of every job you have had or a description of your ultimate goal in life—it is an ad presenting facts and accomplishments relevant to a specific position.

2. **The goal of a résumé is to secure an interview, not a job.** Few, if any applicants, are hired solely on the basis of a one- or two-page document. The goal of a résumé is simply to generate enough interest in the applicant to prompt the employer to schedule an interview. Present only the highlights of your career and education.

3. **Applicants usually benefit from having more than one résumé.** Just as companies design different advertisements to market the same product to different consumers, you may have three or four résumés. An accounting major may have one résumé emphasizing auditing expertise and another stressing tax experience. Because they are read quickly, highly targeted résumés addressing a single job are more effective than general statements.

Strategies for Writing Résumés

1. **Realize that there are no absolute rules in writing effective résumés—only guidelines.** You may have heard that a résumé must be only one page, that it is useless to list hobbies, or that you should never mention your age. Because there is such a range of jobs and applicants, there are instances in which "breaking" the rules may be the only effective way of getting attention.

2. **Focus your résumé by carefully reading the want ad or job description.** Note the key requirements employers seek, and highlight those skills. Pay attention to key words and phrases, and determine whether you can repeat them in your résumé.

3. **Include your full name, address, telephone number with area code, or e-mail address.** If you are in the process of moving, you can list two addresses.

4. **Provide a clear, objective statement describing the job you seek.** Avoid using general statements, such as "a position making use of my skills and abilities," or one that lists too many job titles: "Sales Manager/Marketing Manager/Advertising Director." Broad objectives make applicants appear indecisive or desperate. It is better to have specific statements:

   A position in publishing design making use of my experience in graphics
   Assistant Sales Manager

5. **Use a short *summary* or *overview* statement to encapsulate key elements in your background.** A short paragraph describing your background, goals, and skills can personalize a résumé. It can encourage the reader to view your experience in a certain light, showing how seemingly unrelated jobs or education would be relevant to the job you seek. You may find it easier to write the summary last, after you have identified your key strengths.

6. **Open your résumé with your strongest and most recent credentials.** If you have professional experience, you may find it more effective to highlight your recent job than to emphasize a new degree. If you are unsure which area to highlight, prepare two résumés, one emphasizing experience and the other stressing education. You can use either résumé, selecting the version that best matches a particular job.

7. **Arrange education and experience chronologically, beginning with the most recent.**

8. **If you are a recent graduate with little professional experience, list significant courses, awards, grade point averages, and honours.** If you have worked as an intern or completed clinical work, place this under the heading Experience rather than Education.

9. **Stress individual accomplishments.** Briefly list dates of employment, title, and general job description; then provide examples of specific skills and experiences.

10. **List training seminars, volunteer work, hobbies, and military service only if directly related to the position.** A résumé is a fact sheet listing your key skills and experiences. Secondary information can be included in a cover letter or mentioned at a job interview.

Professional Résumé

SAMUEL BENJAMIN
537 MEADOW LANE
VANCOUVER, BC
(604) 879-8989
sbenjamin@sfnet.com

OBJECTIVE	**CONTROLLER**	Goal
SUMMARY	More than five years experience as controller of firm with $50 million in sales. Adept at financial reporting, payroll, benefits, insurance. Highly skilled in managing personnel expenditures.	Summary blends experience
EXPERIENCE 2000–Present	FISHERMAN'S MUTUAL INSURANCE COMPANY, Vancouver, BC *Controller* responsible for accounts receivable and payable, finance reports, quarterly and annual statements, payroll and benefits, and insurance purchasing.	
	■ Created new payroll system, reducing costs 15%. ■ Developed employee benefits manual. ■ Selected by president to purchase computer and all software for accounting and billing services. ■ Wrote computer program to centralize personnel files.	Verb phrases highlight specific accomplishments
1993–2000	CITY OF BURNABY, Burnaby, BC *Personnel and Safety Director* directed by mayor and city council to serve as first safety director of personnel in Burnaby. Supervised payroll operations, risk management, and insurance.	
	■ Served on team negotiating contracts with firefighter and police unions. ■ Oversaw all city insurance programs, including life, health, liability, and casualty. ■ Established self-insured health program resulting in first-year savings of $100,000.	
1988–1993	BURNABY ENGINEERING COMPANY, Burnaby, BC *Industrial Engineering and Human Resources Director* responsible for risk management, job classification, and training in firm with 2,000 employees.	Less space devoted to early experience
	■ Created videotape training series, reducing accident rate 22% in six months. ■ Worked directly with president, controller, and auditing team to centralize records.	
EDUCATION	SIMON FRASER UNIVERSITY BS in Business Administration, 1988	Education listed last

References Available on Request

Student Résumé Including Previous Experience

BLYTHE NOEL
1732 St. Charles Avenue
St. John's, NL A2B 4I6
(709) 455-5767
bnoel@fairfieldcc.ca

Goal	OBJECTIVE	Management position in retail printing with opportunities for advancement
Overview blends education and previous experience	OVERVIEW	Five years experience in retail sales management. Fully familiar with state-of-the-art printing equipment and methods. Proven ability to lower overhead and build customer relations. ■ Certified to service all Xerox copiers.
Most recent credential	EDUCATION	FAIRFIELD COMMUNITY COLLEGE, St. John's, NL Associate Degree, Printing and Publishing, 2006 Completed courses in graphic design, editing, high-speed printing, and equipment repair. ■ Attended Quadgraphics seminar. ■ Assisted in design and publication of college newspaper.
Corporate training		XEROX, St. John's, NL Completed service training program, 2004.
Current student job	EXPERIENCE 2004–	FAST-PRINT, St. John's, NL *Retail Sales* Work twenty hours a week assisting manager in counter sales, customer relations, printing, and inventory.
Previous job description emphasizing skills related to desired job	1999–2004	CRESCENT CITY MUSIC, St. John's, NL *Manager* directly responsible for retail record outlet with annual gross sales of $1.2 million. ■ Reduced operating costs 15% first year. ■ Hired and trained sales staff. ■ Prepared all financial statements. ■ Developed advertising plan generating 35% increase in sales in first month.
	HONOURS	Deans List, 2004, 2005, 2006

References and Transcript Available

COVER LETTERS

Cover letters can be as important as the résumés they introduce. Résumés submitted without letters are often dismissed by employers because they assume that applicants who do not take the time to address them personally are not serious. Résumés tend to be rather cold lists of facts; cover letters allow applicants to present themselves in a more personalized way. The letter allows applicants to counter possible employer objections by explaining a job change, a period of unemployment, or a lack of formal education.

Strategies for Writing Cover Letters

In most instances, cover letters are short sales letters using standard business-letter formats.

1. **Avoid beginning a cover letter with a simple announcement:**

   Dear Sir or Madam:
   This letter is to apply for the job of controller advertised in the *The Moncton Times* last week. . . .

2. **Open letters on a strong point emphasizing skills or experiences:**

   Dear Sir or Madam:
   (if possible, it is always better to have an actual person to direct a cover letter to, rather than a generic "Dear Sir or Madam"—and it is always worth the extra effort to do some web research or call the company to get a real contact person to address your cover letter to)
   In the last two years I opened 58 new accounts, increasing sales by nearly $800,000.

3. **Use the letter to include information not listed on the résumé.** Volunteer work, high school experiences, or travel that might not be suited to a résumé can appear in the letter—if it is career related.

4. **Refer to the résumé, indicating how it documents your skills and abilities.**

5. **End the letter with a brief summary of notable skills and experiences and a request for an interview.** To be more assertive, state that you will call the employer in two or three days to schedule an appointment.

Letter Responding to Job Announcement

BLYTHE NOEL
1732 St. Charles Avenue
St. John's, NL A2B 4I6
(709) 455-5767
bnoel@fairfieldcc.ca

May 24, 2008

J. & J. MacAdam's Printing
500 Water Street
St. John's, NL A1B 2G7

Identifies position

RE: Manager position Faxed to Fairfield Placement Office
May 18, 2008

Dear Sir or Madam:

Opens with strong point
Refers to résumé

This month I will be graduating from Fairfield Community College with an associate degree in printing and publishing. As my résumé shows, I have been trained in state-of-the-art publishing and equipment repair. I received additional training in printing at Quadgraphics and Xerox.

Explains relevance of previous experience

Before choosing printing and publishing as a career, I managed a high-volume record store in St. John's. I hired, trained, and supervised 30 employees. In addition to decreasing turnover, I lowered overhead and increased sales.

Close and request for interview

Given my training in state-of-the-art publishing and my extensive background in retail sales, I think I would be an effective store manager. I would appreciate the opportunity to meet you to discuss my abilities at your convenience. I can be reached at (709) 455-5767.

Sincerely yours,

Blythe Noel

Putting Your Résumé to Work

Like any advertisement, a résumé is effective only if it reaches the appropriate reader. Don't limit your job search to obvious sources such as the want ads or Internet listings. Talk with instructors in your major courses, contact local recruiters and employment agencies, and investigate professional organizations for networking leads.

Strategies for Successful Professional Writing

1. **Establish a goal for each document.** Ensure your main point is clearly stated.
2. **Address the needs and concerns of both immediate and extended readers.**
3. **Make sure your writing does not conflict with the policy or image of the organization you represent.**
4. **Review your document for legal liability.** Avoid making commitments or promises you cannot keep.
5. **Conform to the standards used in your organization or industry.**
6. **Use peer review to evaluate documents before submission or publication.**
7. **Test-market documents before mass distribution.** After peer review, submit copies to a limited audience and evaluate the response before sending the document to every reader.

COLLABORATIVE WRITING

We often think of writers as solitary workers, but some academic courses and many professions require people to work with others to produce a single document. Two business partners may cowrite a sales brochure; a group of engineers or accountants may submit a team report; or a committee investigating a problem or proposing a solution may issue a single document. Even when produced by an individual, writing often incorporates the ideas of a group.

Because writing is a social act and collaborative writing is common in many jobs, an increasing number of composition teachers require students to work in groups.

Whether writing alone or in a group, the basic process is the same. The completed document must address the issue, meet the needs of the readers, and respect the conventions of the discipline, or situation. To be effective, writing groups must achieve the "Three C's" of group dynamics: cohesion, cooperation, and compromise. Members of a group must be able to meet, communicate, and work together, and must be willing to accept the views and criticism of others. Members must understand that not all of their ideas will be represented in the final product and that their individual opinions will not always prevail.

Strategies for Collaborative Writing

1. **Establish cohesion by stressing the common goal, intended readers, and the needs of the discourse community.** Introduce members who may not know each other and focus on the task at hand. Ensure every member has a copy of the assignment.

2. **Keep the group focused on the task by creating a timeline.** People enjoy talking, but discussions can easily degenerate into forums for heated debates or gossip. A timeline can help keep the group on track by outlining expected outcomes and reminding members of the upcoming deadline. The timeline should mark stages in the writing process. Ensure your group allows time for revision and editing.

3. **Use prewriting strategies to develop topics and explore ideas.** Members can take time to individually freewrite, brainstorm, or cluster ideas and then participate in group prewriting.

4. **Designate one member to serve as moderator or recorder.** One member of the group should serve as chair or recorder to document the progress of the group and keep the discussion on target. Use the assignment as a reference point for organizing the group's actions.

5. **Avoid topics that are too controversial, require too much research, or cannot be adequately explored in the allotted time.** If members of your group have strikingly different opinions, or if you find precious time being consumed by arguments and debates, suggest the group select a topic that will prompt cooperation and compromise.

6. **Make meetings productive by setting goals and assigning tasks.** Meetings can become repetitions of previous discussions. Members will have second thoughts and want to express them. Members also may become bored if the group does not seem to make progress.

   ■ Keep the group on track by opening each meeting with a brief summary of what has been accomplished and a list of what has to be achieved in the current meeting.

   ■ Summarize points that have been agreed to; then announce tasks for the next meeting.

   ■ Ensure each member is assigned work and knows what is expected at the next meeting.

7. **Avoid personalizing disagreements.** It is important to discuss opposing viewpoints in neutral terms. Avoid personalizing ideas (attaching ideas to individuals), which leads to "*us* vs. *them*" conflicts.

8. **Experiment with different writing methods.** Groups can produce writing in a number of ways:

   ■ *Individual drafting.* If the writing is short and not too complex, you might ask each member to prepare a draft and bring copies to the next meeting. Members can then select the best version and suggest alterations, adding items from other drafts.

   ■ *Parallel drafting.* For longer documents or those that include specialized information, divide the paper into sections, assigning each one to a different group member.

■ *Team drafting.* Assign two or more writers to the document or each section. A lead writer begins the first draft, then passes the writing onto subsequent authors when he or she gets stuck or lacks knowledge or data to continue. Drafts are then reviewed by the group.

9. **Take advantage of technology.** Professionals and students alike frequently have difficulty scheduling common times to meet. Use telephone conferences and Internet chat rooms for long-distance meetings. Use e-mail to distribute drafts so that members can read and post comments. There are a number of web-based collaborative writing solutions available now, such as writeboard.com and Zoho Writer (zoho.com), and even Google Docs has collaboration features.

Online Writing Groups

Many students and professionals use the Internet to expedite the writing process by posting drafts for others to read, criticize, and revise. Online writing groups allow writers to elicit responses from people who cannot meet in person and allow members to respond to a posted draft at their convenience. Students who find it difficult to voice comments in class may feel more comfortable expressing their opinions in writing. Because writing requires more concentration than talking, online writing groups can prompt more thoughtful responses about a draft than a discussion. Members can easily make revisions and suggest alternative versions.

Strategies for Working in Online Writing Groups

1. **Allow time for members to respond.** Unlike those working collaboratively, members of online writing groups respond individually. Don't post the draft of an essay at midnight and expect to receive feedback the next morning. Budget your time carefully.

2. **Label your documents and restate goals.** If members receive a number of assignments or documents, they can become confused. They will be in a better position to respond to your work if you remind them of the assignment or the purpose of your document.

   You might attach a thesis statement or goal to guide members' responses.

3. **Proofread your document before posting.** Errors in spelling and punctuation will be distracting and influence the quality of response. The better edited your writing, the more likely that readers will respond thoughtfully to the content and analyze your ideas.

4. **Direct responses by asking questions.** To focus the revision process, provide readers with questions about specific problems or shortcomings you detect in your draft. Encourage readers to make suggestions and possible revisions.

5. **Use alternative communications.** Posting and reading e-mail can lead to static exchanges. The work of online writing groups can benefit from personal meetings, chat room conferences, and telephone calls.

(Continued)

6. **Print and save hard copies of posted drafts.** Hard copies allow you to preserve different versions of documents and work while away from your computer.

7. **Observe standards of netiquette.** When you send e-mail or post messages, follow the basic guidelines for electronic messages:

   ■ *Write responsibly.*

   E-mail is real mail. Although it can seem informal and casual, e-mail sends messages to readers that cannot be retrieved. Think before you send anyone anything that you might later regret. Consider your academic or professional role and potential extended audiences. A printed letter might be photocopied and passed around to a few people, but an e-mail can easily be reproduced and circulated to thousands.

   ■ *Keep subject lines brief.*

   The subject line of your e-mail serves as a title. It should be short and clearly identify the purpose of the message.

   ■ *Keep line length short.*

   Many monitors display only 40 characters in a line. State messages concisely in short paragraphs using tightly worded sentences. Use attachments to transmit longer, more complex documents.

   ■ *Follow standard capitalization rules.*

   Use lowercase and capital letters as you would in a print document. Using all caps is considered shouting and viewed as rude and unprofessional.

   ■ *Proofread your messages.*

   Review the spelling and grammar of electronic communication with the same rigour you would apply to a standard letter or research paper.

   ■ *Respect copyrights.*

   Do not electronically distribute copyrighted material, including e-mail from others, without permission. Document use of outside sources.

   ■ *Sign your e-mail.*

   Include your name, affiliation, and e-mail address at the end of your message.

8. **Remember that you are writing as a representative of a group, not as an individual.** Do not make any statements in official correspondence you will not be able to explain or defend to other members of the group.

9. **Clearly distinguish personal opinion from passages expressing ideas of the group.** If you insert personal views in a business letter, clearly label them and indicate to your reader that your views do not reflect those of the group.

10. **Never use official letterhead for personal communications.** Employees have been terminated for using company or government stationery for personal messages. Never write anything on office stationery you would not want your supervisor or manager to read.

11. **Never make profane or even humorous comments that will compromise your professional position.** Even if you are sending a memo to your best friend, be aware that others may read it out of context and draw negative conclusions about your performance or professionalism. Remember that many people who will never see

you will see your writing. Whatever you write should reflect the image you wish to project in your career.

12. **Model your writing style on existing documents.** Large organizations provide employees with style manuals containing samples of letters and reports. If official guidelines do not exist, ask your supervisor or fellow employees for examples of what they consider good writing.

ORAL AND MULTIMEDIA PRESENTATIONS

Many academic courses and careers will require oral or multimedia presentations. In some instances, the presentation will consist of simply an introduction or a brief overview of a document. In other instances, it may be a complete alternative to a written report.

Public speaking and writing call on very different skills. An oral presentation occurs in a specific location at a specific time. Environmental factors, such as noise and seating arrangements, affect how messages are received. Listeners' reactions often are shaped by the responses of the people around them. Readers can study a document at their own pace, taking as long as they wish to read and reread. All listeners, however, receive the message at the same rate and cannot alter the flow of information. Studies reveal that even the most attentive listeners retain much less than readers.

Strategies for Giving Oral and Multimedia Presentations

1. **Study the environment.** The more you know about the time, place, and conditions of your presentation, the more comfortable and effective you will be.
   - If you are unfamiliar with the location, visit it beforehand if you can. If you cannot survey the site in person, ask what kind of room it is—a seminar room, an auditorium, a lounge? What kind of seating arrangement will be used for the speech? Does it lend itself to a formal or informal presentation? What kind of presentation aids, such as a computer and projector, chalkboard, or microphone, will be available?

2. **Learn as much as you can about your audience.** A speech is a public event, an interpersonal exchange. Learn as much as you can about your listeners and their perceptual world so you can tailor your presentation to address their needs, answer their concerns, and confront their objections.

3. **Isolate the key points of your document.** Listeners are unable to grasp the range of details usually presented in written form. Highlight and number the key points of your paper, emphasizing your thesis, most important evidence, and actions you wish the audience to take.

(Continued)

4. **Prepare a range of presentations.** If you are not sure how long your presentation should be, ask. If you are given 30 minutes, prepare a 30-minute, 20-minute, and 10-minute version. If you are pressed for time or recognize that the audience is restless and bored, it is better to deliver a clearly organized short version of your presentation than subject them to the full text.

5. **Try to avoid reading your speech.** Reading a written document—except for key quotes—can have a deadening effect on listeners. Written language, no matter how clear and eloquent on paper, is often difficult to present orally or remember. Spoken English, even in formal circumstances, is usually simpler and delivered in shorter sentences.
   - Do not attempt to memorize your speech—talk to your audience, using a few notes as reminders.
   - Practise your delivery, especially pronunciation of difficult words or phrases.

6. **Maintain eye contact.** The most important skill effective speakers develop is maintaining eye contact with listeners.

7. **Use visual aids.** People retain more information if they receive it in more than one medium. Even motivated listeners will recall only about one-third of what they hear. A simple outline, a list of talking points, a diagram, or the table of contents of your report can help people follow your presentation.
   - If giving a speech makes you nervous, a handout can reduce stress because people will be viewing the document instead of looking in your direction.
   - Keep handouts, transparencies, and PowerPoint images simple and direct. Avoid distracting artwork. Keep verbal statements short. Emphasize key words that appear in the text of your presentation.

8. **Provide distinct transitions between main points.** In writing, you can use visual indicators such as paragraph or page breaks, titles, or chapters to signal transitions between ideas. Give your audience clear signals of when your presentation changes course.
   - Numbering points makes your speech easier to follow and remember. If you tell people there are five points to consider and they can recall only three, they will realize they have lost something and are more likely to ask questions or refer to your document.

9. **Encourage listeners to write.** One way of getting people to become active listeners is to encourage them to take notes.

10. **If you plan to take questions, mention it at the outset.** If listeners do not know beforehand that they can ask questions, they may fail to pay attention, dismiss difficult or confusing ideas, or interrupt and distract you during your talk.

11. **Motivate listeners to read your document.** Unless your document is a brief letter or memo, no oral presentation is likely to communicate the complete message. Urge your audience to read the paper.

12. **Do not waste the audience's time.** Arrive in good time to prepare the presentation. During the talk, be ready to pause between main points to give people an opportunity to absorb ideas but avoid long moments of silence. If you have misplaced or forgotten something, do not take time to search for it; instead, move to the next point. Be flexible and ready to adapt to last-minute changes.

FOR FURTHER READING

Baugh, Sue L., Maridell Fryar, and David A. Thomas. *Handbook of Business Writing.*

Beatty, Richard. *The Perfect Cover Letter.*

Bell, Arthur. *Complete Business Writer's Manual: Model Letters, Memos, Reports, and Presentations for Every Occasion.*

Brock, Susan L., and Beverly Manber. *Writing Business Proposals and Reports: Strategies for Success.*

Brown, Leland. *Effective Business Writing.*

Clover, Vernon. *Business Research Methods.*

Frailey, L. E. *Handbook of Business Letters.*

Griffin, Jack. *The Complete Handbook of Model Business Letters.*

Hansen, Katherine. *Dynamic Cover Letters for New Graduates.*

Kupsh, Joyce. *How to Create High Impact Business Reports.*

Ryan, Robert. *Winning Resumes.*

Tepper, Ron. *Power Resumes.*

E-SOURCES

Professional Writing Handouts and Resources
http://owl.english.purdue.edu/handouts/pw

A Beginner's Guide to Effective Email
http://www.webfoot.com/advice/email.top.html

Writing Résumés and Cover Letters
http://www.utoronto.ca/writing/applic.html
http://jobsearchtech.about.com/od/resumes

Oral Presentations
http://www.calss.utoronto.ca/pamphlets/oral.htm

Collaborative Writing
http://www.stanford.edu/group/collaborate

Supporting Your Talk with Visuals
http://www.engineering.utoronto.ca/English/page-1-2080-1.html

Presenting Effective Presentations with Visual Aids
http://www.osha.gov/doc/outreachtraining/htmlfiles/traintec.html

Microsoft Office PowerPoint 2007
http://office.microsoft.com/en-us/powerpoint/FX100648951033.aspx

COMPANION WEBSITE

See **http://www.transcanadawriter.nelson.com** for additional information about special writing contexts.

CHAPTER 25

Writing for Essay Examinations and Literary Purposes

This chapter provides guidance in writing for two special academic purposes: essay writing and writing about literature. It examines the purpose of essay exams and how to study and heighten writing performance for them. It also provides an overview of major literary terms and offers strategies for reading literature through the eyes of a writer and guidance in writing about fiction, poetry, and drama.

Vigorous writing is concise.

—WILLIAM STRUNK JR.

WHAT ARE ESSAY EXAMS?

Throughout your academic experience you will most likely face essay examinations. Essay exams, unlike essays or reports you write outside class, force you to truncate the writing process to meet a deadline. Learning to write essay exams can teach you to work under pressure in your profession, when you may have to provide immediate answers to questions or draft statements to manage a crisis with little time for reflection.

To help you feel confident about writing under pressure, here are strategies that can improve your performance.

The Purpose of Essay Examinations

Instructors use objective tests consisting of multiple-choice and true-or-false questions to measure the ability to recall factual information. Essay questions go beyond memorization to accomplish additional goals:

- measure your understanding of facts by asking you to restate information in your own words

- evaluate your ability to assimilate and analyze material

- analyze your critical thinking skills in diagnosing problems, proposing solutions, comparing situations, outlining causes, and predicting outcomes

- judge your ability to discriminate or classify ideas by isolating essential information from incidental details

- determine your ability to apply knowledge to test cases or hypothetical situations

In asking essay questions, instructors seek more than a simple recital of memorized facts. The literature student who provides an accurate definition of *dramatic irony* in his or her own words better demonstrates an understanding of the concept than one who simply remembers enough from the textbook to recognize a familiar statement appearing on a multiple-choice test.

Strategies for Studying for Essay Examinations

1. **Determine the scope of the examination.** Recognize that many instructors are reluctant to answer the direct question, What's on the test? But most will respond favourably to two critical questions that you should ask: What does the examination cover? What is the best way to prepare? Asking these questions can help you target your studying and avoid reviewing the wrong material.

2. **Begin studying at once. Don't attempt to cram the night before.** If you spread your studying over a week, you will have more opportunity to learn and recall information than attempting to absorb the same amount of information in a few hours of last-minute cramming.

   - If you delay studying until the night before the examination, you run the risk that an unexpected problem will disrupt your plans and leave you unprepared.

   - Studying in advance gives you the opportunity to ask questions before the examination. If you discover that your instructor defines a term differently than the textbook, for example, you can ask which one he or she thinks is accurate.

3. **Talk to other students about the upcoming examination.** Discuss possible topics, methods of studying, and lecture notes. When you talk to classmates, you may realize that you have forgotten or misunderstood information or failed to recall an instructor's recommendation.

4. **Consider the nature of the discipline.** The kind of response that instructors expect is determined by the discipline. In the humanities, students are trained to base well-supported arguments on individual interpretations of a work of art or historical event. In such fields as law, psychology, sociology, and nursing, students are expected to advance only ideas that follow specific standards and practices and that can be scientifically proven.

5. **Review your syllabus, notes, textbooks, and handouts.** Highlight important passages for easy review just before the exam. Note significant facts, statistics, and quotations that may serve as support for your responses.

   - Take notes as you study. Essay exams require that you state ideas in your own words, not simply identify what you have read. If definitions are important, close your book and write a brief version of your own and then compare it to the text. Writing about the material is the best way to prepare for an essay test.

   - If you are taking an open-book examination, highlight passages and use labelled bookmarks so you can quickly locate information while writing. Familiarize yourself with the book's index.

(Continued)

6. **Recall the types of questions your instructor has asked in class.** The kinds of questions asked to prompt class discussion may provide a clue about the way the instructor may word questions on essay examinations.

   - Does your instructor focus on comparing issues, analyzing problems, or debating alternative interpretations or theories?
   - Does he or she concentrate on presenting in-depth analysis of narrow topics or providing a sweeping, inclusive overview of the subject?

7. **Think in terms of the modes.** Most essay questions use prompts that ask students to *define* elements, *compare* related topics, *explain* a process, or detail *causes* or *effects*.

   - In reviewing your notes and textbook, consider what major items require definition, which subjects are often compared, which processes require explanation, and what ideas are presented as causes or effects.

8. **Prewrite possible responses.** Select the key issues or topics you expect to appear on the examination and freewrite, cluster, or brainstorm possible essays. List possible thesis statements.

   - Remember that an essay test requires that you express what you know in writing. Fifteen minutes of prewriting can help you assimilate information, identify facts, generate ideas, and reveal knowledge that you may have overlooked more quickly than hours of reading and memorizing. *Prepare yourself to write.*

9. **Get as much rest as possible the night before.** Late-night cramming may help you identify facts and figures that appear on multiple-choice tests, but essay questions demand thinking. If you are not rested, you may find yourself unable to quickly analyze issues, generate ideas, make connections, and present your thoughts in an organized fashion.

Strategies for Writing an Essay Examination

Writing under pressure can frustrate even the most prepared student. If you tend to become rattled or nervous, you may wish to take a walk between classes, call a friend, eat a high-energy snack, or listen to your favourite song just before the test to put you in a positive frame of mind.

1. **Come to the examination prepared to write.** Bring two pens, paper, and, unless prohibited, a dictionary and handbook.

2. **Read the entire exam.** Go over *all* the questions carefully before starting to write. Determine how much each question is worth. Some instructors will indicate the point value of each question.

3. **Budget your time.** Determine how much time you should devote to each question. Give yourself enough time for planning and editing each question.

4. **Answer the easiest questions first while thinking about the more difficult ones.** The easiest questions will take less time to answer and may stimulate ideas that will help you confront more challenging questions.

5. **Read each question twice.** Students often miss points by failing to fully read the question. They respond to a word or phrase out of context and begin writing an energetic essay that does not address the question.

6. **Study the verbs or command words that direct your response.** Most essay questions contain clues to the kind of response the instructor expects:

QUESTION	DESIRED RESPONSE
List reasons for the rise of labour unions in the 1930s.	A series of reasons rather than an in-depth analysis of a single factor
Distinguish the differences between ancient Athens and Sparta.	A comparison/contrast, highlighting differences
What led to the collapse of the Soviet Union?	A cause-and-effect essay, perhaps related in a narrative or organized by division or classification
Describe three common forms of depression.	Three short definitions or descriptions organized by division
Discuss the effects of global warming on the environment.	An essay consisting of cause and effect, process, description, or division

7. **Study questions that require more than a single response.** Some essay questions contain more than one command and require a two- or three-part response:

QUESTION	DESIRED RESPONSE
Provide a definition of chemical dependency and explain why treatment remains problematic.	1. Define term. 2. List causes for problems in treatment.
Select three key economic proposals made by the prime minister in his address to the country and predict how they will affect both the trade deficit and unemployment.	1. Describe or define three points. 2. Discuss each point, listing effects on trade deficit and unemployment.

8. **Provide a clear thesis statement.** Your response should do more than simply list or discuss ideas. A strong thesis statement will give your response direction and can help organize ideas. This is very important if instructors present you with general questions or topics.

Question:

How has the concept of separation of church and state affected Canadian society?

(Continued)

Possible Thesis Statements:

The separation of church and state has allowed Canadian public schools to accommodate students from diverse religious backgrounds with little of the conflict found in other countries.

Unlike state-supported religious institutions in other nations, Canadian churches are independent and able to take active roles in criticizing government policies regarding discrimination, Canadian foreign policy, and abortion.

9. **Explain or justify your response to broad questions.** Sometimes instructors ask sweeping questions that cannot be fully addressed with a brief response. Avoid responding with a detailed explanation of one factor or presenting a list of a dozen factors. Instead, justify your response in a balanced context:

Question:

What led to Canadian Confederation?

Justified Response:

There were numerous political, social, economic, and philosophical causes that led to the Confederation of Canada. But clearly the most significant and enduring cause for the union was the problem of growing economic autonomy . . .

Although many Canadians would cite the need for stable autonomy as the main reason for the Confederation of Canada, it is difficult to isolate a single factor as a cause for the union. To understand the impulse toward federation, one must appreciate the full range of social, economic, commercial, internal politics and foreign policy issues at play at the time . . .

10. **Keep an eye on the clock.** Pace yourself. Don't "overdo" a response simply because you are knowledgeable about the topic. Provide enough information to address the question, and then move on.

11. **Keep writing.** If you become blocked or stalled on a question and can't think, move on to other questions or review what you have answered. Often, rereading the response to one question will spark ideas that aid in another.

12. **Provide space for revisions.** Write on every other line of the page or leave wide margins. You will not have time to write a full second draft, but you can make neat corrections and slip in ideas if you give yourself space for changes and additions.

WRITING **ACTIVITIES**

1. Review essay exams you have taken in the past. How could you have improved your responses? Read the question and write a fresh response within the time limits of the original test.

2. Select one of the following questions and write for 15 minutes, drawing on your personal experience, reading, and past courses.

What, in your opinion, is the principal cause of poverty in Canada?

How has immigration shaped Canadian society?

What effects has the Internet had on education?

Identify the key abilities needed for someone to succeed in your future profession.

Examine your completed response.

- Is the thesis clearly stated?
- Is the thesis supported by detail?
- Is the response logically organized?
- Are there irrelevant ideas that should be deleted?
- How effective is the conclusion?

How could you improve your ability to write under pressure?

3. Select a textbook chapter you have recently studied and use one of the questions at the end to prompt a 15-minute response. If your book does not offer questions, summarize one or more of the chapter's key points in a short essay without looking at the book.

- Were you able to develop a thesis and support it with detail?
- What problems did you encounter in writing?
- How could you improve your studying?

WHAT IS LITERATURE?

Literature consists of works of imagination. Poems, short stories, novels, and plays present writers' visions of the world. Chaucer's poetry, Shakespeare's *King Lear*, Michael Ondaatje's *The English Patient*, Emily Dickinson's "Because I could not stop for Death," and Michel Tremblay's *Les Belles-soeurs* are all examples of literature.

Writing about literature can be challenging, especially if you are accustomed to reading only for pleasure or information. Literature courses require you to understand not only what happens in a work but also how it is stated.

Writers who study literature, like writers in any discipline, use technical terms to discuss their subject. In order to write about a work of literature, it is helpful to understand definitions of key words and concepts.

Major Literary Terms

genre   A form or type. In literature, genres include poetry, the short story, the novel, the play.

tragedy   A work of literature in which the protagonist moves from a position of power and respect within a society downward to destruction, usually marked by exile, death, or suicide. In literature tragedy involves choice, not random disaster. A character killed in an airplane crash is not considered "tragic." Macbeth, however, makes a decision to kill the king and sets into motion the forces that ultimately destroy him. Traditionally, the tragic hero is a nobleman or person of high standing. In classic Greek tragedy the heroes often suffer from hubris, or pride, which leads them to assume that they can break laws and control events. Often, as in *Oedipus Rex,* the hero learns too late that no mortal can control destiny.

comedy   A work of literature in which the characters, often a pair of young lovers, overcome obstacles to form a new society, often culminating in a wedding, festivity, or new understanding. Comedies, although they usually have "happy" endings, may not be filled with jokes. Chekhov, for instance, labelled *The Cherry Orchard* and *The Seagull* comedies, even though one play involved a family's being dispossessed and the other involved suicide.

Characters

characters   Individuals appearing in a story, novel, poem, or play.

protagonist   The main figure, often called the hero—Hamlet, Huckleberry Finn, Hedda Gabler.

antagonist   A person or force working against the protagonist. This could be a villain or a hostile environment or element like the sea or a blizzard.

stock characters   People representing recurring types—the hard-boiled detective, the innocent child, the vengeful spouse, young lovers.

foils   Minor characters who serve to define the qualities of another figure by contrast. The idealism of a young attorney can be demonstrated to readers by surrounding him or her with cynical or uncaring coworkers.

flat characters   Minor characters who are two-dimensional. Unlike the major figures, they are only superficially developed.

Plot

plot   The events that occur in the work.

conflict   The struggle or tension that is a key element of the plot. The conflict can be between individuals, an individual and society or nature, or between contrasting forces within a character.

climax   An event signalling a turning point in the plot, usually when the conflict reaches its greatest intensity.

setting   The time and place of the work.

Theme

theme   The major issue, problem, or controlling idea. Ralph Ellison's *Invisible Man* concerns racism. Margaret Lawrence's *A Jest of God* reveals the petty cruelty, loneliness, and deceit that small-town life can generate. An author's treatment of theme may include political commentary or a call for social reform.

tone   The author's attitude toward events, characters, or plot. The tone of a play, story, or poem can be somber, humorous, sarcastic, or sympathetic.

social and cultural context   The influence of social and cultural forces—such as gender, economic class, race or ethnicity, age, religion—on the characters, plot, and conflict.

Point of View

point of view   The perspective from which the story is told.

first-person narrator   A narrator who experienced or witnessed the events in the story. The narrator may be the protagonist or a bystander.

unreliable narrator   A narrator who may have biases or misunderstandings that distort the way readers perceive events.

third-person narrator   In third-person point of view, the narrator may be **omniscient,** or all-knowing, entering the minds of several characters, or may have **limited knowledge** of characters and events. Often the third-person narrator may show the inner thoughts and feelings of major characters and report only the actions and dialogue of minor figures.

Technique

exposition   Supplies readers with background information about setting, characters' past lives, or events that occurred before the plot begins. Exposition is challenging to develop in drama because details have to be communicated to the audience through dialogue.

foreshadowing   Clues or hints of action to follow.

flashback   A scene in a novel, play, story, or poem that returns to earlier events to suggest a character's memory, provide a historical perspective, or clarify the present.

allusion   A casual reference to a famous literary or historical event or figure. Biblical allusions might include a character receiving "thirty pieces of silver" to betray a friend or "parting the Red Sea" to overcome an overwhelming obstacle.

irony   The contrast between anticipated and actual elements. **Verbal irony** consists of remarks in which the spoken words differ from their intended meaning, often for comic or sarcastic effect. An undercover officer arresting a drug dealer might state ironically, "This is your lucky day." In **dramatic irony** there is a discrepancy between what a character believes to be true and what the author or audience knows. In *A Doll's House* Helmer tells his wife that most criminals have mothers who lie, unaware that his wife has been living an elaborate falsehood.

image   A person, object, scene, or situation that creates a strong impression, usually one that relies on the senses.

symbol   A person, object, scene, or situation that represents something else: an idea, quality, or concept. A lion might symbolize courage. A cross represents Christ. Symbols may be obvious or complex.

simile   A comparison of two unlike things using the words *like* or *as:*

The unpaid bills hit him *like* a tidal wave.
The coffee was *as* cold as ice.

metaphor   A direct comparison of two unlike things made without using *like* or *as:*

He was hit by a tidal wave of unpaid bills.
We drank ice-cold coffee.

stanza   A unit of poetry named for the number of lines it contains:

couplet: two lines	sestet: six lines
triplet: three lines	septet: seven lines
quatrain: four lines	octave: eight lines
quintet: five lines	

epiphany   A sudden realization or burst of insight.

Strategies for Reading Literature

1. **Survey the work and read available biographical or introductory material.** Many literary anthologies include headnotes similar to those in the reader portion of this book. Examine the biography carefully and review any questions that might appear after the text. Consult an encyclopedia or search the Internet for background material about the work, including biographical information about the author.

2. **Read the work once to get a first impression.** Allow yourself to read for pleasure. Enjoy the poem or story, noting passages you find interesting, difficult, powerful, or confusing.

3. **Review the overall work and ask questions.**

4. **Examine details in context.** Avoid allowing personal or contemporary attitudes to colour your perceptions of the work or the author's intention. Statements by a 19th-century writer may strike you as being racist or sexist. Poetry by someone of another culture may puzzle or offend you. Don't allow isolated statements to distort your impression of the entire work.

5. **Identify possible topics for discussion or writing.** Highlight significant passages for easy reference.

6. **Note aspects of the work you find puzzling or confusing.** Sometimes an author will present an image or make a historical reference you do not understand. Characters may use regional or slang expressions you are unfamiliar with. Look up confusing words in a dictionary. Discuss the work with other students. They may know the meaning of a word or the significance of a reference or detail. Another reader may have an alternative interpretation that sharpens your analysis of the work.

☑ QUESTIONS FOR LITERARY ANALYSIS

✔ What significance, if any, does the title have? What does it suggest?

✔ What is the time and setting of the story? Is it significant or only incidental?

✔ Who are the principal characters? Do they remind you of characters in other works? What motivates their actions and influences their thoughts?

✔ How would you characterize the protagonist? Does he or she have internal or external conflicts? Does the protagonist appear to represent a group of people, a cause, or a set of values? What motivates the protagonist?

✔ How is the plot developed? What is the central conflict? Does the author use devices such as foreshadowing?

✔ Does the writer use imagery and symbols? What are they? What impact do they have?

✔ Who is the narrator? Is the story related in first or third person? Does the narrator have limited or full knowledge of events and characters? If told in the first person, is the narrator the protagonist, a minor character, or simply a witness or recorder?

✔ What seems to be the author's message? Is the author making a social or political statement?

✔ What are the significant themes in the work? What is the central theme?

✔ What lasting impression does the work create?

Strategies for Writing about Literature

Students often make the mistake of beginning to write about something they have read without giving themselves time to think and analyze the work. If you finish reading Atwood's "Death by Landscape" and start writing, you are likely to want to recapture what you have just experienced and produce little more than a plot summary. But retelling each twist of the tale adds little to anyone's knowledge or appreciation of the story.

1. **Avoid summarizing the work.** Although most writers analyzing a story, play, or poem will refer to the text, they do more than restate the plot.
   - Assume that everyone you are writing to has already read the work. Your job, then, is not to retell the story but to reveal something that other readers may have missed.

2. **Narrow the scope of your response by answering questions.** If you focus on answering specific questions about a character, the author's use of symbols, or the point of view, you prevent yourself from merely writing a summary.

3. **Prewrite to explore the topic and develop a thesis.** Use brainstorming, clustering, or freewriting to investigate your topic. As you sketch out ideas, you may have to narrow or expand your approach.

4. **Develop a working thesis.** Your thesis should express a clear opinion about the meaning, structure, or style of the work:

   In *Shape of a Girl*, Joan MacLeod dramatizes the murder of Reena Virk to explore the effects of bullying on high-school-aged girls.

   The Great Gatsby presents a world in which marriage, the stock market, and even the World Series are corrupted by selfish greed.

5. **Support your thesis with evidence from the text.** Works of literature are subject to a variety of interpretations—but they should not be viewed as abstract sculptures that can mean anything you want. Your opinions must be based on evidence presented in the story or poem. If you assert that a character is mentally ill, you must cite passages where the individual's speech, actions, or thoughts exhibit symptoms of a psychological disorder.

6. **Avoid extensive direct quotes.** Because your readers have read the work, there is no reason to repeat large sections of the text.
   - Use quotations when the author's image or a character's statement is so impressive that a paraphrase would weaken its impact.

(Continued)

- Refer to passages or statements rather than quote them. Assuming your reader is familiar with the work, you can provide reminders rather than reproduce text.
- Abbreviate longer quotations by selecting key words or phrases.

7. **Quote poetry accurately.** Unless a poem is very long, you can present the full text within your paper or a section in a block quotation. When you quote a few lines within a paragraph, use slash marks to indicate original line breaks:

Eliot's Prufrock muses at one point, "I should have been a pair of ragged claws/ Scuttling across the floors of silent seas."

8. **Write in the present tense.** Although most works are stated in the past tense, writers usually describe an author's views and a character's action in the present tense:

Shakespeare *presents* his audience with a dramatic dilemma. How *does* an indecisive character like Hamlet *avenge* his father's death? Hamlet *muses* and *ponders* long before taking action to confront the king.

9. **Identify the most effective mode to organize your supporting details.** You can structure your analysis by comparing two characters or events, defining a problem the protagonist faces, or discussing the causes or effects of a character's actions.

10. **After writing a first draft, review the work and then examine your thesis and support.**
    - Does your paper have a clear focus? Should the topic be narrowed?
    - Does your paper have a clear thesis?
    - Do you support the thesis with sufficient evidence from the text?
    - Is the support clearly organized? Would another mode be a better method of structuring the essay?

WRITING ABOUT FICTION

Read the following story; then review the questions on page 568. Though short and starkly told, with little reference to time and setting, "The Bread" presents a strong plot marked by both a climax and anticlimax.

WOLFGANG BORCHERT

Wolfgang Borchert (1921–1947) was born in Hamburg, Germany, and worked as an actor and bookseller. During the Second World War he served in the German army in Russia and was wounded. An anti-Nazi, he was twice imprisoned for expressing defeatist views. He captured the despair and deprivation of the war in poems and short stories. Borchert died of a fever contracted during the war the day after the premiere of his play **Outside the Door.**

The Bread*

Borchert wrote this story when food was strictly rationed, forcing many families to survive on a few slices of bread a day.

Suddenly she woke up. It was half past two. She considered why she had woken up. Oh yes! In   1
the kitchen someone had knocked against a chair. She listened to the kitchen. It was quiet. It
was too quiet and as she moved her hand across the bed beside her, she found it empty. That
was what had made it so particularly quiet: she missed his breathing. She got up and groped
her way through the dark flat to the kitchen. In the kitchen they met. The time was half past
two. She saw something white standing on the kitchen cupboard. She put the light on. They
stood facing one another in their night-shirts. At night. At half past two. In the kitchen.

On the kitchen table lay the bread-plate. She saw that he had cut himself some bread.
The knife was still lying beside the plate. And on the cloth there were bread-crumbs. When
they went to bed at night, she always made the table-cloth clean. Every night. But now there   10
were crumbs on the cloth. And the knife was lying there. She felt how the cold of the tiles
crept slowly up her. And she looked away from the plate.

"I thought there was something here," he said and looked round the kitchen.

"I heard something, too," she answered and thought that at night, in his night-shirt, he
really looked quite old. As old as he was. Sixty-three. During the day he sometimes looked
younger. She looks quite old, he thought, in her night-dress she really looks pretty old. But
perhaps it's because of her hair. With women at night it's always because of their hair. All at
once it makes them so old.

"You should have put on your shoes. Barefoot like that on the cold tiles! You'll catch
cold."   20

She didn't look at him, because she couldn't bear him to lie. To lie when they had been
married thirty-nine years.

"I thought there was something here," he said once more and again looked so senselessly
from one corner to the other, "I heard something in here. So I thought there'd be something
here."

"I heard something, too. But it must have been nothing." She took the plate off the table
and flicked the crumbs from the table-cloth.

*Borchert, Wolfgang, "The Bread" translated by David Porter, from *The Man Outside*, Copyright © 1971 by New Directions Publishing Corp. Reprinted by permission of New Directions Publishing Corp.

"No, it must have been nothing," he echoed uncertainly.

She came to his help: "Come on. It must have been outside. Come to bed. You'll catch

30 cold. On the cold tiles."

He looked at the window. "Yes, it'll have been outside. I thought it was in here."

She raised her hand to the switch. I must now put the light out, or I shall have to look at the plate, she thought. I dare not look at the plate. "Come on," she said and put out the light, "it must have been outside. The gutter always bangs against the wall when there's a wind. I'm sure it was the gutter. It always rattles when there's a wind."

They both groped their way along the dark corridor to the bedroom. Their naked feet slapped on the floor.

"It is windy," he said, "it's been windy all night."

As they lay in bed, she said: "Yes it's been windy all night. It must have been the gutter."

40 "Yes. I thought it was in the kitchen. It must have been the gutter." He said it as though he were already half asleep. But she noticed how false his voice sounded when he lied.

"It's cold," she said and yawned softly, "I'll creep under the covers. Good night."

"Night," he replied and added: "Yes, it really is pretty cold."

Then it was quiet. Many minutes later she heard him softly and cautiously chewing. She breathed deeply and evenly so that he should not notice that she was still awake. But his chewing was so regular that it slowly sent her to sleep.

When he came home the next evening, she put four slices of bread in front of him. At other times he had only been able to eat three.

"You can safely eat four," she said and moved away from the lamp. "I can't digest this

50 bread properly. Just you eat another one. I don't digest it very well."

She saw how he bent deep over the plate. He didn't look up. At that moment she was sorry for him.

"You can't eat only two slices," he said to his plate.

"Yes, I can. I don't digest this bread properly in the evening. Just eat. Eat it."

Only a while later did she sit down at the table under the lamp.

☑ | QUESTIONS FOR ANALYSIS

✔ Consider the title. How does it shape your understanding of the story?

✔ The author presents no details about time and location. Would they be helpful? Does the author seem to assume his readers understand the significance of a few slices of bread?

✔ What characterizes the conflict between the husband and wife?

✔ Review the dialogue between the two characters in the kitchen. Why doesn't the wife confront her husband? Why does she go along with his obvious lie?

✔ How do you interpret the wife's final gesture?

✔ Which event would you label the climax? Which scene represents an anticlimax?

✔ What point of view does the author use in telling the story?

STUDENT ESSAY

Denial

At first reading Wolfgang Borchert's story about an old couple and a few slices of bread seems trivial, especially when cast against the mass murder and suffering of the Second World War. But by focusing on this small incident, Borchert is able to create a tightly focused drama that explores the toll hunger and deprivation can take on a person's character, morality, and self-respect.

More pointedly, Borchert's story is a study in denial, demonstrating the defense mechanisms people employ to protect themselves from something too painful to acknowledge.

"The Bread" presents a classic case of what current psychologists call "enabling." Awakened by a noise, a woman enters the kitchen and discovers clear evidence that her husband has cut a slice of bread, stealing food from her. Her husband, whom she knows is lying, offers a childishly clumsy explanation, claiming to be investigating a noise in the dark.

Instead of confronting her husband, the wife changes the subject, abruptly scolding him for not wearing shoes. When her husband haltingly explains that he heard a noise, she quickly agrees, enabling his deception. To leave the scene of the crime—the kitchen with its signs of his betrayal—she urges him to come to bed. Even when she hears him chewing the stolen bread, she remains silent.

In helping him lie, in going along and playing dumb, the wife is masking her pain and anger. It is a form of denial, a way of wishing this theft not to be true. This behaviour is common in spouses who discover their partners are unfaithful or parents who encounter a child's drug abuse. The wife certainly must feel betrayed on many levels.

First, her husband was stealing food from her. Suffering severe hunger, he evidently did not ask for more bread or even discuss it with her. Instead, he stole. Second, when caught, he did not admit his guilt but lied. She must feel anger at this betrayal and perhaps disgust at his weakness, his inability to control his hunger and his failure to muster the courage to tell the truth and apologize.

The wife's final gesture is a wordless confrontation, letting her husband know that she is aware of his theft. Guilt-stricken, her husband cannot look her in the eye and asserts that she needs to eat more than two slices. The wife lies, claiming to have digestion problems. Her inability to sit at the table, however, reveals the extent of her anger. After decades of life together, the couple can only communicate with shared acts of deception.

Borchert's point is that hunger will drive one to steal from a loved one, to break the trust and love that held a couple together for almost forty years.

☑ QUESTIONS FOR REVIEW AND WRITING

✔ How adequate is the student's title?

✔ What is the student's thesis? Is it clearly stated?

✔ Does the student provide enough support from the story?

✔ The student introduces a psychological term. Is it suited to this essay? Should it be better explained?

✔ Do any passages need expansion? Are there needless details that should be deleted?

✔ How would you improve this commentary? Do you have an alternative interpretation of the woman's final gesture?

WRITING ABOUT POETRY

Poetry is a literary form many students find challenging to analyze. You can compare poems to paintings. Unlike the sweep of fiction, which offers a movielike flow of events, a poem usually captures a scene, a moment, or a mood, like a painting or still photograph. Some poems are narratives and can be analyzed almost like a short story. Other poems, much like impressionist or abstract paintings, offer images and statements that resist literal interpretations.

Strategies for Writing about Poetry

1. **Read the poem aloud.** Poems rely on subtle relationships between words and meanings. You may find it easier to understand the patterns and language devices the poet uses by hearing the way the poem sounds. Read difficult lines several times, emphasizing different words.

2. **Use peer review.** Ask other students or friends about their understanding or interpretation of a poem, line, or image.

3. **Prewrite by writing a prose summary if possible.** Put the meaning or basic action of the poem in your own words. This may help you identify the literal meaning of the poem as well as topics for writing.

4. **Review the rhyme, meter, and form of the poem.** Notice how the cadence of words affects the poem's meaning.

5. **Look up key words in a dictionary.** Words may have subtle meanings or associations you may be unfamiliar with. Because poems are brief, almost every word is significant.

EDWIN ARLINGTON ROBINSON

Edwin Arlington Robinson (1869–1935) was born into a wealthy family in Maine and began writing poetry at the age of 11. After attending Harvard for two years and enduring a series of tragic losses, he moved to New York City where he began writing in earnest. Spurred on by the support of President Theodore Roosevelt and later by the widow of composer Edward MacDowell, Robinson eventually won three Pulitzer Prizes. This poem, Richard Cory, was set to music many years later by Simon and Garfunkel.

Richard Cory

Whenever Richard Cory went down town,   1
We people on the pavement looked at him:
He was a gentleman from sole to crown,
Clean favored, and imperially slim.

And he was always quietly arrayed,
And he was always human when he talked;
But still he fluttered pulses when he said,
"Good-morning," and he glittered when he walked.

And he was rich—yes, richer than a king—
And admirably schooled in every grace: **10**
In fine, we thought that he was everything
To make us wish that we were in his place.

So on we worked, and waited for the light,
And went without the meat, and cursed the bread;
And Richard Cory, one calm summer night,
Went home and put a bullet through his head.

☑ QUESTIONS FOR ANALYSIS

✔ What kind of person is Richard Cory? What attitude does the narrator have toward him?

✔ The narrator refers to himself or herself as representing the "people on the pavement." What kind of people would they be?

✔ What does this poem say about wealth and envy?

✔ What impact does the final line have? What does it leave unanswered or unexplained?

STUDENT PAPER

One Calm Summer Night: Contrast and Irony
in Robinson's "Richard Cory"

"Richard Cory" endures as one of the most memorable and widely anthologized American poems, largely because of its surprise ending. The "lesson" of the poem—that you can't judge a book by its cover—is quite simple but so powerfully stated that it makes a profound impression on most readers. Robinson uses contrast and irony in both content and form to maximize the impact of the unexpected and unexplained suicide of his admired protagonist.

First, there is the ironic contrast of Richard Cory's wealth and his eventual suicide. The title character is handsome, slim, wealthy, elegant, yet "always human." The poem, told from the standpoint of the "people on the pavement," celebrates Richard Cory as someone who embodies everything people admire. Cory, though wealthy and aristocratic, appears modest and graceful. Although poor, the townspeople do not resent Cory's wealth. Like a celebrity, Cory has the power to flutter their pulses by simply acknowledging their presence when he passes them on the street. Working, waiting for the light, living without meat, these common people continue with their pedestrian lives while on a calm summer night the admired Cory shoots himself. Seeing his wealth and grace only from a distance, Cory's poor admirers had no knowledge of his inner life, no hint of the turmoil or depression that led him to commit suicide.

Second, the impact of the poem is heightened by the contrast between syntax and subject matter. In telling the story of a suicide, Robinson writes in the unadorned language of a children's poem. The lines read easily in the simple hum drum pattern and flow of a Mother Goose rhyme. The sing-song effect of the poem makes the violent ending unexpected. In addition, the tone and mood of the poem is largely positive and cheerful. The royal connotations of words describing Cory—"king," "imperially," and "crown"—all contrast with the despair and desperation associated with suicide. All these elements work to create a stunning and memorable ending, making both townspeople and readers perplexed by the mystery of Cory's suicide.

✔ QUESTIONS FOR REVIEW AND WRITING

✔ What is the student's thesis?

✔ Does the student provide enough detail from the poem to support the thesis?

✔ How do you interpret the poem's meaning?

✔ Robinson entitled the poem with the protagonist's name. Would a more descriptive title give the end away and weaken the impact of the last line?

✔ The reasons for Cory's suicide are never explained. What is Robinson's point?

✔ How would you improve or expand this student's analysis?

▣ WRITING **EXERCISE**

Read the following poem, and then write a short analysis of its meaning, structure, or imagery.

My Life Had Stood—A Loaded Gun—*

My Life had stood—a Loaded Gun—
In Corners—till a Day
The Owner passed—identified—
And carried Me away—

And now We roam in Sovereign Woods—
and now We hunt the Doe—
And every time I speak for Him—
The Mountains straight reply—

And do I smile, such cordial light
Upon the Valley glow—
It is as a Vesuvian face
Had let its pleasure through—

And when at Night—Our good Day done—
I guard my Master's Head—
'Tis better than the Eider-Duck's
Deep Pillow—to have shared—

To foe of His—I'm deadly foe—
None stir the second time—
On whom I lay a Yellow Eye—
Or an emphatic Thumb—

Though I than He—may longer live
He longer must—than I—
For I have but the power to kill,
Without—the power to die—

—*Emily Dickinson*

*Dickinson, Emily, "My Life Had Stood—A Loaded Gun" reprinted by permission of the publishers and the Trustees of Amherst College from *The Poems of Emily Dickinson*, Thomas H. Johnson, ed., Cambridge, Mass.: The Belknap Press of Harvard University Press, Copyright © 1951, 1955, 1979, 1983 by the President and Fellows of Harvard College.

WRITING ABOUT DRAMA

Although most plays relate a narrative with a strong emphasis on plot and character development, they differ from stories and novels because the events must be presented through dialogue. If you are unaccustomed to reading plays, you can easily become lost in the interplay between characters.

Strategies for Writing about Drama

1. **Study the set and character descriptions.** Read and review the opening descriptions of each character so you can easily identify each one.

2. **Review the playwright's biography, other works, or information about the time and place.** If you know something about the writer's concerns or the setting of the play, you may be able to more easily identify key themes or appreciate subtle details.

3. **Visualize the set and actors.** Plays are meant to be seen, not read. Study the set descriptions and imagine what the stage would look like. Is this a living room, warehouse, nightclub, or battlefield? Would it be darkly or brilliantly lit? Does the background suggest a conflict with or between the characters? After reading descriptions of the characters, imagine the actor or actress who might play the part. If you can imagine faces instead of names, you can more easily follow the plot and understand the interplay between characters.

4. **Read important lines aloud.** Hearing the words of a protagonist's final speech can bring the text to life and help you appreciate the impact it would have on a live audience.

5. **Study the structure of the play.** Plays are usually divided into acts and scenes, many of which end with an important turn of events, revelation, or conflict. Focus on the way each act ends.

WRITING EXERCISE

Read this scene from Clifford Odets's 1935 play *Paradise Lost** and write a short analysis of one of the following: the conflict between characters, the exposition of the plot, the struggle between the two partners, or the author's implied message.

Background: *Paradise Lost* follows the decline of a middle-class family. The protagonist, Leo Gordon, is a small manufacturer who has mortgaged his house to keep his struggling business afloat. A deeply moral man, he has increased wages for his impoverished workers, unaware that his partner of 20 years has been embezzling funds. In this scene, his partner, Sam Katz, has brought home a professional arsonist, hoping to convince Gordon to set fire to their business to collect the insurance money. The arsonist, Mr. May, speaks with a slight Swedish accent and is described as a neatly dressed man carrying an umbrella and briefcase.

Sam: I brought May on a little business.
May: There you got it in a nutshell, Mr. Gordon. Assimilated: business!
Leo: What kind of business?
May: *(May has the quality of apricot cordial):* Well, there is a historical perspective in these things. Delicate!
Leo: What?
Sam: Delicate!

May: For these last three years I handled upward of fifty-three cases. Some of them will pay as triflin' a fee as two hundred dollars. These are cheap jobs—adulterated, what we call. *(Hastily adds):* But don't misunderstand, no prices now. The recommendation is purely suggestive, what we call. *(Leans back with satisfaction. Sam waits with bated breath. Leo does not understand a word of the speech.)*

Leo: *(finally):* I see, but what is your business?

May: *(leaning forward):* You don't ever know who's listening, do you?

Leo: Listening to what?

May: Mr. Gordon. Tell the truth—you're a puzzled gent.

Leo: If you don't mind my saying . . .

May: Business with us is what we call purely a state of mind. You take the average small manufacturer. He pays his bills on the first of the month. Right? *(Answers himself.)* Right! *(Again lowers voice.)* Suppose when the first comes, he can't pay. What then?

Leo: *(after waiting for the answer):* Yes . . . ?

May: Won't it make a state of mind?

Leo: Without doubt.

May: "Without doubt!" The manufacturer will not sleep! Won't eat! Irritation in the business and at home. The wife who is often a thing of beauty, he hits her! In this condition the respected citizen makes a werry foolish mistake. Some charlatan will sell him headache pills.

Sam: *(in an outburst):* But a smart man—!

May: *(chiding Sam gently before continuing to Leo):* Mr. Katz! But the man of sensitivity, does he leave unturned the rare gold and silver of experience? Does he? No! Six feet away stands the safe. A certain drawer within those swinging doors. Therein he finds what we call "insurance policy." Protection against theft . . . against fire, Mr. Gordon . . . *(Leans back again.)*

Leo: Fire . . . ?

May: Purely suggestive . . . *(Waits for Leo, who first looks to Sam, and then begins to scrape crumbs with his fingers.)* Yes, you guessed it: Should the respected citizen take aspirins? *(Leo continues to shovel nutshells together. The two watch him closely. Finally Leo says):*

Leo: Your profession is making fires?

May: Incorrect! No! *(Suddenly throws orange from table to Leo.)* See how quick you catched it? Not a thought in your head and you catched it! Fires happen like that.

Leo: In the last three years you made fifty fires—*happen*?

May: Fifty-three.

Leo: Human life is not important?

May: *(with flashing pride):* Nobody was burned—ever! *(Leo slowly replaces the orange.)* Don't be afraid, Mr. Gordon. In every case—

Leo: *(quietly, trembling):* Please leave my house.

Sam: Don't be in such a hurry, Leo.

May: Everything has a first time, my friend. The respected citizen . . .

Leo: Please leave!

May: Don't take umbrage, my friend. Tomorrow's another day. Here's my card—Edgar F. May. *(Places card on table.)* Purely suggestive . . .

(Continued)

Leo: *(shouting):* Get out of here!!

Sam: Don't insult humanity with your ignorance!!

May: No, he's right. It's his prerogative in his own house. *(Puts his glasses in their case now.)*

Sam: *(bitterly):* Any day now he won't have a house!

May: *(at the door):* Remember . . . May—between April and June—May. Good night . . .

*Odets, Clifford, "Paradise Lost" from *Waiting for Lefty and Other Plays* by Clifford Odets. Copyright © 1935 by Clifford Odets, Copyright © renewed 1963 by Clifford Odets. Used by permission of Grove/Atlantic, Inc.

☑ LITERARY PAPER **CHECKLIST**

Before submitting a literary paper, review these points:

✔ Have you selected an appropriate work for the assignment?

✔ Does your paper *analyze* or only *summarize* a literary work?

✔ Does your paper focus on a specific element of the work, such as the imagery, structure, character development, or plot—or does it attempt to explain everything the writer presents?

✔ Is the thesis clearly stated and supported by details taken from the text?

✔ Do you avoid reading passages out of context?

FOR FURTHER READING

Barnet, Sylvan. *A Short Guide to Writing about Literature.*

Burns, Richard. *Pass Exams and Write Top Essays.*

Callaghan, Patsy, and Ann Dobyns. *Literary Conversation: Thinking, Talking, and Writing about Literature.*

Frye, Northrop. *The Educated Imagination.*

Galica, Gregory. *The Blue Book: A Student's Guide to Essay Exams.*

Griffith, Kelley. *Writing Essays about Literature: A Guide and Style Sheet.*

Kurata, Marilyn Jane. *Models and Methods for Writing about Literature.*

Lesyk, Susan Burgess. *The Blue Book: Achieving Success on Essay Exams.*

McMahan, Elizabeth, Robert Funk, and Susan Day. *The Elements of Writing about Literature and Film.*

Meyer, Michael. *Thinking and Writing about Literature.*

Proffitt, Edward. *Reading and Writing about Literature: Fiction, Poetry, Drama, and the Essay.*

Roberts, Edgar. *Writing Essays about Literature: A Guide and Style Sheet.*

 ## E-SOURCES

Writing about Literature
http://owl.english.purdue.edu/handouts/general/gl_lit.html

Literature
http://www.unc.edu/depts/wcweb/handouts/literature.html

Poetry Explications
http://www.unc.edu/depts/wcweb/handouts/poetry-explication.html

Drama
http://www.unc.edu/depts/wcweb/handouts/drama.html

Common Words Used in Essay Questions
http://gwired.gwu.edu/counsel/asc/index.gw/Site_ID/46/Page_ID/14566/

The Essay Exam
http://web.uvic.ca/wguide/Pages/ExamEssays.html
http://www.studygs.net/tsttak4.htm
http://www.unc.edu/depts/wcweb/handouts/essay-exams.html

COMPANION WEBSITE

See **http://www.transcanadawriter.nelson.com** for additional information about writing about literature.

PART FIVE

Grammar and
Handbook

CHAPTER 26

Grammar

WHAT IS GRAMMAR?

Grammar, for many students, is off-putting. To them it means complicated rules, obscure terms such as "nonrestrictive elements," and memories of high school drills about capitals and commas. Some mistake grammar as merely a set of arbitrary conventions, a form of etiquette. But when students realize that grammar is the basis of meaning-making in language and that all those so-called rules and regulations exist to serve communication and human understanding, it can become a much more compelling subject of study.

Grammar consists of patterns that organize words into sentences to express ideas. Grammar affects how well you communicate and how well your readers interpret your writing. The following sentences are grammatically correct, but each creates a different impression of the same incident:

> Dr. Green, along with angry patients, protested the closing of the clinic.
> (Emphasizes the role of Dr. Green in the protest)

> Dr. Green and angry patients protested the closing of the clinic.
> (Indicates that the doctor and patients were equally significant)

> Angry patients, along with Dr. Green, protested the closing of the clinic.
> (Dramatizes the action of the patients and places the doctor in the background)

Grammar does have rules and definitions. Although it is not necessary to memorize each detail of this chapter, reviewing and understanding the basic building blocks of grammar will help you not only avoid errors but also improve your ability to write effective sentences.

PARTS OF SPEECH

English consists of nine parts of speech or types of words: nouns, pronouns, adjectives, verbs, adverbs, articles, prepositions, conjunctions, and interjections.

Nouns

Nouns are names of people, places, concepts, and things:

child	dog	automobile	computer
religion	month	ship	university

Proper Nouns

Names of specific people or specially designated places and objects are capitalized:

Nancy	Bichon	Buick	Apple
Islam	April	Titanic	King's College

Gerunds

Gerunds are nouns formed from verbals, usually ending in -ing:

Swimming is good exercise. He gave up *running*. She finds *singing* relaxing.

Pronouns

Pronouns take the place of nouns. They form a kind of shorthand so that Michelle can be referred to as *she*, and the Treaty of Versailles can be called *it*. The noun that the pronoun represents is called the "antecedent."

Personal Pronouns

Personal pronouns refer to specific people, places, or things:

Singular:

I, you, he, she, it   me, you, him, her   mine, yours, his, hers, its

Plural:

we, you, they   us, you, them   ours, yours, theirs

(Antecedents and pronouns must match in number.)

Indefinite Pronouns

Indefinite pronouns refer to general or nonspecific people, places, or things. Because they don't refer to specific nouns, they do not require an antecedent:

"Can *anyone* help?"

all	any	anybody	anyone	anything
everybody	everyone	everything	few	many
one	something	somebody	someone	some

Demonstrative Pronouns

Demonstrative pronouns point to antecedents:

This is my book.   *That* is her car.   *These* are our cards.   *Those* are the boys.

Interrogative Pronouns

Interrogative pronouns introduce questions:

Whose is that?   *Which* is yours?   *What* are you talking about?

Reflexive Pronouns and Intensive Pronouns

Reflexive pronouns add *self* or *selves* to a pronoun to indicate that the subject is also the object:

"He implicated *himself* by lying."

Intensive pronouns add *self* or *selves* for emphasis:

"She baked it *herself*."

Adjectives

Adjectives modify or describe nouns and pronouns. Adjectives may precede or follow the word they modify:

red car	*old* house	*expensive* tastes	*white* cloth
he was *tired*	she is *young*	they are *angry*	it was *broken*

Verbs

Verbs express action or link ideas.

Action Verbs

Action verbs express both visible action such as running and invisible action such as listening or contemplating:

argue	create	destroy	purchase
run	sing	support	think

Action verbs are transitive or intransitive. Transitive verbs express action directed toward nouns or pronouns called "direct objects":

She *purchased* mutual funds.
  Transitive verb   Direct object

Intransitive verbs express action that is not directed to nouns or pronouns:

She *purchased* recklessly.
  Intransitive verb   Adverb

Linking Verbs

Linking verbs express a state of being or relationship. You can think of linking verbs as an equal sign (=), connecting ideas:

Jacques *is* seventeen.	Jacques = seventeen.
They *are* lost.	They = lost.
Anya *seems* tired.	Anya = tired.

Auxiliary and Modal Verbs

Auxiliary verbs, often called "helping verbs," accompany verbs:

had worked	*has* helped	*is* walking

Modal verbs also accompany verbs to add meaning and indicate tense or time:

should work	*might* help	*will* walk

Time and Number

Verbs are important words in any sentence because they not only express action or a connection but also provide information about the time of the action and whether the subject is singular or plural.

Paul *works* at Starbucks.	(singular present tense)
Paul and Joan *work* at Starbucks.	(plural present tense)
Paul and Joan *will get married* in June.	(future tense)
Paul and Joan *worked* last semester.	(past tense)

Using singular or plural verbs can help shape meaning:

A desk and chair *is* on sale.   (indicates the desk and chair are one unit)
A desk and chair *are* on sale.   (indicates the items are sold separately)

(Subjects and verbs must agree in number. See pages 602–606 for guidelines on subject-verb agreement.)

Adverbs

Adverbs modify verbs, adverbs, adjectives, and entire sentences. They often, but not always, end in -ly.

He ran *quickly*.   (*Quickly* modifies the verb *ran*.)
She sang *very* well.   (*Very* modifies the adverb *well*.)
He bought the *freshly* waxed car.   (*Freshly* modifies the adjective *waxed*.)
Evidently, they refused the offer.   (*Evidently* modifies the whole sentence.)

(See pages 619–620 for guidelines on using adverbs properly.)

Articles

Articles are a form of adjective that limits nouns.
The is a definite article, indicating a specific noun:

We took *the* train to *the* city.

A and *an* are indefinite articles, indicating a general or nonspecific noun.

■ *A* generally precedes nouns beginning with consonants:

She ate *a* banana.   He read *a* book.   They bought *a* tent.

■ *An* generally precedes nouns beginning with vowels:

She ate *an* ice cream.   He read *an* article.   They bought *an* umbrella.

Prepositions

Prepositions express relationships in space and time:

about	beneath	into	outside	under
above	between	like	over	until
among	down	near	past	up
below	during	of	to	with

Prepositions and their objects form prepositional phrases:

above the city   into the night   during the game
near the car   to the school   until next week

It is important to recognize prepositional phrases because the subject of a sentence will not be part of a prepositional phrase:

The *cost* of books *is* rising.

(The subject is *cost*, not *books*, so the verb is singular.)

Conjunctions

Conjunctions are connectors.

Coordinating Conjunctions

Coordinating conjunctions—*and, or, yet, but, so, nor, for*—join equivalent words, phrases, and clauses:

Darren *or* Kevin   (*or* connects two nouns)
take the bus *or* walk home   (*or* connects two phrases)
I live in Charlottetown, *and* she lives in Gander.   (*and* joins two clauses)

Subordinating Conjunctions

Subordinating conjunctions—*after, although, because, since, though, when, where*—connect main clauses with subordinate clauses:

She failed *because* she did not study.
After the game, we went home.
Though he spoke no French, he moved to Paris.
We moved to Windsor, *where* we opened a cafe.

(Note that when the subordinating clause introduces the sentence, it is set off by a comma.)

Interjections

Interjections are words or phrases that express strong or sudden emotions:

Wow! That's expensive.
Oh! I had no idea.
The paramedics, *alas*, arrived too late.

UNDERSTANDING PARTS OF SPEECH

Words are not automatically nouns or verbs. Parts of speech are determined by the word's role in the sentence. The word paint, for example, can be a noun, verb, or adjective:

I bought red *paint*.	(noun)
I will *paint* the bedroom yellow.	(verb)
The brushes are stored in the *paint* room.	(adjective)

A verbal phrase, for instance, can serve as a noun and subject:

Walking along the beach under a full moon is romantic.

Understanding a word's role in the sentence can help you focus on main ideas, avoid common grammatical errors, and write more effective sentences.

Strategies for Determining Parts of Speech

1. Read the sentence aloud.
2. Locate the verb, which either expresses action or links ideas.
3. Determine the subject (noun) that performs the action or is linked to other ideas.
4. Use adjective to modify nouns—subjects, direct objects, or indirect objects.
5. Remember that adverbs modify verbs, adverbs, and adjectives.
6. Use conjunctions to link words, phrases, and clauses—*and, or, yet, but, so, nor, for.*
7. Recall that prepositions express relationships in time and space and often form phrases—*in the mood, around the corner, during the night.*

PHRASES AND CLAUSES

Phrases

Phrases are groups of related words:

Diet and exercise are important.	(noun phrase)
He *sang and danced*.	(verb phrase)
She put the book *on the shelf*.	(prepositional phrase)

Clauses

Clauses are groups of related words that include at least one subject and one verb.

Independent Clauses

Independent clauses can stand alone because they state a complete thought. They are sentences:

We bought a new car.   (subject: *We* verb: *bought*)
She speaks Farsi.   (subject: *She* verb: *speaks*)
Italy produces wine.   (subject: *Italy* verb: *produces*)

Dependent Clauses

Dependent clauses, though they have a subject and verb, do not express a complete thought and cannot stand alone. They are sentence fragments:

after we bought a new car . . .
because she speaks Farsi . . .
since Italy produces wine . . .

You can often detect dependent clauses by reading them aloud. (See pages 594–596 for guidelines on fragments.)

Sentences

A sentence contains a subject and verb and expresses a complete thought:

Mary bought a hat.
Swimming is good exercise.
Take cover! (The subject *you* is implied.)

✔ COMMON SENTENCE PATTERNS

✔ Subject 1 Predicate (Verb)
(*Predicates* consist of verbs and related words that express what the subject does.)

Actors rehearse.

✔ Subject 1 Predicate (Verb 1 Complement)
(*Complements* complete the predicate.)

Actors rehearse daily.

(Continued)

✔ Subject 1 Predicate (Verb 1 Direct Object)

(*Direct objects* are nouns or pronouns receiving the verb's action.)

Actors rehearse dialogue.

✔ Subject 1 Predicate (Verb 1 Indirect Object 1 Direct Object)

(*Indirect objects* are nouns or pronouns that receive the action described by the verb and direct object. They usually precede the direct object.)

Directors give actors suggestions.

✔ Subject 1 Predicate (Verb 1 Direct Object 1 Complement)

Directors make actors content.

Types of Sentences

There are four basic types of sentences:

Simple Sentence

A simple sentence consists of a single independent clause:

George moved to Alberta.
Quebec City is the capital of Quebec.

Simple sentences can have compound subjects and verbs:

George and Nancy moved to Regina and *opened* a store.
Subject   Subject   Verb   Verb

Compound Sentence

A compound sentence consists of two or more independent clauses. You can think of it as a double or triple sentence. It contains more than one simple sentence:

George moved to Calgary, and *Philip returned to Summerside.*
Independent clause   Independent clause

Dublin is the capital of the Republic of Ireland; Belfast is the capital of
Independent clause   Independent clause

Northern Ireland.

There are two methods of joining independent clauses to form a compound construction:

- Link the independent clauses with a comma and a coordinating conjunction—*and, or, yet, but, so, for, nor:*

Independent clause,	*and*	independent clause.
	or	
	yet	
	but	
	so	
	for	
	nor	

- Link the independent clauses with a semicolon:

Independent clause; independent clause.

Incorrectly punctuated compound sentences can result in run-ons and comma splices. (See pages 597–598 for guidelines on run-ons and comma splices.)

Complex Sentence

Complex sentences consist of one independent clause and one or more dependent clauses:

The team won the game because Daniel made two touchdowns.
   Independent clause   Dependent clause

After they lost the game, *the team demanded the coach resign.*
   Dependent clause   Independent clause

Note: When dependent clauses begin a complex sentence, they are set off with a comma. (See pages 621–625 for comma rules.)

Compound-Complex Sentence

Compound-complex sentences include two or more independent clauses and at least one dependent clause:

After she appeared on Broadway, *Fran McCarg opened a jazz club in*
   Dependent clause   Independent clause

Montreal, but *she never matched her early success.*
        Independent clause

Jack Kerouac wrote *On the Road* based on his American travels; he wrote

Independent clause

Satori in Paris *after visiting France,* where he sought to learn the origin of his

Independent clause   Dependent clause

family's name.

William Shatner first achieved success as an actor at the Stratford Festival,

Independent clause

but he *became nationally famous when he joined* Star Trek, playing Captain

Independent clause   Dependent clause

James T. Kirk.

Note: Dependent clauses are set off with commas when they open a sentence.

WRITING **ACTIVITY**

Label each of the following sentences as simple (S), compound (C), complex (CX), or compound-complex (CC).

1. _____ Charles Jackson was born in New Jersey in 1903.
2. _____ He attended Syracuse University but dropped out after his freshman year.
3. _____ While working odd jobs, he developed symptoms of tuberculosis, but he hid his condition from his family.
4. _____ When he was no longer able to conceal his illness, Jackson sought treatment, and he entered a sanitarium in Davos, Switzerland.
5. _____ While he was recovering from tuberculosis, Jackson began drinking to deaden the pain and boredom.
6. _____ Jackson became an alcoholic.
7. _____ Unable to find work during the Depression, he drifted for years, depending on his younger brother for support.
8. _____ In 1936 Jackson entered a hospital; he made a serious effort to stop drinking.
9. _____ Sober, Jackson began writing short stories and radio soap operas.
10. _____ Jackson recorded his experiences in *The Lost Weekend;* the novel became a bestseller, inspiring the Academy Award–winning film starring Ray Milland.

Other Ways of Looking at Sentences

Sentences can also be classified in rhetorical and functional terms.

Rhetorical Forms

Rhetorical sentences can be categorized as *periodic* or *cumulative.*

Periodic sentences end with the main idea, usually stated in an independent clause. Most complex and compound-complex sentences that open with dependent clauses are periodic:

> After he studied for weeks, *George panicked and refused to take the bar exam.*
> Developed by scientists in the 1950s, *the drug, which many thought had little value for decades, now is considered a breakthrough in AIDS research.*

Periodic sentences are useful to build tension or highlight a surprise or climactic ending. **Cumulative sentences** open with the main idea, usually an independent clause, and add further details in phrases or clauses:

> *Al Capone was tried for income tax evasion* because prosecutors doubted that a Chicago jury would convict him of Prohibition charges.

Cumulative sentences communicate clearly because they state the most important idea first, followed by supporting details. They can be read easily and are less likely to be misinterpreted than periodic sentences.

Alternating between periodic and cumulative sentences can increase the variety in your writing style, reduce repetition, and more clearly emphasize important ideas.

Functional Forms

Functional sentences can be classified as *declarative, imperative, exclamatory, and interrogative.*
Declarative sentences make a statement:

> Ottawa is the capital of Canada.
> Once banned, absinthe is now legal in some countries.

Imperative sentences give commands:

> Bring your books to the exam.
> Don't attempt this at home.

Exclamatory sentences state strong feelings:

> That is ridiculous!
> He should be fired!

Interrogative sentences ask questions:

> Can you help?
> Where have you been?

✔ GRAMMAR REVIEW

Remember these key aspects of grammar to avoid common sentence errors:

- ✔ Sentences must contain a subject and a verb and must express a complete thought.
- ✔ Compound sentences join independent clauses either with a comma and *or, and, yet, but, so, for, nor,* or with a semicolon.
- ✔ When dependent clauses open complex sentences, they are set off with commas.
- ✔ Personal pronouns—*he, she, they, we, it*—must be clearly linked to nouns (antecedents).
- ✔ Singular nouns take singular pronouns (*he, hers, it*); plural nouns take plural pronouns (*they, theirs, them*).
- ✔ Singular subjects have singular verbs; plural subjects have plural verbs.

COMPANION WEBSITE

See **http://www.transcanadawriter.nelson.com** for additional information about grammar.

CHAPTER 27

The Handbook

THIS CONCISE HANDBOOK FOCUSES ON THE MOST COMMON WRITING PROBLEMS.

Strategies for Using the Handbook

1. Review this chapter to become familiar with its layout.
2. Examine previous assignments to identify mistakes in your writing. Note repeated errors.
3. Highlight sections in the handbook addressing your problem areas.
4. Review these sections while editing and proofreading papers.
5. Refer to the handbook when instructors return papers with errors in grammar and mechanics.
6. See the Companion Website http://www.transcanadawriter.nelson.com for additional information on mechanics.

CONTENTS

SENTENCE PROBLEMS

There are three common sentence errors:

Fragments	incomplete sentences
Run-ons and comma splices	improperly punctuated compound sentences
Faulty parallelism	words or phrases presented in pairs or lists that do not match in form

You can overcome many errors if you understand basic sentence structure. Review the definitions of *simple* and *compound* sentences on pages 588–590.

Fragments

Fragments are incomplete sentences. They lack a subject or full verb, or fail to state a complete thought. The term *fragment* is misleading because it suggests something short. But even a long group of words can be a fragment:

Sentences:

> Duck! (Note: The subject *you* is implied)
> Ann sings.
> She is seventeen.

Fragments:

> Located by the side of the road just two miles from the main highway.
> (a phrase lacking a subject and verb)

> Worked and toiled for weeks to prepare a new budget before the annual meeting.
> (a verb phrase and complement lacking a subject)

> Kim working until midnight every weekend.
> (incomplete verb. Note: *ing* verbs cannot stand alone.)

> Because Sharon was angered by the voters' lack of support.
> (dependent clause. Note: Although there is both a subject and full verb, the statement does not express a complete thought.)

Writers often intentionally write fragments in fiction and personal essays for special effect:

> He looked out the window. The blizzard had obliterated the farm. There was nothing but snow. Snow in all directions. *Snow on the fields. Snow in the road. Miles of blinding snow. White and unforgiving snow.*

Fragments are to be avoided in formal academic, business, and technical writing.

Fragments often occur when you write quickly and either skip a needed word or accidentally break off part of a sentence that cannot stand alone:

> Working at Mister Paul's was frustrating. I had to supervise six employees. *Most of them teenagers.* They had poor work skills and usually arrived late. On the busiest weekend of the year, three waiters failed to show up. *Because they decided to attend a rock concert.*

Strategies for Detecting and Revising Fragments

1. Read your paper, pausing after each period. Ensure all sentences have a complete subject and verb. Each sentence should express a complete thought. Fragments, especially dependent clauses, sound like introductions to unstated ideas:

   > After the game ended.
   > Because the examination was cancelled.
   > Before the Internet was developed.

   (Continued)

2. Revise fragments in three ways:

- **Add missing elements**

  The house~~is~~completely filled with visitors and relatives.

  ~~Are~~ They are unable to locate the source of the pollution.

- **Turn dependent clauses into sentences by deleting subordinating elements (usually the first word or words):**

  ~~Because the~~ The prime minister failed to warn the House.

  ~~Although the~~ The union had won two bitter strikes.

- **Connect fragments to related sentences.** Often fragments are just that, pieces of another sentence you have accidentally broken off:

  Companies must provide day-care services to recruit employees/ ~~Who~~ who have preschool children.

  The museum purchased works by some of Europe's greatest painters: Manet, Monet, Degas, and Chagall.

  Even though he was born in Nigeria, Derrick had little knowledge of African politics.

WRITING **ACTIVITY**

Locate and revise the ten fragments in the following passage:

The word "Harlem" conjures up a variety of images. To some the neighbourhood is one of New York's most distressed slums. While others recall the heyday of the Harlem Renaissance. Cradle of black writers, poets, and jazz musicians. But few realize the unique history of this famous black community. Harlem, ironically, began as an upper-class white residential area. In the late 1800s Harlem was open country. Featuring ponds, woods, and pastures. South of Central Park, Manhattan growing. Additional housing was needed. Because of the new streetcar lines. The land north of Central Park was within easy commuting distance to Manhattan's offices, stores, and businesses. Real estate developers seeing great opportunity. Constructed blocks of expensive townhouses. Unfortunately, speculators overbuilt. Demand had been greatly overestimated. When upper-income white people failed to take interest in the new community. Landlords subdivided the units and rented to blacks. Who traditionally had been forced by discrimination to pay higher rents. Within a decade or so, the planned reserve of white executives became a thriving black community. Its collection of artists, musicians, and intellectuals made it the capital of African American culture. However, as landlords continued to subdivide houses to increase rents. Harlem became overcrowded and began to decay.

Run-on Sentences and Comma Splices

Run-on sentences and *comma splices* are incorrectly punctuated compound sentences. *Compound sentences* (see pages 588–589) consist of two or more independent clauses (simple sentences) joined by a comma and *and, or, yet, but, so, for, nor,* or by a semicolon:

> The teachers edited the magazine, and the students designed the illustrations.
> The runway is closed; it will reopen at noon.

Run-ons occur when two sentences run together without the proper punctuation:

> Administrators are struggling with budget cuts, ⌃*and* they hope private industry will donate computers.
> Patience is important in parenting; ⌃children are often defiant.

Comma splices (also called "comma faults") occur when two sentences (independent clauses) are joined with a comma instead of a semicolon. In writing quickly, you may instinctively sense that two complete ideas should be separated but fail to use the proper punctuation:

> The city is responsible for the bridge; ⌃the province must repair the on-ramps.
> Sean Nelson served in the Navy, ⌃*but* he never learned to swim.

Strategies for Detecting and Revising Run-ons and Comma Splices

- Read your sentences. If they contain more than one complete idea or simple sentence, ensure the independent clauses are joined by a comma with *and, or, yet, but, so, nor, for,* or by a semicolon.
- Revise run-ons and comma splices in four ways:

  1. **Add missing elements:**

     Celluloid is unstable, ⌃*and* many early films have been lost.

     or

     Celluloid is unstable; ⌃many early films have been lost.

  2. **Determine if you have used a comma instead of a semicolon.** In revising sentences, you may wonder if a comma should be a semicolon. To determine if you need a semicolon, follow these steps:

     a. Read the sentence aloud. Does it sound like more than one complete idea? Are independent clauses properly joined?

(Continued)

---

b. If a comma seems to join two independent clauses, ask yourself if you can replace the comma with a period and have a complete sentence on the left and on the right. If you can create two simple sentences and a word such as *and, or, yet, but, or, so,* or *nor* is not used, use a semicolon.

3. **Revise the wording of the sentence.** It may be better to stress the relationship between clauses by making one of them dependent:

Because celluloid is unstable, many early films have been lost.

4. **Separate the independent clauses to form two or more simple sentences.** You may have accidentally run together sentences that are not closely related and should be separated. Ideas are given greater emphasis when stated in simple sentences:

Comma splice and run-on:

Creditors were demanding payment, *and* employees were threatening to strike. Bricklin Motors declared bankruptcy.

■ **Read your revisions. Do your new sentences avoid run-ons? Do they effectively express your ideas?**

WRITING **ACTIVITY**

Revise the following comma splices and run-ons. You may add missing elements, separate independent clauses, or reword the sentences for clarity and emphasis.

1. The first computers were large machines they filled entire rooms.

2. They contained thousands of tubes, the tubes blew out constantly.

3. Graduate students ran up and down the computer room they pushed shopping carts filled with replacement tubes.

4. These monstrous computers were marvels they had less power than today's handheld calculators.

5. An early computer expert predicted the United States would need only five computers he could not anticipate the revolution to come.

6. Computers remained mysterious and somewhat sinister machines, most North Americans saw them only in science fiction movies.

7. Computers have revolutionized society some experts see problems.

8. The 1960 census was computed on massive reels of tape no modern computer can accommodate them.

9. Only one computer from that era is still operational it is located in a museum.

10. Years of data may be lost future researchers will face a daunting task to retrieve information processed on obsolete equipment.

Faulty Parallelism

When you write about pairs or lists, the words or phrases must match — they have to be all nouns, all adjectives, all adverbs, or all verbs in the same form:

Nancy is *bright, creative,* and *funny.* (adjectives)

Mary writes *clearly, directly,* and *forcefully.* (adverbs)

Reading and *calculating* are critical skills for my students. (gerunds)

She should *lose* weight, *stop* smoking, and *limit* her intake of alcohol.

(verbs matching with *should*)

Mistakes with parallelism are easy to make. If asked to describe your best friend, you might come up with nouns (*a student*), adjectives (*smart*), or verbs (*sings*). It is often difficult to combine all these ideas into one list and keep them in the same format.

The concert was loud, colourful, and ~~many people~~ ^well^ attended.

(The adjective *well attended* matches the adjectives *loud* and *colourful.*)

John failed to take notes, refused to attend class, and ^wrote an unreadable^ ~~his~~ final exam ~~is unreadable~~.

(The verb *wrote* matches the verb phrases *failed to take* and *refused to.*)

Quitting smoking and daily ^exercising^ ~~exercise~~ are important.

(*Exercising* and *quitting* are both gerunds, or *ing* nouns.)

Strategies for Detecting and Revising Faulty Parallelism

Examine any sentences that include pairs or lists of words or phrases to ensure that they are parallel by applying this simple test:

1. Read the sentence and locate the pair or list.

2. Make sure each item matches the format of the basic sentence by testing each item.

Example:

Students should read directions carefully, write down assignments accurately, and take notes.

Students should read directions

Students should write down assignments accurately

Students should take notes

(Each item matches *Students should* . . .)

This sentence is **parallel.**

(Continued)

Computer experts will have to make more precise predictions in the future to reduce waste, create more accurate budgets, and public support must be maintained.

Computer experts will have to make more precise . . .

Computer experts will have to create more accurate . . .

Computer experts will have to public support must be . . .

(The last item does not link with *will have to*.)

This sentence is **not parallel.**

Review of Faulty Parallelism

Test each of the following to identify unparallel elements:

1. Unemployment can lead to marital problems, alcohol and drug abuse, feelings of depression, and bouts of irrational behaviour such as gambling.

2. Maintenance costs are based on labour rates, availability of spare parts, and are subject to inflation.

3. My job entailed word processing, filing, and sales orders had to be verified.

4. An effective resume, a confident interview, and being realistic about hiring salaries will increase your chance of being hired.

5. Born in Montreal, jazz pianist Oscar Peterson was discovered in 1949, played the same year in Carnegie Hall, and went on to become one of the greatest "swing" musicians of the 20th century.

Answers

1. Correct

2. Not parallel: *are based on . . . are subject to inflation* do not match. Substitute *inflation* so the list is composed of all nouns.

3. Not parallel: My job entailed . . . sales orders had to be verified do not match. Substitute verifying sales orders.

4. Not parallel: Being realistic does not match with the nouns resume and interview. Substitute a realistic attitude about hiring salaries.

5. Correct

A Tip on Parallelism

In many cases it is difficult to revise long sentences that are not parallel:

> To build her company, Shireen Naboti is a careful planner, skilled supervisor, recruits talent carefully, monitors quality control, and is a lobbyist for legal reform.

If you have trouble making all the elements match, it may be simpler to break it up into two or even three separate sentences:

> To build her company, Shireen Naboti is a careful planner, skilled supervisor, and lobbyist for legal reform. In addition, she recruits talent carefully and monitors quality control.

The first sentence contains the noun phrases; the second consists of the two verb phrases. Remember, it is often easier to create two short parallel lists than one long one.

⌨ WRITING **ACTIVITY**

Revise the following sentences so that the pairs and lists are parallel. You may break the sentences into two if you are unable to make a single list of items match.

1. The Knights of Labour fought for higher wages, shorter hours, and opposed unsafe conditions.

2. Farmers must anticipate prices, decrease production costs, maintain accurate records, and willing to take risks.

3. The team faces three major problems: the coach's retirement, recurring injuries, and fans unwilling to purchase season tickets.

4. Computers allow entrepreneurs to market products worldwide and competing with major corporations.

5. They saved money to repair the house, purchase a new car, and repayment of debt.

6. Applicants must be intelligent, creative, flexible, and work with little supervision.

7. They decided to drop out of school and seeking adventure in Europe.

8. The employees will be either fined or demotions may be announced.

9. Parents and teachers must agree on the best methods to discipline rude conduct, instruct children with learning disabilities, and determining the role of extracurricular activities.

10. She was spirited, witty, charming, and showed knowledge about the school.

Strategies for Revising Sentence Problems

1. Read your paper aloud. You can often hear incomplete statements, indicating possible fragments or confusing ideas signalling possible run-ons. Some errors such as comma splices, however, may sound correct because both a comma and a semicolon denote a pause.

(Continued)

2. When you locate sentence errors, do not think of them as a puzzle or math problem you have to solve or "fix." Poorly written sentences may not be easily revised. Reconsider what you were trying to say and express your ideas in a new sentence. Often, trying a fresh approach will lead you to not only avoid errors but also create more effective and interesting sentences.

3. Keep track of errors instructors note in your writing and highlight or tab these areas in the handbook for future reference.

COMPANION WEBSITE

See **http://www.transcanadawriter.nelson.com** for additional information on sentence structure.

AGREEMENT

Subjects and their verbs and nouns and their pronouns must agree or match in number. Singular subjects have singular verbs; plural subjects have plural verbs:

Singular: The *boy* next door *plays* the piano. (*boy . . . plays*)
Plural: The *girls* across the street *play* the violin. (*girls . . . play*)

Note: An *s* is usually added to indicate plural nouns (cats) and singular verbs (purrs). Singular nouns take singular pronouns; plural nouns take plural pronouns:

Singular: The *boy* next door rides *his* bicycle. (*boy . . . his*)
Plural: The *girls* ride *their* bicycles. (*girls . . . their*)

Maintaining these patterns of agreement emphasizes the relationship between ideas and prevents confusion. Although the concept is basic, agreement problems are very common.

Subject-Verb Agreement

Although matching singulars and plurals appears easy in simple sentences, choosing the right verb can be challenging in longer and more complicated structures. Many words can be singular or plural depending on context. Long noun phrases can easily be misread and assigned the wrong verb form. There are eight common situations that present problems for writers:

1. **Nouns ending in *s*: Many words that appear plural because they end with *s* are in fact singular:**

Singular: mathematics   physics   economics

Words like *statistics* can be singular or plural:

Singular: *Statistics requires* a keen sense of logic.

Plural: These *statistics* about homelessness *are* alarming.

2. **Collective or group subjects: Collective nouns *and* phrases are singular when they act as a unit:**

Singular:

United Technologies appears to be gaining market share.
(United Technologies is a single corporation.)

The *jury deliberates* this weekend.
(The 12 members act as a unit.)

Twenty Thousand Leagues under the Sea is my favourite adventure book.
(the title of one book)

The *number* of dropouts *is* less than anticipated.
(one number or figure)

Five dollars is not enough for lunch.
(a single amount of money)

Collective or group nouns are plural when items in the group act separately:

Plural:

A *number* of parents *were* unable to come.
(Parents act separately.)

Five dollars were spread on the table.
(individual dollar coins)

3. **Subjects joined by *and*: Subjects linked by *and* are plural if they refer to two separate items:**

My *mother* and *father are* going to Florida.
(two people)

His *intelligence* and *hard work are* admirable.
(two separate qualities)

Subjects linked by and are singular if they refer to a single item:

My *friend and partner is* a skilled designer.
(a person who is both friend and partner)

Her *drinking and driving is* very disturbing.
(a single action)

4. **Subjects joined by *either . . . or*: The words *either* and *or* indicate that one or the other subject, but not both, is linked to the verb.**

If both subjects are singular, the verb is singular:

My *father* or *mother is* driving us to the airport.
(Only one parent will drive.)

If both subjects are plural, the verb is plural:

Parents or *teachers* supervise the playground.
(In both instances, more than one adult watches the playground.)

If one subject is singular and the other is plural, the verb agrees with the subject nearer the verb.

Either the *letters* or *the package is* insured.
Either the *package* or *the letters are* insured.

5. **Inverted word order or *There* verb constructions: In some sentences the normal word order is inverted so that the verb comes before the subject. In other instances such words as *there, here, when, how, what, which,* and *who* begin constructions that can be singular or plural:**

Singular: *There goes* my best friend.
            What is your problem?
            He is a person *who loves* money.
            When is she coming?

Plural: *There go* my best friends.
            What are your problems?
            He is one of those people *who love* money.
            When are they coming?

6. **Indefinite pronouns: The words *anybody, anyone, someone, each, either,* and *everybody* are singular.**

Singular: *Everybody is* encouraged to participate.
            Someone travels downtown every day.

The words *all, any, some, none, most,* and *half* can be singular or plural, depending on the noun preceding the verb:

Singular: *All* of the money *is* missing.
            Some of the snow still *remains* on the field.
            Half of my income *depends* on bonuses.

Plural: *All* of the books *are* missing.

               Some of the children *remain* on the field.

               Half of the stores *close* early on Sunday.

7. **Prepositional phrases: Prepositional phrases are groups of related words linked to such words as *above, around, over, under, before, after, while,* or *during*. The subject of a sentence is not included within a prepositional phrase. The key word or subject usually precedes the prepositional phrase.**

Singular: One of *my friends* is absent.

                (The subject is *One*, not *friends*.)

Plural: Children *with a love of poetry* are attracted to these programs.

                (The subject is *Children*, not *a love*.)

8. **Subjects with possessive forms: Subjects that include a possessive form can be easily misread:**

Singular: The parents' main concern *is* school security.

                (*concern* is the subject, not *parents'*.)

               The Europeans' love for American music *is* well known.

                (*love* is the subject, not *Europeans'*)

Plural: Paul's clothes *are* stylish.

                (*clothes* is the subject, not *Paul's*)

               Kim's books *are* overdue.

                (*books* is the subject, not *Kim's*)

Strategies for Overcoming Problems with Subject-Verb Agreement

1. Recognize sentences that may pose problems—sentences with compound subjects, collective nouns, *either . . . or* constructions, or inverted word order.

2. Locate the verb or verbs.

3. Ask who or what is associated with the verb's action or linked to the subject. The answer will be the subject.

In some instances you may have created a long or awkward sentence that should be restated rather than simply repaired. Consider your ideas and express them using different constructions that will avoid agreement errors and state your ideas more clearly.

WRITING **ACTIVITY**

Circle the correct verb in the following sentences.

1. Children's clothing (is/are) designed for durability, not style.
2. The goal of the parents and teachers (remain/remains) the same.
3. Either the teacher or the substitute (supervises/supervise) the testing centre.
4. Neither the lawyers nor the investigators (are/is) confident about solving the case.
5. *Nine Stories* (is/are) on the summer reading list.
6. There (are/is) guests waiting.
7. Either the cities or the federal agency (oversees/oversee) new construction.
8. The teacher's guidelines (provides/provide) strategies for using the library.
9. Fifteen minutes (give/gives) us enough time to evacuate the building.
10. The movies, especially ones filmed before WWII, (was/were) usually in black and white.
11. The lifespan of birds (vary/varies) greatly.
12. Anyone who is interested in helping (is/are) invited.
13. In a small office, located in a battered safe, (lie/lies) secrets of a major conspiracy.
14. The audience, which included teachers and students, (was/were) restless.
15. Half the class (is/are) interested in attending summer school.

Pronoun Agreement

Pronouns must agree or match with their antecedents—the nouns or pronouns they represent:

1. Pronouns should agree in number and gender with antecedents:

Bill took *his* time.   *Nancy* rode *her* bicycle.   The *children* called *their* mother.

2. Compound nouns require plural pronouns:

Both the *students and the teachers* argue that *their* views are not heard.
Tom and Nancy announced that *they* plan to move to Colorado next year.

3. Collective nouns use singular or plural pronouns:

Singular: The *cast* played *its* last performance.
            (The cast acts as one unit.)

Plural: The *cast* had trouble remembering *their* lines.
            (Cast members act independently.)

4. ***Either … or* constructions: The words *either* and *or* indicate that one noun or the other, but not both, is linked to the verb.**

   If both nouns are singular, the pronoun is singular:

   Either the city council *or* the county board will present *its* budget.
   (Only one group will present a budget.)

   If both nouns are plural, the pronoun is plural:

   The board members or *the city attorneys* will present *their* report.
   (In both instances, several individuals present a report.)

   If one noun is singular and the other is plural, the pronoun agrees with the nearer noun:

   Either the teacher or students will present *their* findings to the principal.

   Note: Place the plural noun last to avoid awkward statements or having to represent both genders with *he and she, his or her,* or *him and her.*

5. **Avoid shifts in person or point of view: Pronouns should maintain the same person or point of view in a sentence, avoiding awkward shifts:**

   Awkward shift: To save money, *consumers* should monitor *their* (third person) use of credit cards to avoid getting over *your* (second person) head in debt.

   Revised: To save money, *consumers* should monitor *their* use of credit cards to avoid getting over *their* heads in debt.

6. **Indefinite pronouns. In speaking, most people use the plural pronouns *they, them,* and *their* to easily include both males and females. But in formal writing, most writers follow the established rule that singular indefinite pronouns agree with singular pronouns:**

   Singular:

anybody	everybody	nobody	somebody
anyone	everyone	no one	someone
either	neither	each	one

   Anybody can bring *his or her* tax return in for review.
   Everybody is required to do the test *himself or herself.*

   Plural: If *many* are unable to attend the orientation, make sure to call *them.*

   Indefinite pronouns like *some* may be singular or plural depending on context:

   Singular: *Some* of the ice is losing *its* brilliance.

   Plural: *Some* of the children are missing *their* coats.

Strategies for Avoiding Sexism in Pronoun Use

Singular nouns and many indefinite pronouns refer to individuals who may be male or female. Trying to include both men and women, however, often creates awkward constructions:

If a student has a problem, *he or she* should contact *his or her* adviser.

In editing your writing, try these strategies to eliminate both sexism and awkward pronoun use:

1. **Use plurals:**

   If students have problems, *they* should contact *their* advisers.

2. **Revise the sentence to limit or eliminate the need for pronouns:**

   Students with problems should contact advisers.
   Advisers assist students with problems.

WRITING **ACTIVITY**

Circle the correct pronoun in the following sentences:

1. The cable television industry or the local stations are responsible for the messages (it/they) convey to children.
2. An attorney should focus on the needs of (his or her/their) clients.
3. The attorney and her advisers claimed (her/their) meeting had to be delayed because (they/it) could not be scheduled before the judge's ruling.
4. A child or (his and her/their) parents may sign the release form.
5. The causes of heart disease demand extensive research because of (its/their) complexity.
6. The jury made (their/its) decision.
7. Neither Canada nor any European country is willing to risk (its/their) prestige.
8. Half the merchandise could not be delivered because of (its/their) cost.
9. Either Mom or Dad can let you into (his or her/their) house.
10. If prices of wheat cannot remain stable (it/they) will drive investors from the market.

COMPANION WEBSITE

See **http://www.transcanadawriter.nelson.com** for additional information about agreement.

VERBS

Irregular Verbs

Most verbs are *regular: -d* or *-ed* is added to indicate the past participle.

pass/passed walk/walked create/created adopt/adopted

Other verbs are *irregular:* other spellings or words indicate the past and the past participle.

swim/swam/swum drink/drank/drunk sing/sang/sung

Common Irregular Verbs

Review this list and highlight any verbs that have given you trouble in the past:

PRESENT TENSE	PAST TENSE	PAST PARTICIPLE (USED WITH HELPING VERB)
arise	arose	arisen (e.g., have arisen)
be	was/were	been (e.g., have been)
bear (carry)	bore	borne (e.g., were borne)
bear (give birth)	bore	borne/born
beat	beat	beaten
become	became	become
begin	began	begun
bend	bent	bent
bet	bet	bet
bite	bit	bitten/bit
blow	blew	blown
break	broke	broken
bring	brought	brought
build	built	built
burst	burst	burst
buy	bought	bought
catch	caught	caught
choose	chose	chosen
come	came	come
do	did	done
draw	drew	drawn
eat	ate	eaten
fall	fell	fallen
find	found	found
fly	flew	flown
forbid	forbade/forbad	forbidden

freeze	froze	frozen
get	got	got/gotten
give	gave	given
go	went	gone
have	had	had
lay (to place)	laid	laid
lie (to recline)	lay	lain
lose	lost	lost
pay	paid	paid
ring	rang	rung
say	said	said
shine	shone/shined	shone/shined
show	showed	shown/showed
sleep	slept	slept
strike	struck	struck
swear	swore	sworn
take	took	taken
tear	tore	torn
tell	told	told
throw	threw	thrown
wear	wore	worn
write	wrote	written

Verb Tense

Verb tense shows the time of an action or event. English verbs have three simple and three perfect tenses or times.

Simple tenses indicate that the action is restricted to one specific time.

Past: I *was* sick.
           (suggests the illness was limited to the past)

Present: I *study* French.
           (indicates the speaker is currently studying)

Future: I *will take* algebra next semester.
           (indicates a future action)

Perfect tenses indicate that the action is not limited to one time period.

Past: I *had been travelling* for several months before I met my family.
           (suggests travelling ended before a past date)

Present: I *have been studying* French.
           (indicates recent and current action)

Future: I *will have completed* algebra by the time I graduate.

(indicates that a future action will be completed by a date further in the future)

Strategies for Using Verb Tenses

1. **Shift tenses in writing to indicate changes in time:**

   I was born in Toronto, but I live in Victoria.

2. **Shift tenses to contrast past with ongoing action or unchanging status:**

   The conference *was* in Regina, which *is* the capital of Saskatchewan.

   Note: Stating *was the capital* suggests that the capital has changed.

3. **Add clarifications to prevent confusion:**

   Capone *sold* liquor, which *was then* illegal.

   Note: indicates a subsequent change in the law

4. **Avoid inappropriate shifts in time:**

   Inappropriate: Janet *hosts* lots of dinner parties. They ~~were~~ *are* elegant.

5. **Use either past or present tense to describe actions in a work of art, such as a novel, play, or film.**

PAST	PRESENT
Hamlet *pondered* his fate. He *was* haunted by the death of his father. Yet he *could not bring* himself to avenge his murder.	Hamlet *ponders* his fate. He *is* haunted by the death of his father. Yet he *cannot bring* himself to avenge his murder.

WRITING **ACTIVITY**

Revise the following sentences to avoid incorrect tense or inappropriate shifts in tense.

1. Translators work for years to produce the 1989 edition of *War and Peace*.
2. Students who currently worked full time will be eligible for loans next year.
3. The Lafontaine Tunnel was congested, so we call to postpone our meeting.
4. He wait a full day before calling a doctor, a delay that was almost fatal.
5. The children can't come this weekend because they were sick.

(Continued)

6. Counties in Louisiana were called parishes.

7. Students hated his take-home exams so much they call them "brainkillers."

8. Telephone when you needed a ride.

9. My father was born in Halifax, which was a major city on the East Coast.

10. He speaks Greek better than he spoke Turkish.

COMPANION WEBSITE

See **http://www.transcanadawriter.nelson.com** for additional information on verbs.

PRONOUNS

Pronouns take the place of nouns and other pronouns. Because pronouns can refer to a number of words, they must be used carefully to avoid confusion.

Pronoun Reference

Pronouns should clearly refer to specific antecedents. Avoid unclear references:

> Crime is ruining the community. Cars are stolen. Stores are vandalized. Windows are smashed. *They* just don't care.

Who does *they* refer to? Criminals? Residents? Police? Politicians?

Note: *They* is probably the most often misused pronoun. When editing, make sure that each *they* can be clearly linked to a specific noun or pronoun.

Strategies for Using Pronouns

1. **Ensure pronouns have clear antecedents.** Avoid constructions in which a pronoun could refer to more than one noun or pronoun, creating alternative possible interpretations.

   Unclear: Nancy was with Sharon when *she* got the news.
   (Who received the news—Nancy or Sharon?)

   Revised: When Sharon received the news, *she* was with Nancy.

2. **Replace pronouns with nouns for clearer references.**

   Unclear: The teachers explained to the students why *they* couldn't attend the ceremony.
   (Who cannot attend the ceremony—teachers or students?)

Revised: The teachers explained to the students why *faculty* couldn't attend the ceremony.

The teachers explained to the students why *children* couldn't attend the ceremony.

3. **State *either . . . or* constructions carefully.**

Either George or Jim can lend you *their* key.
(George and Jim share one key.)

Either George or Jim can lend you *his* key.
(Both George and Jim have keys.)

Either George or Anna can lend you *a* key.
(avoids need for *his or her*)

4. **Avoid unclear references when using *this, that, it, which,* and *such*.**

Unclear: Many people think that diets are the only way to lose weight. *This* is wrong.

Revised: Many people mistakenly think that diets are the only way to lose weight.

Unclear: Sharon used a company car and drove to the airport, *which* was illegal.

Revised: Sharon illegally used a company car to drive to the airport.

5. **Avoid awkward use of *you*.** *You* is acceptable for directly addressing readers. Avoid making awkward shifts in general statements.

Awkward: Highway congestion can give you stress.

Revised: Highway congestion can be stressful.

Pronoun Case

Pronouns have different forms—or cases—depending on how they are used in a sentence:

Subjective Case:

I/we   you   he/she/it   they   who/whoever

Subjective pronouns are used as subjects:

I can drive. *You* look great. *She* is here. *They* are moving.
Who is there?

Objective Case:

me/us   you   him/her/it   them   whom/whomever

Objective pronouns are used as direct or indirect objects and objects of verbals or prepositions:

He drove *me*. Here's to *you*! Give it to *her*. Help *them*!
To *whom* it may concern

Possessive Case:

my/ours   your   his/hers/its   their   whose
mine/ours   yours   his/hers/its   theirs

Possessive pronouns indicate ownership:

Take *my* car.   Is that *your* hat?   She likes *her* house.
Their car is stalled. *Whose* hat?

Strategies for Using Proper Case

Your use of case is usually automatic. Nevertheless, there are a few areas that most writers find confusing:

1. **Using who/whom:**

   Who and *whom* are often confused because they are typically used in questions:

   (Who/Whom) did you call?
   (Who/Whom) called last night?

   To determine which pronoun to use, answer the question, substituting *they* or *them*:

   I called *them* (objective case needed)
   Whom did you call?

   They called last night (subjective case needed)
   Who called last night?

   When *they* is appropriate, use *who*; when *them* is appropriate, use *whom*.

2. **Using whoever/whomever:**

   Whoever and *whomever* often introduce dependent clauses:

   The director shouted at (whoever/whomever) crossed the stage.
   The director shouted at (whoever/whomever) she liked.

   To determine which pronoun to use, isolate the dependent clause and substitute *they* or *them*:

   they crossed the stage (subjective)
   she liked *them* (objective)

   The director shouted at *whoever* crossed the stage.
   The director shouted at *whomever* she liked.

   When *they* is appropriate, use *whoever*; when *them* is appropriate, use *whomever*.

3. **Using we and *us* before a noun:**

   (We/us) girls can win this game.
   They'd better give that trophy to (we/us) winners.

   To determine which pronoun to use, delete the noun to see which sounds appropriate:

   We can win this game. (subjective)
   They'd better give that trophy to *us*. (objective)

   We girls can win this game.
   They'd better give that trophy to *us* winners.

4. **Using the right pronoun case in compounds:**

   Although you may automatically choose the right pronoun in isolation—*I* gave the money to *her*—you may find compounds confusing:

   Tim and (I/me) worked with Sandy and (she/her).
   We wanted Sharon and (she/her) to attend the seminar.

   To determine which pronoun to use, simplify the sentence by isolating each pronoun:

   I worked with *her*.
   We wanted *her* to attend the seminar.

WRITING **ACTIVITY**

In the following sentences, apply the strategies to identify sentences with correct use of pronouns and sentences with pronoun problems. In some instances you may correct the problem by simply substituting a word; in others, you may have to rewrite the sentence.

1. Sarah and Nancy spent the day looking for parts for her antique car.
2. The government announced that they should pay their taxes.
3. To prevent workers from being injured by tools, make sure they are examined before each shift.
4. In Martin Luther King's article, he states that people deal with oppression in three ways.
5. Children and parents often feel their feelings are being ignored.
6. The coach rewarded whomever could hit a home run.
7. I give money to whoever needs it.
8. I hate the way they treat we students.
9. Sharon borrowed my report and made copies for everyone. That was unfair.
10. When Jack and her first opened the store, I was convinced they would be successful.

COMPANION WEBSITE

See **http://www.transcanadawriter.nelson.com** for additional information on pronoun use.

DANGLING AND MISPLACED MODIFIERS

Modifiers—adjectives, adverbs, prepositions, and verbals—are effective only if they are carefully placed in a sentence:

> She wore a ribbon in her hair, which was *red*.
> (What is *red*, her hair or her ribbon?)

> *Drained yesterday*, the guests were disappointed that the pool was empty.
> (Were the guests *drained*?)

Dangling Modifiers

Modifiers that serve as introductions must describe what follows the comma. When they do not, they "dangle," so that what they modify is unclear:

Grounded by fog, airport officials ordered passengers to deplane.
(Were airport officials *grounded by fog?*)

Revised:

Grounded by fog, the passengers were ordered by airport officials to deplane.
Airport officials ordered passengers to deplane the aircraft, which was grounded by fog.

Strategies to Detect Dangling Modifiers

Sentences with opening modifiers set off by commas fit this pattern:

Modifier, Main Sentence

To ensure the sentence is correct, use the following test:

1. **Read the sentence, then turn the modifier into a question, asking who or what in the main sentence is performing the action:**

   question, answer

2. **What follows the comma forms the answer.** If the answer is appropriate, the construction is correct:

   Hastily constructed, the bridge deteriorated in less than a year.

   Question: What was *hastily constructed?*
   Answer: the bridge

   This sentence is **correct.**

   Suspected of insanity, the defence attorney asked that her client be examined by psychiatrists.

   Question: Who was suspected of insanity?
   Answer: the defence attorney
   This sentence is **incorrect.**

   Revised: Suspecting her client to be insane, the defence attorney asked that he be examined by psychiatrists.
   The defence attorney asked that the defendant she suspected of insanity be examined by psychiatrists.

Misplaced Modifiers

Place modifying words, phrases, and clauses as near as possible to the words they describe:

Confusing: Scientists developed new chips for laptop computers *that cost less than 50 cents.*

Do laptop computers cost *less than 50 cents?*

Revised: Scientists developed laptop computer chips that cost less than 50 cents.

Confusing: Jogging often reduces stress.

Does this mean that frequent jogging reduces stress or that jogging has proven often to reduce stress?

Revised: Frequent jogging reduces stress.
           Jogging can reduce stress in some instances.

WRITING **ACTIVITY**

Revise the following sentences to avoid dangling and misplaced modifiers. In some instances, you can merely move phrases; in others, you may have to rewrite the entire sentence.

1. Spinning out of control, the aeronautical engineer struggled to advise the troubled pilot.
2. She is teaching a course at McMaster on plane geometry.
3. Fearing contamination, all food products were ordered destroyed by inspectors after the flood.
4. Hoping to pass with flying colours, the exam grade stunned Michelle.
5. Shocked by his falling blood pressure, Sam was treated by paramedics.
6. Once regarded with suspicion, marketers see the Internet as a way of increasing sales.
7. No longer endangered, tourists can easily see lions in their natural habitat.
8. Popular with customers, the kitchen staff at the Coffee Trader felt overwhelmed.
9. Chewing often provokes headaches.
10. She designed restorations of old houses that people just loved.
11. The almost developed lots sold for a million dollars.
12. Developed only recently, scientists still doubt the efficacy of the new drug.
13. Demanding a refund, car dealers tried to calm the angry consumers.
14. Understanding these notes completely prepares students for the LSAT exam.
15. Children only learn what they can experience.

COMPANION WEBSITE

See **http:// www.transcanadawriter.nelson.com** for additional information about dangling and misplaced modifiers.

ADJECTIVES AND ADVERBS

Adjectives modify nouns and pronouns, and can be formed from nouns and verbs:

Nouns:	*car* insurance	*field* glasses	*book* report
Verbs:	*steamed* rice	*iced* tea	*dyed* shirt

Adverbs modify verbs, adverbs, adjectives, and sentences. Most adverbs are formed by adding *ly* to adjectives:

poor/poorly   angry/angrily   heated/heatedly

Strategies for Using Adjectives and Adverbs

1. **Understand differences between adjectives and adverbs:**

   She gave us *freshly sliced* peaches.
   (The adverb *freshly* modifies the adjective *sliced*, meaning that the peaches, whatever their freshness, have just been sliced.)

   She gave us *fresh sliced* peaches.
   (The adjectives *fresh* and *sliced* both describe the noun *peaches*, meaning the peaches are both fresh and sliced.)

2. **Review sentences to select the most effective adjectives and adverbs. Adjectives and adverbs add meaning. Avoid vague modifiers:**

Vague:	The concert hall was *totally inappropriate* for our group.
Revised:	The concert hall was *too informal* for our group.
	The concert hall was *too large* for our group.

3. **Use adverbs with verbs.**

Incorrect:	Drive *careful*. (adjective)
Revised:	Drive *carefully*.

4. **Avoid unnecessary adjectives and adverbs.**

Unnecessary:	We drove down the *old, winding, potholed, dirt* road.
Revised:	We drove down the *winding, potholed* road.

   (Continued)

5. **Use *good* and *well*; *bad* and *badly* accurately.** Good and bad are adjectives and modify nouns and pronouns:

The cookies taste *good*. (*good* modifies the noun *cookies*.)
The wine is *bad*. (*bad* modifies the noun *wine*.)

Well and *badly* are adverbs and modify verbs, adjectives, adverbs:

She sings *well*. (*well* modifies the verb *sings*.)
He paid for *badly* needed repairs. (*badly* modifies the adjective *needed*.)

WRITING **ACTIVITY**

Revise adjective and adverb use in the following sentences:

1. I ruined my shoes walking across the fresh tarred parking lot.
2. He played so good last night.
3. That is such a high stressful job.
4. Radical diets are unfortunate popular with teens who feel bad about their appearance.
5. Drive slow because of the ice.
6. He suffered a severely injury in the accident.
7. The soup tasted badly.
8. Without glasses, she sees poor.
9. I was upset at the sloppy decorated banquet hall.
10. That tastes so well.

COMPANION WEBSITE

See **http://www.transcanadawriter.nelson.com** for additional information on adjectives and adverbs.

PUNCTUATION

Punctuation can seem trivial. But missing or misused punctuation marks, like misspelled words, not only detract from your message and your credibility as a writer but also can alter meaning:

Instructors, say students, complain about the grading policy.
        ∧   ∧

Without commas, faculty members report that students are complaining about the grading policy. With commas, the sentence means the opposite, suggesting that instructors are the ones who are complaining.

, Comma

Commas serve as road signs signalling a change or transition in a sentence. Commas indicate pauses that prevent confusion:

> When we reached the theatre, patrons were leaving.

Commas are used for ten basic reasons.

1. **Commas come before a coordinating conjunction that joins independent clauses in compound and compound-complex sentences:**

> Independent clause, *and* independent clause
> (simple sentence)   *but* (simple sentence)
>   *or*
>   *nor*
>   *for*
>   *yet*
>   *but*

2. **Commas follow introductory words, phrases, and clauses:**

> Angered, the committee read the complaint letters.
> Opened in 1912, the bridge remains the only link to the island.
> Earning ten million dollars in less than a year, she became the highest paid player on the tour.
> To avoid becoming infected, avoid contact with patients.
> Prepared to take decisive action, the firefighters waited for the wind to change.

Commas follow dependent clauses introducing independent clauses:

> When she graduated from law school, Corinne decided to move to Edmonton.
> Because prices rose faster than investors anticipated, additional stock offerings were postponed.

3. **Commas separate lists of parallel words, phrases, or clauses:**

> Words: The gym was *old, dark,* and *musty.*
>   She *ran, swam,* and *danced.*
>   *Pens, pencils, paper,* and *books* were supplied to refugee children.

Phrases: *He exercises daily, eats lightly, and drinks moderately.*

Parents of small children, small business owners, and real estate developers met with the zoning committee.

The changes were developed too late, explained too poorly, and implemented too quickly to solve the problem.

Clauses: In the ideal company *the customers receive respect, the employees are appreciated, and the investors are enriched.*

The students were frustrated, the faculty was confused, and the alumni were dumbfounded by the president's speech.

We were convinced that *most of the children were malnourished, the parents were overworked, and the community was nearing collapse.*

4. **Commas come between coordinate adjectives. Coordinate adjectives modify the same noun or pronoun and can be joined by a coordinating conjunction. One test is to reverse the order of the adjectives. Another is to place the word *and* between them. If you can include *and* without changing the meaning or creating an awkward phrase, insert a comma:**

Examples: It was a *hot humid* day. It was a *hot and humid* day. (no change)
       add comma
       It was a hot, humid day.
       I bought a *hot apple* pie. I bought a *hot and apple* pie. (awkward)
       no comma
       I bought a hot apple pie.

5. **Commas set off nonrestrictive phrases or clauses. *Nonrestrictive phrases and clauses* provide nonessential information about a noun or pronoun. They can be eliminated without changing the meaning of a sentence.**

Restrictive phrases or clauses restrict or limit the meaning of nouns or pronouns. They cannot be eliminated without changing the meaning of a sentence.

Because the terms *nonrestrictive* and *restrictive* are difficult to remember—think of the words *extra* and *ID*. *Nonrestrictive* elements don't *identify* words; they add *extra* or parenthetical information. *Restrictive elements* help *ID*, or *identify*, words:

Nonrestrictive: Tom Green, *who wants to quit smoking,* should consider hypnosis.

(The proper noun *Tom Green* is clearly identified and the phrase *who wants to quit smoking* merely adds additional or *extra* information. Eliminating the phrase does not alter who should consider hypnosis—Tom Green.)

Restrictive: Anyone *who wants to quit smoking* should consider hypnosis.

(The pronoun *anyone* is restricted or further *identified* by the phrase *who wants to quit smoking*. Eliminating the phrase alters the meaning, suggesting that everyone should consider hypnosis.)

NONRESTRICTIVE

Extra
George, who is my friend, will help.

Extra
Frank's car, which was repaired
last week, broke down.

Extra
Marquette University, located in
Milwaukee, will conduct the research.

RESTRICTIVE

ID
Anyone who is my friend will help.

ID
The car that was repaired last week,
broke down.

ID
A university located in
Milwaukee will conduct the research.

In some instances the use of commas depends on the writer's meaning:

Teenagers, who like rock music, love this store.
(implies that all teenagers like music and love the store)

Teenagers who like rock music love this store.
(implies that only teenagers who like rock music love the store)

6. **Commas set off appositives, absolutes, and contrasted elements.** *Appositives* **provide additional information about a noun or pronoun. Appositives giving nonrestrictive or *extra* details are set off with commas:**

Sir John A. MacDonald, *Canada's first prime minister,* was born in 1851.
Pennsylvania, *the Keystone state,* has a new lottery.
Morphine, *a highly addictive drug,* is prescribed carefully.

Contrasted elements: Books, *not television,* should inspire our children.
Absolutes: *Designed for speed,* the car was not practical for most drivers.

7. **Commas set off parenthetical expressions, interjections, and direct address.**

Parenthetical expressions:

The conduct of the judge and, *thus,* the attitude of the jury shocked the defence attorneys.
Her statement to the press, *no doubt,* alters the whole investigation.

Interjections: *Say,* that is a good idea.
   She refuses, *I bet,* to share her thoughts.

Direct address: *Mother,* are you coming?

I suggest, *Dr. Wilson,* that you talk to the parents.

8. **Commas set off geographical names, items in dates, addresses, and numbers.**

Geographical names: The office in *Summerside, Prince Edward Island,* processes all bills.

He was born in *Ottawa, Canada.*

Items in dates: She retired on *December 15, 2002.*

Addresses: Cheques can be sent to *Committee for Refugees,*

700 Division Street, Kingston, ON K72 3N6.

(Note: No comma between province and area codes.)

Drive to Henri Maltrec's warehouse at *3737 North Lakewood, Victoria.*

Numbers: Commas set off units of three numbers: We sold 425,987 cars last year.

Note: Do not insert commas in page numbers, area codes, Social Insurance numbers, decimals, street addresses, or telephone numbers.

9. **Commas set off quotations.**

Winston Churchill said, "Never give in."

10. **Commas are inserted in sentences to prevent confusion. Writers often add commas simply to prevent readers from being confused.**

We assume that by 2005, 500 computers will have to be replaced.

Strategies for Eliminating Unnecessary Commas

Because commas have so many uses, you may easily place them where they are not needed.

1. **Do not set off prepositional phrases from what they modify:**

The boy/ *in the last row/* has a question.

2. **Do not put commas between subjects and verbs unless setting off nonrestrictive elements:**

The mayor/ spoke with the press.
The mayor, *who denied he was resigning,* spoke with the press.

3. **Do not set off titles in quotation marks with commas:**

I read/ "The Gold Bug/" last night.

4. **Do not put commas after a series unless it ends a clause needing to be set off from the rest of the sentence:**

They brought *food, water, and clothing/* to the church.
They brought *food, water, and clothing,* and they offered to take the supplies to the flood victims.

5. **Do not separate items in a compound verb unless there are three or more.**

We *talked/* and *danced* all night.
We *talked, danced,* and *played cards* all night.

6. **Do not set off dependent clauses that end a sentence:**

He sold the house/ because it was too expensive to maintain.

WRITING **ACTIVITY**

Insert commas where needed in the following sentences.

1. Henry Woo who majored in history applied to law school.
2. We can accept cash credit cards and cheques for any rentals leases or purchases.
3. She insisted the documents were filed on January 15 2000.
4. Warner Oland who played Chinese detective Charlie Chan was Swedish and he translated the works of Strindberg into English.
5. Exercise not diet is the key to losing weight.
6. They played tennis ran marathons and lifted weights to stay in shape fight boredom and avoid chores.
7. At what point Shelly wondered would her family accept her decision?
8. Teenagers including those who show no outward signs often suffer from depression.
9. The small book shop is threatened by Internet booksellers chain bookstores and discount retailers.
10. She was hired because of her willingness to take risks drive to make changes and ability to improvise solutions.

COMPANION WEBSITE

See **http://www.transcanadawriter.nelson.com** for additional information about commas.

;   Semicolon

Semicolons link related independent clauses and separate items in lists containing internal commas.

1. **Semicolons link related independent clauses. Compound sentences without coordinating conjunctions use semicolons:**

   Lewis drove to Pickle Lake; Frank flew to Winnipeg.

   He visited France often; however, he never learned French.

2. **Semicolons separate items in a list containing internal commas:**

   The Big Three consisted of Franklin Roosevelt, president of the United States; Josef Stalin, leader of the Soviet Union; and Winston Churchill, prime minister of Great Britain.

The inclusion of semicolons prevents readers from counting an item twice, thinking, for instance, that Roosevelt and the president of the United States were two different people.

When you encounter semicolons in a list, all the words and phrases between them are considered one item.

🖳 WRITING **ACTIVITY**

Circle each of the six ingredients of milk chocolate as listed on the wrapper of a Hershey's chocolate bar:

MILK CHOCOLATE CONTAINS SUGAR; MILK; COCOA BUTTER; CHOCOLATE; SOYA LECITHIN, AN EMULSIFIER; AND VANILLIN, AN ARTIFICIAL FLAVOURING.

🖳 WRITING **ACTIVITY**

Add the missing commas and semicolons in this passage from Bruce Catton's "Grant and Lee." After completing the exercise, check your corrections against the original text on pages 269–271.

Lee was tidewater Virginia and in his background were family culture and tradition . . . the age of chivalry transplanted to a New World which was making its own legends and its own myths. He embodied a way of life that had come down through the age of knighthood and the English country squire. America was a land that was beginning all over again dedicated to nothing much more complicated than the rather hazy belief that all men had equal rights and should have an equal chance in the world. In such a land Lee stood for the feeling that it was somehow of advantage to human society to have a pronounced inequality in the social structure. There should be a leisure class backed by ownership of land in turn society itself should be keyed to the land as the chief source of wealth and influence. It would bring forth (according to this ideal) a class of men with a strong sense of obligation to the community men who lived not to gain advantage for themselves but to meet the solemn obligations which had been laid on them by the very fact that they were privileged. From them the country would get its leadership to them it could look for the higher values—of thought of conduct of personal deportment—to give it strength and virtue.

COMPANION WEBSITE

See **http://www.transcanadawriter.nelson.com** for additional information about semicolons.

: Colon

Colons are used to introduce elements and separate items such as numerals, titles, and time references.

1. **Colons introduce a list, explanation, or an example. Note that colons are used only after an independent clause.**

   We need/ computer paper, pens, and pencils.
   We need office supplies: computer paper, pens, and pencils.
   We could resolve all the problems but one: pollution.

2. **Colons introduce long quotations:**

   Though Harry Truman is highly regarded today, Smith argues that he disappointed many in Washington when he assumed the presidency:
   Truman lacked the polish and dignity that marked the Roosevelt era. He was a plain-spoken, sometimes earthy Midwesterner who had only a high school education. He struck many as woefully unprepared to conclude a world war and lead the country forward after victory.

3. **Colons are used in common notations:**

Time references:	10:15 a.m.
Ratios:	They chose our product by a 4:1 margin.
Titles and Subtitles:	His book is called A Whole New Mind: Moving from the Information Age to the Conceptual Age.
Biblical references:	Ecclesiastes 12:12

" "   Quotation Marks

Quotation marks are used for direct quotations, titles of short works, and highlighted words.

1. **Direct quotations. When you copy word for word what someone has written or said, enclose the statement in quotation marks:**

   Martin Luther King said, "I have a dream."

   Note: The final mark of punctuation proceeds the final quotation mark, unless it does not appear in the original text:

   Did Martin Luther King say, "I have a dream"?

   Note: The identifying phrase is set off with commas:

   Maria argued, "We cannot win."
   "We cannot win," Maria argued.
   "We cannot win," Maria argued, "unless we practise!"

   Note: Commas do not set off a quotation if the quotation is blended into the sentence:

   They "do unto others" by volunteering at the clinic.

   Note: Quotations within quotations are indicated by single quotation marks:

   The president said, "I was only a child when Martin Luther King said, 'I have a dream.'"

   Note: Final commas are placed inside quotation marks:

   The letter stated, "The college will lower tuition," but few students believed it.

   Colons and semicolons are placed outside quotation marks:

   The letter stated, "The college will lower tuition"; few students believed it.

   Note: Indirect quotations or paraphrases do not require quotation marks:

   Martin Luther King stated that he had a vision.

2. **Titles of short works. Quotation marks are placed around the titles of articles, poems, songs, short stories, essays, individual episodes of television shows, and other larger works. (Titles of longer works such as magazines or books are underlined or placed in italics.)**

   Did you read "When Are We Going to Mars?" in *Macleans*?

Note: In titles, capitalize the first and last words, and any middle words that are nouns, pronouns, adjectives, verbs, adverbs, or subordinating conjunctions (such as *if, because, and that*). Do not capitalize middle words that are prepositions, articles, or coordinating conjunctions (such as *and, but,* and *or*). The "to" in infinitives should also not be capitalized in middle words of titles.

3. **Highlighted words. Quotation marks can be used to focus attention on items, words, or phrases:**

> I still don't know what "traffic abatement" means.

☐ WRITING **ACTIVITY**

Insert quotation marks where needed in the following sentences.

1. John F. Kennedy stated, Ask not what your country can do for you, ask what you can do for your country.
2. The film seems to be a modern adaptation of Willa Cather's story Paul's Case.
3. Nancy Lowe argues, The most famous saying of the Depression was Roosevelt's statement We have nothing to fear but fear itself.
4. I can't go, James said, until I register these documents.
5. Advertisements aimed at children should not mention the word sex.

COMPANION WEBSITE

See **http://www.transcanadawriter.nelson.com** for additional information about quotation marks.

' Apostrophe

Apostrophes indicate possession, missing letters or numbers, and some plurals.

1. **Possessive forms:**

Add *'s* to show possession for most singular nouns:

> a boy's hat   the book's cover   the dog's collar

Add *s'* to show possession for plural nouns ending in *s:*

> two boys' hats   the books' covers   the dogs' collars

Add *'s* to show possession for plural nouns that do not end in *s:*

> women's clothing   children's games   men's shoes

Add apostrophes to the last noun to show joint or mutual possession:

Smith and Baker's travel agency is providing the tickets.

Add apostrophes to all nouns to show individual possession:

The parents' and the teachers' statements were reported by the press.

2. **Missing letters and numbers. Omitted letters in contractions are indicated by a single apostrophe:**

can't for cannot   *he'll* for he will

Note: Only one apostrophe is used, even if more than one letter is deleted. The apostrophe is placed over the missing letter or letters, not where words are joined:

do not = don't   *not*   do'nt

Deleted numbers are indicated by a single apostrophe:

He was embued with the Spirit of '76.
Back in '29, Wall Street collapsed.
My brother is restoring a '65 Mustang.

Apostrophes indicate letters dropped to reproduce dialect or slang:

The London cabby shouted, "'E ain' goin' nowhere!"

3. **Plurals of letters, numbers, or symbols:**

She got all A's last semester.
I need a lot of size 7's this week.

Note: Common abbreviations such as UFO and ESP do not require apostrophes:

They claimed he stole two TVs and three VCRs.

Note: Apostrophe use in referring to decades is optional; be consistent:

Incorrect: I grew up in the *1980s* but loved the music of the *1960's.*
Correct: I grew up in the 1980s but loved the music of the 1960s.

Remember: *it's = it is*   *its = possessive*
            It's raining.   The car will not start because *its* battery died.

WRITING **ACTIVITY**

Add apostrophes where needed in the following passage.

Charles Lindbergh will always be remembered for 1927s famed flight to Paris. However, his influence on American politics, science, aviation, and medicine cant be underestimated. Fame seemed to follow Lindberghs every move. He pioneered new air routes over some of the worlds most remote areas. Lindberghs marriage to the daughter of Dwight Morrow brought him more fame. The kidnapping of Charles and Annes first son thrust the young couples grief into the headlines. The newspapers lurid coverage and the reporters intrusive behavior soured Lindbergh on America. He moved his family to England in the late 1930s because he felt Britains more genteel society would provide a safe haven. During those years, Lindbergh worked with Dr. Alexis Carrel, a Nobel Prize winning scientist. Lindberghs and Carrels creation of an experimental artificial heart in the 1930s signaled an achievement in medical engineering. Lindberghs visit to Nazi Germany and his opposition to Americas entry into the Second World War led many Americans to question his loyalty. Lindbergh did serve in the South Pacific as an advisor, showing US pilots how to extend their planes range by lowering gas consumption. Though he spent most of his life working with aircraft, Lindbergh opposed the SSTs development in the 1960s because he felt it would damage the earths atmosphere. In his last years, Lindbergh devoted his life to environmental causes, sharing the younger generations concern about pollution.

COMPANION WEBSITE

See **http://www.transcanadawriter.nelson.com** for additional information about apostrophes.

. . . Ellipsis

An *ellipsis*, composed of three periods (. . .), indicates that words have been deleted from quoted material:

Original text: The mayor stated, "The city needs a light rail system to overcome highway congestion and provide efficient transportation between the airport and the convention centre."

With ellipsis: The mayor stated, "The city needs a light rail system to . . . provide efficient transportation between the airport and the convention centre."

Note: Do not omit words that will alter or distort the meaning of the original text. Delete only extra or parenthetical material.

Note: When deleting words at the end of a sentence or an entire sentence, add the final period to the ellipsis, creating four periods:

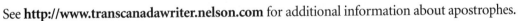

The mayor stated, "The city needs a light rail system to overcome highway congestion. . . ." (The quotation marks follow the ellipsis.)

Note: Do not use ellipses when omitting words from the beginning of a quotation:

The mayor stated the city needs light rail to facilitate "efficient transportation between the airport and the convention centre."

Note: If omitting words alters the grammar of a sentence, you may change a verb or pronoun to maintain agreement:

Original: The mayor said, "The convention centre and the new hotels are the lifeblood of downtown development."
With ellipsis and alteration in brackets:
The mayor said, "The convention centre . . .[is] the lifeblood of downtown development."

( ) Parentheses

Parentheses enclose nonessential but related ideas. Parenthetical information can be located anywhere in a sentence except at the very beginning. It should be placed just after the idea it refers to.

1. **Use parentheses to set off additional or illustrative matter and to enclose abbreviations, explanatory letters, or numerals:**

   Students took the Scholastic Aptitude Test (SAT) last week.
   George Wilson (later joined by Jan Sullivan) argued for a policy change.
   Michael Collins (1890–1922) remains one of Ireland's greatest heroes.
   Primary diagnostic methods (such as blood tests and X-rays) are fully covered by the new insurance policy.
   Because Tom graduates in December (he took a semester off to travel), he won't look for a job until after New Year's.

Note: When parenthetical comments appear after a word or phrase set off by commas, the commas follow the parentheses:

Star Trek, which lasted only three seasons (1966–1969), became a TV classic.

2. **Use parentheses to enclose nonessential sentences:**

   College and university instructors assume students will use computers to conduct research and prepare research papers. (Most professors refuse to accept handwritten documents.) Most colleges and universities guarantee students access to computers.

Note: The parentheses enclose the entire sentence, including the final mark of punctuation.

[ ]   Brackets

Brackets are used to enclose words inserted into a quotation.

1. **Brackets set off clarifications or explanations:**

   "The main plant [located in Oshawa] will be expanded next year."

   "During the Gulf War, the President kept in touch with Professor Sarah Bush [no relation] at the Middle East Institute."

   "The ambassador stated she could not deliver the message until he [Frank Wilson] completed the annual report."

2. **Brackets indicate grammatical alterations or corrections:**

   Original: "The United States, Canada, and Germany are among the most promising markets."

   Quotation with brackets containing alteration:

   "The United States . . . [is] among the most promising markets."

   Original: "After Rosevelt's death, Harry Truman became president."

   Quotation with brackets noting error:

   "After Rosevelt's [*sic*] death, Harry Truman became president."

   (The Latin term *sic* is used to indicate that an error appears in the original text.)

-   Hyphen

A *hyphen* consists of a single short line used to separate or join words and other items.

1. **Use hyphens to break words:**

   We attempted to tele-
   phone her last night.

2. **Use hyphens to combine words into adjectives:**

   Grossman made a last-ditch attempt to save his job.

3. **Do not use a hyphen after an adverb ending in *ly*:**

   Grossman issued a quickly drafted statement to the press.

4. **Use a hyphen to join words forming numbers:**

   The company was forced to pay twenty-two million dollars in back taxes.

5. **Use a hyphen after some prefixes:**

   It is dangerous to take these drugs based on a self-diagnosis or the advice of an ex-doctor.

6. **Use a hyphen between a combination of a number and a word:**

> He drove a 4.5-tonne truck.

— Dash

A *dash* is used to set off words in a sentence. Sometimes a dash appears in print as two hyphens (--) but usually it appears as one continuous line (—) that is about the length of two hyphens. Dashes are dramatic marks of punctuation that emphasize words and phrases:

> The college changed the tuition schedule—driving it to near bankruptcy.
> The college—long pressured by student groups—changed the tuition policy.

Note: Do not place spaces between the dash and the words it connects.

/ Slash

The *slash* is used to separate words when both are applicable and in quotations to signal line breaks in poetry:

> A student should study his/her lessons.
> To test the microphone, she began reciting the simple refrain, "Mary had a little lamb / Its fleece was white as snow / And everywhere that Mary went / The lamb was sure to go."

? Question Mark

Question marks are placed after direct questions and to note questionable items:

> Can anyone truly predict the stock market?
> He read a disturbing article, "What Is to Be Done?"

Note: In the preceding example, the question mark is placed within the quotation marks because it is part of the title.

> Did you read Poe's "The Tell-Tale Heart"?

Note: In the preceding example, the question mark is placed outside the quotation marks because it is not part of the title.

> The children reported they waited two hours (?) for the police to arrive.

Note: To indicate that you doubt the accuracy of a fact, number, or idea, place the question mark in parentheses after the item in question.

! Exclamation Point

Exclamation points are placed after emphatic statements:

> I can't go on!
> Get out!

Exclamations, like dashes, should be viewed as special effects that lose impact if overused.

. Period

Periods are used after sentences, in abbreviations, and with decimals:

> They moved to Kamloops.
> We gave the report to Mrs. Chavez and promised to give an estimate by Jan. 15.
> We promised to pay $134.45 a share.

Note: When a sentence ends with an abbreviation, only one period is used.
Note: Some abbreviations such as CSIS, NBA, CAW, and UBC do not require periods.

WRITING **ACTIVITY**

Insert punctuation where needed in this passage from Armond Budish's "Fender Benders: Legal Do's and Don'ts." After you finish editing the section, review the original text on pages 309–311.

Call the Police

Its obvious that if its a serious accident in which someone is injured the police should be called immediately. Thats both the law and common sense. But what if the accident seems minor. Say youre stopped another car taps you in the rear. If its absolutely clear to both drivers that there is no damage or injury you each can go your merry way. But thats the exception.

Normally you should call the police to substantiate what occurred. In most cities police officers will come to the scene even for minor accidents but if they wont you and the other driver should go to the station of the city where the accident occurred to file a report. Ask to have an officer check out both cars.

If you are not at fault be wary of accepting the other drivers suggestion that you leave the police out of it and arrange a private settlement. When you submit your $500 car repair estimate several weeks later you could discover that the other driver has developed amnesia and denies being anywhere near the accident. If the police werent present on the scene you may not have a legal leg to stand on.

(Continued)

> *Even if you are at fault its a good idea to involve the police. Why. Because a police officer will note the extent of the other drivers damages in his or her report limiting your liability. Without police presence the other driver can easily inflate the amount of the damages.*

MECHANICS

The writing context can dictate or influence the rules of mechanics. Ensure your writing follows the accepted style used in your discipline or profession.

Capitalization

Capital letters signal the beginning of a new sentence and denote proper nouns such as *Alberta, Chevrolet, Dublin, Islam,* and *Dark Ages.* Capitals also help prevent confusion by making distinctions:

> They drove the Dodge to ford the stream.
> We bought china made in Japan.
> The Liberal candidate supported conservative principles.

Capitalize proper nouns and their abbreviations and acronyms.
Names of people, specific objects, and trademarks:

Michael Collins	Malcolm X	Coca-Cola	Buick
Xerox	Apollo	Ford Mustang	Apple computer
Titanic	Tommy	Lucky Jim	

Geographical names:

Maple Avenue	Laval	Lake Huron	the Prairies
Asia	Mars	Mexico	Lee Valley
Grant Park	Cherry Beach		

Peoples, nations, and languages:

Asians	Jews	Italian	Chinese
Mexican	Kurds	Germany	Canada
Haida	Iran		

Corporations, organizations, institutions, and government agencies:

RCMP	Trinity College	NASA	Calgary
Stampeders	CRA	Microsoft	YMCA
KLM	RCMP	Campbell Soup	

Historical documents, eras, events, and movements:

Charter of Rights and Freedoms	the Dark Ages	the Civil War
Existentialism	the Feminist Movement	Nazism

Days of the week, months, and special days:

Monday	October	Victoria Day	Labour Day

The seasons—winter, spring, summer, fall—are not capitalized.

Religions and their followers, sacred texts, holidays, and names for the Supreme Being:

Presbyterian	Islam	Roman Catholic	Hinduism
Muslim	Jews	Buddhists	Mormons
Bible	Talmud	Koran	Book of Mormon
Easter	Christmas	Ramadan	Kwanza
Allah	God	Immanuel	Christ

Special events:

World Series	Grey Cup	Winter Olympics	Mother's Day

Common or generic words when used in titles or part of proper names:

Huron College   *Children's Hospital*   *Toronto Police Department*

but

"The police took him to a children's hospital after the accident."

Titles of books, films, paintings, and other works of art:

Hamlet   *Starry Night*   *Moon for the Misbegotten*   *"Moonlight"*

Professional titles preceding a personal name or when used in place of a person's name:

"Get Doctor Wilson" but "Get the doctor."
The delegation met with a mayor and Senator James.
The following morning former Prime Minister Clark met with the president of France.

Words derived from proper nouns:

Orwellian   Marxism   French

Breeds of animals are not capitalized unless they refer to a geographical region, such as *Irish terrier*, *French poodle*, and *Labrador*.

WRITING **ACTIVITY**

Edit this opening passage from Joe Rodriguez's "Mexicans Deserve More Than La Mordida" and add capital letters. After completing the exercise, review the original text on pages 209–211.

"i wouldn't give you a dime for mexico!"

my father used to tell us that every time mexico broke his heart. he was *muy indio*, with dark reddish brown skin, huge calloused hands and a handsomely hooked nose. on our occasional trips to tijuana to visit relatives, he'd see indian women begging on the streets, indian kids selling chiclets chewing gum, and white-skinned mexicans owning and running everything.

"not a dime for mexico!"

he was more mexican than i'll ever be, more mexican than any harvard-educated technocrat, any spanish-looking *gachupin*, any middleclass zapatista guerrilla-intellectual, or any bald-headed ex-president crook from mexico city's ritzy polanco district. my father wasn't referring to the nation's people, but to a political and social system that still fosters extreme poverty, discrimination and injustice, and to the privileged and the ruthless who benefit by it.

i should have remembered my dad's dime recently when two mexico city policemen pulled me over for making an illegal left-hand turn at the monument of cuauhtemoc on the famous paseo de la reforma boulevard.

i was driving back into the giant city after three days in the countryside.

i had escaped a traffic accident only minutes earlier. i was hot, tired, grumpy and jumpy. i was driving a rental car. these conditions made me the perfect *pollo* for these two uniformed coyotes.

both cops got out. the older one checked out the rental plates. the younger one wanted to see my driver's license.

"where's your hotel?" he asked.

right over there, i said, the maria cristina hotel on rio lerma street.

COMPANION WEBSITE

See **http://www.transcanadawriter.nelson.com** for additional information about capitalization.

Underlining and Italics

Traditional typewriters could not change type, so writers used *underlining* to indicate text that would be *italicized* in print. The advent of changeable type and computers have made underlining unnecessary, but MLA still requires its use.

   Underlining and *italics* serve to highlight words and phrases for special reasons:

1. **Underlining or italics is used for titles of long works of art. Books, magazines, newspapers, plays, television programs, and recordings are underlined or italicized:**

We saw <u>The Drawer Boy</u>.   *Or*   We saw *The Drawer Boy*.

Note: Underline the entire title, including spaces between words.
Note: Religious texts and historical documents are not italicized: The Bible, The Bill of Rights.

2. **Names of ships, trains, aircraft, and space vehicles:**

My grandmother sailed on the <u>Titanic</u>.
My father took the *City of New Orleans* to Chicago.

3. **Words being emphasized or highlighted:**

Patients <u>must</u> sign a release before receiving treatment.
Your paper is hard to read because the *1*'s and *7*'s look alike.

4. **Uncommon foreign words and phrases:**

Hitler demanded <u>Lebensraum</u>.
The hero was undone by his overwhelming *hubris*.

Note: Once foreign words enter popular English usage, they are no longer underlined or italicized: kindergarten, tortilla, rotisserie, or lasagna. Consult your dictionary if you are unsure.

Abbreviations

Abbreviations are shortened versions of words or phrases:

1. **Names of organizations, names of products, and common phrases:**

CSIS	UPS	GM	NATO	IRA
USA	VCR	CBC	COD	CFL

Note: Capitalize all letters and do not separate them with periods.
Note: Some writers insert periods between letters or numerals: W.W.II. Consult your handbook or professional style manual. Always be consistent.

2. **Abbreviations of single words:**

Mon.   Dec.   pg.   fwd.   ms.

Note: Most abbreviations use lowercase letters except for abbreviations of proper nouns.

3. **Professional titles:**

Dr. Smith   Ms. Wong   Jim Chavez, M.D.   Rick Gross, Esq.

Note: Professional titles preceding names are followed by a period. Professional titles following names are set off with commas.

Note: Avoid using abbreviations unless associated with a name:

We saw Dr. Green.
> *or*

We saw the doctor.
> *not*

We saw the Dr.

Note: Do not use double titles:

Dr. Green *or* Sandy Green, M.D.
> *not*

Dr. Sandy Green, M.D.

4. **Geographical regions:**

Do not use periods between letters in province or state abbreviations used in addresses:

Haddonfield, NJ   Ancaster, ON   Trois-Rivieres, PQ

Note: Use periods in *Washington, D.C.*, and *U.S.* when these are used to modify another word, as in *U.S. regulations.*

5. **Latin expressions:**

etc.   e.g.   i.e.   vs.   et al.

6. **Certain terms used with dates or numbers:**

80 B.C.	A.D. 95	*or*	80 B.C.E	95 C.E.
35 kph	10 a.m.	*or*	35 KPH	10 AM

Note: Be consistent with alternate forms.

You do not have to identify commonly known abbreviations such as FBI, NYC, or RCMP. When you use an abbreviation your readers may not understand or may misunderstand, define it after its first use:

We reported the incident to the Center for Air Pollution Studies (CAPS).
She worked for the CIA (Canadian Insurance Adjusters) for two years.

Numbers

Numbers are either written out (*twenty-two*) or presented as numerals (*22*).

1. **Numbers presented as words.** Write out numbers if they appear infrequently in your writing, can be written in one or two words, or when they begin a sentence:

   We drove *forty-two* miles.
   Three hundred seventy-five students graduated last week.

   Note: Hyphenate numbers between 21 and 99 (except for round numbers such as *forty* and *sixty*).
   Note: To avoid long and awkward phrases, avoid opening sentences with large numbers:

   Last week, 8,998 students graduated from the city's high schools.

2. **Numbers presented as numerals.** Use numerals to represent dates, addresses, large or often repeated numbers, page numbers, most percentages, decimals, and identifications:

   She accepted the post on January 25, 2000.
   Send the car to the garage at 700 Victoria Street.
   Last year 32,987 complaints were received.
   Look on page 23.
   Sales rose 34% last year.
   The average subject slept fewer than 7.5 hours a night.
   You can find the offices of Channel 36 in Room 300.

3. **Numbers presented in combinations of words and numerals:**

4646 North 47th Street	or	2323 Second Avenue
4 PM	or	four o'clock in the afternoon
$24,000,000	or	24 million dollars

Spelling

Spelling errors, even in the age of computer spell-checks, remain one of the most common and most annoying errors. Poor spelling detracts from the impact and authority of your writing. Readers interpret spelling mistakes as indications of haste, sloppiness, and ignorance.

Understand the Limits of Spell-Checking Programs

If you write on a computer, you may be lulled into the belief that you can rely on a spell-checking program to locate errors.

1. Spell-checkers do not find missing or misused words.

2. Many programs will not detect problems in usage, for example, mistaking *there* for *their* or *conscience* for *conscious*.

3. Spell-checkers often flag correctly spelled words, especially proper names. If your spell-checker keeps flagging a repeated word, click IGNORE ALL or customize the program by adding the word to its list of correctly spelled words.

Strategies for Improving Spelling

1. Review the guidelines in the chapter, noting words that you have found confusing.

2. Review the list of commonly confused words on pages 645–648. Underline or highlight pairs that you have found troublesome.

3. Review the list of commonly misspelled words on pages 648–650. Underline or highlight those that you recall misspelling.

4. As you are introduced to new terms in college or university courses, readings, or your career, make sure to get the correct spelling. If you learn to spell a word correctly as soon as you learn it, you will not have to unlearn or correct a habitual error. Refer to glossaries in your textbooks and specialized dictionaries.

5. Develop a list of words that you commonly misspell.

Spelling Guidelines

1. **Prefixes:** *Prefixes* are added to the beginning of words to form new words. *The spelling of the base word does not change:*

im + moral	=	immoral
re + entry	=	reentry
anti + biotic	=	antibiotic
mayor + elect	=	mayor-elect

Note: Some combinations use hyphens, especially if the base word is capitalized: *un-American, non-Lutheran, anti-Communism.*

2. **Suffixes:** *Suffixes* are added to the end of words to form new words.

If the word ends in a silent *e* and the suffix begins with a vowel, drop the *e:*

continue + ous	=	continuous
pure + ist	=	purist

If the word ends in a silent *e* and the suffix begins with a consonant, do not drop the *e:*

state + ly	=	stately
state + ment	=	statement

Note: There are some exceptions to these guidelines:

dye + ing = dyeing *not* dying
true + ly = truly *not* truely

If a word ends in *y*, change the *y* to an *i* if preceded by a consonant:

easy + ly = easily

Note: If the suffix is *-ing*, the *y* is always retained:

cry + ing = crying

Add *-ly* to adjectives to create adverbs. For most words ending in *-ic* add *-ally*. Retain the final *l* in words ending in *l*:

regular + ly = regularly
tragic + ally = tragically
cool + ly = coolly

Double the last consonant if the word ends with a single accented vowel and a single consonant and is joined to a suffix beginning with vowel:

stop + ed = stopped
begin + ing = beginning

3. *ie* **and** *ei* **words:**

When words sound like *ee* as in *see*, write *ie* except after *c*:

belief   field   brief   yield   shield
receive   ceiling   perceive   conceit

When words sound like *ay* as in *ray*, write *ei*:

weigh   rein   neighbour   eight   vein

Exceptions: ancient, either, foreign, height, science

4. **Plurals:**

Most words in English simply add *s* to create plural forms, but there are a few exceptions: When words end with a consonant and *y*, add *-ies:*

theory/*theories*   mystery/*mysteries*

When words end in *s*, *sh*, *ch*, *x*, or *z*, add *es:*

bus/*buses*   bush/*bushes*   fox/*foxes*

Many words ending in *f* or *ef* change to *ves:*

leaf/*leaves*   calf/*calves*   self/*selves*

Some words do not have a separate plural form:

deer/*deer*   sheep/*sheep*

Latin and Greek terms ending in *on*, *um*, or *us* change to *a* or *i:*

medium/*media*   alumnus/*alumni*

Add the *s* to the first word in hyphenated words:

mother-in-law/*mothers-in-law*   court-martial/*courts-martial*

WRITING **ACTIVITY**

Read and correct the spelling errors in this passage from George Orwell's essay "Shooting an Elephant." When you complete the exercise, examine the original text on pages 182–187 to see whether you located all the misspellings and errors in usage.

In Moulmein, in Lower Berma, I was hated by large numbers of people—the only time in my life that I have been impotant enough for this to hapen to me. I was sub—divisonal police oficer of the town, and in aimless, petty kind of way anti-European feeling was very bitter. No one had the guts to raise a riot, but if a European women went through the bizarres alone somebody would probably spit betel juice over her dress. As a police officer I was an ovious target and was bated whenever it seemed safe to do so. When a nimble Berman tripped me up on the football field and the refere (another Berman) looked the other way, the crowed yelled with hedious laughter. This happen more then once. In the end the sneering yellow faces of young men that meet me everywhere, the insults hooted after me when I was at a safe distance, got badly on my nerves. The young Budhist priests were the worst of all. Their ere several thousands of them in the town and none of them seemed to have anything to do but accept stand on street corners and jear at Europeans.

COMPANION WEBSITE

See **http://www.transcanadawriter.nelson.com** for additional information about spelling.

Appendix

COMMONLY CONFUSED WORDS

accept	to take	Do you *accept* cheques?
except	to exclude	Everyone *except* Joe went home.
adapt	to change	We will *adapt* the army helicopter for civilian use.
adopt	to choose or accept	They want to *adopt* a child.
adverse	unfavourable	*Adverse* publicity ruined his reputation.
averse	opposed to	I was *averse* to buying a new car.
advice	a noun	Take my *advice*.
advise	a verb	Let me *advise* you.
affect	to influence	Will this *affect* my grade?
effect	a result	What is the *effect* of the drug?
all ready	prepared	We were *all ready* for the trip.
already	by a certain time	You are *already* approved.
allusion	a reference	She made a biblical *allusion*.
illusion	imaginary vision	The mirage was an optical *illusion*.
all together	unity	The teachers stood *all together*.
altogether	totally	*Altogether,* that will cost $50.
among	relationship of three or more	This outfit is popular *among* students.
between	relationship of two	This was a dispute *between* Kim and Nancy.
amount	for items that are measured	A small *amount* of oil has leaked.
number	for items that are counted	A large *number* of cars are stalled.
any one	a person, idea, item anybody	*Any one* of the books will do.
anyone	anybody	Can *anyone* help me?

brake	to halt	Can you fix the *brakes*?
	a stopping mechanism	
break	an interruption	Take a coffee *break*.
	to destroy	Don't *break* the window.
capital	money	She needs venture *capital*.
	government centre	Regina is the *capital* of Saskatchewan.
capitol	U.S. legislative building	He toured the Ohio *Capitol*.
cite	to note or refer to	He *cited* several figures in his speech.
site	a location	We inspected the *site* of the crash.
sight	a view, ability to see	The *sight* from the hill was tremendous.
complement	to complete	The jet had a full *complement* of spare parts.
compliment	express praise, a gift	The host paid us a nice *compliment*.
conscience	moral sensibility	He was a prisoner of *conscience*.
conscious	aware of/awake	Is he *conscious* of these debts?
		Is the patient *conscious*?
continual	now and again	We have *continual* financial problems.
continuous	uninterrupted	The brain needs a *continuous* supply of blood.
council	a group	A student *council* will meet Tuesday.
counsel	to advise/adviser	He sought legal *counsel*.
discreet	tactful	He made a *discreet* hint.
discrete	separate/distinct	The war had three *discrete* phases.
elicit	evoke/persuade	His hateful remarks will *elicit* protest.
illicit	illegal	Her use of *illicit* drugs ruined her career.
emigrate	to leave a country	They tried to *emigrate* from Germany.
immigrate	to enter a country	They were allowed to *immigrate* to Canada.
eminent	famous	She was an *eminent* eye specialist.
imminent	impending	Disaster was *imminent*.
everyday	ordinary	Wear *everyday* clothes to the party.
every day	daily	We exercise *every day*.
farther	distance	How much *farther* is it?
further	in addition	He demanded a *further* investigation.

fewer	for items counted	There are *fewer* security guards this year.
less	for items measured	There is *less* security this year.
good	an adjective	She has *good* eyesight.
well	an adverb	She sees *well*.
hear	to listen	Can you *hear* the music?
here	a place/direction	Put the table *here*.
imply	to suggest	The prime minister *implied* he might raise taxes.
infer	to interpret	The reporters *inferred* from his comments that the prime minister might raise taxes.
its	possessive of it	The car won't start because *its* battery is dead.
it's	contraction of *it is*	*It's* snowing.
lay	to put/to place	*Lay* the books on my desk.
lie	to rest	*Lie* down for a nap.
loose	not tight	He has a *loose* belt or loose change.
lose	to misplace	Don't *lose* your keys.
moral	dealing with values	She made a *moral* decision to report the crime.
morale	mood	After the loss, the team's *morale* fell.
passed	successfully completed	She *passed* the test.
past	history	That was in my *past*.
personal	private/intimate	She left a *personal* note.
personnel	employees	Send your résumé to the *personnel* office.
plain	simple/open space	She wore a *plain* dress.
plane	airplane/geometric form	They took a *plane* to Chicago.
precede	to go before	A film will *precede* the lecture.
proceed	go forward	Let the parade *proceed*.
principal	main/school leader	Oil is the *principal* product of Kuwait.
principle	basic law	I understand the *principle* of law.
raise	to lift	*Raise* the window!
rise	to get up	*Rise* and shine!

right	direction/correct	Turn *right*. That's *right*.
rite	a ritual	She was given last *rites*.
write	to inscribe	They *write* essays every week.
stationary	unmoving	The disabled train remained *stationary*.
stationery	writing paper	The hotel *stationery* was edged in gold.
than	used to compare	I am taller *than* Helen.
then	concerning time	We *then* headed to class.
their	possessive of they	*Their* car is stalled.
there	direction/place	Put the chair over *there*.
they're	contraction of *they are*	*They're* coming to dinner.
there're	contraction of *there are*	*There're* are two seats left.
to	preposition/infinitive	I went *to* school to study law.
too	in excess/also	It was *too* cold to swim.
two	a number	We bought *two* computers.
wear	clothes/damage	We *wear* our shoes until they *wear* out.
where	a place in question	*Where* is the post office?
weather	climatic conditions	*Weather* forecasts predict rain.
whether	alternatives/no matter what	You must register, *whether* or not you want to audit the class.
who's	contraction of *who is*	*Who's* on first?
whose	possessive of who	*Whose* book is that?

COMMONLY MISSPELLED WORDS

absence	address	appreciate	basically	calendar	commitment
accept	adolescence	approach	basis	candidate	committee
accident	advertisement	arctic	beautiful	career	competition
accommodate	a lot	argument	becoming	carrying	completely
accumulate	amateur	article	beginning	celebrate	complexion
achieve	analysis	assassination	belief	cemetery	conceive
achievement	analyze	assistance	believe	challenge	consistent
acquaint	annual	athletic	benefit	characteristic	continually
acquire	anonymous	attention	breakfast	column	control
across	apparent	attitude	business	coming	controversial

criticism	fascination	identically	maneuver	particularly	recede
curious	favourite	identify	marriage	perform	receive
dealt	February	immediately	martial	permanent	reception
decision	feminine	importance	material	permission	recognition
definite	field	incidental	mathematics	persistent	recommend
deliberate	finally	independence	meant	persuade	refer
dependent	foreign	influence	mechanical	persuasion	regulation
description	forgotten	intelligence	medieval	philosophy	relation
difficult	forty	interest	mere	physical	religious
disappear	fourth	interpret	miniature	playwright	remember
disappoint	frequent	interrupt	mischief	politician	repetition
discipline	friend	involvement	misspell	positive	responsible
discuss	frighten	irrelevant	mortgage	possession	restaurant
dominant	fulfill	irresistible	necessary	possible	rhythm
dying	fundamental	irresponsible	ninety	precede	ridicule
efficient	further	judgment	noticeable	preference	roommate
eighth	generally	judicial	obligation	prejudice	sacrifice
eligible	generous	judicious	obvious	presence	safety
embarrass	government	knowledge	occasionally	primitive	scene
enough	gradually	label	occupation	probably	schedule
environment	grammar	laboratory	occurred	procedure	seize
equipment	grateful	language	omit	prominent	separate
essential	guarantee	leisure	operate	psychic	sergeant
exaggerate	guard	libel	opinion	psychology	severely
excellent	guidance	library	opportunity	publicly	significance
existence	happiness	license	oppose	qualify	significant
experience	height	lightning	optimism	quality	similar
explanation	heroes	loneliness	ordinarily	quantity	simplify
extremely	holocaust	luxury	original	query	sincerely
fallacy	huge	lying	paid	quiet	situation
familiar	humorous	magazine	pamphlet	quizzes	skillfully
fantasy	hypocrite	maintenance	parallel	realize	sociology

sophisticated
sophomore
special
specimen
stereotype
straight
strict
studying
success

Add other words you often misspell:

_____ _____ _____
_____ _____ _____
_____ _____ _____
_____ _____ _____
_____ _____ _____
_____ _____ _____
_____ _____ _____
_____ _____ _____

summary			
surprise			
synonymous			
technique			
temperament			
tenable			
tendency			
thorough			
thought			
throughout			
tomorrow			
tragedy			
tremendous			
truly			
unfortunate			
uniform			
unique			
until			
unusual			
useful			
using			

ESSAY TOPICS

stalking	standardized tests	student unions	ideal job
dieting	privacy laws	day care	women in combat
Internet fraud	lawyers	soap operas	prisons
AIDS	being fired	gay bashing	Iraq war
depression	Employment Insurance	life after death	bilingual education
spring break	fads	funerals	gambling
family values	blind dates	success	pornography
new cars	disabilities	being a victim	airport fees
exercise	Security Certificates	voting	gangs
gun control	job interviews	hybrid cars	bloggers
racism	oil	wearing fur	minimum wage
immigration	adoption	high school	CFL teams
latest hit movie	drug testing	living wills	camera phones
local singles bars	sex offenders	fast food	the homeless
charity	role models	Bay Street	reality TV
friendship	Bollywood	dreams	car insurance
music videos	Christmas	tobacco	birth control
pensions	summer jobs	terrorism	graffiti

cults
drinking age
eating disorders
talk shows
morning-after pill
baseball
single parents
toxic waste
sexual harassment
health care
digital TV
banks
lawsuits
twelve-step programs
sex on the web
child abuse
stadiums
churches
pets
suburbs
China
images of women
steroids
surveillance cameras
hazing rituals
relationships
alcohol
teen smoking
the Olympics
comedy clubs

video games
people you admire
nuclear power
feminism
car repairs
employment equity
hate speech
illegal immigration
marriage
work ethic
fatherhood
credit cards
censorship
ski resorts
Islam
romance
grand juries
the insanity defense
the Pope
slavery reparations
child labour
The Senate
married priests
coffee bar
foreign aid
mutual funds
bad habits
addiction as disability
art museums
profanity in public

world hunger
owning a business
child support
gay rights
jealousy
worst jobs
conspiracy theories
politicians
drunk driving
professors
space exploration
commercials
suicide
local restaurants
best teacher
jogging
crack cocaine
being "in"
the Holocaust
doctors
Africa
TV news
favourite film or book
the American Dream
future career
adultery
animal testing
night clubs
children's TV
seatbelts in school
  buses

stereotypes
sex education
divorce
the glass ceiling
right to die
interracial dating
labour unions
welfare reform
plea bargaining
military recruiting
poverty
first apartment
addiction
chat rooms
fashion models
celebrities
animal rights
cable TV
urban sprawl
legalized prostitution
school choice
ethnic conflict
e-mail
casinos
nationalism
alternative fuels
NBA salaries
nostalgia
the prime minister
discrimination

Credits

Ericsson, Stephanie, "The Ways We Lie" copyright © 1992 by Stephanie Ericsson. Originally published by *The Utne Reader*. Reprinted by the permission of Dunham Literary as agents for the author.

Fawcett, Brian, "Politics and the English Language (1991)" from *Unusual Circumstances, Interesting Times* by Brian Fawcett, published by New Star Books 1991. Reprint by permission of the publisher.

Fraser, John, "Universities Need Money, Yes, But a Social Mission, Too" *The Globe and Mail*, March 26, 2005. Reprinted by permission of the author.

Gatto, John Taylor, "Why Schools Don't Educate" from John Taylor Gatto, *The Underground History of American Education* (Mr. Gatto accepts e-mail at www.johntaylorgatto.com). Why Schools Don't Educate. © 1991 John Taylor Gatto. All rights reserved.

Hébert, Jacques, "Eulogy by Jacques Hébert" reprinted by permission of Jacques Hébert.

"Homicide" definition reprinted from *Black's Law Dictionary, 6th ed.*, 1990 with permission of Thomson West.

Iyer, Pico, "In Praise of the Humble Comma" copyright © 2001, Time Inc. All rights reserved. Reprinted by permission.

Jacobs, Jane, "Streets that Work" from *Canadian Heritage*, 13, 2 (May/June 1987). Copyright © 1987 Jane Jacobs.

Kenna, Peggy and Lacy, Sondra, "Communication Styles: United States and Taiwan" from *Business Taiwan* by Peggy Kenna and Sondra Lacy. Copyright © 1994. Used with permission of The McGraw-Hill Companies, Inc.

King Jr., Martin Luther, "Ways of Meeting Oppression" reprinted by arrangement with The Heirs to the Estate of Martin Luther King Jr., c/o Writers House as agent for the proprietor New York, NY. Copyright 1958 Martin Luther King Jr., copyright renewed 1986 Coretta Scott King.

Klein, Naomi, "The Beginning of the Brand" excerpted from *No Logo: Taking Aim at the Brand Bullies* by Naomi Klein. Copyright © 2000 by Naomi Klein. Reprinted by permission of Knopf Canada.

Lutz, William, "With These Words I Can Sell You Anything" reprinted by permission of the Jean V. Naggar Literary Agency.

MacLennan, Hugh, "The Halifax Explosion" selection from *Barometer Rising* by Hugh MacLennan © 1941, 1958. Published in Canada by McClelland & Stewart Ltd. Used with permission of the publisher.

Malcolm X, "My First Conk" from *The Autobiography of Malcolm X* by Malcolm X and Alex Haley, copyright © 1964 by Alex Haley and Malcolm X. Copyright © 1965 by Alex Haley and Betty Shabazz. Used by permission of Random House, Inc.

Moaveni, Asadeh, "Maman and America" from *Lipstick Jihad* by Azadeh Moaveni. Copyright © 2005 by Azadeh Moaveni. Reprinted by permission of Public Affairs, a member of Perseus Books Group.

Munro, Alice "A Walk on the Wild Side" copyright © by 1989 by Alice Munro. Reprinted by permission of William Morris Agency, LLC on behalf of the Author.

Odets, Clifford, "Paradise Lost" from *Waiting for Lefty and Other Plays* by Clifford Odets. Copyright © 1935 by Clifford Odets, Copyright © renewed 1963 by Clifford Odets. Used by permission of Grove/Atlantic, Inc.

Orend, Angela, "Corporate Logo Tattoos: Literal Corporate Branding?" reprinted by permission of Angela Orend.

Orwell, George, "Politics and the English Language" from *Shooting an Elephant and Other Essays* by George Orwell. Copyright © George Orwell, 1946. Reprinted by permission of Bill Hamilton as the Literary Executor of the Estate of the Late Sonia Brownell Orwell and Secker & Warburg Ltd.

Orwell, George, "Shooting an Elephant" from *Shooting an Elephant and Other Essays* by George Orwell. Copyright © George Orwell, 1936. Reprinted by permission of Bill Hamilton as the Literary Executor of the Estate of the Late Sonia Brownell Orwell and Secker & Warburg Ltd.

Pearson, Lester B., "The Implications of a Free Society" from *Words and Occasions* by Lester B. Pearson (Toronto: University of Toronto Press, 1970). Reprinted by permission of University of Toronto Press.

Prager, Emily, "Our Barbies, Ourselves" copyright © 1991 by Emily Prager. Reprinted by permission of the Wylie Agency.

Pringle, Heather, "The Way We Woo" reprinted by permission of Heather Pringle.

Rodriguez, Joe, "Mexicans Deserve More Than La Mordida" © McClatchy-Tribune Information Services. All Rights Reserved. Reprinted with permission.

Rosenberg, Don, "What Is Depression?" reprinted by permission of the author.

Shields, Carol, "The Same Ticking Clock" first published in *Language in Her Eye: Views on Writing and Gender by Canadian Women Writing in English,* editors Libby Shier, Sarah Sheard and Eleanor Wachtel (Toronto: Coach House, 1990), is reprinted with the permission of the Carol Shields Literary Trust.

Simpson, Eileen, "Dyslexia" from *Reversals* by Eileen Simpson. Copyright © 1979, 1991 by Eileen Simpson. Reprinted by permission of Georges Borchardt, Inc. on behalf of the Estate of Eileen Simpson.

Staples, Brent, "Black Men and Public Space" originally titled "Just Walk on By: A Black Man Ponders His Power to Alter Public Space" in *Harper's Magazine,* 1986. Reprinted by permission of the author.

Suzuki, David, "Living with Nature" reprinted by permission of David Suzuki.

Taylor, Drew Hayden, "Pretty Like a White Boy" from *An Anthology of Canadian Native Literature in English,* ed. Daniel David Moses and Terry Goldie (Toronto: Oxford University Press, 1992). Reproduced by permission of Drew Hayden Taylor.

Trudeau, Justin, "Eulogy by Justin Trudeau" reprinted by permission of Justin Trudeau.

Waisglass, Sean, "*The New City* is an Old Photoblog" reprinted by permission of the author, Sean Waisglass.

Wallace, Bronwen, "An Auction at Mother's Childhood Home" from *Arguments with the World: Essays by Bronwen Wallace,* ed. Joanne Page (Kingston: Quarry Press, 1992). Reprint by permission of Quarry Press.

White, E.B., "Once More to the Lake" from *One Man's Meat,* text copyright © 1941 by E.B. White. Copyright renewed. Reprinted by permission of Tilbury House, Publishers, Gardiner, Maine.

Winn, Marie, "TV Addiction" from "Cookies or Heroin" from *The Plug-In Drug, Revised and Updated—25th Anniversary Edition* by Marie Winn, copyright © 1977, 1985, 2002 by Marie Winn Miller. Used by permission of Viking Penguin, a division of Penguin Group (USA) Inc.

Zinsser, William K., "Simplicity" copyright © 1976, 1980, 1985, 1988, 1990, 1994, 1998, 2001, 2006 by William K. Zinsser. Reprinted by permission of author.

Index